Irina

University Press of Florida

Florida A&M University, Tallahassee
Florida Atlantic University, Boca Raton
Florida Gulf Coast University, Ft. Myers
Florida International University, Miami
Florida State University, Tallahassee
University of Central Florida, Orlando
University of Florida, Gainesville
University of North Florida, Jacksonville
University of South Florida, Tampa
University of West Florida, Pensacola

Irina

Ballet, life and love

Irina Baronova

University Press of Florida

Gainesville · Tallahassee · Tampa · Boca Raton
Pensacola · Orlando · Miami · Jacksonville · Ft. Myers

Text copyright 2005 by Irina Baronova Tennant
First published by Penguin Group (Australia), 2005
Printed in the United States of America on acid-free paper
All rights reserved
Copyright notices continued on page 521

11 10 09 08 07 06   6 5 4 3 2 1

A record of cataloging-in-publication data is available from
the Library of Congress.
ISBN 0-8130-3026-9

The University Press of Florida is the scholarly publishing agency
for the State University System of Florida, comprising Florida A&M
University, Florida Atlantic University, Florida Gulf Coast University,
Florida International University, Florida State University, University
of Central Florida, University of Florida, University of North Florida,
University of South Florida, and University of West Florida.

University Press of Florida
15 Northwest 15th Street
Gainesville, FL 32611-2079
http://www.upf.com

In loving memory of
my mother, Lydia, and my father, Michael,
and my beloved husband, Cecil Tennant

and to my children,
Victoria, Irina and Robert,

and my grandchildren,
Natasha, Hugh, Finn, Katya, Nikolai and Laurie,
and my great-granddaughter, Zoe,

with love.

CONTENTS

FOREWORD

*I*rina Baronova's life was, from its beginnings – as an infant refugee in her parents' arms, fleeing the Russian Revolution – extraordinary. There is, though, little exceptional in the idea of a child who dances well. The world is full of them, and they usually amount to nothing in the great scheme of balletic things. But a child dancer who was one of a trio of Russian émigrée prodigies holding the world's attention by their artistry when they were barely teenagers? This is astonishing.

The glamorous creativity of Serge Diaghilev's Ballets Russes had taken Paris by storm early in the twentieth century, but had ended abruptly when Diaghilev died in 1929. When, in the early 1930s, the Ballets Russes were reborn in Monte Carlo, the new troupe soon acquired a truly significant image due to the dancing of these three young girls, soon to be known as the Baby Ballerinas, whose skill and beauty astounded audiences. Ballets were made for them by the greatest choreographers of the time. Critics and audiences were enraptured by their gifts. The youngest of them was Irina Baronova.

She was blessed with beauty, intelligence, a *joie de vivre* (and a *joie de danser*) that have never left her, and she grew up to live a life where art, private emotion and public attainment were fascinatingly mingled. Irina Baronova's story, as it unfolds in these pages, is told with modesty, and with a security in her identity that is central to the character of this delightful, heart-warming woman.

A ballet-goer for more than sixty years, and a critic for more than fifty, I have cursed the cursedness of fate that meant I never saw Baronova dance on stage, although I often saw Tamara Toumanova and Tatiana Riabouchinska, who were the other two Graces of this youthful and prodigious trinity. I knew Baronova from film, and was thrilled by the grandeur and warmth of temperament that shone in her interpretations. I knew critics who had charted the careers of these three marvels, and they spoke with huge enthusiasm and delight about their performances.

Then I met Baronova on her return to London in the 1970s. The years seemed to have ignored her. She was the Baronova of the performance photographs: beautiful still, the glorious vitality, the entirely natural and absolutely knockout charm that I knew from film and commentary, all there and all-conquering. (She certainly conquered me!) What struck me at our subsequent meetings, and what shines through her story, is how she greets the world, how fundamentally yea-saying is her attitude, and how the tremendous disciplines of the ballet, and a huge respect and reverence for her art, have shaped her temperament.

You need no insider's knowledge of ballet to understand what sort of woman emerged from the career of the young star-blessed girl who helped bring fresh audiences to the theatre (not least in Australia during the tours of the Ballet Russe). There is, in essence, a double narrative in these memoirs. There is the story of a child, truly a child, given that most dangerous of gifts, phenomenal skill, and that equally dangerous gift, public adulation. There is also the story of how that child copes with the gift, trusts it, and reconciles it with her inner self as she grows to womanhood.

The ballet is a hothouse world, and its finest blooms are protected and nurtured if they merit such care. Once away from the hothouse, vulnerability, even innocence, can be liabilities, and the personality may be damaged. Baronova was – is – sustained by an emotional strength (she is not of a good Russian family for nothing) and by a dignity that reflect exactly her identity as a youthful star of ballet, loved by the world, and loving the world. Her dancing inspired audiences worldwide by its grace and life-affirming generosity.

Irina, dear friend, I never saw you dance. In these pages I know how you danced, and how you touched the hearts of everyone who saw you, and everyone who knows you today.

Clement Crisp

PROLOGUE

OUR FLIGHT FROM RUSSIA

'*W*here do you come from?'

I am asked this question constantly, and have been throughout my life, by taxi-drivers, salespeople, tradespeople and total strangers. What intrigues them all is that they cannot place me. My unusual accent and intonation leave them with no clues. I shed the typical Russian accent, but a hint of it still colours the other languages I speak. So to that eternal question I reply, 'I'm Russian.'

'Oh . . .' they stare at me in curiosity and suspicion. It used to embarrass me, but now it just amuses me. I always hasten to add, 'I am a "White" Russian, a refugee from communist USSR.' My questioners then relax and ply me with more questions, especially the taxi-drivers, and we end up telling each other our life stories and parting in friendship and goodwill!

So, anticipating your question, 'Where do you come from?', dear reader, I shall go back in time to my grandparents' days and recount where I come from and how, due to the 1917 Russian Revolution and its tragic consequences, my parents and I found ourselves stateless refugees. My father, Michael Baronov, hardly ever talked about his family. His pain at being separated from his mother, who was a widow, three brothers and sister, and not knowing their fate, was too great. As I grew up, I noticed that if and when his family was mentioned, his eyes would fill with tears and he would leave the room, unable to speak.

My mother, Lydia, on the other hand, reminisced readily about her early youth, her parents and her schooldays whenever I asked her questions. She talked about old Russia with pride, and of her happy times with her father with a smile and love in her eyes. She would always end her tales by saying, 'For me, today's Russia does not exist. My Russia is dead!' Then she would sit in silence, deep in thought, for a long, long time.

My maternal grandmother, Eugenie Engalytcheva-Engels, married a much older man, Alexander Vishniakov, a general in the Imperial Guards Regiment. My mother was their only child. She was brought up in the nursery by a nanny and later by a German governess and then a French governess. My mother adored the French governess and had great fun with her. My grandmother was very prim and proper, like her own mother. It gave her an aura of being cold and distant, but beneath the surface was tucked away a very warm and understanding nature. She was very beautiful, with enormous eyes and chiselled features. The last time my mother saw her, Granny was only forty-two!

My grandfather was tall, with a proud head and a big moustache. He was open, gay and affectionate. My mother adored him; he was her friend, her soul mate. She felt free to jump into his arms, hug him and be hugged in return. That was not the case with her mother, to whom she was brought by her nanny every morning for a kiss on the forehead. But my grandmother did, without fail, tuck my mother into bed and kiss her goodnight.

Mama used to tell me how much she loved seeing her mother dressed for dinner, looking beautiful and smelling of her lovely perfume. They lived in a very big apartment that occupied the entire first floor of their building – 20 Panteleymonovskiya Street, around the corner from the Neva River and near the Summer Gardens in St Petersburg. The household comprised a cook, kitchen maid, parlour maid and Granny's personal maid, plus the nanny or governess. My grandparents had their own carriage and horses, and a coachman who lived above the stables at the back of the building's big courtyard. My grandfather had two batmen, one for the heavy work around the house and to serve at table, the other to accompany Grandfather in his duties and help him at home. The batmen slept in the barracks and reported to Grandfather first thing each morning.

Each January, my grandparents went to Paris and then on to the south of France or to Italy, and sometimes to the Swiss Riviera on Lake Como, where the Russian dowager empress had a grand house called Villa d'Este (nowadays a luxury hotel). The empress's bodyguards were Russian Cossacks, which explains why there were so many children in the area with blonde hair and blue eyes! At these times, my mother was, of course, left at home in the loving care of the household. Mother went as a day girl to a prestigious private school where all the classes were conducted in German. She had a tutor at home for Russian and learned French with her governess.

My grandfather had three brothers and two sisters. Both sisters were old maids – both were over-prim, over-proper and dry as Melba toast! Grandfather loved to tease them and pull their legs. My mother hated them because they hated her fox terrier dog. The dog would get his own back, however, by creeping under their chairs when they came round for tea and noisily farting, surrounding them with a nasty pong. My grandfather would roar with laughter and pay no attention to his wife's disapproving glances. Grandfather also had a black labrador, and the dogs always had the run of the house. Loved by everyone, they were part of the family.

Two of Grandfather's brothers were retired admirals, both full of the joys of life and alcoholic refreshments. They were fun and frequent guests for lunch or dinner, or both. The third brother was the black sheep of the family. My mother described him as a good-for-nothing with strong leftist ideas who was always causing trouble. In the end he was despatched to oversee my grandfather's small country estate of 2000 acres. Grandfather's household spent each summer there in a vast wooden *dacha* (summerhouse). On her third son's rare visits to St Petersburg, Grandmother would ask him, 'What are you doing tonight?' to which the black sheep would reply, 'Don't question me. You're invading my privacy. It's none of your business!'

The estate and summerhouse were near Schlisselburg, some forty miles from St Petersburg by Lake Ladoga, from which the large, beautiful, deep and at times rough River Neva springs on her course through St Petersburg. In the cold Russian winter months, the Neva freezes solid – people skate on it and in the old days horse-drawn sleighs were used to cross from bank to bank.

The neighbouring estate and *dacha* belonged to the Baronov family, long-standing friends of the Vishniakovs. They also lived in St Petersburg and spent summers at their *dacha*. Theodor Baronov was the director of the Imperial Bank. His wife, Varvara, a jolly, unaffected person, had five children: four boys and girl. She doted on them and showered them with love and attention. A true 'mother earth' – that's how my mother remembered my paternal grandmother.

When the children were still very young, tragedy struck the family. Grandfather Theodor came home from a day out shooting with friends and settled down to clean his gun, forgetting to check if it was loaded. The gun went off. Grandfather was later found dead. That's all my mother could tell me. She hardly knew him, being knee-high to a grasshopper at the time.

But my mother reminisced with evident pleasure about the great times she had with the Baronov children in summer. She particularly liked the company of the four brothers and her own four cousins, all boys, who were frequent visitors. She felt like a queen, she would say – laughing, ordering her 'knights' around, riding bareback like a tomboy, to her mother's alarm but her father's delight. Growing up with eight boys as her playmates influenced her relationships with women throughout her life. She did not like women and always preferred the company of men. Mother would say, 'Women are either cats or rats!' Once one of my daughters asked her if she was a cat or a rat. Mother was taken aback, then after a moment coyly replied, 'I'm a pussycat.'

One summer she fell in love with one of the Baronov brothers. The next summer she transferred her affections to the youngest brother, Michael, my father-to-be. Mother was sixteen, Father twenty-one. Having finished his studies at the Naval Academy in 1913 and done his duty as a midshipman, by then Father was a lieutenant serving on a minesweeper and about to be transferred to a battleship with the Black Sea Fleet under the command of Admiral Koltchak.

In August 1914, Russia declared war on Germany and World War I began its bloody run. In those old days there was time for courtship, followed by a long engagement. A decent time lapse had to be observed before the marriage ceremony – a hurried wedding aroused suspicions. But during the war, Father's shore leaves were few and far between. There was no time for courting, so my parents were allowed to get engaged and their parents also agreed that their wedding could take place sooner than originally planned. Mother was seventeen-and-a-half when she married my father on one of his shore leaves. After their wedding, my father had to report back to his ship, so they both went to Sevastopol, where the Black Sea Fleet was based. Mother told me that it was agony to watch the ships leave, not knowing when or if they would return. When my mother got engaged, Grandfather started to build a *dacha* for her and Papa on his estate. But it was never finished, because of the Revolution, which spelt the end of the life they had known.

By order of the Tsar, out of wartime patriotism, St Petersburg was renamed Petrograd. The meaning was the same – Peter's City – but it was now expressed in Russian rather than German. A little later, the Bolsheviks renamed it Leningrad, but now it has been restored to its original, rightful name.

The news from the front-line of the war was alarming. There was tension in Petrograd – rumours, speculation and uncertainty. Then in February 1917, like an exploding bomb, the Revolution took hold of Russia. Fights raged between those loyal to the Tsar, called the 'White Army', and the Bolsheviks, the 'Red Army'. In Petrograd bullets whistled in the streets – there was chaos and all services were stopped. The Tsar and his family were arrested and whisked away from the capital. Soon after, the Tsar, his wife and all their children were murdered, shot by the Bolsheviks.

From the start of the Revolution, the Bolsheviks removed those in high positions and replaced them with their own people. For example, the director of my mother's former school was replaced by the door-man! These people had no idea what to do when entrusted with the 'boss's' responsibilities. Factory workers, sailors, soldiers and public serv-ants were led to believe, and did believe, that they had been exploited by the bourgeoisie and could run the country without the 'upper classes'.

In my father's case, the sailors took over the ships. Drunk with power, they shot a great many of the officers or tortured them sadisti-cally. My father was put on the reserve list by the naval commissar and sent back to Petrograd to await orders. Uncertain as to what his future held, for the time being my father had to be grateful that he was still alive. When my parents returned to Petrograd, they found that their families' homes had been requisitioned, their owners restricted to one or two rooms according to the whim of the appointed district commis-sar. The rest of the rooms were occupied by people of the commissar's choice – total strangers.

Food was hard to find, money was worthless. If one was lucky enough to find something to eat, it was obtainable only in exchange for valuables, preferably jewellery. Freezing in the cold Russian winter, people smashed their furniture and burnt it to keep warm. When there was nothing left, they just froze. People dropped dead in the streets from hunger and cold. Skeletal horses would also drop dead, attracting a frenzied crowd who would hack off pieces to obtain a meagre meal. Churches were shut, religion forbidden, the clergy prosecuted. An early separate 'peace' was signed with Germany, and the 'Iron Curtain' came down, cutting off the USSR from the rest of the world.

My parents shared their two rooms with my maternal grandpar-ents. Each morning, my father and grandfather ventured out to look for food. Their best bet was, by some means, to get to a village where the peasants had extra food from their farms that they were willing to part with for an item of value.

Soon Father was recalled and assigned to 'shore duty' with the Baltic Red Fleet, which was anchored in Kronshtad. It was very near Petrograd, and he was back most nights. By then my mother was preg-nant with me. Cold and hungry, she had a miserable time. In the middle of a freezing March night, Mother went into labour. Supported by my father and Granny, she walked and slid on the icy roads to the hospital, which at that time was taking care mainly of the battle-wounded. After thirty-two hours of labour, through which my mother told me she screamed solidly, early in the morning, on 13 March 1919, I was born.

My father was again relieved of his duties in Kronshtad and told to await new orders, so it was decided that my parents and I should go to Grandfather's *dacha* in the country. Although the estate had been pilfered and requisitioned, the commissar-in-charge allowed us to use a couple of rooms, and even agreed to leave one cow on the farm as long as my father would milk it. Father readily agreed! We made our way to the *dacha* and my grandparents stayed in Petrograd. My parents' days passed in search of food, milking the cow and looking after me. And waiting . . . Father awaited new orders, not knowing what was in store, what to expect or when.

There was still a train from Petrograd that was running at no fixed hours. My grandparents, at great risk to themselves, managed to get on that train, intending to visit us and see their baby granddaughter. As the train neared our station, a soldier walked into the compartment. Eyeing the occupants, he noticed my grandfather's black military overcoat, which was lined in red, an indication of the wearer's rank.

'Aha! You're a general!' said the soldier and, producing a revolver, shot my grandfather in the head. He died instantly. Grandfather's body and Granny, numb with shock, were brought to the *dacha*.

The effect on my mother was terrible. Devastated by her grief at the loss of her father, she fell to pieces, developed a very high fever and lost her milk. In bed for days, she was unable to attend her father's funeral. He was buried quietly in the village cemetery, with only Granny and my father there to say a prayer.

My mother told me that when they returned from the cemetery, she did not recognise her mother. The beautiful woman she had known was no more. Her hair had turned grey, her face was sunken and wrinkled. She looked like an old lady but was only forty-two. But Granny did not lose her strong character, and calmly looked after her daughter and infant granddaughter while my father was absent, on duty at naval headquarters or searching for food. I owe my survival during those terrible days to the dear cow, no doubt hungry herself, whose milk nourished me with no ill effects, and kept me healthy and content.

My father's family, meanwhile, remained in Petrograd. Before we went to the *dacha*, my father visited his mother, sister and eldest brother, who was studying to be a surgeon. They were living, restricted, in their requisitioned home. As for his other two brothers – one was fighting the Bolsheviks with the White Army, but the other, a cadet instructor at the Naval Academy, had disappeared from view. Granny Varvara had no word from him and worried a great deal. Time went by, each month bringing new restrictions and hardships, along with endless violence, hunger and misery.

One day an officer friend of my father's arrived at the Kronshtad base from Petrograd, bringing him the latest news of his family. The news was bad. The brother who was fighting with the White Army was killed, and his sister's fiancé had been tortured and shot in front of her. She was in bad shape. There was no news of the missing brother – he had just disappeared. My granny Varvara was broken-hearted but stoic and courageous in her grief. It was a hard blow for my papa. Being cut off from his family and unable to give moral support to his mother and sister added frustration to his grief.

In March 1920 my father was transferred to the Red Fleet base on the Sea of Azov, in the town of Mariupol. My mother and I were allowed to go with him, but Granny returned to Petrograd. On the trip to Mariupol we were in a carriage with several other naval officers and some of their wives. We were all under the commissar's supervision. This particular commissar was well known for his brutality, especially towards children, whose heads he smashed against trees or walls to assert his power over their parents. As he paced up and down the carriage, he always stopped to ruffle my hair and call me *Goluboglazka* (Blue eyes). Mother later told me she was terrified each time he touched me.

At one point, when I was standing up by holding onto my papa's knees, the commissar motioned to me saying, 'Come on, *Goluboglazka*, walk to me!' I let go of my papa and made my first ever wobbly few steps straight into the commissar's arms. He lifted me high over his head, roaring with laughter. Apparently I was laughing too! My parents were not amused, their nerves at breaking point.

Again my father was put on shore duties, where he made friends with a sailor who took to Father, confiding in him that he was not a revolutionary but had to play along with them to save his skin. He begged my father not to go anywhere alone, only with him – to go alone would be too dangerous. Father felt the young man was genuine and trusted him. Mother later told me that whenever Father went to sea she worried whether he would return safe and sound. Now that he was stuck on shore duty, she still worried as much, wondering if he would return to their room in the evening. The random shooting of officers by the Bolsheviks continued. They were brainwashed, propaganda-fed and full of hatred. There was no further news of our families. Communication with Petrograd was non-existent.

The Whites were still fighting the Reds. By October 1920, the White Army was successfully approaching Mariupol, and the Azov Sea Fleet was ordered to evacuate to Odessa. All those serving at general staff headquarters were bundled onto a train of cattle wagons. We sat and slept on bare, filthy boards, obtaining scraps of food and water at prolonged stops near villages. We were dirty, hungry, cold and continually surveyed by commissars. What in normal times would have been an overnight trip took our train three weeks. Upon arrival in Odessa, we were distributed to our allocated billets. A couple of days later, my father met a young woman in the corridor. They greeted each other and stopped for a chat. She turned out to be Yelena Smirnova, a ballerina at the Maryinsky Theatre. She and her husband, Boris Romanov, a character dancer and choreographer, occupied the room next to ours. One day, after making sure the commissar was out of earshot, Yelena confided to my father that they had found a way to escape from Russia to Romania and urged him to do the same. She thought she could arrange it with the person who was to smuggle them across the River Dniester to the Romanian bank, but my parents would have to make up their minds fast. It was a difficult decision to make, but it became easier when my father's young sailor friend told him that his name was on the list of officers to be shot if the White Army approached Odessa.

'Take your wife and child and try to get away,' he pleaded.

That evening, my parents gratefully accepted Yelena's offer to help. She gave Father the instructions for finding the *isba* (peasant cottage) near the River Dniester, where the smuggler was to meet them, and the date on which we should turn up. It was now up to my father to find a horse and cart and to forge the passes.

Yelena and her husband left and soon it was our turn to follow. On a cold dark night at the end of November 1920, my father, dressed as a sailor and carrying me and his violin, and my mother, dressed as a peasant and carrying a bundle of our effects, walked to the outskirts of the city and climbed into the cart. Father took the reins and we set off, my parents consoling themselves with the thought that the Revolution could not last and that within a year we would return to our home and family. But first we had to make it to Romania.

We trotted by night and kept out of sight by day. Wherever we went, we were well received by the villagers, who were kind to us and our horse. They shared their soup with us, asked no questions of us and expected nothing in return. Simple, warm Russian hospitality still prevailed among the peasants in the villages far away from the cities. Mother and I would rest but Father would always help the peas-ants with their chores. As dawn broke on the last leg of our journey, Father found the *isba*. The elderly peasant couple let us in then led the horse away.

'Thank God, you made it!' exclaimed Yelena, embracing my mother. She introduced us to the man who was to take us across the river. He questioned my parents at length before finally agreeing to smuggle us into Romania. He named a price and Mother took down her bun and parted with a piece of her jewellery she had hidden in her hair. Yelena and her husband were going across that night. The man said he would come to fetch us from the *isba* the next night. Meanwhile we were to stay put with the peasant couple.

However, our rescuer was not very happy about having me on board. He explained that we were the last people he was to take across. He himself was staying in Romania, having already transferred his entire family there. If, during the crossing, I made any noise, he risked being caught by the Romanian patrol, arrested and delivered to the Bolsheviks.

'I have to warn you,' he told my parents coldly, 'if your child cries or makes any noise, I'll have to throw her overboard. My life comes first.'

Once again, my parents faced a dilemma. What to do? Late that night, the man, Yelena and her husband started the long walk to the river, and we were left alone with the old peasant couple. My mother went to pieces; the kind old peasant woman tried to comfort her. Finally my parents came to a decision – they would play it by ear, and if things were to go wrong, my father would shoot me, Mother and himself. To remain in Russia was certain death at the hands of the Bolsheviks; our survival depended upon me keeping my mouth shut. The old peasant woman came to the rescue. Taking her few remaining lumps of sugar out of a box, she gave them to my mother, saying, 'Stuff them, piece by piece, into Irina's mouth as you cross the river. It will keep her quiet.' Mother always remembered that kind old lady.

The next night, as it neared midnight, the man appeared as promised. My parents thanked the old couple for all their help and kindness, then started on the one-hour walk through fields and forest to where the man's rowboat was hidden. Before letting us climb aboard, the man asked Father if he had a revolver. Father hesitated, but finally admitted that he did. The man ordered Father to hand it over and Father, feeling cornered, had no option but to give it to him.

The lumps of sugar did their work and kept me quiet. As we reached the Romanian side, it started to pour with rain, and as we got off the boat, the sound of approaching steps alerted the man, who whispered to Father, 'It's the Romanian patrol. All of you lie down on your stomachs and keep quiet.'

So there we were, lying in the mud in the pouring rain while Mother stuffed the last lump of sugar into my mouth and hoped for the best. The patrol passed, and when the man considered it was safe, we got up and followed him through the trees along the river bank to a waiting carriage. As the man helped us into the carriage, he told Father we would be taken to a safe house to spend the night and that in the morning my father should go and make himself known to the police. Then he wished us good luck and disappeared into the night.

We were well received in the safe house, given a welcome plate of hot soup and a room with a comfortable bed. In the morning Father presented himself at the police station. The police officer in charge was obviously used to the regular appearance of Russian refugees, but he questioned my father endlessly. Sometimes the Bolshevik commissars, pretending to be refugees, would appear in search of genuine refugees, whom they would drag back to Russia or simply shoot on the spot.

At midday the Romanian police officer told Father to wait a while, as he had to go home and would return in a couple of hours. Over lunch, he told his wife that another Russian family had crossed the border and that he wasn't yet certain whether they were genuine refugees. His wife had been married to a naval officer who was killed during the war, leaving her a widow. She had managed to escape into Romania and eventually married the Romanian police offer. 'What's the name of the new arrivals?' she asked.

'Baronov,' he told her.

'Oh,' she exclaimed. 'I know Michael Baronov. He served on the same ship as my husband.' The police officer was delighted with the news and asked his wife to come to the police station to identify my father. The moment she walked in, they recognised each other. They embraced warmly and my father received permission to stay in Romania.

So now we had a new life to begin, but how? We spoke no Romanian and had no money. The only profession my father knew was that of a naval officer in the Imperial Fleet. Now we were on our own.

I

CHILDHOOD, 1920–1931

1

MEMORY

My life has been lived out of suitcases, in foreign lands, with foreign people. Home was just the place where I unpacked for a short while or, early on, the place where others unpacked for me.

In my first clear memory I am on Romanian soil, at a place called Argeş. I can see it still, clearly and sharply. I stand in the middle of a garden, between two narrow beds of brightly coloured flowers – later I learned that these flowers were snapdragons. I stand very still and stare at them. I long to touch them. As my fingers are about to close on a flower head, I hear footsteps. My hand shoots behind my back and I turn towards the disturbing sound. I see at the end of the path a small whitewashed cottage, the sun beaming hard on it from a bright blue sky. I half close my eyes and wait. My mother (I just know it is my mother, although I do not know or understand what 'mother' means) appears through the low wooden door and walks towards me. I keep still and stare at her. She is blonde, like me, round-faced, young and pretty. I stare at her but do not see any response in her eyes.

Later I understood why she always had that vague look – she was very short-sighted. Then, at the age of three-and-a-bit, I did not know or understand, and her non-seeing look scared me. As she stooped to my level, she pointed at the flowers and told me I must not touch them or gather them. Then she turned and walked back to the cottage. I remember standing still, staring at the flowers. I was puzzled. *Which ones mustn't*

I touch? The matter had to be clarified. Slowly and deliberately, I picked a flower of each colour. Squashing them in my fist, I went indoors and displayed the mutilated flower heads to Mother, asking her, 'Is it these I mustn't pick?' The result of my enquiry was far from pleasant.

From this time in my life I have no recollection whatsoever of my father. He was out looking for work, washing carriages or doing any odd jobs to bring in the few pennies we needed to survive. I do not remember anyone else around that cottage, no other grown-ups or children – just a garden, the flowers, the silence and the vast emptiness.

My next clear memory is of standing up on my bed and drawing on the wall. We are not in Argeş any more, we have moved to Kishinev (which is now in Moldova). Mother obviously did not appreciate my drawing talents, and the result – not only were my feelings hurt, but so was my bottom! I took great umbrage at the situation and decided to run away from home. I slipped out the front door in my nightshirt, and with great difficulty negotiated a dark, wide flight of stairs. The door giving onto the street was huge. With much effort, I finally managed to reach and turn the handle, and walked out into a grey, freezing winter's day. I felt nothing – I just walked.

The local cobbler saw me through his shop window, rushed out to grab me and brought me home. A strange vision I must have been: barefoot in my nightshirt, trotting up the snowy street. He took me gently by the hand, then in total silence lifted me in his arms and carried me back to Mother. Mother whacked me.

Not long after, we moved to Bucharest. Now I am sitting on a long fence dangling my legs into the street. Opposite stands a dirty-looking, enormous, strange building. I know it is a factory because that's what I've heard the grown-ups call it, but I have no idea what the word means. I am wondering about it. I know my father works there. *Papa.* The thought makes me feel good. Papa is gentle and has such nice, kind blue eyes. *I love Papa.* He is my friend. It is fun to be with him. He sharpens sticks for me so I can draw in the muddy path that leads from the gate to the front door. I do not remember having any toys then – we were very, very poor. There were no other children to play with, only silence and my fantasies.

I would wander back and forth on the path to our small rickety house, which had two rooms that were almost empty except for the beds, a table and chairs. In the winter, large icicles hung from the roof almost to the ground. I used to break them off and suck them, to my mother's horror when she caught me. The toilet was outside in the wooden shed, just a hole in the ground, with a box-like wooden seat over it with a hole in the middle. There was no running water and I do not recall there being any bathroom or kitchen.

So I am sitting on the fence, dangling my legs, just looking. A lady walks down the street towards me. I observe her with great interest. She looks different. I have never seen anyone like her. I stare at her as only children can stare, with all their curiosity and total innocence. The lady stops in front of me, smiles, reaches into a big bag and takes out a round, purple box on which are printed two flowers and some writing. She hands me the box and says, 'It's for you. They're chocolates.' Timidly, I take the box from her gloved hand and murmur, 'Thank you.' I suddenly realise that I can speak Romanian. As I watch her walk away, she turns and waves to me. I wave back and then scramble off the fence and run indoors to Mother to show her the box and ask her what chocolates are. That was the first time I tasted a chocolate. For my parents, chocolates were a luxury they could no longer afford. Instead, for a treat they would sometimes give me a lump of sugar, just as they had on that night we escaped from Russia. To this day, although I love chocolate, I would rather have a lump of sugar.

On another day, my fantasies are not functioning and I am bored. Suddenly I have a brilliant idea. I promptly take my mother's scissors, dash to the outside toilet and close the door. It is great fun chopping off my hair. It is nice hair, very light blonde, below my ears, with a fringe. When I have had enough, I go back to the house to return the scissors to Mother's box. As I enter the room, my mother gives a most unpleasant shriek – the kind I know means a spanking. I am puzzled. *What have I done?* Mother grabs a mirror and sticks it in front of my face. I stare at the image of a very red-faced little girl, the right side of whose head is barely covered by ragged wisps of hair, while the left side looks perfectly normal.

I suppose I was often naughty, sometimes innocently, as puppies are. But sometimes my pranks were thought-out and deliberate. I knew instinctively what I was not supposed to do, although I did not yet understand why it was forbidden. But I had to do it – slowly, solemnly, silently . . . and then, of course, get spanked.

I see Mama, Papa and me sitting at the table, eating. It is so grey outside. Papa looks grey too, or perhaps he is sad. Mama is silent. I have a bowl of semolina in front of me. They have only tea in front of them. I want to ask them why they are not eating semolina too, but I do not dare. I feel shy and uncomfortable and I hate semolina.

We had only one change of clothes each. I remember them hanging on hooks on the wall – there was no wardrobe. One day, Mother and I were out, Father working at the factory across the street. When we came back, all the spare clothes were gone. Mama cried and Papa was silent, his blue eyes very sad. I did not fully understand what had happened, but I felt crushed and wanted to hide. I crept to the outside toilet, sat on the dirty floor and cried until I had no more tears, only loud hiccups and gulps that seemed to go on forever.

One day soon afterwards, Father told us he had another job at another factory and we were soon to move. For me it was a great excitement, a big event, and I could hardly contain my curiosity. The big day arrived and I fussed around my few belongings, getting under my parents' feet and no doubt making a thorough nuisance of myself. A final look at the rooms, a final click of the wooden gate and we were on our way.

After a thrilling drive in a horse-drawn cart through strange, unfamiliar streets, while we held onto our bundles so they wouldn't fall off onto the road, we finally arrived at our new home. When I remember it now, seventy-eight years later, I can only describe it as a sore to the eye and death to the soul. It was as depressing and grey as a prison or factory anywhere in the world. I had never seen anything so big – or perhaps I was just small and it only seemed big. Facing this monstrosity, across a big courtyard, stood the factory, heavy and crushing.

We rode in through a side gate. To the left of the gate were some small derelict wooden outbuildings. In one of them lived a family with two small children and a newborn baby. On the right was a long two-storey building, with many concrete steps leading to the doors of the blocks in which the factory workers and their families lodged. These blocks were infested with bedbugs, while the derelict outbuildings were crawling with rats as well. The children were covered in lice. There sure were plenty of insects and vermin in that place, not to mention the starved cats that rummaged in the garbage bins, competing with the rats for the best smelly discards of human misery!

We were lodged in two rooms on the second floor of one of the blocks. The stairs were like a dark tunnel, and at the end of passage was our new home. One room was occupied by my parents' bed; the second was the room we used for everything else. There was a wooden table on which my mother cooked with a primus and around which we ate or sat when friends of my parents, who like us were Russian refugees, occasionally dropped by of an evening to sip a cup of tea and share their sad experiences.

In one corner of that room stood my bed. My father curtained it off with a sheet to give me some semblance of privacy and to dim the light of the oil lamp that stood on the wooden table. I loved it when the grown-ups talked; I would lie in my bed behind the curtain and listen, fascinated by their stories. The reality of these stories escaped me, of course, but my fantasy painted pictures that were very real to me, mysterious and horrific. In a strange way I felt proud to be a participant in it all – I felt a sense of self-importance. Gradually the voices would seem to come from further away, then become a murmur and then I was asleep.

Mother had a terrible time learning how to cook. Not that there was much to cook – food was limited and we had only the cheapest items. Mother had never been required to go anywhere near the kitchen in Russia. Indeed, it had been out of bounds to her. Faced with the hateful primus, a couple of pots, dirty dishes and no idea whatsoever how to go about producing a dinner, she became very bad-tempered. She took a violent loathing to it all, and her hatred remained for the rest of her life. On the rare occasion she would decide to make a real effort and produce a treat, it usually ended in catastrophe and tears of rage.

I remember one instance clearly. One afternoon Mother decided to make some doughnuts. The pot of boiling oil was on the primus and as Mother prepared the dough and rolled it into ball shapes, I watched with my mouth watering. Pleased with herself, she started dropping the pieces of dough into the boiling oil, which spluttered like a fountain right into her face, burning her badly. It was an immediate cue for me to get out of her way, be out of range. I scuffled off the chair and ran like a rabbit until I found myself in the courtyard, where I pondered the intricacies of the culinary art as I took a nice stroll around the garbage bins.

Another time a few years later, when Mother was the proud but totally unthrilled possessor of an oven, somebody gave her a rabbit to cook. It was dead all right, but unskinned. Mother almost fainted with horror, but it was food, so somehow it got skinned and shoved into the oven. But the beast shrank with the heat, and when Mother opened the door to take a disgusted look at how the cooking was progressing, she suddenly shrieked with terror and started to shake all over. The rabbit was sitting up, staring at her with its glassy eyes. She never made any more special efforts with cooking.

Bedbugs devoured us every night. It was really horrible. One day Mother got a flame-throwing gadget from somewhere, poured petrol onto the iron frame of their bed and set it alight to burn the bugs, forgetting to remove the mattress. When the mattress caught fire, my fast-thinking mama found the strength to push it through the window and into the courtyard, but there it consumed itself together with the bedbugs. And although my parents' bed was now minus a mattress, enough bedbugs survived to multiply their population. The war against those bloodsucking beasts was lost.

In winter there was no heating, no hot water and grey, dirty snow in the courtyard – even the icicles hanging down from the roofs of the outbuildings were dirty and no longer attracted me. I was cold and bored. When spring finally came, I was thrilled to see nettles, so green and fresh, growing by the sides of the wooden huts. I found out very soon that I must keep my hands off them, but the fact that they hurt did not diminish my interest in their growth.

One morning as I approached the wooden hut in which the poor family lived, I saw a small crowd of women at the door, all talking at the same time, crying and gesticulating. Being very curious, as all kids are, I went to investigate from a closer vantage point. I pushed my way through the women's skirts and found myself staring inside the room. A man was howling and beating his chest, tears pouring from his distorted face. A woman was on the floor with her arms around a wooden box, making sounds I had never heard before. A chill went through my body and terror stuck me to the ground. I wanted to run but my poor legs would not obey me. My eyes shifted to the box. Inside, among bloody rags, lay a baby – still, still. It had only half a face. The voices were penetrating now and I finally understood. The rats had eaten half the baby's face during the night. The baby was dead.

I sat for a long time under the concrete stairs in the darkest corner. Dead! Of course, by that stage of my life I had seen a dead bug, a dead mouse, a run-over cat, but a baby! My little mind was distraught; I could not comprehend the horror of what I had seen. Why, why, why? There was no-one who could give me an answer, and the thought of running to Mother or Father never occurred to me. I was born to bottle things in, as indeed I have done all my life. That night I could not sleep. Then I suddenly remembered how Mother had tried to burn the bedbugs and I knew what had to be done. My mind made up, I fell into an uneasy sleep, emotionally exhausted. Next morning I was all set for the execution of my plan. When Mother's back was turned, I grabbed the bottle of spirits she used for the primus and the box of matches, and tiptoed down to the yard. I walked straight to the hut; all was quiet now and no-one was around. I hid the bottle and the matches behind the hut and turned my steps to the garbage bins, where I collected all the bits of paper I could find then gathered them all behind the hut.

Now to work. Slowly, meticulously, tidily, I pushed the paper into the cracks of the wooden walls. Then I poured the spirits over it and, mustering all my courage, lit my first ever match – at home I was not allowed to touch them. The flames spread quickly through the dry, rotten wood of the hut. Feeling proud to be ridding humanity of the rats,

I marched back home without a backward glance, without any realisation of what the consequences of my act might be, nor how miraculous it was that no-one was in the hut at that moment or that my clothes did not catch fire.

The hut burned to the ground and the poor wretched family was now without any roof over their heads. It was not difficult for Mother to come to the sad conclusion that her daughter was guilty of arson, and I was so certain that I had done good that I did not deny it. I was sure I had been helpful, avenging the baby's death, ridding everyone of rats. But instead of a pat on the head, I got a beating that I have neither forgotten nor forgiven.

I think that every living being, be it human or animal, has an inborn sense of dignity. It is an instinct, a respect for one's own soul, and no matter who we are or what we are, no-one has the right to squash or smash this dignity. It is so fragile in children, and they have no way to defend it. An adult can fight for their dignity, a grown animal can bite, but children and puppies can be destroyed for life. The seed is planted, and complexes grow and sicken the soul. I had always accepted my spankings as a way to make me learn right from wrong, but this time it was different. When one is too young to understand why one is being punished, the terror and mental turmoil are such that one's life is not long enough to live it down. I do not think that my father was aware of what happened. If he noticed, he didn't say anything, at least in my presence. And I just could not tell him. I remember nothing more about what happened after that episode.

Before I go on, I must stand in defence of my mother and father. What I have just said sounds bitter, I know, self-pitying and cruel. Each coin has two sides, and one must never forget it. Here they were, two young people whose lives had not prepared them for the cruel events that had befallen them. They had been tragically torn away from their country and family, and from the way of life they had been born to. They were on foreign soil, with no language in which to communicate, no money, no profession and responsibility for a small child. Their living conditions were squalid and they were hungry and cold. The pain in their soul could not help their morale – it is human to go to pieces at least some of the time. Father was strong, physically and psychologically, so he was better able to control his moments of despair, insecurity and bitter loss of faith. No hard or dirty work frightened him; he took on any work so we could survive. We did survive, and at least that must have helped Father's morale.

For Mother I think it was much worse. She was a young woman robbed of her youth, robbed of looking pretty, of having fun and enjoying life. She suddenly found herself in rags, scrubbing, washing my dirty pants and sodden sheets and, in general, living in conditions she could not have suspected existed on our miserable earth.

My father had humility. Mother did not. Everyone's genes are different. She took her anger out on me, not because she did not love me or did not want me, but because she did not know what she was doing to me when her nerves snapped and her anger had to come out. How can a 22-year-old girl know when she is totally submerged by the misery around and inside her? So I do not blame her, I do not sit in judgement, I understand – I only wish I could forget.

DAYS WITH DIDINA

My next memory opens up in new surroundings. We have moved again, but we still live in Bucharest. I'm sitting at the table eating *gogol-mogol*, a Russian dessert made from egg yolks beaten with sugar. Mother says, 'Drink up your milk.' I hate milk but I have to drink it. Blimey, it's hard to be a kid!

I survey the room over the rim of the glass. The table is black, as is the huge matching sideboard. I know that behind me are two big black wooden chairs, and I wonder why they are so big and especially so very, very black. Above the sideboard hangs a big poster. On the top left-hand corner of the poster are some writing and some numbers. I stare at the poster to the last drop of the detestable milk. Then, in a loud voice, I slowly read the inscription. It says, 'The Year of 1924.'

'Irischka, you can read!' Papa's voice is excited and happy and we all laugh. Papa promises to get some Pushkin fairy tales for me. Mama promises to teach me the Russian alphabet and give me dictation. I prefer Papa's proposition – it sounds more fun.

'You can go outside and play now,' says Mama.

I hurry off my chair and dash to the adjoining room, which is our bedroom. My parents' bed occupies one corner, mine the other. In between stands a piece of mirror leaning against the wall and all sorts of fascinating bits that Mother uses to make herself pretty. At the foot of my bed is a low, large box. Inside are all my treasures – it is 'my corner'. I dash to my corner, fish out my catapult, throw myself a quick glance in the mirror and dash through the door into the kitchen, then through another door into the corridor. Sharp left, left again and I am out the front door. Sliding down the uneven concrete stair rail I rip, as usual, my knickers and land in the front courtyard. There is no-one around.

I cross the yard to the tall grey wooden fence that runs around the entire compound in which the factory workers live. The factory is just outside the fence, looming large and hiding the sky. I peep through a hole in the fence to see if the little bad-tempered dog is around, so I can tease him and make him cross (one day he bit my nose) but no, there is no dog. I march around the corner of the house and through a narrow alley to the backyard. Here I am sure to find life and things going on. It is my favourite spot; it holds many attractions.

In the right-hand corner of the yard stand several overflowing bins of *gounoy* (Romanian for 'garbage') – it smells and looks familiar. Right next to the garbage stands a small wooden shack. Its occupants are a mother and three daughters – the two eldest exercised the world's oldest profession, but at my age I did not know of these things. To me they were two young ladies who always laughed, sang saucy songs and when they had arguments shouted at each other so that one could hear them a mile away. Listening to them, my Romanian vocabulary enriched itself considerably with four-letter words and colourful expressions. Their younger sister might have been seven or eight. Her name was Didina and she knew so many fascinating things.

Didina was my first encounter with other children. She taught me how to climb the tree that grew on the other side of the fence by clambering on anything handy. We would hoist ourselves up onto a branch and then make our way to the treetop to steal *corcoduşe* (cherry plums).

Climbing trees with Didina, who had lice in her short, messy blonde hair, and visiting their shack to watch the two elder sisters dress and paint their faces for work, was strictly forbidden by Mother, but I managed to sneak some delightful times in their company until Didina's lice found their way into my hair. Mother was not amused, and very distressed and angry. In those days, getting rid of these beasts was a long and tiring procedure. I suffered it stoically and in silence. Even after that I could not keep away, and Didina and I became firm friends.

On the far left-hand side of the yard stood a second wooden shack occupied by a German family who did their best to keep it clean. The two kids, a girl and a boy, were very friendly, and so were their parents. I liked them very much, but somehow it was more fun with Didina and her big sisters.

After my visits to the back courtyard, I would come home rather filthy, and Mother would wash me while I stood in the basin in the kitchen. There was no bathroom, running water or heating. That winter, Father bought a heating stove and it was a big event. There was one communal toilet on each floor, and needless to say the state of it was permanently most unhygienic. I was forbidden to go anywhere near it. I had my own private potty – although it was well hidden in the kitchen, I still felt very embarrassed and unhappy about it.

In the flat facing ours lived Mr and Mrs Dragna and their two children: Lenoutza, the eldest, and her little brother, Mircha. They kept away from the rest of the inhabitants but were always very friendly to us. On the rare occasions my parents went out of an evening to visit some friends, I was left in the care of Mrs Dragna and slept with them, everybody in the one bed like sardines. It was great fun for me. Everything about them was impeccably clean, and I greatly admired their heavy old linen sheets with white embroidery, no doubt from Mrs Dragna's dowry. She was very proud of them, and indeed of her profusion of treasures, like little vases with paper roses in them, boxes covered in shells, and other bric-a-brac.

One day Lenoutza dashed in, grabbed me by the hand, dragged me into the courtyard and excitedly whispered that a man outside was about to cut off a chicken's head. We installed ourselves on top of the concrete stair rail to watch, our hearts beating fast. The unfortunate bird was lying on the ground, fluttering its wings and desperately trying to get up, its legs tied up with string. The man picked up an axe, placed the chicken's neck on the block of wood and chopped off its head. As a jet of blood sprang up, the man pulled the rope off the legs of the bird and threw the beheaded body on the ground. I watched in horror as the bird's body stood up and started to run all over the courtyard. For a long time afterwards, almost every night, I had nightmares and would wake up shaking and crying.

The first Christmas tree I remember will always be the most beautiful Christmas tree of my life. Papa brought the tree in and fixed it in the corner of the main room. It was so big it touched the ceiling. It smelt so good. Then Papa brought out lots of crepe-paper rolls of different bright colours, yards of thick silky thread, sheets of cardboard, paper, paints, glue and many other magical things. Arranging it all on the big black table, Papa said, 'Now, Irischka, we shall make lots of things to decorate the tree.' We all sat around the table and Papa and Mama taught me how to make lovely little baskets, gold-painted stars, crackers, and paper chains with each link a different colour. It was so exciting!

The next day Papa brought home a box of coloured baubles to hang on the tree, and candles of different colours – electric Christmas tree lights did not yet exist. Finally the evening came to decorate the tree with all the beautiful things we had made. We filled the little baskets with sweets, tied up fresh tangerines with red silk thread, and when all was hung, fixed the candles. I stood back to admire this fairy tale vision, deeply moved, intensely happy. As I lay in bed that night, too excited to sleep, I could see through the open door the shiny balls on the tree glowing faintly in the darkness and smell the aroma of pine and tangerines that filled our tiny little flat. It was a very happy little girl that finally fell asleep. I did not know then how hard my father had had to work and how hard my parents had had to save to be able to give me such a beautiful Christmas tree.

My father had an enormous natural talent for drawing and painting, and it had got him the job at this factory, which printed posters. Papa was one of the designers. He also learned the art of engraving in no time at all, and the engraving he did of King Ferdinand I of Romania's profile was presented to His Majesty and was said to hang in his study.

To earn more money, Father started to bring home work doing engravings. I can see him now, sitting hunched over the table with the engraver's enlarging glass in one eye and a small bright light on his work, fighting off sleep and working far into the night while Mother and I were asleep. I would watch him from my bed and waves of tenderness for him would come over me. I loved him so much and I felt so sad. I prayed to little Jesus that Papa should not fall asleep, because I knew that if he did, the sharp engraving instrument might ruin his work. When I could not watch any more, I pulled the sheets over my head and would finally fall asleep. When I woke up in the morning, Papa had already gone to the factory, and I missed him all day.

At about this time I saw my first movie. It was called *La Bataille*, with the great Japanese actor Sessue Hayakawa. I was riveted to my seat and terribly impressed. When it ended I did not want to leave, so I begged Mother to stay on so we could watch it again. As she loved the cinema, she readily consented, but my most beloved films of that time were the comedies with the two Danish characters Pat and Patachon. Pat was very tall and thin, Patachon was short and fat. They were the European counterparts of Laurel and Hardy, and I adored them.

At this time Mother also started to take me to Russian church services. The church was old, from pre-revolutionary days, big and very beautiful. I loved listening to the choir, watching the multitude of candles flickering in front of every icon, making the expressions of the saints they depicted grave and mysterious. I observed with interest the intense looks on the faces of the people praying and wondered why they looked so sad, why some were even crying. At some point, Mother would approach one particularly big icon on the magnificently carved wall of the altar. She would kneel down, rest her forehead on the palm of her hand and stay like that for what seemed to me a very long time.

After having had my own short talk with God, my knees would ache, so I would slump onto my haunches and then, to do something, would stick my index finger into the carvings of the altar and follow the design – well, it made the time pass. On one occasion I stuck my finger too far into a recess and could not get it out again. I pulled and twisted and was about to burst into tears when Mother finally noticed my peculiar antics. With her help, the inquisitive finger was finally freed, but it was rather bruised and skinned.

One Sunday, a beautiful sunny day in spring, Father was at the church with us. Suddenly the big chandelier hanging in the middle of the church started to shudder and then swing slightly. A wave of uneasiness went through the congregation, the choir faded out and there was total silence, all faces staring up at the increasingly swaying chandelier. Then a low, roaring sound penetrated the stillness and a voice screamed, 'Earthquake! Everybody get out into the street.' Father grabbed me in his arms and we made our way out. Everyone crossed the churchyard and massed in the street while the growling from the bowels of the earth became louder and louder.

Then everything around – the buildings, the street, the people – seemed to capsize and sway. I hung fast to my father's neck, burying my face, but still curious enough in spite of my fright to survey the incomprehensible with one eye. When it was over, I pestered my father with questions, barging into the grown-ups' agitated conversations. We walked all the way home, surveying the destruction and hoping we would find our factory intact.

I have one more memory connected with the church, from my first midnight Easter service. As the Romanians are of Russian Orthodox faith, quite often the members of the Romanian royal family came to the services at our church in Bucharest. On this occasion, Queen Maria and her little son, Prince Carol, were there. They had their own special pew, to the right of the altar, away from the crowd.

My parents and I were standing right in front of them, and my mother whispered to me who the little boy was. As far as I was concerned, princes and princesses existed only in fairy tales, so I was most intrigued and could not stop looking at the royal party. I suppose the little prince was getting a bit bored with the long service, so he started to fidget and his eyes roamed all around.

Inevitably, our eyes met and we stared at each other for a while, as only children can stare. Then he stuck his princely tongue out at me – and I did not wait to stick mine out at him. We passed the rest of the service sticking our tongues out at each other and competing as to who could make the most disgusting grimace! What fun! Years later, when the former King Carol II lived with Mme Magda (later Elena) Lupescu in Mexico, I was introduced to him. I could still chat in Romanian then, although I have totally forgotten it now, and I asked him if by any chance he remembered an occasion at the Russian Church in Bucharest when a little girl and he had made the most disgusting faces at each other. He looked puzzled, then laughed and said, 'Yes, I do.'

'Shall we try again?' I said, and we chatted for the rest of the evening. It was the last time I saw him – he died soon after – and it was the last time I spoke Romanian.

SUMMER HOLIDAYS

As Mother had promised, she started teaching me to read and write the Russian alphabet. These Russian lessons, which took place every afternoon for an hour, were the torture and terror of my life. Mother had no patience and a short temper. The more she raised her voice, the less I understood. One day, when it ended in a particularly catastrophic way, all I could think of was running far, far away and never coming back.

I found a piece of rag in my box and used it to wrap up a few particular treasures, tying up the corners. Hugging my bundle to my chest, I slipped silently out of the flat and onto the street, turned left and walked to the corner. *Now what?* I sat on the kerb and pondered. Although

I was only six years old, I was fully aware that one cannot exist without money. I had none. I pondered again: *I am a little girl. Someone like the old cobbler will take me back home. I am trapped. I will have to wait until I'm grown up. And if I hide, where will I hide? Papa will be sad if I'm gone. Papa is my friend.* At the thought of Papa, I started to cry.

Scared that someone would notice me, I stood and ran up the street and into the church on the corner. It was empty and dark inside, except for something in the middle, by the altar – a long box on a table with a big candle at each end. My curiosity took over. Slowly, I went forward to see what it was. In the flickering candlelight I made out a face. I was staring at an old man with a very hooked nose, his nostrils stuffed with cotton wool. His eyes were closed and he was very still inside that long box. Fear seized me. I backed away with my teeth chattering, then turned and ran out of the church and down the street as if all the devils were after me. When I reached the alleyway that connected the street with our courtyard, I stopped and threw myself onto the dusty ground to catch my breath. Then I slowly made my way home.

Once a week Mother would take me with her to the former Russian Consulate, where our Consul and his wife still lived in what seemed to me to be royal splendour. I do not know what the Consul did now that he was no longer a representative of his country, but he looked very pompous and important. His wife was a tall, thin lady, with buckteeth, a little white spitz dog and a maid in a black dress with a white apron.

Mme la Consule received on Wednesdays at teatime. I loved going there, not least because it was fun to catch the horse-drawn tramcar from the corner of our street. In the winter the carriage was closed in; in the summer it was all open, with benches across it. I loved sitting right in front so I could watch the horses. We drove along our street, then through a big square that was a flower market, a truly beautiful one, then across the bridge over the River Dambovita, which was always brown and dirty, and on to a very wide space with imposing buildings, one of which was the Opera House. That's where we got off.

A block away was the Consulate, standing in its own garden. There was always a doorman at the gate. He looked like a man but had a voice like a woman, and a podgy face, smooth like a baby's bottom. I was most intrigued. I discovered much later he was a eunuch. We came up a large staircase with very impressive striped burgundy-coloured wallpaper and were announced by the maid as we entered the beautiful living room. Mme la Consule was already seated behind a largish table, graciously pouring tea for her visitors. On the sofa by her side was her little dog. I was allowed to play with it.

One day I had to go to the toilet. From then on, Mme la Consule's toilet became my favourite place in the whole world. Just imagine, there was a huge bathroom with a marble sink, a big white bathtub with taps – you simply turned them and water ran from them, just like that! – wall-to-wall carpet, sweet-smelling soap in different colours and, in the middle of one wall, this throne. You went up three steps and sat on a bench padded in red velvet with a hole in the middle. From then on, Madame's tea, delicious pastries and even her dog lost all interest for me – all I wanted was to sit on that throne!

One afternoon Mme la Consule gave me a present, a lovely little red umbrella. It took my breath away. I would not part with it, not even to go to the bathroom, so I sat on the throne with my red umbrella open over my head and felt like a fairy tale princess. My beautiful umbrella had a sticky end though. My parents had friends called Colonel and Mrs Ignatov, who were refugees like us. The Colonel worked as a photographer at the Bucharest mental asylum. They had a son, Volodia, my age and we used to visit them in their apartment on the top floor of the asylum. I liked playing with Volodia and listening to his father playing the accordion. Besides, it was fascinating and also a bit scary to see the asylum inmates walking around the garden. These were the ones who were considered harmless; there were also some others who walked around the fenced-in compound dressed in long white shirts, and still others who hung onto the bars of their windows and yelled at those outside.

One day Volodia and I, sporting my open red umbrella, were walking down the path, minding our own business, when suddenly one of the inmates took umbrage at my umbrella, grabbed it out of my hand and beat me over the head with it until it broke. I cried for days.

Another time Volodia and I were naughty. We went nosing through the corridors of the big building, even though we were forbidden to do so. Somehow we lost our way and, hearing steps around the corner, dashed through the nearest door and quickly closed it behind us. The steps passed by, we relaxed and turned around to inspect the premises. It was the morgue. A couple of corpses lay on the tables. Panic! We heard steps again and threw ourselves under an empty table, hugging each other, shaking with fright. The steps stopped by the door, a key turned and the steps went away. Now we were locked in with the stiffs! We were in such a dreadful state when the grown-ups finally found us that we were not even punished.

Then there was another earthquake. This time we were all at home and I was curled up on my bed reading a fairy tale. Everything shook and swayed and the big wardrobe started to fall towards me. Papa must have been very strong – he checked the fall of the wardrobe halfway and held it there to give me time to get away. I was very impressed and kept telling everyone how strong my papa was.

My parents had friends who lived just outside Bucharest, by a river in a village called Chitila. Going there was great fun for me. I loved playing in the water and watching the grown-ups swim. They had funny outfits, or so I thought. The ladies had one-piece bathing costumes with pants that came below their knees, and sometimes with little skirts as well. One lady was very chic – she sploshed about in boots laced up to her knees, while making coy sounds and constantly adjusting her frilly bonnet, which had a big bow on the front. I thought she was smashing! The men? Well, I did not think much of them in their one-pieces down to their knees and hair all over!

I made frequent trips with my mother to pawnshops. The little jewellery she had managed to carry out of Russia in her hair kept going and coming back over the counter. A small haughty man with a pince-nez on his long nose kept the shop. On these occasions Mother was subdued, silent and sad, and she passed this mood on to me. Although I could not possibly understand why, I instinctively knew better than to ask her questions.

Gradually my parents made new friends or re-met old ones, mostly from among the other navy men who had escaped to Romania, but also among Russians who happened to be living in the Romanian province of Bessarabia (now Moldova) at the time of the Russian Revolution and now lived peacefully on their properties, although in rather reduced circumstances.

We were invited to spend a summer holiday with one of these families and it was my first time in the real countryside (I had been too young to remember my grandparents' *dacha*). The trip by train from Bucharest to Bessarabia was a thrill. I sat with my nose glued to the window and marvelled at fields of corn, large sunflowers and deep green forests that flickered by the train window in quick succession. It seemed so adventurous to sleep the night on the hard bench in third class and to see the sunrise bathing the large horizon in pink mist. It made me daydream of enchanted things and cleaned my little mind of the sordidness of the factory yard. Inside I was exploding with joy.

We were met by a carriage with benches on three sides and drawn by two horses. The luggage loaded and secured, we started the hour's journey to our friends' estate. I was allowed to sit on the high bench with the coachman; I was delighted but a little alarmed too. From this unusual vantage point I surveyed the horses while holding on tight to the railings around the bench. One horse lifted its tail and noisily did its plop! I went red with embarrassment. The coachman winked at me, unwound the brakes, clicked his tongue at the horses and we were off. It did not seem to take long to get to the estate, along a little country road bordered with poppies, fields of corn, wheat and buckwheat.

We were greeted by the owners of the estate, the parents of Papa's friend, who was a former naval officer. They were adorable, warm people who made us feel welcome and at home. The house was a typical big Russian *dacha*, with very large terraces at the front and back. We lived on these terraces, eating at a very immaculately set table, and lounging around on comfortable garden furniture. The rooms were large and cool, and an atmosphere of happy serenity reigned over it all. There were lots of people, family and friends, including the daughter of my father's friend, who was my age and also called Irina. At mealtimes everyone was summoned by someone playing the bugle very loudly. We two Irinas were in constant competition to arrive at the kitchen first for the enjoyable task of blowing the bugle.

At the back was a farm, orchards and a vegetable garden. The farm was my favourite spot. I loved throwing grain to the chickens, and watching the pigs wallow in a mud patch and the ducks in the little pond. But I did have unfortunate encounters with a goat and a goose. The goat and I stood staring at each other, then it decided to take action. It charged me and butted me in the stomach, making me fall on my back. I lay in the grass a long time without moving, too scared to get up. As for the goose, it was so bad-tempered! It chased me around the farmyard until it caught up with me and bit my behind. I have never been near a goose since.

All too soon it was time to return to Bucharest and the factory. In town we met two other families. The two mothers were sisters, one married to a doctor and with two children, a girl my age and her younger brother. They had a German governess they called Schnooky – which impressed me greatly. The other sister was married to a Romanian cavalry officer and had a little son. We saw them often and I sometimes spent the night with them and joined them in their German lessons with Schnooky. She was nice but kept very strict discipline and one did not argue with her. Before going to bed, the kids all had a bath. The first time I sat in a real bath it was so wonderful I did not want to get out. The other attraction was a very big rocking horse; I would rock on it for hours until one of the other kids would start whimpering their protests and run to complain to Schnooky that I was not giving them their turn.

The kids' grandparents on their mother's side also lived in Bessarabia, and the following summer we were invited to stay with them all. Their estate was much bigger than the one we had stayed on the year before, with large stables for horses, carriages of all shapes and sizes, and an enormous underground larder filled with blocks of ice and stocked with so much food of all kinds that my mouth fell open when I first saw it.

They owned a big vineyard, and when we visited them the children were allowed to pick the grapes and eat as many as they wanted. I immediately made a pig of myself, eating and eating until I could no longer stand up. Then I lay down under another bunch of delicious black grapes and ate them too. Oh boy, was I sick that night!

Schnooky was in complete charge of us and organised our days. We rose early, washed and had breakfast, then trotted to the schoolroom and had a German lesson. After a few minutes' rest, long enough to eat some delicious fruit from the orchard, we went back to our long table and Schnooky taught us to do all sorts of things with whatever we had collected in the fields or the woods on our walk the afternoon before. That was great fun and we all loved it.

Mid-morning, Schnooky took us all to the riding ring just below the terrace. We played with a ball while we waited for the smallest boy's father, a Romanian cavalry officer, to give us each a riding lesson. He would appear, tall and strong, in his riding pants and high boots, a whip in his hand, his batman leading a saddled horse. The beast was enormous, white with grey spots, and I was as scared of it as I was of the man with the whip. First we just rode around on a lead, then soon afterwards on our own. We learned to trot and gallop. Towards the end of the session the saddle was removed and we each had to ride bareback and do a trick. By the side of the ring grew a big old oak tree with one long branch sticking out above the ring. We had to get into a kneeling position on the horse's back as the horse trotted around the ring. Then, as we reached the branch, we had to clasp it with both hands and let the horse trot away from under us. We then had to hang in the air until the horse came back under us, and drop back onto its back.

All went well until one morning, when I fell back from the branch onto the horse's back just at the moment one of the other kids threw their ball into the air. The horse promptly bolted and ran out of the ring towards the stables with me hanging under its belly. I was properly shocked, to say the least. In spite of my protests, the horse and I were brought back to the ring immediately and I had to do the trick with that tree branch once more. Swallowing my tears, with hatred in my heart for the man with the whip, I did it all in silence, shaking with fear. But from then on those riding lessons lost all charm for me, and I have never lost my fear of horses.

Our lunch, which we ate separately from the grown-ups, occasionally ended with homemade ice-cream, which we were allowed to eat only when it was almost melted on our plate, for fear we should get sore throats if we ate it sooner! After lunch we had to go to bed and rest for an hour, which was a monumental bore. The other kids would immediately fall asleep, leaving me wide awake, thinking up fantastic and improbable stories. An hour later, Schnooky would reappear, tidy us up and take us for a long walk, sometimes with some of the grown-ups. Someone would start a song and all would join in. We would go to the woods to gather mushrooms or pick wildflowers in the fields and collect funny-shaped twigs, stones and acorns. We would return to the house happy and starving, have a wash, eat supper, play for a bit and off to bed.

One day, though, I rebelled. I did not pay attention during the morning lesson, and my thoughts were far away at that other Bessarabian summer, where there was no governess, where I had freedom to roam, where I did not have to rest after lunch or mount detestable horses. Schnooky got annoyed with me. I got annoyed with everybody. So on the way to the riding ring I snuck onto the terrace, got out at the other end, made for the orchard, climbed a plum tree and hid at the top, treating myself to its juicy fruit. I heard Schnooky calling me but I did not respond. More voices called. I did not respond. Now some grown-ups were searching for me. I could see them from the top of my tree. I just picked another plum and stuffed it in my mouth, the juice dribbling from my chin and onto my clothes. Then I saw Papa coming down the orchard, calling my name. I sat still. Papa lifted his head and saw me. Filthy dirty and red in the face, I had to make my way down the tree, ripping some of my clothing in the process. I was not popular for the rest of that day, definitely in the doghouse with everyone. Well, that's life.

All the following winter, Father worked very hard, bringing home work to do at night. I suppose he was trying to make enough money to send Mother and me to Constanza, a resort town on the Black Sea where we stayed as paying guests the following summer with some other friends of my parents who lived there. Father joined us a bit later then went back to work, letting us stay on a little longer. It was my first sight of the sea. I could not understand how there could be so much water and why it was so salty and so beautiful.

I immediately adored the lady of the house, whom I came to call 'Mamotschka Tania', and we became fast friends. I corresponded with her for the next fifty-eight years until her death. I never saw her again after the age of seven-and-a-half; although I dearly wanted to go back to Romania after the war just to see her, something always prevented me from going.

There was the most beautiful beach at nearby Mamaia, with mountains of white sand. I had a great time playing there with two new friends, Russian boys who were always around. Again, I got myself into trouble. One day, walking along a railway track with the boys, I found a packet of cigarettes on the ground. We decided to smoke one. I pinched some matches from my mother's bag and we retired to a secluded spot and lit a cigarette each. In no time at all one of the boys started to vomit. Then the other one followed suit. I was fine. I cannot say that I enjoyed my first smoke, not really, but I was fine. However, I threw the rest of the pack into the bushes. Back home, I rinsed my mouth with Mother's cologne, which made me really sick – big mistake; you live and learn. The rest of the day went on peacefully and I slept through the night, unworried by thoughts of tomorrow.

Next day all hell broke loose. One of the boys had been sick all night and had told his parents I made him smoke. The parents arrived, kicking up a stink and yelling that I was corrupting their little darling. Mother was persuaded that I had stolen her cigarettes and that I had lied about finding them on the ground, and I ended up being spanked and punished. I felt there was no justice in this world, no friends and no point telling the truth. From then on I decided to trust no-one and never tell the truth. It took many long years for me to trust again and stop lying.

That autumn my parents decided it was time for me to go to school, and enrolled me in a school near enough for me to walk. I looked forward to it out of curiosity and the thrill of putting on the school uniform, which consisted of a blue dress with white cuffs and collar, and a black bibbed apron tied at the back with a bow. Around my neck I wore a ribbon in the three colours of the Romanian national flag – red, yellow and blue – from which hung a two-inch cross with the name of the school written on it. In summer we wore white linen hats, in winter navy ones with the school badge on. Father bought me a satchel, a pencil box and exercise books. Mother labelled the books for me, attached blotting paper and covered them in thick blue paper.

When the big day finally arrived I got up very early, too excited to sleep. Once I was rigged up in my uniform, very proud, satchel in my hand, Mother took me to school. I waved goodbye to her at the gate and stepped into a courtyard full of noisy and unknown faces. *No, no, I mustn't cry. I'm a big girl now.*

I did not cry. I moved to one side of the courtyard, put my satchel on the ground and waited. *What next?* A few ladies came out and took their positions in front of the big school building. The lady in the middle I recognised as the one who had filled in my enrolment papers when Mother took me in for the interview a few weeks before the beginning of term. She was the headmistress. On a chain around her neck hung a whistle, which she blew long and loud. All chattering stopped and everyone turned to face her, standing very still. She pronounced a few words of greeting, then said she hoped everyone had had a splendid holiday and was ready to apply themselves to some good work and their studies. I noticed a few girls making faces behind other girls' backs. Then she called out the new girls' names and told them to come forward. *Here we go*, I thought, embarrassed to death, going redder and redder, feeling dozens and dozens of pairs of eyes scrutinising me. I approached the headmistress along with the other new girls, who were just as miserable as I was. Another whistle and the remaining girls fell into columns of two abreast in front of their respective class mistresses. We, the new miseries, were directed to our columns and, in total silence, class by class, the children entered the building, hung their hats on pegs and walked up a wide staircase to their classrooms.

I was directed to a desk at the back of the room, which I was to share with another girl. As we emptied our satchels and arranged our books inside the desk, my hand holding open the desk slipped and the lid fell and hit the fingers on my other hand. It was painful, vexing and produced delighted giggles from my beastly neighbours. I wished I had never been born.

I cannot recall our class mistress at all, what she was like or what she looked like. Strange! But I remember very vividly three of our teachers. There was the priest who told us stories from the Bible and made me wonder and daydream about what he said for the rest of the day – he was so kind, cosy and approachable. There was the German mistress, who was tall, thin, middle-aged, like dry toast, with fuzzy wisps of blonde hair and a very bad temper. However, I did not fare too badly with her; the German lessons from Schnooky stood me in good stead and most of the time she left me alone. On one occasion, she even said, '*Sehr gut*' (Very good).

The French teacher was more than my favourite, I adored her. In short, I had a crush on her. She was young and very pretty, with dark hair and a lovely petite figure. Always beautifully dressed, she oozed femininity, charm and kindness. I would have done anything for her – jumped out of the window if she asked me to, but she never did. The next best way to show her my love was to reach the top of her class. I promptly did so and, until the day I left that school, I was always first in French.

I liked school – it took me away from home for the best part of the day. I also liked it because I enjoyed learning new things and because I loved my French teacher. Unfortunately, I made no friends among the girls at school, not one. I was a foreigner, and in some spheres foreigners were not popular. My deep, inborn shyness also prevented me from even trying to break through the barrier of being different. Of course I did not understand or yet know the meaning of racism, I just felt unwanted by the little Romanian girls. It did not really bother me. I never really suffered from it. I just retreated more and more into my own world of daydream and fantasy.

Although we were little, we were given a great amount of home-work each day. That, on top of the unavoidable Russian lessons with Mother after school, kept me busy until bedtime, so my fun and games with Didina in the factory courtyard were drastically reduced, and I must say I missed her and the antics of her two sisters.

One day when I did manage to get away from my studies for a moment, Didina and I sat at the top of the plum tree, stuffing ourselves with the unripe fruit and competing as to who could spit the stones furthest from the tree. Didina informed me that when we got older we would bleed once a month. I was horrified at this prospect, choked on the plum and almost fell off the tree. But then curiosity took over and I plied Didina with questions, to which she replied with misinformation and gruesome answers. Fascinating!

I could hardly wait for our next visit to my 'posh' (well, they had a governess) friends to prove to my little girlfriend how knowing I was about life! When I told her, she burst into tears and rushed to her mother. She came back sniffing and was not friendly – she did not even demand her turn on the rocking horse. My mother was not friendly either. What had I done now? The rest of the day at home was heavy with silence. My parents whispered in the kitchen. I felt guilty without knowing why. Thankfully bedtime came and I turned my face to the wall, pretending to be asleep. I felt Papa standing by my bed looking at me, then he said softly, 'Irischka, I know you're not asleep. I want to talk to you.' *Whatever it is, here it comes*, I thought to myself as I sat up in bed and faced Papa. 'Tell me now,' he said, 'what did you tell the little girl this afternoon and where did you get it from?' So I had to tell Papa.

'Is it not true then?' I added as I finished.

'Yes, it is true. But you're too young to know about these things. It's most unfortunate. Now I feel I must tell you how and why this thing happens to ladies, because the information you got from Didina is somewhat wrong.'

As Papa proceeded to explain to me the workings of female anatomy, I could feel his deep embarrassment and distaste at having to talk to me about it. As he finished he said, 'Now I don't want you ever to speak to anyone about this subject. It's unattractive and dirty.' Mother never said a word. The incident was closed. But was it really? Some seven years later I found myself in that 'unattractive', 'dirty' predicament and was in a disgusted despair. I tried to hide the fact. I was ashamed. Later, when normal sexual feelings started to awaken in me, that too, because it was connected with the same part of my body, became in my mind something to be ashamed of. It took a very long time before I could accept womanhood and all the natural instincts in a normal simple way, and find in them tenderness, love and beauty.

FIRST BALLET LESSONS

*M*y mother's dream, her love, her passion, was ballet. Because she came from an upper-class family, she had not been allowed to become a dancer herself – to appear on stage was out of the question. Now that she was in exile from her homeland and had lost the social status she had known from birth, there was no earthly reason to prevent her from transposing her dreams onto me and living through me. She was determined that I, her daughter, would become a ballerina.

'Ballerina?' I queried. 'What is that?'

I was soon to find out – if not what a ballerina was, at least what kind of bewilderment would be produced by my first lesson in an art I had never seen with a finished product I could not imagine.

It was 1927 and I was almost seven-and-a-half years old. My teacher, Mme Majaiska, had been a member of the *corps de ballet* in the Maryinsky Theatre Ballet. Refugees like us, Mme Majaiska and her husband lived in a one-room house at the other end of Bucharest. In that room, where one could not swing a cat, I received my first ballet instruction. For my first exercises at the barre, I held onto the small kitchen table. Two other girls, both older than me, also participated in the lessons. For the exercises away from the barre we used the small space between the table, the bed and the two chairs. Mme Majaiska and my mother sat on top of the bed like Turks, my mother humming some tunes to give us rhythm and tempo.

What did I think of all these capers? Not much. To be perfectly honest, I did not like it at all, although I had no difficulty turning my toes and heels out, keeping my knees straight and pointing my toes. I could not see any sense in what I was learning nor to what end I was made to move in such a strange, boring, ridiculous way. And I missed the fun of climbing trees with Didina.

Another aggravation was that whenever we returned home from a lesson, my mother would check how well I had listened to Mme Majaiska's instructions and corrections. It was like an examination after each lesson, and if it turned out that I had been inattentive or absentminded, Mother would punish me. To avoid this most unpleasant experience, I tried my very best to be a model pupil. I now bless my mother for her severity, insistence and determination to make me take up ballet. In time, I came to love and respect it, and I worked hard at it, fiercely and willingly. But in those early days it seemed that I was really only a lottery ticket clutched in Mother's hand – it was yet to be seen if she clutched a winner.

One day after a class at Mme Majaiska's, Mother was displeased with me. 'Why do you not express anything?' she asked. 'Why this po-face? Why don't you ever smile?' I did not know what to say. I felt scared and my mind went blank. 'Answer me!' Mother shouted. Tears filled my eyes as I stared at her in silence. 'Idiot, idiot, idiot,' yelled Mother, and I got a whacking.

I was gulping, crying, choking. When my crying stopped, I lay in the corner on the floor, hiccupping, not knowing whether to stay there, get up or what. After a while, out of the corner of my eye, I saw Mother fill a washbasin with cold water. She then ordered me to undress and stand in the basin. It was cold in the room and my teeth were chattering, but I did what I was told. Mother started to sponge my body and my face. Then she dried me and told me to dress and sit quietly and read my Pushkin book.

These episodes were to recur from time to time, and I considered myself lucky when only my face was slapped, which was the way Mother usually expressed her anger. Each time, I expressed my misery and humiliation in tears and hiccups. I was never smacked in front of my father, so I sensed that I should hide my heavy heart when he was around. When he came home from work I would set my face into a permanent smile, which must have looked odd, because Mother would hiss at me when Father was out of earshot, 'Stop making that idiotic face!' I do not know if Father ever noticed anything, but the long silences between my parents became more frequent and I felt like it was all my fault.

But things were not always bad. Sometimes there was laughter and my heart would leap with joy. One day when Mother was pleased with me after my ballet lesson, I told Papa excitedly that I had learned to do a *grand jeté* (a large leaping movement from one extended leg to the other) and demonstrated it in the space between our two rooms. 'Great!' said Papa. 'Now let me try it.' It was very funny and, as he jumped, his slipper flew out of the window. I was in stitches and so was Mother. We had such a nice evening.

One day, on our way to my ballet class, Mother pointed out a poster with great excitement. It announced the forthcoming appearances of Tamara Karsavina with her dancing partner, Keith Lester. Mother explained to me that Tamara Karsavina had been a great ballerina in Russia before she, too, left because of the Revolution. She said I simply had to see Karsavina perform. That evening Mother told Papa all about it, and Papa said he would do his best to buy us some tickets. He did, my wonderful papa, and I could hardly wait for the great day, when I would discover what a theatre was and what a ballerina was.

When the day finally arrived I could hardly contain my excitement. The hours at school dragged on and I could not concentrate. My parents were just as excited as I was. They had seen Mme Karsavina dance at the Maryinsky Theatre in St Petersburg before the Revolution, and this would be their first theatre outing since we had become refugees. It was a red-letter day for all of us.

Putting on our best clothes to go to the theatre was great fun. Mama had made me a beautiful outfit: a wide skirt in navy velvet, a white blouse and a navy bolero. She was a good seamstress, and I thought I looked smashing. Mama herself looked beautiful and Papa very handsome. As we walked down the street to catch our tram, I placed myself between them and held their hands. I felt proud and happy.

When we got off the tram, I could hardly stop myself running towards the theatre, which I could see a short distance away. Crowds of people, oh so beautifully dressed, were streaming through the big open doors and I was agog. When we were finally in our seats I stared around the vast (or so it seemed to me) auditorium. Its red plush seats and boxes seemed to me to be occupied by very important people.

'But where will Mme Karsavina dance?' I asked Papa.

'You see that big curtain in front of you and the orchestra pit below it? When the musicians come and take their places, the lights in the auditorium will go off, the lights called footlights in front of the curtain will go on, the conductor will take his place and the overture will begin. Then the big curtain will part and you will see the stage – a big space – and that's where Karsavina will dance. Here, see, the lights are dimming and here comes the conductor. Now sit down, Irischka. Can you see?'

'Yes,' I murmured as the orchestra struck up the overture. It made me jump and almost fall off my seat; I had not expected such a volume of noise.

At the end of the overture the great curtain slowly parted, and to a thunder of applause Karsavina appeared. She was a vision of beauty, magic and light, and seemed unreal. I was transfixed, overwhelmed. To this day I remember it all like photographic snapshots, which have not faded with the passage of time: Karsavina's solo variation, a stylised Russian dance on points, her costume a knee-length tutu, beautifully embroidered, with a Russian boyar *kokoshnik* (headdress) on her beautiful head. Her smile was dazzling and her gaiety infectious.

I can still see her classical *pas de deux* with Keith Lester too – it bowled me over. I had never imagined that a man could dance like that, look like that, hold and lift his partner like a magician. It was all so wonderful. Walking out of the theatre I was in a daze, full of new, beautiful impressions, the magic of Mme Karsavina and my amazement at Keith Lester.

On our way home from the theatre, Mama kept telling me that if I worked hard at my ballet lessons, one day I might, like Karsavina, dance in theatres all over the world. I still did not understand what she was on about, because I could not at all connect what I was doing at my ballet lessons – hanging onto the kitchen table while Mme Majaiska and Mama sat on the bed singing – with the magic and beauty I had seen that evening. There was no connection at all, I decided. My poor mama was going cuckoo.

But my dreams were sweet that night – in them Karsavina was dancing. From that day on, for all of my life, I have loved ballet.

FIRST PERFORMANCES

Not long after, a great excitement came into our dreary lives – a concert and ball in Constanza for the benefit of invalid Russian refugees in helpless circumstances. The idea came from the Russian refugees who lived in Constanza, some of whom were navy people and friends of my parents. The grown-ups often gathered at our place to discuss their various plans, and I listened to their conversations from my bed, spellbound. The director of the casino in Constanza had kindly agreed to donate the ballroom, which also had a stage. But who would perform? It was out of the question and financially impossible to approach professional artists, so the entertainment would have to be provided by willing, enthusiastic amateurs who were armed with homemade costumes and a rich imagination.

Papa volunteered to design sets and make props. Mama was thrilled to be able to perform, and was to sing with some of the men. The men decided to form a choir, and a Russian professional soprano who lived in Constanza was also keen to participate, as was Colonel Ignatov who was an amateur but virtuoso accordion player. The concert would have to be held during the summer months, when the men could take two weeks' holiday from their jobs, and when the tourists would flock to Constanza and the beautiful nearby beach of Mamaia.

At one of the evening gatherings, Mama suddenly had an idea. From my bed in the adjoining room I faintly heard her saying my name in an excited voice. Sleep flew out the window and I sat up in bed, listening intently.

'Wouldn't that be wonderful?' Mother was saying. 'Irina could perform three dances, two on her toes – she's already quite good on her toes, she has strong ankles. Mme Majaiska could devise two variations for her, and the third number should be a *kazachok*' (a Russian folkdance) 'with Volodia – he can do the *prisyatki*' (squatting dance) 'very well – and I'll arrange the dance.'

'But what about the music?' Papa queried.

'The Colonel will play for them on his accordion.'

'But Irischka is quite shy. She might not want to perform,' I heard Papa say.

'I do, I do, I do,' I screamed, and everyone burst into laughter.

Mama came to my bed beaming and gave me a hug and a kiss. I felt so happy that she was pleased with me.

'I'll make your costumes and Papa will decorate them with glittering paints. It will be such fun!'

'Oh yes,' I murmured. 'Fun!'

'Now, go to sleep. We'll talk about it all tomorrow.'

Sleep eluded me now though. I was too excited about the concert and by the fact that Mama had hugged me. It felt so good – I longed for her to hug me again. If I tried hard to please her in the concert, maybe she would.

The next day, as soon as I came home from school, Mama and I set off to Mme Majaiska to tell her about my forthcoming performance and to ask her to arrange two dances for me. She readily agreed.

For music, Madame suggested Delibes' 'Pizzicato' from *Sylvia* and a nocturne by Anton Rubinstein. She hummed the music to us – between alternating fits of asthmatic coughs and puffs on her brown cigarettes, whose smell hung heavy in the small room. Luckily Mama knew the tunes and could hum them while Madame started to devise the dances on me. For the first time, I enjoyed going to her classes, because they ended in her taking me through my dances, which was quite different from doing exercises while hanging onto the kitchen table or doing combinations in the middle of the room and trying to avoid the chairs and bed.

I took to my recently acquired toe shoes like a duck to water and had no difficulty getting up onto my toes. The very next time we went to spend Sunday with the Ignatovs, Volodia and I did not go roaming around the nuthouse in the afternoon but rehearsed instead. The Colonel played for my two dances on his accordion – which sounded so wonderful that it made my insides bubble – and Volodia was agog seeing me on my toes, while our parents smiled their approval. I was enjoying myself and did not once think about Didina or wish for her company. It was then time for Volodia to join in and for Mama to teach us the *kazachok*. The Colonel's accordion burst into the gay tune and Mama executed the dance to show us how it was done. She was terrific – full of spirit and animation. Volodia was shy at first but soon took up the general enthusiasm, and we learned the dance in no time. Everyone was pleased, including Mama, and I wondered if I might get a hug that night. I do not remember if I did.

Mama bought some tarlatan (stiff open-weave muslin) at the market to make me tutus: yellow for 'Pizzicato' and black for the nocturne. She also bought some red cloth to make me a *sarafan* (a traditional Russian pinafore dress) to wear for the *kazachok*. Volodia's mother made him a Russian shirt and *sharavary* (baggy knee-length pants), with which he wore his shiny knee-high boots.

For 'Pizzicato' Papa made me a lovely wreath of yellow flowers as a headdress. He decorated the black tutu with painted glittering stars and made me a headdress with a crescent moon. He painted folkloric motifs on the Russian costume and on my *babushka* headscarf. When they were ready I tried them on in front of the mirror; if I overlooked my pointed elbows and one skinned knee, I thought I looked smashing!

The grown-ups rehearsed at each others' houses in the evenings, but the Russian Church allowed the choir to rehearse in the church hall. Rehearsals were also going on in Constanza, and a few days before the event everyone was to gather there for the final rehearsals and staging. Everyone had three months in which to save enough money for their train tickets (third class, naturally). It was a day and night trip to get there, and then we would be lodged with local Russian families. My parents and I were going to stay at the same place we had stayed the winter before. I was looking forward to seeing Mamotschka Tania, basking in her warmth and kindness, and playing with her fox terrier, Pic, whom I adored and who slept on my bed.

Meanwhile, there was also excitement in our backyard, near the overflowing and overpowering garbage corner. Didina and her friends from the tenement down the street were planning a performance of their own. Their idea was triggered by my accounts to Didina of Mme Karsavina's concert, and by our preparations for the grand occasion in Constanza. Didina and her friends invented comic sketches at their parents' suggestion. I offered to dance my 'Pizzicato' but they met my offer with suspicion and some reservations.

'You'll have to show us first what you do in this "pizzi-something",' said the tallest girl, who seemed to be in command.

'You can't dance without music,' put in the little fat girl.

'I can hum it to you and you can all learn it and be my orchestra,' I responded, and proceeded to sing them the melody. I got an instant response.

'Shit, it sounds terrible,' they chorused.

'It's not shit, it's Delibes,' I protested.

'What's Delibes?'

'*Vai de capul meu*' (Oh, my poor head) I retorted. 'You are an ignorant lot.'

'And you're a dirty *rusoika*' (Russian).

I went red with rage and was about to hit the tall girl, but Didina stepped between us, yelling, 'Stop, stop, don't fight! We'll get in trouble.' Didina was right. We backed off, glaring at each other.

'You can take your fucking dance somewhere else. We don't want you in our performance,' snapped the tall girl.

I turned to Didina. 'What is fucking?' She obligingly informed me. I was stunned, disgusted and bewildered. Thus I learned how babies are made. *Ai!* I needed time to digest this information.

I turned my back on them all and marched away. In the days that followed I hid around the corner in the late afternoon and watched them rehearsing by the garbage bins. In one particular sketch, a huge cardboard spider dangled above the heads of a couple supposedly having dinner, then landed on their plates. Didina wore one of her big sisters' dresses and copied all her sisters' mannerisms – I thought it very amusing. The little fat girl, dressed as a man with a painted moustache, was hysterically funny as she tried to catch the spider. They had rigged up a curtain using two sheets that had seen better days strung on a rope, one end attached to Didina's hut, the other to the tall fence.

At the end of the sketch, they closed the sheets across the garbage corner (the stage) and there was a pause while they removed the props. Now I saw a way to show the gang that I was not to be dismissed so easily. Behind the chairs they had arranged for parents to sit on there was a strip of concrete. I was determined to perform my dance there.

The day of the performance by the garbage bins arrived. It was due to start when all the fathers had returned from work, so there was plenty of time for me to come back from my ballet class, drink my detestable glass of milk and be allowed out into the yard. I stood around the corner from where the crowd had gathered and awaited my chance. '*Messieurs et Mesdames*,' I shouted, running onto the concrete strip. (I thought getting attention in French was more classy.) All heads turned and I announced, 'Now I shall dance for you.' Singing the tune at the top of my voice, I attacked my 'Pizzicato'. I could see puzzled expressions on the audience's faces, replaced by broad smiles, then giggles and laughter when my singing became a farce. I carried on to the end and finished with a flourish, keeping the pose still as Mme Majaiska had taught me. The applause was thunderous. As I made my curtsy, I caught sight of the tall girl's furious face watching me through the sheets. I could not resist sticking my tongue out at her as I ran back to my side of the yard and out of sight.

That night I lay in bed: *So, they laughed at me. They thought I was funny. It's vexing, but they also applauded, which means they liked me.* It was strange and confusing, but in any case I had got my own back!

The much-awaited day arrived when everyone gathered at the railway station to travel to Constanza. Vania Zabeline, 'Uncle Vania' to me and one of my favourites among my parents' friends, whisked me away to go and inspect the steam engine. How big and mighty she looked; she hissed periodically, letting off great puffs of steam from her underbelly. Uncle Vania was my special friend after my papa. In exile he had become a jockey in trotting races and married a Romanian lady. She was nice, jolly and made scrumptious chips, which I thought the best food in the world. He gave out free passes on the Sundays he was in the races and I would cheer him on, willing him to come first. It was all so exciting at the racecourse, and there was always a big plate of chips to look forward to at the end of the day. Uncle Vania told me stories of life on a battleship, of big storms and waves as tall as houses. He played catchings with me in the yard using a ball he had given me – it was my treasured possession.

The third-class carriages in the train had thick, hard wooden benches, which were agony for bums on long journeys, but I was happy sitting between Papa and Uncle Vania and listening to their stories about the passing panorama as we sped into the night. We arrived in Constanza the following afternoon. As the train pulled into the station, I spotted Mamotschka Tania, who had brought Pic with her to greet me. It was a happy day.

The next day everyone gathered at the casino to start putting the performance together. I had the time of my life watching Papa making the props, and observing the rehearsals on the stage. Mother was in her element, fully participating in the staging of the show. She took particular care rehearsing Volodia and me, working out where we and the Colonel should be and doing the lighting with Papa. She was happy, kind and helpful.

On the afternoon before the concert, after the run-through in the morning, I was told to rest, but I could not relax. The anticipation was too great and the butterflies in my stomach were fluttering quite a bit. I lay on my bed going over my two variations, reminding myself to point my toes, stretch my knees, make my arms and my body from the waist up sing with the music. That's what Mme Majaiska had told me to remember. 'How can my arms sing?' I had asked her.

'Listen to the music with all your being and they will,' she replied.

It all seemed so difficult! I glanced at Pic. He was asleep, curled by my side, with no worries. *Happy little fella. Lucky doggy! He doesn't have butterflies in his stomach.*

Later Papa came to fetch me and then I felt reassured and started to look forward to the performance. It was fun backstage – people putting on make-up, asking each other for advice, getting into their costumes, shouting and laughing.

Mama was looking beautiful in her costume for the Don Cossack's beloved in the song 'Volga, Volga', which tells the story of an *ataman* (chief), his Cossacks and the beloved in a boat. The men are singing 'Volga, Volga'. At the end of the song, the River Volga gets stormy and the boat is in danger of sinking. To lighten the load, the *ataman* throws the beloved overboard as a pacifying present to the Volga. What a cheery tale! But Mama looked beautiful and Papa had made a splendid boat and waves on the mighty river. The lighting effects made the storm look quite real, but I wished that Mama was not thrown out, even though she landed on a mattress hidden behind the boat.

Mama got me ready for my first variation, the 'Pizzicato'. The show was about to start, so Papa took me into the wings to watch. Holding onto his arm, I did some *échappés* (jumps in which the feet spring apart from a closed to an open position) to warm up as I waited my turn. While my stage fright mounted, Colonel Ignatov appeared on the stage with his accordion, sat down and made me a sign to run in and pause in the centre.

'*Ne poohoo ne pera*' ('No down, no feathers', the Russian way of saying 'Break a leg') whispered Papa.

'*S Bogom*' (Go with God) said Mama, appearing from nowhere.

I ran in, all fear gone as if by magic, and happily started my variation. At the end I was rewarded by long and loud applause. Elated, and grateful that the audience had not found me funny, I hurried to Mama to change into my black tutu for my second number, while the Colonel kept playing on his accordion.

My second variation met with the same loud approval from the audience. Now totally relaxed and happy, I had plenty of time to change into my Russian costume – our *kazachok* was the last item on the program. I was looking forward to my jolly dance with Volodia. Jolly it was! As the Colonel's accordion gaily attacked the tune, I dashed in first, then Volodia had to run in. He did, but slipped and fell, skidding on his bum. Jumping up, he burst into tears and ran off stage. I started laughing and the Colonel roared, 'Go get him!'

I did. I dragged Volodia back on stage and whispered, 'Dance or I'll kill you!' Volodia resisted. The audience was roaring with laughter. '*Dourak!*' (Stupid) I went on. 'Make them think you're meant to fall. It's a comic dance. Wipe your nose on your sleeve and let's start.' To make my words more convincing, I pinched his arm.

It worked. He danced with gusto and his *prisyatki* drew loud applause. We were a big success. As we took our bows, I was presented with a big doll, Volodia with a big basketful of toys.

Then we stayed on for the ball, having the time of our life watching the grown-ups and giggling. But all good things come to an end. Too soon for my liking, we were back on the train to Bucharest.

GOODBYE BUCHAREST, HELLO PARIS

Mme Majaiska told Mama she thought I had potential as a ballerina, but that if I stayed with her, she would ruin me. If Mama wanted me to continue my ballet studies seriously, she said, she should take me to Paris to study with Mme Olga Preobrajenska. What great honesty on the part of Mme Majaiska! I am eternally grateful to her for it.

But now Papa had a difficult decision to make. He and Mama discussed the matter for several evenings and I was all ears. For Papa it meant struggling all over again in a new country, finding a job, plunging once more into the unknown. There was also the question of obtaining visas to enter and reside in France. As Russian refugees, we had been issued with Nansen papers, but we had no passports. Nansen papers were looked upon with suspicion by many countries. It was also difficult to obtain the transit visas necessary to travel through the other countries on the way to France – Hungary, Austria and Germany. Then there was the question of money. Train tickets for a three-day journey were not cheap, even in third class. And then we would have to survive until Papa found a job.

Not long after, Papa came home from work looking determined. 'Irischka, you must have a chance in life,' he said. 'We shall go to Paris, God willing.'

They started saving every penny possible and, in between his extra work, Papa made the round of consulates, obtaining the necessary visas. Mama was in a good mood; our Russian dictations went smoothly and I even enjoyed the extra French she started to teach me. They decided that Papa would go to Paris alone, find work and then send for Mama and me. Luckily, the factory boss allowed Mama and me to remain in our lodgings until we departed. He was obviously a kind man who appreciated and liked Papa.

Weeks went by but finally the day came for Papa's departure, and we saw him off at the railway station. As I hugged him goodbye, I felt devastated by the fear of never seeing him again and burst into tears. I hung onto him and would not let go. Papa promised that we would join him soon, soon, until my tears subsided into hiccups and I let go of his neck. The carriage door slammed shut, a whistle blew, we gave a last wave, and Papa was gone. I felt sad and worried remaining alone with Mama.

The next day, Mama came with me to school to tell the headmistress that I would be leaving in the near future. As I followed my class mistress up the large staircase with my classmates, we heard raised voices angrily shouting at each other. The door to the headmistress's study flew open just as we went past, and my furious-looking mother emerged, shouting over her shoulder, 'You are an uncultured, stupid woman!'

The headmistress's voice replied from within the study, 'And you are an idiot to want your daughter to take up such a disreputable profession when she could be a schoolteacher.'

'It's you who's an idiot!' shouted Mother. Then she caught sight of me. 'Irina, come here immediately,' she said. 'We're going home.'

Red with embarrassment, I obeyed. She almost dragged me down the staircase to the courtyard and out on to the street, then she stopped to catch her breath and looked me up and down, muttering, 'You, a schoolteacher? Ha! Over my dead body!'

She took my hand and we walked home. My Romanian education was over, but now that I was at home all day, Mama's Russian lessons were longer and she made me read Pushkin's poems and Gogol's short stories aloud. I enjoyed that very much – it fed my fantasies and made my own dream world more exciting.

In the afternoons Mama attacked me with French verbs. That was not exciting at all. I could hardly wait to escape to the yard and join Didina up the tree. I missed Papa and looked out for the postman every day in the hope of a letter from him telling us to join him in Paris. And finally it came. What joy!

Mme la Consule gave me a present, a little suitcase all of my own, to carry my books and treasures. It was all so thrilling. The day before our departure I went to say goodbye to Didina and her sisters. That was sad; I was so fond of them. I often wonder now what became of Didina, my only real childhood friend. A special place in my heart is hers forever.

On the day of our departure, Uncle Vania arrived with a horse and carriage to take us to the railway station and install us on the Trans European Express. There were no reserved places in third class, so one had to come early to grab seats by the window. After lifting our cases onto the racks, Uncle Vania kissed us goodbye fondly and gave me a packet of sweets. Dear Uncle Vania – I did not realise then that I would never see him again. The door slammed shut, the whistle blew and the train, gathering speed, was on its way to Paris. With my nose glued to the window, I thought to myself: *Paris! In three days, we'll be in Paris and I shall see my papa!*

'What are you smiling at?' asked Mama.

It was still daylight when the Carpathian Mountains, the first real mountains I ever saw, came into view. I was much impressed. I remember our picnic basket packed with food for three days – bread, sausages, hard-boiled eggs and fruit. Water was available in the carriage corridor. I also remember the couple in our compartment; they were very friendly and offered us some of their cheese. Mama then offered them some of our sausages. When night came, the man put the suitcases between the benches so we could lie down, head on one bench, feet on the other, body on the suitcase. We rolled up our coats for pillows. I slept like a log, waking only occasionally, when the train jerked or the man snored loudly.

I was terribly excited as we pulled into a big station and I saw a board saying 'Vienna'. 'Mama, Mama, we're in Vienna!' I cried. 'That's where the waltzes come from.' I still love waltzes. The train stopped there for an hour, so everyone got out and stretched their legs on the platform. People with trolleys laden with delicious-looking pastries, buns, sandwiches and coffee, walked up and down the platform selling their wares. Mama bought me a great big bun and herself some coffee – she even let me have a sip, my first taste of coffee. As we strolled on the platform, I kept looking at the boards saying 'Vienna' and felt very proud that I could now say to everyone that I had been there, if only inside the railway station.

Then it was time to get back on. The door slammed, a whistle blew and we were on the last leg to Paris. Next day, as we approached our destination, the sky turned heavy grey and it poured with rain. I was getting impatient – soon, soon I would see my papa. And there he was on the platform, just under our window. I could not contain my joy and ran along the corridor towards the exit, bumping into people. I jumped onto the platform and hung on Papa's neck. A porter took our luggage and Papa hailed a taxi.

'What's that, a taxi?' I asked.

'A car that you can hire to take you where you want to go,' Papa explained.

'What, no horse and carriage?'

'No,' Papa smiled. 'It's different here. They even have trains running underground all over Paris – they call it the Metro.'

On the way to our apartment in a place Papa called Buttes-Chaumont, Papa explained that it was only small and cheap. We had one room, a sink and a stove, and it would have to do until he found a better paid job. At that time he was working in the printing business and looking for something better.

When we got to the apartment it was dark and raining. The room was very small – a double bed, a camp bed for me, a table I had to climb under to get to my bed and two chairs. There were hooks for hanging up our clothes, a sink in a small recess, and a two-plate gas cook top on the shelf. The communal toilet was on the landing.

We brushed our teeth in the sink, but to wash our bodies we had to go to the public baths once a week. There was no money for three baths, so we shared a cubicle. The attendant filled the tub and locked the taps, then I washed first, followed by Mama, and then Papa inherited our far-from-limpid bath. Not nice! But when you are poor, you can't be choosy.

Papa had found out the address of Mme Preobrajenska's studio and had found me a district school not far from the hotel. The morning after our arrival, Mother, not wasting any time, took me on the Metro to the Place de l'Opéra – Papa had explained to her how to get there. Mme Preobrajenska gave classes in a big studio on the top floor of the Théâtre Olympia. We were told that she gave two classes in the afternoon, and that if we wanted to see her we would have to wait for the last class to finish. As we waited, we could hear a piano behind the closed doors of the studio. *Hmm*, I thought. *Mama won't have to hum the tunes. Here they have a pianist.*

Over the sound of the piano, a loud, irritated voice shouted something, correcting a student. I started to feel intimidated and did not look forward to meeting Madame. Finally, the door of the studio opened and the students filed out, chatting happily, their faces covered in beads of perspiration. A few mothers emerged and eyed Mama and me with unrestrained curiosity.

We were shown into the studio and I was taken aback by its vastness: there were barres along three walls and the fourth wall was a solid mirror – a far cry from Mme Majaiska's small room in Bucharest. A tiny lady came towards us; her manner was reserved but not unfriendly. I stared at her as only children can stare, in awe of this great, legendary ballerina of whom I had heard so much from my parents. After exchanging greetings with my mother, Madame turned to me.

'Why do you stare at me like that?' she asked in a gruff voice.

I blushed to the roots of my hair, but her face suddenly lit up with a kind and mischievous smile and she stroked my hair. This kind gesture and her beautiful smile went straight to my heart. From that moment, I adored her. And I adored her through all the years to come, as she screamed at me, encouraged me, taught me. Whether she was demanding, irritable, cross or kind, I adored her, and will adore her memory to the day I die. She has my eternal gratitude.

She spoke to my mother and asked me a few questions, which I answered shyly, then said that I could start when we were settled – she did not ask me to dance. For a short while, she said, I could take a class three times a week but, if I were to take my training seriously, I would have to come every day. Mama was so excited that Madame had accepted me as her student, and I could tell that Papa was pleased too.

Now my education had to be sorted out. The next day we had an interview with the headmistress of the district school. Mama spoke French fluently, but in spite of being top in French in Bucharest, I discovered to my dismay that in Paris my French was non-existent. I could not converse or understand other people's conversations. For some peculiar reason, I was amazed that even the woman who sold her wares in the milk bar spoke French!

Mama and the headmistress spoke for what seemed to me a very long time, while I just sat and stared at them, wondering what would happen to me. As we took our leave, Mama prompted me in Russian, 'Say thank you to Madame.'

'*Merci, Madame,*' I said, and added off my own bat, '*Au revoir.*' The headmistress had agreed that I could have the afternoons off on the three days I had my ballet class, on condition that Mother taught me French verbs at home. *Verbs with Mama! Ai-ai-ai!* My heart sank. I knew only too well what to expect. Since I also anticipated with terror going to school, I hoped that my ballet classes would prove less painful.

My class mistress at school was very kind to me. She installed me by her desk and took great pains to explain and guide me through the lessons. Within three months, I was able to start conversing and take my place with the other girls at my own desk. At that point, thankfully, my lessons with Mother could stop.

My ballet classes were at first scary but also exciting. Being shy, I tried to hide behind the piano at the back of the class, but this manoeuvre did not escape Madame's eagle eye and she promptly put a stop to it. The star pupil in the class was Tamara Toumanova. She was my age, but she already had four years' training – she was quite strong technically and very beautiful, with dark southern looks in complete contrast to my blonde northern features. At the end of the class, only a few of the students were able to execute thirty-two *fouettés* (spinning turns in which the raised leg whips the body around) like Tamara, who did them beautifully. Beginners like me were, of course, not allowed to attempt them yet – there was so much to learn first.

Mme Preobrajenska's students were almost all Russian refugees, and so had limited financial means. Madame too was poor, and could not afford to rent a studio for her sole use. This meant that her classes could not be graded, and there was quite a mixture of advanced, intermediate and beginner students in the same class. Madame would alter some combinations to suit each category, and never allowed a weaker student to attempt a more difficult step or combination before they were well prepared and ready for more advanced work. It must have been a colossal pressure on Madame, but we learned fast and worked hard.

In the evenings, Madame held a class and gave private lessons at another studio in Rue de la Pompe in the 16th arrondissement, near her flat. There she taught some very poor students free of charge. She told their parents laughingly, 'You can pay me when your daughter becomes a ballerina!'

Not long after our arrival in Paris, Papa got a new job at the Agence Havas, an advertising and news agency, designing advertisements, posters and so on. His salary allowed us to move out of the flea-pit apartment and into a flat in Rue Lamblardie, near the Bois de Vincennes. Two other Russian families, friends of my parents, lived in the building. One of them was another ex-naval officer who had escaped from Russia at about the same time we did. His beautiful wife worked as a model at Chanel, and his stepson, Aliosha, became my buddy. The other family was Dr Nemtchinov and his wife, a middle-aged couple. This was handy, as the following month I came down with every sickness that in those days children could not escape. Dr Nemtchinov looked after me with patience and kindness.

It was a great treat moving into the flat. It had a real little kitchen – although that was no thrill for Mother – and a bathroom with a bathtub and a loo. Just for us! Magic! There were two adjoining rooms, one for my parents and the other with a divan bed for me, and a table and two chairs and a dresser. The flat had no central heating, so Papa bought a salamander (portable) stove. It was luxury to be warm in the winter, but the bedbugs that had the run of the building were unwelcome nightly visitors, and we usually had to wake up a couple of times a night to hunt them.

I had to go to a new district school, in the Rue Picpus, which luckily was just around the corner. My new headmistress, Mme Bizet, was great. She agreed to me attending school only in the mornings, but the afternoon lessons were added to my nightly homework. There was a lot of it every day, including a piece to learn by heart and maps of things like the French rivers to draw. Often, I would start to fall asleep and Papa would draw the maps for me. I got highest marks for my map-drawing. Cheating? Yes! But Papa and I were unrepentant.

The girls at my new school were less hostile than the Romanian lot. But although a few were friendly, the majority called me a *sale étrangère* (dirty foreigner). They were no doubt parroting what they had heard their parents say. I was puzzled. I was a foreigner, yes, but I was not dirty – we had our own bathtub! I washed every day. I felt hurt. When

I asked Papa why the girls called me dirty when I was not, he explained that it was just an expression that meant we were not liked because we came from another country. Once more, I was puzzled.

Eventually Madame had to move from the Théâtre Olympia to another studio – Salle Wacker, on the Rue de Douai near Place de Clichy. After that, I started to go to classes every day. The studio was a little smaller than the one in the Olympia, and had no recess in which the mothers could sit to watch the class. So Madame had a bench placed at the back of the studio, by the door, where the mothers had to sit in silence. Madame did not tolerate any chattering or whispering during her classes.

I would dash home after morning school, swallow a horse-meat steak in a hurry (Dr Nemtchinov said I was anaemic and must eat horse meat), and then Mama and I would take the Metro to the studio. Mme Preobrajenska would come in with a little watering can and water the floor, so we would not slip. She would then proceed to feed the sparrows waiting for her on the ledge of the long window above the barre. And only after that would the class commence. Ballet lessons were much more diverting than school – I was quite indifferent towards my classes at regular school, even though I was a good student.

A dear fat Russian man, who looked like Taras Bulba the Cossack warrior, came by the studio every day with an enormous basket of a delicious Russian version of Danish pastry called *vatrushki*. The aroma of freshly baked *vatrushki* made our mouths water. Mama always bought me one after the class.

One day Mme Preobrajenska remarked to Mama that I had difficulty breathing, and Dr Nemtchinov suggested I have my adenoids out. Mme Kasskova, a friend of my parents, was the matron of a children's clinic in the poor district of Vaugirard. With her help, they agreed to operate on me and a day was set. Mother was told to bring a towel.

'What for?' I asked.

'I don't know,' answered Mama, shrugging.

Off we went to the other side of Paris on the Metro. When we arrived at the clinic, Mme Kasskova took me to a group of children queuing by a closed door. From behind the door came horrible sounds of screaming, spitting, crying and gulping. We stood in the queue, frozen to the ground with fear, clutching our towels. But at least it was quick – no sooner was I in, than the nurse grabbed me, sat me on her lap and immobilised me by wrapping her legs and arms around me. A big lamp on the surgeon's forehead shone in my face, blinding me.

'Open your mouth wide and keep it open,' ordered the voice with the lamp.

I felt something metallic and cold in my throat then horrible pain. There was a jet of blood and my head was pushed into a bucket already containing the other kids' blood. Then my towel was slammed into my mouth and I was pushed out the door as the next victim was pushed in. Shaking and crying, I was conducted back to Mama. Mme Kasskova and Mama then promised me lots of ice-cream, which helped. We caught the Metro back home, while I sat clutching the bloody towel to my mouth. It was awful, but it was worth it – after that I had no more problems with breathing.

No sooner was I over that episode than I needed an operation for an umbilical hernia. I went to a small Russian hospital in Villejuif. The surgeon, Professor Yakovlev, was kind. I marched to the operating table, argued about being strapped to it, which I did not like, then was silenced by the ether mask. As I fell asleep, I saw myself falling from the moon into my bed, through black skies down to the earth far below, which looked like a small blue ball. Afterwards, Papa came to see me and brought me a red rose.

But these episodes were both mercifully short, and soon I was back at my ballet classes and enjoying every minute of it. On Sundays, when there were no classes, Papa took me walking through Paris along the Seine. I treasured these Sundays. We often stopped at different stalls, looking at books or paintings. Sometimes he took me to the Grand Palais and Petit Palais on the Champs Elysées to see the exhibitions there. I would listen fascinated as he explained who the painters were and pointed out the beautiful details to look for. At a Salvador Dalí exhibition I was amazed by the paintings depicting watches that were sliding, distorted, out of drawers.

'Why?' I asked Papa.

'Why not?' Papa replied.

On Sundays Papa also cooked the dinner – herrings and boiled potatoes with dill and butter. It was a great treat, and a change from sausages and cheese, the usual dinner Mama cooked on weekdays.

One day a white convertible car was parked in front of the entrance to our building. The roof was down and the seats were bright red. I was fascinated – I had never seen such a fabulous car. I longed to sit inside to see how it felt. I was about to find out and climb over the door of the car, when an angry voice yelled, 'Hey, little girl, get off my car!' I turned and saw a furious-looking young man on Dr Nemtchinov's balcony. The doctor stepped out and, seeing me, laughed, saying in Russian, 'She's my patient, the daughter of my friends upstairs.' Then, addressing himself to me, he called out, 'Irinotschka, leave Jerry's car alone. Get ready for your ballet class or you'll be late!' Embarrassed, I dashed through the front door, disgusted with the rude young man. But in just a few short years our paths were destined to cross again, with turbulent consequences.

THE FRONT OF THE CLASS

By the end of my second year with Mme Preobrajenska, I had graduated to the front of the class, next to Tamara Toumanova – a red-letter day for me! I was now ten and had mastered many of the difficult technical aspects of ballet.

At that time, it was fashionable among the society ladies to hold tea parties with entertainment in their sumptuous, grand townhouses. These ladies – Baroness de Rothschild, the Countess de Polignac and the Countess de Beaumont, among others – often asked Mme Preobrajenska to supply some of her students for their parties. Tamara Toumanova and I often performed for them. There was a promise of remuneration, which was always welcome, and Mme Preobrajenska thought it was good for us to get used to performing in public.

I started taking evening classes with Madame so that she could choreograph a few numbers for me to perform. She gave me two of her own costumes – one for the *Danse d'Anitra* (music by Edvard Grieg) and one for a Russian dance. Mama made me two tutus for the other numbers. Tamara and I would arrive early with our pianist and our mamas and be received by the butler, who would conduct us to a room adjoining the ballroom, for us to use as a dressing room. A long table with mirrors would be set up for us, where we would sit to put on our modest make-up. Eventually the hostess would come in to greet us politely. At a fixed time, the butler would appear and escort our pianist to the grand piano in the ballroom, where the guests sat at a multitude of pretty round tables sipping their tea.

When we heard our short introduction played, Tamara or I would run into the ballroom and take our position for the start of our number. As I ran in, I would notice the guests eyeing me with curiosity and amusement, because I was so very young. I always tried not to look at them and concentrated on my dance. And we often needed to concentrate very hard, because the floor of our performance space was usually covered with a thick, deep rug. It was hellish for doing *pirouettes* and *fouettés*, because one's toe shoes sank into the rug. I had to force each turn and concentrate on my balance. It was good experience, though, for coping well in difficult conditions.

Our tea party audiences were always warm and appreciative. Once our performance was over, the butler would bring tea and pastries to our make-shift dressing room. When we were ready to go, our hostess would appear to tell us we were adorable and bid us goodbye. The butler, ready to escort us to the door, would hand us an envelope of money each. The sum was left to the discretion of the hostess but, on some occasions, much too often really, we would be given a brace of pheasants or something similar instead. Mother was disgusted at having to cart unplucked birds, hanging from a string, all the way home on the Metro.

Soon after, one of the mothers managed to secure for several of us a month's engagement at the Théâtre Femina on the Champs Elysées. Mme Preobrajenska gave this her blessing and said it was all good experience. We performed in a children's play, *François le Bossu* by the Countess de Ségur. The same mother choreographed (if you could call it that) our dance sequence – it consisted of *petits jetés* (small springing leaps taking off on one leg and landing on the other), hand-clapping and not much else. And we were dressed as lobsters. Lobsters! We thought it was hilarious and giggled through each performance. Six happy lobsters! Six happy mothers! The money we earned was most welcome.

For my twelfth birthday, Papa gave me a *doumka*, a 'thinking pillow' (from the Russian word *doumatz* meaning 'to think'). He said it was a Russian custom to have one. I took it everywhere and I still have it. Wherever I go my *doumka* goes – I am never without it.

By then the Russian refugees had organised themselves into clubs and associations, including regimental clubs and an invalid association. Papa was a member of the Naval Officers Club. Each club organised a yearly charity ball, and Preobrajenska's students were much sought after as performers. Our mothers were put to work too, making our costumes under Madame's supervision. They excelled themselves and we always looked lovely at minimum cost.

Occasionally Mme Preobrajenska herself performed a beautiful Russian dance and her famous dance from *Le Matelot* (The Sailor) for the Naval Club. I have never heard ovations like those Madame received – they were full of adoration and gratitude. Some had tears running down their face; they remembered the much-admired and beloved ballerina on the Maryinsky stage in their forever-lost homeland.

For these occasions Madame would use a great number of her students. We would rehearse in the evenings at her big studio in the Rue de la Pompe. She recreated ensemble numbers from *The Sleeping Beauty* and *Paquita*, and some of us also danced solo numbers. It was such fun.

The first time I had a solo to dance, a lovely gay gallop, I felt very nervous, paralytically nervous. As I ran onto the stage, I saw the famous ballerina Vera Nemtchinova sitting in the front row. She smiled at me encouragingly, nodding her head in approval. My nerves disappeared – I smiled back and was filled with happiness. Madame was pleased with my performance and I was in seventh heaven.

On another occasion, a Russian gypsy troupe was among the performers. They were very popular, not only with us Russians, who loved gypsy songs, but also with the French. They had many engagements in the nightclubs around Paris. I noticed among the musicians a youth playing the guitar; he had an unruly mop of black hair and a slightly Asiatic look – he looked different from the others. Later in the evening I bumped into him at the buffet table and told him how much I had loved their performance.

'Thank you. What's your name?' he said.

'Irina. What's yours?'

'Yul. You danced well. How old are you?'

I still had my make-up on, so I risked a lie. 'I'm fifteen.' I was still only twelve.

'Ha! You look younger.'

I was crushed and mortified. Mumbling an excuse I dived into the crowd, blushing with vexation. As the saying goes, it's a small world. Many years later, we worked together and became very good friends. By then Yul Brynner had lost his unruly locks, but he still played the guitar and would tell delightfully far-fetched stories. That was before he became a film star, before *The King and I*, and before he sometimes forgot to take off the King of Siam's crown when he left the stage door and continued to play his kingly role, much to the embarrassment of the people in his company. To the end he remained my good friend and never ceased to shock, amuse or be different. He was a free spirit. But I am digressing. Let us return to those days in Paris.

The Count St Martin, a much-respected musician who played the organ with great success and toured France each year giving concerts, asked Mme Preobrajenska if she could spare a few of her students to come with him on tour and provide entertainment between his numbers. Madame agreed and chose three of us – two girls called Elena and Natasha, and me. She started rehearsing solo numbers and trios with us immediately. The first performance was in Paris, in the huge old Théâtre Trocadero (since pulled down and replaced by the equally impressive Palais de Chaillot). It was my first encounter with a real stage in a huge theatre. To dance to the powerful sounds of the organ was exhilarating; my 'nun' number to music by Rachmaninov took on a special meaning, and I learned how to portray the emotions of my character.

Our three-week tour was very pleasant. The charming count lodged us and our mothers in good hotels, we ate at good restaurants and he often invited us to supper, where he liked to show us off to his friends – he seemed to have friends everywhere. Our pay was excellent and everyone returned to Paris happy and with good memories.

Our next engagement came when Mlle Frank of the Paris Opera came to a class and asked Madame if Toumanova and I could join her students in a limited season of a short ballet she was putting on at the Palais Garnier (the Grand Opera House). It seemed a fantastic opportunity. Madame agreed and we rehearsed in the big studio under the dome of the Palais Garnier. Tamara was the star and I was in a group of four soloists. Mothers were not allowed at the rehearsals, but Mama Toumanova said that if she could not come, Tamara could not dance. So Mama Toumanova sat perched on her chair and her big dark eyes burnt holes in all of us. Serge Lifar, the leading dancer with Serge Diaghilev's company, had been invited to head the Opera Ballet as *maître de ballet* and choreographer after Diaghilev's death. Lifar often paid a visit to our rehearsals. He was handsome and eccentric. He did a great deal to elevate the standard of the Opera Ballet and nurtured many talented French dancers who became great stars. He always had a few nice words for me and I felt very flattered.

But on the whole my memories of this venture are not pleasant. The place was vast, cold and unfriendly, and we had to walk to rehearsals through miles of long, scary, very dimly lit corridors, the sides of which were lined with props from operas and ballets. Sometimes the boys would hide in great big urns (were they from *Aida*?) and jump out at us with screams and grunts. I was petrified walking alone through these corridors and always hoped for another dancer's company. I also was intimidated by the goings-on in the anteroom to the stage where, all dressed in our costumes, we warmed up. It was the custom, in those days, for men with special privileges to come into that foyer and eye the dancers through their monocles, talking to their favourites or even inviting them to supper, hoping for more I bet. Thank heavens none of these dandies ever approached me. I suppose it was too obvious that I was only twelve years old, in spite of my make-up and costume. But they scared me. I was truly glad when the curtain came down on the last performance. Even now, as I write these lines more than seventy years later, I hate remembering that time. It still seems like a bad dream.

II

THE BALLET RUSSE DE
MONTE CARLO, 1931–1936

ROYAL OPERA HOUSE

COVENT GARDEN,

W.C.

COLONEL W. DE BASIL
AND THE MEMBERS OF HIS COMPANY OF
BALLET RUSSE,
being anxious to show their appreciation of the Support that they
have received from the Great British Public during their Present and
Past Seasons in London, have it in mind to organise a

Grand Rout & Cabaret Entertainment

to take place upon the Stage of the ROYAL OPERA HOUSE
after the usual Performance on

THURSDAY, AUGUST 22nd, 1935.

DANCES AND OTHER DIVERSIONS
Specially devised and arranged for the occasion by the principal
Choreographers and Artists of the Company will entrance the eyes
of the spectators, while a

DELECTABLE BUFFET SUPPER,
Accompanied by Malt beverages and other cordials
will charm their palates.

Such an occasion should not be missed, and the moderate price
fixed at **6s.** is calculated only to cover the cost of the Refreshments.

So that nothing be omitted that might add to the brilliance of the
occasion, the Players of the

LONDON PHILHARMONIC ORCHESTRA
Have graciously consented to give their services, and the Public will actually
be afforded the unique privilege of Dancing to the strains of this illustrious
Orchestra, under the direction of SIR THOMAS BEECHAM, BART., who
will himself conduct a Series of VIENNESE WALTZES for their delight.

☞ **All parts of the House will be thrown open
and all lovers of the Ballet will be welcomed.**
*Early booking is advised, as the number of tickets
available will obviously be unequal to the demand.*
EVENING DRESS IS OPTIONAL.

DANCING.	"Nunc est bibendum : nunc pede libero" "Pulsanda tellus . . . ." HORACE. ODES. God Save The King.	SINGING.

Printed by BURRUP, MATHIESON & COMPANY, LTD., 114, Southwark Street, London, S.E.1.
Established 1628.

3

THREE BABY BALLERINAS

One day in 1931, Mme Preobrajenska told us that some important visitors would be coming to watch the class, and warned us that she would conduct the class slightly differently. Next day we had just finished at the barre when the visitors appeared. Loving, warm greetings were exchanged between Madame and her guests, then she turned to us and said, 'This is my darling Georgi Melitonovich Balanchine and Colonel Wassily Grigorievich de Basil,' and to the visitors, 'Meet my students.'

We were agog. We had heard of Mr Balanchine – renowned choreographer for Diaghilev's Ballets Russes – but we knew nothing about Colonel de Basil, although we later learned he had been a director of l'Opéra Russe à Paris.

The two men gestured to us in greeting, there were smiles all round, and then they sat near Madame while the class proceeded. Madame was obviously showing us off. When the class ended, our visitors lingered, talking to several of us and our mothers. They then told us what it was all about. Colonel de Basil and René Blum were forming a new ballet company in the hope of continuing in Diaghilev's footsteps. They were acquiring repertoire, scenery, costumes and orchestral scores with the assistance of Léonide Massine, who had been a soloist and choreographer with Diaghilev's Ballets Russes.

Mr Balanchine was to be the choreographer; his idea was to assemble the majority of Diaghilev's dancers, who knew the repertoire, and to introduce young dancers straight from ballet school and entrust them with leading roles. It was an unheard-of thing to do, but Balanchine was adamant. He chose three young dancers: Tamara Toumanova, Tatiana Riabouchinska and me! We were lucky to be in the right place at the right time. During our first London season, the critic Arnold Haskell called us the 'Three Baby Ballerinas'. When we reached our early twenties, we each tried to shed this tag, but with no success – we were destined, each in turn, to appear at the pearly gates as one of the 'Three Baby Ballerinas'. We made ballet history.

The company would be based in Monte Carlo; they planned to start rehearsals in October 1931 and give their first performance in Monte Carlo in January 1932. René Blum, the other director, was a man of culture and humanity who was much liked and respected. We all admired him and were deeply fond of him. Approachable, caring, friendly, dignified and a gentleman of the old school, he contributed greatly to our art and our beginnings. Without him, the Ballet Russe de Monte Carlo might never have existed. Most people now choose to forget this wonderful man's involvement – how ungrateful!

In 1931 he was already fifty-three and had been associated with the theatre for some time. When Diaghilev died in August 1929, leaving an unexpired contract with the Théâtre de Monte Carlo for his Ballets Russes, the director of the Monte Carlo Opera hoped to carry on the company, and appointed Blum director of ballet. However, the debts of Diaghilev's company were too heavy – it was disbanded, and the costumes and scenery dispersed.

Blum was eager to revive the Russian ballet. He sounded out possibilities for a new company to be based in Monte Carlo, writing to Massine, Balanchine, Lifar, Boris Kochno and Diaghilev's *régisseur général* (rehearsal director), Serge Grigoriev. Nothing was resolved. Then he met Colonel de Basil and the rest, as they say, is history. Blum was impressed by de Basil's energy and initiative, and discussed his cherished scheme of forming a Russian ballet at Monte Carlo. Blum had the most to offer the new venture – the Monte Carlo connection, a theatre as a headquarters, rehearsal rooms and storage space, and financial backing. He had some dancers and so did de Basil, but everything depended on their being able to recruit good choreographers and principals.

Blum was to be artistic director, de Basil administrator. By the end of 1931 de Basil had followed up Blum's groundwork and signed contracts with Balanchine as *maître de ballet* from 4 January 1932, and Kochno, Diaghilev's librettist (story-writer) and artistic counsellor, for six months from 15 December 1931. The conductors for the first season were to be Marc-César Scotto from Monaco, Diaghilev's orchestral director Roger Désormière, and Pierre Kolpikov. Serge Grigoriev was an important acquisition for the new company, which with such young dancers needed to maintain discipline and traditions. Blum and de Basil approved Balanchine's idea to include very young dancers, and de Basil in particular, with his instinct for audience reaction, recognised immediately what excellent publicity the policy would create.

Now, let us get back to my story! In spring 1932 Mama took out two brown cardboard suitcases and started packing for our journey to Monte Carlo. She took me shopping for a new spring coat and shoes, and to my delight she decided I could have a coat that came well below the knees, not above them, and shoes with little heels. She also bought me my first stockings and suspenders, and a beret. It all made me feel like a *mademoiselle* – oh, bliss!

My initial excitement was soon dampened by the realisation that I would have to leave Papa all alone in Paris and not see him again for many weeks. I felt sad – I knew I would miss his comforting presence, especially now that I had to face the unknown world of a ballet company and being alone with Mama. As he stood on the platform at the Gare de Lyon, seeing us off and trying to look cheerful, I felt guilty. The train moved off and I opened the window of our compartment to wave to Papa until I could see him no more.

'Shut that window and sit down.' There was slight irritation in Mama's voice, so I promptly obeyed.

It was an overnight journey, so as the evening came we tried to make ourselves as comfortable as possible on the hard third-class bench for the long night ahead. After daybreak we went through Marseilles and the train began travelling along the coast – I was riveted by the sight of the Mediterranean sparkling in the bright sunshine under a cloudless, blue sky.

My spirits rose and I started to look forward to discovering the 'new world' of Monte Carlo. We were met at our destination by Serge Grigoriev's son, Vova Grigoriev, and wife, Mme Lubov Tchernicheva. Vova was Colonel de Basil's secretary and Mme Tchernicheva, who had been a leading artist in Diaghilev's company, conducted the company's daily ballet classes. Vova took us to our pension and said he would come back in two hours and take us to the rehearsal studios to meet Serge Grigoriev (whom we soon called 'Papa' Grigoriev) and the company. It was only a short walk to the theatre, through beautiful surroundings, the air filled with the aroma of mimosa and jasmine.

Monte Carlo was a lovely place then, discreetly elegant, with no high-rise buildings, so that behind the town one could see the mountains that are now almost totally obscured. The focal point was the Casino Square, with the old and very chic Hôtel de Paris. Across the square stood the Café de Paris, which was elegant and beautifully appointed. These days there are tourist buses permanently parked right in front of it, and one carries one's food on plastic trays. But the casino and its theatre thankfully have not changed. It is a glorious building in the grand old manner, and the gardens surrounding it are just as beautiful. In those days Prince Rainier was a little schoolboy; now he has left us forever – nothing ever stays the same but our memories.

At the theatre Serge Grigoriev received me warmly, but he was obviously taken aback by my childish appearance. 'Oh, my angel,' he said, 'what shall I do with you?'

'I look older in my make-up,' I responded, hating my blonde northern looks and baby face. How I envied Tamara her dark southern beauty!

Meeting the company was not as scary as I had anticipated. Everyone was very friendly and helpful, and the older dancers from Diaghilev's company took me under their wing in no time. Some of them soon became very special friends and remained so for many years until their death. There were Marian Ladre and his wife, Lara Obidenna, Edouard Borovansky and Tatiana Lipkovska. Each morning Tatiana would smother me with kisses and pinch my cheeks. I grew to love these people with all my heart; I could confide in them, ask their advice and rely on their support. Marian, soon after my arrival, started calling me Bouboule ('Little ball', or perhaps 'bubble') and in no time at all it became my nickname among most of the company. I suppose it was my round cheeks that made Marian think of that nickname, but I liked it – it sounded friendly and fun.

The morning after our arrival I reported nervously at nine o'clock for a company class with Mme Tchernicheva. She was beautiful, tall and very regal in her bearing, with piercing, expressive amber eyes and a commanding manner. She greeted me warmly and watched me intensely during the class. Her class was pure Cecchetti (the great Italian dancer who taught for many years at the Imperial School in St Petersburg), and I found some of it restrictive after Mme Preobrajenska's freer method, but I soon got used to it and enjoyed feeling thoroughly warmed up and ready for rehearsals.

After class we had twenty minutes to change for rehearsals; there was a big change room for girls, and the men had two change rooms at the other end of the big studio. There was a smaller studio beyond these change rooms where we could practise alone or with our partner, while we waited until we were needed in the main rehearsal. We usually had to be at rehearsals all the time. Apart from anything else, it was useful to watch the choreographer composing a new ballet, so that we could get acquainted with the style and mood of the production before we started work on it ourselves.

The mothers who accompanied us teenagers sat on a bench inside the entrance to the big studio or outside on the path leading to it. If only that bench could talk! So many mums' bottoms sat on it – as these women gossiped, argued or reminisced about their lives in Russia and told the story of their escape from the Bolsheviks.

We broke for lunch from one to three p.m. and then there would be an afternoon rehearsal until seven. On performance days, our afternoon rehearsals would stop at five or five-thirty. Sometimes, during the opera season, which preceded the ballet season, some of us were required to perform sequences in the operas, which meant we also had to do evening rehearsals.

By the time I arrived in Monte Carlo, rehearsals were already well under way. Massine had been and gone, having choreographed the lovely *Jeux d'enfants*. Balanchine, who we called Mr B., was starting work on *La Concurrence*, having already finished *Cotillon*. These ballets were timeless little jewels, and it is most unfortunate they have fallen into oblivion. *Cotillon* was a tender, mysterious dream of youth, while *La Concurrence* was inventive and funny, with brilliant choreography. Many years later, when I asked Mr B. why he did not revive these two ballets for his company, the New York City Ballet, he looked pensive, then answered, 'I don't remember them.' I did not believe him for a moment!

At one point in *La Concurrence*, Mr B. lined up Toumanova, Tatiana Riabouchinska and me: Tamara in the middle, Tatiana on her right and me on her left. In this arrangement, the three of us had to execute thirty-two *fouettés* in unison, a thing never seen before. For us it was not a problem – we could do the *fouettés* on one spot, travelling in any direction or *en diagonale*. In rehearsals the company always applauded us at the finish, amazed and amused by what was considered then an unusual tour de force. The audiences reacted in the same way – it was great fun.

That first season I also had to learn the first waltz in *Les Sylphides* and the part of a shuttlecock in *Jeux d'enfants* right away. Otherwise there was not much of any importance for me to do. In *Chout*, choreographed by Boris Romanov in 1921, a ballet best forgotten (which it soon was), I was dressed as a boy servant in boots two sizes too big and had to bring a samovar onto the stage. At the first performance I managed to trip and fall flat on my face, samovar and all. The audience laughed, but I did not. Papa Grigoriev could hardly contain his laughter and asked me to fall in the other performances – he said it would lighten the proceedings. It did nothing to cheer me up, but I obliged him for the short life of that ballet.

I made friends with Tatiana Riabouchinska right away. She had been a student of Mme Kshessinska, who was Mme Preobrajenska's great rival. Tania, as I called her, was nice, a little bit shy, petite, graceful and light as a feather, with a delicate, beautiful face she inherited from her delightful mother. They were a striking contrast to mother and daughter Toumanova. Mama Toumanova was forever telling whoever cared to listen that Tamara was a genius, that there never was anyone like Tamara, and never there would be, that no-one could walk on high heels like Tamara, and so on. Marian Ladre once said to Mama Toumanova when she cornered him, 'And no-one farts like Tamara.' Mama Toumanova looked stunned but shut up. Poor Tamara was constantly told by her mother that she was unique in every way and, not unnaturally, Tamara behaved accordingly. She was aloof with most of us except the small entourage that her mama invariably managed to collect. Her mother told her how to prepare for her roles and took over her life in every way. If one asked Tamara a question, Tamara would look at her mama and it was Mama who would answer. Tamara adored her mother and they were inseparable for as long as Mama Toumanova lived.

Mama Toumanova had a habit of glaring at Tania and me as she stood in the first wing during performances, which was rather off-putting. Once, Tania and I decided to annoy Mama and get our own back. One night during our Monte Carlo season we decided to squeeze Tamara during our *fouettés* in *La Concurrence* and give Mama Toumanova the vapours. We knew it would not hamper Tamara, since we had no intention of colliding with her – it was strictly for her mama's benefit. Our plan was to move closer to Tamara during the first eight *fouettés*, then the next eight we would move back to our places, the third eight we would move back towards her and in the last eight we would go back to our places and finish as usual. All went according to plan and, to our delight, we could hear Mama Toumanova getting hysterical, gulping and whimpering, 'They will kill my Tamarotschka.'

Then all hell suddenly broke loose. During the last eight *fouettés*, a prop – a dressmaker's dummy – that was badly secured fell on top of Tania, knocking her down. The dummy and Tania were rolling on the floor, while I was in trouble too – my black wig flew off my head but remained attached by one hairpin, so that the wig slapped my face with each turn. Tamara stoically and beautifully finished the *fouettés* as if nothing had happened. Tania and I had already been punished for our unprofessional behaviour, but as the curtain came down Colonel de Basil, Papa Grigoriev and Mr B. were waiting for us.

'What the hell were you doing?' roared Colonel de Basil. Bursting into tears, we confessed. The Colonel ticked us off in no uncertain terms and so did Papa Grigoriev. Mr B. said nothing, but his eyes were laughing. When Tania and I retreated to our shared dressing room, ready to face our mothers' wrath, we found to our relief that they were in stitches. They scolded us, but they could not keep a straight face. As for Mama Toumanova, from then on she glared at us twice as hard. Eventually we got used to it and it no longer bothered us.

Just before the opening night of *Cotillon*, David Lichine, who was dancing the lead, hurt his ankle and was not able to dance. Mr B. volunteered to dance Lichine's part himself. Having seen him demonstrate the choreography to Lichine during rehearsals, it was obvious to us all that he would be wonderful. And he was. We were all thrilled to have the privilege and opportunity of watching this great artist perform. He was only twenty-eight, but he had given up dancing due to health problems. He was a choreographer for the rest of his long life, and produced countless works, many of which are performed around the world to this day.

Many of us regularly went to a small Russian restaurant down in Monaco for lunch – it was cheap and we could count on delicious *borscht* and Russian *kotletki* (patties). Once a week, for a treat, Mother would get me some super pastries from the famous Pâtisserie Pasquier.

But the real excitement for me was seeing the Monaco Grand Prix for the first time. I was hooked immediately, and to this day I'm an avid follower of the Formula One Grand Prix, no matter where I might be or if I have to get up in the middle of the night to watch it. On the day of the race there we had no rehearsals, because the streets of Monte Carlo were barricaded with bales of hay and access to the studio was tricky. The racing cars of that time bore no resemblance to the monsters of today. The drivers' helmets were leather caps and they wore goggles. My hero was Louis Chiron, although I admired the courage and skill of all the drivers. But I still wonder why they do it – risking their lives every time they get into their racing machines. Obviously they love it and do not think of death, like gamblers who want to win and do not think of bankruptcy. The teamwork and pit stops always keep me on the edge of my seat. They give a performance in the same way as we dancers, and I feel certain that we experience the same butterflies in our stomachs. One small difference – we could break a leg, but they could get killed.

When Russian Easter came, Colonel de Basil organised buses to take the entire company to the midnight service at the Russian Church in nearby Menton. Afterwards, in the big studio, we had an Easter feast with *paskha* (cheese pressed in a mould with fruit and nuts), *koulitch* (Easter raisin cake), coloured eggs and other great food. As is the Russian custom, we all kissed each other three times on the cheeks, saying, 'Christ has risen,' the other person responding, 'Indeed risen.' Everyone was in evening dress. Mother bought me my first long evening dress for the occasion and I was so thrilled. I wished Papa could be with us – I missed him and was sad that he was alone in Paris.

When the season in Monte Carlo ended, we were due in Paris for our first season at the Théâtre Champs Elysées, opening on 9 June. I was glad to be back in Paris with Papa and to take classes with Mme Preobrajenska, but I felt dejected that I had so little to do in the company and that what I did have was of no great interest or importance. An inferiority complex was getting hold of me. I hated seeing my baby face with its round cheeks in the mirror – it embarrassed and annoyed me. I wondered if I would ever be given the chance to do more and to be taken seriously.

One day after class, I opened my heart to Mme Preobrajenska. She sat me down and, holding my hands, said, 'Irinotschka, what counts in our art is what you give from your heart, your ability to touch the audience, not your looks. The looks you need for a role you can achieve with make-up. Be patient. Observe, learn, work intelligently, and soon you will have a chance to prove yourself. Now wipe your nose and no more nonsense!'

The Paris season was a smashing success. As they say, *le tout-Paris* was at our opening night – including the princesses and countesses on whose carpets I had once struggled to perform. We had been worried about how we would be received and accepted by Paris, where Diaghilev's Ballets Russes and his glorious dancers had been gods. But the critics praised us unanimously and our audiences were just as enthusiastic. We were acknowledged as Diaghilev's successors. The audiences took us to their hearts and we were feted by Diaghilev's devotees and friends.

For Colonel de Basil and René Blum, the season was a morale boost, and the company was encouraged and happy. But Mr B. was not happy. The rumour was that Colonel de Basil had asked Massine to join the company as resident choreographer and leading dancer, and that was not in Mr B.'s plans. Towards the end of our Paris season, we learned that the rumours were true. I felt sad at this news; Mr B. was such a lovely person, and since I had not met or worked with Massine, I was a little scared of the unknown. The season in Paris closed on 21 June and we were then free until mid-September, when we were to reassemble in Paris for rehearsals before leaving on 1 October for a tour of Belgium, Holland, Germany and Switzerland. After that we were to return to Monte Carlo on 5 January 1933.

I was looking forward to a rest from all the emotions of the past month, to resuming classes with Mme Preobrajenska and to my week-end walks through Paris with Papa. But it was not to be. A few days before our closing performance in Paris, I was sitting in my dressing room with Mama when Serge Lifar came in with Pierre Vladimirov, who had been a leading dancer in Russia and had partnered Pavlova. Now in his middle years, he was a renowned teacher and Lifar's great friend. I already knew Mr Vladimirov; Mother and I often had tea at his flat with his wife Felia Doubrovska, one of Diaghilev's ballerinas who was also a childhood friend of my mother's.

So Lifar and Vladimirov came into my dressing room with an extraordinary, most flattering proposition. Lifar was forming a small group to tour the fashionable sea resorts of France during July and August and wanted me to join his group and dance *Le Spectre de la rose* and his *Promethée* with him, and the solo waltz in *Les Sylphides*. It was impossible to refuse such an honour and such a chance at the age of thirteen. Rehearsals were to begin immediately. The other members of the troupe were Felia Doubrovska, Roman Jasinski, Léon Woizikowski, Kira Nijinska (Nijinsky's daughter), Natalia Vranitskaya and her husband, Jan Hoyer. The impresario was Arnold Merkel and the whole venture was to be financed by Lifar's friend Sir Edward James.

Without consulting Papa, my mother agreed on the spot. I was speechless, two thoughts and feelings conflicting in my mind. On the one hand I was thrilled that Lifar had chosen me to partner him. On the other I felt guilty about leaving Papa again so soon. When we got home and told Papa about Lifar's invitation, he was surprised but genuinely happy for me, and his supportive reaction made me feel better. The next day Mother and I told Mme Preobrajenska about Lifar's invitation. She smiled and said she knew all about it, as Lifar had consulted her about me. 'It will be very beneficial to you and you will learn a great deal,' she said.

At the end of the Paris season, Mr B. left us officially, taking Toumanova and several of the young dancers with him to form a company called Les Ballets 1933. I asked Boris Kochno why Mr B. chose that name. In his dry, cynical manner, Kochno replied, 'Because it did not exist in 1932 and will not exist in 1934.' He was right!

Léonide Massine was to join us in Monte Carlo in January, and I was now looking forward with trepidation to meeting and working with him. But the immediate challenge was the tour with Serge Lifar.

A BIG BREAK

Our rehearsals took place at the Salle Wacker in Mme Preobrajenska's studio, which was home turf to me and was a great comfort. Pierre Vladimirov coached everybody, and it was a totally new experience to me to be led through the roles assigned to me with attention to the smallest of details.

He taught me how to polish my work, how to grasp the mood and convey the role physically and emotionally. Vladimirov was still in great condition and would demonstrate a point by jumping and pirouetting, his profuse sweat spraying around him in the process. Sometimes he would simply make tender, passionate or heroic noises as he encouraged us to give our all. As we rehearsed *Le Spectre de la rose*, Vladimirov and Lifar, both unbridled extroverts possessed of fiery temperaments, would dance themselves into near frenzy. Having completed the famous jump to exit the stage, Lifar would collapse on the floor and Vladimirov onto his chair, both exuberant and happy. They were an inspiration, and the enthusiasm with which they attacked every rehearsal was infectious. It was an unforgettable experience.

Lifar was in his prime as a dancer. He was handsome and fiery, with great presence and impeccable technique. In my opinion, though, he was self-centred and conceited, showing off at the expense of his partner. Opinionated and touchy, he quarrelled with many people, but he was a vibrant, colourful person who loved himself and fanatically loved his art. He choreographed many works and wrote over twenty books on ballet; he devoted his entire life to his art.

The only person in our group I did not know was Kira Nijinska. At our first meeting I was struck by her resemblance to her father, Vaslav Nijinsky, whose photos I had seen in many ballet books. She was stocky, with muscular legs, very short brown hair and a pretty, vivacious face full of mischief and with a ready smile. We struck up a friendship immediately. Kira's ambition was to dance her father's roles, an unrealistic *idée fixe*. She was not a man, she was not her father, she was an eccentric – adorable Kira. Strong in her movements and able to perform a high jump, she disliked putting on her toe shoes and tried her best to persuade Lifar to allow her to dance the mazurka from *Les Sylphides* in soft shoes.

Lifar, of course, would not hear of it. But Kira tried to have her way and at our first performance, after the first three jumps *en diagonale*, discarded her toe shoes right there on the stage and continued the variation barefooted. Lifar was livid! Whatever he said to her must have been very strong, as she never did it again.

In *Promethée*, Lifar was the only main character, while Roman Jasinski and I danced the parts of the Man and the Woman. Roman was a beautiful classical dancer, elegant and dignified. He was also a considerate partner, with whom I enjoyed dancing in classical roles for many years. We learned our parts quickly, and the rehearsals, under the eagle eye of Vladimirov and with the exuberance of Lifar, were a joy. Doubrovska danced the *Adagio pas de deux* from Act II of *Swan Lake* and the *pas de deux* waltz from *Les Sylphides* with Lifar. Her beautiful line and lyrical style were poetry. Léon Woizikowski, an outstanding character dancer, brought contrast and variety to the program with his solo numbers.

Our first stop was Le Touquet-Paris-Plage in the north near Calais, followed by Deauville in Normandy near Le Havre, and finally Biarritz, on the south-west coast. Sir Edward James, our sponsor, joined us for the performances. He was a young English gentleman of the old school and instantly charmed those of us who were meeting him for the first time. He drove everywhere in his new sports car – a sensation! It could do 100 kilometres an hour. He gave us all a demonstration, and when my turn came I was relieved to return to base – 100 kilometres per hour terrified me. Not so my mother – she climbed out of the car ecstatic and asked for another go.

Sir Edward also was the proud owner of a small four-seater aeroplane, which his pilot brought along, and we were invited to experience the joys of flight. One morning everyone assembled at a small airfield and Sir Edward, dismissing the pilot, took the controls while Lifar, Kira and I climbed aboard. It was the first time I had ever been near an aeroplane, let alone flown in one, and my heart was pounding. The rest of the party stayed on the tarmac, awaiting their turn.

No sooner were we in the air than the engine caught fire and tongues of flame began to leap around the propeller. Sir Edward landed the plane as fast as he could, with admirable skill and composure, Lifar loudly encouraging him with 'Oh, ohs', 'Ah, ahs' and 'Ha, has', Kira shrieking, 'Eeeee', and me paralysed into silence. Down below, Mother was in hysterics, while Vladimirov slapped and shook her, yelling, 'Shut up, shut up!'

Upon seeing me in one piece, Mama quickly resumed her composure and asked Sir Edward to take her up next, but there was no question of any further flights. Sir Edward took us all to lunch instead, during which Lifar kept us in stitches re-enacting the events of the morning.

Our performances were a big success with the audiences, and in every town we danced to sold-out houses. Lifar and Vladimirov were pleased with me, and I was in heaven dancing with Lifar and gaining invaluable experience. In our free time, Kira and I went to the beach for a swim, doing back flips in the water and jumping on the wet, firm sand. In Biarritz, however, I almost drowned. The waves there are always big. One of them knocked me over, pulling me under and, as hard as I tried, I could not find my footing and kept being dragged under with each oncoming wave. Fortunately, Woizikowski was with us that day. He noticed me struggling and dragged me out to safety. After that I developed a great respect for the mighty sea.

After we returned to Paris, I went with Mama and Papa to Colonel de Basil's office to sign a new contract for the Ballet Russe de Monte Carlo. My parents asked for an increase in my salary, but the Colonel said he could not possibly afford any pay increases. Mother argued that surely now that I had danced with Lifar I was entitled to an increase. The Colonel stood his ground. Papa finally said, 'In that case we're not signing.' I looked at Papa, tears welling in my eyes.

The Colonel was sitting cross-legged and I noticed something about the state of his shoe. Jumping off my chair, with tears now streaming down my face, I grabbed the Colonel's leg and lifted it up, pointing out to my parents a big hole in the sole of his shoe.

'Look, Papa, he's poor. He has holes in his shoes. He really cannot pay me more.' There was a moment of silence then everyone started laughing. Finally Papa agreed to sign.

As we were leaving, the Colonel told me that since Toumanova had left the company, Mr Grigoriev, Mr Blum and he had decided that I would take over her roles in Balanchine's ballets and the spinning top in Massine's *Jeux d'enfants*. Mother's displeased expression softened then, but as we stepped out onto the street, she looked at me in disgust. 'You were a great help, idiot!'

But I did not care if she thought I was an idiot. I was happy – I was in the company and there was much to look forward to.

I started rehearsing *Cotillon*, *Concurrence* and *Jeux d'enfants* with Mr Grigoriev right away. I have much to thank Mme Tchernicheva for: she took me under her wing; taught me how to apply make-up; showed me how to do my hair for different roles; and through all my years in the company was always there for me to discuss my roles, to guide and to coach me. I spent many happy and interesting hours with her, listening to her stories about the Maryinsky Theatre School in St Petersburg, from which she had graduated, her career with Diaghilev, the dancers of those days, the people she knew outside the ballet, and her personal adventures. She was a passionate, temperamental person and a dramatic dancer – tall, beautiful and commanding.

In mid-October 1932, the company gathered early one morning in front of Colonel de Basil's office to board the two big coaches that were to transport us on our six-week tour of four countries. The coaches were rented at cut price, courtesy of Lichine's uncle, who managed a transport company in Paris. Papa had to go to work, so I had said my goodbyes to him at home.

The scenery and costumes for three ballets were stacked on the roof of the coaches and covered with tarpaulins. Mama and I were sitting right behind the Grigorievs. When everyone had settled, Papa Grigoriev put his hand on the driver's arm and said, '*Un moment*,' then turned to us and said, 'Shhh. God speed.' For a moment there was silence, then everyone crossed themselves – a Russian custom – then he signalled to the driver to start.

Colonel de Basil, driving his own car, brought up the rear. He wore glasses with very thick lenses but he was still extremely short-sighted. How well he saw was questionable, which made his driving alarming to other drivers as well as to his passengers. Tooting horns and rude exclamations saw us out of Paris and northwards onto the Route National to Liège and Brussels. It was fun on the coach – we talked, read and sang, chorusing Russian gypsy songs. Lichine tied his long scarf to the luggage rack in a loop and rested his head on it to sleep. The Colonel sometimes drove on ahead if he had business to attend to with the manager of the theatre we were heading for. On these occasions, he would greet us with a mountain of sandwiches, a gesture we much appreciated.

When nature called, we would yell, '*Essence, s'il vous plaît*' (Petrol, please). The driver would stop at the next bushy spot and everyone in need would spend a penny among the bushes or behind a tree. On days when there was no time for a proper class on stage, Papa Grigoriev would be on the look-out for a level stretch of grassy verge with a fence to keep the cows off the road. Once he spotted such a stretch, he would tell the driver to stop. We would change into our practice clothes, and wrap our towels around the barbed wire to form a makeshift barre. Mme Tchernicheva would then give us an hour of barre work, arousing much curiosity among the cows, who would bunch up by the fence, their velvety eyes staring at us. The passing motorists were also intrigued, and many came to an abrupt halt to stare at us.

For food we would stop at small roadside cafés. Some days, if the next destination was a long distance away, we would climb back into the coaches after the performance and drive on through the night, sleeping slumped in our seats. Our drivers had slept while we performed. They became our friends, part of our tribe, and always drove safely and considerately.

In Holland, my best friend, Tatiana Semenova, one of our dancers, whom I always called Tassia, and I went to the theatre for a nine a.m. class via an open market. There we bought ourselves delicious herrings displayed in large wooden buckets, dill pickles and some cheese. These we hungrily consumed after class as we changed for rehearsal.

Our mothers were our chaperones. At times, there were nine mothers travelling with us, but Tassia chaperoned her mother. Tassia was the boss! Her mother would ask Tassia's permission if she wanted something. The most usual request was for beer. 'Tassinka, can I have some beer?' her mother would ask in supplicant tones and then look hurt when Tassia would bark, 'No!' They were such a funny pair, Tassia protective and loving, her mama loving and childlike – and so they remained until the end of their lives.

On one occasion, after the last performance in a particular theatre, the manager would not allow us to load the scenery and costumes onto the coaches, maintaining that the Colonel had not paid him in full. A big argument ensued outside the stage door while the company stood around awaiting the outcome. Finally the Colonel approached Mama Riabouchinska, who was known for having reserves of cash on her person, and led her into the alley by the stage door. After a brief conversation, we saw Mama Riabouchinska pull up her skirt, reach inside her long bloomers with elastic below her knees, pull out a thick envelope, and count out of it the funds owed to the manager. We all cheered her loudly.

With the property loaded on the roof and the company in their seats, we were about to depart when we saw a woman running towards us carrying a huge basket and shouting, 'Stop, stop!' The lady turned out to be the manager's wife. She had brought the 'starving' dancers biscuits, sandwiches and fruit – bless the lady and her kind heart. There was much merriment on our coaches that night.

Germany flitted by, our success undiminished after Belgium and Holland, and at the end of November we reached Switzerland. We performed there under the auspices of the Société de l'Orchestre de la Suisse Romande, with Ernest Ansermet himself conducting. Ansermet had at one time been Diaghilev's musical director, and we were excited and flattered to be working with him.

When we returned to Paris, we had a short break before we were expected to return to Monte Carlo for the 1933 season and our first rehearsals with Massine.

LA DAME EN ROSE

It was great to be back in Mme Preobrajenska's classes. After the experiences of the past year I felt more assured, stronger and freer in my movements. This did not go unnoticed by Madame, who once in a while would quietly say to me, '*Horosho*' (Good). It was so rewarding.

At home I played endless exercises on the piano, which I had abandoned for so long, read Russian classics and resumed dictations in Russian with Mother. Thankfully Mother was in a good mood, and it was bliss not having to go to school any more. In the evenings we had long talks with Papa, and for the first time in my young life home felt good. As the holidays came to an end, I started to look forward to Monte Carlo, but I was sad at the thought of parting from Papa again.

The company assembled at the Gare de Lyon, a long night on our hard third-class benches ahead of us. Mama and I found ourselves in the same compartment as the Grigorievs. It was a marvel to me how still Mme Tchernicheva sat throughout the night, and in the morning she had not one hair out of place, not a wrinkle in her suit. The rest of us looked a mess.

A strange-looking man slid the door of our compartment half-open, stuck his head in and bade the Grigorievs good morning. His broad face was badly marked by smallpox and on his shaven head he sported a beret. Yellow teeth protruded from a wide mouth and his breath smelled of vodka. He grinned at Mama and me and disappeared down the corridor.

'Who's that?' Mama asked Vova.

'Ah, it's Wassiliev. He's quite a character. He was a soldier in the Colonel's Cossack regiment and the Colonel's batman. They fought the Bolsheviks together, and when the White Army collapsed, Wassiliev followed the Colonel into exile and has been looked after by him ever since.' His job from now on was to supervise the loading and unloading of the scenery, baskets of costumes, shoes and books. 'Wassiliev's devotion and loyalty to the Colonel is total, as is his love for vodka,' concluded Vova, laughing.

When we arrived at Monte Carlo, it was so good to feel the warmth, and to smell the aroma of mimosas and jasmine in the air. Vova gave us a list of pensions at various prices, as we had to pay for our own lodgings. Mama picked the cheapest, up a hill in Beausoleil, as did several of the other dancers. Lugging our suitcases, we all marched merrily up the hill and found the pension to our liking. The rest of the day was free, so we had ample time to settle down and have a good night's sleep before reporting the next morning for class and rehearsals.

During the break after our first class, Léonide Massine arrived with his wife, Eugenia Delarova, escorted by the Colonel and René Blum. My first impression of Massine was chilling. He was of medium height, with a sombre, cold expression on his handsome face, with thin lips and huge, beautiful dark eyes – the most beautiful I have ever seen. He greeted the assembled company and said he looked forward to working with us. The Colonel beckoned to me and introduced me to Massine, who shook my hand, saying, 'Aha,' with the same closed, cold expression that seemed fixed on his face from the moment he came in.

Massine's wife, Eugenia Delarova, a character dancer, was to be a member of our company. She seemed well acquainted with most of the dancers and greeted them all with hugs and kisses. What a contrast to her illustrious husband! Delarova's charm, her vivacious smiling face, and her warm hug when I introduced myself to her immediately endeared her to me, a feeling that grew in time to friendship and deep respect.

Massine took the rehearsal that morning for our revival of his *Beau Danube*. As he emerged from the change room he was a different man. In high-waisted Spanish-style trousers, an open-necked white shirt, with a jumper draped over his shoulders, and carrying his books and notes, he was in his element – relaxed, even occasionally smiling as he took one of us by the wrist to demonstrate the steps or point us in the right direction.

Rehearsals were also scheduled for Massine's new works, *Scuola di Ballo*, *Beach* and his first symphonic work, to Tchaikovsky's Fifth symphony, *Les Présages*. I was cast in all of them, so both my work with Massine and my career started in earnest. I had to learn very quickly those things that make one professional and worthy of the title 'ballerina' – hard work, long hours, total dedication to and love for one's art, respect for the audience, and constant striving for new ways to improve one's technique and portrayal of a role. A ballerina may be tired and hungry, and her toes may be skinned and bleeding from many hours in toe shoes, but all that does not matter. She copes with it smiling because she loves every minute of what she is doing and would not have it any other way.

Massine, like all choreographers, had a definite idea of what he wanted at the start of rehearsals for a new work, but his imagination was immense. He had in his mind several variations on the same sixteen bars. I really had to concentrate and struggle to remember the seven different variations on my entrance in *Beach*, where I was La Dame en Rose, the belle of the beach. Massine would look at each composition in turn, then ask me to start with number one for four bars, then go into number three, then five, then finish with number two. But I soon learned to remember and string the required steps together. I enjoyed these rehearsals with Massine, although I felt totally drained afterwards.

When the company was first formed, Alexandra Danilova, who had been a leading member of Diaghilev's company, expressed a desire to join. But Mr Balanchine, with his mind set on very young dancers, said, 'No, you're too old.' Good grief, Danilova was only twenty-eight! When Balanchine left and Massine took over, the doors were open for Danilova to join the company. She arrived some time after the start of rehearsals.

I had met Danilova in Paris at Doubrovska's house when I was eleven. At the time I thought I'd never seen a more elegant, pretty woman in my life. As she entered the studio now with Colonel de Basil, she looked as lovely as I remembered. Of course, she knew all of Diaghilev's dancers and felt at ease with them, but for a time she kept her distance from us young ones and assumed a patronising manner. She called us by our first names while we called her by her first name and patronymic – a mark of respect for someone older. However, after a time she asked us to call her Choura (a pet name for Alexandra), and gradually her patronising manner disappeared.

Thinking back, I realise now how difficult it must have been for Choura to accept the fact that Tania and I, twelve and fifteen years her junior, were leading members in the company and even shared roles with her in some ballets. This went against all established rules, an unprecedented system instigated by Balanchine. But at the time, I did not ponder such matters.

Her attitude to the mamas was one of bemusement. The morning after her arrival, Choura came to class looking just as elegant in her practice clothes. Her tunic was of lovely printed silk; instead of tights she had pale beige hand-knitted leggings of fine wool, and she wore a headband in the same material as her tunic. A beautiful diamond brooch was pinned at her shoulder. She wore pastel-green eye shadow above her cat-like, beautiful eyes, and bright lipstick. I could not take my eyes off her and I wished Mama would let me put on a bit of lipstick.

I watched Choura in class with great interest. Her technique was clean, her *batteries* sparkling, but her turns were modest – her arms and hands lacked grace. Her personality and chic, however, were abundant. At the rehearsal that morning, Choura was learning the part of the Street Dancer in *Le Beau Danube*. It was obvious from the start that the role was tailor-made for her. She was superb in it and made it her own. At these rehearsals, I also discovered Massine the dancer. In the role of the Hussar his magical presence, the inner nobility of his bearing and his fiery nature, were such a contrast to the remote, cold man he seemed off stage.

Rehearsals for *Les Présages* were exciting for all of us. It was new, different and unusual, the first ballet by Massine set to a symphony. The first movement, 'Action', superbly suited Nina Verchinina, who admired Mary Wigman (the German modern dancer) and preferred modern to classical dance. Massine's choreography for her was sharp, angular but based on the classical. In that first movement, the very young André Eglevsky was striking. He was tall and strongly built; his jumps were high and his landings soft as a leopard's. His *pirouettes* were spectacular. Slowly, his arms closing very gradually in perfect balance, he would do ten to fourteen *pirouettes*, music permitting. It was his special trick. I have seen no-one since André who could turn like him. In a very short time he became one of our leading dancers, alongside Lichine, Roman Jasinski and Paul Petroff.

The second movement was 'Passion'. Lichine and I were playing lovers, with Woizikowski, as Fate, trying to separate us. The choreography for Lichine and me was purely classical, very beautiful, lyrical and romantic. At one moment, as the music swelled to *fortissimo*, I ran towards Lichine and he would lift me high above his head, holding me under my right thigh and left side of the torso for six bars. It was torture! He would not just hold me up as he was supposed to, but would sink his fingers into my flesh and grab. I was covered in bruises, but it did not occur to me to complain. In the third movement, 'Frivolity', Tania Riabouchinska was light and graceful, a beautiful vision. The final movement was strong – man's struggle against his destiny, with a victorious finale.

The scenery and costumes were designed by the surrealist painter André Masson. They were expressionistic, with strong, brash symbolic colours. Masson was quick-tempered and had many rows with Colonel de Basil. When he came to Monte Carlo to watch the rehearsals and oversee the set-building, his fiery temper landed him in the local jail on one occasion, much to our amusement.

Henri Matisse, who was a great friend of Masson, often came to our rehearsals, and could be very helpful in pacifying his young temperamental friend. In the end, Matisse took Masson away to his home in Nice until the 13 April premiere of *Les Présages* in Monte Carlo. The ballet was a great success everywhere it was performed, and it has a very special place in my heart, as it was the first leading part choreographed for me and on me. It gave me my first big success at the age of fourteen, firmly cementing my status as a leading member of our company.

We had many other visitors during that period of rehearsals. One was the Count Etienne de Beaumont, socialite and designer for *Le Beau Danube* and *Scuola di Ballo*. He was tall, lanky and enthusiastic, endlessly exclaiming in a high-pitched voice, '*C'est miraculeux,*' and complimenting us. In Paris, the Count and Countess entertained lavishly in their huge garden, where they would erect a platform and invite famous artists to perform.

During our Paris seasons, we too performed at these grand occasions and joined in the party afterwards, mingling with *le tout-Paris*, gorging ourselves on (for us) exotic food and dancing to a super band until the wee hours of the morning. Mother did not mind that she was not present on such occasions, as some of the dancers were at the same hotel as us, and she knew they would see me safe – and sober – back home. I so enjoyed occasions like this, when I was unchaperoned and could feel free to pretend I was a grown-up. In reality, I was a mixed-up kid: I lived with grown-ups, I worked as a grown-up, I was subjected to the same demands, both physical and mental, as a grown-up, and yet I was fourteen but treated by my mother as if I were eight.

A feeling of rebellion was building up inside me – I needed a bit of trust and respect. Mother's constant surveillance irritated and humiliated me. So, what's new? Now, in my eighties, I know that most teenagers go through stages of rebellion against a parent for one reason or another. The main thing is how both parties come out at the other end. It needs a lot of understanding on both sides, but that only comes with the passing of time. They either achieve communication, love and friendship, or they end up resenting each other for the rest of their lives – heavy baggage to cart through life! My mother and I lacked the ability to communicate with each other, I through my fear of her disapproval and my shyness. *What's stopping her?* I wondered in those faraway days. *A cold heart?* No, I am certain she did not have a cold heart, and even through a cold heart, warm blood flows. I shall never know.

As you have gathered, dear reader, I do have a hang-up about my dear mama. I wish our relationship had been different but it was not, which is a regret and sadness I shall carry to my grave. I have this habit of diverging from my story and getting carried away by my searching, interfering thoughts and feelings. Forgive me. So, where were we? Oh yes, with the visitors to our rehearsals.

Also popping in and out were Jean Françaix, who composed the music for Massine's *Beach*, and Raoul Dufy, who designed the scenery and costumes. Françaix would often take over at the piano while Dufy watched the choreography and the dancers, making notes for his costume sketches. They were approachable and friendly, and there was a great spirit of collaboration. René Blum would bring groups of Monaco dignitaries and his social acquaintances to watch. Several times Pierre Grimaldi, Prince of Monaco, came – a handsome man with a reserved but charming manner. On one occasion he brought his son, Prince Rainier, with him. The little chap was at first bemused by the goings-on, then after a while looked bored. To relieve the boy's boredom, Marian Ladre started to catch the little chap's eye, and when no-one was looking his way, pull funny faces. The Prince cheered up and a contest began as to which could outdo the other in grotesque face-pulling. It inevitably came to the notice of everyone and the Prince was escorted out of the studio by his (I suppose) governess. As they left, we all applauded the little chap and he looked delighted. Massine did not seem to mind these interruptions. If he did, he did not show it, remaining calm, remote, polite, and as serious and focused on his work as ever.

I was very intrigued by the diagrams in Massine's books, which were always by his chair. He consulted them often, especially when he was devising groupings or big ensemble movements. Whenever I found myself near the books, I tried to peep at them and figure out what it all represented. Massine must have noticed my interest, as one day he asked me if I would like him to teach me how to understand and use these diagrams. I thought it was extremely kind and generous of him, and so did Mother.

From then on, until the pressures on Massine got too great as our season opening approached, he and his wife, Eugenia, would take me for a picnic in the lunch break and, installed on some rocks by the sea, the great man would painstakingly explain to me what was in his books and how it worked. The books he had were from Russia, but he also had a collection of diagrams and notations he had devised and drawn himself.

It was fascinating and made me observe his choreography with more understanding and increased interest. I can still see us on those rocks, Eugenia, her face tilted to the sun, tanning herself, Massine and me sitting on a flat rock surrounded by books, munching on a sandwich, the cool, remote, generous, great artist giving me his precious free time. It's a memory I treasure with gratitude.

As our opening approached, we started dress rehearsals on the stage with the orchestra. One particular morning the rehearsal was for *Beach*. As La Dame en Rose, I wore a slick bathing costume in pale blue, with a pink motif on my left shoulder, and pale body make-up, in contrast to Lichine's deep tan. His bathing trunks had a decorative strap over one shoulder exposing his bare chest, which had to be shaven – aesthetics demanded it. In our *pas de deux*, his chest felt very prickly and scratchy whenever I came in contact with it.

After his athletic variation, Lichine would sweat profusely, and in our *pas de deux* his tan body make-up left brown marks all over me. One could not stop him sweating, so I had to put up with it, and apparently it was hardly noticeable from the audience. But on one later occasion, in Paris, Lichine finished his brilliant variation as usual, taking a run across the stage and swallow-diving into the wings. We heard a loud crash and moans – the stagehands had forgotten to put out the mattress for Lichine to land on and he crashed onto the floorboards, bruising and skinning his chest. So, after that I was covered in his blood as well as his sweat and make-up during the *pas de deux*. Disgusting!

As the dress rehearsal for *Beach* started, I noticed Danilova positioning herself in the wings to watch the run-through. When my variation took me to the side of the stage where she was standing, she whispered loudly to the person next to her, 'Look at her, La Dame en Rose – ridiculous! Flat as a board, no boobs. What man would look at her?!' It was like a knife in my heart. I could barely contain my tears. Somehow, I got through the dress rehearsal, then I ran into my dressing room, locked myself in the loo and cried my eyes out. As I was taking off my make-up, a thought occurred to me. *Hey, Danilova is right. My body, dammit, is not sexy. I must do something about it. But what? How?*

In those days falsies did not exist. So I thought of a way to give myself sexy boobs. We all wrapped lamb's wool around our toes before we put our toe shoes on: lamb's wool was the answer. On the night of the first performance of *Beach*, I put my dressing gown over my bathing costume and pretended to Mother that I had to spend a penny. I dashed to the loo, where I had previously hidden a box of lamb's wool, then I padded my chest, making, I thought, two shapely boobs. Covered by my dressing gown, my construction went unnoticed by my mother. At the last minute, just before I went on stage, I shed the dressing gown and triumphantly made my entrance. 'Oh my God,' I heard hissed from the wings. Success, I told myself. When Lichine approached me for the *pas de deux*, his eyes were popping out in disbelief. At the end of the *pas de deux*, one of the boobs went askew and dropped well below the other one. The people in the wings, including my mother, were in stitches.

After the curtain came down, Papa Grigoriev approached me with a grin and told me that Massine wanted me in his dressing room. 'Ah, Irinotschka. Hmm. Hmm.' Massine was slightly embarrassed. 'The idea is good, but remember, you are La Dame en Rose, not Mae West.' He asked Mme Larose, the wardrobe mistress, to make me some proper shapely pads and sew them firmly into the bathing costume. I was happy – I had boobs. Thank you, Mme Danilova!

Our performances in Monte Carlo went well, and we were thrilled to hear from Colonel de Basil that we would be going to Spain to open on 12 May at the lovely old Teatro del Liceu in Barcelona, an engagement secured with the help of Joán Miró. This would be followed by a season in Paris, starting on 9 June at the Théâtre du Châtelet, and then at the Alhambra Theatre in London from 4 July. Thus began a string of continuous engagements, voyages and performances around the world for many years to come.

THE STAGE BUG

When we arrived in Barcelona we dispersed to our lodgings, some to a pension and the others to the Hotel Liceu, which was almost next door to the theatre on the lovely Rambla – a long avenue with a multitude of flower stalls. In the mornings, as we walked to the theatre for class and rehearsals, it was a joy to pass each stall, to look at the colourful display of flowers covered in droplets of water and to smell their fresh aroma, which filled the air.

The theatre was old and very big, beautifully appointed with a vast stage. It had an atmosphere of elegance. But as we gathered on stage for class, our hearts sank. The stage had a steep rake, very steep. We felt completely off-balance and had to practise hard in rehearsals to adjust. Surprisingly quickly we did get the hang of it, and without any further worry we were ready for the opening night.

To our amusement, but not Colonel de Basil's, the theatre manager told him he must hire the '*claque*' to be part of the audience. This was another cost on top of the rent for the theatre. The Colonel argued that his company did not need a *claque*, so the manager patiently explained that no-one could afford not to accept their obviously unnecessary services, because the *claque* would then ruin the performance, covering the stage and performers in rotten eggs, tomatoes, oranges and any other suitable projectile, thrown from the balcony.

'It's blackmail!' protested the Colonel.

'No, no. It's not against the law. It's tradition. I'll explain,' retorted the manager. 'The *claque* was invented by Nero. He thought of himself as a great actor and musician, and his vanity required applause and noisy acknowledgement. He made sure he got it. It became a tradition in Latin countries.'

So we had to have the *claque*, who often applauded and cheered at the wrong moments and were a bloody nuisance. In some Latin countries the tradition persisted in the 1930s and the following year we had to have them in Madrid as well as Barcelona. We also endured them in Italy; they had complimentary tickets to all performances – a racket called tradition.

Nevertheless, our season was a huge success, and seasons in Barcelona, Madrid and Valencia were assured for the following year. The audience members who had permanent subscriptions to a box at the Teatro del Liceu were diplomats, socialites and the wealthy. They soon made friends with de Basil, who brought them backstage to meet the leading dancers and extend their congratulations. Friendships developed, and they frequently invited us to supper after performances and to their homes on our free days. They entertained us generously, enthusiastically and with great warmth.

Other audience members showed their appreciation by crowding outside the stage door and waiting for us to emerge, applauding each of us in turn and asking for our autographs. It was my first close encounter with audience members who had been seated 'in the gods'. At first I felt bewildered by their attention, but their smiling faces soon put me at ease, and I felt deeply touched by their appreciation. In years to come, in every country or city in which we performed, they would queue for hours, on their little folding canvas stools, waiting for the box office to open. When the doors to the gallery were eventually unlocked, those at the head of the queue would brandish their tickets and race upstairs to grab the best seats.

I would watch them as I arrived at the theatre, usually three hours before curtain, from my dressing-room window. They were young people in the main, but there were also many elderly ones. I learned that these dear enthusiasts dipped hard into their modest purses for the price of a ticket, spent many long hours queuing, and then patiently waited for us to emerge from the stage door. This showed a genuine interest in and appreciation of our art, and a love for us dancers. I always had a tender feeling and much gratitude for the people in the gallery.

In the little spare time we had, we explored the beautiful city of Barcelona. After the performance we usually went to small, typically Spanish restaurants, where we could admire the gypsies dancing, with their proud postures and fiery temperaments. Often Massine came along with us.

On a tour of Barcelona a couple of years later we went again to see the gypsies dance, and a young gypsy boy took our breath away with his *faruca*, a flamenco dance. Massine was so impressed that he sent the boy a note via the waiter, inviting him to join us at our table. The note read, 'I am Massine. Please join us – we'd love to meet you.' But the waiter returned with the response: 'I am Antonio. So what?' Antonio did not join us.

At about that time, Mr Sol Hurok, the great American impresario, arrived in Barcelona to see our performances and discuss with de Basil the details of our forthcoming American tour. Massine urged Hurok to come with him to see Antonio dance. Hurok was impressed, insisted on meeting Antonio and his cousin Rosario, and spent most of the night persuading their entire family to sign a contract with him and come to America. They finally agreed, and that's how the world discovered Rosario and her great Spanish dancing partner, Antonio. The rest is history.

Despite being completely happy with my work with Massine, the excitement of our performances and the multitude of new experiences and impressions, I began to miss my papa dreadfully. So I was happy when our season in Barcelona ended and we were on our way to Paris and the comfort of Papa's presence.

Paris . . . how good to hug my papa! So much to tell him. Home. Our little flat felt strange and seemed even smaller. Or was it me who was bigger? We talked and talked – about my trip with the company, where we had been, how we had got there and what we had seen. He was interested in hearing all my new impressions.

We had over two weeks' rehearsals before our opening at the Théâtre du Châtelet on 9 June. Massine rehearsed and polished his ballets, while Grigoriev rehearsed Michel Fokine's and Balanchine's ballets. Paris, where Diaghilev's company had reigned supreme, was very important to us. We had had a big success there in 1932. Now, in 1933, we had not only to maintain our good reputation but to build on it. I was learning fast that the better one gets, the harder one has to work, not only to maintain one's standards but to improve on them. There were always some details to work on to make my performance richer emotionally and better technically. After morning class we sometimes rehearsed high up on the flat roof of the theatre. It was spring, and it was fun looking down onto the roofs of Paris stretching on and on.

The opening night went brilliantly – Massine's *Les Présages* made a huge impression and the audience went wild. We brought Massine onto the stage as the audience shouted his name, and he got a long standing ovation. The notices next day showered much praise on Massine and on us, the leading dancers, as well as the company as a whole. The rest of the season was sold out and we felt that our hard work of the past months was paying dividends – a wonderful feeling.

At this time I was privileged to meet Alexandre Benois, the celebrated Russian painter and designer, a person of great culture and knowledge. He had collaborated in St Petersburg in 1899 with Diaghilev, costume designer Léon Bakst and music critic Walter Nouvel, co-founding the art magazine *Mir iskusstva* (*The World of Art*). The magazine was responsible for the Paris exhibition of Russian art and for the first Russian ballet season in Paris in 1909, as a result of which Diaghilev's Ballets Russes was born. Benois remained Diaghilev's artistic director until 1911. The scenery and costumes he created for Diaghilev are legendary, as are those created by Léon Bakst.

Benois' designs for Lichine's *Graduation Ball* in the late 1930s were truly enchanting. As I grew to know Benois better, I found him approachable and sympathetic, and I plied him with questions about Russia, Diaghilev, Karsavina, Nijinsky, the ballets he collaborated on with Michel Fokine, and the roles that now I danced in those ballets. I loved hearing his stories and learned so much from him.

If I was not needed immediately after the lunch break, Mother and I would dash to Mme Preobrajenska's studio to pay her a visit. Unfortunately there was never enough time for me to join her class, but Madame came to most of our performances, and I listened carefully to her observations and the precious suggestions she gave me. My father came to every performance and loved all he saw. On the way home in the Metro, we would talk of his impressions of the evening, which were always of great interest to me. He told me what had impressed him most in the performance, and made observations on the scenery and costumes. He was always interested in how we worked with a choreographer and what differences I experienced in working with different choreographers.

Our first London season was looming. We were due to open at the Alhambra Theatre on 4 July 1933. Our last performance in Paris was on 30 June, leaving us hardly any time to get to London and be ready for the opening night. London was very important for us – there as in Paris, Diaghilev's Ballets Russes had been much admired, so we had to be very good in order to establish ourselves and earn success in our own right. We were fully aware of the challenge but, encouraged by our success in Paris, looked forward to it. Tania had been to London before, performing in impresario Nikita Balieff's Russian revue, *La Chauvesouris*, which was very successful in those days.

But most of us young people had never been to England, nor could we speak the language. Again, I was sad leaving Papa – for some reason I felt sadder than ever before. *Is this how it's going to be*, I asked myself, *always saying goodbye, not seeing much of Papa?* I could not bear the thought. Yet I could not think of a solution. Of course, I could always stop dancing and stay at home, but deep down I knew that was impossible. It was too late – the stage bug had got me.

'PERFIDIOUS ALBION'

In my childhood I had often heard England referred to as 'perfidious Albion'. I did not understand what this meant, but I was impressed by those mysterious words. As our train approached London, the thought crossed my mind that I was in 'Albion' and it felt exciting.

As we emerged from Victoria railway station, I was astonished by the sight and shape of London taxis – all black and so tall! Later it was explained to me that the reason the cabs had such high roofs was to accommodate gentlemen wearing top hats. Very considerate!

Tassia and I and our mamas shared a taxi to Russell Square. As we drove along, I was agog at the red double-decker buses and promised myself to take a ride on an upper deck as soon as possible. Our bleak and unwelcoming boarding house was in Montague Street, which ran down the side of the British Museum. On both sides of the road stood absolutely identical, narrow, three-storey houses glued together wall to wall. All of them had green doors and zero personality. *Oh la la*, I thought, I hope all of London is not like this! I was soon to find out that indeed it was not. London was a beautiful city. On Sundays, when we had no performances and absolutely everything was closed, even the cinemas, I loved to take long walks with Tassia and discover the rich history attached to certain buildings or sites, and the 'personality' of London – which was so different from anywhere I had been so far.

Our lodgings were modest – we had a room with a basin, but the loo was in the narrow dark corridor, and the bathroom firmly under lock and key. If you wanted a bath, you had to ask the person in charge, and if the bathroom was vacant, for half a crown (two shillings and six pence) they gave you the key. You even had to clean the tub after use, and then lock the door and promptly return the key.

There was great excitement in the company at the news that Anton Dolin was to be a guest artist for our London season. Most of our dancers knew Dolin well from the days of Diaghilev's company, where in the last few years before Diaghilev's death, Dolin and Lifar were the two great young leading artists. His real name was Patrick Healey-Kay, but Diaghilev had given him the stage name Anton Dolin. Those who knew him well always called him Pat. It was obvious that he was much liked by everybody as a person and admired as a dancer, so I for one looked forward with curiosity and trepidation to meeting him.

The Alhambra Theatre was in Leicester Square, with the stage door entrance on Charing Cross Road. It ceased to exist soon after our season – it was pulled down in 1936 and replaced by the Odeon Cinema Leicester Square. In 1933 the Alhambra was a lovely theatre with an old-fashioned, warm atmosphere and a good stage, but to my astonishment there were no footlights. This proved at times to be a hazard, but also cause for laughter.

On one occasion Danilova was ill and I had to step in for her in *The Firebird*. The Firebird first appears with three big jumps across the dark stage. The only light was the spotlight on me, which blinds one completely, and with no footlights I had no indication of where I was going. Someone would stand in the wings and click their fingers so that I would jump towards the sound. At one particular performance, the person clicking their fingers was late or forgot, so I had no sound to direct me into the first wing. With my last jump I overshot the edge of the stage and crashed down into the musicians, to the hilarity of all. No harm was done. I was pushed back on stage and continued with the performance.

Each morning we had a company class on stage followed by rehearsals. The morning after our arrival in London, Colonel de Basil appeared at the end of our class with Dolin. Dolin was greeted warmly by his former colleagues, and then the Colonel introduced him to us, the young ones. Dolin greeted us as equals, with no trace of the condescension Danilova had initially displayed towards us. He was handsome, with jet-black hair, an Irish twinkle in his merry eyes and a friendly manner that conquered me on the spot.

In the short period before the opening night we rehearsed long hours. Not only was it important for us to impress our London audiences, but Sol Hurok was arriving from New York for our opening night, and much depended on him being impressed enough to want to present us in America.

The day of the opening night arrived. Class, rehearsals all day, no time for a meal, sandwiches on the go, make-up time, butterflies in my stomach fluttering, seven p.m. warm-up on stage, last directions from Massine, 'No down, no feathers' from the Colonel, back in the dressing room with Tania, our mothers helping us with the last touches to our costumes, shaking hands pinning my little Russian cross inside my bodice.

'Everyone on stage, please,' calls Papa Grigoriev's booming voice. Mama kisses me; 'No down, no feathers,' she says. Everyone takes their place, I hear three hard knocks on the stage, the overture begins. A little prayer, a sign of the cross, the curtain slowly goes up. The moment so dreaded, so desired, has come. I am on, nerves gone, lost in that magic world of being someone else.

Our opening program was *Les Sylphides* followed by *Les Présages* and *Le Beau Danube*. Tania and I danced in all three ballets, Danilova in *Les Sylphides* and *Le Beau Danube*, in which her role as the Street Dancer became the one for which she was always best remembered.

The performance was sold out. As the curtain parted, there was a feeling of electricity in the air. It was no ordinary audience – they had admired Diaghilev's company, loved the art of ballet and filled the theatre with good vibes. London audiences had a reputation for being ardent balletomanes. Knowing and appreciative, if they liked you it was for life. As the years went by I experienced this for a fact.

The big test of the evening would be *Les Présages*. It had already been mentioned in the press and discussed in an article by the leading music critic of the time, Ernest Newman. Newman disapproved of the use of symphonic music for ballet; serious music was not be trifled with! Much later his wife, Vera, confided that Newman had said, 'I dread sitting through the performance of *Les Présages*. Still, I can always shut my eyes and just listen to the music!'

Les Sylphides, Fokine's masterpiece, went well. We all received tumultuous applause at the end of each of our variations and at the final curtain calls. As we assembled on stage for *Les Présages*, Massine installed himself in the first wing in his dressing gown and made up for his role as the Hussar in *Le Beau Danube*. He was visibly tense. I said, 'No down, no feathers,' to which he replied, 'God willing.'

As the ballet unfolded and each scene received loud, prolonged applause, it became clear the audience loved the work and that Massine had scored a triumphant success in his very first symphonic endeavour. We all received a standing ovation, and the audience shouted Massine's name. Lichine and I dashed into the wing and brought Massine onto the stage to wild applause. This warm recognition of Massine's genius brought tears to my eyes, and I thought to myself how wrong those people were who said the English were cold. They are not, once they drop that certain reserve they consider to be good manners.

Le Beau Danube made a happy end to the evening. As was the custom in those days, people from the audience came to our dressing rooms to congratulate us – friends, strangers, people brought to meet us by Colonel de Basil, fans who later became friends – all were welcome, and the corridors by the dressing rooms were full of smiling people and the sound of complimentary exclamations.

That first night Tania and I had many visitors. The ones we were thrilled to meet were Ninette de Valois, Lydia Lopokova, Lydia Sokolova, Adeline Genée and Mimi (Marie) Rambert, all former Diaghilev ballerinas – we knew their names and reputations. To meet them in person meant a great deal to me. Tania and I introduced our mothers to our illustrious visitors and our mamas beamed, happy to hear the compliments showered upon us and so obviously proud of their daughters.

When all our visitors left, Tania and I, exhausted but happy, were about to take off our make-up when there was a knock on the door and Colonel de Basil appeared again showing a beautiful lady into our dressing room. As I am about to recount to you, dear reader, my memory of meeting this 'beautiful lady', I feel the echo of the emotion I felt on that night sixty-eight years ago!

'Tania, Irina, Tamara Platonovna Karsavina wants to meet you!' the Colonel said.

Karsavina! The unattainable magic princess of my childhood! Here she was – real, shaking my hand, her beautiful big eyes smiling at me as she complimented me on my performance with warmth and simple sincerity. My mind was in turmoil and so were my emotions. My eyes filled with tears and I blurted out, gulping, 'I saw your concert in Bucharest when I was seven years old. You are my magic princess forever!'

Karsavina put her hands on my shoulders, gently kissed my cheek and murmured, 'Thank you.' She always remained my magic princess, but in the years to come I learned to adore and revere her as a human being and great artist. She generously guided me through the roles that had been created for her by Fokine, so I can say I learned Fokine's intentions for and conception of these roles from the 'horse's mouth'. Later, when Fokine was with our company and rehearsed us in his ballets created for Diaghilev, he asked me from whom I had learned the interpretation of the roles.

'From Mme Karsavina,' I answered.

'Aha!' he nodded in approval.

But that first night I met her, when we finally got to our lodgings, I felt emotionally drained and physically exhausted. Sleep eluded me.

I just lay in my bed going over the events of our opening night, and our meetings with so many great people – I could still feel Karsavina's kiss on my cheek. It was a sleepless but happy night, what was left of it, before I was up and dashing to class at eight-fifteen a.m.

The newspapers the next day were unanimous in their praise for Massine's *Les Présages*, and for the leading dancers and the company as a whole, for our freshness and vitality. Our London season was supposed to last three weeks. As the first week ended to glorious notices and sold-out houses, the theatre management asked the Colonel if he could extend our season by a month. The Colonel gladly agreed (we had no other engagements). To cut a long story short, we came for three weeks and stayed, by popular demand, four months. Sol Hurok signed the contract with Colonel de Basil and our American tour was in the bag.

Anton Dolin's first performance for us was with Danilova in *Swan Lake*. At that time the female lead, Odile, was exclusively Danilova's, and in the past she had been partnered by David Lichine. Positioned in the first wing to watch Dolin, I was mesmerised from the moment he appeared on stage. His presence, his strong personality and the elegance of his bearing made a great impression on me.

His partnering of the beautiful Danilova was a revelation. He showed total regard for his ballerina and her comfort; his touch ever gentle but secure, he lifted her effortlessly, never breaking the flow of the movement, never stepping out of character due to physical effort. The *pas de deux* breathed tenderness and anguish, and was beautiful to watch.

At curtain calls Dolin was a perfect gentleman (unlike some!), presenting his ballerina as he took a step back. *Wa-oo*, I thought to myself as I ran to my dressing room to get ready for the next ballet, *to dance with Dolin must be the dream of every ballerina!*

That night after the performance, Tania had an unexpected visitor to our dressing room.

'Good God!' she shrieked. 'Jerry, what are you doing in London?'

'On holiday, going back to America after tomorrow. Meet my hosts, Tony and Gladys Diamantidi,' replied the tall, handsome young man.

Tania introduced them and Jerry Sevastianov to me, saying, 'Jerry and I are sort of related through marriages.'

As all this was going on, I was searching my memory. I was sure I had seen that man, Jerry, before. 'Jerry, do you know a Dr Nemtchinov in Paris?' I asked.

'Yes, why?'

'Do you remember standing on his balcony and yelling at a little girl to stop climbing all over your car?' I asked.

'Ye-e-es, I do . . .'

'Well,' I laughed, 'that little girl was me, and you were very rude!'

General amusement ensued, and after complimenting us on our performance our visitors left, Jerry saying, 'See you in America.'

We met many others during that first London season, many of whom became firm friends. There was Arnold Haskell, the ballet critic who later wrote many books and was a much-loved and respected director of the Royal Ballet School. He became Tassia and my most enthusiastic supporter, friend and accomplice in our escapades. It was he who gave Tamara, Tania and me the tag, the 'Three Baby Ballerinas'.

Another ballet devotee, Philip Richardson, became a wonderful friend. The flourishing of the magazine *Dancing Times* is due to him. It survives to this day, expanded and thriving in the capable hands of Mary Clarke. I can still see the tall, lanky Philip in those faraway days – with a cigarette always hanging from the side of his mouth, only to be removed when it started to scorch his moustache and then immediately replaced by a new one, the front of his suit eternally covered with dropping ash.

He, with Adeline Genée, Tamara Karsavina, Phyllis Bedells and other leading dance personalities, had founded the Association of Operatic Dancing in Great Britain in 1920. Their aim was to improve teaching standards in England, which were not up to scratch at the time. They introduced examinations for ballet students, for which Karsavina composed the syllabus. These wonderful, caring people sowed the seed that has grown into the Royal Academy of Dance, which now has members in eighty-two countries, embracing different branches of ballet, dance and education – it is now a formidable institution.

Another lifelong friendship begun in London was with Florrie Grenfell, soon after to become Lady St Just, when her husband was knighted for services to his country. Lady St Just had been a friend of Diaghilev and of many members of his company. She was a very good-looking woman with immense charm, a deep voice and a wicked sense of humour. She often organised supper parties for us at her beautiful townhouse at 4 Cavendish Square, at which we met lots of her friends, like Sir Oswald Birley and Simon Elwes, both painters of renown. In subsequent years, Sir Oswald did a lovely portrait of Sono Osato, one of our dancers, capturing her exotic beauty to perfection, and Simon Elwes painted a full-length canvas of me in a simple black rehearsal tunic. I wonder where these beautiful paintings are now. Lady St Just was instrumental in arousing the interest of the royal family in our company. In our subsequent yearly London seasons at the Royal Opera House, the royal box was very often graced by their presence.

But that first season in London in 1933 kept us very busy, as we learned and rehearsed works that Fokine and Massine had created for Diaghilev's company. Massine also started rehearsals on his new ballet, *Choreartium*, set to Brahms's Fourth Symphony.

By then, Toumanova was back with us, along with the rest of the dancers who had chosen to go with Balanchine's Les Ballets 1933. Boris Kochno's prediction was correct – after deciding, wrongly, to hold their season in London at the same time as us, Les Ballets 1933 ceased to exist. Balanchine went to America, the 'defectors' returned to us. It was good to have them back, especially my friends from Mme Preobrajenska's school.

Halfway through our season, Danilova became sick. The morning she informed Colonel de Basil she would have to take a few days off, he came in towards the end of our class and I observed him in earnest discussion with Papa Grigoriev by the side of the stage. The class over, they asked David Lichine and me to join them. Colonel de Basil told us that Danilova was indisposed, that the program was set for that week and could not be changed, and that he was asking me to help out and dance *Swan Lake* the next night.

'You must know it pretty well,' said Papa Grigoriev. 'You've watched every rehearsal and every performance.'

'Yes, but I've never rehearsed it.'

'David will rehearse with you all day today and tomorrow. So, will you do it?'

What a challenge! By now my mother had joined us, to discover what this little conference was about. Lichine stood in silence all this time, looking at the floor, but then all hell suddenly broke loose! David started screaming that he would not dance *Swan Lake* with someone who was only 'three inches higher than a chamber pot' (a Russian expression used to slap down a cocky youngster). I was only fourteen, but his comment was unfair. I burst into tears, Mama started screaming at Lichine, Colonel de Basil tried to pacify everyone, and Papa Grigoriev offered me his hanky.

At that moment Anton Dolin appeared – at what must have looked and sounded like a Turkish bazaar. He approached us and asked what the matter was, so Colonel de Basil explained the situation. Dolin, looking Lichine up and down, exclaimed, 'I never heard such nonsense! I'll dance with Irina myself.'

Everyone looked happy except Lichine. I was overflowing with gratitude for Dolin's generosity. After his vote of confidence, I could not refuse the challenge. It was settled – I was to dance *Swan Lake* the next night.

Dolin took me to his studio, having phoned ahead to ask his pianist to meet us there. We rehearsed all day. His partnering was a wonderful new experience – he made it all so easy and let me into the 'secrets of the trade', as he laughingly called them. I was learning far more than just *Swan Lake*. We then took a lunch break, and a nice-looking young man, whom Dolin introduced to me as his student, brought us some delicious sandwiches and drinks. We sat and talked – I felt totally at ease with Dolin and greatly amused by his sharp sense of humour and the pidgin Russian he had learned while he was dancing with Diaghilev's company. After class, I raced back to Dolin's studio and we kept on working until the early afternoon.

'Now,' said Dolin, 'you're going to be fine. Try not to be nervous. You know the role – enjoy it. Go and put your feet up for a couple of hours. See you later.' With that, he gave me a hug and I thanked him with words that sounded hardly adequate to express my gratitude. Back at our lodgings, I lay on my bed hugging my *doumka* and thinking of Papa. How I wished he could be there tonight. How I missed him.

I could not relax, not on that bed, not in that boarding house! My refuge, my 'home' was my dressing room at the theatre. My mother understood my feelings and we set off at once. Stretched on the couch while Mother busied herself with my toe shoes and tights, I felt more relaxed and in control of the butterflies that started to flutter in my stomach. I took my time over my make-up, changed into practice clothes and went on stage to do a long set of barre exercises and practise the solo variation, which requires clean work and good balance.

When I returned to my dressing room, I found Mme Tchernicheva waiting to help me with my hairdo and headdress, talking to my mother, Tania and her mother. They were all so nice and encouraging.

Luckily the costume fitted me all right – well, sort of – but it was Danilova's tutu and I put it on with reverence. Colonel de Basil and Papa Grigoriev came to say, 'No down, no feathers,' while a voice yelled, 'Fifteen minutes, please.' Oh dear, oh dear.

On stage, behind the curtain, I practise the *pirouettes* with Dolin, and as the overture strikes he says, 'No down, no feathers.' I take my place in the wings for my first entrance. *I think I'm going to be sick* . . . but I am not. The curtain goes up, I count the bars, run down the ramp, *grand pas de chat* – I am on!

As I recall this moment, sitting at my desk, it is three-thirty p.m. on an autumn day in 2005. Seventy-odd years have passed, but it is all so vivid, so present. My old heart is pounding as it did then, long ago! I must pause, get a drink, a cigarette, calm down. Back with you, dear reader, in a moment . . .

So I ran down the ramp, leaving my nerves behind. I am not Irina any more. I imagine I am Odile. I am where I am happiest, in my imaginary magic world. Anton Dolin's sensitive response to Odile and his superb partnering made the technical passages easy. As the curtain came down, I felt as if we had danced together for a long time, not the first time.

The audience, surely disappointed at the announcement that Mme Danilova was indisposed and that the role of Odile was to be performed at twenty-four hours' notice by Baronova, now demonstrated their approval with noisy and prolonged applause! As I made a deep curtsy to Dolin, he took my hand and kissed it. It took my breath away and meant more to me than all the applause in the world.

Oh, what a happy night it was. Exhausted after all the emotion, I gratefully stretched in my bed clutching my *doumka*, and my thoughts were with my papa and Mme Preobrajenska. How I wished that they could have been with me that night! My mama was happy with me – she said, 'Well done,' and hugged me, and I felt satisfied with my perform-ance. Suddenly, I could hear Mme Preobrajenska's voice.

'Irinotschka, don't ever be satisfied with yourself – it's a dead-end road. There's always room for improvement. Think of details, work hard and use your brain.'

Yes, of course, I know I will, but just tonight, what the heck, I'll be satisfied!

FREEZING IN PLYMOUTH

During the week that followed my debut in *Swan Lake* I performed it twice more before Danilova returned. The ballet critics gave me won-derful notices, and Mme Tchernicheva believed that I was ready and able to tackle the old classics. Dolin agreed. Massine decided that from now on I would alternate with Danilova in *Swan Lake*, and asked our wardrobe mistress to make me my own costume. I heard through the grapevine that Danilova was furious, but Colonel de Basil stood firm on Massine's decision.

Danilova did not say a word to me, never mentioned the circumstances that propelled me into dancing *Swan Lake*, and did not acknowledge the flowers I sent her to wish her a speedy recovery. I felt embarrassed – like a thief. When I confided in Mme Tchernicheva, she told me not to be silly. 'The theatre world is hard and cruel,' she said. 'Disappointments come alongside successes. Learn to take it in your stride, ignore pettiness and jealousies, rise above all that and concentrate on your work.' Throughout my career I tried to remember Mme Tchernicheva's good advice, but it was not always easy.

When the season was extended our morale was high. We were also rehearsing old and new ballets to enlarge our repertoire, which was interesting and exhilarating. And our new English friends filled our free time, limited as it was. My buddy Tassia always provided laughter and silly pranks. One morning as we walked to the theatre, she pointed out a shop with a display of fruit on the footpath. 'Poupa, I dare you to steal a banana without stopping,' she said.

'If you pinch one tomorrow,' I replied.

'It's a deal,' giggled Tassia.

Bracing myself, fixing my eyes on the bananas as we walked past them, I tore one from the bunch and dropped it down the front of my dress. Mission accomplished! But as we approached the theatre laughing our heads off, a terrible thought occurred to me. 'Tassia, suppose I was caught. Can you see the newspapers printing "BALLET RUSSE'S BABY BALLERINA ARRESTED FOR STEALING BANANAS"?!'

'*Oh la la!* Hurry, get rid of the banana!' was Tassia's advice.

'You bet I will!' I cried.

Fishing the offending banana from inside my dress, I promptly dropped it inside Tassia's. As we passed by the stage doorman's cubicle, Tassia produced the banana and shoved it into the astonished keeper's hand, saying, 'Good morning, have a banana!'

Often at lunch break, Tassia and I and our mamas would go for a light meal at the Lyons Corner House. There were many of them all over London; the food was cheap and adequate. For the first time I became acquainted with Heinz Tomato Ketchup and Heinz Salad Cream, which adorned each table alongside the salt, pepper and toothpicks. They sold lovely buns, and cakes one could take home. Alas, this great establishment ceased to exist a long time ago. Instead, we now have, in London and all over the world, thousands and thousands of McDonald's.

Our work on *Choreartium* was going well. Massine's choreographic imagination, power and inner depth made it a stunning work. Brahms's Fourth Symphony is in four movements, each conveying a different mood – the first movement majestic, the second with religious undertones, the third a light-hearted pastoral, and the fourth heroic. Massine's choreography fused completely with the music.

The costumes were designed and beautifully produced by Barbara Karinska, who had made all our costumes since the company began. At first she lived in Paris, but then she moved to London, where she acquired Reynolds House and turned it into her *atélier*, employing many seamstresses. Later, she moved to New York and became the most sought-after costume-maker not only for ballet, but on Broadway and in films. Karinska was tall, distinguished-looking, elegant and commanding. All the great artists who designed our costumes always listened to her advice and suggestions, and all the costumes she made for us were real works of art.

Now Toumanova was back with us, she was cast in the first movement of *Choreartium*, Nina Verchinina for the second, Danilova and Tania for the third, and everyone was to participate in the fourth. Massine asked me to come to the rehearsals to learn Toumanova's part, in case she left us again. I learned her part and, as it turned out, ended up dancing it permanently when she did leave us again.

Before the premiere of *Choreartium* in October, it was shown to an invited audience after the evening performance, in front of a cyclorama and in rehearsal clothes. The concentration was on Massine's choreography – there were no costumes or scenery to distract from his handling of groups, the beauty of his composition and the total synthesis with the music. This preview was a huge success, and Ernest Newman had no more doubts about the suitability of symphonic works for ballet. He praised Massine to the skies.

After our London West End season ended, leaving us with happy memories, we danced at the Golders Green Hippodrome from 6 to 9

November, before a month-long provincial tour of England, ending in Plymouth, where we were due to embark the ship *Lafayette* for our voyage to America. How exciting! But it was dampened by the thought that I would not see my papa for a long, long time.

One morning after class, Colonel de Basil beckoned to me. 'Irina,' he said, 'I'm going to Paris for a few days. I want to talk to your father and offer him the job of keeping our scenery in good condition – they need retouches constantly. It's a full-time job. Do you think he'll be interested?'

My voice was shaking with emotion when I replied, 'We have no phone in our flat. Can you call him at the Agence Havas?' Then I added, 'Papa, if he accepts, will he come to America?'

'Yes, of course,' replied the Colonel. 'I know it will make you happy. Now, I must have a word with your mother.'

My heart was full of hope. *If Papa agrees it will be a dream come true!* I waited impatiently for a letter from Papa. My mother did not say much about the possibility of him joining us – it made her neither happy nor unhappy. I was puzzled by her unenthusiastic reaction. Because I was unwilling and I suppose incapable of understanding her feelings, I felt annoyed and tried not to think about it.

Colonel de Basil returned from Paris at the beginning of November, bringing a letter from Papa telling Mother and me that he had accepted the Colonel's offer and would embark our ship at Le Havre, its port of departure, meeting us in Plymouth. I was overjoyed!

Our one-month English tour went well, but our lodgings were freezing. The English did not seem to believe in central heating. All we had in our rooms was a small gas fire, and we had to insert a shilling before we could light it. That shilling lasted two hours, and then the fire switched off automatically. If we ran out of shillings we froze. Another novelty to me was my first encounter with the thick English fog. Most of us found it fun to grope through it to the theatre and back to our lodgings, but at times it was scary and you felt as if you had plunged into a bottle of milk. You could not see the fingers on your own out-stretched hand!

By December, we had reached Plymouth. It was perishing cold, with icy winds. The theatre was huge, unheated and smelled of damp. High up on the back wall of the stage was a long range of windows, all broken. We were freezing, and no amount of exercise, woollen tights or jumpers could warm us.

To our surprise, our performances were sold out – the English are hardy! On the opening night, I danced *Les Présages* with André Eglevsky, who was replacing Lichine. Our entrance was from the far back corner of the stage, which we would then cross diagonally in a slow walk. We warmed up in the corner with our coats over our costumes as we waited to go on stage.

As the first movement ended, I shed my coat and took my place, waiting for Eglevsky to come and stand behind me. The music struck up and we were on. As I turned to face him at the end of our *diagonale*, I saw with horror that he had kept his coat on – and it was a long, thick navy winter coat! 'Andriouschka, your coat!' I whispered.

'I know, it's cold!' came the reply.

Papa Grigoriev dashed furiously from wing to wing, whispering loudly, 'André, coat!' But our placid André paid no attention and resolutely kept his coat on.

He did, however, make one concession. Whenever he struck a sustained pose, he would open his coat and show the audience his costume. Massine and everyone else were furious at Eglevsky, and he was fined five guineas – a fortune in those days, especially for underpaid ballet dancers.

On 9 December we gave our last performance. I was now looking forward to boarding our ship for America, to being reunited with my papa, and to a whole new adventure.

4

AMERICA

*I*t was already dark when we assembled at the docks in pouring rain and icy wind. We saw our ship anchored at some distance from the pier – it could not dock due to a high swell. We were going to be transported to the ship on tenders, which made it a lengthy procedure.

I stood under the roof of the customs shed looking in wonder at our huge ship so brightly lit, its portholes shining like stars in the dark night. When we were finally helped onto the tender, I glanced at my mother – her expression was worried as the tender rolled from side to side. The rolling got worse once we were on our way. Mother held her face in her hands muttering, 'Oh, *Gospodi*!' (Oh, God!). She was not a good sailor, poor Mama.

As we got nearer and nearer, I could see people on the ship's deck observing our arrival. With mounting excitement, I strained my eyes, trying to find Papa among them. I found him and shouted with joy, 'Papa, Papa!', waving my arms to draw his attention.

'Oh, *Gospodi*, behave yourself!' Mama said.

Then I was finally on board, hugging Papa – he looked happy, I was happy, Mama was seasick. We were all in one cabin. I bagsed the top bunk, a novelty – what fun! Mama went straight to bed and remained there for most of our journey. Papa and I went to explore the ship and then we joined some other members of our company in the large sitting room.

In the days that followed, the sea was rough, very rough. Papa and I spent a lot of time on the covered deck, watching the mountainous waves lift our ship to the summit then plunge us down as the next wave loomed high above. It was exciting but at times, I must admit, I was frightened.

Practically everyone on board was seasick. From our company, the only ones who appeared in the dining room and did not miss a meal were my father, Marian Ladre and me. We ate heartily and laughed a lot. Instead of the seven days it usually took to cross to New York, it took us nine. The ship shivered, the propellers rattled when thrust out of a wave, our personal effects in the cabins slid and banged, and Mama Riabouchinska moaned from her bed, 'Tania, call me a taxi. I want to go home!'

The day before we were due to dock in New York, the weather calmed down and passengers started to emerge on deck – pale, exhausted but cheered by the thought of reaching terra firma the next day.

As the dawn broke we were all on deck, eager to watch New York appearing on the horizon. It was a clear, crisp, winter morning, the sun just rising, its pale rays illuminating the sky in the palest of pinks. A magical sight greeted our eyes – Manhattan Island, the skyscrapers of New York, an unreal city rising from the water. I had never seen buildings with roofs that seemed to touch the sky.

We passed the Statue of Liberty – its colossal size was so impressive that I felt I had arrived in a fairy tale world. All too soon I discovered not to trust my first impressions, but my first impression on that morning was unforgettably beautiful.

The tenders arrived at the ship and Mr Hurok and the press were transferred on board, along with the customs officials who were to check our passports in the big lounge. The press bustled around us noisily, asking questions that Mr Hurok did his best to translate for those of us whose English was not good enough to grasp American slang.

One reporter, with his photographer in tow, said to Toumanova, Tania and me, 'Let's have some cheesecake, girls.' We responded that we were not hungry.

Mr Hurok came to the rescue and explained to us that the press man meant for us to pose in a more sexy manner: 'He wants you to lift your skirts above your knees in a coquettish way.' We were appalled and chorused together, 'No, no! We're ballerinas!' Danilova joined us and the photos were taken without 'cheesecake'.

Another reporter dashed around the deck shouting at the top of his voice, 'Calling Mr Diaghilev, calling Mr Diaghilev!' Vova Grigoriev, who spoke perfect English, caught up with the man and explained to him that Diaghilev was dead and that the head of the company was Colonel de Basil. The reporter retorted with, 'You're kidding!' and carried on running around calling, 'Mr Diaghilev.' *Oh la la*, I thought to myself, *we have a lot of pioneering to do!*

We were given the addresses of cheap, small flats to rent. A number of us settled in the same large brownstone building on the West Side of New York, not far from the docks. The street was ugly and shabby, a far cry from the New York we had admired from the ship. The mother of Olga Kobseva, one of our dancers, came up with a proposition: 'Let's club together for food and I'll do the shopping and cook lunch for us all every day,' she offered. This was accepted with enthusiasm! We could not afford restaurants and there was no time to cook for ourselves between rehearsals. Mama Kobseva was a great cook and we were economically but very well fed.

On 22 December 1933 we opened at the St. James Theatre, just off Broadway on West 44th Street. In spite of the publicity before our arrival, the auditorium looked half-empty. When the curtain went up on *Les Sylphides*, we noticed a man in the front row reading a newspaper! He glanced at the stage from time to time, but obviously we could not capture his undivided attention. During intermission, Colonel de Basil asked the theatre manager if he enjoyed *Les Sylphides*. 'It's okay,' he replied. 'The girls are pretty, but what's that guy doing there? Take him out, take him out!'

Yes, there was a lot of pioneering work awaiting us! We took on the challenge in good spirits and were recompensed by seeing interest grow, tickets starting to sell and balletomanes emerging.

We discovered a great establishment, Thompson's Cafeteria, to which we all flocked after our performances for a bite to eat. Like Lyons Corner House, they had branches all over the city. We were amused by row upon row of glass compartments containing different sandwiches, cold plates, compotes and pastries. You had to insert coins in a slot, then the little glass door would click open and, as you removed the dish, it was immediately replaced as if by magic. Well, it was food, it was cheap and we were content.

Tassia and I walked around New York with our mothers, admiring the imposing Empire State Building, Chrysler Building and other skyscrapers; elegant Fifth Avenue with its expensive shops; and Park Avenue, where the rich resided. But we were shocked by the sudden contrast as we turned the corner into a side street and found shabbiness, deprivation and ugliness, especially on the West Side. Remember, it was 1933, during the Depression.

Jerry Sevastianov (who later changed his name to Severn) appeared, as he said he would when we last saw him in London. Jerry was obviously drawn to us, his compatriots, and in no time at all had made friends with everyone in the company. Colonel de Basil took to him in a big way, and Jerry was around all day every day, from morning till night. A romance blossomed between him and Danilova. Colonel de Basil persuaded Jerry to give up his job as a ranch manager in Colorado and join the administration side of the company. When Jerry called his boss, Senator Mayo, to inform him that he would not return, the senator was surprised and asked him if there was a problem. There was not. Did Jerry want more money? No, he did not. In fact, he was going to work for Colonel de Basil for far less. He just wanted to be with his fellow Russians, and he was in love! And so our 'tribe' acquired one more member.

After our New York season, we were off on a long tour of the United States. Sol Hurok did things in a grand manner – he arranged our own special train, on which we lived for the duration of the tour. That year we visited one hundred cities. In big cities like Chicago, St Louis, Los Angeles, San Francisco, Denver, Philadelphia and Boston, we performed for at least a week or ten days. Those were the only times we lodged in hotels and had the luxury of sleeping in a bed that did not shake and sway, unlike our bunks on the train, and of having a hot bath! The rest were one-night stands.

Our special train had many carriages – by now there were almost a hundred of us. Our small orchestra, provided by Sol Hurok and which we called the S. Hurok Symphony Orchestra, had twenty-five members. In big cities we used the local symphony orchestra with their own conductor for one or two ballets. Our own permanent conductors, who travelled with us, were Efrem Kurtz and Antal Dorati, both of whom later achieved international fame as heads of symphony orchestras in the United States and Europe.

Several carriages contained our scenery and baskets of costumes, toe shoes, books and props, as well as our personal trunks and suitcases. These were delivered to our hotels in the cities, but we carried a small suitcase ourselves for the one-night stands. There was a permanent restaurant car and the food was good, especially when we travelled through the southern states. We were assigned permanent places in a designated carriage and could leave our belongings there. When we reached a town we would dash to the theatre. Dressing rooms assigned, we changed for a class on stage or a quick warm-up, depending on how much time we had before the performance. We had to clear the stage in time for the stagehands to hang the scenery and for Papa Grigoriev to do the lighting. The chief electrician and three stagehands, who travelled with us and knew the set-up, would direct the local stagehands. The scenery for three ballets was hung efficiently and quickly, and we never had any problems.

Some small towns did not have a theatre, only a small cinema. We then had to improvise as to how to deal with the scenery. The stages were small and narrow, slippery or full of holes, or both. We all had some toe shoes fitted with rubber soles for slippery floors, but nothing could be done about the holes, so we learned to navigate around them and watch our step! In one of the cinemas, there was nowhere that could be used as a dressing room. The local manager suggested the basement. When we got there, we were greeted by one naked electric bulb hanging from the ceiling and illuminating mountains of coal. Well, *à la guerre comme à la guerre*. We laid great quantities of newspaper over the mountains of coal and stood up as we dressed. As there were no chairs or tables, we had to manage the best we could. We carried our toe shoes to put them on on stage, but the hems of some costumes became very grubby.

In university auditoriums, we had to contend with just a backcloth and no wings to enter from, just steps on either side of the platform. Despite the chaos, the audiences, bless them, were most enthusiastic.

We had to present a new ballet or two, if possible, on our spring return season in New York, so the question was how and when we could rehearse them. Massine solved the problem, giving rise to a new daily routine. After each performance, we all had a bite to eat at the corner drugstore – each town in America had one – then we would report to the 'best' hotel in town, where the Colonel would have rented the 'ball-room' or biggest space available. A piano was always available and our dear pianist, Rachel Chapman, always waiting.

Massine, always full of inexhaustible energy, would choreograph and rehearse until four or four-thirty a.m., then we would go to the railway station and climb back onto our train – everyone had to be on the train by five-thirty a.m. We had our breakfast in the restaurant car. After breakfast, the girls in our carriage would gather in the washrooms located at either end. We would wash our tights and smalls, festooning them around the carriage on all available hooks, lamps and towel rails to dry, then we would wash ourselves the best we could. There was lots of joking and laughter.

We would climb into our bunks – mine was the top one, Mama was below – and soon we would be asleep. The coaches were wide, with two tiers of bunks on either side, each curtained with thick green cloth on which there was a glow-in-the-dark number in white, so we could not mistakenly climb into someone else's bunk. It happened, but it was no mistake, that's for sure. There was no sex segregation, and the bunks, which turned into seats in the daytime, were allocated to us by Vova Grigoriev, who was very good at knowing who to seat where, according to friendships and marital status.

The distances between the towns were large, so we could sleep long hours and grab some food before we arrived in the next town, somewhere between five and six p.m. Then we would dash to the theatre, warm up, perform, go to the drugstore, then the hotel for rehearsal, then the train. Day after day after day! Tiring? Yes, a bit, but we were young, strong and loved what we were doing.

I enjoyed watching the ever-changing landscape from the train as we travelled through different states. There was a different feel at the small stations we passed. Occasionally we would stop for half an hour or so, jumping onto the platform to stretch our legs. In the South we were fascinated by the Indians crowding onto the platforms selling beautiful Indian jewellery. When we crossed the bridge over the Mississippi River, the first sight of paddleboats sent me into a daydream of older times. New Orleans somehow did not seem to fit into the United States. It was so different in architecture, feel and atmosphere – so Latin and very beautiful. There was never much time at our disposal to see much of the places we passed through, but even looking out the coach window at the sliding world made my life interesting and richer.

In St Louis, one beautiful, crisp, snowy night, bad luck struck me. After the performance, many of us, in great spirits, were throwing snowballs at each other in the large space outside the theatre. Even Massine could not resist joining us in this horseplay! The snow was deep – I was buried in it up to my calves. Massine threw a large hunk of snow at me, I lost my balance and fell awkwardly while my feet remained standing in the snow. Result – fractured ankle, the worst injury that can happen to a dancer. I was in despair! In pain, my ankle swollen, hobbling, I was despatched with my mother to New York, where we were met by our dear friend Dr Appelbaum, who took me to hospital for an X-ray, where my leg was encased in plaster up to my knee.

I was stuck with Mother in the same flat we had before, my leg up as I cried, read, listened to the radio and cried, worrying and missing being with the company. Dark thoughts would assail me – would I be able to dance again? I would be out of practice. How long before I would be in good form again? Dr Appelbaum's reassurances did little for me, and my mother was also gloomy. We lived on sandwiches, and coffee in carton cups that Mother bought from the drugstore.

One night I turned on the radio and heard Tchaikovsky's Fifth Symphony – *Les Présages*, my *Présages*! It was like a knife in my heart! Danilova had to learn it quickly and replace me in it. How it hurt! *Les Présages* was mine, mine, mine! I felt so possessive of that role. I raged, I hurt, I cried! Hearing the music of 'my *Présages*' on the radio devastated me. Now (in my eighties) I understand Danilova's feelings when I replaced her in *Swan Lake*.

Mother put her arms around me, rocking me gently. 'You'll be all right, Inoussia' (one of her names for me). 'Be patient,' she said. Her calm reassurance helped – I stopped crying and felt grateful that she understood and was with me. I missed Papa but he had to go on with the company and look after the scenery.

Finally, after three weeks, the plaster was taken off and I had another shock! A thin stick emerged from the plaster – the calf muscle was gone. It looked terrible! I was reassured that it would all come back when I started exercising and walking, and so it did. Mama and I rejoined the company, and after a week of taking class with Mme Tchernicheva and working out during every available moment, I was back performing, with a greater appreciation of my role and a new sense of responsibility.

From then on, however, my ankle tended to grow adhesions, which had to be snapped off every eighteen months or so. It was a minor twist of the wrist for the doctor!

MOVIE STARS AND FORBIDDEN FRUIT

Our train was heading towards Los Angeles! Hollywood! Film stars! I pictured it as a mysterious, glamorous place, and I was full of expectation. Our theatre was in the centre of Los Angeles and our hotel was just across the square. It was handy, but there were no film stars to be seen in the streets. What a disappointment! The beautiful, mysterious people lived in the exclusive parts of Hollywood – Beverly Hills and

Bel-Air, an hour away from downtown Los Angeles and reachable only by an ordinary road (the freeway had not yet been built).

My disappointment did not last long. Before the curtain went up on our opening night, an excited David Libelius, our company manager from Sol Hurok's office, appeared backstage naming the many film stars he had spotted in the audience. That sent our adrenaline up! Sol Hurok had come down from New York for the opening night. Always on the look-out for good publicity, he busied himself introducing Colonel de Basil to film stars, and the newspaper photographers had a field day.

Our success that night was tremendous. Charlie Chaplin came backstage to meet the leading dancers and convey his admiration and enjoyment. We were thrilled to meet this great man, who was so vivacious and charming. Colonel de Basil and the leading dancers received numerous invitations to supper parties. My mother could hardly object to me going to them, and so I had the thrill of meeting many people whose faces were familiar but who were total strangers – what a funny feeling!

At one party, at the house of character actor W.C. Robinson, I spotted a young Cary Grant seated at a small, round table with a stack of photos of himself and a pen in hand, waiting for takers. I was shocked and dismayed that anyone could be, in my view, so undignified. But to this day, I try to watch Cary Grant's films whenever they are on television, just as I never missed seeing them on the silver screen in the old days. I adore him!

Tania, Tamara and I were very impressed by the female film stars we met at these Hollywood parties. They were so different in looks and personality, but in our eyes they were all beautiful, glamorous and elegant! They were 'cut from a different cloth' to us, but cloth or no cloth we tried (in secret) to 'glamorise' ourselves. I had good eyebrows but decided to pluck them into a thin line. My parents were very upset! So was I eventually, when it became clear that I had lost my eyebrows for ever. They never grew properly again.

There were some Russian actors in Hollywood, all of them refugees like us, who were trying to carve a place for themselves in the film industry. We met most of them, since they attended many of our performances and spent lots of time backstage, happy to be with their fellow Russians.

Jerry introduced us to Akim Tamiroff and his wife, Tamara, and the Chaliapin brothers, Boris and Fedia, sons of the famous bass baritone Feodor Chaliapin. They were friends of Jerry's from the days when they were all living in Paris, struggling and saving to go to the United States, the country of great opportunities.

Akim Tamiroff came from Moscow, where he was a young actor and member of the Konstantin Stanislavsky's Moscow Art Theatre. Akim was a great character actor and had a big career in Hollywood until his death in the 1970s. He was on the short side, podgy and terribly funny, even when he was serious, preoccupied or upset. Tamara was great. It was such fun to be in their company, and we became close friends for life. The Chaliapin brothers were like fixtures in the Tamiroffs' house, and Tamara cooked endless *kotletki* for all and sundry.

Boris Chaliapin enjoyed a long career as a portrait painter and news artist, while Fedia's ambition was to be a great actor. He never became 'great' but he acted all his life (as Feodor Chaliapin Jnr) in occasional bit parts, always cursing and criticising the way the world was run. Both brothers were larger-than-life characters – wonderful storytellers, temperamental, moody, emotional and hysterically funny. These wonderful people became my cherished close friends.

As all good things have to end, so did our LA season. We gave a few performances in lovely nearby Santa Barbara, and from there resumed our one-night stands and life on our special train.

Around this time it became clear that Mama Riabouchinska was not well. She was in obvious pain and even gave up playing poker with the boys. Colonel de Basil took her to New York to have tests, and the prognosis was alarming. It was decided that she should return to Europe to the care of her eldest daughter, Tania's half-sister Elena Komarova. Elena was a great deal older than Tania and a former member of Diaghilev's company. Elena readily agreed to care for her mother, but she did not do so for long – Mama Riabouchinska died soon after of advanced cancer.

Tania received the sad news of her mother's death while we were on the road. She was distressed and so were we all – her mama was much loved by everyone.

With her mama gone and no more chaperoning, Tania and David Lichine openly became an 'item'. No-one blinked an eyelid – we had all known of their romance. They remained together all their lives and many years later had a lovely daughter, also Tania, who is now happily married. 'Little' Tania gave 'big' Tania three wonderful grandchildren, who were her pride and joy.

Colonel de Basil still had a commitment to René Blum and Monte Carlo that spring, but our American tour did not end in time for us to fulfil that engagement. A compromise was reached: Blum would engage a number of dancers in Europe, and some of our dancers would join them in Monte Carlo, with Bronislava Nijinska (Nijinksy's sister) as ballet master/choreographer and Papa Grigoriev as *régisseur*. We were to be reunited with our dancers in Barcelona for our opening on 9 May 1934. Our American tour was coming to an end, and we were glad to reach New York for the farewell season. There we had a bed that did not rock and a hot bathtub to stretch in.

One night after a performance, Choura, Jerry and another couple decided to go to a Russian restaurant for supper. Choura asked my mother's permission to take me along. My mother liked and admired Choura, so permission was granted. I was surprised but pleased by this invitation and looked forward to *borscht* and *piroshki* (small meat pies)! I love Russian cooking!

As we drove to the restaurant, they were all in great spirits, teasing me about my age and baby face. It was a sore point with me, but I was determined not to show it, so joined them in laughing at myself. Suddenly, Choura asked me, 'Irischka, would you like to marry Jerry?' She had noticed my crush on Jerry and was teasing me.

Yes!' was my flippant reply, greeted by loud laughter.

The restaurant was small and cosy, all red plush and soft seats. Choura and Jerry made me drink vodka with the *zakouski* (an hors d'œuvre). It was the first time I had ever drunk vodka and I did not like it, refusing the second tumbler. Over the *borscht*, I glanced at Jerry with a newfound interest, silly thoughts going through my mind (it must have been the vodka) as I consumed a great number of *piroshki*. It was a fun evening.

Choura did not sail with us back to Europe, but took a leave of absence to participate in a Broadway musical. Perhaps she needed to get away from the 'Baby Ballerinas'. Jerry stayed behind with her and they both came to see us off. We all stood on the upper deck to wave to them as the ship slowly moved away. As I watched Choura and Jerry disappear from view, their arms romantically linked, I felt a pang of envy. Would I ever have romance in my life? *Fat chance*, I decided – my mother appeared next to me at the railing and we watched New York disappear into the misty night. Soon we were back in Barcelona and reunited with our friends. They had so many stories to tell us about their work in Monte Carlo and the terrifying Nijinska!

Choura's Broadway venture did not last long. She was soon back with us and so was Jerry, but something must have gone wrong in their relationship. Jerry seemed cold and distant towards her whenever she tried to get his attention.

One morning in class, Choura asked me, 'Why don't you wear a bit of lipstick?'

'Mama doesn't allow it,' I replied. 'She says I'm not old enough to wear make-up off stage.'

'But you're an artist, it's different. I'll talk to her,' she promised. Mother granted me permission, and Choura bought me a lipstick called 'Tangee'. It looked yellow, but once on the lips turned the palest pink. I was thrilled, and grateful to Choura for her lovely gesture.

Colonel de Basil had been approached for us to give an extra performance at the bullring, the proceeds to be given to a charity organisation. *Bullring?! Well, that should be fun*, I thought. Massine decided we would perform *Les Sylphides*, *Petrushka* and *Le Beau Danube*.

A big platform was built at one end of the ring, closest the matadors' dressing rooms, where we would have to change. The dressing rooms were as austere as monks' cells, with a crucifix on the wall, a prie-dieu, a table and a chair. Of course, there was no scenery and no public seating behind us. The only prop was the magician's booth for *Petrushka*. We did our make-up at the theatre and brought only a hand mirror and the absolute essentials with us. Buses transported us from the theatre to the ring, with our costumes, dressers and stagehands.

The bullring *habitués* honoured us with their presence – the ring was packed but, as ballet and bullfights are not quite the same thing, most were not sure what to expect. The orchestra sat in the ring below the stage. As Antal Dorati made his way to the conductor's rostrum, we climbed the few steps onto the stage in well-rehearsed order, and took our positions. The audience sat in total silence throughout *Les Sylphides*. The ballet's creator, Fokine, would have been delighted, as he forbade the dancers to acknowledge applause after each individual variation in this particular ballet. Quite rightly, he considered that such interruptions ruined the mood and continuity. Usually we ignored any applause during the ballet, and after a very slight pause, the music continued and the applause stopped. But our bullring audience sat in total silence. Were they utterly bored?

Hoping for the best, we attacked *Petrushka*. I was dancing the Doll. The curtain of the magician's booth parted and we, the three puppets on our hangers, started our fast footwork. To my horror I felt the elastic that held up my pantaloons snap and then, slowly but surely, they slid down my bum and finally down my legs. As we ran out of the booth towards the middle of the stage, my pantaloons were around my ankles! Without a pause, I shook them, freeing my feet and kicking them to the side. A tremendously loud '*Ooolé*' cheered me on! The ice was broken and the rest of our performance was received with applause, cheers and loud *olés*!

Our next destination was Paris, where we were due to open on 28 May 1934 at the Théâtre Champs Elysées. It felt strange returning to Paris and not going to our flat – for me it represented home. There was no 'home' any more. Instead our taxi took us to a small hotel in Rue de Parme, near Place Clichy. Lots of theatrical people dwelt around there, as it was across the way from Casino Paris and not far from Les

Folies-Bergères. It was also not more than five minutes' walk from Mme Preobrajenska's studio, and I was looking forward to taking a few classes with my beloved teacher.

Having settled in at our hotel, we visited our friends for dinner whose flat was below our old flat. Riding in the Metro to Daumesnil felt so familiar, as did walking up to 20 Rue Lamblardie. I had a strange feeling of belonging, and yet I was totally removed from these familiar surroundings – I had no feeling of attachment, no regrets. It was not home any more and I was glad.

As we squeezed ourselves into the narrow screeching lift, I noticed Papa's face contort in a strange way. As we got out of the lift, Papa made for the staircase and collapsed, sobbing, tears streaming down his face and across the steps. Mama and I froze in shock.

'Papa, what's the matter?' I blurted, choking with fright. I turned to Mother. She was leaning on the banister, her back to Papa, a look of disgust and annoyance on her face. What was going on?

A feeling of helplessness and pity for my papa invaded my being. I went and sat by him on the step and pulled him into my arms. Not knowing what to say, I kept patting his shoulder in silence. Eventually he calmed down and sat up beside me, wiping his face on his handkerchief. He patted my knee and then gave me a kiss.

'All right, let's go now,' he said, standing up. Mother threw him a glance, walked to our friends' door and pressed the bell. The evening was animated, our friends full of questions about our travels, and we caught the last Metro to our hotel.

But what was it all about? What was the matter with Papa? At the time, I could not understand or figure it out. Now, as I write and recall that episode, which remained profoundly etched in my mind, I know, I understand. Do you? You will, dear reader.

Our opening night went brilliantly well, and it was nice to have familiar faces coming into the dressing room afterwards with greetings and compliments. The Count de Beaumont was organising a big party for the company and *le tout-Paris* was invited. Panic stations! My evening dress did not fit me any more – I was taller and had finally developed feminine curves! Mother and I dashed to Galeries Lafayette, the department store, and found a very pretty evening dress, white with pastel flowers. Straining our budget, Mama also bought me a pair of white satin evening shoes. I was delighted!

The Count asked us, the leading artists, to give a short performance in his beautiful garden. Massine was in great spirits and on the morning of the party we had huge fun rehearsing our numbers in the Count's garden, on the platform specially constructed for the occasion. The Countess saw to our comforts and provided delicious 'elevenses'.

That night, after our usual performance in the theatre, we went to the Beaumonts'. The garden, magnificently illuminated, was already full of guests. The heady aroma of flowering bushes filled the air on this warm spring night. I thought, *It's just like in the films!*

The guests enthusiastically applauded each of us as we stepped onto the platform to perform, and loud bravos saw us off. The guests were merry and getting merrier, and after our performances we had great fun dancing the night away to a fabulous band. I don't recall what time it was when Massine said, 'Irischka, class at nine a.m! Time to go!'

Massine and Eugenia were leaving too, and told me they would give me a lift. Our hosts came out to see us to the car. The Count and Massine did the polonaise all the way to the car, Massine jumping on and off the bumper bars of the parked cars in front of the house, both roaring with laughter. I was astounded! I had never seen Massine drop his reserve, his solemn seriousness and laugh so heartily! Never before . . . and never after! But I enjoyed the privilege of this glimpse into his hidden humanity.

A couple of days later, as Mother and I were leaving the theatre after morning rehearsal, we bumped into Jerry at the stage door. He told us he was off to the cinema to see a new film that was all the rage.

'Irina, would you like to come with me?' he inquired.

I glanced at my mother, as I was taken aback and did not know what to reply. I never went anywhere alone without her or her permission. To my surprise, my mother said, 'You're free this afternoon,

Inoussia. Go if you want to see this film.' Then she asked Jerry to see me back to our hotel afterwards.

It felt strange to be out alone with a man. I felt shy, but Jerry soon put me at ease. I asked him how old he was. He laughed and with a sigh told me he was twice my age. So, he is thirty, I mused – funny, only five years younger than Mama. During the intermission he bought me an *Esquimau glacé* (ice-cream). The film was great and I enjoyed my afternoon very much. As we were leaving the cinema, a couple in the queue for the next screening called out to Jerry. They exchanged greetings and then Jerry introduced them to me. On the way back to my hotel, he told me that these people were old acquaintances he had not seen in years and did not particularly like. Once back at the hotel, I told my parents all about my afternoon and that Jerry was twice my age! For some reason that really impressed me – I was flattered that he was showing me any attention at all.

Next morning I was ready early and was chatting to the girl at the reception desk as I waited for my parents. A tall blonde woman came in and asked the girl at the desk if Irina Baronova was in. The girl at the desk pointed at me, saying, 'Here she is.' The tall blonde lady looked at me with astonishment and disbelief.

'But you are only a child!' she said. 'Are your parents here? I must see them immediately.' Puzzled, I went up to fetch Papa.

'I must talk to you in private, without your daughter,' the lady demanded. Papa told me to wait downstairs and took the lady up. I sensed trouble. Who was she? What did she want? *Oh bother, I'm going to be late for class!*

As it happened, I missed class altogether. When the lady finally left, Papa asked me to come upstairs. My parents looked grim. They told me that the lady was Jerry's wife. She had told them that her friends had seen me at the cinema with Jerry, so she wanted to see me and warn me that Jerry was bad company, a man who had been through 'fire, water and copper pipes' (a Russian saying used to degrade someone). He was lying when he said that his divorce from her was in order and valid. Seeing how young I was, she had to speak to them.

'But Papa, how does all this concern me? Whatever her quarrel is with Jerry, it's of no interest to me, nor any of my business. What does she want with me?' I asked, baffled.

Papa then told me that I was too young to understand and had a lot to learn about life and people. He and Mama forbade me from talking to Jerry or having anything to do with him. Next time I saw him, I was to tell him to leave me alone. I protested that I had no cause to be rude to him.

Mama lost her temper and shouted, 'You will obey our order or else!'

Wrong move, Mama and Papa – forbidden fruit. From that day on, Jerry became, in my eyes, fascinating. I felt totally confused by this strange episode and my mood was dark when I arrived at the theatre for rehearsal. When Mme Tchernicheva asked me why I had missed class, I confided in her, telling her of the morning's happenings and asking her what should I do.

'Tell Jerry what happened and ask for his cooperation so that you don't get into trouble with your parents,' she said. 'It will all blow over,' she assured me.

'But how can I tell Jerry? Mama is watching me all the time!'

'Would you like me to tell him?' she offered.

'Oh, yes please!' What a relief!

Mme Tchernicheva was as good as her word and talked to Jerry. He was furious, she said, and would have a word with my father. As we were leaving the theatre for lunch, Jerry was at the stage door, waiting. To his request for a talk, Papa replied that there was nothing to discuss, just to keep away from Irina, and marched out the door. I felt deeply embarrassed and bewildered. I had never seen Papa being so unpleasant to anyone. It was so out of character. What had happened to my papa?

Jerry looked at me, shrugged and walked away. *Why am I treated like an imbecile?* I mused, *no explanations, do as you're told.* Anger rose in me and a little voice in my head said, *I will not obey!*

Our very successful Paris season ended on 16 June 1934. I was looking forward to London and this time had no regrets about leaving Paris – it was not home any more and I was not leaving Papa behind. We had only three days before our opening in London. As soon as we arrived on 17 June, we dropped our suitcases at the same lodgings near the British Museum and rushed to the Royal Opera House Covent Garden to settle in to our dressing rooms and rehearse the opening-night program on stage, to get familiar with its size and the backstage layout.

When the trucks started to arrive with all the scenery and baskets of costumes, we moved to the rehearsal room on top of the building. I loved the theatre immediately – it had the right atmosphere for me. The auditorium was elegant, red and gold, with beautiful brackets on the walls and crystal chandeliers. The stage curtain, in dark red velvet, was lovely in its fullness and simplicity. It was always my favourite theatre – to this day I feel very sentimental whenever I think of it as it was then, untouched by 'modernisation'.

At first I was dismayed that the Opera House was right in the middle of the fruit and vegetable market! Rows and rows of warehouses, squashed oranges on pavements, trucks being loaded with crates of fruit, jamming the narrow streets, making access to the Opera House by car or taxi almost impossible. The men working at the market were noisy, cheerful and friendly. The aroma of ripe and squashed fruit penetrated the open windows of the dressing rooms.

Before a matinee, as I watched the men in the markets working, they would wave to me. I would wave back and joke with them, shouting across the street. After a while they started to throw oranges through my window, and I had a regular supply of free oranges throughout the season. Oh, it was fun! Whenever I could obtain complimentary tickets, I would give them to my special chaps. By the end of the season, each one would have seen a performance, and they became quite a bunch of balletomanes. The chaps and I kept up this ritual for five years. During those years, the Royal Opera House became our 'home', as did London.

It was with joy that we would return there each year from our seasons in other countries.

As one entered the stage door, immediately to the right was the counter, behind which sat Mr Jackson, the stage doorkeeper. He was a friendly, dignified gentleman with a kind twinkle in his eye. Many great artists went in and out of Mr Jackson's stage door. I noticed how observant he was – that twinkle in his eye could be amused or veiled by a look of silent disapproval. Always calm and courteous, he was respected and liked by all in our company. Often, I would go to the Opera House earlier than usual, just for the great pleasure of spending time with Mr Jackson, plying him with questions and listening to his descriptions and stories of artists and audiences. Dear, dear Mr Jackson.

Each opening and closing night of the season was listed as a 'gala' performance, as were the occasions when new ballets were performed for the first time. For these premieres, the men in the stalls wore tailcoats with medals on their chest while the ladies wore tiaras to complement their usual long evening dresses. As I peeped through the special hole at the side of the curtain as the audience took their seats, I was most impressed by these glamorous English customs. It made the performance a very special occasion for everyone, charging our inner batteries to the full.

As the curtain went up on that first night in Covent Garden, the audience greeted the first appearance of each one of us with tumultuous applause, as one greets an old, beloved friend. We were touched and grateful. We also received an enormous number of flowers from friends and admirers. From then on and throughout the season, our dressing rooms and lodgings always looked bright and gay, embellished with these offerings.

At this time, two people entered our lives who were to play a very important role in securing the company's financial stability, so that we could commission new ballets and work with Fokine, Nijinska and Massine. These wonderful people were Captain Bruce Ottley and Baron Frederic d'Erlanger. Captain Ottley had fought in Europe and the Far East in World War I. He was a director in the banking firm Erlanger's

Ltd and was a close friend of Baron d'Erlanger. They shared a love of ballet and opera, and both were accomplished musicians and composers. Baron d'Erlanger had already had two of his operas performed in the Royal Opera House Covent Garden and, although he was the vice-chairman of Erlanger's Ltd, his heart was in the arts and music. Captain Ottley was much younger than Baron d'Erlanger, who was then in his mid-sixties. Both had seen us perform at the Alhambra Theatre the year before and had fallen in love with our company. They had met Colonel de Basil and a solid friendship had developed between them.

Besides offering their friendship and introducing us into English society and artistic circles, they actively set about helping the company in every possible way. Captain Ottley organised committees, headed by Lady Deterding and Florrie St Just, to raise funds for new productions. We acquired sponsors, and Baron d'Erlanger started to compose a ballet score for me, *Les Cent Baisers* (A Hundred Kisses), which he was to fund. The 'boss' of the Royal Opera House Covent Garden at that time was Sir Thomas Beecham, the acclaimed conductor who, with the assistance of Lady Cunard, had taken over the lease of Covent Garden with the rights to sublet. Captain Ottley and Baron d'Erlanger were instrumental in helping Colonel de Basil negotiate the contract for our season at Covent Garden with Sir Thomas Beecham. This was a great help, as Sir Thomas was not an easy person to deal with, in the office or the orchestra pit.

It was a great feeling to be such a success in London. We worked hard, reviving Massine's ballets for Diaghilev, and Fokine's *Thamar* and *Scheherazade*. The last two were revived for Mme Tchernicheva, who came out of retirement to dance the title roles. They were a great addition to our repertoire, dramatically strong works in which Mme Tchernicheva was superb. Her dramatic strength, beauty and sex appeal obliterated the fact that she was approaching forty. For us youngsters it seemed a great age. Ah, cruel youth! But we all admired her immensely.

Our Sundays were free from work, and we rarely lacked for invitations to house parties held for us by our many friends. Many of these I shall always remember – for different reasons.

One beautiful sunny Sunday, Nancy, Lady Astor invited the entire company to spend a day at her sumptuous home by the Thames in Berkshire, Cliveden House. In 1934 her ladyship had a powerful voice in politics and a strong dislike of Winston Churchill, which was reciprocated. Lady Astor was a strong personality and an impressive figure of a woman. The buses collected us all at ten-thirty a.m., and we were driven to the most impressive Cliveden House. When we arrived, Lady Astor came out to greet us, regal and charming. She took the arms of Colonel de Basil and Massine, and welcomed everyone into her home.

She showed us into a huge sitting room, where her butler presided over the champagne, and uniformed servants offered us delicious canapés. She introduced us to her friends who were there for the weekend, and soon happy, loud chattering filled the room and spilled onto the large terrace through the tall, wide, open French doors. From the terrace, amid beautiful gardens, broad steps ran down the slope to the Thames, where in those days the water was clean and people enjoyed swimming.

I noticed at the far end of the terrace some of our boys hoisting two ladies on their shoulders, showing them balletic lifts, and my incorrigible friend Tassia teaching a bewildered English gentleman how to hold her while she did *pirouettes*, holding the gentleman's finger above her head. *Oh dear!* My eyes went in search of Lady Astor – she was not far away, watching and roaring with laughter. I relaxed. Well, you never can tell – our tribe could be too boisterous at times.

Amid all the merriment a gong sounded and the butler approached Lady Astor, announcing loud and clear, 'Lunch is served, milady.' As the wide doors into the dining room opened, her Ladyship took Colonel de Basil's offered arm and, with a sweeping gesture that included everyone, exclaimed, 'Please come and help yourselves.'

While Colonel de Basil escorted our hostess into the dining room, my tribe shot past them on the double like locusts, surrounding the long table covered in huge, beautifully presented dishes of exquisite foods. By the time the Colonel, Lady Astor and her house guests approached the table in a restrained, polite English manner, half the food was gone!

The oh-so-dignified butler, visibly bewildered, sent his underlings to the kitchens to bring refills as he eyed my colleagues in disbelief. Although I felt a bit embarrassed about my tribe, I could not help finding the whole scene hilarious.

As we sat around sipping after-lunch coffee, Lady Astor suggested that those who wished to swim in the river should do so. Swimming costumes were kept in two big wooden chests on the half-landing of the staircase leading to the first floor. The chests were huge, made of magnificently carved dark wood. One contained ladies' swimsuits, the other men's. They were full to the brim with swimming gear of all sizes and colours.

As I stood at the foot of the stairs watching the dancers crowd around the two chests, pulling out garment after garment in search of one they preferred, the scene reminded me of a sales day at a big department store. English hospitality in the grandest manner? No, I felt that for some this was just a normal way of life. For someone like me, who knew only the hardships of life, the discovery of how wealthy people lived was mind-boggling, but that Sunday at Lady Astor's topped everything I had seen and experienced before.

As most of the company and house guests made for the river, the rest of us gathered on the terrace around our hostess. She plied us with questions about our work and travels, and we in turn asked her about England and its politics, careful not to show our ignorance in these matters, only interest. It was an enjoyable afternoon.

That night, back at our lodgings, after describing our day to my parents – but omitting to report that Jerry and I did not ignore each other (although our conversation had been inconsequential) – I sat in my small room on my squeaky bed thinking about the events of that day. As was my habit, I engaged myself in conversation. *Cliveden House – wa-oo! Would I like to live there, have a big room, with a beautiful, soft four-poster bed, lobsters every day (oh, I love them), chests full of bathing suits and clothes? Magic! Well, would I like that?*

No. Nice, but not magic. My magic world is inside the stage door. It's every night, it's when the curtain goes up and I can be a queen, a princess, a doll, a farm girl, La Dame en Rose, and I can feel joy, passion, sorrow – that's magic, my own magic. And I like my squeaky bed, I muttered in defiance as I fell asleep.

A small group of us often spent Sundays at Lydia Deterding's mansion outside London. Her husband was rarely present, kept away on business. Her home was as grand as Lady Astor's but the atmosphere was strikingly different. It was cosy, relaxed and informal, in spite of the butler, and full of laughter, initiated by our hostess. She was Russian, a striking, voluptuous, vivacious blonde, oozing charm and fun. As I learned later, the English considered her an eccentric and sometimes 'not cricket'. In my book, she was fun to be with. But then, I am a Russian too!

We soon noticed that Lydia had a thing about engraving, embroidering or forging her monogram on simply everything imaginable, and we teased her about it a great deal. She would laugh and say, 'Oh, I love monograms!' Besides doing a wonderful job raising funds for the company, she herself subsidised two of our new productions.

Out of all the grand ladies who showed us such generous hospitality and enveloped us in their friendship, my very favourite was Lady St Just. Lord St Just, like Lord Deterding, was distinguished, quiet and rarely present.

Florrie, as we called her, was truly one of us. She was very tall, thin and lovely, with a protruding chin that gave her a commanding look. She had a terrific sense of humour and a wealth of hilarious stories. Florrie was a close friend of Diaghilev's ballerina Lydia Lopokova, who had retired early to marry John Maynard Keynes, the well-known economist. I met Lopokova on many occasions at Florrie's, her presence always promising a delightful and funny experience. Lydia was short and wore no make-up, with her pale blonde hair pulled into a small bun at the back of her head. Her dresses, as she boasted herself, were made of old discarded curtains, skirt upon skirt which she proudly lifted, displaying each layer with a running commentary on which room and which window that particular material had come from. Her English was perfect, but she delighted in Russifying certain expressions and putting on, for better effect, a thick Russian accent.

I noticed that she could not stand people who monopolised the conversation or bored her. She said what she thought, but in a funny way that was meant to startle and confuse the offender and make them shut-up. She was an eccentric, intelligent, witty, funny, unpredictable, adorable person. Massine told me that Lopokova's endearing personality had shone in her dancing and made her a favourite with the audiences. How I wished I could have seen her dance!

One lunch party at Florrie's sticks in my mind. There were about a dozen guests – Lopokova, Tania, Lichine, me, Sir Oswald Birley and his wife, some friends of Florrie's and a chap who was a politician. As we entered the spacious dining room, everyone's attention was drawn to a very large window, outside of which was a very large aviary with a multitude of colourful birds. We took our places at the table, Lopokova with the politician on her right. The general conversation soon withered, as the politician took over, expounding his views on world affairs and not letting anyone else speak. Lydia had had enough. She stared at Florrie and in a loud voice, cutting into a half-finished sentence of the vocal guest, announced with a heavy Russian accent, 'Florrie, what beeaauutiful ovaries you have! But birds not happee!'

After a second of stunned silence everyone laughed, our hostess exclaiming over and over, 'Lydia, you are so delightfully naughty!' Lydia looked smug. Taking advantage of this most welcome interruption, everyone turned to their neighbour and engaged in earnest conversation. The culprit of Lydia's displeasure was left in limbo but, after a few mouthfuls of lobster mousse and a sip from his wine glass, he became a model guest.

Soon after our opening night, the premiere of Massine's new work, *Union Pacific*, took place. We had rehearsed it nightly during our tour of America. Massine had been keen to do a ballet based on American folklore ever since he first visited America with Diaghilev. Hurok, always on the look-out for good publicity, was enthusiastic and helpful in every way. Nicolas Nabokov was commissioned to write the music, which was based on folk songs of the period in which the Union Pacific Railway was being built. The libretto was by Archibald MacLeish, and the three of them worked together to adapt it into a ballet. The sets were by Albert Johnson and costumes by Irene Sharaff.

Massine himself played the Barman. My role was Lady Gay, the belle of the camp. I was thrilled with this new role, which was so different from the classics or the symphonies. And it was a character role, something I loved to work on. I wanted to portray my Lady Gay as saucy, tarty but not vulgar. As rehearsals advanced, Massine gave his blessing to my interpretation, and I concentrated on details. It was such fun!

I also loved my costume – a canary-yellow crinoline with lots of *broderie anglaise* frills on the skirt, a velvet bodice, a yellow velvet top hat, long yellow gloves and yellow suede ankle boots with high heels (it was strange at first not wearing toe shoes). A bright red wig completed the elegant but tarty look. I was delighted. It was wonderful not being a princess or sylph for once!

Meanwhile, Boris Kochno was back with us and working with Baron d'Erlanger on the libretto for *Les Cent Baisers*, fitting the music to the action of the story. I was immensely happy that Kochno was collaborating with d'Erlanger, as I admired his knowledge of our art and felt that I could learn a great deal from him.

Danilova, Toumanova and I were rehearsing *Aurora's Wedding*, in which we were to take turns in the role of Aurora. There is one moment in the *pas de deux* where Aurora *bourrées* (makes tiny running steps in which the feet are kept close together) forward and *pirouettes* while her partner holds her. This is repeated three times. Papa Grigoriev and Mme Tchernicheva, who were reviving the ballet, showed us this passage, doing one *pirouette*, then two and finishing with three.

One day Boris Kochno was watching the rehearsal when Toumanova took her turn to rehearse. Instead of one, two, three *pirouettes*, she did two, three, four *pirouettes*. Not to be outdone, when my turn came to rehearse, I did the same. Rehearsal over, Kochno, looking very displeased, called Toumanova and me to one side and asked, 'What the hell do you think you're doing distorting Petipa's choreography? He wanted one, two, three *pirouettes*. He had his reasons – style and musicality. Respect the choreographer and pay attention to the style and period of the old classics. No circus, please!'

I hung on his every word and liked him for his dry humour, admiring his capacity to see what was unsatisfactory in a new work and how to make it right. I think he appreciated my endless questions and the fact that I followed his advice. We became close friends. Kochno liked his drink, which at times made his behaviour rather eccentric. A free spirit, a very private person, he also could be very touchy. He could not stand bad manners or coarseness – in public he was quiet and observant, which was at times disconcerting. Dear, unforgettable Boris Kochno.

Baron d'Erlanger – by then I was calling him 'Uncle Freddie' – would fetch me twice a week after the morning rehearsal and I would spend the lunch break at his home in Rutland Gate, listening to him play the music he was composing for *Les Cent Baisers*. I loved these occasions – the atmosphere of his beautiful drawing room, with a view through tall, large windows onto the garden, was so calming and restful.

A small table was always set for me by the grand piano, and Uncle Freddie's butler would, discreetly and very quietly, serve me a most delicious cold lunch. Uncle Freddie played, explaining how each passage fitted into the ballet. I loved the music he was composing; I also loved his company and wished I could spend all afternoon with him. However, rehearsals awaited, and too soon it was time to go back to them.

All this time, my parents remained vigilant and watched me closely whenever Jerry was around. But at parties, out of their sight, we talked. I felt flattered by his marked attentions – it made me feel so deliciously grown up! I had a real crush on him now, and I probably imagined that I was in love with him. The company, of course, knew I was disobeying my parents by talking to Jerry, but they were my friends and I knew they would not tell on me. I was not so sure about Danilova, but I considered it a risk worth taking.

I do not like blowing my own trumpet, but for once I will put modesty aside – our London season was a tremendous success, and all of us, individually and together, were applauded, admired and loved to bits. It was of great satisfaction to us, a reward for all our hard work, and it showed in our performances. They were full of joy, life, energy and total dedication. After our last performance, a supper party was organised on stage, for the company and special invited guests.

The scenery from the last ballet was packed away and carted off to the trucks outside the stage door. The caterers then invaded the stage and set the tables, leaving space for the dance band and after-supper dancing. The invited guests, meanwhile, had drinks in the Opera House's Crush Bar. Vova Grigoriev was busy with the seating plan and place cards. The leading dancers were seated at different tables with our special guests, while the rest of the company had their own tables and sorted out the seating among themselves.

When everything was in place and the company assembled on the stage in formal attire, Vova Grigoriev gave the signal for the curtain to be raised, which indicated to Colonel de Basil that we were ready to greet our guests and welcome them onto the stage. The empty auditorium looked immense in semi-darkness and made a beautiful background for the stage, which was transformed into a nightclub and decorated with flowers. We were honoured by the presence of the Duke and Duchess of York and the Duke and Duchess of Kent. They came onto the stage first, escorted by Colonel de Basil and his wife, Captain Ottley and his wife, Baron d'Erlanger and Lady St Just. The guests followed and a happy chatter filled the air. Immaculate waiters in white gloves got busy and the party took off. As the night progressed, everyone mingled with everyone else, wandering from table to table.

At one point I observed several of our character dancers, among them Léon Woizikowski and Jan Hoyer, seated at the royal table and teaching the Duke of Kent how to drink vodka the Russian way, in a small tumbler, neat and swallowed in one gulp. Before coffee was served, everyone stood up to drink a toast to the King and Queen – that was the protocol. That done, we relaxed with coffee and most, including the Duchess of Kent, lit a cigarette. Oh yes! In those days smoking was an acceptable habit and pastime. Of course, we dancers did not smoke. We needed our lungs, as all athletes do. It amazes me that many young dancers now smoke and drink!

The band attacked a waltz and Colonel de Basil and the Duchess of York took to the floor. Everyone danced into the wee small hours of the morning. The party was such a success that at the end of each season at the Opera House we held a wonderful party.

HOLIDAYS AND PLOTS

We were due for a holiday before embarking for Mexico City, where we were to open on 25 September 1934 for the inauguration of the beautiful Palacio de Bellas Artes. A group of us departed for the South of France in great spirits, looking forward to relaxing on the beach, swimming and catching up on our sleep. My parents and I booked into a pension run by a Russian couple, not far from Cap d'Antibes. It was a lovely villa with a garden, and from there it was a short walk across a field to Bijou Plage, an almost deserted, lovely beach (but nowadays a commercial, overcrowded hell). My friend Tassia and her mother joined us, and Arnold Haskell booked his room there too. Harold and Lesley Good, some darling friends from London, were driving down to join us, so the holiday promised to be great fun. As you see, our tribe stuck together, even on holidays.

When we arrived at the pension, I had a nasty shock. There on the terrace sat a man I hated with all my guts, Mr Ian Blake. One of our many acquaintances from London, he was always around, annoying as a mosquito. He had big dark eyes like oily black olives and was always trying to get in my good books – or so I thought. But slowly the penny started to drop – it was not me the creature was after, it was my mother! I could not stand him.

The first thing I had noticed was the most unusual absences of my mother during afternoon rehearsals. Usually she would watch or would be busy in my dressing room, dealing with my toe shoes and tights or doing other chores. Then there was my father's preoccupied, sad look . . . *why?*

Two days before the last London performance, Tassia and I returned to our lodgings in the late afternoon and noticed at the far end of our street, on the corner, Mother and Ian Blake deep in conversation, then embracing in a way that left no doubt as to the nature of their relationship.

'Ai-ai-ai!' muttered Tassia.

'*Oh la la*!' I muttered in response. 'Thank God we're leaving in two days!'

I felt embarrassed and hurt for my papa, and made Tassia promise not to gossip. Mama, being short-sighted, did not notice us until we were on top of each other at the door. I did not feel like tea with her and returned to the theatre to keep Papa company in the props room, where he was working late. Tassia came with me. She loved my papa and he was very fond of her too. On the way we bought coffee and buns. Papa was pleased to see us. Swallowing mounting tears, I acted jolly, thankful for Tassia's presence and her friendship.

Later, as I was doing my make-up, I had consoled myself with the thought that we would soon be away from London for almost a year and that all this unpleasantness would blow over. And now, there he was, Ian Blake, on the terrace of our pension in France! I glanced at Papa. He wore a look of pained astonishment and dismay. Tassia was by my side, dragging her suitcase. 'Ai-ai-ai. *Merde*!' she hissed, in perfect tune with my own thoughts. Mother looked delighted and acted coy.

As I unpacked in my room, I had only one thought: to get rid of Mr Blake! That evening, as we all had dinner around a big table on the terrace, Mr Blake told us about his drive down from London in his sports car. As I listened, an idea slowly started to germinate in my head. Chewing my *kotletki*, I devised a plan of action. Knowing I could count on Tassia's cooperation, I kicked her under the table and, pretending to wipe my mouth with my napkin, whispered, 'I have a plan. Cooperate.'

Tassia grinned as she whispered, 'Okay.'

When Mr Blake finally finished telling us about his trip, I addressed myself to no-one in particular and exclaimed, 'Oh, how I wish *I* could learn to drive!' Then, as an afterthought, I turned to him with the most charming smile I could muster. 'Ian, won't you teach me?'

He looked taken aback by my sudden show of friendliness, but then he swallowed the bait and said, 'I shall be delighted!'

Mother protested that I was underage. I protested that I would soon be sixteen. Papa said if I was caught I would be in trouble and so would Mr Blake. I insisted, arguing that if we went on the little untarred road behind the villa, where cars were seldom seen, it would be quite safe. Finally my parents consented, although Papa looked doubtful.

'Oh, thank you, thank you,' I enthused. 'Tassia, you must come, it will be such fun!'

The first stage of my plan successfully achieved, I relaxed. It was agreed that I would have my first driving lesson the following afternoon. Later that night, in the privacy of my bedroom, I told Tassia my plan. '*Magnifique!*' she said, but then added with a worried look, 'I hope it works.'

The next day I forced myself to act civilly and be friendly to Mr Blake, but it was not easy. I did not enjoy our day on the beach; I felt impatient and nervous. Papa, Tassia and I swam to the raft anchored a little way out to sea and lay there in the sun, occasionally diving in to cool off. I was risking sunburn, but it was better than watching Mother flirt with that creep. Papa showed no sign that he noticed the goings-on – the only way I knew he did, was that his silences were deep and his eyes sad. My poor papa.

Finally the hour of reckoning came, and Mr Blake, Tassia and I were on our way to the back road. Once there, I took the driver's seat. The familiar little road ran straight. At the far end of it, on the left, stood a villa well away from the road, surrounded by a wall made of big raggedy stones. My aim was to get there.

After practising shifting gears and pressing the right pedals, listening intently to the creep's instructions and Tassia's encouragements, I was finally allowed to put what he hoped I had learned into practice. After a few hiccups and stalling the engine, I got the hang of it and slowly proceeded up the road. Mr Blake relaxed a bit, but Tassia grew silent.

When the car reached the villa wall, I turned the steering wheel sharply to the left and pressed the accelerator pedal a little harder – at that, the front of the car went smack into the wall. There was a nasty sound of crunching metal and broken glass grating our ears as we jerked to a stop. The second step of my mission was accomplished! I braced myself for the finale.

'Why did you do that? Oh my God, you silly girl! Why did you swerve?' yelled Mr Blake.

'I will tell you why, Mr Blake,' I answered icily. 'You are disgusting! I find your behaviour with my mother despicable. You are making a fool of my father. I will not allow you to hurt him. Now you have a good excuse to leave tomorrow and get out of our lives. Your car needs repairs.' (I had rehearsed that speech all day!)

'I don't know what you're talking about!' wailed Blake.

'Tassia and I saw you and Mother in London, in the street by our lodgings. Your behaviour left no doubt as to the nature of your relationship.' Then I lost my cool and shouted at him, 'Go away, get out of our lives!'

Tassia and I got out of the car and could not resist inspecting the damage. The bumper bar? Well, it needed replacing. The glass in both headlights was smashed and the paint on one wing was scratched. No big deal – I had been going very slowly. But I was satisfied. It was enough of a nuisance to teach him a lesson.

Tassia and I walked back and waited for Blake on the road by the villa. He took his time. Everyone was on the terrace when we approached. I hastened to inform them what a stupid, rotten learner I was and how clumsy I had been to drive the car into a wall. Acting very apologetic, I said to Mr Blake, 'You will have to take the car to Nice or Cannes tomorrow for repairs.'

He did not answer, just muttered. My father was embarrassed and kept apologising for me. Mother looked annoyed as hell. Tassia's mama loudly demanded a beer. Arnold Haskell eyed Tassia and me suspiciously while he sucked his pipe and stifled a grin. Dinner was awkward, but next morning Mr Blake left.

As we swam to the raft that day, Tassia asked me, 'What would you have done if he hadn't left?'

'Killed him!'

We both laughed. The rest of our holiday was looking good. Papa found his voice and joined in our fun. Mother looked annoyed with me for a few days and then reverted to her normal behaviour.

We went to Monte Carlo to gorge ourselves on the best pastries in the world at the Pâtisserie Pasquier. Haskell made Tassia and me compete over who could eat the most pastries. Tassia stopped after her eighth piece; I won eating twelve, but I could not face dinner that night!

But, as all good things come to an end, the time soon came for us to pack our bags and start thinking about Mexico City. I was looking forward with great anticipation to discovering a new country.

5

TROUBLE IN THE FAMILY

The members of our company who had holidayed in England boarded the ship at Tilbury, but the rest of us joined it on its brief stop at Le Havre in France. It was a happy reunion, as everybody compared notes on their holidays, rested and looked forward to the Mexico season.

My parents were entrusted with the care of the youngest member of the company, Kira Strakhova (real name Patricia Thal – we called her Patka), whose mother could not come with us. She was a Preobrajenska student like me, and we had been friends since I was eleven. I was glad to share a room with her. She was a good dancer but as thin as a stick – she ate chocolate cake and drank Guinness every day in the hope of putting on some weight. In Mexico she would pinch *pesos* from my father's pockets at night so that she could buy ice-cream the next morning. Patka had the most hilarious sense of humour, which to this day she has not lost, bless her.

Upon arrival in New York, we transferred to our special train and steamed to Mexico City. In Laredo, the frontier village between the United States and Mexico, we had to stop for three hours, parked on a siding. Night was falling and dim lights popped up here and there, illuminating the buildings near the railway tracks. Loud music and singing attracted our attention. It came from a dwelling with a sign above the doorway proclaiming 'Bar'.

By morning, we had arrived in Mexico City. First impression: clean, limpid air – we were at 10000 feet altitude – large squares; big beautiful churches; gaily decorated stalls selling flowers and food, the kind you find only in Mexico; Latino–Spanish buildings that reminded me of Barcelona; lively but not-at-all-crowded streets, with traffic that did not bring out the worst in people, no bumper-to-bumper queues, no traffic jams, plenty of elbow room for everyone; lots of beggars, many of them children and nursing mothers.

The minute you sat down in an outside café, boys would assail you and offer to clean your shoes. The obvious poverty was disturbing and sad. One afternoon, as we sat with a Mexican friend, a woman clutching a baby wrapped in a blanket approached our table begging. I had reached for my purse when our friend said that the woman was faking her baby. 'Look,' he said sharply, pulling at the blanket. Out rolled two cabbages! The poor woman ran away on the double.

Our theatre, the Palacio de Bellas Artes, a beautiful building in the grand manner of the Opéra Garnier in Paris, graced one end of a large square in the centre of the city. But although the building had just been completed after many years of building, the foundation on one side was already sinking, giving the structure a look reminiscent of the Leaning Tower of Pisa! Amazingly now, seventy-odd years later, it is still standing in all its glory!

As we took our first class the morning after our arrival, we realised with dismay how quickly we ran out of breath due to the high altitude. I tried to take deep breaths of air every time I had to stand still in a pose, and tried not to let my body sag. Deep breathing helped a bit, but none of us had expected to undergo such terrible, excruciating pain in the chest and lungs as we endured during the first couple of weeks. At first, after each exit into the wings, we would double up with pain, gasping and hanging onto anything handy, but we gradually became acclimatised and got the hang of it.

As we were inaugurating the Palacio de Bellas Artes, our first performance was a special gala affair. The performance was sold out, the boxes occupied by dignitaries and foreign diplomats with their most elegant wives. The audience in the stalls was just as impressive. We eyed them with great satisfaction as they took their seats. As the performance proceeded, the audience's approval grew and grew. When the curtain came down on the last ballet, we received a standing ovation that seemed to last an eternity! Curtain call after curtain call, together, separately, together again, it went on and on – the audience would not let us go! It was a great morale-boost and made it worth suffering the excruciating pains in our lungs.

We were asked to remain on stage to meet the 'important people', who came escorted by Colonel de Basil. The general informal chatter was most jovial and we felt that we would make many good friends in that lovely city. The first invitation came from Don Pedro Corcuera. He wanted to take the Massines, Choura, Tania, David and me to see Diego Rivera's famous mural paintings in Cuernavaca, a small town near Mexico City. On a lovely sunny morning, we set off. Don Pedro reminded me very much of Uncle Freddie – tall, lean and aristocratic-looking. He was in his late fifties, perhaps – anyone over thirty-five seemed elderly to me. He was a charming host and soon became a very special friend.

Cuernavaca was a lovely small, mostly residential town. I remember many, many oleanders bordering the roads. Diego Rivera's murals depicting Mexican rural life, in a long arched gallery opening onto a simple, neat garden, were magnificent. After a splendid lunch on the terrace of a local taverna, we drove back to the theatre for our afternoon rehearsal.

A group of us, including Patka and my parents, went to Xochimilco, just outside the city. It was famous for its canals, which were flanked by fields of wild flowers, and on which one could go boating. Over the long, narrow boats were arches covered in beautiful flowers that perfumed the air. The boatman, in white clothes and a sombrero, pushed the boat with a long pole, like a gondola or a punt. Gliding along, with the sky reflected in mirror-like water, and surrounded by flowers, it felt so romantic. I remember wishing I had someone to hold hands with.

We hoped our next visit would be longer and that we would be able to see more of this fascinating country and its rich ancient history and culture. Our last performance, on 17 October 1934, was a gala, and the farewells were touching. I, for one, was sorry to leave, but we had to open in Montreal, Canada, on 25 October, and so it was back onto our special train for the long trek across America.

Montreal seemed very tame after Mexico City. Golden trees lined the street from our hotel to the theatre. There were wooden footpaths and many shops selling fur coats – we were told that even on our meagre salary we could afford to buy a fur coat in Canada, so all the girls went for it. We could afford squirrel, sheepskin or skunk. My parents bought me a grey squirrel coat and I was so very proud of it.

Our performances in Montreal, Toronto and Quebec were all a great success – full houses, wonderful press. The Canadian countryside we saw from the train was beautiful, but there was no socialising, no sightseeing, just total concentration on rehearsals for our rapidly growing repertoire.

The American tour that followed was just as gruelling as the previous one had been. Chicago, the windiest city on earth, was a joy. The Auditorium Hotel, where we usually slept over Christmas, was huge and very comfortable. We rehearsed in the hotel's west ballroom, which was connected by a passage to the theatre. We did not have to go out into the street at all if we did not want to. On cold, windy or blizzardy days, it was a blessing not to have to show one's nose outside.

All this time, Jerry kept his distance, sort of – let's say, from ten yards it came down to five yards. Looks were exchanged and notes found their way into my hands. I replied in lipstick on loo-paper, scribbling away locked in the loo. It was scary, thrilling, fun – a game!

It was in Chicago that we met Dr Alexander Gabrielianz (Sasha to us). He became a close friend of the Colonel and took great interest in the company's health, plying us with vitamins and instructing Colonel de Basil on how to inject us with B12. Sasha used to follow us whenever we went to Cuba. He would shut his surgery, then call in his barber to shave his entire body. I once asked him why on earth he would do that. He informed me, his big fat body shaking with laughter, that he was very, very hairy all over and children on the beach used to pull his hair and call him a monkey, until their embarrassed parents would rush to pull them away. He adored pretty women but was single (no wonder!) and was simply adorable. I corresponded with him until his death – his fun letters, full of *joie de vivre*, brought humour into my life and, at a sad moment, a smile. Dear Sasha, may you rest in peace.

At the end of our American tour we had our season in New York. We lodged in the same unattractive furnished flats and again Mama Kobseva cooked for us. For some reason I could not understand, Mother told me I would be sleeping in the bedroom with her (twin beds, thank God!), while Papa slept on a mattress in the sitting room. Before, it had always been me in the sitting room. I was puzzled but did not ask questions. One did not ask Mama questions.

One night I was already in bed, exhausted and sleepy, when I was jolted fully awake by my parents' raised voices coming from the next room. Mama was asking for a divorce! I sat up in bed bewildered, straining to hear my parents' every word.

'What do you intend to do?' asked Papa.

'Go to London and take Irina with me.' I froze and started to shake. Panic took hold of me, my head swam and only snippets of their conversation reached my ears.

'Ian Blake?'

'Yes, and Irina could join the English Ballet,' was Mother's reply.

'No, Irina's place is here and you will not break her heart by taking her away from our company. For her sake, we must stay together. I shall never consent to a divorce!'

Silence . . . then I heard Mama crying.

So, I had achieved nothing by crashing that creep's car – silly, naïve me. I had an urge to run to Papa and beg him to let Mama go, to tell him that I would never leave him or my company, that Mama could not force me, that I was almost sixteen! But I did not. I was afraid. Of what? I did not know.

Papa's steps approached the bedroom and I dived under the covers, turning my face to the wall and pretending to be asleep. Papa came in. I felt him kneel by my bed, put his head on it and start to cry. How

I longed to take him in my arms, talk to him, but I did not. Lost, embarrassed, I pretended to sleep. Now, seventy-odd years later, as I relive that traumatic night, I am ashamed of myself. If only I had spoken out, our lives could have taken a different course, a happier one for us all. Why oh why did I not speak out?

From that night on there was no more talk of divorce.

MEETING NIJINSKA

Our life at the flat was now more silent than ever. I was grateful I had to spend most of my time in the theatre. My heart was heavy and it was an effort to concentrate on my work. I could not share my anxiety with anyone, not even with Tassia or Mme Tchernicheva. Some things I simply could not talk about.

Our season ended with rave notices for everyone, but I was glad to embark the liner to Le Havre, from where, via Paris, we were to travel by train to Monte Carlo. To get away from that ugly flat in New York and its unhappy memories was in itself a relief. Before we left, I had my sixteenth birthday. I had awaited it eagerly and, although it was just another day, it felt great to turn sixteen. My parents gave me a lovely present of two pairs of earrings, one of white crystal, the other pendants of pear-shaped topaz. They made me feel so grown-up!

On board ship I had a wonderful surprise: a cabin to myself with a connecting door to my parents' cabin – usually we had one cabin for three people. I thanked Colonel de Basil profusely. He smiled and said, 'Well, you're sixteen now, and I thought you'd like some privacy.'

Indeed, I liked it and badly needed it, being still upset by recent events between my parents. I felt very tired throughout the trip, and spent most of my time stretched out on a deckchair on the upper deck, covered with a thick blanket, dozing, reading or just looking at the ever-fascinating ocean. Papa was always by my side, sketching or reading.

The news that in Paris I was to meet Bronislava Nijinska, Vaslav Nijinsky's sister, lifted my spirits. She was to choreograph *Les Cent*

Baisers. Colonel de Basil had arranged for Boris Kochno and me to go straight to his office when we arrived in Paris. There Uncle Freddie, having flown from London, would meet us and play her and her husband, Nicolai Singaevsky, the finished music for *Les Cent Baisers*. In the evening we were to meet up with the company at the Gare de Lyon and catch the Paris–Lyon–Méditerranée train to Monte Carlo, where we were to open on 4 April 1935.

We arrived at Colonel de Basil's office in good time. Uncle Freddie was already there – I was so happy to see him again. While we waited for Mme Nijinska, Uncle Freddie played the 'Finale' for us. We were all in such high spirits! Mme Nijinska and her husband arrived on the dot and were shown into the office by Mme Bouchonnet, the Colonel's assistant in his Paris office. I immediately felt intimidated – strange, disturbing vibes filled the room.

Nijinska was small and broad, sort of four by four. She wore a severe black suit over a white shirt, her mousy hair flat over her ears and secured in a tiny bun at the back of her head. She had a broad face, slightly slanty eyes and full lips. She greeted the Colonel and Kochno with a faint smile – but then, of course, she knew them both. Her blank expression as I was introduced to her was very off-putting.

Once Uncle Freddie had been introduced, he expressed his pleasure (in perfect French – Nijinska's English was practically nonexistent) that Madame had agreed to choreograph his ballet, which he had written for Mlle Baronova. In response, Nijinska snapped back, 'I don't want Baronova. I want Danilova!'

In the ghastly silence that followed, Nijinska's husband – a tall, lean, charming man – tried to murmur something into Madame's ear. She brushed him away with some measure of irritation. Colonel de Basil wiped his specs and was about to say something, Kochno gazed pensively at the floor, Uncle Freddie packed his music back into his briefcase and left the room, saying quietly, 'I'm going back to London.'

The Colonel ran out after him, Kochno ran out after the Colonel. I was left alone with Nijinska and her husband, wishing I were dead! No-one spoke. Nijinska sat down and nonchalantly reached in her handbag for a cigarette, inserted it into the longest cigarette-holder I have ever seen, then sat poised, waiting for her husband to light it. The silence was loud and unfriendly – Nijinska totally ignored my presence. *Well, I thought, this is ridiculous. I must do something. What the hell – I have nothing to lose!*

I approached her chair, sat on my haunches and put my hands on her lap while she stared at me with a mixture of incredulity and astonishment. 'Bronislava Faminishna' (this is a customary Russian form of address) I quietly began, 'I know you have worked with Danilova before, and I understand your reluctance to work with me, but you do not know me. Please, please try me. I have looked forward so much to working with you, ever since Baron d'Erlanger told me that he was composing a ballet for me! He thought of you as the choreographer and I felt so excited that I would have the honour of working with you! Please give me this chance!'

Nijinska half turned towards her husband, who was standing rather bewilderedly by her chair, and said, 'Nicolai Nicolaevich, what did she say?' *Oh dear*, I thought, *she must be hard of hearing*, and so I repeated my little speech in a loud voice. When I had finished, Nijinska snapped at me, 'Don't shout, I'm not deaf!' But a shadow of a smile crossed her face and she added, 'I heard you the first time. All right. I will try to work with you.'

I jumped up and kissed her on both cheeks, thanking her for her change of heart. Then I dashed to the open window, aware of arguing voices in the courtyard below. There they were, Uncle Freddie pacing up and down, while the Colonel and Kochno kept pace with him, gesticulating, all three obviously upset. I called and waved, shouting, 'Come back, come back. Mme Nijinska says she'll work with me! It's okay!'

They came back; Uncle Freddie eyed Nijinska with suspicion but Madame was all smiles now and asked to hear the music. She liked what she heard, we all relaxed, and a date was set for her arrival in London to do some preliminary work with Uncle Freddie and Kochno. We saw Nijinska and her husband to their car, and they departed in a friendly, civilised way.

Then Colonel de Basil, Uncle Freddie and Kochno plied me with questions. Why had Nijinska changed her mind? What had happened? As I recounted the farcical scene to them, even Uncle Freddie had to laugh, in spite of his lingering anger. 'Strange lady,' he commented, as he departed for the airport.

While Colonel de Basil returned to his office, Kochno and I went for a stroll and had an early dinner at a brasserie he knew. He then conveyed me to the Gare de Lyon and into the arms of my parents, who were anxious to know how my meeting with Nijinska had gone. When I told them, Papa laughed and said, 'Well done!' but Mother did not share his sense of humour. Diaghilev's dancers laughed and were amazed at my daring, but they warned me that working with her would not be all roses. So did Papa Grigoriev and Mme Tchernicheva. As the train rolled towards the South of France, rocking me into slumber, I relived my strange encounter with this lady over and over again.

Monte Carlo was always a pleasure to return to, and I settled down to rehearsals and performances. Massine started work on his third symphonic ballet, *Symphonie fantastique*, based on Hector Berlioz's narrative music in five movements. It was going to be a big production, with designs by Christian Bérard, costumes for the second, third and fourth movements by Mme Karinska and for the first and fifth movements by Mme Larose, our own wonderful wardrobe mistress.

The premiere was scheduled for 24 July 1936. Efrem Kurtz, one of our conductors, had his hands full working with Massine on the music, while our other conductor, Antal Dorati, collaborated with Baron d'Erlanger on the orchestration of *Les Cent Baisers*.

After Monte Carlo, we returned to beautiful Barcelona. On 9 May 1935, the opening-night audience was brilliant, and at the end there were bouquets of gorgeous flowers for us all. We were showered with flowers thrown from the balcony and gallery amid shouts of bravo that warmed and thrilled our hearts. Let's face it, it's rewarding to be appreciated and makes it all worthwhile – the hard work, the sweat, and the homeless, gypsy existence! It also made me realise that our great choreographers, Fokine, Massine and Balanchine; the legacy Diaghilev left us;

our ballet tradition; our constant search for the new; and our collaboration with great painters and composers, all made our company unique. I felt so privileged and grateful to be a part of it all. Yes, of course I enjoyed being successful immensely, but above all I loved the work that got me to the top.

One free afternoon, Paul Petroff volunteered to come with me to the docks in search of a playmate for my little marmoset, Miky, which Arnold Haskell had bought for me in Harrods. The docks were swarming with people gazing at cages full of colourful birds, mostly parrots. There were some furry creatures, but Paul and I did not know what they were. We wandered along, almost losing hope of seeing a marmoset, when suddenly there one was, in a tiny cage tucked between a parrot and a stall selling beverages. As I dashed towards the cage, Paul restrained me. 'I'll bargain,' he said, 'I'm better at it than you.'

He was, bless him. The little monkey looked scared and shy – it was a little smaller than Miky. 'Maybe it's a girl,' I ventured.

'God forbid! What would you do with the babies?'

The vendor had no clue which gender the marmoset was. *Never mind*, I thought. I had to have it – and I got it! Paul and I returned triumphantly to our lodgings and my parents' worried looks soon disappeared at the sight of the newcomer's cute face. 'Is it a girl or a boy?' my father asked.

Paul had an idea. 'There's a pharmacy next door, the man could surely tell us!'

We grabbed the cage and ran to the pharmacy, then pushing the cage towards the bewildered pharmacist, demanded, '*Señor o Señorita?*'

The man must have thought we were nuts. Wildly gesticulating, he kept shouting, '*Veterinario*,' and almost pushed us out the door.

We were none the wiser – what should we do? We let the newcomer into Miky's cage and they immediately had a fight. We distracted them with a banana, but decided we had acquired another boy. We called him Peki. Miky and Peki were friends by the end of the day and lived happily through thick and thin for nine years – a record: marmosets usually do not live more than five or six years. One morning Miky's dear old heart gave way and he died. Peki, grieving for his friend, refused food and the next morning died too. They were affectionate, intelligent little creatures, and my parents and I sorely missed them.

Our Spanish friends told us the small tailor shops in Barcelona would make us some wonderful suits and coats to measure. The cloth was of high quality and very, very cheap, as was the workmanship. Off went Tania and I to the supplied address, where we were indeed amazed by the quality and choice of different cloths and colours. We ordered a suit and a coat each. They were ready inside a week, fitted perfectly and cost next to nothing! Toumanova bought Spanish earrings – beautiful pieces that looked great on her. Most girls went for shoes, beautifully made from fine leather. The men also favoured shoes, and big bottles of Jerez sherry. In each country we visited, there was some specialty that was welcome and affordable on our meagre salary.

One afternoon when I went to the theatre to see Papa, I found him in deep conversation with Pablo Picasso, who had surprised us by coming unexpectedly to see how his designs for *Le Tricorne* were faring. Picasso found my father busy working on the scenery. Knowing how thrilled Papa must have been to have these moments with Picasso, I stayed in a dark corner of the stage and observed them. They talked in French – Picasso said he was pleased with the colours, which Papa had mixed in separate containers to match the originals, and then the discussion switched to the Russian Revolution. Picasso wanted to know how we had escaped. Listening to Papa, he became pensive, then taking off his jacket and rolling up his shirt sleeves, he chose some brushes and joined Papa, crawling around the backdrop spread on the floor. Since I knew that I would be seeing Picasso later that evening at supper and did not want to disturb them now, I left them to it, thinking what a nice man Picasso was.

The next night *Le Tricorne* was on the program. We had a run-through with the orchestra in the afternoon, conducted by Antal Dorati. The overture over, the curtain went up and Picasso appeared, walking briskly across the stage holding a small pot of paint and waving a brush at Dorati, 'Maestro, Maestro,' he cried. 'Stop!'

The orchestra faded away. There was an astonished silence, and all eyes turned to Picasso. He reached the side panel of his backdrop then crouched to 'refresh' his signature in the lower right-hand corner. Stepping back, he looked at it for a moment, then satisfied with the result, turned to Dorati, made a grand gesture with his brush and said, 'Maestro, *continuez!*' and disappeared into the wings. Oh, how we laughed!

Barcelona is in Catalonia and we soon realised that there was no love lost between the Catalonians and the rest of the Spaniards. Our next stop was Valencia, the capital city of Valencia Province, near the mouth of the Guadalquivir. It is a beautiful old city, with great character of its own. When we were in Barcelona, Colonel de Basil had met a former Russian officer who had fought in the White Army during the Revolution. He was captured and tortured, and his wife and baby were shot in front of his eyes. He was so traumatised by these experiences that he could hardly speak – his stuttering was appalling. When we met Kolia, he was jobless.

While we were in Spain, Colonel de Basil offered Kolia a temporary job selling souvenir programs in the theatre foyer. In Barcelona all went well – Kolia had written the price of the programs on a piece of card to show the purchaser. On the first night in Valencia, Kolia could not find his card. A member of the audience asked for a souvenir program, but poor Kolia could not get a word out, stuttering, 'A-a-a-o-o-a,' getting nowhere except into a panic, which was no help at all. The would-be purchaser lost patience and barked, 'And your accent is Catalonian too!' Poor Kolia was so distressed he returned to Barcelona the next day.

As the end of our Spanish season approached, I grew more and more impatient to get to London and meet my next challenge: Mme Nijinska and a totally new work.

A HUNDRED KISSES

How good it was to be back in London and in my dressing room at the Royal Opera House. It was home. We were to open on 11 June 1935, so rehearsals were intense. Those for *Les Cent Baisers* were held at the Drill Hall in Chenies Street, which was around the corner from Goodge Street Station, not far from the Opera House.

Les Cent Baisers is Hans Christian Andersen's story (usually published in English as 'The Swineherd') of a fey and capricious princess who is prepared to kiss a swineherd, really a disguised prince, for material gain but fails to recognise the treasure of true love with the prince. The ballet shows that some things that do not glitter are gold. I played the Princess, Edouard Borovansky the King, David Lichine the Prince, Roman Jasinski the Gardener, and Yurek Lazowski the Birdcatcher.

We all awaited Mme Nijinska's arrival with trepidation, but when the day of the first rehearsal finally arrived, the call was for me alone – the rest of the cast were not needed until the next day. I was pleased to have a chance to be alone with Nijinska so I could concentrate fully on grasping her way of working, and I hoped to end the day without tears. I went to the Drill Hall straight after morning class and braced myself for this first encounter.

Our pianist, Rica, arrived and settled down at the piano while I warmed up. Mme Nijinska and her husband arrived punctually. I rushed to the door to greet them and saw, with great relief, that Boris Kochno was with them. Mme Nijinska greeted me in a very friendly way, as did her husband, and I relaxed, all tension gone. After kissing Boris, I introduced Rica to Madame, who silently shook hands with her.

Nijinska had her working clothes on – black slacks, loose white shirt, and soft leather ballet shoes on her tiny feet. Two of the chairs against the wall were to be hers: one for her to sit on, the other for her cigarettes, long cigarette-holder, lighter and ashtray. Lastly, she pulled out of her handbag a pair of white cotton gloves, which she proceeded to put on. I watched, fascinated. Her cigarette lit, she looked satisfied and turning towards me said, 'Let's start, shall we?'

For my first entrance, she explained, I would whirl through the large gates of the castle, starting with *chaînés* (continuous turns on alternating feet *en diagonale*) well out of sight of the audience and finishing with *pirouettes* and non-stop whirling to the other side of the stage – whirl,

whirl, whirl! Very effective to look at, technically very difficult, but I always loved a technical challenge. It was gratifying to master the technical side so I could give my thoughts and feelings to the role and so that the audience would believe I was the character I was supposed to represent.

As we worked on Nijinska's steps, I observed that from the waist down it was pure classical but from the waist up it was stylised – the posture, the angle of the shoulders, the turn of the head, the arms slightly bent at the elbows with the hands bent back from the wrists. This posture immediately established the haughty, capricious personality of the Princess. I loved it! It was different, exciting, and it was an inspiration to watch Nijinska demonstrate; her movements were so expressive, she was so wrapped up in her vision and what she wanted.

We worked in a friendly, happy atmosphere, Nijinska only pausing from time to time to light yet another cigarette. All aloofness gone, she emerged as a lovely human being – eccentric, yes, but wonderful to work with. I felt that I would learn a great deal from her. I also felt that I was not on trial any more. She said as much when we finished work at lunchtime. Patting my cheek she said, 'You'll be very good in this role.'

Over lunch with Kochno, I asked why Nijinska wore white gloves at rehearsal. 'She hates touching sweaty bodies with her bare hands,' he replied.

The afternoon rehearsal was very productive. I assimilated Nijinska's style quickly and, at the end of the day, my entrance and solo were choreographed. I looked forward to the next day's rehearsals with great anticipation. The whole cast was to be there, and Papa Grigoriev would be at every rehearsal from then on. Boris Kochno divided his time between our rehearsals and visiting Jean Hugo in France to see how he was progressing with the designs for our costumes and scenery.

Next morning after class we all dashed to the Drill Hall. Papa Grigoriev had warned us all to be ready before Mme Nijinska's arrival or there would be big trouble; she was a stickler for punctuality. When Nijinska arrived with her husband, as usual on the dot, Papa Grigoriev greeted her with a certain coolness, to which she responded with double coolness. I later heard that when they were both in Diaghilev's company their relationship had been far from amicable.

I approached Nijinska to bid her and her husband good morning. She patted my arm and proceeded to arrange her smoking implements on her chair. Finally, having donned her white gloves and lit a cigarette, she asked Grigoriev to call the dancers forward. She exchanged a brief muttered greeting with those she knew; the others received a silent nod as Grigoriev told her their names

Mme Nijinska started with the maids of honour. At the start she seemed calm, but very soon she began to show signs of impatience and irritation, picking on individual dancers, throwing unkind remarks and sarcasm at them in a brusque manner, as saliva accumulated at the corners of her mouth. Tamara Tchinarova, Anna Volkova and Galia Razoumova, when they had come back to work with Nijinska in Monte Carlo during our American tour, had all been reduced to tears. They had told us how terrifying it was to be picked on by Nijinska and were dreading having to work with her again. Suddenly Nijinska stopped and demanded that all three come forward. My poor friends' faces expressed utter misery in anticipation of Madame's tongue-lashing. Nijinska, addressing herself to the rest of the dancers, shouted, 'These are my girls! Look at them – they are doing exactly what I want.' Their faces were now a picture to behold!

As I observed Mme Nijinska at this first rehearsal with the cast, I tried to figure out her neurotic behaviour, the sharp contrast in her demeanour from the previous day. She fascinated me, in a strange way. Balanchine was relaxed, charming; Massine was dry, highly focused, controlled; Nijinska? Alarming! I just watched.

Borovansky looked imposing as the King. A character dancer and excellent mime with a strong personality, no-one could intimidate him. All was peace between him and Mme Nijinska. Madame knew David Lichine and obviously liked him, which was a great relief to me when we started to work on the very intricate *pas de deux*. I did observe one thing: Nijinska was much nicer on the whole to the boys than she was to the girls. But her impatience and temper were always lurking just beneath the surface, ready to explode at the drop of a hat. Nevertheless, as the days went by, everyone including Nijinska became considerably more relaxed.

Meanwhile Mme Karinska started making the costumes in Paris. As Jean Hugo could not leave his home to supervise her, Christian Bérard, a designer of great repute and a close friend of Kochno, volunteered to help and work closely with Karinska. Bérard was also working on his designs for Massine's *Symphonie fantastique*, and was a frequent and much-loved visitor at our seasons in London. From the day I met him in 1932, when he designed the costumes and sets for Balanchine's *Cotillon*, I liked him immensely. He was in his early thirties, and had good stature and a warm personality. He was sentimental, kind and hugely talented, his work invariably beautiful. His friends called him 'Bébé' – soon I had the privilege of counting myself among them.

Mme Karinska had the measurements of all in our company and could start work on the costumes without us. For final fittings she came to London, bringing her two head seamstresses and all the costumes. The final work on them was done in the wardrobe at the Opera House. The following year she established her *atélier* in London, leaving her daughter in charge of her Parisian business. As Karinska was constantly busy making costumes for our company's new productions, it was great to have her in London, where our seasons were lengthy. Being a perfectionist, Karinska often delivered our costumes at the last minute.

Time seemed to fly and the first rehearsal with the orchestra was upon us with Antal Dorati conducting. It was always exciting to hear the music played by a full orchestra. Dorati was a joy to work with – his verve and humour encouraged and uplifted us, and we knew he would watch and follow us carefully.

We were about to start. Dorati was going through his tempos with Nijinska, who was standing with Uncle Freddie. Kochno, Bruce Ottley and several other people, including Jerry, were talking to Bérard some distance away. I saw Colonel de Basil come in escorting the Duchess of York! I was really touched by her interest and, whoops, my stomach was full of butterflies!

'Curtain down, please,' shouted Papa Grigoriev. We took our places, the curtain came down and we waited for the overture. I crossed myself and prayed. *Please, God, help me not to fail Uncle Freddie and Mme Nijinska!*

My papa and mother were in the wings; I glanced at them and they nodded and smiled at me encouragingly. A wave of tenderness and love surged in my chest – I owed them so much! Pulling myself together, concentrating on my role, I waited for the first sounds from the orchestra.

The first run-through went well. Just a few times Nijinska stopped Dorati for a few minor adjustments. In the *pas de deux* I was happy with Lichine's, for once, lovely partnering. No pinching, no bruising! Nijinska called a fifteen-minute rest and then requested a full non-stop run-through.

Afterwards, Colonel de Basil called to me to join him and the Duchess of York (much later the Queen Mother). As I did my curtsy, the Duchess asked me to sit beside her. She loved *Les Cent Baisers* and said she hoped it would be performed at a matinee, so she could bring her daughters, Elizabeth and Margaret, to see it. (It was, and she did.) She then asked me how I was planning to do my make-up for the role, adding, 'I just thought that if you had one eyebrow curved up higher than the other, it would give you a capricious expression just right for the role!'

'I shall try that. Thank you – a wonderful idea!' I did try, it looked good, and that's how I kept it.

The costumes had an Elizabethan feel – frilled ruffs, tight bodices, long sleeves with puffed tops, knee-length skirts held up by hoops. My costume was black satin and chiffon, with snow-white buttons forming a garland at the edge of the skirt and in straight lines down the sleeves. It was beautiful and so effective. A very light, blonde wig coiffed in Elizabethan style adorned my head, with a small crown on top, out of which sprouted colourful ostrich feathers. I also wore white gloves. That morning, Karinska tried the costume on me and it fitted perfectly. It needed only a few minor adjustments and was ready for the next day's dress rehearsal.

The girls' dresses were in the same style but in beautiful autumn colours. The men's costumes were handsome and the King's, rich with embroidery and appliquéd motifs, looked fit for Henry VIII. Karinska's execution of Jean Hugo's designs was magnificent!

Uncle Freddie's composition, played by a full orchestra, sounded enchanting, and he and Dorati were satisfied. After the dress rehearsal, Lichine and I talked to Nijinska for a while, discussing some small details. On my way to my dressing room I came face to face with Jerry. He hugged me with a kiss, saying, 'Well done.' It felt so good! By that time, in my naïve teenage way, I was sure I was in love. But I did not linger – Mother was never far away. In my dressing room, I excitedly discussed the rehearsal with Papa and Mother. They loved the ballet and praised my work – that felt good too.

The rest of the day I remained in my dressing room, trying two different ways of doing my make-up until I was satisfied with the result. I wanted to look haughty and capricious but avoid exaggeration, as I also had to look pretty. I tried on my wig to find the best way to secure it to my head. With all the *pirouettes*, I could not risk the calamity of my wig flying off! When I finished sorting all that out, it was time to start getting ready for the regular evening performance. Did I feel tired? I do not know, I did not think about it. Life was too exciting!

The next day, 18 July 1935, was the gala premiere of *Les Cent Baisers*. I woke up thrashing in my bed in despair! I had dreamt I was running up and down some twisting stairs, corridors and more stairs, trying to get onto the stage, which I could not find! I could hear my entrance music approaching as I ran and ran, trapped in that maze of stairs and corridors. My screams woke me up. They also woke my parents. As I sat up in bed dazed, they came to my side, shaking me. When I could finally share my horrid dream with them, we laughed and Papa decreed that I had had an attack of first-night nerves.

It was still very early, just after six a.m., but I was in haste to get to the theatre and the reassuring safety of my dressing room. I wanted plenty of time to get ready for the full dress rehearsal with orchestra scheduled for eleven a.m. That morning, as we assembled on the stage, admired each other's costumes, checked the wings for our entrances and exits, and commented on the scenery, we had a lovely surprise – Mme Nijinska appeared on stage with none other than Jean Hugo! At the last minute, he had decided to leave his home in Lunel, southern France, and come to London for the premiere. No doubt he also wanted to see how his scenery and costumes looked! It was a thrill to meet him, an illustrious artist, whose great-grandfather was Victor Hugo. It was very impressive for me, as I avidly read Victor Hugo's books.

A quiet, gentle person with beautiful old-fashioned courtesy and charm, he was very pleased with Mme Karinska's execution of his costumes but thought the scenery representing the castle looked a bit sinister. He decided to modify it on the spot. My father took him to the prop room and helped him find the right paint and brushes, and right there on the stage, standing on a ladder, Hugo painted pigeons and nests in the archways. It immediately gave the backdrop a different look. He worked quickly, without delaying the dress rehearsal a minute.

As he descended from his perch we applauded him heartily! Boris Kochno was beaming, and even Nijinska smiled approvingly. Everyone's good spirits calmed my butterflies, and as the curtain was lowered, I was ready to twirl and *pirouette* onto the stage and do my very best for Uncle Freddie and Mme Nijinska. I wanted so much to please them!

After the first run-through, Nijinska came on stage from the audience and made some corrections and adjustments. Dorati dismissed the orchestra for half an hour, Kochno checked the lighting. All dancers not in the cast started to gather in the audience to watch our second and final run-through. Massine appeared on stage, talking to Jean Hugo. I spotted my parents in the wings and went over to ask them to watch the second run-through from the audience. I wanted to hear their impressions and comments.

The second run-through went well. Nijinska, Kochno, Uncle Freddie and Dorati were satisfied, and after a thankyou from Mme Nijinska, we were free to go and rest. Back in my dressing room, chatting to my parents as I took off my make-up, I was pleased by their favourable comments. I declined their offer to bring me something to eat – I could never eat before a first night – so they went out together for a bite and to fetch my evening dress for the reception after the performance and for the supper party Uncle Freddie was giving at Boulestin afterwards.

A big night was in front of me – what would it bring? The thought brought the butterflies back into my stomach. Clad in my dressing gown, I stretched out on the couch, propped up my legs and closed my eyes, trying to relax and rest. Rest, yes – my feet were up. Relax? Impossible! My thoughts jumped like crazy rabbits from one thing to another in anticipation of the evening ahead.

By five o'clock, Mother had returned and was quietly busying herself with my toe shoes and tights, checking, cleaning, getting them ready for that night and the next day. I started on my make-up, wanting more time for a good long warm-up on stage. As I was getting into my practice clothes, Mme Tchernicheva came in and offered to give me a short class. I felt so grateful. In spite of her return to the stage and the great success she achieved in *Scheherazade* and *Thamar*, she never stopped being there for me. Her care, coaching, advice and support never diminished. Like Anton Dolin, Mme Tchernicheva was a generous artist – a rarity, I found out through my many years in the theatre.

Finally, the much-anticipated moment arrived. There, gathered on stage, waiting for us to assemble and to wish us luck, were Colonel de Basil, Uncle Freddie, Nijinska, Kochno, Hugo, Ottley, Massine and Jerry. As Jerry and I exchanged a glance, he winked at me. Uncle Freddie held my hand and, I could feel that he was as nervous as I was. Mme Nijinska took me aside and, making the sign of the cross over my chest, kissed me lightly on the forehead and murmured '*S Bogom*' (Go with God).

All except Nijinska disappeared through the side door into the audience. She remained in the wings while we, the cast, said 'break a leg' to each other in the French way: '*Merde, merde, merde!*' In places, curtain up. '*S Bogom*,' I whispered, crossing myself . . . and *pirouetted* through the castle gates.

As the curtain went down again we heard tumultuous applause and knew that *Les Cent Baisers* was a success. I felt utter happiness for all concerned. During the more than twenty-five minutes of curtain calls, I got baskets of flowers and the female dancers each got a bouquet; the men received laurel wreaths. Mme Nijinska, when Lichine and I brought her on stage, received a standing ovation, a basket of flowers taller than her from Uncle Freddie, and a multitude of other floral tributes. She beamed, applauded the dancers, and hugged and kissed Lichine and me. Her dignified charm and modesty, her courtesy towards Baron d'Erlanger when we brought him on stage to another ovation – I could hardly believe that this charming woman could ever be a dragon or reduce dancers to tears! Uncle Freddie was visibly moved. If Hans Christian Andersen could have seen us, surely he would have been pleased by the way we had transformed his fairy tale into a lovely ballet.

Back in my dressing room, friends started to arrive to express their approval and it seemed like ages before they all left. Among the multitude of baskets and bouquets was a basket of special beauty from Uncle Freddie. In the middle of the flowers was a white soft toy elephant – with his upturned trunk and beady eyes, he seemed to smile at me. After reading the card from Uncle Freddie, which brought tears to my eyes, I untied the little elephant and held him tight, silently saying, 'You'll come with me wherever I go and sit on my *doumka* for as long as I live!'

While I changed, my happy mama unpinned all the cards from the flowers for me to read later and write my thanks. In the following days, as I did just that, I noticed that some bouquets were from total strangers, members of the audience who had left no address. If, by some wild chance, any of these kind people happen to read these lines, here is my opportunity to say how much I appreciated their flowers and good wishes, how touched I was and that I have never forgotten it!

Finally, Uncle Freddie escorted me to the reception; we entered the foyer to applause. The super party that followed was a happy ending to a day that was of great importance to my career and reputation as a ballerina. Yes, I worked hard, but the chance to further my standing as an artist was given to me by Baron d'Erlanger, who showed faith in me; Mme Nijinska, who developed new, enriching qualities in my work; and Boris Kochno, who guided us so well. To these three I owe my success on that unforgettable night.

The notices in the next day's newspapers were fabulous for everyone concerned. I was so happy that Ernest Newman praised Uncle Freddie's music. This praise, coming from the leading music critic in England, must have gladdened his heart! Colonel de Basil promptly suggested that Uncle Freddie should think of composing the score for a new ballet, and asked Kochno to think of a libretto. Smart move on Colonel de Basil's part! Having achieved a big success with his first ballet score, Baron d'Erlanger could easily be persuaded to compose another and subsidise the ballet's production. According to Kochno, that was what the Colonel hoped for. His hopes were realised.

Kochno suggested the story of *Cinderella*. Uncle Freddie liked the idea, and what's more, we had a perfect Cinderella – Tania Riabouchinska. Her delicate physique and personality were just right for portraying the role. The following year, Uncle Freddie and Boris Kochno set to work on this new project. Kochno also suggested approaching Michel Fokine to do the choreography. If Fokine accepted, our company would boast new works by the four great choreographers of the time – Balanchine, Massine, Nijinska and the greatest, Michel Fokine.

Several days after the first night of *Les Cent Baisers*, Uncle Freddie took me out to lunch. Afterwards, instead of going back to Covent Garden, to my surprise I found myself whisked to Cartier in Bond Street. 'Irina, choose whatever you want, as a souvenir of our ballet,' Uncle Freddie said as he led me towards the jewellery section, where a gentleman in striped trousers and with a most charming manner enquired what Mademoiselle wished to see. I felt embarrassed – I did not want anything; Uncle Freddie's present to me of *Les Cent Baisers* was the most precious thing he had given me. I told him so! The gentleman in the striped trousers looked puzzled, but Uncle Freddie smiled, saying it would make him happy if I did not argue. 'Show Mademoiselle a few brooches and perhaps these bracelets,' said Uncle Freddie, gently pushing me towards the counter.

As the gentleman in the striped trousers displayed some lovely items for my inspection, a most unusual-looking vanity case in the glass cabinet behind him caught my eye. 'Well, Uncle Freddie, all right,' I said, 'but could I please see that vanity case?' The gentleman in the striped trousers looked questioningly at Uncle Freddie, who nodded. The case was about a foot tall, and when the top was lifted, the front opened up like a gate. Everything inside looked golden – the two hairbrushes, a round mirror with a handle, beautiful crystal bottles, four jars, each item in its special compartment, and a multitude of accessories in boxes. There were also long drawers and, what thrilled me most, a very secret drawer. That was it – I wanted it! 'Can I have it?' I enquired.

'Of course you can,' Uncle Freddie replied. He then told the gentleman in striped trousers that he wanted my initials to be engraved on the handle of every item and a plaque with an engraved inscription from him to be fixed on the inside of the case. I was so thrilled and thanked Uncle Freddie profusely.

The inscription said, '*À ma chère interprète de mon ballet "Les Cent Baisers", ma merveilleuse princesse, avec mon admiration et ma gratitude,* Frederic d'Erlanger.' (To the dear interpreter of my ballet 'A Hundred Kisses', my marvellous princess, with my admiration and gratitude.)

That vanity case travelled with me all over the world. I still have it, and occasionally I take it off the shelf to look at it and remember. By now the strap has rotted away, the hairbrushes have lost a lot of bristles and the round mirror is about to fall off its handle. One crystal bottle is cracked and the drawers are parting at the seams, but the plaque with Uncle Freddie's inscription to me, when I give it a good polish, shines as it did then, seventy years ago.

THE SHOW MUST GO ON

A few days after the premiere of *Les Cent Baisers*, Nijinska had to return to America. There was talk that she might revive *Les Noces* for us sometime during our American tour, which was to start at the Metropolitan Opera House, New York, on 9 October 1935, with visits to Canada and Cuba before a return season at the Met in April. When I was talking to Nijinska before she left, she asked me if I knew she had choreographed the 'Finger' variation (as we call it) and the dance of the 'Three Ivans' for Diaghilev's revival of *The Sleeping Beauty*. Yes, I did know.

'I want to show you how it should be danced, my way!'

That evening, instead of my usual warm-up, in the dim light of the pilot lamp on stage, Nijinska showed me her way. We had no pianist, so Nijinska hummed, sang, roared and mimicked the music of the variation. The steps were the same, but the execution of them was totally different. This seemingly ordinary variation became an extraordinary and devilishly difficult one. It had life, style and *brio*. The only major change was the run-in from the wings and a pause before the start of the variation.

Papa Grigoriev and Mme Tchernicheva had shown Toumanova and me to run on from the top left to the middle and stop, arms extended, fingers pointing. Nijinska said that was totally wrong, that the eight beats preceding the start of the variation must bring me from the down-stage wing, sweeping by the footlights – left arm extended – turning to centre stage and stopping sharply from a deep *plié* (bending move-ment of the knees), arms together, and then up with a twist of the body, throwing the arms sideways, fingers pointed. It made a strong, dramatic entrance. In the variation itself, from the waist up the body and shoulders were never static, the arm movements rounded, elbows slightly raised, the jumps long rather than high. What was an ordinary little variation became a vibrant, unusual, fascinating one. There, on that semi-dark stage, Nijinska singing and shouting, I learned a great lesson. Not a step was altered but it was a different cup of tea!

As Mme Nijinska was leaving, Papa Grigoriev appeared. They nod-ded to each other in silence. I thanked Madame and hugged her, wishing her bon voyage, and then she was gone. I dashed to Papa Grigoriev and told him excitedly that Nijinska had shown me what she wanted in the 'Finger' variation. I was stunned by his hardly contained fury. Spraying me with saliva (his habit when excited), he forbade me to dance the variation Nijinska's way. *Wa-oo!* On the spot, I determined to disobey his orders!

Toumanova and I alternated in *Aurora's Wedding*: when I danced Aurora, she danced the 'Finger' variation, and vice versa. I marched to

Toumanova's dressing room and told her what had happened, also adding that I would show her Nijinska's way.

'Ai-ai-ai,' chorused Tamara and her mama. 'We cannot go against Grigoriev's wishes!'

'I am!' And, nose in the air, I went to my dressing room.

Two days later *Aurora's Wedding* was on the bill and it was my turn to do the 'Finger' variation. I told Mme Tchernicheva what had happened and asked her why her husband, Papa Grigoriev, had forbidden me to dance the variation the way its choreographer, Mme Nijinska, wanted. Mme Tchernicheva gave me a pensive smile, but she did not give me a direct answer. Instead she asked me, 'So-o-o . . . what have you decided to do?'

'Do it Nijinska's way – she's the choreographer!' was my reply.

With a mischievous grin, she wished me good luck.

When the curtain went up, Toumanova and her mama were curious to know what I would do. 'Watch and see,' I replied.

My parents supported my determination to dance the variation Nijinska's way but worried about Papa Grigoriev's reaction. As for me, my adrenaline pumped joyously as I figured out how to outwit Papa Grigoriev, who had stationed himself in the first wing (aha – he knew!), to prevent me making my entrance from there. I lingered in the middle of the wing.

As the variation preceding mine ended and the dancer exited after her bow, I made a mad dash past Papa Grigoriev and was on! Nijinska's way! My colleagues on stage were popeyed, surprised, smiling. Those in the wings applauded as I exited. The audience's applause was loud and lengthy. Once the curtain came down, I went straight to Papa Grigoriev. 'I'm sorry to anger you,' I said, 'but you can see yourself how much more effective the variation has become.'

He sighed, shaking his head sadly. 'What shall I do with you, my angel? You are a bad, naughty girl.'

The matter was never mentioned by anyone again and I continued to dance the variation Mme Nijinska's way while Toumanova always stuck to the old way.

One mid-morning, Salvador Dalí and his wife, Gala, came to watch our rehearsal. At the time, Massine was discussing a new project with Dalí. Introductions over, I sat by Gala. She was Russian and very talkative, inquisitive and friendly. While we talked, in whispers, as the rehearsal resumed, I eyed Dalí with great curiosity. He had a great reputation as an artist and his paintings were much admired, but in some quarters he provoked controversy and heated discussion. I loved his work, no doubt influenced by my papa's admiration, and was fascinated by Dalí's unique imagination. It astonished, shocked and, at times, moved me profoundly.

Dalí was slim and elegant, and I found him devastatingly handsome – in a Latin, romantic way. His moustache was then in its infancy, compared with its ludicrous length in much later years. Curved upwards, the beautifully groomed and waxed moustache was as unusual-looking as Dalí and his work. He sat quietly, intensely observing the dancers.

After the rehearsal, Dalí joined in the general conversation. He was easy to talk to and courteous, but what struck me were his eyes – beautiful, intense, never empty, as if in constant thought and searching. The Dalís were off to America, so I made plans to meet Gala in New York.

My friendship with Tassia was as close as ever, but due to my ever-increasing workload, we had less time to spend together. As we stayed in the same boarding house, at night, ready for bed, Tassia would come to my room. Sprawled on my bed, we would gossip, share our thoughts and laugh a lot. Some evenings after the performance, if Tassia's mother was not in the theatre, we would go with my parents to the pub on the corner to fetch her. If she was not there, it meant she was being looked after by the kind officers at Bow Street Police Station across the road.

Docile and friendly, she was no bother. After a few beers she simply could not walk or find her way back to Tassia's dressing room. Dumped by the barman at Bow Street Police Station, where she was known as the 'regular', she awaited collection by her daughter and friends. Yes, London was such a friendly place!

One day Tassia lost patience with her mother. That morning Tassia had told her mama that if she made one more excursion to the pub she would make arrangements for her to live permanently in Paris, no more travelling with the company. Her mama burst into tears and promised to be good. That evening she wanted to stay at home, complaining she had a bad headache. When we returned to our lodgings, I went with Tassia to her room to see if her mama was feeling better. An extraordinary sight greeted us. The room was in darkness but a faint light came from a single candle on the table at the foot of her mama's bed. The bed was covered in flowers from the bouquet Tassia had received from an admirer the previous night. In the middle of the flowers lay Tassia's mama in her nightshirt, her eyes closed, her hands crossed on her chest. 'Oh my God,' I whispered, riveted to the floor, with goose pimples invading my body.

'Relax,' said Tassia. 'It's her way to punish me, watch! Olga Alexandrovna,' she said, 'I brought you a bottle of beer.'

I could never imagine anyone rising from the dead with such speed! Flowers flew in all directions and Mama was on her feet, all smiles, asking us how the performance went! I left them – the mama to her beer, Tassia to her glass of chianti.

The previous year, at the recommendation of Anton Dolin, the company had engaged Eva Brigitta Hartwig. Her father was German, her mother Norwegian; she had studied ballet in Berlin but come to London to further her studies. When Brigitta became a member of our tribe she was eighteen, on the tall side, blonde, with a beautifully chiselled face, big blue eyes, and sex appeal oozing from every pore! The men panted at her sight, competing for her attention, but Brigitta ignored their advances with cool indifference. Brigitta aimed high; she knew what she wanted – she wanted Léonide Massine. The fact that he was married, seemingly happily, to Eugenia Delarova, did not count either for her or for Massine, who fell for Brigitta in a big way. We all watched the situation progress with dismay and felt deeply sorry for Delarova, who looked more and more miserable.

As was the custom in Diaghilev's day, the non-Russian dancers had to russify their names when becoming a member of our company. The only one who stoically refused was Sono Osato. Her name was unusual, sounded beautiful and looked good in print, so the Colonel made an exception for her. Of the several names suggested to Brigitta, she chose Vera Zorina. She was nice and friendly, not prima ballerina material, but a very good soloist with a charming personality.

Brigitta's mother did not travel with us. She lived in Berlin and occasionally visited her daughter when we were in Europe. But being of the theatrical *milieu* herself, she kept a close watch on Brigitta and her career, and had great ambitions for her. Their relationship was very close – they were a team – and Brigitta adored her. When her mama visited, she did not fraternise with the other mothers, nor with the dancers. She watched the performances from the audience and kept company with Colonel de Basil and his entourage.

We had hopes that *Muthin* (the endearing way Brigitta called her 'mummy') would use her influence over Brigitta and stop the unhappy situation with Massine. But *Muthin* did not do anything about it. I thought of Massine as a genius, a balletic god, different from us mortals, but came to the conclusion that even geniuses are human.

When our London season closed on 22 August 1935 we again held a big party. The Dukes and Duchesses of York and Kent had accepted the invitations, as had the Prince of Wales. We were thrilled! There was a buffet supper and we put together a cabaret-style entertainment. The London Philharmonic Orchestra, conducted by Sir Thomas Beecham, played Viennese waltzes for the guests to dance to.

The company, changed and looking great, gathered on stage. I marvelled at the beautiful flower arrangements, which blocked out the view of the wires, pipes and cables backstage. There were long and round tables, all covered in white linen, with crystal glasses, silver cutlery and place cards. Who sat at the royal table was dictated by protocol.

I felt very proud at the sight of my parents – Mother looked beautiful in a simple long black evening dress with a big pink silk rose tucked in her bodice, and Papa, in a dinner jacket – the first time I had seen him in one – looked so different from the person I was used to seeing in his working smock, paintbrushes in his hands. That Papa's dinner jacket was rented only for the occasion suddenly mattered to me – I felt a pinch in my heart and promised myself that when I had some money, I would buy him a dinner jacket of his very own!

My slightly sad and wandering thoughts were cut short by the appearance of Colonel de Basil escorting the royal party. The greetings over, they were conducted to their table and the curtain went up, which was the signal for the guests to come on stage and take their places. Once everyone was seated, Colonel de Basil stepped into the middle of the stage and, in his funny pidgin English, made a short, charming speech of welcome and thanks to our wonderful English friends.

Once dessert was cleared away, Colonel de Basil stood up and proposed a toast to His Majesty the King, as was obligatory at such functions. Everyone arose and said, 'The King,' and drank His Majesty's health. Now coffee could be served, cigarettes lit and guests could change places to talk to other guests and friends.

After the toast to the King, we dashed to our dressing rooms to change into our costumes, which did not take long. Rica was at the piano in the orchestra pit, and we got on with our little performance. It was much appreciated by our guests, and great fun for us. Back in our evening clothes, we rejoined our guests. The orchestra was now in the pit, and Sir Thomas Beecham appeared at the rostrum, heartily applauded by us all. Beautiful melodies filled the Opera House as Baron d'Erlanger sedately waltzed around the stage with the Duchess of York, then everyone joined in. Protocol commanded that no-one could leave the party before the royals, but they were obviously having fun and did not seem in a hurry to leave.

One of our dancers was drinking vodka with the Duke of Kent. The Duchess of Kent was waltzing away with Cecil Beaton. Even the Duke of York looked relaxed, protected by Captain Ottley from having to talk too much, which made him uncomfortable because of his stutter. He was just content to observe the dancers.

The Prince of Wales gallantly danced with several of us. When we took to the floor, I immediately noticed that, in my high heels, I was taller than him. It was not easy to waltz on half-bent knees, and a couple of times I stepped on his toes. Apologising, I explained that ballerinas are used to leading, but in ballroom dancing it's the man who leads, so we don't make very good ballroom dancers. He laughed, replying that he did not mind having his toes crushed by a Russian ballerina! Most of the time, the Prince of Wales sat in earnest discussion with Lady Cunard who, as the gossip ran, was cultivating his friendship with Wallis Simpson.

It must have been about three o'clock in the morning when the royal party left. We all stopped dancing and waved to them, but once they were gone, the atmosphere relaxed even more. I found Tassia and asked her if she had noticed how Miss Frances D., a well known cabaret singer, had danced with Jerry.

'Yes, it was rather disgusting,' replied Tassia. 'Sort of climbing all over him.'

'Yes, he didn't seem to discourage her,' said I with pangs of jealousy. At that moment we noticed Frances making her way to the ladies' room in the stalls.

'Let's go after her,' said Tassia. As we entered the ladies' room, Frances was reapplying her lipstick in front of the mirror. She was a tall platinum blonde, beautiful in a flashy way, but I noticed that the curls piled up on top of her beautifully coiffed head were a hairpiece.

'Miss D.,' I said, 'it was disgusting the way you danced with Jerry.'

She looked at me with a smile and nonchalantly said, 'Piss off.'

I did not know that expression, so I turned to Tassia and asked her in Russian if it was something rude. Tassia replied in the affirmative so, without stopping to think, I grabbed Miss D.'s false curls and gave them a good pull. Having successfully parted the curls from her head, I dropped them on the floor with disdain. My poor victim shrieked and Tassia and I left the ladies' room, killing ourselves laughing. Miss D. did not reappear at the party.

It was a smashing party. When we got back to our lodgings, dawn was about to break. Luckily the company was free the next day. We were looking forward to our three weeks' holiday, before embarking for New York. As usual, Massine went to the little island he owned – a gift from Diaghilev – Isole dei Galli, in southern Italy, opposite Positano.

Colonel de Basil was needed at his office in Paris, and many members of our company were also headed for the French capital. Tania and Lichine went to stay with friends in Florence. The rest of us made a beeline for the South of France.

Before we all dispersed, I had an opportunity to see Jerry without my mother around. Tassia and I were shopping for bathing suits and bumped into him at one of the entrances to Selfridges in Oxford Street. Tassia, who of course knew of our arm's-length flirtation, gave me a wink, said she would meet me in fifteen minutes at that same door, and disappeared into the shop.

Jerry told me he was remaining in England for the holidays and staying with the Diamantidis at their house in the country. He said he would miss seeing me, even from a distance. After a few more sweet nothings, Tassia reappeared. Jerry and I wished each other a good holiday and, after a hug and a kiss, went about our business. After our holidays were over, I found out that Danilova had spent her holiday at the Diamantidis' as well. It surprised me – I thought their affair was over, since Jerry, at least in public, was avoiding her. I was puzzled, but that day I was happy – looking forward to a good rest, swimming and just relaxing all day on the beach.

The holiday was soon over, and I was happy to join my friends and colleagues on board the ship to America. To be away was nice, to be home was better – the company was my home. We spent the five-day crossing to New York as usual. On the third day out, Tassia passed me a note from Jerry. He asked me to manage somehow to come to his cabin after dinner; he had something very important to discuss with me and would be waiting for me.

I showed the note to Tassia. How could I escape Mother's surveillance? Impossible! But where there is a will, there is a way! That evening after dinner, as we sat in the big lounge having coffee, I suggested to Tassia, within my parents' earshot, that we go to the upper deck for a breath of fresh air.

'Girls,' said Mother, 'put your shawls on. It will be cold out on the open deck.'

I asked Tassia to come with me and stand guard in the corridor, so she could knock on Jerry's door in case of danger and I could make a quick escape. We found the cabin easily – it was on the deck below. I knocked softly, Jerry opened the door. 'You're going to get me into trouble,' I muttered.

'Sit down.' He motioned me towards a chair. 'I want to marry you,' he said. 'Do you want to marry me?'

'It's impossible,' I replied. 'My mother told me I can't marry until I'm thirty.'

After a moment's silence, Jerry asked, shaking his head incredulously, 'Are you stupid? Or are you being funny?' I did not know what to say. 'Am I supposed to wait for fourteen years until you're thirty?' he asked.

But before I could find an answer, the door opened and in stepped Danilova! We stared at each other, she made as if to go, I jumped to my feet. 'Don't go,' I said. 'I was just leaving.' Without a glance at Jerry, I left his cabin. Where the hell was Tassia? Ah – there she was, around the corner by the stairs.

'Sorry, sorry. I couldn't warn you. Danilova's cabin faces Jerry's – she was out and in. There was nothing I could do!'

As we hurried back to the lounge, I asked Tassia if she noticed what a beautiful pale pink satin dressing gown Danilova was wearing – it was absolutely gorgeous. I wished I had one like that . . . *One day.*

'Never mind the dressing gown,' Tassia said impatiently. 'What happened? What did Jerry want?'

I relayed our short conversation verbatim.

'Were you being funny?'

'No! Mother said —'

Tassia interrupted me, barking, 'Then you *are* stupid!'

We reached our coffee table in the lounge and I had no chance to defend my mental capacity. The whole episode seemed unreal, disturbing and puzzling, and a horrible thought crept in as I was getting ready for bed. What if Danilova told my mother she had found me in Jerry's cabin? This thought gave me nightmares in the days to come.

Danilova stopped talking to me. I felt utterly out of my depth and guilty – why? Of course, I had disobeyed my parents, deceived them, lied to them – at the time it seemed like a bit of exciting, romantic fun. *It's no fun now. Is Tassia right? Am I stupid?* My days were poisoned by fear as I waited for an explosion, and I could not concentrate properly on my work.

I had long discussions with Tassia. She thought I was shy by nature, but that when it came to the crunch I was not afraid of anything or anyone, except my mother. Why was that? I could not really explain why. Could I not talk to my father, she asked. Could he not help me sort out my relationship with Mother? No, I could not talk to him. Papa I adored – we could talk about everything, except Mother. I had a strong feeling that subject was taboo.

I struggled to pull myself together, knowing we would soon be opening in New York. Since, so far, Danilova had said nothing to Mother, my fears diminished. Jerry made no reference to the awkward episode in his cabin, and his unromantic marriage proposal did not take hold of my mind. It was unreal and impossible; I was not thirty yet, I was only sixteen.

As the ship sailed into New York, we were all on deck as usual, watching the unique sight of skyscrapers rising from the sea through the early morning mist. This time some of us stayed at a big hotel in Times Square. It was so much nicer than the usual dreary lodgings. In those days, Times Square was nice, lively without being the overcrowded, noisy, smelly bazaar it is today. Not far from the Met either, which was an advantage. The (old) Metropolitan Opera House was not much to look at on the outside, but great inside. It was a large auditorium in red and gold, with a very big, good stage, and old-fashioned dressing rooms in shabby corridors. It had an atmosphere of great tradition.

The opening night was a glamorous occasion. The Mayor of New York, high society, those not mentioned in the *Who's Who* but genuinely interested in our art – everyone was there. The critics were all there, as was the American dancing world – they were curious about and not particularly friendly towards what they called 'the Russian invasion'.

The leading American critic at the time was John Martin. I learned to respect him and read his notices. Although he was a great admirer of Martha Graham and 'modern' dance, he was without doubt knowledgeable in classical ballet, fair and objective. His notices were constructive and often helpful.

The opening night was a great success, and we were well received everywhere we performed on our long tour of the United States and Canada. Massine's symphonies were much discussed and praised, as was all his older work. His performances thrilled the audiences. What a great artist he was!

Not long after our opening in New York, Danilova appeared on the darkened stage as I was warming up for the evening performance. She came straight to me and asked me to come to her dressing room, as she wanted to talk to me. Instinctively, I knew that the subject would be Jerry. I wasn't looking forward to it, but I had no option but to follow her. She motioned me towards the sofa and sat down at her dressing table, turning the chair towards me. She looked kindly at me, hesitating for a moment. 'Irischka,' she said, 'you're so young. You will meet – as you get older – someone who's your age, who'll be the right person for you to fall in love with. Jerry's not right for you. Please stop this flirtation with him. Jerry belongs to me. Leave him alone!' Danilova's mouth and chin were trembling and tears filled her eyes. 'Promise me you'll tell him you don't want his attentions.'

I felt utterly out of my depth, embarrassed. As I stared at her face, thoughts flashed in disorder through my mind – *Jerry . . . makes me feel important . . . secrecy . . . excitement . . . leads nowhere . . . must wait until I'm thirty . . . upsets Danilova . . . not nice . . .*

'Irischka?' Danilova put her hand on my knee, waiting for my response.

With a feeling of compassion and warmth for Danilova, I stood up, hugged her and promised to abide by her wishes. Feeling gratified by my conduct, I hurried out of her dressing room and came face to face with Jerry in the corridor! *Oh God!* Here was my chance to execute my promise to Danilova. In a loud voice, hoping she could hear me, getting more and more out of control, I almost shouted at Jerry, 'Leave me alone. I don't want to talk to you ever again. You belong to Choura. Go to her!'

Danilova's door opened as I made to go. Jerry grabbed my arm and turned me around as he shouted furiously, 'Don't you tell me what to do! I don't belong to anyone and I do what I want!' Upon which he walked towards the stage and out of sight. By now, the other dressing-room doors were open, and curious faces were staring at us, including my mother's. For once I was not scared of her. What she may have over-heard could only please her.

When I was back in my dressing room, she smiled. 'Well done. Finally!'

No . . . not well done. I had a strong feeling that I had made a mess of it. Danilova did not raise the matter with me again; she remained friendly yet somewhat distant, but Jerry ignored us both. Mother relaxed her vigilance, while Tassia teased me, telling me I must practise checking my impulses. As for me, I soon got over the sorry incident and concentrated fully on my work.

On tour in Canada we got snowed in – our train stopped and we had to wait for the snowplough to come and get us moving again. Three days passed before the snowplough arrived. It was fun the first day, playing in the snow. It was the first encounter with snow for our Cuban dancer, Alberto Alonso. He was so excited that he jumped out of the carriage, but being quite short, he totally disappeared in the snow and had to be dug out by his laughing, teasing colleagues.

On the second day, the heating started to give up and the restaurant car ran low on food, but we still had fun and were in good spirits. On the third day there was no heating at all and food was reduced to a minimum, so we sat around clad in coats, hats, scarves and whatever was available, hungry and freezing, getting seriously worried. But at the end of the afternoon the snowplough finally appeared. It was amazing how quickly it got us moving. Later that evening we finally arrived at our destination, where we had been scheduled to perform that night, but we were hours and hours late and so secretly hoped that the performance would be cancelled.

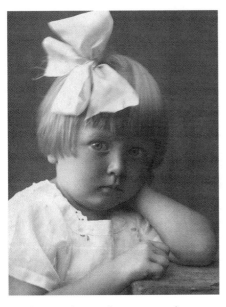

At the age of two, when we were living in Romania.

My papa, Michael Baronov, in his Imperial Navy uniform, 1919.

My mother, Lydia Baronova, and me in 1923.

On Christmas Day 1925, with our first Christmas tree behind me.

My beloved teacher, Mme Olga Preobrajenska, with a lovely note from her in Russian.

Mme Tamara Karsavina, as she was when I saw her dance in Bucharest in 1926.

One of my first ballet poses, aged nine in Paris. (Studio-Iris, Paris)

George Balanchine, who in 1931 was our first choreographer. (© Martha Swope)

In Cotillon *(1932), one of Balanchine's timeless little jewels that has fallen into oblivion.*
(Gordon Anthony, London)

Serge 'Papa' Grigoriev (left), the régisseur général of the Ballet Russe de Monte Carlo, with director Colonel Wassily de Basil (centre) and choreographer and principal dancer Léonide Massine (right).

Mme Olga Preobrajenska with Colonel de Basil, who has my eternal love and respect. These two people had an enormous impact on my career. (Studio-Iris, Paris)

Paul Petroff and me in Michel Fokine's Spectre de la Rose. (Maurice Seymour, Chicago)

The Doll in Michel Fokine's Petrushka *in the 1930s.* (Gordon Anthony, London)

In Aurora's Wedding, *in the role I shared with Alexandra Danilova and Tamara Toumanova.* (Maurice Seymour, Chicago)

Lady Gay in Massine's Union Pacific, *1934.* (Spencer Sitier, Melbourne)

With Marc Platoff in Massine's Symphonie fantastique, *1936.* (Maurice Seymour, Chicago)

As Swanilda in Coppélia, *which I first danced with Massine's Ballet Russe de Monte Carlo in 1940.* (Foto-Semo, Mexico)

*Léonide Massine, the creator of the
first symphonic ballet,* Les Présages,
in which I had my first major role.
(Maurice Seymour, Chicago)

In Massine's Les Présages, *1933.*
(Studio-Iris, Paris)

With David Lichine in Les Présages.
(Batlles, Barcelona)

The legendary choreographer Michel Fokine and his wife, Vera, 1931.
(Lazaro Sudak, Buenos Aires)

As the Queen of Shemakhan in Fokine's magnificent restaging of Le Coq d'or, *1937.* (Maurice Seymour, Chicago)

Tatiana (Tania) Riabouchinska as the Golden Cockerel in Le Coq d'or, *1937.* (Gordon Anthony/V&A Images, The Victoria & Albert Museum)

Mme Bronislava Nijinska, from whom I learned so much.

Rehearsing Les Cent Baisers *with the choreographer, Mme Nijinska, in 1935.*

As the Princess in Les Cent Baisers. *The costume was designed by Christian Bérard.* (Maurice Seymour, Chicago)

Baron Frederic d'Erlanger, 'Uncle Freddie', who composed the music for Les Cent Baisers *with me in mind.* (Harrods, London)

As Lise in Nijinska's La Fille mal gardée, *1940.* (Maurice Seymour, Chicago)

Dinner with Massine's ballerinas; (clockwise from left) Massine, me, Tania Orlova (Massine's third wife), Alexandra Danilova, Mia Slavenska and Alicia Markova, 1940.

Anatole Vilzak, whose wonderful classes I took regularly in New York.
(Michael Kidd, New York)

George Zoritch, so beautiful in
Le Spectre de la Rose. (Castro)

The three 'Baby Ballerinas', Tania Riabouchinska (left), me (centre), and Tamara Toumanova (right), in a publicity shot, American-style, 1933.

With my first husband, Jerry Sevastianov (later Severn), in around 1938.
(National Library of Australia, MS8495, Series 23, Special Album No. 1)

Fooling around with Tania Riabouchinska (left) and David Lichine in Esther and Henry Clifford's Florence garden, 1937.

At Jacob's Pillow in Massachusetts, with Alicia Markova (centre) and Nora Kaye (right), during our first rehearsals for Ballet Theatre, 1940.

My best friend during my Ballet Russe years and beyond, Tatiana (Tassia) Semenova. (G. Nelidoff)

With my collection of soft toys and dolls, including the white elephant Uncle Freddie gave me, before its watery end. (National Library of Australia, MS8495, Series 23, Special Album No. 1)

With Alicia Markova at the opening of an art exhibition in London. (London News Agency Photos Ltd, London)

With Shirley Temple at MGM Studios in 1940; I was shooting Florian *at the time.* (Keystone-Nemes, Madrid)

With Florian, the Lipizzaner horse that starred in MGM's Florian, *1940. This was my first foray into film.* (Editorial Sopena Argentina)

A still from Yolanda, *filmed in Mexico in 1942 with Manuel Reachi producing.*

Anton (Pat) Dolin as Bluebeard and me as Boulotte, in Fokine's 1941 ballet choreographed for Ballet Theatre.
(Maurice Seymour, Chicago)

Lucia Chase, who founded American Ballet Theatre in 1941.

Lucia Chase's son, Alexander (Sandy) Ewing, and his wife, Sheila, in Ireland in 2004.

The manager of the theatre met our train and informed us that the audience, upon hearing that we had been snowbound for three days but were now on the way, had refused his offer to reimburse them and cancel the performance, electing to wait for our arrival, no matter how late it might be! We took it as a compliment and rushed to the theatre, despite our hunger and the lack of time to warm up. By the time the scenery was in place, the costumes were unpacked, we were made up and everything was ready for curtain-up, it was almost midnight! The audience was terrific, and so generous with its applause. I felt like hugging every one of them and thanking them for their understanding, patience and interest in our art.

Back at the railway station in the wee hours of the morning, we flocked to the restaurant cars, where an extra-good breakfast was waiting. Satisfied, we fell into our bunks just as our train moved on. The rhythmic, muffled noise of the wheels soon lulled me into sleep. One gets used to anything and takes it in one's stride, especially when one is young and loves what one is doing.

After cold and windy Chicago and freezing Canada, it was lovely to get to Los Angeles and feel warm again. Spending time with the Russian film 'colony', who by now were our great friends, was always fun and a source of much laughter. Akim Tamiroff kept us in stitches with his stories of how he began in Hollywood. There also was the flamboyant Gregory Ratoff (a noisy version of Peter Ustinov) – he always ended his fantastic stories by declaring, 'Everything I said is ninety-nine per cent not true!' Flaming red hair crowned his head; he had fat pink cheeks, a large stomach that incessantly shook with laughter, and a booming voice – all of which made him endearing. He fascinated Darryl Zanuck, a big boss in the film industry, and was close friends with him, thanks to which Gregory could secure jobs for his less fortunate compatriots.

One name that even the youngest reader will have heard of was Marlene Dietrich, a huge film star in a category all of her own. She was blonde and dazzlingly glamorous, with a low husky voice tinted by her German accent, and a languorous, seductive manner. Her strong but very ladylike personality commanded awe and respect.

She became a fixture backstage, sitting in the first wing as quiet as a mouse. We were mesmerised by her; she was mesmerised by Léonide Massine. On one occasion, as I was standing by her chair waiting for my cue, she turned to me with a smile. As I smiled back, I noticed that half of one of her false eyelashes had detached itself from her top eyelid and was sticking up at a crazy angle! I had no time to warn her, as I had to make my entrance, but it dawned on me that this 'goddess' was just as vulnerable, as human, as the rest of us.

A few days later, one of the ballets in the program was *Union Pacific*. Panic stations – we were short two dancers, who were sick with flu. At one stage in the ballet they were usually entirely enclosed in brown sacking, to represent sleepers being laid across the rails. Papa Grigoriev asked for volunteers among the mamas to be put into the brown sacks to save us. My mother seemed to be the only one of the right height and size, but one more beam was needed. Marlene Dietrich came forward and offered to be the missing beam! Her offer accepted with gratitude, she slid into the sack and saved the day. That's what I call a trooper!

Massine acquired a trailer, which he attached to his Lincoln car. He was soon travelling in it with his wife, Zorina and, for a short time, Marlene Dietrich! We seldom saw him on our train from then on, except for long hauls. He engaged a young Russian man as his chauffeur and this young man's mother as his cook – they slept in hotels. A new resident in the trailer was Smoky, a kerry blue terrier, who became Massine's constant companion and sat like a good doggy in his dressing room during performances. We all loved Smoky – he was a big dog with grey–blue, slightly curled hair, a moustache and a friendly disposition. It was interesting to observe the dry, serious Massine, his eyes smiling as he stroked Smoky with so much affection – which Smoky openly reciprocated, happily wagging his bum and tail. Yes, Massine had a big heart – it showed in his work, he showed it to his dog – but he camouflaged it when it came to people.

But soon Marlene Dietrich went back to Hollywood and the tour continued calmly. We gave a few performances in Detroit. It was a treat to get to the hotel and plunge into a hot bath! One afternoon I was free and told my parents I was going to watch the rehearsal. 'All right,' said Mother and continued reading her book. I hurriedly left their room and went to the ballroom. I had no intention of watching the rehearsal – I was hoping I might see Jerry. I still felt guilty for being so unfairly rude to him in New York and I wanted to apologise. There was no sign of him at the rehearsal, so I thought I would go down to the café where Colonel de Basil, Jerry and the tour manager liked to talk. They were not there. I sat down at the counter, ordered a coffee and waited in the hope that Jerry would appear. He did not. Two cups of coffee and half an hour later, I returned to my room.

As soon as I closed my door, Mother's angry voice from the adjacent room commanded me to come over. 'Where have you been?' she shouted.

'At the rehearsal,' I responded, my face flushing.

'Liar, liar!' shrieked Mother. Trembling with rage, she slapped my face with such force that I reeled backwards, losing my balance. Papa, getting up to restrain Mother, who was about to hit me again, told me to go to my room and close the door.

My face was on fire and my cheekbone painful. I felt shattered, humiliated and ashamed. Ashamed of myself, ashamed of my mother. I wanted to crawl into a corner and melt away into the wall. I stood in my room, numb, not knowing what to do. My face hurt, so I went to the bathroom to splash cold water on it. What I saw in the mirror filled me with disgust: Mother's wide wedding ring had made a purple mark on my cheekbone. It was swelling, as was the corner of my eye. I hated that face in the mirror; I hated myself. I wished I did not exist. *How can I go on? How can I cope?* I asked myself, plunging my face into the basin. The thought of going to the theatre, showing my face, performing, sent a cold shiver down my spine. *I cannot do it.* All I wanted was to get away from it all, from everyone, to hide.

Papa came and stood in the bathroom doorway, watching me in silence. I lifted my face out of the water and mumbled that I had been in the café. Papa did not respond. 'Please,' I asked him, 'call Papa Grigoriev and tell him I can't dance tonight. He must let Toumanova know that she'll have to take over.'

Papa shook his head. 'No way. If you want to be a good artist, you must exercise discipline over yourself. So relax, rest for an hour. I'll come to the theatre with you.'

'But, Papa,' I insisted, 'look at my face!' A shiner was on the way.

'You're good at make-up,' was Papa's curt response as he left the room.

I dropped on my bed and tried to get a grip on myself. Papa was right. As the saying goes, 'The show must go on!' At the theatre I got some curious glances but no questions. I was grateful for this tactfulness. Only Tassia remarked, 'Ai-ai-ai! I suppose you walked into a lamp post!' I did not reply. I could not tell her what had happened – I was too ashamed.

I wish I could skip this miserable event now, but I cannot do so. It was the trigger for the fast-coming, unexpected events that radically changed the course of my private life.

III

MARRIAGE, 1936–1939

6

ON THE RUN

*A*s I put on my make-up, trying to steady my trembling hands, Mother arrived and busied herself in silence with my tights and toe shoes. We avoided looking at each other – you could have cut the air with an axe! Somehow I managed to get through that night's performance, painfully aware of the doom in my heart, which I unsuccessfully tried to lighten.

That night sleep was eluding me when a very faint sound of someone knocking on my door made me sit up in bed. I switched on the bedside lamp and glanced at my alarm clock. It showed one forty-five a.m. *Oh God, please, spare me more trouble!* The faint knocking persisted. Terrified that my parents might hear it, I got out of bed, rushed to the door and opened it a crack, half expecting to see Tassia. To my surprise, I was facing Colonel de Basil! 'Shh, shh!' I begged, pointing to my parents' room.

'I was just informed that you have a black eye and seemed upset during the performance. I had to see for myself. What happened?'

'I slipped in the bathroom and knocked my face on the basin,' I replied, wishing he would go before my parents heard us.

He looked at me intently for a long moment. 'It's late now. I'll talk to you tomorrow after class and I'll expect to hear the truth.' I felt ill at ease and remained silent. 'Try to sleep now,' he said, ruffling my hair, then left.

In a strange way this unexpected visit comforted me – someone cared. Next morning as I was getting dressed, it dawned on me that some of my colleagues would undoubtedly ask me how my face got bruised. I decided to stick to my bathroom story.

I thought my parents should know this story, in case they, too, were asked. I knocked on their door before going to class. Papa opened the door; Mother ignored me. I told them what I would say when people asked me about my face. Papa, with a sad expression, said, 'All right.' Mother continued to comb her hair. I went off to class. I told my story when asked and acted cheerful – although I was far from it. I actually could not have cared less whether people believed me or not!

I was fully aware that Colonel de Basil knew exactly what was going on among the people in his company, but he only interfered when he felt he had to. When he appeared at the end of our class, I knew I was in for a difficult discussion. As we walked slowly up and down the corridor outside the ballroom, he came to the point: 'The truth, please!' I could not control my need to unburden myself, so I told him what had happened. He stopped walking and looked at me through his thick lenses. 'You'll be seventeen soon?' he asked.

'Yes, in March,' I replied.

'Jerry wants to marry you. Do you want to marry him?'

'Yes!' This impulsive statement flew out of my mouth before I had time to think of all its consequences. It just seemed like the perfect way to get away from Mother.

'All right then, I'll talk to Hurok. We'll sort out where and when your elopement should take place. Meanwhile, you must not tell any-one, not a soul, about the plan. Understood?' As an afterthought, he added, 'Jerry is best out of the way just now. I'll tell him to go to New York and wait there. I'll tell you as soon as we've decided on a plan.'

And so, to my total bewilderment, in less than fifteen minutes my fate was decided. I stood speechless, staring at the Colonel's back disappearing down the corridor. For the next few days, thoughts whirled chaotically in my head. Nothing seemed real. Elopement? A crazy fantasy – it could not possibly happen! Surely I would never get away from my mother! The Colonel disappeared, so I asked Vova Grigoriev where he was. Vova told me the Colonel and Jerry had gone to New York on business. Strangely, though, I never gave my parents a thought during those days. It never occurred to me to ask myself what their reaction would be if the elopement came to pass.

The tour took its course and soon we were in Cleveland. Before the last performance I was warming up on the dimly lit empty stage when Hurok's tour manager, Mr Libidins, came over to me. Looking around to make certain we were alone, he whispered that he had instructions for me. 'Tomorrow we perform in Columbus,' he said. 'The company's staying overnight in hotels. You're performing in the first ballet only, then you should hurry to change and tell your mother that you want to see the next ballet from the stalls. I'll wait for you by the side door and take you through to the street, where Jerry will be waiting in a taxi. You'll drive to the airport and fly to Cincinnati. You'll get married the next morning, before the company arrives early in the afternoon. Write a note to your parents telling them what you're doing and give the note to me. I'll pass it to them when they raise the alarm at your disappearance and try to pacify them. The Colonel will be in Cincinnati before the company arrives. Good luck!'

His tall, imposing figure disappeared through the side door before I could make any comment or ask questions. *So, it's for tomorrow. What the hell am I doing?* was my first reaction. I continued to warm up automatically, but my thoughts were elsewhere. *Papa, poor Papa, he'll be so upset. Mother?* A wave of resentment swept over me, even anger. *You'll be enraged, Mother, but you won't be able to hit me again! I'll be a married woman!* That thought elated me so much that I put too much force into a *pirouette* and threw myself sideways. *Ai-ai-ai, that's enough ruminating. Concentrate on the performance now!*

As I went back to my dressing room, I wished I could talk to Tassia. But I could not. I knew I must not involve her. That night as I was trying to sleep, it occurred to me that I could not take an overnight bag with me on the flight to Cincinnati. I could only take what would fit into my handbag: not much – it was not roomy. Nightshirt, slippers, face cream, forget it! The only things I could take were my toothbrush and hair curlers. In those days hair curlers were made of wire wrapped up in wool and fitted into a string-bean-shaped leather pouch. I could fit a dozen into my handbag easily. It would have to do. Toothpaste? I would borrow Jerry's. I tried again to sleep but with no success, so I got up and wrote the letter to my parents.

As I walked towards our railway carriage the next morning, a thought crossed my mind. *Good thing it's today. A few more days and I would have lost courage. But it's today – too late to back out.* In the carriage, curled up in my seat, my coat under my head, I tried if not to sleep, at least to doze. I did not want to talk to anyone – I felt emotionally drained. The snow was falling steadily over Columbus as we pulled into the station; the frosty air revived me and cleared my head. Once at the hotel, I had a quick bath, a sandwich, a cup of coffee, and it was time to go to the theatre.

As I started on my make-up for *Aurora's Wedding*, a nervous excitement got hold of me, mixed with fear and butterflies in my stomach. As the theatre was small, several of us shared the same dressing room, which provided welcome distraction. Everyone chatted and laughed, and I did not have to cope with the lingering tension between my mother and me. We could not warm up, as the stage was occupied by stagehands hanging the scenery, so Tania and I held onto our chairs and tried to do a short set of barre exercises the best we could. Zorina, with none of her costume on except her tights, teased my monkeys, Miky and Peki, who were in their cage on the end of my table. Miky got very excited – hanging onto the bars and emitting his funny 'koo-koo' noises, he peed in an arc onto Zorina's stomach! General hilarity!

'Fifteen minutes, please,' called Grisha, knocking on our door. (Grisha was Gregory Alexandroff, one of our dancers, whose job it was to call everyone on stage.) Boom, went my heart. *That's it – in a little more than an hour, I'll be on the run. Concentrate,* I told myself, *and give a good performance. On stage and off!*

As the curtain went up and we made our entrance, circling the stage in a polonaise, I felt a terrific surge of energy and enjoyment in performing. Mother, as usual, was watching from the wings. Back in the dressing room, as she helped me out of my tutu, she said, 'Well done. You were full of life tonight!'

Tears welled in my eyes. I longed to put my arms around her neck to say how I wished things were different between us. My poor mama. I was about to cause her more distress . . . and to my papa too . . . *I am sorry, so, so sorry* . . . Filled with these unhappy thoughts, I hurried to take off my make-up, get dressed and be ready before the start of the next ballet. 'Five minutes, please,' called Grisha, knocking on the door.

'Mama, I'm going to watch the next ballet from the back of the stalls.'

'All right,' said Mama, busy packing up my make-up and bits and pieces. I threw my coat over my shoulders, took my handbag hanging underneath it and made my way to the side door. I caught a glimpse of my papa on the other side of the stage. He was telling the stagehands where to put some props.

'Come quickly,' whispered Mr Libidins, grabbing my hand as I came out the door. The lights in the auditorium were already dimmed and we reached the street door unnoticed. It was snowing heavily. I gave him the letter for my parents.

'See the taxi across the street?' asked Mr Libidins. 'Jerry's inside it, waiting for you. See you tomorrow. God speed!'

As I stumbled into the taxi, I was greeted by a, 'Hi, you made it!' Jerry's voice came from somewhere below the seat. He was hiding on the floor of the cab, which immediately took off while he tried to get himself up off the floor. In the process he knocked his head hard on the doorhandle. We sat in tense silence for a while.

'I wish it would stop snowing,' I ventured.

'Why? It's nice.'

'The aeroplane might be grounded.'

'Stop worrying – it won't.'

I noticed through the rear window that a car was right behind us – a police car. I panicked! 'Police, look, police! My parents sent police after us!'

'Keep your voice down and don't be silly!'

I kept on predicting doom until Jerry lost patience and offered to turn around and take me back. We quarrelled the rest of the way to the airport. Not until the plane was in the air did I finally relax. Jerry explained to me why our marriage had to take place in Cincinnati – in that state one could marry at eighteen without parental consent.

'But I'm not eighteen.'

'Say you are and leave the talking to me.'

Jerry seemed confident, so I did not argue any more. I do not remember exactly how long our flight was – not long. Checking into the hotel as 'Mr and Mrs' felt odd, being in the same room with Jerry even odder. 'You must be hungry,' he said. He phoned room service and ordered sandwiches and a bottle of wine. He took a toiletries bag out of his suitcase and handed it to me. 'Use whatever you need,' he said kindly. He gave me a hug, remarking that I must be exhausted.

The sandwiches arrived, looking delicious. Jerry poured the wine and tried to put me at ease. He did not succeed very well, but the wine did! We talked for a while about the past few weeks, our present situation and my parents' reaction, which we were going to have to face the next day. There was nothing romantic in our conversation; my main thought was still that Mama and Papa might send the police after me. Finally, Jerry suggested I use the bathroom and get ready for bed.

And so I did – brushed my teeth, wound my hair on the twelve hair curlers, took my skirt and jumper off but kept the cardigan over my slip, and stuck my feet back into my snow boots (I hate walking barefoot on strange carpets). As I emerged from the bathroom, I found Jerry changed into his pyjamas and dressing gown, smoking a cigarette. An expression of startled incredulity appeared on his face as I walked into the room. Then he burst out laughing and laughed and laughed!

Early next morning we were on our way to the marriage bureau. It had stopped snowing; pale sunrays were breaking through grey clouds. The taxi-driver was cheerful and talkative. 'So, you two are getting married?' he enquired. After an affirmative from Jerry, he looked at me through his rear-vision mirror. 'How old are you, Miss?'

'I'm s—,' a dig in the ribs from Jerry, 'Oh, I'm eighteen!' The taxi-driver grinned and winked at me.

We stopped in a nondescript street lined with small shops. 'Here we are,' announced the taxi-driver, pointing to what looked like just another shop. 'Will I wait for you?'

'Yes, good idea, thank you,' replied Jerry.

Then the driver got out of his cab and said he was coming in with us! Outside the entrance to the marriage bureau, I noticed a woman with a big basket in front of her. 'Buy my peanuts, Miss?' she called out to me.

'Later, when we come out,' I called back, waving to her.

Inside was a small, dingy room with a counter running along one side. Behind the counter, at a desk, sat a man smoking a cigar. He asked us questions – Jerry supplied the answers while the man made notes on what looked like official papers. Then, removing the cigar from his mouth, he asked me how old I was. 'Eighteen,' I said, feeling my face flush.

'Do you have your birth certificate or passport with you?'

To my relief, Jerry stepped in and explained that we were with the Russian ballet company and our tour manager kept all our passports, but he would not be in town until later that afternoon. 'As for birth certificates, they're lost in Russia. We're refugees from the Revolution.' As an afterthought, Jerry added, 'We're opening tonight. You should come and see the performance. I'll leave two tickets at the box office for you. Please come!'

'Oh, thank you. My wife would love that!' He gave his card to Jerry, stuck his cigar back in his mouth and asked where our witnesses were. Apparently we had to have two. The taxi-driver immediately volunteered to be one, and I suggested we ask the peanut lady to be the other. Jerry and the cabbie dashed into the street, where Jerry bought all her peanuts! They reappeared in no time, the peanut lady beaming.

The man deposited his cigar in an ashtray on his desk and called us to the counter: the ceremony could begin. Flanked by the cabbie and the peanut lady, we stood solemnly, in attentive silence. The cigar man cleared his throat and began. I had only ever been to Russian Church weddings before, which were so beautiful, so romantic! This one, mine, was far from either. When the cigar man asked me something about 'Taking this man . . .', it took me a minute to realise he was waiting for me to reply. So I said, 'Yes, sure!'

The peanut lady pulled my sleeve. 'You must say, "I do"!' she said.

'Oh, sorry – I do,' I corrected myself. When the same question was asked of Jerry, a thought crossed my mind: *How silly! We wouldn't be here if we 'didn't'!* Pronouncing us 'man and wife', the cigar man handed me the marriage certificate, in a pretty folder embossed with flowers. We shook hands and thanked him.

I was glad to get out into the fresh air. I could not have borne the smell of stale cigars for much longer. The peanut lady gave me a hug and I told her to keep her basket of peanuts. She was delighted! The cabbie bowed to me and, with a theatrical gesture, opened the taxi door. We all laughed! What lovely, kind people they both were.

It was one o'clock by the time we returned to the hotel. Colonel de Basil had arrived from New York an hour before and was waiting for us in the lobby. With great joviality he congratulated us and suggested we go and have lunch. The company was not due until three o'clock. I felt nervous, not hungry. 'You must eat, you need strength. It will be a taxing day and you have a performance tonight.' With these words, Colonel de Basil shepherded us into the restaurant.

On the way to our table, we saw Eugene Goossens and his wife, who were tucking into their lunch. Colonel de Basil told them that Jerry and I had got married that morning. Congratulations, kisses, good wishes. The Cincinnati Symphony Orchestra was playing for us and Goossens, their musical director and head, was guest conductor for some of our ballets. We knew him well, liked him enormously and admired him as a conductor. He was one with us dancers, watching, following, and inspiring us as well as his musicians.

As we finished lunch, a bellboy came to our table and handed me a beautiful bouquet of flowers with a lovely card that said they were from the Goossens. What a beautiful gesture! Back in our room, I sat on pins and needles waiting for the company to arrive and for the call from

Mr Libidins informing me of my parents' room number. When the call finally came, Mr Libidins warned me that my parents were highly distressed and angry, and that we must brace ourselves for a most unpleasant afternoon. As we knocked on my parents' door, my heart pounded and my knees shook. Jerry, however, seemed calm. My papa flung the door open and I had a shock. I had never seen Papa angry. I had never heard him raise his voice. This enraged person who pulled me into the room, pushed Jerry out into the corridor and slammed the door shut, was a complete stranger. I went numb, dumb and speechless. Papa was shouting and pointing at my mother, who was lying on the bed, her face to the wall, ignoring me.

Jerry banged hard on the door and shouted, 'Let my wife out!'

Papa shouted back, 'Your wife? She's not your wife!'

'I am!' I protested, pulling the marriage certificate out of my handbag. Papa snatched it out of my hands. I snatched it back.

Now there were loud, insistent knocks. Colonel de Basil's voice asked Papa to open the door and talk things over calmly. Papa turned to me, shouting, 'You're stupid! Can't you see? It's all a plot, a conspiracy to ruin your career! To stop you dancing!'

This, to me, outrageous remark pulled me out of my paralytic, dumb state. It was not my papa talking – Mother's words were coming out of his mouth. I glanced at her. She did not move, her face to the wall, silent. 'You're wrong, Papa. Please open the door.' I forced my voice to sound calm and steady.

Papa fell silent, then after a moment of hesitation opened the door and let Colonel de Basil and Jerry in. Accusations flew back and forth like ping-pong balls. Mother, her face to the wall, did not move, persisting in her silence. Finally, the Colonel asked Papa how old Mother had been when he married her.

'The same age as Irina is now, but the circumstances were different. We were at war and we had the full blessing of our families,' answered Papa, adding, 'This man is twice her age and totally unsuitable!'

'Wait a minute,' parried Colonel de Basil. 'It may seem so now, but when Irina is thirty, Jerry won't be sixty – he'll be forty-five!'

But Papa had had enough. He opened the door and asked us all to leave. As we made our way to our rooms, Colonel de Basil said, 'Don't worry too much. It'll sort itself out.'

The afternoon was gone and it was time to go to the theatre. Jerry came with me but we walked in silence. At the theatre, I met with a mixed reception. The older company members were shocked, and disapproved of my behaviour. The young ones giggled, saying, 'Well, well, well!' Massine muttered, 'That was unexpected!' Papa Grigoriev shook his head and said, 'Oh, my angel!' Mme Tchernicheva was amused and kind. Tassia was annoyed that I had not shared my decision with her, but she soon forgave me.

As I started on my make-up, a bouquet was brought to my dressing room. To my astonishment, it was from my parents. The card said, 'We wanted to call the police but finally decided not to darken your name. Be well, be happy. Mama and Papa.' A little later, they came to my dressing room and I thanked them for the flowers. Papa went backstage to get on with his work. Mother busied herself as usual, arranging my tights and shoes. She looked calm and composed but did not speak. I was at a loss, utterly uncomfortable. After the performance Jerry asked my parents to have supper with us. They did, but it was anything but jovial.

And so ended my wedding day.

HEARTBREAK

Whenever we stayed in a hotel, my parents requested a connecting room with Jerry and me. They said we had to live together as a family. Connecting rooms consisted of a bedroom for my parents and a sitting room with a sofa bed for us. The sofa bed invariably had springs under a thin mattress that poked us in the ribs. Soon Jerry had had enough of this 'family life' and told my parents I needed to rest in a proper bed. It did not go down well with them and created bad vibes. I could see and sense that Papa was just as unhappy with the situation as I was, but he could not do anything about it. Mother was being difficult.

It was hard to leave my problems in the dressing room and not let my performances become automatic and lifeless, but my love for what I was doing and the discipline it taught me helped me through these difficult weeks.

How did the marriage go? Under the circumstances, far from being a romantic, happy time, it brought home to us the fact that we really did not know each other or what made us tick at all. Our courtship, if one could call it that, had been at a distance – exchanged looks and notes, but hardly words. Like strangers thrown together, we had to get acquainted with each other's personality in the disapproving and hostile atmosphere maintained by my parents. Jerry kept his calm and was kind and patient towards me. I was grateful but wondered why he had married me. Did he regret it now? I couldn't tell. I didn't know him at all.

My seventeenth birthday came and went, unnoticed by any of us except my papa. He brought me a red rose and put it on my make-up table that evening, silently kissing the top of my head. I felt so sad. I don't remember Jerry marking my birthday in any way; if he did, I was too preoccupied to notice.

Philadelphia was a welcome change from one-night stands. All our rehearsals now concentrated on Massine's *Symphonie fantastique*, which promised to be a great work and do justice to Berlioz's music. Proper, full rehearsals were to start in the early northern spring in London, and the premiere was scheduled for 24 July 1936, during our season at the Royal Opera House Covent Garden.

Hector Berlioz wrote *Symphonie fantastique* under the influence of drugs and inspired by his fixation on the actress Henrietta Smithson. There was a story or 'program' in Berlioz's music, which made it appropriate for a ballet. Massine's role as the Young Musician required purely dramatic acting. Toumanova, with her languorous dark beauty, was perfect as his Beloved. Boris Kochno collaborated on the libretto and Christian Bérard designed the scenery and costumes – it promised to be another great symphonic work by Massine.

Besides our usual conductors, Efrem Kurtz and Antal Dorati, Leopold Stokowski was our special guest conductor for a couple of ballets. The flamboyant maestro was chief conductor of the Philadelphia Orchestra, which played for our Philadelphia performances. He was handsome, with flowing white hair – imposing, authoritarian, stubborn and eccentric. On the night Stokowski conducted *Petrushka*, we had a morning orchestral rehearsal. Massine danced Petrushka, Lichine the Moor and I the Ballerina. From the start, the tempos Stokowski chose were too fast. When the three of us were dancing in the magician's booth, the tempo became impossibly fast. Massine called a stop and an argument ensued that got hotter and louder until Lichine and I joined in. Stokowski yelled that we were wrong, we argued he was! Didn't he know that Stravinsky and Fokine had worked on the ballet together?

Stokowski stormed out of the orchestra pit and the rehearsal was cancelled. Massine followed the maestro to his dressing room, where they had a civilised discussion, and Massine assured us that all would go well at the performance. It did go well, very well, and there were no hard feelings. As was the custom, at the end of the ballet we brought Stokowski on stage, where he beamed happily at us and acknowledged our applause as well as the applause of his adoring audience.

Next morning, as I arrived for class, I was greeted by Mr Libidins brandishing the morning papers. On the front page was an article with the headline, 'BARONOVA SAYS STOKOWSKI STINKS!'

'Oh my God, I never said that!'

'I know, I know, it must be that reporter who sneaked in yesterday morning and heard you arguing. I asked him to leave.' Mr Libidins looked annoyed.

I asked him to give me Stokowski's telephone number, so Mr Libidins took me to the office to make the call. When I was put through, the maestro roared, 'Ah, Irina, so you think I stink?'

'No! I never said that!'

Stokowski burst out laughing. 'I know you didn't,' he laughed again, 'I was there!' After dismissing reporters as 'that cheap lot', he invited me to come to lunch. It was a jolly lunch and I was reminded once again that every coin has two sides. Like Nijinska, he too could be impossible and also loveable, depending on which way the coin fell.

That evening I was performing in two ballets, the first and last on the program. The second was *La Boutique fantasque*, a fun work Massine had choreographed for Diaghilev's company. It was the story of a toy-shop selling animated dolls. When it was revived for us, Toumanova and I alternated in the 'Tarantella', partnered by Lazowski. As our repertoire rapidly grew, the 'Tarantella' was passed on to Olga Morosova.

At the start of intermission, as I was changing for the last ballet, Colonel de Basil and Jerry came to my dressing room. Apparently, Morosova was doubled up with pains in her stomach and the Colonel asked me, as a favour, to dance the 'Tarantella' in her place. I immediately agreed, of course, no problem. But there was a problem: my parents angrily stepped in, prohibiting me to do so. Surprised, I asked why. 'Can't you see? We told you so. They're set on ruining your career! They're using you, destroying your standing. Can't you see?' raged my mother.

'No, I can't see how helping out in an emergency could harm me.'

'Why didn't you ask Toumanova?' Papa asked Colonel de Basil.

Before the Colonel could answer, my mother shouted at me. 'I forbid you to be a fill-in for Morosova. If you dare disobey me, I'm through with you!'

Everyone was looking at me – my parents angrily, Colonel de Basil and Jerry expectantly. I felt my parents were unfair and wrong, so turning to Jerry, I asked him to tell wardrobe to hurry and bring me Morosova's costume and my character shoes. I thought Mother would explode with rage. In a menacing tone, her face close to mine, she said, 'You'll regret this one day!' She motioned to Papa to follow her and they left my dressing room.

Colonel de Basil and I sat in silence until Jerry returned with Mme Larose, who brought me the costume. 'Mr Libidins will announce that you're dancing the "Tarantella" before the curtain goes up,' said the Colonel. As he left, he kissed me and said, 'Thank you.'

I had no time to dwell on what had happened. With Mme Larose's help, I was ready as the ballet started. Jerry stood in the wings, but there was no sign of my parents. I decided to wait until the next morning before going to their room to make peace with them.

Jerry did not say much over supper, just, 'Oh, don't worry, it will pass,' but I did worry and felt scared to face Mother. The next morning, just as I was about to call my parents and ask if I could come to talk things over, the phone rang. It was Mr Libidins; my parents had just advised him that they were leaving for New York. He wanted to know if I was aware of it. No, I was not!

'When?' I asked.

'In a few minutes. Your mother's checking out, your father's gone to the baggage room to collect their suitcases.'

I dropped the phone and raced to the baggage room in the basement. As I stepped out of the lift, I saw Papa at the far end retrieving their big suitcases. I ran towards him calling, 'Papa, Papa.'

Papa turned around and his arm shot up in a forbidding gesture. 'Don't come near me. Go away, go away!' he repeated, raising his voice.

I stopped. 'Papa, please,' I begged. The porter appeared with a trolley. As Papa pointed out the cases for the porter to collect, I took a few steps towards him.

'I told you to keep away from me! Go away!' His voice was icy.

'Taxi, sir?' asked the porter.

'Yes, please,' said Father. Then, ignoring me, without a glance, my papa was gone. My insides were shaking, tearing apart with pain and despair. I had lost my papa, the person I loved above all others. My papa did not want me! I slumped onto someone's suitcase in tears. *Oh God, what have I done? My fault, all my fault. I am stupid, selfish, a bad, bad person! Bad, bad!* These thoughts burnt in my head with a feeling of unbearable guilt. I hated myself. I was still sitting on the suitcase crying when Mr Libidins and Jerry appeared.

'Come on, pull yourself together,' said Jerry.

'Let's go and have some coffee,' said Mr Libidins.

Then they both reminded me that I had a matinee and soon it would be time to go to the theatre. Pull myself together? How does one do that when one's heart is breaking? But performances do not wait for one's heart to heal. That curtain must always go up and one must be there, ready.

I was there, ready, on time, as usual. My despair concerned only me. It was nobody's business and had to be hidden. The show must go on!

WAR LOOMS IN SPAIN

Our tour took us south. As we progressed towards Miami it got warmer, and the towns had different, distinct personalities. There was a reminder of the old world, with colonial architecture and food prepared in old-fashioned Southern ways. Even in our restaurant carriage, the meals became different: delicious corn muffins, fried bananas with tender chicken cooked in breadcrumbs, and other appetising dishes.

Just before we reached Miami, Smoky, Massine's dog, escaped from his dressing room and appeared on stage during *Prince Igor*, gambolling and chasing after the girls, pulling at their veils in a playful, happy mood! The audience laughed, while Massine unsuccessfully tried to call Smoky to him in the wings! Finally, one of the dancers caught Smoky by the collar and dragged him off stage. It was not on to impose a fine on Massine for his dog's misbehaviour, which would have been the usual procedure, but we all decided that Massine should not get away scot-free, and so clamoured for him to organise a picnic for the company when we arrived in Miami. Massine was a good sport and we had our picnic at the beach.

Our stay in Miami was also marked by a less pleasant event. Vera Zorina checked into our hotel. She was not in Massine's trailer any more; something had gone wrong in their relationship, that much was clear. It became even clearer when the phone in our room rang at two a.m. and Mr Libidins asked Jerry to go immediately to Zorina's room. While Jerry was gone I sat up waiting, anxious, wondering what had happened. When Jerry came back, he asked me to get dressed quickly. As I dressed, he told me that we were to take Zorina to a doctor friend of Mr Libidins. No, she was not sick – she had done herself an injury. Thank God she came to her senses and called Mr Libidins for help! She needed a few stitches.

Zorina was obviously distressed but calm. Mr Libidins saw to every-thing, bless him. A taxi was waiting. I sat next to her, holding a towel tightly wrapped around her wrist. We reached the doctor in silence. He turned out to be youngish, good-looking and charming. He soon put Zorina at her ease and she even managed a smile, looking as beautiful as ever. Stitches in, bandage in place, he recommended a few days off from performances. He refused payment for his services but said he had a favour to ask of Miss Zorina. Turning to her he asked sweetly, 'Would you do me the honour of having dinner with me tomorrow night?'

'With pleasure!' responded Zorina. 'What time will you pick me up?'

The incident was closed. None of us ever spoke of it again. The next day I was warming up on stage, hanging onto the spotlight stand, while Massine did the same nearby. Without stopping his *grands batte-ments* or *petits battements*, he said, 'Irina, I hear that Brigitta (Zorina) was a nuisance last night.'

'No, she was not a nuisance,' I answered.

He paused and looked like he wanted to say something, but then changed his mind, turned around and continued his *battements* with the other leg. A couple of years after this drama, Zorina left the com-pany. It was the right decision – ballet was not her road to success.

Miami over, we steamed towards Cuba. All this time I tried to find out how my parents were and where they were living in New York. The few Russian friends I contacted were surprised that my parents were not still with me, and knew nothing of their whereabouts. From Miami I called Dr Appelbaum and finally got some news of them. He told me that upon arriving in New York they went straight to his house and he helped them to find a room to rent on the Upper West Side.

'But how will they survive? I must send them some money. I must have their address!'

'Irina, for the moment don't worry,' he replied. I kept plying him with questions, so he told me that Papa had found work at the graphic design studio of a Russian acquaintance by the name of Bobri. He was a designer himself and was glad to take Papa on board to cope with a large number of commissions. 'So for the moment don't worry. Your father has a job and, under the circumstances, he wouldn't accept any help from you,' was Dr Appelbaum's advice to me. As to giving me my parents' address, he firmly refused, saying that at my father's request he had given his word not to.

As I sat on the deck of the steamer, I went over and over my conversation with Dr Appelbaum, sad thoughts floating in my head. Then Havana Harbour came into view, and I felt that never-failing excitement of arriving in a new country. The sky was intense blue, the air very hot; Alberto Alonso, our funny Cuban, hopped about joyfully and waved to people on shore, his family no doubt. He was back home at last – we were in Cuba.

As we came ashore we were greeted by the director of the Pro-Arte Musical theatre and a nice Russian gentleman, Nicolai Yavorsky, who turned out to be a ballet teacher. Amazing, one encountered Russian refugees all over the world, but a ballet teacher in Cuba?!

Havana in those days was a friendly, peaceful place with narrow streets and old houses. In the evenings its inhabitants sat on the footpath, gossiping with neighbours and watching the passers-by, who were mostly American tourists. There were squares surrounded by lots of trees where we often sat after a performance, drinking freshly squeezed juices of watermelons, pineapples and oranges, or eating delicious ice-creams sold from small kiosks on wheels. There was a casino and a very smart nightclub, but we were too poor and tired to frequent them. The residential part of Havana had lovely old houses with a profusion of flowering shrubs in their gardens. The beaches were very beautiful, but we had hardly any free time in which to enjoy them. The Cubans themselves were good-looking, either sleepy or boisterous, always friendly and colourful.

Pro-Arte Musical was a large theatre, and its big stage accommodated our productions well. It had that wonderful atmosphere which, for me, is completely lost in the magnificent modern theatres of today, where concrete, steel, glass and vastness have eliminated that certain magic of entering a fairy tale world.

The audiences in Havana were most enthusiastic, and we performed to sold-out houses. One day Mr Yavorsky asked Jerry and me to come and watch a young girl in his class whom he considered very, very talented. Tania and Lichine came as well, as they were always interested in seeing new talent. The young student was just fourteen, beautiful to look at, already quite strong technically, and possessed that elusive special quality that a person is born with – either you have it or you do not. That young girl had it all. Her name was Alicia Ernestina de la Caridad dei Cobre Martinez Hoyo. What a mouthful!

While she was still in her teens she married the Cuban dancer Fernando Alonso, the brother of our Alberto Alonso. As Alicia Alonso, she left Cuba to study abroad and became a beautiful classical ballerina, internationally famous and much loved. Her other great achievement was that of creating her own ballet school in her native Cuba and founding what is known as the National Ballet of Cuba, of which she was the prima ballerina and director. She worked closely with her by then ex-husband, Fernando Alonso, and her brother-in-law, Alberto, who choreographed for her company with great success. I love remembering that morning of 1936, when we watched a very serious and shy young girl dance.

There was only one thing in Cuba that I found trying – its high level of humidity. We all sweated profusely twenty-four hours a day. At night it was even more trying – lying on wet sheets drenched in sweat and propped up on pillows sticking to our necks. The humidity also made us out of breath when dancing, but we soon got used to it, as we did to every difficulty and discomfort we encountered on our travels.

After our last performance in Havana, some of us were invited by the theatre management to supper at a posh nightclub – the Buena Vista Club, I think. In our best evening attire, we had a great time and danced rumbas till the wee hours. It was a treat to relax and have fun.

When my thoughts were not on rehearsals or performances, they were constantly fixed on wondering and worrying about my parents. I stayed in touch with Dr Appelbaum, who kept assuring me that my parents were all right, but he still would not give me their address. I remained in the doghouse.

When we returned to New York for our second season at the Met, all-day rehearsals were to start with Nijinska, who was, as planned, reviving *Les Noces* for us. I thought I would learn a great deal if I was allowed to participate in this ensemble work, which was so different in movement and style. The fact that there was no leading role and no ballerina required was of no consequence to me. I just wanted to learn more from Nijinska. Jerry was against what he called, 'Your silly idea . . . a whim!'

I retorted, 'You civilians do not understand us dancers!' and stuck to my guns.

The first thing I did when we arrived in New York was phone Mme Nijinska to get her to accept me as one of the girls in the ensemble. Her husband answered the phone and I explained to him the reason for my call. As I waited on the line, I heard him say, 'Brouitschka, it's Irina, with a strange request!'

After a little while, Nijinska herself came to the phone. 'Aha, Irinotschka, why do you want to be in *Les Noces*?'

'To be able to work with you,' I answered.

'Ah, all right, but Grigoriev and Colonel de Basil will object.'

'I'll talk to them,' I said.

'All right then. Good luck!'

Good, I thought. *Now I have to corner Papa Grigoriev and Colonel de Basil.* The next morning I got my chance when I found them talking outside the stage door of the Met. After I explained to them why I wanted to participate in *Les Noces*, Papa Grigoriev kept saying, 'It's not done.'

Colonel de Basil stroked his chin and looked amused, finally turning to Grigoriev and saying, 'Let her do it. Just don't mention her name in the cast list.'

Papa Grigoriev shrugged. 'Oh, my angel, what shall I do with you?' he sighed, looking at me with disapproval.

But I had won! I was delighted. The dancers did not bat an eyelid when I joined them in rehearsals. Jerry kept saying that all I would achieve would be to give my parents more ammunition to accuse him and the Colonel of destroying my career. I mentioned that it did not matter now; one day they would realise that it was not so.

Les Noces was most interesting to rehearse. I learned a great deal and was treated by Nijinska in the same, at times harsh, manner she used for everyone else. It did not matter. I felt I was learning something new and precious. Nijinska and Stravinsky were obviously great friends and showed enormous affection for each other. Her face would light up in welcome as Stravinsky's small, slight figure would enter the studio, beret perched on his head. He would sit for a while by Nijinska's chair, watching us intensely through his old-fashioned spectacles, but before long would sidle up to the piano. He took evident pleasure in playing himself and in taking an active part in the rehearsal. Intense, serious, charming, this great composer was a lovely human being and a true gentleman of the old school. The score of *Les Noces* is not easy, so to have the composer himself playing for us, explaining the difficult passages, was of enormous help, so much so that we got to know the music well enough not to have to count any more, and could concentrate on the intriguing style of the choreography.

When Stravinsky asked why I was rehearsing, Nijinska told him that it was at my request.

'*Umnitza*' (Clever girl) he said in Russian, patting my shoulder.

The premiere of *Les Noces* took place on 20 April 1936 and it was an enormous success. It was different from anything American audiences had seen before and was acclaimed by the critics.

A few days before our last performance in New York, I made another attempt to persuade our Dr Appelbaum to give me my parents' address. I could not bear the thought of sailing back to Europe without seeing them, but my pleas were in vain. I was not allowed to know where they were. I was not wanted. As our ship pulled away from the pier, streamers dangling from decks to shore, people waving, horns tooting, I stood on the upper deck watching the skyline of New York slowly disappear. I felt crushed, longing for my papa, and in a strange way for Mother. I felt like I had lost my parents, and did not know if or when I would ever see them again. I felt guilty about leaving New York. I felt lost for the first time in my life, going so far away alone, like an orphan. At that moment Jerry appeared at my side.

'Hi, here you are. I was looking everywhere for you! Why this miserable face?' I told him what I felt – the sadness, the loss . . . 'You must let go of your parents. You're a married woman, not a child!' He looked irritated as he spoke. *He doesn't understand*, I thought to myself, *he just doesn't understand.*

My best friend, Tassia, had left. She felt she was not getting anywhere in the company and she wanted to open her own school. In Baton Rouge, Louisiana, she was given the chance to do just that, so she left us. I missed her so much. She would have understood. There was no-one else with whom I could or wanted to share problems of such a personal nature. Bottling in my troubled thoughts, I looked forward to Barcelona, where we were due to open in mid-May. I loved Barcelona, but when we arrived we felt a strange tension in the city and heard from friends that some political trouble was brewing. Not being interested in politics, we felt it was none of our concern.

The opening night was, as usual, a grand occasion, a big success, with bouquet after bouquet of flowers and joyous reunions with friends in our dressing rooms once the performance was over. Shortly before our closing performance, we were told that a general strike was going to start the next day. How long it would last no-one knew. We were taken by surprise, totally ignorant of what 'general strike' meant and totally unprepared for the situation we found ourselves in the next day. Everything came to a total standstill. The theatre was shut, there was no service at the hotel, no transport of any kind, all restaurants, bars and cafés were shut, all shops closed. In short, no food to be had anywhere – and we were getting hungry! We were also stuck in this 'ghost town', as the trains to France were cancelled. The telephones did not work either.

Tania and Lichine wandered the streets with Jerry and me in the hope of finding some food to buy, but without success. On the way back to our hotel, we encountered crowds of people assembling and marching in rather angry demonstrations. It was getting unpleasant. Back at the hotel, we found Colonel de Basil, the director of the Teatro del Liceu and a few members of our company eager for news. The theatre director told us he was taking Colonel de Basil to see a friend of his, a high-up member of the government, to ask for his help in getting the company over the border into France. When we asked how long this strike would last, he threw his arms to the sky, saying, 'Who knows?'

Everyone dispersed to fend for themselves. The four of us toyed with the idea of going to the docks to see if we could persuade a sailor from a foreign merchant ship to sell us some food. Before leaving on this expedition, Tania and I asked the boys to go and see if Danilova and Toumanova were in their rooms and would like to join us in our quest for food. They were not in, obviously pursuing their own agendas.

At the front door of the hotel, we bumped into our Russian program-seller, Kolia, who by now was our special friend. Excited, out of breath, it took a while before he could make us understand through his terrible stuttering what he was trying to convey. Kolia was glad he had found us. He knew we would not find food anywhere, but he knew a courtyard, not far from the hotel, where a man kept chickens. He would take us there and perhaps we could persuade the chook owner to sell us one. If the man was not there, we could steal one! Tania and I were shocked at the idea of stealing. Lichine and Jerry were all for it!

'But how shall we cook it?' Our hunger was, by then, starting to undermine our sense of honesty. Kolia, with a triumphant gesture, retrieved from a big brown paper bag a primus and pot that he had brought from his dwelling.

The boys decided that we girls should stay at the hotel while they attempted this expedition. I sat with Tania in her and Lichine's room waiting, our stomachs grumbling with hunger. A good hour went by and no sign of the boys. Half-worried, half-laughing, we imagined what would happen if they were caught in the process of stealing the coveted chicken. Finally the boys reappeared. Success! In the brown bag was a dead chicken. 'We had to steal it!' they confessed, and Kolia had had to put the poor chicken out of its misery.

'Hey,' cried out Tania. 'Who's going to pluck its feathers?'

Again, that unpleasant task fell to Kolia. Installed in the bathroom, newspapers on the floor, he gingerly got on with the job while Lichine produced a bottle of Jerez from the wardrobe. Scrambling for our bathroom glasses, we had the drinks ready to toast the chicken as it was plunged into the pot of boiling water sitting on the primus, which we placed in the bathtub to save making a mess on the carpet.

While Tania and I sat on the rim of the bath watching the chook boil, the boys cleared up the mess on the floor. The Jerez went to our heads quickly, as we were not used to drinking wine, and our little party became very happy, to say the least!

We cut the cooked chicken into chunks with a penknife, and sat in a circle on the bathroom floor eating it with our fingers over newspaper, laughing our heads off, oblivious to the seriousness of the situation and the dark clouds gathering over Spain.

It's useful to have friends in the government. Not only did Colonel de Basil and the Liceu director reappear in the evening with a mountain of sandwiches, but they also came with the good news that the next day the company would be taken over the border into France and all the way to Perpignan in a special train. Our scenery and baskets would be transported to Bologne by truck and shipped to England in plenty of time for our London season.

Next day we trooped to the station carrying our suitcases. In those days no-one had thought of putting wheels on them, so it was heavy going! Groups of people in the streets stopped their loud discussions and eyed us with suspicion as we went by. But we made it! We breathed a sigh of relief as the train pulled out of the station. We loved Barcelona and felt sorry to leave in such an abrupt way, without having a chance to say goodbye to the nice friends we had made there. I was especially sorry to leave our dear stuttering friend, Kolia. He came to see us off. My last vision of him is of a sad figure standing alone on the empty platform, waving his big handkerchief to us in farewell. We never saw him again.

We reached France and Perpignan without incident. While arrangements were being made to get us to Calais, we all went in search of a good meal. The next afternoon we reached Calais and boarded the Channel ferry. Thankfully the sea was calm on our crossing to England, and the beautiful sight of the white cliffs of Dover soon greeted us. It was late when our train pulled into London. We dispersed to our lodgings in high spirits, looking forward to our season at the Royal Opera House Covent Garden and to seeing our dear friends again. It felt like coming home!

Next morning on my way to class, I exchanged warm greetings with Mr Jackson at the stage door and asked him if there was any mail waiting for me. He handed me quite a few letters, but not the one I was hoping for, from Dr Appelbaum, with news of my parents. No news, not a word. Disappointed, worried, saddened, I went to my dressing room to change for class, promising myself I would write to Dr Appelbaum that evening and beg him to drop me a line. All my worries about my parents did nothing to help my relationship with Jerry.

Backstage was coming alive with familiar sounds – the scenery being unloaded from the trucks onto the stage; the baskets carted to the wardrobe; the company assembling for class, heels clattering on the concrete staircase, dressing-room doors slamming, shouts, calls and laughter. It lifted my spirits and switched my thoughts to happier things. There was so much to look forward to in that London season.

While Massine rehearsed *Symphonie fantastique* on stage all day, Lichine began rehearsals for his new choreographic effort, *Le Pavillon*, in the upstairs studio. His first two attempts at choreography had been failures, entirely subsidised by Count Etienne de Beaumont, who believed in the young man's talent and gave him a chance to experiment. But Lichine needed guidance and cultural development, of the kind Massine and Balanchine had received from Serge Diaghilev. Although Massine always encouraged Lichine, he simply did not have the time to do more than be supportive.

When Boris Kochno returned as the company's artistic advisor, it was a godsend for Lichine. Guided by Kochno in the choice of music, subject, era, style and construction, he finally had the chance to use his evident talent for choreography in a positive way. Lichine grabbed this chance with all his heart and *Le Pavillon* became his first success as a choreographer.

Good-looking, with a strong personality, Lichine was an inspiring performer. He was a free spirit, a naughty boy and an incorrigible womaniser, to which Tania chose to shut her eyes. She adored him! I am sure he loved her too, since in spite of his gallivanting, he stuck to her firmly all his life. He had a great sense of humour and a capacity to laugh at others as well as himself, but off stage he never displayed any deep feelings of tenderness, except to the dogs that he and Tania both loved. In the ballets he eventually choreographed, it became clear he was no stranger to feelings of drama, sadness, love, tenderness and pure young fun, which he displayed so well in *The Prodigal Son, Francesca da Rimini* and *Graduation Ball.*

It was a joy for me to have Kochno with us again; it was so reassuring to be able to run to him for advice. He would soon sort out any problems for me and everything would fall into place. Christian 'Bébé' Bérard came from Paris with Kochno to supervise Mme Karinska's making of the costumes for *Symphonie fantastique.* It was great to have Bébé, our dear sweet friend, around. He was always gentle, smiling and fascinating to talk to. He would talk readily on any subject, often getting emotional; Russian gypsy songs would bring tears to his eyes! What a contrast they were – Kochno, who always viewed the world with a cynical eye; and Bérard, a sentimentalist at heart. Yet they were devoted to each other.

The story Kochno conceived for *Le Pavillon* was set in the late Romantic period. The music was chosen by Kochno and Dorati. They wanted to use lesser known pieces by Alexander Borodin and decided on chamber and piano works, to be orchestrated by Dorati. The scenery and costumes were by Cecil Beaton, a great friend of Kochno. Colonel de Basil was delighted, as he had wanted English artists to collaborate with our company for some time. For us, the company, the pavilion that Beaton designed to stand in the middle of the sombre garden was reminiscent of the Parisian *pissoirs* along the Boulevard Haussmann!

Lichine played the Poet, I played the Maiden, and Tania the Chief Spirit. The Maiden's solo was truly wonderful, my *pas de deux* with Lichine touching and quite beautiful, and Tania's lightness and grace well used. It was in his moving and grouping of the spirits of the garden that one might have discerned Lichine's lack of assuredness. But he was a keen and fast learner.

In the *Daily Telegraph*, Arnold Haskell complimented Lichine's ability to exploit the best qualities of his cast, showing 'Baronova's long line, her rare poise and poetical feeling' and 'Riabouchinska's lightness and rapidity'. All the other critics praised Lichine's talent, and *Le Pavillon* remained in our repertoire for many seasons.

Before the premiere of *Le Pavillon*, the much-anticipated premiere of *Symphonie fantastique* took place, on 24 July 1936. Massine's third and most ambitious symphonic work to date attracted much interest from critics and audiences alike, although the sceptics still argued that Berlioz's great symphony was too 'holy' to be used for a ballet.

Clad in my dressing gown, I installed myself in the first wing to watch the premiere, excited, nervous, with butterflies in my stomach and wishing Massine success. He stood in his corner, silent and concentrating, incredibly handsome in his skilfully applied make-up, which gave him a slightly haunted look without interfering with his own expressive face and strong acting ability. It always amazed me, that transformation from the 'real-life' Massine – distant, cold, rarely smiling, heavily serious – to this vibrant, expressive artist whose strong personality and artistry took one's breath away.

In the middle of the stage, Mama Toumanova fussed around Tamara, making signs of the cross over her and everyone else – her usual ritual. Toumanova looked beautiful, a perfect 'vision', stunning and mysterious.

Papa Grigoriev, having checked that everyone was present, gave the conductor the green light to proceed to the orchestra pit and waved his arms at the dancers to clear the stage and take their places. We heard the applause greeting the conductor's appearance in the pit then 'Curtain, please' from Grigoriev. As the curtain parted, thunderous applause greeted Massine as the Young Musician, who sat at his table composing, his mind distracted and tortured by visions of his Beloved. The impact of his acting was magical!

Toumanova, gliding suspended high up above the stage in the pastorale scene, was most effective. Danilova was Gaiety, Tania a child and George Zoritch a young shepherd – all were superb. But it was Massine's ballet. In my mind, this was the greatest role he had devised for himself to date.

At the end, Massine received a standing ovation. The ballet was pronounced a great achievement, and even the critics who argued that symphonies should not be used for ballet capitulated. The notices the next day fully acknowledged Massine's greatness as a choreographer. He had taken a symphony meant for the ears and transposed it for the eyes, without losing any of its impact.

We have a superstition in the ballet that at the second performance something might go wrong and, indeed, this time it did. As Toumanova glided suspended across the stage, the cables faltered and she came to an abrupt stop, stuck in mid-air. Without forward motion, she could not sustain her flying pose. No matter how hard she tried, she sagged in a helpless heap, her face expressing dismay and fright. Her mama was getting hysterical in the wings; the audience started to giggle.

The stagehands tried to pull the cables manually and finally, with a few jerks, they pulled Tamara across to safety. From then on the flight was cancelled, and instead Toumanova had to cross the stage gracefully in small *pas de bourrées*. It was a pity, but it did make sense, since in America it would have been too difficult to stage the Beloved's flight in so many different theatres.

The new invention, television, in its infancy at this time, was much talked about. We received an invitation from the BBC to appear on the program they were to broadcast from their studios at Alexandra Palace. We put together a short program for the leading dancers and on the given day, bubbling with curiosity, we were picked up by the BBC for a morning rehearsal at Alexandra Palace and a live transmission in the afternoon.

We were dismayed to find that the space in which we had to dance was very, very small, and worried when we were told that our performance would be recorded in total darkness, with horizontal white lights flickering in front of us. Imagine dancing with no reference points – keeping your position, your balance, without being able to see your partner!

We rehearsed that morning in these conditions, determined to succeed. I was to dance the spinning top from *Jeux d'enfants*, an unfortunate choice, as it is based on *pirouettes*; and a *pas de deux* from *Aurora's Wedding* with Paul Petroff, which was much easier. Another surprise was that our faces were made up white with black lipstick. Thankfully it all went well. The BBC considered it a success and we were invited again, this time choosing a more suitable program for total darkness.

At this time Colonel de Basil was looking into the possibility of taking the company to Australia. He had received an offer from Nevin Tait of J. C. Williamson for the northern autumn of 1936 and the following spring. As we were already contracted to appear in America, Colonel de Basil decided to honour the Australian engagement by forming a smaller second company, headed by several of our dancers and complemented by new ones, under the leadership of Léon Woizikowski. This venture proved very successful, and the following year Colonel de Basil began firm negotiations to take the full company to Australia in 1938. For once we were going to miss our American tour which, frankly, did not bother us, and we looked forward to discovering faraway Australia.

At that time rumours were circulating that Massine did not see eye to eye with Colonel de Basil and might be leaving us, enticed by offers from America to start another company. If he went, Danilova would also leave us, as would Toumanova, who perhaps had different reasons for doing so. It was also rumoured that the Colonel was negotiating with Michel Fokine to be our permanent choreographer. My feelings were mixed: regrets at losing Massine but excitement at the prospect of working with the great Fokine.

Our London season ended with the usual last-night gala and supper party on stage. We truly loved being in London, and whenever we had to leave, it was always with regret. Now we had a rare event – just over a month's holiday. It would be a much-needed rest for all of us before we assembled in Berlin in mid-September for our opening there on 1 October. Jerry's friends, the Diamantidis, insisted that he and I spend the holiday with them at their country house in Effingham, Surrey, one hour from London.

Although I would have preferred to go to the South of France and spend my days on the beach, on reflection I decided not to argue. Staying near London meant I could take classes at least three times a week with Nicolai Legat, a much-esteemed teacher, ex-leading dancer of the Maryinsky Theatre Ballet, and a partner of Mme Preobrajenska in the pre-revolutionary days. It would help me to keep in good shape for the opening in Berlin.

Before going to the Diamantidis I wrote to my parents care of Dr Appelbaum, expressing my concern for them, my sadness at not hearing from them, and my news about our London season. I enclosed my address in Effingham in the hope that they would relent and send me a few words. I had no response.

Grove House, Gladys and Tony Diamantidis' Georgian house, was vast, with ivy-covered walls, and typical English flowerbeds surrounding a big stretch of lawn, at the far end of which was a tennis court. Beyond it were fields of grazing cattle. It was a peaceful place, except on some Sundays during our London season, when a few of us regular visitors, 'adopted' by Gladys and Tony, would roll in to stay until Monday morning. We were a happy, boisterous bunch – Jerry and me, Tania and Lichine, Sono Osato, Roman Jasinski, Zorina, and Jerry's four cousins, the two Knoop brothers and two Alexeiev brothers. The neighbours would also occasionally pop in, fascinated by the ballet dancers. Sono Osato was wonderful, entertaining them with stories of our travels.

The day we moved to Grove House for our holiday and it sunk in that I had no performances to give for several weeks, I suddenly felt all the physical and emotional tiredness that had accumulated during that year. Like a stretched-to-the-limit rubber band, I snapped. Not able to explain my tears and sobs, made to sip some brandy by dear, solicitous Gladys, I collapsed into bed and slept solidly for thirty-six hours. My hosts and Jerry were worried and about to call the doctor, when I finally woke up fresh as a daisy and full of energy.

Every morning Gladys, driven by Tony, went to London, where she had a fashionable establishment in Mayfair making ladies' dresses and hats. Tony went about his varied businesses – it was never quite clear to me what they were.

This holiday gave Jerry and me a chance to get to know each other better. I did not know anything about his family, his childhood or his early days as a refugee, first in Yugoslavia then in France. Jerry was a good storyteller, and I spent endless hours listening to his accounts of his large, eccentric family in pre-revolutionary Russia. As I got to know him I grew fond of him, but I did not love him the way a wife should love her husband. My love was still ballet.

Jerry's mother was born into the Alexeiev family, very rich textile magnates who exported their wares all over Europe. She had a sister and two brothers. The brothers were expected to enter the family business but one of them stubbornly refused. His inclinations were artistic and his ambitions to act and direct were unshakeable. His father finally had to give in, but the old man made a condition: that the good name of the Alexeievs must not be dragged onto the boards. He ordered his rebellious son to take a pseudonym. Konstantin obliged and became Konstantin Stanislavsky, the inventor of the Stanislavsky method of acting and, in time, the founder of the world famous Moscow Art Theatre.

According to Jerry, Konstantin's brother, Volodia, was artistically inclined as well, but caved in and entered the family business. Every holiday he would travel to Spain to study Spanish dancing and learn to play the castanets. When he arrived back home, he would gather the family together and, sticking a rose behind his ear, draping a Spanish shawl around his tall figure, and taking up the castanets, would throw himself into a frenzied dance, oblivious to all present. The children just adored him.

Jerry remembered his grandmother Alexeiev as a gentle, kind person, a contrast to the severe, serious Grandfather Alexeiev. She helped the needy, built an orphanage and a hospital in Moscow, and spoilt her grandchildren. Jerry's mother also had artistic ambitions; she wanted to be an opera singer. She was very beautiful, wilful, charming and adored by all. Her voice was pleasant enough, but did not have the capacity for her to become an opera diva. This fact did not deter her. Being rich, she rented a theatre, enticed singers to join her in the venture and sang the lead roles in her two favourite operas, both by Tchaikovsky, *Eugene Onegin* and *The Queen of Spades*. Men were at her feet!

She married three times. From her first marriage she had three children, from the second (Jerry's father) also three children, and from the third one child – the Revolution then put the brakes on any further additions. A friend once asked Jerry's mother, 'Why do you have so many children?' She replied, 'I collect them!'

The family's living arrangements were unusual. They occupied three large flats on the same floor of a building in Moscow. One flat was for Mama, her husband of the day and their child; the second was for the children by her first husband, their nannies and governess; and the third, connected by a door to the second, was for the children of the second marriage, with their nannies and governess. Mama also had a flat at the Hotel Metropole, where she preferred to live, entertain and vocalise.

Jerry's father, the second husband, was a celebrated tenor and had two older sisters. Jerry's mama fell in love with his father when he sang the role of German (pronounced 'gairman') in *The Queen of Spades* – which is why Jerry, whose full name was German, had been given that name. A tall, flamboyant figure, he was much loved by the children. When their mama announced that she was leaving him for the third husband-to-be, it broke his heart, and he forever lost his singing voice.

After the Revolution, he was asked to take on the directorship of the opera company in Odessa. He wanted to take his children with him, as it seemed safer in the south than in Moscow. Their mother left it to the children to decide who would go with him and who would stay in Moscow with her. She herself wouldn't hear of leaving. The girls decided to stay with their mother because they said, 'Mother is fun.' Jerry decided to go with his father.

After a while, Odessa became as unsafe as anywhere else, and the Red Army was advancing. Jerry's father joined the Red Cross train as a volunteer and Jerry remained alone in Odessa, where he was studying at the Naval Academy. Jerry, with the rest of the Academy, was evacuated under difficult conditions and eventually found himself in Yugoslavia. Somehow his father managed to get out too.

A few years later, father and son were finally reunited in Paris. News from the family in Russia was scarce and they never knew if their letters reached Moscow. After World War II, Jerry heard from a friend that his mother had died of starvation in Omsk. His father didn't live long and died in Paris. After the war Jerry made a trip to Belgrade to be reunited with his two sisters and his youngest half-brother. Since Yugoslavia was a communist country, the Soviets allowed Jerry's siblings to visit Belgrade for two weeks.

Our Effingham holiday drew to a close and Jerry and I flew to Berlin. It was a good feeling to be among my tribe again. The Scala Theatre was very nice, with a good audience capacity, a big stage, good dressing rooms, and, importantly, an excellent large rehearsal studio on the top floor.

The director of the Scala Theatre, Edward Duisberg, had a Russian wife; both received us warmly, and were always helpful and hospitable. Through them we met a giant of a man with a red moustache and jovial manner, by the name of Dr Krause. He fell in love with our company and became a self-appointed guardian of our health and wellbeing. He attended every performance, watching, entranced, from the audience or from the wings.

With daily classes and constant rehearsals, we did not have much time to explore Berlin. I remember it as a clean and orderly city with sturdy buildings, and wide streets and boulevards; the massive Reichstag was very impressive. Everyone was extremely polite. Our hotel was just around the corner from the busy Kurfürstendamm, a wide avenue with many outdoor cafés, shops and some nightclubs (soon to be shut under Hitler's orders). My favourite shop was Rosenthal, famous worldwide for its exquisite, fine china. I often gazed at its window displays thinking that if I ever had a home of my own and plenty of money, a Rosenthal dinner service would grace my table. *Well, no harm dreaming!*

Germany in 1936 was more inclined towards modern expression in dance. In Germany, Mary Wigman was what Martha Graham later became in the United States: the flag-bearer of modern dance. I wondered how the German audiences would respond to our classical style, but to my surprise, delight and relief, the packed auditorium on the first night gave us a standing ovation. People ran forward to the rails of the orchestra pit shouting bravo and applauded on and on with vigorous enthusiasm. The critics were just as enthusiastic. Our season was sold out and we were invited to return the following year.

Just as in all the other countries, after the end of each performance a crowd would gather around the stage door waiting for us to come out. Some would ask for autographs, some just wanted to have a look at us. But here, unlike everywhere else, no member of the audience was allowed to come backstage. If we had friends in the audience, we had to give their names to the stage doorkeeper and request him to show them to our dressing room. As we knew hardly anyone in Berlin, we did not keep the nice people at the stage door waiting long!

The Duisbergs, one night at supper, told a few of us that Herr Goebbels, the propaganda minister, had indicated his intention to attend a performance, perhaps with Herr Hitler. Although none of us took much interest in politics, we were aware of the impact of *Mein Kampf*. Our non-dancer friends were outraged. I listened to many heated discussions and speculations, which aroused my curiosity, and I started reading the newspapers and paying attention to the *Pathé News* shown at cinemas before the feature. I would see Hitler on these newsreels, orating to mesmerised, adoring crowds and party members. As he spoke, forcefully, his voice would rise and rise to an almost hysterical pitch, but it had a rhythm that made one listen, as if hypnotised. I saw Hitler as fierce and unpleasant, and Goebbels as small, thin and lugubrious.

One night halfway through the season, before the last ballet on the program started, Papa Grigoriev asked Massine, Danilova, Tania, Lichine and me to remain on stage after the final curtain. (Toumanova had not come to Berlin with us.) Important guests had requested to meet us. We stood waiting on the empty stage for quite a while. When, by the sound of it, the public had left the auditorium, the guests arrived through the side door onto the stage. In came Hitler, Goebbels and Goebbels' wife, escorted by the Duisbergs and Colonel de Basil, followed closely by half a dozen SS (*Schutzstaffel*) or the 'Blackshirts'. They stood around motionless, eyes alert.

Herr Duisberg and the Colonel conducted the guests towards us. The ladies were introduced first and Hitler, with great charm, gallantly kissed our hands. He then shook hands with Massine, Grigoriev and Lichine, Goebbels following suit, introducing his wife. Both complimented us in German, while Herr Duisberg translated. I was struck by Hitler's blue eyes, intense and penetrating. He thanked us for our beautiful performance, and with a wave they left through the stage door, where their cars were waiting, protected by more Blackshirts. Goebbels kept sending Tania and me bunches of mauve lilacs, always with the same inscription on his card: 'With thanks. J. Goebbels.' Now when I remember this encounter, it immediately evokes the horrors and tragic events that these men inflicted upon humanity.

For some time, I had been experiencing a nagging pain in my stomach. I tried to ignore it and did not mention it to anyone. I also disliked posing for publicity photos and the photo calls on stage – they were so tedious and boring! One morning we had such a photo call, on stage, in costume and make-up, for *Aurora's Wedding*. The pain in my stomach was particularly sharp that morning, which did not help my already sour mood. I was on time and on stage, ready and waiting. The photographer was fussing with the lighting; I eyed him in utter frustration. I pulled myself together, trying my best to cooperate and hide my pain. We were almost through when a sharp stab of pain hit my right side. I doubled up in agony. Dear Papa Grigoriev rushed to me.

'What's the matter, my angel?'

All I could say was, 'Ai-ai-ai!'

Jerry appeared from the wings where he had been chatting with Dr Krause and, half-annoyed, half-amused, told Papa Grigoriev I was shamming! 'She hates being photographed, you know that!'

'Ah, my angel.' Papa Grigoriev was not sure what to believe.

Furious with Jerry, I screamed, 'I am not shamming.'

Dr Krause came to my rescue. 'Irina is not pretending,' he barked at Jerry.

He picked me up and carried me to my dressing room, where my dresser helped me out of my costume while he, ordering me to lie still on the sofa, rushed out to make a phone call. Jerry followed him. When they returned, Massine was with them, hotly arguing with Dr Krause.

'No, no, it's impossible!' I heard him say. 'I need her to dance *Symphonie fantastique* at the opening night in New York!' (As Toumanova was not with us, Massine had asked me to take over her role.)

'What's going on?' I enquired, feeling apprehensive.

Dr Krause informed me that he was taking me to the Augsburg Clinic in Berlin to see his friend Professor Gorband and that, if he was right in suspecting I was suffering a bad case of appendicitis, Professor Gorband would operate on me that afternoon.

'No, no, this is impossible!' insisted Massine.

Dr Krause lost his temper. He lifted Massine clear off the floor by the lapels of his jacket, and stared into his eyes, murmuring, 'The whites of your eyes are yellow. Trouble with your gall bladder?' As he deposited Massine back on the floor, Dr Krause reassured him, 'I promise you, Irina will be fine, in good shape and dancing in New York.'

Massine backed towards the door. 'Oh well, all right then,' he said. Then, hesitating for a moment, he added, 'Will you check my gall bladder, please?'

'I will, I will,' Dr Krause reassured him, barely containing his laughter.

Still stunned by this unexpected turn of events, I was driven by Dr Krause to the clinic, where the professor examined me and confirmed that my appendix was in urgent need of removal. I liked Professor

Gorband immediately; he was gentle and reassuring. He had seen me perform, and complimented me warmly. That lifted my morale, which by then had begun to sag. I was to remain at the clinic and be prepared by the resident, Dr von Ondarza, and the nurse assigned to look after me.

Dr von Ondarza was young, tall, dark and devastatingly handsome. In his immaculately tailored white coat, he was to die for. No wonder the girls visited me daily during the eleven days I spent at the clinic! They obviously hoped to bump into him in my room or in the corridor.

The operation was to take place at five p.m. Installed in my room, I gave Jerry a list of things to bring me from the hotel and picked on him unmercifully for accusing me of shamming. Dr Krause promised to be back by three p.m. and said he would assist the professor at the operation. I felt so grateful to this gentle, understanding, caring man.

To my surprise, a camp bed was installed in my room. It turned out to be for my nurse, who was to be with me twenty-four hours a day. I felt so pampered! She turned out to be a most adorable, fun person and great company. I soon began to call her 'Schwester Ou-Hoo', my nickname for her. In the end, everyone at the clinic was calling her 'Ou-Hoo'! She was a tiny person, but very strong.

Soon after four p.m., the professor appeared with Colonel de Basil, who had charmed Professor Gorband into allowing him to be present at the operation and to hold the dish into which the offending piece of my gut was to be deposited. The Colonel was thrilled, the professor amused. The whole affair was turning into a party, and I was actually beginning to enjoy being the focus of attention.

Jerry returned from the hotel with my bits and pieces. He was acting jittery and seemed anxious to leave. As he was about to do so, he said, 'Well, good luck. See you tomorrow.'

I expressed surprise that he was not staying with me. His explanation was that he could not stand clinics and hospitals, as they gave him panic attacks, and he couldn't deal with being around sick people – they made him feel awkward and nervous. And so, wishing me good luck again, he hurriedly left. I was beginning to discover what made Jerry tick – or not, as the case may be.

Ou-Hoo told me later that once the operation was over, Colonel de Basil, clutching the dish containing my appendix, ran up and down the corridors showing it to everyone he encountered, poking his finger into it with great excitement, scandalising the staff and 'amusing' the other patients and visitors.

These days, after such an ordinary operation, one would be walking around on the second day, but in the old days one was kept in bed for a week, and then only gently taken out to walk a few steps. They were amazed that I did not have difficulty walking and did not feel weak. I kept telling them that there was nothing amazing about it and that we dancers were not ordinary people like them. Due to our rigorous training and discipline, we were more resilient. I have such good memories of my stay at the clinic – I had lots of visitors and, once everyone had gone, peace had been restored, and a delicious dinner had been eaten, Ou-Hoo would reach under the bed and produce a bottle of port, which would get emptier and emptier at an alarming rate, as we chattered endlessly and laughed a great deal. I never slept better!

On the eleventh day after the operation, I was out of the clinic, and that same night went to see the circus, where the internationally famous clown Grok was performing. He was truly a great artist, and I loved his antics so much that the friends who were with me were worried that I would split my fresh new scar!

I was very much intrigued by the Zeppelins and had often expressed a desire to fly in one. As a surprise for me, Jerry managed to get us onto a Zeppelin flight back to London but, due to the delay caused by my operation, we had missed the flight. As I remember it, there was a terrible accident when the Zeppelin landed, so I blessed my appendix, which saved our lives.

Our embarkation for America was not far off, and we hurried to London, so I could take a few classes with Legat before rejoining the company on board ship and bracing myself for another gruelling tour.

Since my parents were not with me any more and I therefore did not require two cabins, Jerry and I now travelled first class. The cabin was roomy, with a real bed, wood-panelling, nice-looking armchairs and a full-length mirror on the wardrobe door. It was very cosy. Not used to such luxury, I felt like the Queen of Sheba! But the enjoyment of the crossing was watered down each day that brought us nearer to New York. Anxious about my parents, not knowing what to expect, my mind was troubled.

As our ship docked, I scrutinised the pier below, looking out for Dr Appelbaum. He was there, as usual, to greet us. I braced myself to hear from him what was happening with my parents. But the news was worse than I expected – my papa had suffered a heart attack and was still in bed. Two months before, they had been burgled and Papa's treasured gold pocket watch, his mother's present upon his graduation from the Naval Academy, was stolen, along with some money he had saved and kept at home. He had never had a bank account.

Papa, Dr Appelbaum thought, would love to see me – it would do him good – but Mother was being difficult and objected when Dr Appelbaum suggested it. I listened with a sinking heart. Under the circumstances, the doctor did not need much persuasion to give me my parents' address. He knew that I had to see my papa, whether Mother liked it or not!

Once I was settled at the hotel, I asked Jerry to give me all the money in his wallet, which he did, then I grabbed a taxi, giving the driver my parents' address. I was worried about appearing without warning, but they had no telephone. I arrived at a brownstone house with a 'Rooms to Let' sign and, my heart in my mouth, knocked on their door. My mother opened and for a moment we stood there facing each other in silence. I wanted to hug her but did not dare – something in her expression stopped me. Then I heard Papa's voice enquiring who was there. I couldn't stay outside any longer. I brushed past Mother and entered the room. 'Papa, it's me . . . can I come in?'

Papa stretched his arms to me and I ran to his bedside, tears flooding my face. He held me in his arms until I stopped crying, then offered me his handkerchief and said, smiling, 'It's good to see you.'

I glanced at Mother. She stood in the middle of the room watching us. 'Do you want a cup of tea?' she asked me.

'Yes, please,' I answered gratefully.

The silence was broken. There was so much to ask, so much to tell. At first all three of us felt awkward, but as the hours ticked by it became easier, and Mother's tone of voice more friendly. I noticed that Mother now wore spectacles. I also had a chat with Miky and Peki, who were well and looked happy. Papa told me that in a couple of days he would be allowed to get up and would soon go back to work. Not once was Jerry's name mentioned.

As Mother saw me out, I gave her the envelope with the money and, to stop her arguing, said we would talk about it later. She thanked me and even gave me a kiss. The worst was over and I was full of hope that our relationship was on the mend. Back at the hotel, Jerry was waiting for me. I told him briefly how things stood and that I needed to talk to him at length about my parents' situation.

'All right,' he said, 'but dinner first,' and took me to the Russian Tea Room, which became our favourite restaurant in New York. I was too preoccupied with my own thoughts to enjoy a meal out. Food did not tempt me. All I wanted was to go back to the hotel and have a serious talk with Jerry about the plans that were formulating in my mind concerning my parents. Finally back at the hotel, we did have a long talk. My dearest wish was to persuade my parents to move out of New York to Long Island, where they had several Russian friends living in Sea Cliff and Locust Valley. Forty-five minutes from New York and by the seashore, Sea Cliff constituted a real Russian colony. I knew my parents loved the place and enjoyed visiting their friends there. Jerry agreed that it was a good idea.

I knew it would benefit Papa's health to be by the seaside. And since he told me he worked at home most of the time, going to Bobri's design studio no more than twice a week, my idea made sense to me.

The task now would be to persuade them to make the move and to accept my financial assistance.

The extent of my financial help had to be worked out. Until my marriage, my parents had always taken care of my earnings. Now, since I was still only seventeen, Jerry was in charge of them. I never paid bills and had no idea about money matters. My purse only contained the amount I asked for if I was in need of more make-up, stockings or toiletries. But although I was a minor by law, my signature invalid, I was working and earning my living. I thought this situation was unfair and now I had to assert myself. I knew what my salary was; I had no idea what Jerry's was. I told Jerry that from now on I wanted him to give me two-thirds of my monthly earnings, which I would put towards helping my parents until such time as my father was well again, working and independent. We would have to economise, stay at cheaper hotels, I ventured.

To my relief, Jerry made no objections. To cut a long story short, with the help of Dr Appelbaum, Papa finally agreed to move to Long Island. But it took some persuasion for him to accept my financial help – Papa was a proud man and always dealt with financial situations on his own. With the help of friends, we found a nice flat in Sea Cliff. The only other flat in that house was occupied by my parents' friends. It had a big garden, was near the sea, and was immediately available, which meant my parents could get away from New York and their depressing lodgings straightaway.

Papa was up and getting better by the day. He and Mama still never mentioned Jerry's name; it was as if he did not exist. And whenever I told Jerry about Papa and how the arrangements for my parents' move were progressing, he would listen in silence, without comment. Soon I stopped telling him anything and he did not ask. I felt trapped between two parties who fiercely disliked each other – not a nice feeling, not a comfortable situation to be in.

One night at the Russian Tea Room we bumped into George Balanchine and Vera Zorina who were together by then. 'I suppose I should congratulate you two,' was Balanchine's greeting. Then he added, 'But I don't give your marriage more than a couple of years.'

We laughed politely but a thought crossed my mind: *He might not be far wrong . . .*

Only that morning, Jerry had said to me, 'You always put your parents first. What about me?' He was obviously resentful. He was right, of course, but I could not change my priorities.

Our season at the Metropolitan Opera House was proceeding with the usual great success. Massine was relieved that I was fit again, and pleased with my interpretation of his Beloved in *Symphonie fantastique*. I had to think hard about it; there was no way in my mind I could copy Toumanova – a copy is never as good as the original. I had to portray the role with my own feelings. I tinted the Beloved's remoteness with a tenderness that was gradually replaced by harshness.

The notices for my own interpretation were excellent, and Massine scored another triumph. But soon he was to leave us to start his new company – which he chose to call Ballet Russe de Monte Carlo – with the financial assistance of Julius Fleischmann. He was to be the sole artistic director and Serge Denham, a Russian businessman, the director. Endless litigation went on between Massine and Colonel de Basil regarding the ownership of Massine's ballets and who had the rights to which works. Massine's choice of name meant that we had to change our name – over the years we became known as the Colonel de Basil Ballet Russe, the Covent Garden Ballet Russe, the Original Ballet Russe and the Educational Ballet Russe.

Many friends in both camps who liked to interfere got the idea that our company and Massine's should merge. Colonel de Basil was under pressure from Sol Hurok to merge, but it was in Hurok's interest. Baron d'Erlanger and Captain Bruce Ottley were against this merger, and so was Jerry, who by now had great influence over Colonel de Basil. And Massine had his ambition of being the artistic director *assoluto* and the one and only choreographer. It was clear that the idea of a merger was doomed from the start, but Sol Hurok and Serge Denham still did not give up.

Serge Denham (I found out years later), unbeknown to Sol Hurok, thought that if Jerry could be eliminated from the picture, Colonel de

Basil could be pressured to agree to the merger. As part of his research into Jerry's past, Denham got in touch with my parents and invited them to spend the weekend at his home in the country. My parents happened to mention Jerry's previous marriage and his ex-spouse's visit to them at our hotel in Paris.

Totally oblivious to all these goings-on, and frankly not interested, I was busy with my performances and helping my parents with their move to Sea Cliff. All I knew was that I did not want any mergers – I was happy with our company as it was and wanted it to go on like that forever. Although I regretted Massine's departure, I was so looking forward to Michel Fokine joining us.

The New York season over, we went on tour, at the end of which we were due for another season at the Metropolitan Opera House before sailing back to Europe, first stop Florence. Tamara Toumanova was back with us, beautiful as ever, if very thin, slightly tired and a little green in the face. On our train hops she looked exhausted and slept a lot, but she was still dancing beautifully. I admired her tenacity and willpower, but then she too was a pupil of Olga Preobrajenska – she taught us both DISCIPLINE!

One crisp, wintery day in Philadelphia, I was sitting in my dressing room, putting on my make-up for the matinee performance. I was relaxed, my mind finally at rest concerning my parents. Papa was back at work, feeling well again and pleased with their move to Long Island. There was a brief knock on the door and, as it was flung open, my papa rushed in brandishing a newspaper. Surprised and alarmed by his unexpected appearance in Philadelphia, I asked him if anything had happened to Mother.

'Mother is all right,' he reassured me and then, getting agitated, he slammed the newspaper down on the dressing table in front of me, almost shouting at me, 'I've come to take you home!' He pointed aggressively at the startling front-page headline: 'IRINA BARONOVA'S HUSBAND ACCUSED OF BIGAMY!'

I couldn't believe my eyes. I was totally dumbfounded. I felt as if something had hit me hard on the head, and I couldn't think. Then the realisation slowly came that I would have to undergo a horrible confrontation with my parents. At that point there was another knock on the door and a worried-looking Sol Hurok walked into my dressing room. He was obviously taken aback when he saw my father. Dropping onto a chair, he said in his funny Russian, 'Well, now you know. Calm down, it's an obvious frame-up. Let's talk civilised.'

'There's nothing to talk about,' retorted Papa. 'Irina's coming home with me.'

'A moment, please,' muttered Hurok, standing up and looking squarely at Papa. 'It's up to Irina to decide whether she goes home with you or comes to New York with me.'

Papa calmed down and they both stared at me questioningly. I sat in a daze until Grisha's voice in the corridor, calling, 'Half an hour, please,' pulled me out of this state and into frantic action. I was dancing in the first ballet on the program. I had to get ready, do my hair, put my costume on, no time for a warm-up . . . 'Please, please, I'm on in half an hour, let me get ready,' I pleaded.

Starting to shake with nerves, I pleadingly looked at Papa, but it was Mr Hurok who put his arm on Papa's shoulder saying, 'Let's go. You and I need to talk. We'll see you at intermission,' he added then, giving me a pat.

As they left, Mme Larose dashed in to help me dress. 'I thought they'd never go!' she muttered. 'Couldn't they wait to upset you until after your performance?'

Oh God, if she knows, everyone knows – how embarrassing! As Mme Larose hooked me into my costume, I realised what I had to do. I had to believe it was a frame-up. There was no need to be embarrassed; Jerry would be cleared in no time and I would have to go to New York with Mr Hurok. Running away to my parents would be a shabby thing to do. Hoping Papa would understand, I went on stage in a defiant mood. As I waited in the wings for my entrance, doing a few *échappés* to warm up, Papa Grigoriev came over to me and, patting my hand, said, 'Ah, my angel, don't worry. *Promolitea i mooka boudet.*' It is a Russian proverb: 'It will grind and become flour.'

I was touched by his kindness. My colleagues showed their regard for me by not mentioning the 'news', which no doubt was setting many tongues wagging around the dressing rooms. I wondered why Jerry had not phoned to warn me of the unpleasantness to come. Two days before he had gone to New York on business with Colonel de Basil, and I had not heard from him since. Now I was wondering, *What business?*

The overture over, the curtain went up. Now was not the time to wonder. I had to concentrate on the present moment and give a good performance. Papa and Mr Hurok were waiting for me in my dressing room. The men looked away as Mme Larose helped me out of my costume. For no reason that I could explain, the situation struck me as grotesque. I started to laugh as three startled pairs of eyes looked at me in dismay. 'Shall I bring you some *valerianka?*' (valerian drops), murmured Mme Larose. I reassured her that I was not in need of *valerianka*. I gave her a kiss and she departed, shaking her head in doubt.

'Where's Jerry?' I asked Mr Hurok.

'Talking to my lawyer, who has agreed to take his case. The Colonel is with them. Jerry's ex-wife is in New York. She went with her lawyer to the police claiming that Jerry had committed bigamy. The police came to my office yesterday, making inquiries. There'll be a warrant for his arrest. It must be avoided until this is sorted out. My lawyer wants you out of reach of the press, so I came to fetch you and take you to my flat. What's your decision?'

I looked at Papa. He was calm now. With a resigned, sad look on his face, he said, 'I suppose you've made up your mind. You're not coming home with me, are you?'

'No, Papa, I can't.'

'Well, if things turn bad, will you remember that my home is your home too? Will you come then?'

'Yes, Papa, you know I will. I'm sorry to bring you so much grief and worry – to Mama too – she'll be so cross with me . . . again.'

Glancing at his watch, Papa stood up, 'I must go. Nikita' (his friend and neighbour) 'will be waiting for me. He offered to drive me here.' Papa shook hands with Mr Hurok, asking him to take good care of me.

Then he hugged me. I loved him so much, so much . . . Papa made a sign of the cross over my chest. 'God be with you,' he said, and was gone. I burst into tears.

'Hurry up and change, Irinotschka, we have a train to catch,' said Mr Hurok softly. He left my dressing room in search of Papa Grigoriev, to warn him I would be absent for several days and that some adjustments would have to be made to the casting. When I was ready, I found Mr Hurok pacing up and down the corridor.

We had to dash into the hotel on the way to the station, to collect my case and pay the bill. When I came down, having hurriedly packed my belongings, I found that Mr Hurok had dealt with my bill. What a nice gesture! We caught the train to New York with a few minutes to spare. We were alone in our compartment, but neither of us felt like talking. Mr Hurok pulled *Time* magazine out of his coat pocket and skimmed absent-mindedly through the pages.

I shut my eyes in search of privacy. I had to sort out in my mind what stance to take when I saw Jerry. I felt as if I had been given a role in an intriguing play. *How will I play this role? As an outraged wife, or as a good sport? But . . . but how do I really feel?* The answer was, *Relieved that my papa was so reasonable and kind to me.* That was of prime importance to me, more important than this 'mess'! *Am I upset? No, not really.* After the initial shock, I felt like I had landed myself in an exciting adventure. Yes, exciting . . . and I had a lead role!

Was Jerry a bigamist, or was he not? At that moment, sitting on the train speeding towards New York, it did not matter to me. I came to the conclusion that it would be more fun to play my role as a good sport. Then, whichever way this mess turned out, I would be liked and no-one would throw rotten tomatoes at me. Having come to this conclusion, I relaxed and opened my eyes. Mr Hurok was dozing in his corner and the New York suburbs were flying past. I tapped him on the knee. 'Wake up, we're arriving in a few minutes.'

'Jerry and the rest will be at my flat,' Mr Hurok warned me. 'Are you going to make a scene?'

'No.'

'God be praised!' he said, making a pious face.

As we entered Mr Hurok's sitting room, the three men stood up with uncertain looks on their faces. I went over to the Colonel to give him a kiss. Mr Hurok introduced me to his lawyer. Then I looked at Jerry; he was tense, obviously feeling uncomfortable.

'I'm not going to bite you!' I laughed, giving him a peck on the cheek. Everybody relaxed. We sat down.

'I'm sorry you've been dragged into this mess,' said Jerry, adding that he would understand and not blame me if I left him there and then and went back to my parents.

Assuming my role of good sport, I laughed, 'And miss all the fun?' Nobody else laughed, so I sensed that flippancy was out of place and quickly added, 'I'm not going anywhere. I'm staying with you.'

Jerry came over and sat by me, took my hand, kissed it and said thank you. Mr Hurok's lawyer proceeded to put me in the picture, explaining the situation and what had so far been done about it. Apparently, some people had found out the whereabouts of Jerry's ex-wife, who had readily supplied them with useful information. She maintained that their marriage in the Russian Orthodox Church had never been dissolved. It was a perfect scenario for stirring up mud! She agreed to come to New York, all expenses paid, lawyer provided, and lodge a complaint against Jerry.

Jerry maintained that they were legally divorced in the Civil Court in Paris, but conceded that he had been negligent and forgot to obtain the ultimate document from the Russian Church, signed by the Patriarch, to certify that the annulment had been granted. In Russia, the church divorce counted; in most other countries it was of no consequence – the civil divorce was. Jerry had to produce his civil divorce documents, but where were they? In a suitcase left at Colonel de Basil's office in Paris. A frantic call was made to Mme Bouchonnet to force the case open, find the documents and send them express to the lawyer's office. As Jerry had a Yugoslav passport, another call was made to his brother-in-law in Belgrade, begging him to see the head of the Russian Church in Belgrade, explain the situation and persuade His Holiness to issue the document needed to annul the marriage.

Jerry's brother-in-law, Vuk Dragovic, was a much-respected journalist and political figure, but he was also an atheist and did not have much time for the clergy. However, he adored Jerry and promised to do his best, even kiss the Patriarch's ring if pushed!

The wheels were in motion. Now we had to wait for the documents to arrive and in the meantime dodge the police. It all sounded terribly complicated to me, and as far as I was concerned, half of what the lawyer said could have been in Chinese! I nodded wisely, pretending I understood.

Finally, the lawyer decreed that Jerry and I must get out of New York State and go to New Jersey, where Jerry would be safe for the time being. He was going to take us to a remote motel, whose proprietor was a friend of his and discretion itself. We were to stay in our room, take no phone calls and only open the door to him or his friend. They would use a code word. As for food, his friend would take good care of us.

'My parents will be worried not hearing from me,' I ventured.

Mr Hurok reassured me, promising to phone them and put their minds at rest. Colonel de Basil looked gloomy. Perhaps he was sick and tired of our marital complications on top of his own problems. He had caught his wife being unfaithful and was discreetly arranging a divorce. The company did not know about it – I knew about this sorry affair from Jerry. I felt sorry for the Colonel.

'Well, let's go,' urged the lawyer. Mr Hurok produced two packs of cards, which he handed to me together with a couple of books. 'To pass the time,' he said, patting my cheek. The Colonel gave me a hug. Collecting our little bags, Jerry and I obediently followed the lawyer to his car and set off for New Jersey. We drove in silence. I felt tired, and a feeling of resentment was creeping in towards Jerry for being so sloppy about his divorce papers. I wished I was back in my dressing room in Philadelphia, not missing performances. The good sport was turning sour!

It seemed to me that we drove for ages. When we finally turned off the main road, we stopped in front of a good-looking building surrounded by a garden, which seemed to me to be in the middle of nowhere. Above the entrance a large electric sign read 'Motel'. The proprietor, a jovial-looking man, stepped out to greet us.

'Ah, here you are. Is everything okay?'

Our lawyer assured him that everything was fine and made the introductions – the man's name was Leo. He showed us to a room that was down the corridor, behind the reception desk. I remarked how unusual that was for a motel.

'This is a special room, more private, and you don't see the cars parked outside,' replied Leo with a grin.

The room was big, a bedsit, nicely furnished, quite cosy. 'What's the password?' I enquired.

'You choose,' said Jerry.

'All right . . . you say "Five minutes, please" as you knock on the door.'

'Okay,' they chorused.

The lawyer departed, promising to come as soon as there was news. Leo also left, promising to bring us something to eat soon. That was the first good news of the day!

The next two days passed in endless games of gin rummy and patience. Jerry won every game. Between these two pastimes, at which I was equally inept, I tried to read but was constantly interrupted by Jerry voicing his thoughts and worries. I was getting edgy, bored and longing to get out into the fresh air.

On the third day our lawyer appeared with the good news that the documents from Paris were on the way. The church annulment was progressing well and, according to Vuk Dragovic, should be ready and despatched in a couple of days. Good news indeed, but it meant more days spent in hiding, boredom and niggling, constant worry.

The next evening, as we were playing gin rummy and for a change I was winning, we heard Leo give the password as he knocked. It was unusual for him to knock at this late hour. 'He must have some news for us,' said Jerry, getting up to open the door.

Leo walked in, accompanied by a total stranger. 'Don't panic, it's okay,' he said.

'Hi,' said the stranger. 'We must talk.' Jerry and I assumed he was someone from the lawyer's office. Leo left the room as the rest of us sat down. 'May I introduce myself?' said the man, pulling something that looked like a small, flat wallet out of his breast pocket. As he flicked it open in front of our faces, Jerry and I froze in shock. The man was a New Jersey police inspector. 'Relax, relax! I'm not here to arrest you. I'm here as a friend.'

We sat speechless. 'Hey, relax! I'm off duty. Let's have a drink. By the looks of you two, you need it. Then we'll talk.' He produced a bottle of scotch from his coat pocket, found three tumblers and poured the drinks. Jerry and I surveyed him with suspicion and disbelief as he settled into the armchair. Pushing the drinks towards us, he lifted his own and, with an amused smile, said, 'To your good health!'

It was only then that I noticed this slight man had his hat on, pushed backwards over his dark mop of hair. *He has no manners*, I thought. 'Take your hat off!' I said curtly. He laughed, but obliged. Jerry gave me a disapproving look.

'Let me put your minds at rest. Leo didn't give you away. You can trust him.' The police inspector went on to explain that the New York police were inclined to believe that the bigamy accusation was a frame-up.

'Yes, and I'll prove it,' said Jerry.

'In that case, why are you hiding?'

Jerry explained his situation and assured the inspector that as soon as his lawyer received the documents proving that he was legally divorced, he would go to New York and contest the ridiculous accusation of bigamy. 'By the way,' asked Jerry, 'how did you discover we were here?'

'Ah,' the man shook his head. Then he became stern and snapped, 'We have our ways!' We all fell silent. The inspector looked thoughtful as he reached for his glass, 'Hey,' he said, 'you haven't touched your drink, Miss Ba-ronova.' He struggled with my name.

I pointed out to him that dancers do not drink – bad for the muscles. He nodded his head approvingly then announced that he was prepared to give us a helping hand in order to avoid us being found before the documents arrived from Europe. 'You can't stay here any longer,' he said. 'I'll take you to a place where you'll be okay until you're ready to go back to New York.'

'How will my lawyer know where we are?' asked Jerry.

'Leo will let him know. Now go and pack. We must get going.'

Pulling my untouched drink towards him, he settled back into his armchair and watched as we packed our few belongings. As we were collecting our toothbrushes in the bathroom, Jerry whispered to me in Russian, 'I don't know if we can trust him.'

'Do we have any choice?' I whispered back.

As we were about to leave the room, I asked the inspector why he was being so nice to us. His reply was most unexpected.

'My wife and I saw you perform in Newark. Great company! You were in a ballet called, oh dear . . . something about a wedding . . .'

'*Aurora's Wedding?*' I prompted.

'Yes, yes, that's the one! You were beautiful. So when I read in the newspapers that you were in trouble, I became interested and made some enquiries.' Turning to Jerry, he added, 'I'm trying to be helpful for her sake. If she wasn't involved in your mess, I wouldn't have bothered.'

Jerry looked vexed and annoyed. I hastened to thank the inspector for his concern about me. 'You should be performing, not hiding!' he muttered. I felt touched and at the same time bewildered. It all seemed so unreal. Jerry settled the bill, then Leo saw us to the inspector's car and wished us good luck. When we reached the main road we turned right and I noticed the sign saying 'Jersey City'. None of us spoke. About forty minutes later we pulled up in front of what looked like a small hotel. It was called Riverside.

The inspector took us to the reception desk, where he was greeted like an old friend by someone I assumed was the manager. We were introduced: 'Meet Mr and Mrs Green, friends of mine in need of a few days' rest. I recommended your place.'

The manager greeted us with a cheerful, 'Welcome!' No, we did not have to register. We were 'friends' visiting.

As the manager was busy at the pigeonholes looking for a key, the inspector turned to us with instructions. 'Don't go outside. Come down to the restaurant for your meals – quite safe, really good food! As far as you two are concerned, we never met! Understood?'

'Yes,' we nodded, thanking him.

'That's okay.' And with a wave to us, and a 'See you' to the manager, he was gone. What a nice person! I wish we had met him again under normal circumstances, but we never did.

Our room was on the first floor, overlooking a nice-looking garden and the river beyond. The cosy restaurant, on an enclosed veranda, served excellent food. But our mood was deteriorating. We sat mostly in silence, preoccupied with our individual thoughts, waiting . . . I tried to do some barre work by holding on to the door handle, but it was not a very satisfactory pastime. It frustrated me no end, as did not having any change of clothes – it made me feel grubby.

The mail from Europe was coming by ship – we had to be patient. But patience was running thin, and Jerry and I would become snappy at the drop of a hat. Finally, as we were going back to our room from dinner on the seventh day, we heard a cheerful voice calling, 'Hey, hello, wait for me!'

It was Mr Hurok's lawyer climbing the stairs after us. The documents had arrived; all was ready to clear Jerry's name. We had to return to New York immediately, where Jerry was needed for a few days. As for me, I could catch the sleeper train that evening to Cleveland and rejoin the company. I felt ecstatic and called my parents to tell them the good news, but their reaction was somewhat cool. I promised to call them from Cleveland the next day.

While the lawyer and Jerry were working on some papers, I packed my small holdall and went down to explore the garden. What joy! It felt as if I had been let out of prison. After settling the bill, the manager of the Riverside Hotel saw us off with good wishes. People can be so nice! We reached New York in time for dinner with Mr Hurok at the Russian Tea Room. At the end of dinner Mr Hurok handed me my ticket and reservation for the sleeper compartment on the night train.

I arrived in Cleveland and took a taxi straight to the theatre to be in time for class. Papa Grigoriev had been notified of my return and my dressing room was ready for me. Mme Larose had even unpacked my make-up, which I found tidily arranged on the dressing table. It felt so good to be back with my tribe.

7

ADVENTURES WITH BORIS KOCHNO

*O*ur tour went on as usual. Colonel de Basil and Jerry rejoined the company and life was never dull. When such large groups of people are thrown together, year in, year out, confined to their own enclosed world, some hiccups and dramas are unavoidable. There are always one or two black sheep in big families.

On one occasion, someone played a nasty prank that was meant to ruin my performance in *The Firebird*. By then Danilova had left our company to join Massine's new venture, so Toumanova and I now alternated in the role of the Firebird. My turn coincided with our opening night at the Met. Paul Petroff, as the Tsarevitch, was my partner.

As the curtain goes up, the Firebird crosses the stage with three *grands jetés en diagonale,* from the back to the front wing, and disappears. The same thing is then repeated from the other side of the stage. The third time the jumps end in the middle of the stage facing the magic apple tree. She picks at the apples in flight, then picks one in her mouth, runs to the front and throws it out of sight. That's when the Tsarevitch, having climbed the wall into the Enchanted Garden and hidden in the shadows, comes forward and catches the Firebird. A very long *pas de deux* ensues – very, very long!

Well, on my second set of jumps across the stage, the right elastic shoulder strap holding up my bodice snapped. An audible 'Oh!' from the audience! No time to do anything about it. On the third set of jumps

I start picking at the apples and, horror of horrors, my second shoulder strap snaps, to a louder 'Oh, oh!' from the audience. I am faced with the very long *pas de deux* becoming a public exhibition of my naked boobs! *Should I run off stage in search of safety pins? Ruin an important* pas de deux? *Unthinkable!* I altered the position of my arms and hands to try to hold the bodice up. At that moment I felt a rush of adrenaline, a challenge to rise above the unfortunate situation and give, in spite of everything, a good performance.

Paul Petroff was magnificent! As he caught me, he placed his hands over my boobs instead of on my waist, whispering in his funny Russian accent, 'My God, my God, I'll hold it, I'll hide you when I can!' He did, bless him, lifting me by my bosom instead of by my waist and helping me all he could to keep me decent, all with his usual elegance and aplomb. The audience, of course, followed the proceedings with interest, and I was told that some were betting on whether my boobs would pop out. The end of the *pas de deux* was met by an ovation! The critics praised our performance. Whoever sliced halfway through the elastic of my shoulder straps badly misjudged the effect it would have. Instead of ruining my performance, it turned it into a great success and generated a great deal of publicity.

During the period Boris Kochno travelled with us, he provided some unusual experiences for me by making me join him in his nocturnal expeditions. Kochno's eccentricity amused Jerry, and the fact that he was gay made my friendship with him acceptable. So I was allowed to go off with Kochno after a performance while Jerry went to bed.

Often, Kochno and I sat up talking after supper in the lobby of the hotel or, if on one-night stands, in our restaurant carriage. I would ply him with questions and listen, fascinated, as he expanded on our art, his collaboration with Diaghilev and all the wonderful artists, painters and musicians connected with that great company. One night he said, 'You're living in a fairy tale world. What do you know of the real world, outside the circle of people around you?'

I pondered for a moment. 'My parents had years of struggle and deprivation. I remember it well. Is that the real world?'

'Yes, one of the many facets of life. But now, as an adult – or almost,' he laughed, 'what do you know? What have you seen, taken on board, felt and thought about? I want to show you some facets of life you've never experienced, enrich your feelings, good or bad, your thoughts, your powers of observation. You'll be a better artist for it.'

It was in San Francisco that my first outing with Kochno took place. 'Dress extra warm tonight. We'll be outdoors for most of it,' he warned, appearing after class one grey rainy morning.

'Where are we going?' I exclaimed, all excited.

'Aha, it's a surprise,' he replied with a mischievous smile. After our supper that night we set off in a taxi. Kochno asked the driver to let us off by the Golden Gate Bridge, which had just been completed that year (1937). In those days, that extraordinary bridge was the longest in the world. There was still all sorts of machinery along the banks, as workmen attended to the finishing touches.

We got out of the taxi and I looked at the deserted, dimly lit shambles around us. As Kochno urged me to follow him, I noticed that he carried a sizeable brown paper bag. My curiosity mounting, I followed him, taking care not to stumble on the debris all over the ground.

It became obvious that Kochno had visited this place before – he knew exactly where he was headed. We reached the cavernous space under the foot of the bridge and there, in the dim glow of embers burning in some kind of metal container, I could discern three figures huddled for a bit of warmth. I stopped, unwilling to approach them, remembering the similar-looking people on the pavements of First and Second Avenue in New York, and the homeless asleep in the doorways of shabby shops. They frightened me. 'Come on, come on,' commanded Kochno sharply.

Not wanting to disappoint him, I braced myself and followed. As we reached the three men, one exclaimed, 'Hey, good to see you again!'

'I told you I'd come and bring our ballerina!' responded Kochno brightly, depositing his parcel on the ground. The man invited us to sit on some spare wooden crates, humorously apologising to me for the lack of better furniture. I was out of my depth and felt at a loss for words. Kochno muttered to me in Russian, 'Act natural, relax!'

I sat on the crate, said thank you, and nodded to the other two men, who displayed little interest in our appearance. But it all changed when Kochno pulled a bottle of whiskey and a pile of sandwiches out of his bag. Then their postures suddenly became animated and their hands, which were encrusted with dirt, stretched out to grab a sandwich. They did not speak to each other or to us, just grunted as their bloodshot eyes roved vaguely over Kochno and me.

Their hunched shoulders, clad in soiled, indescribable garments that stank of unwashed bodies, bore the weight of their misery, home-lessness and tragic fate. I sat there, torn between disgust, compassion, embarrassment and guilt. They drank from the bottle in turns. Kochno was totally at ease and joked with the first man as if they were old friends. That man did not fit in with the other two. I had a good look at him. He seemed very young, in spite of his worn-out clothes. He was not dirty, he conversed easily, and his aura did not project doom and gloom. 'What's your name?' I ventured.

'Jack. What's yours?' He was very talkative, wanted to know about our life in the theatre. He listened, fascinated.

'And you, Jack, tell us about you,' I said.

'Not much to tell . . . family? None . . . lost everything and every-one in the Wall Street crash. I was fourteen then . . . done jobs, got into trouble, short spell in jail . . . Now I'm looking for a job – anything will do. What I really want' (his face lit up with a smile) 'is to become a good painter, like the ones you have to paint your scenery!'

'I am sure you will, Jack,' said Kochno.

We went on talking. The other two men by now were crumpled on some sheets of cardboard, snoring away, mumbling, drooling, a stench of whiskey floating over their drunken slumber. For them there was no hope, poor devils.

Tired, feeling I had had enough, longing for my bed, I suggested to Kochno that perhaps we should go back to the hotel. Kochno gave me a mocking, sly look and pushed a rather dirty-looking piece of cardboard towards me, saying, 'I haven't finished talking to Jack, so curl up and have a snooze.' He was testing me, the devil!

Hiding my displeasure, I grabbed the proffered piece of cardboard and said nonchalantly, 'Okay.' Jack emitted stifled giggles as I turned my back on them. Reflecting on how lucky I was, I fell into a kind of slumber and the time passed. It was five-thirty a.m. when we returned to the hotel and a hot bath – bliss! An hour stretched in bed – bliss! And then it was time to go to class – bliss!

To Jerry's question as to where we had spent the night, I replied, 'We slept with the hobos under the bridge.'

'You're both mad,' he commented dryly.

Another expedition with Kochno was to a boxing match. I hated the brutality of it. Kochno enjoyed it. We argued! Then it was a wrestling match. What a hoot! Two over-muscled, overweight men sweating, making fierce faces, slamming each other onto the floor or tying each other in knots, emitting agonising shouts of pain or rage. They were simultaneously disgusting and funny! Brutal, but in a farcical way.

The only expeditions I really enjoyed were to the small vaudeville theatres and the little bar way downtown in New York, where aged vaudeville performers appeared, very late at night. There, a few down-and-out people, half-asleep over a glass of beer, waited to be cheered up by those old pros, to be taken back to the memories of their lost youth.

The small premises had a floor covered in sawdust, old stained wooden tables flanked by benches and bare of all ornament, pale green walls with damp patches and cracked, blistering, peeling paint. The few customers sat in a brooding silence. At the far end was a small stage, with curtains that had seen better days . . . somewhere . . . a long time ago, like the old pros behind them. And yet, the place was not depressing. The moment the curtains parted and the pianist struck the slightly off-tune piano, everyone sat up, faces smiling in anticipation of being cheered up by ribald songs, risqué jokes and tarnished dance sequences. It was fun, it was touching and their professionalism was admirable. I loved these artists and had great respect for them. But they, too, have disappeared and live only in my memory.

Kochno's last instruction in 'real life' ended in total disaster. It was the last night of our short stay in Seattle. Wonderful friends threw a supper party for us at their home. Our hostess was Russian, married to an American, a lovely jovial person. The supper of delicious Russian food was a treat. Afterwards, in the drawing room, someone started singing Russian gypsy songs. Everyone joined in.

Kochno was restless, in need of a drink. After a while, I saw him at the dining-room door, beckoning to me. 'Look what I've found!' he announced, pointing to a hardly touched bottle of whiskey. He gave me that mocking, sly look I knew so well. 'Let's have a competition – who can drink more, you or me?'

It was a foolish challenge, but I rose to the bait. 'Okay,' I said.

We sat at either end of the table. Kochno poured equal quantities into each glass and muttered, 'What a pity, no ice.' We clinked our glasses and proceeded to drink. Having never tasted whiskey before, I almost choked after the first sip. I found the taste foul and the smell reminded me of medicine, but too proud to back out of the deal, I forced myself to swallow with a smile. The level in the bottle dropped steadily, as did the level of my sobriety. After a while, even the taste became of no relevance. My head became very light and the room seemed to waltz around us. I got the giggles. Suddenly I noticed Kochno's torso getting shorter and shorter until he disappeared under the table. Then I felt two strong hands grabbing my shoulders and Lichine's voice from far away, saying, 'What the hell are you doing?! Tania, go and fetch Jerry.'

In happy oblivion, I felt myself propelled out of the house. As the fresh night air hit me, I muttered to whoever cared to listen that I was going to be sick, and so I was, right there on the flowerbed that adorned my hostess's lovely garden. I was vaguely aware of Lichine holding me by my waist, Jerry holding up my head by my hair, and Tania prancing around us exclaiming, 'Irischka! Ai-ai-yo-ai!'

Our host came to enquire what the commotion was about. I felt too numb to explain, but somehow got the strength to murmur that Kochno was under the table. Our host volunteered to take us back to the hotel in his car, and I vaguely remember Tania in the front seat on Lichine's lap, while I was squashed in the back between Jerry and Kochno, who was making strange noises.

When we arrived at the hotel, two bellboys apparently took charge of Kochno and delivered him to his room, while Lichine, Tania and Jerry took me to the Turkish baths on the top floor of the hotel, which were open twenty-four hours a day. The idea was to sober me up quickly by sweating out the whiskey. Stripped and wrapped only in towels, the boys installed themselves on deckchairs.

Tania took charge of me, making me do a full barre holding onto chairs. If I sagged, she would yell at me. The attendants seemed to enjoy the spectacle. I have never sweated so much in all my life! To finish, my three companions threw me into a cold pool, laughing their heads off at my lack of composure. I had only a couple of hours in bed before we had to catch our special train to the next town. My head was splitting and my hair hurt as I tried to comb it.

'Serves you right, you idiot,' said Jerry, lacking compassion.

Kochno did not turn up at the station, so Vova Grigoriev and the Colonel stayed behind to see what had happened to him. According to Vova, they found Kochno stark naked, asleep in his room. They tried to wake him, only to be told to go away. Colonel de Basil, who liked pranks, dipped pieces of blotting paper in the inkwell on the desk and decorated Kochno's penis with amazing designs. They then left Kochno to sleep it off.

The Colonel caught the train to catch us up at the next town, leaving Vova behind in charge of Kochno. When Kochno finally woke up and discovered his private parts so disrespectfully decorated, he became livid and demanded a ticket back to Paris, stubbornly refusing to return to the company. After several calls to Colonel de Basil, Vova was told to do what Kochno demanded. And so I lost my dear friend and instructor in life matters, never to work with him again. But our friendship continued by correspondence until his death. I never touched whiskey again, but in my old age I drink bourbon.

One other cocktail party that stands out in my memory as most unusual was hosted by Salvador Dalí and his wife, Gala. We were guests – and astounded, fascinated and amused onlookers. The Dalís were like no-one I had ever met. They forever surprised me – their eccentricity was unique, strange, poignant and disturbing. On this particular night it was highly amusing to observe the guests' reactions.

The cocktail party was held at the St Regis Hotel in New York. The large reception room was softly lit, except for a large table in the middle, with very bright lights on it. An amazing array of canapés covered the table, like multi-coloured rock plants in a garden. In the middle of the table was a bathtub, full of what looked like champagne, and in it, reclining gracefully, was a most beautiful naked young woman with green hair!

Gala stood near the door receiving guests. Dalí stood well to the side, solemnly greeting those who approached him, after they had unavoidably spotted the bathtub and its contents. Dalí observed his guests' reactions, himself remaining detached and non-committal. How I wished I could have read his thoughts!

Before our short return season at the Metropolitan Opera House, in some one-night-stand town, Massine left us, with no formal goodbyes, no speech from Colonel de Basil to thank him for all his magnificent work, no chance for us to express our great admiration and gratitude. No-one knew it was his last performance with us. By chance, several of us bumped into him in the street outside the stage door and, as we bade him goodnight, he said, 'I won't see you again. I'm off to New York. Goodbye!'

We were stunned! I embraced him and thanked him, wanting to cry at this sad exit from our lives of someone who deserved a loving send-off, in spite of his quarrels with Colonel de Basil. We owed Massine a great deal for his incalculable contribution to our company's success. As it turned out, Massine did come back for a short time, during our season in London. And then he left to start the new company, which enjoyed great success for several years.

After the New York return season, we sailed to Europe, taking a few days' rest on board ship, before proceeding to Florence, where we were due to open on 5 May 1937. My relationship with my parents was good once more. They attended the New York performances, came backstage and were friendly towards Jerry. Papa's work was going well.

He had obtained his driver's licence and bought a second-hand Ford car. I left for Europe with a light heart, liberated from worries about them.

After the one-night stands in American cities, it was such a pleasure to reach beautiful Florence – a feast for the eyes and nurture for the soul! Our great friends there were Henry and Esther Clifford, American Europeans who spent more time in Europe than in America. Their huge old house in Florence was truly magnificent, surrounded by gardens just as magnificent. They also had a great house in Switzerland above Vevey, with a stunning view over Lake Léman and the French Alps, and another in Philadelphia, where Henry was curator of paintings at the Philadelphia Museum. Highly knowledgeable about art, he was an obvious choice as new artistic director, and accepted with great delight. He loved our company and took particular interest in Lichine's development as a choreographer.

On our one free Sunday, several of us would gather around the Cliffords' pool. Surrounded by cypress trees, with Greek statues placed beautifully among them, one felt transported into a world of beauty and serenity. Tania, Lichine and I had fun in the pool, Lichine lifting us high above his head and throwing us into the water amid laughter, shrieks and encouragement from the onlookers.

Esther Clifford eyed us in silence, a whimsical, amused look on her face. I felt that she watched us as one watches a monkeys' tea party at the zoo! Esther was a very serious lady – an intellectual and very reserved – in total contrast to Henry, who was warm, outgoing and fun. At one point, Lichine climbed out of the pool and pretended to be a Greek god, dancing with great decorum, winding through the cypress trees. Thus Henry had an idea for the libretto of *Protée*, which Lichine choreographed. They set to work on it right away. It was to be a choreographic essay based on Greek classicism. Giorgio de Chirico was approached to design the scenery and costumes. Debussy's *Danse sacrée et danse profane* was chosen as the music.

As Lichine and Clifford were already working on *Francesca da Rimini*, which was scheduled to premiere at Covent Garden that summer, *Protée* was planned for the following 1938 season. Michel Fokine was to join our company in London and immediately start choreographing a new production of *Le Coq d'or*, with Tania as the Golden Cockerel, me as the Queen of Shemakhan, Marc Platoff miming King Dodon and Harcourt Algeranoff as the Astrologer.

Although Fokine had choreographed the opera–ballet version for Diaghilev's Paris Opera season in 1914, he later decided that he would prefer to choreograph the work as a full ballet. We had so much interesting work to look forward to! I welcomed the thrill of working with Fokine with all my heart, although it set the butterflies in my stomach afluttering.

WORKING WITH FOKINE

We arrived in London on a sunny spring day. Jerry informed me that we were going to share a flat with the Colonel and Olga Morosova, one of our dancers, by now officially living with the Colonel (they later married). I was surprised at this arrangement but on reflection decided that it would be rather fun sharing the flat with our eccentric, prank-loving, colourful director! I also liked Morosova – a friendly, giggly young woman – and it would be a nice change from the impersonal atmosphere of hotels.

Through a Russian friend, Jerry found a Russian housekeeper who was also willing to double as my dresser at the theatre. She was already on duty, waiting for us at the flat in Hay Hill, an uphill street of Berkeley Square lined on both sides by beautifully kept old houses. The flat occupied the entire second floor and had three large bedrooms, two bathrooms – one of which Morosova and I declared strictly ours – a large sitting room, a dining room and a spacious kitchen, all beautifully furnished, with everything provided. Not used to such luxury, I was thrilled to bits! Our Russian housekeeper was a happy surprise too.

'I am Fedosia,' she said, as we were introduced, eyeing Morosova and me with a broad smile. I found out later that time had stood still for her from the moment she left her village in Russia during the Revolution, following the family for whom she worked as a nanny into exile in England. At the time I met Fedosia, the children she looked after were grown up, the old people dead. Being of the 'old faith', she stuck with a church group and worked only for Russian families, as she had never learned to speak English properly. With her long skirts gathered at the waist, and her embroidered Russian-style blouses, her rotund body looked almost square. Her round rosy cheeks shone like ripe apples and her grey hair was pulled tightly into a bun on top of her head. She was an adorable vision!

It was immediately clear to me that she adored the Colonel and that he had a special rapport with her. The Colonel loved cooking, Fedosia was a great cook. When the two of them got together in the kitchen to cook lunch on occasional Sundays, it was a scream for all. The results were typical Russian dishes, enjoyed by many of our English friends, who flocked to our Russian flat, its hospitality and its laughter.

Not many people knew that endearing side of Colonel de Basil. Through sharing the flat, I got to know him as he fundamentally was. He was no saint in some business dealings, but he was a good soul, courageous and devoted to his company through thick and thin to the day he died.

That first evening at our new flat, we had a sample of Fedosia's cooking – *borscht*, *koulebaka* (a meat and rice pie) and *kissel* for dessert. Oh dear . . . my mouth waters as I write this. I love Russian food!

Fedosia would arrive at eight-thirty a.m. as we were all leaving for the theatre – Morosova and I for our class, the Colonel and Jerry for the office. By the afternoon she was installed in my dressing room and, under the kind supervision of Mme Larose, soon learned how to deal with my costumes, wash my tights, and clean and put lacquer in my toe shoes. I felt really spoilt. Fedosia did her job beautifully, but was shocked when she discovered what the ballet was about. In her 'old faith', performing was bad enough, but making up our faces and showing our legs was scandalous! She expressed her views loudly, imploring me to quit my occupation, as it came from the devil!

Every time she saw Tania's father, who lived in London, often came to her dressing room and was also of the 'old faith', Fedosia would grumble, 'Shame on him, not stopping his daughter from doing the devil's work!' As the season progressed I had a feeling, judging by the expression on her face as she watched from the wings, that Fedosia secretly enjoyed what she saw. The devil was not mentioned any more – dear Fedosia succumbed to corruption!

Fedosia also disapproved of me not eating before the performance. She could not understand that I could not dance on a full stomach. On one occasion, ten minutes before curtain she plonked two hard-boiled eggs on my dressing table, went out the door and locked it, loudly ordering me to eat them if I wanted her to unlock the door. I had no choice. Trapped, I ate them, but I was really cross with her. After a long talk, I finally made her promise never to pull that stunt again.

In time, we became devoted to each other. When I was sad or worried, she would gather me to her ample bosom and murmur, 'Noo-noo, detka' (There, there, little one) and I felt better. My dear Fedosia – a blessed memory.

Although we had met Michel Fokine before, on his very occasional short visits to oversee and clean up his ballets, this was the first time he would be with our company permanently and choreograph totally new works on us. We were going to become the original cast of Fokine's new ballets, just as Tamara Karsavina and Vaslav Nijinsky had been for his famous ballets first produced by Diaghilev's company.

Fokine arrived in London one spring morning in 1937, ready for our first rehearsal. We were all a bit nervous. Owing to the size of the Le Coq d'or production, rehearsals were held at the Chenies Street Drill Hall not too far from Covent Garden. At ten-thirty a.m. exactly, Fokine and his wife, Vera, accompanied by the Colonel and Papa Grigoriev, walked in. We all stood up and welcomed the Fokines with thunderous applause. Fokine acknowledged us with a smile and a wave, saying, 'Good morning. I look forward to working with you all.'

Several of us approached them to greet them personally. Fokine was calm and reserved, his wife pleasantly remote. In time, we discovered that Fokine could show quite a temper if displeased and did not tolerate excuses or lack of attention to his choreography. He was only fifty-seven at the time, but to those of us still under twenty he seemed of quite venerable age. Ah, cruel youth!

Unlike Massine, he never changed into working clothes. Minus his jacket and tie, his belt slightly below his middle-aged tummy, his feet clad in heavy-looking, round-nosed, old-fashioned shoes, he was surprisingly light and agile in his movements. When he was pleased, his steel-rimmed spectacles would slide halfway down his nose and the tip of his tongue would appear between his teeth, his face expressing approval. When he was displeased, his irritation and impatience were evident. We could see that in his younger days he must have been a very handsome man. What never faded or changed was his strong, electric personality.

Mme Fokine was ever present, ever by his side, ever dressed as for a royal garden party. In her large picture hats, black hair slicked over her temples, heavy make-up, fur cape, diamond earrings, diamond brooch and diamond rings, she was serene, with a slight, enigmatic smile. She sat by Fokine's chair like a benevolent, good-natured Buddha.

Fokine's way of working was very different from Massine's. Fokine brought no books of diagrams, no notes. Both obviously knew exactly what they wanted, having worked it out before the start of the rehearsals, but Massine worked out details on his dancers, trying the movements this way and that. Fokine had every movement, every detail worked out in advance and showed the dancers his new work as if it were already complete – which it was in his head. Having chosen the dancers he wanted for each role – he knew their personality and technical capacity – his choreography brought out the best in them.

It was fascinating to watch Fokine in rehearsal. The way he moved indicated the essence and character of each role or of the ensemble. He metamorphosed so totally from one character to another that one forgot his middle-aged figure, his clumsy boots, his specs sliding down his nose. He became the oriental Queen, with exquisite fluid movements of the arms, then the Cockerel or King Dodon, funny and clumsy in his movements. It was so clear what we had to represent. Learning the movements and the technical side made our work infinitely interesting, satisfying and, for me, thrilling. I was amazed how quickly and painlessly *Le Coq d'or* was choreographed.

Meanwhile, Lichine rehearsed *Francesca da Rimini* on the stage of the Opera House. The premiere was to be on 15 July 1937, ahead of the premiere of *Le Coq d'or* on 23 September. The ballet was subsidised by Miss Parish, Tchernicheva's ardent admirer. Lichine and Clifford had to take poetic licence and turn a blind eye to the fact that Tchernicheva was at that time forty-seven, although still svelte and beautiful. But as it turned out, there could not have been a better choice. Mme Tchernicheva brought to the role a dramatic power of no equal. She was superb, and Lichine's choreography was greatly inspired by her dramatic talent.

The day before the premiere someone overheard Jerry saying that Francesca looked old enough to be Paolo's (Francesca's lover's) mother. It was immediately reported to Tchernicheva, who came to my dressing room fuming. 'Tell your husband to stop his vicious tongue undermining me!'

I tried my best to calm her. I, too, was angry at Jerry's tactlessness and rudeness, so inappropriate for his position in the company. When I tackled him about it, he laughed, saying it was just a funny joke. On that point we did not agree, and I often found his jokes tactless and not at all funny.

Madame had one great superstition. She detested the colour purple. To her, it meant bad luck. For the premiere of *Francesca da Rimini*, Jerry sent Tchernicheva a bouquet of flowers as a peace-offering, but forgot to ask the florist not to tie it with purple ribbon. As fate would have it, the bouquet had a resplendent purple bow! After the last curtain, the masses of flowers Madame received were brought from the stage to her dressing room, where she discovered the offending bow on the bouquet and read who it was from.

Through the open door of her dressing room, where crowds of people were congratulating her, she saw Jerry coming down the corridor. She grabbed the bouquet, pushed her way through all her admirers and threw the bouquet, smacking it hard on Jerry's face. *Good show!* I thought to myself, as I watched this dramatic, regal gesture. My relationship with

Mme Tchernicheva never changed. We were as close as ever and she continued to advise me and I to consult her and share my thoughts with her. But she never spoke to Jerry again unless it was unavoidable, and then only in icy tones.

Francesca da Rimini was a huge success and the critics raved about Tchernicheva's portrayal of Francesca. For Lichine it was a red-letter day. He was recognised by all critics as a young choreographer with a great future.

Now everyone concentrated on *Le Coq d'or*. We started to rehearse on stage, dashing to Mme Karinska for costume fittings. They promised to be sumptuous, with that unique Karinska touch. In spare moments I read and reread Pushkin's poem 'Le Coq d'or' – his rich imagination, colourful descriptions, wit and fairy tale magic, helped and inspired me as I worked on my role. I had been raised on Pushkin's poems, he was my hero, so to portray this Queen of his imagination was a thrill and a joy. In those days I was fulfilled by my work, my success, and the joy of performing. I just brushed aside any marital conflicts.

I wrote many letters to my parents and received many from them. They had settled well in Sea Cliff and Papa's work was going well. At least on that score I had no worries. Our season was also going beautifully. The weather that summer was all sunshine and the men from the market kept throwing oranges through my dressing-room window. The fast-approaching premiere of *Le Coq d'or* sent my adrenaline soaring! It felt great to be alive and working so intensely with Fokine.

Among our audience there was great expectation too. It was quite an occasion, a brand-new work by the legendary Fokine. All the tickets for the gala premiere and the subsequent performances were sold well in advance. At Reynolds House, Mme Karinska's seamstresses were in a frenzy, working late on embroidery and appliqués. Karinska, always so smart, would emerge from our fittings rather dishevelled, her hair – always otherwise immaculate – in disarray, her blouse poking out of her skirt, scissors hanging from her waist.

Dear Mme Karinska, a genius and artist in costume-making. The only snag was, since she was the ultimate perfectionist, sometimes the costumes were delivered late and there would be frantic rushing between her place and the theatre on the day of a premiere. The ballet had a prologue, epilogue and three changes of scenes, with 150 costumes designed by Natalia Goncharova, each one of them a work of art. Some of the designs she based on her originals for the 1914 production; the others had to be adapted for Fokine's new choreography, which was technically more demanding. The designs for the scenery were sumptuous. King Dodon's scenes were all colour and bright lights, while the interior of the Queen's tent had a lush Eastern look, lit in blue–green, subdued light.

The first time the Queen was seen on stage, she was standing still in the middle of the tent, with a richly embroidered cape over her costume. Attendants approached to remove the cape, then I began my variation as the lights gradually got brighter. Unfortunately, Fokine's choreography is often distorted and this scene wrongly staged when his ballets are revived by people who never worked with him and never saw the original work.

Fokine's granddaughter, Isabelle Fokine, a dancer herself, has inherited a treasure – Fokine's notes, letters and other papers, as well as films of some of his ballets. She tries hard to preserve her grandfather's work. With this unique information in her possession, she is the one to turn to, but the nuances, the details, the 'something' that cannot be notated, will be lost forever when the last few of us survivors who worked with Fokine disappear through the pearly gates. The 'soul' of the works for which we were the original interpreters will then be scattered with our ashes.

We have always been eager to coach and pass on to the younger generation what the choreographer wanted from us, but only two artistic directors have ever invited me to work with their dancers. These were Ben Stevenson of the Houston Ballet and Maina Gielgud of the Australian Ballet. They understood and cared; no-one else seemed to.

On the day of the premiere, we had the final dress rehearsal in the morning. But we still had no costumes! Frantic calls to Karinska, and her promises that the costumes would be delivered by late afternoon, did little to assuage our uneasiness about having no chance to get used to our costumes. Usually there are always small adjustments to make so that one feels entirely comfortable in one's movements. I was back in my dressing room by four o'clock, hoping to be able to put the costume on and check that all was in order. Two hours later, still no costumes! I started my make-up and tried not to add to the butterflies in my stomach as the clock ticked closer and closer to Grisha's voice calling, 'Fifteen minutes, please.'

By seven o'clock, still no costumes. I went backstage to warm up and found Colonel de Basil, Papa Grigoriev, Bruce Ottley and Uncle Freddie in an agitated conference. Jerry, who had dashed over to Karinska's place to see for himself what was happening, telephoned to say that the costumes would be ready to be transported to the theatre in half an hour. As it was already so late, Captain Ottley remarked that Karinska would never find enough taxis to transport all the costumes to the theatre. It was an emergency, but in the captain's capable hands, with the assistance of an influential friend, the solution was found. At eight-thirty p.m. sharp, the curtain went up on the first ballet in the program, *Swan Lake* with Danilova. No sign of the costumes for the next ballet.

Clad in our headgear, ballet tights and toe shoes, Tania and I sat together in my dressing room on pins and needles, our nerves at breaking point. Suddenly, we heard the wailing sound of ambulances approaching and stopping just under the window of our dressing rooms. *God, what now?* We dashed to the window, and an extraordinary sight greeted our eyes – the doors of the two ambulances swang open and Mme Karinska and her seamstresses piled out onto the footpath in great agitation, as our wardrobe personnel ran towards them!

There was pandemonium as the costumes were handed out of the ambulances and on the double through the stage door. An announcement was made to the audience to the effect that intermission would be longer. The audience did not mind; the news had already spread that the costumes had been delivered by ambulance. It added to the excitement of the evening, and the Crush Bar did good business. The intermission lasted fifty minutes!

Finally, clad in our costumes, pinned in by Karinska's trembling hands where hooks were still missing, we were ready and on stage. Fokine, calm and smiling, wished us luck. Overture, curtain up, on the darkened stage the Astrologer dances the short prologue, then to tumultuous applause the curtains part to reveal Goncharova's magnificent bright scenery. Oh, what a great moment, one's first appearance – nerves instantly gone, you plunge into your role, the music singing inside you. You belong to that make-believe world where the real world has no place.

We could sense that the ballet had a big impact on the audience. The occasional muted reactions – a laugh, a sigh, a bravo – were so satisfying for us to hear. As the curtain came down and the last note from the orchestra melted into the air, the audience exploded into thunderous applause, a standing ovation and shouts of bravo. There was curtain call after curtain call, as the audience shouted Fokine's name. We brought Fokine on stage and the audience went wild. We, too, lined up behind Fokine, applauding him with heartfelt enthusiasm. Finally and reluctantly, the audience let us go, but we had to remain on stage, line up and await the arrival of our guests from the royal box, who wanted to congratulate the company in person.

Colonel de Basil, Baron d'Erlanger and Captain Ottley escorted the royals onto the stage, and Fokine went forward to welcome them. Although some of us had socialised with the Duke and Duchess of York, now that they had become King George VI and Queen Elizabeth, protocol demanded that we be formally introduced to them all over again.

Of course, we knew nothing about protocol or that one was not to speak to them unless they addressed you first. As Fokine introduced the leading dancers to the Queen, the Colonel followed with the King. Baron d'Erlanger escorted ex-King Alfonso XIII of Spain, Captain Ottley escorted King Carol II of Romania. We curtsied, shook hands and thanked them for their compliments. The Kings were rather stiff, the Queen her charming, lovely self.

Her Majesty moved on to Tania, who was standing next to me, and who, as she rose from her deep curtsy, vigorously shook Her Majesty's hand, saying loudly with a broad, happy smile, 'Hello, Queen!'

This highly un-British way of addressing the sovereign drew every-one's attention. After a split second of stunned astonishment, an amused smile lit up the Queen's face. Everyone relaxed and had the grace to allow a flicker of a smile to cross their faces. Tania was totally oblivious to the sensation she had created. Oh, how we laughed and teased her!

The presence of ex-King Alfonso sent Mme Tchernicheva into a flutter! She lined up with us, looking resplendent in her beautiful evening gown. She had confided in me the story of her brief liaison with the King, so I watched from the corner of my eye, making sure not to miss the moment when, after so many years, they would come face to face again. As the King approached her, Baron d'Erlanger did not have to introduce her, as the King spoke first, 'Ah, Mme Tchernicheva, *aussi belle que jadis!*' (as beautiful as ever). She sank into a deep curtsy, and he took her hand and kissed it tenderly. Happy memories were in the look they exchanged. And then, with a wave, the royals were gone.

Fokine thanked us all and briefly praised our individual perform-ances, but he was not prone to praise, so any praise from him was worth a ton of gold. Happy, exhausted, scratched by Karinska's pins, we dispersed to our dressing rooms to find crowds of people waiting to congratulate us, and crowds at the stage door applauding each of us as we came out. I must admit, it is a great feeling to be a success. But a lot of hard work has to be done to earn, achieve and sustain it. The process of working on a role was the fascinating part for me, the part I loved. If it resulted in success, it was a moral satisfaction, a pat on the back, an acknowledgement that the work I loved doing was done well.

ANTICS AT THE OPERA HOUSE

The end of our 1937 season at Covent Garden was rapidly approach-ing and, as usual, I felt sad to leave London and all our wonderful, dear friends. We sailed from Southampton to New York, where we were due to open at the Metropolitan Opera House on 21 October 1937. It was good to relax. Too exhausted to make whoopee after dinner, I went straight to bed and read a book. It was important to me to be fit and rested for New York. Was I becoming more responsible and reasonable? Or growing old? I was approaching my nineteenth birthday!

I was looking forward to seeing my parents. I missed them, especially my papa, and could hardly wait to spot his dear face, to hug him and to feel that special bond between us, a bond of unconditional love and belonging. As usual I was on deck watching our approach to land, impressed as ever by the sight of New York rising slowly in the mist of early morning.

We came down the gangway and I was relieved to see my mother greet Jerry cordially. It made me hopeful that our stay in New York would be free of bad vibes. Publicity photos over, we were free to catch our breath, settle in at our hotel, have dinner at the Russian Tea Room (naturally), hear all the news and gossip, and be ready next morning for class, rehearsals and preparations for opening night. My parents came to most performances and, at Mr Hurok's insistence, they always sat in his box.

Papa was happy with his work, feeling better and quite at home in Sea Cliff. Obviously my performances and the huge success I had in *Le Coq d'or* contributed to my parents' peace of mind regarding my career. My relationship with my mother improved greatly, except on one occasion, when I recited a rather naughty take-off on the opera *Sadko* that contained some four-letter words and which I thought was really 'cool'. Mother looked shocked and disgusted and, with deep sadness in her voice, said, 'How coarse and vulgar you've become! No doubt it's Jerry's bad influence. I command you never to use such language again.'

I felt deeply embarrassed and, to this day, I am incapable of uttering four-letter words in Russian – but in English, French and Spanish I am fluent in them! They are just sounds to me – meaningless expressions universally used. But said in Russian, these words have retained their true meaning for me, and I agree with my mother that it is the height of vulgarity to use them.

While we were in New York, a strange character, Richard Davis, was a permanent fixture in Sol Hurok's entourage. He knew everyone and had a finger in all sorts of pies. An addicted gambler at casinos and private poker games, one day he was rich and extravagant, with presents for everyone, the next day broke and hysterical. He had a diagonal scar from a car accident that ran from the middle of his balding head to under his chin.

He constantly fell in love with girls young enough to be his daughters and was always in search of his 'Cinderella'. Poor man, his scar was not an asset. He began to cling to Jerry, who liked Richard and was amused by his eccentric ways. The two of them developed a system for finding a 'Cinderella'. The fact that Richard was married to an attractive Russian refugee actress was not an obstacle, and she, also a fanatical gambler, was too busy playing cards to notice or care. His plan was to divorce her and marry his 'Cinderella'.

The system was that when Richard fell in love, he would introduce the subject of his adoration to Jerry and ask him to charm the young woman (no problem) into accepting a supper invitation with both of them at the Russian Casino, which was at the back of the Russian Tea Room, with a shared kitchen between them. A gypsy band provided entertainment and dance music for the patrons. Happily installed for supper, Jerry would ask the particular young woman to take the floor.

While dancing, he would tell the girl that Richard was madly in love with her and to please be gentle and not break his heart. Sometimes it worked, sometimes not. On one occasion, the young woman firmly declared, 'But I'm not in love with Richard. I'm in love with you!'

Obviously, on that occasion Jerry had used an overdose of his charm. He abandoned Richard to sort out his own love life, dashed through the kitchen into the Tea Room and joined the rest of us at supper. There he recounted, with much laughter, the failure of his mission to help Richard. But he wore the air of a flattered ego – although I laughed with the others, deep inside I felt irritated and disgusted.

When the 'system' worked, Richard would eventually take the young woman to Paris, shower her with clothes from Chanel, stay at the George V Hotel and bask in bliss, genuinely in love. The girl, according to Richard, would kiss his hands and pledge her undying love for him.

Richard would plan the marriage and then the girl would disappear, luggage and all, leaving a note of thanks and begging his forgiveness for falling in love with someone else. Richard would return to New York heartbroken but no wiser, and the search for a 'Cinderella' would start all over again.

When Richard started to appear in different towns on our tour and stick to Jerry like a Siamese twin, I could no longer keep silent. I told Jerry I found their charade distasteful and sick, and that allowing himself to be used as bait on Richard's fishing rod was undignified. Jerry, in turn, accused me of needing a sense of humour. I was glad when I heard that Richard was broke, having lost a fortune at roulette, and had to stay put in New York to find a way to remake his fortune.

I was still finding it difficult to adjust to married life with Jerry. We did not see eye to eye on many things and argued frequently, irritated by each other. Sulking silence would then set in. Boring! But it was never boring in my world inside the stage door. Jerry was almost never backstage, so I rarely saw him when we were at work. Backstage everything was vibrant, interesting, exciting. Even the one-night stands on tour were full of laughter and camaraderie. No sulks! Heaven!

Christmas and New Year found us, as usual, in Chicago, where we had a fun party after the performance to see in the New Year. *What will 1938 bring me?* I wondered. I had so much to be grateful for in the year just left behind. The tour over, we returned briefly to New York before sailing back to Europe and our season in Berlin from 28 March to the end of April. I had three free days before sailing, which I spent at my parents' house. Mother made my room look so pretty! We had such a lovely time in those few days together that I felt a deep pang of sadness at leaving them again and being far away from Papa. When I left, Mother cried buckets and remained in bed. Papa saw me to the station, cheerfully wishing me bon voyage, but I knew that he was as sad as I was at parting again.

Lichine was nervous about going to Berlin. He was half-Jewish, so the ever-more-frequent reports of the persecution of Jewish people by the Germans made him uneasy. Telegrams were exchanged with Mr Duisberg, director of the Scala Theatre, who managed to obtain a letter signed by Goebbels stating that 'all members of the company are pure Aryans'. This incident finally made me think about and take an interest in what was happening in Europe. Slowly I started to realise, with a sinking feeling, that all was not well, not well at all, outside my stage door.

When we arrived in Berlin, we could not help feeling and noticing a new kind of atmosphere. There were great numbers of uniformed men and Blackshirts everywhere. Flags with swastikas were flying. Jewish shops were recognisable by the wooden planks nailed across their windows and doors. Some people in the street looked preoccupied, others were in animated discussion, gesticulating with satisfied smiles. And meanwhile the cafés in the Kurfürstendamm were moving their tables outside – spring was in the air.

Mme Begas, a sculptor friend, asked me after the opening night if I would pose for her – she wanted to make a statuette of me in *Swan Lake*. As our season was a month long, I complied with her request with pleasure. I admired her work immensely and liked her as a person. Several casts were made of the statuette, some in bronze, others in china. Now, seventy-odd years later, I still have my statuette in white china. Amazingly, it survived all my years of travels without chips or cracks, wrapped up in my old tights and a nightshirt in my suitcase. All these years later, my statuette and I have reached our final destination – Australia! Unpacked and washed, she stands on a high shelf in my office, out of harm's way, where clumsy hands can't reach her. I am looking at her now, as I write these lines, and wonder . . . Was it really me?

Halfway through our Berlin season, two Blackshirts appeared in my dressing room after the evening performance. Clicking their heels, they congratulated me on my performance and the company's success, requesting, in adequate English, the pleasure of my company for a glass of beer and perhaps some supper at a nearby restaurant. I politely refused, telling them I had a matinee the next day and must go to bed. At that moment, Jerry came in. The introductions over, they repeated their request, this time including Jerry. I declined again, with Jerry's support. One of the men shook his head and said with a smile, 'Sorry, but we must insist – and please bring your passports.'

It was clear we had to obey their 'request'. The men, polite as ever, drove us to our hotel so that Jerry could get our papers. At the restaurant we declined supper. As we sipped our beer, the men flicked without much interest through Jerry's passport and my Nansen papers and, after half an hour of inconsequential small talk, we bade them goodnight and walked back to the hotel. What was it all about? It remained a mystery. When we told Herr Duisberg about this unwelcome outing, he was as mystified as we were. Perhaps those Blackshirts were just having fun – young men pulling rank.

I began counting the days to the end of our season, in spite of our great success and our usual enthusiastic audiences. One morning when we arrived for class, we found both sides of the street jammed with people and the police waving away all traffic. The stage doorkeeper told us that Hitler would be driving through later that morning.

After our class, we rehearsed with Fokine in the large studio on the top floor of the theatre, which was flanked by a balcony overlooking the main street. On Fokine's request, the door onto the balcony was closed, as the crowd was so noisy. He showed mounting irritation.

The noise from the street suddenly changed from a distant roar to an approaching louder and louder one. Some of our dancers who were not at that moment engaged in the rehearsal, dashed onto the balcony to see Hitler pass by. Through the open doors the noise from below was deafening. The pianist stopped playing. It seemed as if all hell had broken loose. Fokine, livid with rage, shouted to Papa Grigoriev to order everyone off the balcony and to shut the door. Stunned by Fokine's rage, the dancers looked sheepish and embarrassed. Fokine, his anger exploding, shouted, 'How dare you walk out on Fokine's rehearsal!'

A little voice timidly ventured, as she burst into tears, 'We only wanted to see Hitler pass by.'

To which Fokine barked, 'Fokine is more important than Hitler!' Then, turning to his very tight-lipped wife, 'Verasha, let's go!'

The rehearsal was over, cancelled. It was the only time I saw Fokine in such a rage. Usually his discontent produced stinging remarks in quiet tones, followed by prolonged displays of disapproval.

Our Berlin season over, my only regret was having to say goodbye to Dr Krause, my true friend, who unfortunately I never saw again. From Berlin we flew to Copenhagen; I was glued to the window, fascinated by the landscape below us. I looked forward to discovering Copenhagen, where we were to have a short season before returning to London. All the same, I have no special memories of the Danish capital. In the week we spent there, we were busy rehearsing for London every day. My impression was of a beautiful northern city – calm, clean and orderly. The theatre was beautiful, in the grand manner, the audiences appreciative. No-one ventured to our dressing rooms, except to Paul Petroff's. He was a Dane, so his dressing room was full of his friends. Coming to his own country as one of the leading dancers meant a great deal to him, and the reception he met with from the audiences was heart-warming. I must admit, I felt envious. Paul had his country, his home. I had no country, no roots, no place to call 'home'. But I did not dwell on it and decided that I was lucky – the whole world was my home (although some immigration authorities would no doubt disagree with me!).

We were met in London by a very agitated Vova Grigoriev. Apparently, Sir Thomas Beecham, who was by then director of the Royal Opera House, was trying to prevent our season from happening by replacing us with Massine's newly formed company. Massine, who was Sir Thomas's great friend, counted on it. As we took it for granted that the Opera House was ours each summer, no-one had bothered or even remembered that Sir Thomas had still to sign the official agreement. Colonel de Basil was furious. Assembling us all on the platform, he issued his orders for a *Blitzkrieg* on the Opera House.

We were to go to the theatre immediately and install ourselves in our dressing rooms, remaining there until he, personally, gave us the green light to go to our lodgings. As we dispersed to grab taxis, the Colonel promised double pay to the truck-drivers, who were loading our scenery and baskets on their trucks, if they would deliver them to the theatre and unload them within two hours. The drivers were delighted to oblige.

We stormed the stage door, but our dear Mr Jackson received us with open arms, unsuspecting of the drama that had caused our arrival en masse and only a little astonished at our unusual appearance.

'Yes, yes, Sir Thomas is in his office,' he replied to the Colonel's anxious enquiry.

Antal Dorati, Vova, Jerry and the Colonel disappeared to ambush Sir Thomas. The rest of us retired to our dressing rooms to wait, worried about the outcome of this unnerving situation and hating Sir Thomas for his treachery.

The trucks arrived promptly. Tania and I were hanging out our windows to watch the stagehands carry the scenery backstage, when we heard a window above us being roughly flung open and Sir Thomas's hysterical voice yelling, 'Police! Police! Russian gangsters!'

Abruptly the yelling stopped, the window banged shut and there was silence! 'Oh my God, they're strangling him!' wailed Tania.

Finally Vova's voice echoed through the corridors, calling us all onto the stage, where the Colonel triumphantly announced that the agreement was signed and we could go to our lodgings in peace. With great relief, we cried, 'Hurrah!' and heartily applauded our Colonel.

'But where were Uncle Freddie and Captain Ottley? Why didn't they deal with Sir Thomas?' I asked Jerry later.

'They're cross with Colonel de Basil at the moment,' Jerry informed me. Then he told me that while in New York the Colonel had been conducting talks, behind everyone's backs, with Massine's financial backers about a possible merger, and about giving away to Massine some of the ballets from our repertoire. The Baron was furious. As he was subsidising our forthcoming trip to Australia, he refused to have anything to do with the Colonel and stipulated that if the trip were to take place, the Colonel must resign his position as director for the duration of the tour and remain in Europe. He would be replaced by Victor Dandré (Anna Pavlova's de facto husband) and Jerry as joint directors of the company.

It was an ultimatum. The Colonel had to bow to these demands and, midway through our London season, went off to the South of France, where he installed himself in a small semi-derelict house in Sospel near the Italian border, with the pockmarked Wassiliev, and Wassiliev's wife, Marguerite.

All these events made quite a stir in the company and produced much food for gossip. I personally did not look forward to the presence of Victor Dandré among us. I did not like him – I felt he was a patronising snob – although other members of the company thought he was nice and supportive. Perhaps my chemistry clashed with his. It happens. I felt I would miss the Colonel in our long months away in the unknown, mysterious, faraway land of Oz!

On 5 July 1938 the premiere of Lichine's *Protée* took place with great success. The critics praised this delicate miniature work and remarked on Lichine's great strides forward as a choreographer. They singled out Sono Osato among the five maidens. Her grace, precision and presence were indeed beautiful to watch. The premiere on 19 July of Fokine's new ballet, *Cinderella*, with a score by Baron d'Erlanger, was now rapidly approaching. Goncharova's scenery and costumes looked beautiful.

Cinderella, like *Le Coq d'or*, was a big spectacle. Watching the dress rehearsals from the auditorium, I was again amazed by Fokine's inventiveness and sensitivity. Tania as Cinderella was infinitely touching, her inborn charm irresistible. The two Ugly Sisters, portrayed by Marian Ladre and Harcourt Algeranoff, were perfect caricatures of human nature and, in Fokine's hands, hilariously funny without falling into slapstick.

The premiere was a resounding success for all concerned. There were endless curtain calls, and Fokine was greeted by an ovation. Tania almost disappeared under the mountain of flowers, and there were happy faces on both sides of the great curtain. I felt happy too, and proud. Proud to belong to this great company, to share the stage with my outstanding colleagues, and to have the ultimate luck of working with Fokine. A merry, happy company assembled at Boulestin for the supper party thrown by Uncle Freddie, and the latest success was celebrated late into the night.

The pressure of intense rehearsals lifted, Fokine now concentrated on revising his many ballets in our repertoire and taking time off to work on his new ballet, *Paganini*, scheduled to premiere in London in 1939. Lichine was also concentrating on his next work, *The Prodigal Son*, which was to premiere in Australia. I welcomed some free afternoons and spent them at matinee performances of plays. I was fascinated by the actors and thought, in my ignorance, how easy their life was. *Once the play opens they are free all day, no more rehearsals, just turn up for the perform- ances.* How wrong I was, I discovered years later when I found myself in close contact with some of the greats of the acting profession!

That summer, our friends the Diamantidis found us a small flat in Shepherd Market, Mayfair, across the alley from their *pied à terre*. With Curzon Street at one end and Piccadilly at the other, it was surrounded by a few very narrow alleys flanked by small old rickety houses and by a pub, which I was told was quite famous.

We had a bit of shopping to do. In those days it took five weeks to cross from England to Australia. On board ship, one wore evening clothes for dinner. With our limited funds, we girls had to be ingenious to create diversity in our outfits. I found clothes I considered practi- cal and economical at Selfridges – three long skirts in different basic colours, six interchangeable tops, one khaki divided skirt and matching shirt for going ashore at our ports of call, and two bathing suits.

As Jerry was in charge of our combined salaries, mine being more than double his, I had discovered, I never had more than a few pounds or dollars in my handbag, just in case. If I needed to buy something my 'just in case' money would not cover, I had to ask him for it. The day I set off for my shopping, Jerry gave me the amount of money he considered adequate for my needs, plus extra to get him a pair of white trousers. When I got back to the flat with all my purchases, I had to tell him that I had spent all the money on myself and needed more money to purchase his trousers. Jerry exploded. 'What do you think? That money goes on trees?'

'No it does not!' I shouted back. 'It grows out of my sweaty, bleed- ing toes, and I'm entitled to a bit of it!'

I saw, with satisfaction, that I had hit a sore spot, his pride. When we calmed down, I asked him to give me the money for his trousers, promising to purchase them the next day. We fell into an unpleasant silence. Next morning he handed me the money for the trousers and asked if I needed more for myself. I could not resist another dig. 'No, thank you. Money doesn't grow on trees!'

I was free after class and went to Bond Street, to the shop Jerry had recommended. Just short of reaching it I stopped, riveted, at the window of a pet shop. There, in the window, a grey Angora kitten was gambolling about. I could not take my eyes off this beautiful, adorable little ball of grey fur with the most gorgeous green eyes! I love animals and missed having one. This little kitten swelled my heart with longing. I went into the shop, played with the kitten, could not part with him and bought him! Once again, no money left for the trousers. Oh dear! I could hear my buddy Tassia saying to me, 'You're too impulsive, you never think before you act!'

By the time I got myself and the kitten to the flat, I started to realise what a mistake I had made. I could not take the kitten to the theatre, let alone to Australia. I was hardly ever home and could not offer what the little animal needed and deserved. By the time Jerry turned up, I had decided that I must find, quickly, a nice home for this little bundle of joy. When Jerry saw the kitten he could not believe his eyes. 'What have you done now?' he moaned.

Embarrassed, apologetic, I tried to explain. It did not go down very well. He paid no attention to the kitten, apart from throwing it resentful glances. The phone rang. It was Vera Newman. She wanted to know if we could have supper with them after the performance. Yes, we could. Then, clutching at straws, I told her about the kitten and how desperate I was to find him a home. Vera's excited voice was an answer to my prayer. 'Oh, darling, Ernest adores cats, so do I. We can collect your kitten tonight after supper. Ernest will be thrilled!'

Jerry, greatly relieved, turned my shopping expeditions into a joke, and I was mercilessly teased at supper. When I saw Ernest Newman, the severe, outspoken music critic, cradling my kitten in his arms, scratching his tummy and cooing, I knew the kitten had found a happy home. 'What shall we call him?' asked Ernest.

'Bouboule, of course!' declared Vera. 'It's the company's nickname for Irina.' And so Bouboule lived to a ripe old age with the Newmans, happy and loved. Specific shopping was obviously not my forte – I was never asked to do it again!

Towards the end of our season, Sir Thomas Beecham conducted a couple of ballets as a special guest. These occasions were very popular with our audiences. As usual, Sir Thomas tried to impose his own tempos. On the day of that evening's performance of *Prince Igor*, Fokine, who lacked Massine's restraint and diplomacy, entered into an over-heated argument with Sir Thomas over the tempos. Of course, Fokine was right to demand the tempos to which he had choreographed his work. Sir Thomas tended to ignore the fact that there were dancers to consider, and pretended that he was conducting a concert of which he was the star and interpreter.

That night was a night to remember. *Prince Igor* was the closing ballet on the program. Fokine and his wife were seated in their usual box, third from the stage on the left. The lights went down and Sir Thomas strode into the orchestra pit. Mounting the rostrum, he faced the audience, who burst into prolonged applause, greeting their great much-loved British conductor. Curtain up.

As the Polovtsian camp awoke, musically all was well. But as the action gathered momentum, all hell broke loose! The music gathered speed, faster and faster and faster – the dancers simply could not keep up with it. Suddenly, a very loud tapping rose above the orchestra. Fokine, on the edge of his box, was furiously tapping the right tempo. Sir Thomas stopped the orchestra. Everyone froze in stunned silence – you could have heard a pin drop. Sir Thomas briskly turned to Fokine's box and, with a great theatrical gesture, invited him into the orchestra pit. He then deposited his baton on the rostrum and marched out.

Fokine took up the challenge. It did not take him long to reach the orchestra pit, mount the rostrum, indicate swiftly to the orchestra from where to start and, making a sign to the dancers, take over where Sir Thomas had left off. Fokine's conducting was impeccable and inspiring. The dancers gave all they had, the audience was electrified. Final chord spent, final pose struck, the curtain came down slowly and the audience went mad! They shouted Fokine's name, stamped their feet, applauded and demanded that he come on stage. Fokine appeared in the wings and was brought on stage by the dancers to tumultuous applause.

In the opposite wing, Sir Thomas was pacing back and forth furiously, waiting to have it out with Fokine. Catching sight of Sir Thomas, Fokine dived over, grabbed the surprised conductor under the arm and propelled him onto the stage. A hush fell over the audience. Fokine stretched out his hand to Sir Thomas in a 'let's make peace' gesture. Taken aback, after a moment of hesitation, Sir Thomas shook his head and accepted the peace-offering with a wry smile. The two great men shook hands vigorously. What a performance! It took some time for the audience to calm down and finally disappear. What an exciting way to end our London season!

8

SAILING TO AUSTRALIA

The legal confrontations between our company and Massine's intensified, and our future tour of the United States hung in the balance because of Hurok's interest in Massine's company. But in my naïve little dream world I was not in the least interested in the intrigues and messy dealings. Jerry did not tell me much, and what he did tell me went in one ear and out the other. I could not imagine anything changing.

The big and important news was that Anton Dolin was joining our company. I was thrilled. It had been one of my dearest wishes to dance with him again, and now it had been granted. He was to arrive in Australia at the same time as us but on a hydroplane, which took only three days. I had so much to look forward to! In this happy, optimistic state of mind, I walked up the ramp onto the ship, which was smaller than the trans-Atlantic ones – all white and inviting. *Australia! The faraway land, what do you hold for me?*

Our cabin was next to Tania and Lichine's – good fun – the doors giving onto the open deck, so much nicer than being stuck in a corridor. After the ritual at the purser's desk, we were assigned our permanent tables in the dining room and given the timetable for meals. Unpacking done, I went to explore the ship. To my delight, I found a large canvas swimming pool and ping-pong tables at the end of our deck, and more games on other decks. These, as usual, were immediately monopolised by our dancers and, unless other passengers made friends with them, they had no chance. Soon everyone became acquainted, and some lasting friendships were made.

Once we passed the Bay of Biscay, which is always rough, and through into the Strait of Gibraltar, we entered the Mediterranean Sea. The sky was blue, the sea calm, ripples sparkling in the sun. We had to exercise every day and rehearse *Paganini* with Fokine. The captain was very cooperative. A big space on the top deck was reserved for our use and the sailors hoisted a piano up there, which Vladimir Launitz, whom we called 'Chichoubamboula', played for us. The proud owner of a snake, he was engaged as the second conductor to Antal Dorati and Efrem Kurtz.

As it was getting hotter every day, the blazing sun roasting us on the open deck, we joined the rising sun to do our class, then rehearsed until ten in the morning, with the rest of the day free. It worked very well. To stand on deck at dawn, holding onto the railings in lieu of a barre, and sink into a *plié* – what could be more enchanting? The afternoons we spent on deck, clad in bathing suits. Some read, some just snoozed on deckchairs in the shade, others gambolled about in the canvas pool, which was shaded by an awning. The water was not exactly refreshing, but it was great fun.

The Fokines kept themselves to themselves and we rarely saw them, but one day Mme Fokine appeared on our deck, fully dressed, with high heels, picture hat and, oh dear, a fur stole over her shoulders! She surveyed us sprawled on deck with a look of strong disapproval and, addressing herself to no-one in particular, loudly said, 'Oh, the youth of today! Disgraceful! No decorum, no modesty, lying about semi-naked!' Upon which, she made her prompt exit. We burst into stifled giggles. If we were shocking in our modest one-piece bathing costumes, what would Mme Fokine say at the sight of topless women these days, with just a G-string for modesty? I hate to think!

The ship docked for a few hours at Port Said before entering the Suez Canal. Here began for me the discovery of a whole new world. It surpassed all my expectations and preconceived ideas of what the other side of our planet would be like. As soon as we docked, most passengers went ashore with strict instructions to be back on board by a certain hour. The ship would not delay its departure for late-comers.

The port was small, with a dusty country road leading to a settlement. A hoard of little boys assailed us – noisy, cheerful kids, proposing all sorts of unclear deals, saying, '*Gulli-gulli*,' and laughing a lot. They knew a few English words, enough to deal with tourists. Some specialised in retrieving coins passengers threw into the water. They were expert divers, never failing to grab the coin and, of course, keep it. One kid approached me asking if I wanted to see a trick.

'Okay,' I said.

He made me understand that I had to put money on the palm of his hand. No, not a coin, paper money. Satisfied, he closed his hand and with a big grin told me to say, 'Go.' I said 'Go,' and the little rascal took off, shouting over his shoulder, 'Good trick, yes?'

There was no time to venture very far from the docks. After a brisk walk along a path shaded by tall bushes and palm trees, it was time to return to the ship. The children were still there, squeezing the last coins out of the passengers. Now some teenagers were holding big baskets full of well-wrapped boxes, the contents of which they proclaimed to be the best *rahat lokum* (Turkish delight) in the world. Many of us bought some. When we eventually opened our boxes, none contained a single *rahat* – they were full of pebbles! So much for Port Said.

One day when I went back to our cabin to change for dinner, I noticed that my little white elephant was not on my pillow. I started to look for it under the pillows, then on the floor. Jerry put down his book and asked me what I was searching for.

'Oh, don't bother,' he calmly informed me. 'I threw that silly toy into the sea.'

I felt stunned, tears welling in my eyes. 'Why did you do that?' I gulped in distress. 'You knew what treasured memories that little elephant held for me!' Anger was rapidly getting hold of me.

'I find your treasured memories annoying. That toy of yours was getting on my nerves. Grow up!' He left the cabin.

I was angry, hurt and puzzled. I could not face dinner. I sat on the deck thinking, trying to figure out what made Jerry tick. Whatever it was, I did not like it. The seed was planted for mounting antagonism between us. I did not bring up the subject again – I hated confrontations; anything for peace – I just could not talk to him for a few days.

After leaving the Red Sea, we docked at Aden in Yemen – small decks, a few sheds, a few children, curious faces. The place seemed lifeless and very, very hot. Hardly anyone went ashore, but I wanted to investigate around the sheds. Kira Abricossova, a vivacious member of our company and always a good sport, volunteered to come with me. With one eye on the discharge of the cargo, we walked around the sheds and exchanged greetings with some men who were going about their business. They were British, stationed in Aden. Two kids appeared from around the corner of a shed, dragging behind them a little gazelle lying on her side, her legs tied with a rope! Kira and I were appalled by the sight and ran towards the kids.

Having no language in common, we mimed our displeasure at such cruelty. The kids promptly mimed back that for half a crown, the gazelle was ours. The deal was struck. The kids ran off, we remained with our purchase and a huge problem. If we set the gazelle free, she would undoubtedly be caught again. We had to keep her! But how to smuggle her on board ship? Kira solved the problem. While I held the gazelle, she took off her blouse and replaced it with the big scarf she had on her head. We tucked the gazelle into Kira's blouse and hurried towards the ship, up the ramp and into my cabin.

Delighted with our success, we sat on the floor admiring and stroking our little animal. What a relief when we heard the ship's engine start and we pulled away from the docks. Our gazelle was safe now. At that moment, Jerry entered the cabin and froze in disbelief. When he found his voice, what he had to say was most unflattering. Offended, we gathered our pet and marched off to Kira's cabin, where we were received with amused kindness by other members of the company. We all put our heads together as to what to do next. We could not keep the gazelle in the cabin, that was clear. The decision was that Kira and I would go to the captain and confess our deed to him. Kira went in search of the first officer, with whom she was on flirtatious terms, to ask him to arrange an urgent meeting with the captain. Within an hour, the charming officer had come to fetch us.

We exchanged cordial greetings, then the captain asked to what he owed our visit. Taking turns, we told him our story and begged for his help. The captain listened in silence, occasionally muttering, 'Oh dear, oh dear!'

We ran out of words and looked at him with begging eyes. The captain shook his head with a sigh. 'What you've done is very irregular – smuggling . . . very naughty, wot?' He pondered for a moment, scrutinising our faces. 'All right, ladies, this is what I'm prepared to do for you.'

The captain's plan was to put our gazelle into a large cage they had on board for the occasional dog travelling with a passenger. The cage was on a lower open deck, where the animal would be looked after by the sailors and we could visit every day. They would send a wire to the Perth quarantine authorities and to Perth Zoo to ask if they would be willing to give the gazelle a home. All we could do now was hope for a positive outcome.

Kira and I were immensely grateful to our kind and forgiving captain. We jumped up and hugged the dear man. Astonished but not displeased, he smiled, but warned us against any further breaches of regulations. We were escorted back to Kira's cabin and our little gazelle to her cage on deck. We called her Aden. The news spread fast and little Aden had constant visitors. She got to recognise Kira and me, and liked to nibble the lobes of our ears. A few days passed, then one morning the captain appeared at our rehearsal to tell us that Perth Zoo had agreed to take Aden and that a van would collect her when we docked in Perth. *Hurrah!*

We steamed through the Indian Ocean on our way to Bombay (now Mumbai). The weather became even hotter – not a cloud in the sky, calm seas and, following us, a multitude of beautifully coloured tiny flying fishes. Our ship approached the Bombay docks as we finished our early morning class. Everyone could go ashore as long as they were back on board by midnight.

Having lived and travelled almost exclusively in the Western world, we now stepped ashore into a world, a culture we knew almost nothing about. After only sixteen hours spent wandering around Bombay I, of course, was none the wiser as to what India was like, but I felt a longing to find out more, return, explore, see and learn about India, which was like no other country I had ever been to. Unfortunately I never had the chance to return. All I have are superficial impressions, but they are vividly engraved on my mind.

Above all, colours! Brilliant colours, from buildings, objects and markets, to the brilliant colours of women's saris. At first glance everything looked so cheerful, but the first impression did not last long. Side by side with opulence was dire poverty and misery – outstretched, begging hands of deformed children, adults, and lepers ground down by their terrible disease. I felt deep pity, distress and guilt, embarrassed as I passed them in the street. But all these people seemed placid, begging in silence.

A procession went by – men in white habits carrying an effigy of the elephant god on their shoulders, surrounded by women and children. They made their way towards a jetty not far off. We followed them. To my surprise, the men threw the elephant god into the sea! Sacred cows wandered at will in some streets, helping themselves to their favourite greens outside a green grocer, plopping on footpaths – that was rather endearing! The big, black bats hanging upside-down in the trees like bunches of black grapes revolted me. I had been scared stiff of bats since childhood, but Western bats are small compared to these jet-black giants! I was really scared when passing under them, but I tried not to show it in front of my companions.

By late afternoon, we had all decided to return to our ship, have a shower, change and return to the most beautiful-looking hotel for dinner. Again, I felt embarrassed and guilty as we trooped in, in our evening attire, through the arch leading to the vast veranda of the restaurant. Outside the arch, squatting on the footpath, were many outstretched hands, beautiful eyes and hungry faces. I cannot say that I enjoyed my dinner. Back on board before midnight, we sat on deck for a while, exchanging our impressions. It is amazing how each individual feels and sees the same things differently!

Back in our cabin, Jerry remarked, 'What a ghastly place! Red spit everywhere – revolting!'

I was about to plunge into an argument but thought the better of it. What was the point? Everyone has the right to their opinion. Pity, we were hardly ever on the same wavelength. I went on deck in my dressing gown and watched the Bombay lights slowly fade into the night. My thoughts were sombre too. Our life on board ship, pleasant as it was, had begun to make me restless. I missed performing, our daily routine in the theatre, and all they entailed. But we were getting there, just one more stop, Ceylon (now Sri Lanka), and then, finally, Australia!

To my disappointment, the ship docked in Colombo for only four hours – no time to explore. After the hustle and bustle of Bombay, the place looked so empty of people and so clean. We hung around a big square by the sea and it was soon time to re-embark. Many, many years later, in another life and different circumstances, I had the luck to return to Sri Lanka and spent an enchanting holiday discovering many wonderful, unforgettable places on this unique and very special island.

As every day brought us nearer to our final destination, the holiday feeling was ebbing away. It was time to drag the suitcases out, to start packing, and to relegate the voyage to a special place in my album of memories.

MELBOURNE

Everyone was on deck watching out for the first sight of the Australian coast. 'There, there – look!' exclaimed an excited voice.

'It must be Fremantle, over there!'

We glided nearer and nearer to shore and docked in Perth. It was an indescribable feeling to land on the other side of the earth, so far away from what we knew. We did not have a clue what to expect.

'Bouboule, look! The van from the zoo is here to collect our Aden!'
Kira exclaimed beside me.

We rushed to little Aden's cage to see her off. Just in time! Two
sailors were lifting her cage to deliver her to the driver of the van. 'She's
a lucky gazelle,' one of the sailors said.

Yes, she was. But so were we, to find ourselves in a country that
extended such an amazing welcome to us and made our stay an unforgettable experience. I am often asked about my first impression of
Australia. Not a simple question to answer – I have so many first impressions, depending on where I was. The only impression that embraces
all of Australia is its sky, a sky of immense beauty and majesty. The
vastness of it, uninterrupted by the clutter of buildings, skyscrapers and
constricted horizons! At night it was like low-hanging, endless navy velvet, dotted with billions of stars, some smaller and more distant, others
huge and so brilliant that I felt I could almost touch them. I was in total
awe of it, and still am.

Everything about Australia was new and yet strangely reminiscent,
in an undefined way, of other faraway places I had seen. I liked the
low buildings and the wide roads – no feeling of being squashed, lots of
elbow room. The wooden footpaths in some Perth streets reminded me
of Montreal. The beautiful wrought-iron work decorating the balconies
had a Latin flavour. There was a feeling of the Wild West, mixed with the
up-to-date – modern (by 1930s standards) luxurious homes and hotels,
and department stores such as Myer. The nature was of a lushness I had
never seen before; there were totally new kinds of trees, bushes and
flowers to discover. I fell in love with koalas immediately and, whenever
possible, made a beeline to places you were allowed to cuddle them.
They stole my heart the way they hung onto my neck, their heads on my
chest. They were probably just imagining I was a eucalyptus tree, but
it made me feel so good! The abundance of snakes did not! Numerous
native animals were to discover but not to touch.

After being used mostly to sparrows and noisy, scruffy pigeons in
European cities, the beautiful, exotic, colourful birds of many varieties
surrounding us in Australian cities and in the country made me feel I

was in an enchanted world. I wondered if all the beauty of Australian nature had some bearing on the characteristics of the Australian people. In some superficial ways, they were a bit similar to the English. They were warm-hearted, but did not hide it under reserve. In other ways, they were totally different and infinitely endearing. Everything felt so peaceful, relaxed and laid-back.

These were my first impressions of this beautiful country in 1938. I loved it. Of course, things have changed in so many ways since those faraway days. The cities have changed beyond all recognition from the way they looked then. But the skies are the same, as are the flora and fauna, and people remain friendly, warm-hearted and caring.

Our opening night on 28 September 1938 was to take place at His Majesty's Theatre, Melbourne. It was in Melbourne that we finally disembarked and were directed to our various lodgings by the helpful people from J.C. Williamson Ltd, our management company for the Australian and New Zealand tours. Jerry and I were driven to a little rented house in a wide street full of trees in Toorak. It had a long veranda, large sparsely furnished but comfortable rooms, and a very nice front garden. I was delighted – it was so much nicer than being stuck in a hotel room.

I had a message from Anton Dolin, who had arrived the previous day with his friend, the sweet baby-faced Otis Pearce, to come to their hotel for lunch. I was overjoyed at the prospect of dancing with Pat again, and to have him with us. We had a jolly lunch with Pat and Otis at their most elegant hotel near our theatre, then went over to inspect the stage and sort out our dressing rooms.

As Toumanova had left us in 1937 and Danilova soon after, Tania and I had to take over their various roles, so we often performed in all three ballets at each performance. Pat had to learn quite a few of Massine and Lichine's roles, besides rehearsing the ballets he already knew with Fokine and me. There was much to do. No time for sightseeing. Not yet.

Our opening night was only a few days away, which we spent solidly in the theatre, practising, rehearsing and getting ready. We did not know a soul in Australia, and we were well aware that the ballet audience was quasi-nonexistent. We could only hope that people would come out of curiosity; then it would be up to us to conquer them and make them want to come again. We had to cultivate an appreciation of our art. When the curtain went up we were ready to give all we had, encouraged greatly by the sight of an auditorium full to capacity. The vibes coming from the audience were all we could have wished for and at the end, the noisy applause was more than we had hoped for.

Our management brought many people from the audience to our dressing rooms to meet us. Their appreciation and enthusiastic compliments were expressed with a sincere simplicity we encountered everywhere we performed in Australia. From knowing no-one, we were suddenly surrounded by keen, admiring friends, great hospitality and the start of friendships that were to last a lifetime. More and more, I came to feel the same sense of wellbeing in Australia that I felt in England.

Among the many people we met and made friends with, one family in particular became like family to us all. They were Dr Joseph and Mary Ringland Anderson and their two daughters, Elisabeth and Nairne. Dr Anderson was an ophthalmologist of repute and the family was passionate about all forms of the arts. In no time at all, ballet became their main passion and Dr Anderson, armed with his cine-camera (a novelty in those days), had the run of the theatre, at front of house and backstage. He photographed our performances from all angles – he was here, he was there, he was everywhere! We loved him. He shot a great amount of film, which after his death Mary donated to the archives of the Australian Ballet. As hardly anyone photographed ballet in those days, Dr Anderson's films of our company are among the very few records in existence of bits and pieces of our performances. Of course, they are in black and white with no sound.

What fun we had when every Sunday many of us spent the day at the Andersons', swimming in their pool, resting and playing in their garden. Mary excelled herself as a most generous hostess, with a good understanding of dancers' appetites. In the evenings we all sat on the floor of their living room, a sheet draped over one wall in lieu of a screen, as Dr Anderson showed us the footage he had shot during the week. We sang the music to fit the action. It was tremendous fun, with teasing remarks and much laughter.

Mary had a nephew, Robert Southey, a bright and delightful school-boy. He obviously enjoyed our company, as he never missed a Sunday, and we looked forward to gambolling, talking and laughing with that great kid. In 1986, forty-eight years later, I was invited by the Australian Ballet and its then artistic director, Maina Gielgud, to come to Melbourne to coach the company and its leading dancers in Fokine's *Les Sylphides*. To go back to Australia, to see my wonderful friends again, filled me with joy. Of course I accepted!

I was in for a big, happy surprise when I arrived in Melbourne. I was met at the airport by the company's administrator, Noel Pelly, who became a very dear friend. The first thing he said was, 'Sir Robert is so excited about seeing you again. Do you remember him? He's Mary Anderson's nephew. Sir Robert and his wife, Marigold, are throwing a big party for you the day after tomorrow.'

Well, he could have knocked me down with a feather! Our dear little Robert of long ago, now the chairman of the Australian Ballet? *Wa-oo!* I was jumping out of my skin with excitement! Noel Pelly took me to the party. Sir Robert and Lady Southey stood on the front steps receiving their guests. As we walked along the garden path towards them, Sir Robert caught sight of Noel and called out, 'Where's Irina?'

'Here she is,' called back Noel, pointing at me. As we reached the steps, the look on Sir Robert's face was of complete surprise and disbelief. I was sixty-seven and fit!

'Oh, I expected a little old lady in a wheelchair!' he exclaimed.

It was a great party, a happy reunion with friends. But that was in 1986. Let us go back to 1938. Our Melbourne season was progressing with flying colours. I was busy rehearsing with Dolin and Fokine; Lichine was working on *The Prodigal Son*; everyone was busy and happy. Some romances even started between our dancers and young Australian men. One afternoon I was taken by our theatre manager to watch the races and was photographed with a beautiful Melbourne Cup contender, a horse by the name of Marauder. I do not remember if the horse won, but I remember it was fun!

I started to notice that Victor Dandré surveyed me with an expression of disapproval. One morning after class he asked me to come to his and Jerry's office. Dandré looked at me sternly. 'You do not behave in the manner your position as a ballerina of the company dictates. You are too pally with everybody. You should conduct yourself with more dignity, to command respect.'

Blood rushed to my face in my indignation. I looked at Jerry, who shrugged and said nothing. Anger rose in me and gave me the courage to speak up. 'Everyone you say I'm too pally with has known me since I was thirteen. I know they're fond of me and respect my achievements. I grew up among them, they're like family.'

It was Dandré's turn to get angry. 'Your married status demands more decorum. You exercise none!'

I glanced at Jerry, who nodded in agreement. I had never liked Dandré, but now I positively hated him. 'What the hell do you want from me?' I blurted out, completely at a loss.

'Now you're being coarse and rude!' snapped Dandré.

Feeling like a guilty schoolgirl, I got up and left their office. Back in my dressing room, as I changed for rehearsal, I decided to unburden my mixed-up thoughts on Pat. I would always receive a frank response and wise advice from him.

'Don't pay any attention to Dandré's views on how a ballerina should conduct herself. He's living in the past. Just be yourself,' Pat laughed, adding a few cracks on the subject of rank-pulling. 'And about your married status,' Pat looked serious, 'it's more complicated. It spells trouble . . . you must be aware by now that Jerry suffers from a destructive affliction called "jealousy". At the moment you're provoking him by allowing Yurek' (Shabelevsky, our leading character dancer) 'to try his choreographic ideas on you. The fact that you're spending time alone with Yurek irritates Jerry.'

Pat warned me that if I did not stop this provocation, Jerry would do something rash. He pointed out that we had a long, successful stay in Australia in front of us and that I must not rock the boat. Remembering the fate of my white elephant, I had to admit that Pat was right. However, it was too late – Yurek was dismissed and returned to Europe by the next boat.

When I angrily attacked Jerry about this dismissal, his response was, 'Don't shout. Be grateful that I didn't dismiss you!'

I was aware after that of the subdued gossip in the company, some of whom presumed I had had an affair with Yurek, which did not help. Jerry's jealousy put me in an intolerable position. Pat's comment was simply, 'Calm yourself and cheer up – a storm in a teacup soon forgotten.'

I knew he was right but I did not forget my anger at the two 'directors' in a hurry and, for the rest of our stay in Melbourne, I gave them a very cold shoulder. Jerry was annoyed. I was delighted that he was annoyed!

Another couple who became friends during our time in Melbourne were Mr and Mrs Paul Duval. Paul was the owner of a cosmetics company; his products enjoyed a high reputation and were sold at Myer. He asked me if I would allow him to name his new line of lipsticks after me. I said I would, with pleasure. Soon after, the lipsticks came out with my name engraved on top of the container. They were in many colours, from the palest hues to burgundy. Each week I received a big box of them, and our dancers were constantly popping into my dressing room to help themselves to different colours. It was a big success. Paul presented me with my favourite colour in a specially made gold container, which I still have. I treasure it!

To my horror I discovered, too late, that my name and photo had been used to advertise a well-known brand of cigarettes. As we dancers did not smoke, this was silly and embarrassing for me. When I was asked about the advert, I protested that I knew nothing about it, but no-one believed me, thinking I had been offered a good sum of money for it and had succumbed to greed. I wondered if Jerry did. When I quizzed him about it he denied it, smiling at my annoyance. Someone allowed it. I never found out who, and Jerry didn't do anything to stop it as I asked him to.

I pondered life a lot in those days. Oh, I had so much to learn about what things and people were like in real life, society's dos and don'ts. Until then I had stubbornly acted upon my selfish feelings, never thinking of the consequences. I had to learn to think of the sensitivities of others. 'Think before you act,' Tassia always said. I missed Tassia so much. How simple, how beautiful my fairy tale world on stage was! How complicated everything was outside the stage door! There were moments I felt so alone and wanted my papa.

A SYDNEY WEDDING

The day before our last performance in Melbourne, Jerry appeared with a second-hand car he had just purchased, declaring we would drive to Sydney to see a bit of the countryside. That really pleased me. We set off very early in the morning, me armed with a map, which I always read wrongly and so proved hopeless at giving directions. Sensing that it would spoil the trip, I soon asked to be relieved of that duty.

It was a long but fascinating drive, the landscape changing from flat and arid to hilly and lush. The deserted, sometimes quite dusty roads, with an occasional snake or big lizard making its way across, or a kangaroo hopping away, were fascinating. We drove through part of a recently burned forest. The charred trees with burnt-away branches and big logs lying about, still with red-hot coals smouldering inside them, looked so unreal, and the air was yellowish with smoke. We stopped in small hamlets to stretch our legs, looking out for a pub that would provide us with sandwiches and tell us where to find a petrol pump. The locals were always helpful and friendly.

Jerry told me an apartment had been rented for us in a place called Elizabeth Bay. Then he added, 'There's a Russian Church in Sydney. I made arrangements with the priest for our church marriage there.'

'Oh?!' That was all I managed to say, I was so taken by surprise.

'I hope the church marriage will mature your outlook on what it's all about.'

I kept silent, at a loss for what to say. Two feelings lodged inside me – guilt and resentment. Fortunately we were, by then, not far from our destination and release from a drive that had suddenly become devoid of any pleasure. *I'll talk to Pat*, I decided. *He'll sort me out!*

Elizabeth Bay was a small, delightful place, with very few houses dotted here and there. Our two-storey apartment block was situated right at the edge of the bay, a small, sandy beach with a net across it to keep the sharks away. Our flat was on the second floor, with a big bay window in the living room overlooking the water, which gave me the lovely feeling of being on board ship. There were two bedrooms, a nice kitchen and a bathroom. As we brought up the last suitcase, Jerry pointed to the guest bedroom and told me, 'That's where you sleep until our church marriage.' This game Jerry was playing suddenly struck me as hysterically funny and I burst into hearty laughter. Taken aback by my reaction, he lamely muttered, 'It will be as if we are starting afresh.'

I unpacked, made my room cosy, and was delighted to have a corner of my very own. When I told Pat, he was amused. 'Indulge him. Pain in the neck as he is at times, he really adores you!'

The news of our successful ten-week season and popularity in Melbourne preceded our nine-week stay in Sydney. Our opening night was sold out and the approval of the audience heart-warming. As in Melbourne, we met with great hospitality and made many new friends.

Daryl Lindsay, Norman's brother, very soon became a friend of the company, and was a familiar sight backstage, sketching us in motion. It was most endearing the care he took not to be in the way, his courtesy and warm smile. I regretted not getting to know him better. He seemed to keep himself to himself, or was it that our tribe was a bit too much for him?

The Fairfax family were frequent members of the audience and played host to many of our company. There was a happy reunion between Jerry and Robert Lewis, a fellow student from the early twenties, when they had both studied the wool business in Leipzig. Bob became a fixture and part of our tribe, a handsome, cheerful man we were all fond of. One of our soloists was more than fond of him. Ah, those were the days!

Sydney was a wonderful place in which to work. The beautiful harbour, the accessible beaches, the whole atmosphere of that city made me feel like I was on holiday! Pat made my work even more satisfying. I was learning so much just talking to him, listening to his experiences and rehearsing with him.

It felt so strange to celebrate Christmas in what was an Australian summer! Pat and Otis found a plant vaguely resembling a Christmas tree and decorated it richly – it looked lovely. We had some great parties around it, as well as at the homes of our new friends. On 30 December, Lichine's *Prodigal Son* premiered with great success. He emerged as a truly inventive and sensitive choreographer, and his work was much admired. Anton Dolin, in the role of the Son, scored great personal success. Afterwards we all welcomed in the New Year, 1939, happy at the company's latest achievement and looking forward to the future.

On the home front, things were gathering momentum. The routine Jerry and I fell into was that of any two friends sharing a flat, but this 'flatmate' arrangement was soon disrupted by ten visits from our Russian priest, as part of the wedding arrangements Jerry had made. He told me about these daily visits only the day before the first priestly appearance. When I asked him the reason for these rather strange visits, he replied, 'Our case is unusual. We need to pray.'

And so the priest arrived, to start what were for me ten days of utter irritation, with a good dose of boredom. The priest (I cannot even remember his name) was of small, meagre stature, with a skimpy black beard adorning his chin, and small dark eyes, cold as ice, gazing at me severely. I disliked him instantly. Declining my invitation to sit down, he asked for a small table to be placed facing the bay, upon which he deposited a cross and a Bible.

Bidding us to stand behind him, he began praying and reading passages from the Bible. He read so fast, in such a monotonous voice, that I soon gave up listening or trying to understand what he was mumbling about. I gazed at the bay, thought about the roles I was to perform that evening, or about people I had met in Sydney, or anything that came into my head to pass the time. The thought that I had to face nine more days of this 'praying' did nothing to cheer me up! That evening when I got to the theatre, I told Pat about the priest. His remarks cheered me up and we ended up laughing.

And so every day, for nine more days, at lunchtime (no lunch!), Jerry and I returned to the flat, the priest and the prayers. It must have been on the third or fourth day that I took a look at Jerry. He was earnestly, deeply immersed in prayer, often making the sign of the cross. A feeling of shame came over me at my flippant attitude, and I tried to concentrate and listen to what the priest was saying. I noticed that my name kept coming up. I pricked up my ears . . . The priest was fervently asking Our Lord to forgive me my sins and put me on the right path to becoming a good and obedient wife!

So that's what all this is about! Thoughts filled my head, jumping around like tiddlywinks, aimlessly, in total confusion. I glanced at Jerry. *What's he thinking?* I wondered. *What's eating him up? What's his problem? Or perhaps it's me with a problem and I don't know it.* So ran my tiddlywink thoughts until the end of that 'praying' hour.

A few days later, Pat told me that Jerry had asked him to be his *shafer* (best man), with Dandré as mine and Otis and Mme Larose as our witnesses. At Russian weddings, the *shafers'* duty is to stand right behind the bride and groom during most of the service and hold crowns over their heads. I naturally would have preferred to have Pat as my *shafer*, but I was not consulted. By then I was not certain if I had any right to be a bit offended. Maybe the problem *was* with me. I did not raise the matter, deciding that it was not important anyway, and that the day was too hot to risk an argument.

The big day finally arrived and all concerned were assembled at the church by eleven a.m. It was a lovely-looking church inside, with candles either side of the doors gently lighting up the faces of the saints on the icons. Dandré greeted me dryly. Jerry seemed nervous. The priest emerged from one of the side doors to the altar and motioned to us to take our places facing the icon of the Virgin Mary holding the baby Jesus, which stood on a high pulpit illuminated by a single big candle in a tall ornate holder.

Dandré and Pat were behind us, Mme Larose and Otis on the side. The small church choir took its place and the priest started the service. I always loved the Gregorian chant in our Russian Orthodox Church and, standing there listening to the beautiful singing, a kind of wellbeing enveloped me as I absently watched the big candle flicker. Then the moment came when the *shafers* had to start holding the crowns over our heads. For a few moments all was well then, oh dear, Dandré emitted a loud hiccup! The crown he was holding over my head made a touchdown and bounced off. More hiccups followed with the same result . . . Otis giggled. I was struggling not to. Dandré's hiccups became louder and had obviously settled in for the long haul. The crown kept bouncing off my head while Otis emitted choking sounds. My own shoulders shook with suppressed laughter.

'Otis, shut up and take over!' commanded Pat, in a loud whisper. There was a bit of a commotion behind me as Otis grabbed the crown and Mme Larose grabbed Dandré and propelled him out into the garden. I glanced at Jerry; with a dignified look he upheld the solemnity of the occasion (even if no-one else did). The priest was impassive, but the choir members wore big smiles. Otis and I stifled our giggles and the ceremony proceeded without further distraction. Dandré was still hiccupping when we left the church, and could not join us for lunch. Our lunch was jolly – it could not be anything else with Pat and Otis there. Even Jerry laughed at their version of the wedding! Then it was time to go to rehearsal.

As we returned to the flat that night, Jerry said, 'You can move into our bedroom now.'

Oh, that was too good to let pass! I made a deep, theatrical curtsy to him as I said, 'Thank you, but I'm very happy in my little room and will remain there!' I had the LAST WORD! It was only the next morning, as I brushed my teeth, that I realised how much I must have hurt Jerry's feelings the night before. Fully expecting to be met by a long, silent face, I went to the kitchen to make some coffee, but to my surprise, Jerry greeted me with a jovial, 'Good morning! Coffee's ready. Just making some toast.'

Relieved, I thought him a jolly good sport! I stood my ground and was to remain in the guest room for the rest of our stay in Sydney. Jerry never brought the subject up. He remained in a good mood and was an easygoing flatmate.

The phone rang. It was Dandré. Having hiccupped on and off all night, he had called a doctor and now asked Jerry to come over to his hotel. He was feeling exhausted. Jerry dropped me at the theatre for class then hurried to see Dandré. Later in the day, it was official – due to indisposition, Dandré was flying on the next hydroplane back to England to be attended by his own doctor. I was sorry he was suffering a nasty attack of the hiccups, but not sorry to see this old trouble-making gentleman go!

One bright morning, Jerry announced that he had a surprise for me. The surprise materialised that afternoon. Parked in front of the stage door was a bright yellow Rolls Royce, its canvas roof folded down. The gears – which were monumental – sat outside the body of the car, resting on one of the running boards. The seats were dark red. 'Isn't it a beauty?!' Jerry exclaimed. 'Built in 1919, the year you were born!'

I had never seen a car like it, and stared at it in amazement. 'Does it work?' I finally ventured. By then a curious crowd had gathered to examine the car, even hopping onto the running boards to look at the dashboard.

'Get in, get in!' Jerry urged me.

After he made several abortive attempts to start the engine, the exhaust pipe finally emitted a loud bang and we were off! It was great fun and I was delighted to be in the open and not sweltering under a roof. But after a while, the fact that the car was drawing constant attention, and that we were stared at everywhere we went, embarrassed me no end. I started to beg Jerry to change it for a simple open-roofed white Ford I had seen for sale at a nearby garage. I argued that, as we were due to go to New Zealand soon, it would be much more practical to have a little Ford rather than drag the big yellow monster around with us. Finally my pleas prevailed. Robert Lewis bought the Rolls and we got the little Ford.

Towards the end of our Sydney season, Lichine sustained a slight injury to his ankle and could not dance for a couple of days. To fill in a gap in the program, Pat offered to dance his 'Bolero', a long solo he had choreographed himself to Ravel's famous piece. Pat had a copy of the orchestration with him, so Dorati summoned his musicians for a quick rehearsal after the matinee and Pat was on that evening. With his comic, straightforward honesty, he warned us, 'It's not Art, but at the end I get an ovation!'

All of us backstage jammed into the wings, curious to see this 'not Art' solo. First reaction – oh dear! What Pat did was *terrible*, but *how* he did it was MAGNIFICENT! His presence and personality were magnetic. Nothing else mattered. I watched in awe, with mounting excitement engulfing all my being. As the last chord smashed at the abrupt end, the audience went wild. It was a clear example of the difference between a good artist and a great artist. Technique is not everything – one has to be born with that 'something', that elusive thing one cannot learn and no-one can teach.

A little while later, Lichine asked me if I would consider learning the part of the Siren in his *Prodigal Son*, as he wanted me to replace Tamara Grigorieva in it for the London and New York seasons. I was delighted. It was, for me, an interesting role to work on – not only the characterisation but also the physical appearance. And of course, to work and dance with Pat would be sheer joy! A new challenge – I loved the feeling.

We were having supper at a friend's house one evening after our performance. A very nice gentleman was sitting next to me, who turned out to be the Yugoslav Consul. We talked of this and that, and our nomadic way of life. I told him how frustrating it was at times not to have a passport, only Nansen papers, which puzzled some passport control officials.

The Consul looked pensive for a moment, then took a sip of wine and asked me, 'Can you come to see me at the Consulate tomorrow morning at nine? Bring your Nansen papers. I might be able to . . .' he leant towards my ear, 'give you a Yugoslav passport.'

Next morning, having skipped class, I was at the Consulate at nine a.m. sharp. At ten-thirty a.m. I walked out clutching a Yugoslav passport! Irregular? Dodgy? I did not care. I was a 'citizen' now!

NEW ZEALAND AND THE PACIFIC

We were on the ship to New Zealand for a seven-week tour of the main cities. The Tasman Sea was rough and the motion of the ship most unpleasant. Even I, always a good sailor, felt seasick. Our scheduled short stop in Milford Sound to unload some cargo had to be abandoned – the sea was too rough for the ship to negotiate the narrow entrance to the docks. I managed to get on deck the better to see and admire the beautiful entrance to Milford Sound wedged between two high cliffs. For some strange reason, a smell of rotting cabbages enveloped the deck. I felt 'icky' and hurried back to the cabin. The steward brought me some tea and I asked him if the crossing from Sydney was always this rough. 'Well, nine times out of ten it's like this. The tenth time, it's the worst!' he answered, lurching sideways and spilling my tea all over the tray. I shuddered at the thought of our crossing back to Sydney.

It was a lovely sunny day when we disembarked gratefully in Christchurch. With Pat and Otis in our open car, we drove to the hotel assigned to us. All along the wide street leading from the docks, on every second corner, were Salvation Army groups playing and singing. At the hotel, we were met by a gloomy-looking theatre manager. Apparently tickets were not selling well at all and it looked like a box office disaster! The theatre was just around the corner, so Jerry went with the manager to see for himself how bad the situation was. The rest of us were about to go to our rooms, when Pat asked me if I could drive. Yes, I could, after a fashion . . . Jerry had taught me. But I had no licence, being underage.

'Oh nonsense, never mind that!' said Pat. 'I want you to drive back to the docks, turn around and drive back to the hotel. Can you do it?'

I knew Pat did not drive. He never did learn. He did not want to. 'But why, Pat?' I asked.

'Don't ask questions, just drive and leave the rest to me!' Pat looked pleased with himself. Otis giggled. I felt a bit nervous but ready for anything Pat might concoct. It was always fun.

And so we set off. There was very little traffic, and I relaxed. We turned around at the docks and were on our way back when Pat said, 'Now, drive as slowly as possible and don't pay any attention to what I do.' Upon which he sat on top of the folded canvas roof and, each time we approached a Salvation Army group, shouted at the top of his lungs, 'I was a sinner, you saved my soul! Don't go to see the Russian Ballet – it stinks!'

The Salvation Army bands stopped playing, the passers-by stared and curious glances came from drivers overtaking us as Pat created havoc in the street. Otis and I were in stitches! Reaching the hotel, Pat urged us to duck inside promptly and tell no-one what we had done. Jerry greeted us with, 'Where the hell have you been?' The news from the theatre was not good. Tickets were not in demand.

Pat, looking utterly innocent, replied, 'We went for a walk, just looking around.'

'I'm hungry,' moaned Otis. So we went to the dining room to have lunch. I kept glancing at the door, half expecting the police to come after us for disturbing the peace. Instead it was our manager who almost ran in, all excited and out of breath.

'A miracle's happened! Incredible! They're queuing for tickets around the block!'

Pat lifted his eyes to the sky and made a solemn face. 'We must thank St Patrick – he must have had a hand in this miracle!' The manager looked blank and hurried back to the theatre. Thanks to Pat's ingenuity our season was saved and all our performances sold out!

New Zealanders had ways that constantly surprised and charmed us. The audiences did not applaud anything. Only at the very end did they express their approval in a subdued, polite way. We thought they did not find us to their liking, which was rather demoralising.

Pat and I were interviewed on the radio one day. As we waited to go on air, Pat asked our very nice interviewer why the audiences in New

Zealand did not applaud. 'Oh, we never do. We don't want to disturb the artists,' was his reply.

'Artists love applause. We need applause, old boy!' burst out Pat.

'Tell them!' laughed the interviewer.

'I most certainly will!' promised Pat.

Our interview went very well and Pat, in his humorous way, begged the audiences to show their approval by applauding as much as they wished. It worked! At times too well! They applauded in the wrong as well as right moments, but it was great to have such enthusiastic participation from the audiences. Dear Pat, he certainly knew how to turn things around.

Due to the hospitality of the people we met in each town, we were able to see a bit of the countryside. It struck me how green the grass was, how vivid the colours of the vegetation in the limpid air and how white the sheep looked, as if they had just emerged from a sheep beauty parlour! It was much cooler than Sydney, hence physically easier on us, although we did have a bit of a problem finding somewhere to have supper after our performances – everything closed at nine p.m. Usually we were able to persuade the hotel management to arrange trays with cold cuts, salad and some fruit to be left in our rooms. It worked well and the food was delicious. But in Wellington we were amazed by the way our hotel responded to our need to eat late. No trays in rooms – instead they laid on for us, every night, a cold buffet in the dining room, with none of the staff present. There was a big urn with tea, kept hot on a burner. The last person out was to switch it off. The truly amazing thing was that we were not charged for the food but asked to pay for the tea! Figure that one out! We did not even try – we were truly grateful and did justice to our daily suppers.

We were taken to see Rotorua, which today must be a very different place. Back then the tourist was a rare bird and Rotorua was a small Maori settlement in a strange, enchanted place. As there were so many of us paying a visit at once, it became a special occasion. We were met by welcoming, smiling faces of men, women and children, all painted and dressed in traditional Maori fashion. They showed us all the sites, explaining and answering our numerous questions.

I felt transported into another world. The paths we walked on were surrounded by hot, bubbling, muddy earth. It puffed and plopped, looking like chocolate melting in a saucepan. The many little lakes, each one a different, vivid colour, looked like precious jewels, and there were little hills like miniature volcanoes that spat when you threw a piece of soap into their mouth! Yes, soap – the Maoris handed it to us to throw.

To finish off the day, the Maori men and women put on a display for us, singing and dancing, the men very impressive in their *haka*. It was an unforgettable day, full of wonderment and unusual beauty. We were privileged to meet the Maori people, who were so welcoming and friendly. There were no souvenir shops! We took our souvenirs with us in our hearts and minds. We left New Zealand with much to remember about that beautiful country and its people.

The crossing back to Sydney was not too bad. I even managed to sit on deck and darn a few pairs of my toe shoes or do some knitting. We proceeded to Adelaide, of which I retain only a limited memory, as we were there only two weeks. It was cold and rainy. I rehearsed a great deal with Pat. The audiences were very good but I had almost no time to meet new people.

Pat had the idea of Lichine, Tania, him and me returning to Europe via Fiji, Samoa and Honolulu, giving a *divertissement* program in each place and hopefully making a bit of extra money. Lichine loved the idea, as did Tania and I. We went to work on Jerry to organise it. After some research, investigation, phone calls and telegrams, Jerry discovered that there was a ship sailing to Los Angeles via Fiji, Samoa and Honolulu that suited our dates. Recitals in Fiji and Samoa were not possible – he had found no contacts or premises, but Honolulu was interested and McKinley High School auditorium was available and interested in booking us for two recitals for which we could have the Honolulu Symphony Orchestra.

As the ship docked in Honolulu for two nights, the plan was perfect, but we had to persuade Antal Dorati to come with us to rehearse the orchestra. That was not difficult; he thought it would be fun. We devised our program carefully, in order to minimise the number of costumes we would have to transport. One of our dancers, Robert Bell (who danced with us as Boris Belsky), agreed to come with us to fill in when we needed a little more time for costume changes. Dear Otis would come and see to our costumes.

Before we left Australia, we returned to Sydney for a special midnight farewell performance. It was a very emotional occasion for us, our friends and our loyal audience. There was the added sadness of parting from members of our company who had decided to remain in Australia, each one with their own particular reason for doing so. The political situation in Europe was grim, and whispers about the imminence of war were growing louder. We were uncomfortably aware that our company's future in Europe could be jeopardised. But most of us, including me, were unrealistic optimists and did not dwell on what the future might hold.

I was especially sad to say goodbye to my dear colleagues Tamara Tchinarova and Edouard Borovansky who, with Kira Abricossova, her husband, Serge Bousloff, and another four dancers, were remaining in Australia. I thought them very brave. They had to build their future all over again. With courage and determination they did so and with great success. Kira Abricossova opened a ballet school in Perth, which gained great success and prestige, many of her students becoming leading dancers. She also started the West Australian Ballet. Although Kira is no more, her company is still flourishing.

Tamara Tchinarova, who was already well known and loved from her previous visit to Australia with our smaller company, eventually helped Edouard Borovansky and his wife, Zenia, when they opened their ballet school. When Edouard started his own company, Tamara helped him revive works from our company, and was one of his leading artists. Borovansky sowed a seed that grew and flourished – after his premature death, his legacy to ballet in Australia emerged as the Australian Ballet, one of the few great companies in the world today.

I am telling you all this, dear reader, because I am so proud of the achievements of my beloved tribe! So it was with a heavy heart and cherished memories that I stood on the top deck and watched the shores of Australia slowly fade away and disappear.

It felt strange to be on board ship without the rest of our company. So quiet! Our first stop was Suva in the Fijian Islands, where there was just time to unload some cargo. The shore was pretty deserted, but there was no time to go further afield. We walked a bit then returned on board for lunch. The next stop was Pago Pago, in American Samoa. As we approached, the shore looked so lush and the white sandy beaches so beautiful. Crowds of people appeared to see our ship dock. They were amazing-looking people, milk-chocolate in colour, with beautiful features and frizzy hair standing high above their heads like huge halos. What astonished me was that some of them had copper-coloured hair and bright blue eyes. They were strikingly, amazingly attractive.

The manager of the auditorium met us in Honolulu and a lovely young girl put leis over our heads – their aroma was more beautiful than any Guerlain perfume. Once we were installed in our lovely hotel, we were taken to see the auditorium; we were greatly relieved to find that the stage was big and had an excellent floor, and that the dressing rooms were cheerful and near the stage. The two performances were almost sold out. The remaining tickets would surely be purchased by passengers on our ship, who – thanks to Pat's advertising – had promised to come.

While Otis and Robert got busy unpacking our costumes, the rest of us returned to the hotel to have a rest. Our two recitals went famously well; we thoroughly enjoyed the experience, and the fact that we each made a tidy little sum of money. Lichine mused that if we could go on giving recitals we would be rich in no time.

After a lovely supper, courtesy of our manager, our new friends escorted us back to the ship, expressing a wish that we would come back soon. Back on board we found many new fans – the rest of the voyage was very social and enjoyable.

From Los Angeles we flew to New York, where we were due to board a German ship called *Europa* for Southampton two days later. I had only two days to see my parents, and spent them in their house in Long Island while Jerry stayed in New York. I had a great time with my parents. There was so much to talk about. My papa was doing well, and Mother was in good spirits and really sweet to me.

The plan, after our London season, was Berlin from 1 October and then New York, so it would not be long before I would see them again. That meant Mother did not cry when I had to leave, which was so much more pleasant for Papa and me. We were sad enough at parting, without Mother sobbing! Poor Mama – now in my old age I deeply regret that I did not find more understanding in my heart towards her. Ah, regrets, regrets – such a painful feeling.

As always, being back in London was like returning home, a wonderful home full of dear friends and familiar faces. With opening night, 19 June, rapidly approaching, Fokine was rehearsing *Paganini* intensely and polishing many staging details of a rather complicated production. Between rehearsals we ran for costume fittings and back on the double. Besides working with Fokine on my role as the Divine Genius in *Paganini*, I rehearsed my role of the Siren in Lichine's *Prodigal Son* with Lichine and Dolin. Two new roles to work on – I loved every minute of it!

The opening night was, as usual, a heart-warming and very special occasion. The 'welcome back' from the audience was touching – they greeted each of our first entrances with loud and prolonged applause. The London premiere of *The Prodigal Son* was a great success for Lichine as a choreographer, and we all received great notices in the press. *Paganini*'s world premiere was on 30 June, so everyone now concentrated on Fokine's rehearsals and the hundred-and-one things to be seen to. Fokine, as usual, was tense but controlled as we made the last adjustments during our two dress rehearsals and worked with Papa Grigoriev on lighting.

Fokine choreographed the Divine Genius in a serene, fluid, slow, purely classical way, based mainly on *bourrées*, to give an impression of floating. It could have been beautiful, but I strongly felt that my clumsy, ugly costume was going to kill the effect the choreography was meant to convey. It was a dreary white tunic with long sleeves, a gold leather harness crisscrossed over my chest, a shoulder-length veil like a balaclava with a hole in it for my face, and two smallish stiff wings hanging lifelessly on my back. It was impossible to show grace of movement and most of all to feel divine in this costume. I felt like a clumsy clot!

I was astounded that Fokine had approved such an ugly costume, but out of my deep respect for him and his judgement I kept my peace and tried to do my best. But the enjoyment of dancing that role was spoilt for me. It was the only occasion a costume did not blend with my vision for a role. It was irritating, but there was nothing to do but try to rise above it and do my best.

On the night of the premiere, everyone interested in ballet was in the audience. There was electricity in the air, excited expectation. It was always the same before the curtain rose on a new work by Massine or Fokine. *Paganini* had a tremendous impact on the audience. Dimitri Rostoff in the completely dramatic role of Paganini was superb, with great acting power and demoniac passion. His tall, lean figure in the eighteenth-century black costume, his make-up grotesque and macabre, the violin ever-present in his hands, sent shivers down my spine.

Tania Riabouchinska's solo as the Florentine Beauty was an unforgettable display of speed, lightness and grace on her part, and mastery on Fokine's. The critics, all of them, acknowledged Fokine's genius, but a couple also found something to criticise in the production. One of them did not like the scenery, another felt it was a bit old-fashioned, but all of them praised the dancers, Fokine's mastery and imagination, and Rachmaninov's beautiful music. *Paganini* was performed with great success to the end of the company's existence.

A few days later, Baron d'Erlanger gave a party to honour and celebrate Michel Fokine's jubilee, fifty years in the theatre! Colonel de Basil was back from his enforced exile in the South of France and was regathering the reins of the company. I was very glad to see him, but Jerry was not. It was evident that something was eating him up – he was less than friendly towards the Colonel. As we began our last week at Covent Garden, I finally asked Jerry what was wrong between them. 'We're leaving the company.' His voice was icy.

I froze as if struck by lightning, speechless. 'But why?' I finally managed to ask.

Getting more and more agitated, he asked me irritably, 'After I have been the director of the company for the best part of the year, do you really expect me to take a back seat again?' I pointed out that his joint directorship with Dandré had only ever been a temporary arrangement for the Australian tour. He had known that and accepted it on those terms. 'Well, I don't accept it now!' he almost shouted. 'So we're leaving!'

I was outraged! 'Your outsized ego didn't find it necessary to consult with me, to give a thought to where I would be without our company! My work, my repertoire is with this company. Don't I count?'

'No, you don't. You're self-centred and selfish. We're leaving and no more discussion!'

I felt crushed. This turn of events was so totally unexpected. At a loss, I could not, did not know how to deal with it. My mind was in turmoil. I had everything I could wish for as a ballerina and in a week's time I would lose it all. *What will I do then?* I burst into bitter sobs.

Jerry walked out, slamming the door. The word 'BASTARD' crossed my mind. The next thing that crossed my mind was that I had to have a talk with Colonel de Basil. I hurriedly washed my face and went to Covent Garden, hoping to catch the Colonel before he left the office. I did. Papa Grigoriev was with him. They looked grim and preoccupied. Tearfully, I told them about the distressing news Jerry had sprung on me, adding that I did not want to leave the company, so I would have to leave Jerry!

'Oh, my angel!' sighed Papa Grigoriev. The Colonel removed his specs and gave them a good wipe with his hanky, replacing them on his nose as he got up from his desk and came to sit by me.

'Irischka, do not do anything rash, not now. Wait and see what happens . . . we're all in trouble.' He got up and went back to his desk.

'Why are we in trouble?' I asked.

The Colonel then told me that our Berlin season had been cancelled, that Hurok was now interested in Massine's company for the American tour, and that so far he had not been able to secure any other engagements but had approached Australia. To stay in Europe was not on the cards – war with Germany was imminent. We were due for three weeks' holiday, but as things stood now we were out of further engagements.

He was going to talk to the company after the performance, to explain where we stood and ask everyone to be in contact with his Paris office.

'So, Irischka, just hang in there. This is not a good moment to make serious decisions.' He hugged me.

Dazed by so much bad news, I went to my dressing room, but as the evening progressed, I began to feel better. Colonel de Basil had cleared the cobwebs in my head. I felt certain that he would find future engagements for our company and I made up my mind that come what may I would not leave my tribe. The gravity of the political situation eluded me and was slow to sink in. My world was on the stage; outside the theatre the world seemed so confusing. The company took the news of our uncertain future with the same optimism I did. Their holiday plans, in most cases, remained unchanged, and no-one seemed particularly worried.

That last week of our season progressed with us all basking in the demonstrative affection of our audiences. The very last performance was unforgettable for us all – and for me in particular. At the end, the curtain calls went on and on and on! No-one in the audience made any move towards the exits; everyone remained firmly in their seats, applauding and shouting bravo. The stagehands grew impatient. They needed the stage vacated to start getting the scenery down, pack it up and get everything ready for loading on the trucks.

Finally Papa Grigoriev ordered the fire curtain to come down, which would have been a sign that no more curtain calls were possible. In response, the audience started to stamp their feet and shout my name, on and on and on! I was already in my dressing room, stripped of my costume, when Papa Grigoriev rushed in and said, 'My angel, quick, the audience wants you. Put your dressing gown on and go speak to them. They won't leave until you come!'

I felt terribly embarrassed to appear in the stalls on my own. I felt that Tania, Dolin and Lichine should have been alongside me – we all contributed equally to the success of our company. Here I was in my nondescript dressing gown, plonked by Papa Grigoriev in the middle of the stalls, embarrassed and having to make a little speech – the first in my life. I thanked everyone on behalf of the company . . . that's all I remember. I was so overwhelmed that back in my dressing room, no matter how I tried, I could not recall what else I had said!

Backstage, our friends crowded into our dressing rooms. It was sad to say goodbye, especially because of our uncertainty about when we might return and see them again. Outside the stage door were big crowds, lots of autographs to sign and words to exchange with those we knew by sight. The French have a saying: *Partir, c'est mourir un peu* (To part is to die a little). How true, how true!

IV

WAR AND CHANGE, 1939–1948

ARMY AIR FORCES
CONVALESCENT CENTER
and
REGIONAL STATION HOSPITAL

MITCHEL FIELD, N. Y.

Certificate of Appreciation

IN GRATEFUL RECOGNITION OF UNSELFISH SERVICE

AWARDED TO

9

WAR

*P*at and I had agreed, some time before, to dance at the Bal des Petits Lits Blancs, a charity event held each year at Cannes in the South of France. Serge Lifar, with his partner from the Paris Opera, was to perform as well. I looked forward to seeing Lifar again, and was curious to see Pat and Serge together. They had been the two young stars of Diaghilev's company during its last years of existence, and I had heard of their 'friendly' squabbles, Pat always teasing outrageously and Serge always taking offence.

Jerry and I had already decided that we would spend our holiday with Pat and Otis a little away from Cannes, which was not restful nor affordable, at Cap d'Antibes, in a small hotel Pat knew, right on the water with its own little beach.

We stayed in London for a few days, then left for the South of France, Otis in charge of the big cardboard box with our costumes for the *pas de deux* from *Les Sylphides*. As I could never stand bad atmospheres – they depress me and make me physically sick – I shoved my bruised feelings into the bottom drawer and managed to be polite and even friendly towards Jerry – to his great surprise, I may add! Certain about my decisions for the future, I relaxed and started to enjoy a well-earned rest, swimming and dozing in the sun. At times I felt like a triumphant predator, biding my time, ready to pounce – and smiled to myself, picturing Jerry's anger and dismay.

On the morning of the ball, the sky clouded over rapidly. We were to perform on a platform built in a big garden, although the ball itself was to be held indoors. It did not look promising. Late morning we went to Cannes to have lunch with Lifar's party. The greetings were jovial, with lots of hugs and kisses and 'you look well!' – as if one wasn't supposed to! Serge immediately started to boast about his achievements and success at the Paris Opera. Pat, fed up with it, interrupted with, 'Serge, why are your nails always dirty?'

Outraged, Serge yelled, 'How dare you! They are not!' slamming his hands on the table for inspection. At that moment, a fly landed on his cheek. Serge brushed it off, the fly promptly paid a return visit. Pat slapped Serge's cheek, killing the fly. Serge, oblivious to the fact that Pat was after the fly, took the slap as a personal assault and was about to slap Pat back when the waiter appeared with plates of hors d'œuvres and got in the way of Serge's arm. His hand missed Pat's face, but swept the plates out of the waiter's hands, showering the people at the next table with our hors d'œuvres! Bedlam . . . confusion . . . excuses.

Pat loudly stated that he was after the fly, not Serge. The rest of us were in stitches! Trust Pat to start a farcical incident, accidentally on purpose! Life was never boring with Pat. After a general clean-up and more apologies, everyone piped down and had a good time. When we returned to Cannes that evening, it had started to drizzle. Greeted by the organisers and the pianist, we checked the tempos of our music then chatted with those people we knew from Paris.

The drizzle became steady rain and then a downpour by the time we were supposed to perform. An announcement was made that, due to the rain, regrettably our performances would have to be abandoned. After the crowd made polite noises of disappointment, we bade everyone a happy night and returned to the peace of Cap d'Antibes. Next morning, Pat and I were first on the beach, rubbing a mixture of olive oil and vinegar onto each other's backs (sunscreens were not around yet). Pat said, 'Jerry told me last night that you two have left the company!'

'*He* has, but *I* have no intention of doing so!' I proceeded to tell Pat how Jerry had informed me of his decision to leave, then about my talk with Colonel de Basil. Pat agreed with the Colonel's advice to me, not to rush into a big decision. He also added that the way things stood today, the company could be defunct tomorrow. Pat firmly believed that it was not a question of if but when – once the inevitable war with Germany was declared, all our plans would go down the drain and we would have to play our future by ear.

'What do you think you'll do?' I asked him.

'I think we should go to America. There we'll have the opportunity to sort out our immediate future. There are many possibilities . . . so Hurok tells me.' After a pause, Pat added, 'On the other hand, I might volunteer for the army!'

I looked at him a bit surprised, but he was deadly serious. After lunch, we all went for a stroll to the village.

'Hey, look . . . that bus is going to Sospel!' cried Otis. 'Let's go and see if we can find Colonel de Basil's farm!'

'Good idea!' we all chorused, including Jerry, who had insisted to Pat that he and the Colonel had not parted as enemies.

It is a beautiful drive to Sospel along the coast, past Nice, Monaco and Menton. As we got off the bus in the small village of Sospel, a figure riding a bicycle shot past us. I recognised it instantly. 'Wassiliev!' I screamed at the top of my lungs. He heard me, turned around and pedalled towards us, his pockmarked face wearing a big smile. He was delighted to see us. 'Is the Colonel here?' I asked.

'Yes, yes, we're all here. Come over, the Colonel will be so glad to see you!'

Showing us the little road going downhill, at the bottom of which was the Colonel's house, he raced down on his bike to warn the Colonel of our visit. When we were halfway down the hill, the so-called farm came into view. There was a small, modest house and a bare yard, in the middle of which was something that looked like a round pond, surrounded by a low wall of bricks. From the opposite side of the little valley rose the hills, on top of which was the French–Italian border. On top of the hill, right above the Colonel's house, stood a hut flying an Italian flag from its roof.

As we approached the gates, we saw the Colonel and Olga Morosova on the porch waving to us. Wassiliev and his wife, Marguerite, seemed to be fiddling with something in the yard. When we entered the yard, a series of loud bangs echoed through the valley. We were being greeted with fireworks. What a lovely welcome. Hugs exchanged, the last of the fireworks extinguished, we were about to step indoors when Pat pointed at the hut with the Italian flag and remarked, 'Look, look! Something's going on!'

Indeed, some uniformed men got into a military-looking vehicle then took off on a narrow road down the slope towards the Colonel's house. 'They probably think the war's started!' giggled Otis.

The Colonel rushed indoors, reappearing at the same time as the Italians rolled into the yard. He was holding a tray with a loaf of bread, a plate of salt, a bottle of vodka and some tumblers. As he stepped forward, he said to us, 'We all bow to them in the old Russian fashion and make noises of welcome!'

The Italians alighted from their vehicle and looked startled at the sight of the Colonel proffering the tray and saying in Russian, '*Dobro pojalovat*' (Welcome), then the rest of us joining in and making deep 'Russian' bows. The three Italians gazed at us with alarm and suspicion. The Colonel then addressed them in French, explaining that he was greeting his guests with fireworks and was very sorry to have alarmed them. The three men conferred in Italian for a moment, then one of them said in French, 'Good, good, but no more noise, please!'

The Colonel insisted they come in and have a friendly tumbler of vodka, telling them we were Russian ballet dancers and he was our director. After another short conference in Italian, they came in. Tumblers were filled, emptied and filled again. Olga produced some salami and dill pickles, and everyone became quite jolly and friendly. The sun was low in the sky when the three Italians, rather unsteady on their feet, walked back to their vehicle and drove back up the hill to their lookout post, where the Italian flag hung limp on the roof.

Marguerite and I wandered around the yard for a bit, talking. When we approached the round pond I noticed quite a number of goldfish floating in it, belly up. 'They're all dead!' I exclaimed.

'Well, yes . . .' replied Marguerite, then added matter-of-factly, 'Wassiliev washes his dirty socks in there.'

We had to catch the last bus to Antibes. Before leaving, I asked the Colonel if there was any news concerning the company's future engagements. 'No, not yet,' he said, but he was due in his Paris office in two days' time and was hoping for some positive developments.

On our way back to Antibes, our bus had to slow down and stop to let a large group of French soldiers pass. They were on horseback and making their way towards the Italian border. By the time we reached our hotel, we had all agreed that none of us wanted to risk being trapped in France, and hence that we must get back to London as soon as possible. The next morning we packed and took the bus to Cannes, where we tried to secure train tickets to Calais. We had a very long wait at the ticket office, where we discovered that because the trains were being requisitioned for the transport of troops, it took time to find out which train would still be taking ordinary passengers to the north. We waited all day, then finally were told that we were in luck and that the night train was available.

Our tickets in our pockets, we went to have dinner in town. We were starving, not having eaten all day. Dinner never tasted better. Later, tired but relieved to get going, we installed ourselves in our compartment (first class – soft seats!) for the long night ahead. There were still two vacant seats in our compartment and we hoped they would remain unoccupied, giving the four of us a bit more room to spread out, but no such luck! The door slid open and in came an old gentleman, whom we immediately recognised but had never met. We had seen him from the stage – he came to every performance and sat in the same seats, front row of the stalls, with a bald, middle-aged man. Curious to know who those two balletomanes were, I had asked Mr Jackson, our stage door-keeper. He knew everything about everybody.

'Ah, those two . . .' Mr Jackson smiled. Apparently, the old gentleman was an English lord, the middle-aged, bald one was his son. They kept themselves to themselves, did not socialise, and seemed very shy. No-one knew much about them.

Small world! Of all places, on a train in France, His Lordship appears in our compartment. 'Good evening,' he said curtly, placing his suitcase on the rack above his corner seat. As he turned to sit down, he had a moment of hesitation, and we could see that he recognised Pat and me.

He sat down, retrieved a book from his briefcase, and engrossed himself in its pages, clearly showing to the rest of us that he did not wish to be disturbed. Pat was obviously too tired to tease the old gentleman. As the train moved off, we removed our shoes and, stretching out our feet on each other's facing seat, were soon dozing off. Next morning, after an uncomfortable night, I felt somewhat stiff. Holding onto the handrail under the windows in the corridor, I discreetly did some *demi-pliés* and bends from side to side.

When we got to our flat in Shepherd Market, we discovered that Danilova was in the flat below ours. She was now one of the leading ballerinas in Massine's company, which was due to start its season at the Royal Opera House at the beginning of September, after their run at Drury Lane. Danilova and I got on well these days – there were no hard feelings between us about Jerry or anything else.

Next evening we had dinner with Uncle Freddie and the Ottleys at the Savoy Grill. They were certain that war was inevitable and would be declared any day. The important buildings were being padded at the base with sandbags. High in the sky above London, barrage balloons, looking like small zeppelins, started to appear. At drill halls and other designated premises, the distribution of gasmasks started. Air-raid shelters were assigned in every district. Instructions on how to black out windows, car headlights and so on were posted everywhere.

And although I was expecting it, I was still incredulous when on 3 September 1939, King George VI's voice told us on the radio that England had declared war on Germany. The horrors of war, for our much-loved England and all our friends, were to commence. Massine's season at the Opera House was cancelled. Quite a few of the dancers from both companies were now stranded in London. All our male British friends immediately volunteered for the army, navy and air force. Pat volunteered and was assigned to Civil Defence.

The proverbial British stiff upper lip and their sense of humour prevailed. Everyone was cool, calm and collected as they busied themselves as individuals and as a nation. Finding myself in this strange situation for the first time in my life, my thoughts were centered on what was happening and what it all meant, rather than on ballet matters or the roles I danced. All that suddenly ceased to be the centre of my universe. The fairy tale world took a serious back seat and left me feeling a bit orphaned.

We queued for hours for our gasmasks. They came in boxes that hung on our necks and had a tag on which we had to write our full name and address. The masks had to be with us at all times, although they were ill-fitting and probably useless. Walking up Piccadilly one day, I ran into André Eglevsky, his mother and his sister. They all had their gasmasks hanging from their necks. I was greatly amused to read on their tags, in Russian letters, 'Mama', 'Tania' and 'Andriouschka'. That's all. No address. Ah, Russians abroad!

No ship was sailing to New York, so we waited aimlessly, not quite knowing for what. 'Irischka, we must keep fit. Let's go to Legat's classes,' suggested Danilova. She was right – we had to stay in shape. From then on, every morning we took the bus to Nicolai Legat's school and attended his classes, which were absolutely wonderful! It was, too, a great pleasure to spend time with this great teacher and dancer, and with his wife, Mme Nadine Nicolaeva.

One night the loud sound of an air-raid warning sent us running to the air-raid shelter in Curzon Street. It was a good-sized cellar with benches that easily accommodated all those who took refuge there that night. After the all-clear, everyone quietly dispersed back to their homes. As it turned out, it was a false alarm. From then on, whenever we went to bed we kept some clothes and a small bag with the items we did not want to lose nearby – just in case!

Some of our friends suggested that we should all get out of London for a bit. The choice fell on Torquay in Devonshire. Off we went, eight of us, including Danilova and Paul Petroff, who by then was her companion. We all stayed at the Balmoral Hotel, a pleasant establishment with a nice garden. But our finances were dwindling at an alarming rate. Somehow we had to find a way to get to New York, so we all returned to London and started making enquiries, pestering some of our in-the-know, influential friends. We sat for hours at the American Embassy filling in our applications for visas. Puzzled by some of the questions on the forms, I needed constant help. Never having been required in the past to deal with visas, I did not have a clue how to answer some of the questions.

Danilova and I also resumed our classes with Legat, Petroff joining in. The good news came just in time, as our financial position was becoming catastrophic. The American ship SS *Washington* was sailing in a few days' time on its last crossing to New York. Thanks to Captain Bruce Ottley's efforts, all dancers stranded in England obtained their passage. There was hurried packing, hurried farewells to friends. My heart was heavy, not knowing when we would meet again. Pat was the last person we saw in London before we left. He was waiting to be discharged from his Civil Defence duties, as the authorities had decided he would serve his country better by continuing to practise his art. Danilova was very funny in her speculations as to why Pat was being discharged. Knowing Pat, we could easily imagine the circus he was creating in Civil Defence. We totally agreed with and were delighted by the authorities' decision to return Pat to us!

To accommodate everyone on the ship, every bed, bunk and space had to be filled. Hence the cabins were divided into women only and men only. I shared a small cabin with Danilova and Alicia Markova. We were warned that the crossing would take longer because the ship would be zigzagging to avoid German submarines; it took us eleven days to reach New York and most of the time the sea was rough. When night fell, every porthole was blacked out and stepping on deck was forbidden. Alicia Markova was not a good sailor, and spent much of the time in bed looking very poorly. The rest of us were all right, thankfully.

It was not long before Pat and Otis surfaced in New York, but I was not to see them for some time as, shortly after we docked in New York and, while I was enjoying a stay with my parents, Jerry called and announced that we were off to Hollywood. He had agreed to sign a contract for me to appear in a dancing–acting role in a film produced by Winfield 'Winnie' Sheehan for MGM. Irritated that again I had not been consulted, and still nursing a hope of rejoining the company, I protested. 'I don't want to be in a film. I'm not an actress, I'm a dancer. I don't belong in films! I don't want to go to Hollywood!' I screamed down the phone.

'Be reasonable.' Jerry's voice was calm. 'The money you've been offered is more than excellent, and we badly need it to tide us over until we sort ourselves out.'

I had to admit he had a point. With no news from the Colonel, I had no choice but to play ball and earn some money. My parents, surprised as they were, on the whole took the Hollywood news in their stride. A few days later I had to leave them and get back to New York to pack and face this new, unwelcome challenge.

FLORIAN

When I got to New York, my first question to Jerry was, 'How did this film producer know where to find me?'

'He called Hurok's office and Hurok put me in touch with Mr Sheehan. By the way, I've joined Hurok's organisation as his promotions manager. He also wants you to be under his personal management.'

I felt like a pawn in other people's games. *Ha!* I mused, *my time will come – in three-and-a-half months I'll be twenty-one! Finally, of age! And to be reckoned with* . . . Looking forward to that glorious day, I started packing for Hollywood.

Before we left New York, the film script arrived with a charming note from the producer. It was to be called *Florian*. As I remember it, Florian was the name of one of two Lipizzaner horses that had been a present from the Emperor Franz Josef I to Maria Jeritza, his favourite opera singer and, in her youth, a famous Viennese beauty. By now she was middle-aged, and married to the producer Winnie Sheehan. Her

Lipizzaner horses, which she adored, lived with them on their ranch. Maria, wanting to show off these pure-white horses, suggested that Winnie make a film featuring Florian. They concocted a story and the scriptwriter did the rest. Bless them! This is how the story went.

At the court of Franz Josef I in the 1880s, a prince is betrothed to a princess, but . . . the prince is in love with a dancer and the princess is in love with the stable master. She sneaks off to the stables; the prince sneaks off to rendezvous with his ballerina. Oh dear! The ballerina is jealous of the princess. She dances at a command performance at court, giving the prince dirty looks. Then she goes to the stables and pats Florian! Anyway, let's skip the middle . . .

It ends with political unrest. The princess and the stable master escape separately, I think to Switzerland. So does the horse, which is instrumental in their reunion. The prince gets the boot from the ballerina and she, too, goes abroad. Well, I suppose everybody lives happily ever after!

This stupid story darkened my spirits further, and I was in a proper bolshy mood all the way to the West Coast. We were met in Los Angeles by a very friendly person from MGM and taken to the Beverly Hills Hotel, where we were lodged in one of the private bungalows dotted around the garden. There were flowers for me from Winnie Sheehan, with a note welcoming us and saying that he was expecting us at his office the next morning. With my spirits in better shape, I made up my mind to take whatever came in my stride, to consider the experience as just a job, and to try to do my best in this genre I knew nothing about. But I could not chase away my apprehension and nervousness.

That night we had dinner with our old friends Tamara and Akim Tamiroff. Akim was, by then, a well-established character actor. He knew all the Hollywood ropes and the way the 'factory of dreams' worked. He offered to help me rehearse my lines and in any other way he could. It was so incredibly generous of him and helped my morale a great deal.

Next morning a car was sent for us and we presented ourselves at the MGM studio gates. At the entrance to the office building, someone was waiting to conduct us to Mr Sheehan's office. Greetings exchanged,

Mr Sheehan paid me and our company enthusiastic compliments, telling us that he and his wife had attended many of our performances.

I liked his gracious manner and the charismatic smile on his podgy face. We sat down to discuss business, but I kept silent, as it was all 'Chinese' to me. Finally, I had a chance to ask when I would be due for the screen test. (Akim had told me that this was the normal procedure.) 'Not until your dresses are ready. Then our cameraman will want you for a short test,' replied Mr Sheehan.

'But suppose,' I insisted, 'I look unsuitable or photograph badly. Better to have a proper test first, no?'

An annoyed look from Jerry clearly conveyed, 'Shut up!'

'Don't you worry about that,' said Mr Sheehan, smiling kindly.

At this point we were interrupted by the appearance of a good-looking young man. He was the well-known dress designer Adrian. The sketches he showed us, meant for my role, were lovely. Then someone took me to the wardrobe department to have my measurements taken. When I returned to his office, Mr Sheehan gaily exclaimed, 'We have a deal. Your contract is signed!' Jerry looked well pleased. 'To celebrate,' continued Mr Sheehan, 'you're both coming to dinner at my house. Maria's looking forward to meeting you!'

Then he told me that the next day I would meet Mr Waxman, the musical director, and the Latvian choreographer for my solo variation. He also told me that Robert Young was starring as the Stable Master; a Miss Gilbert, a newcomer, as the Princess; Lee Bowman as the Prince; and that we would be directed by Edwin L. Marin. The only name I knew was Robert Young. I had seen him in many films and liked his personality.

Before we left, I was given a timetable for my appointments – the days to come promised to be very busy. The contract was signed, there was no way out. I had to make the best of the situation.

Maria and Winnie Sheehan's house was beautiful, as was our hostess. Blonde, statuesque and youthful, with lovely looks and a Viennese accent, she was European through and through. Her charm conquered me right away. Several of their friends were present, all easy to talk to.

That made me feel less tied-in-knots, and I enjoyed the evening, thinking that perhaps it would all turn out better than I had feared.

My experiences the next day proved that my optimism was misplaced. My first meeting was with the musical director, Mr Waxman. His first question to me was, 'What's your specialty?'

I was totally taken aback. 'I don't have a specialty. I'm a ballerina, not a circus performer!' Specialty indeed! It took me a while to sort that one out.

He listened with interest to my explanations of classical ballet and the differences between classical, demi-character and character. We even had a few laughs. That matter out of the way, Mr Waxman outlined how he saw my variation at the Emperor's court – me in a white tutu and tall white wig, the other dancers around me in similar costumes, except with ankle-length skirts. The music? 'Let's have something lively!' he said. 'The famous Hungarian *chardash*.'

I thought he was joking, but no, he was deadly serious. I decided it was better to let the producer deal with that *chardash* idea. I felt I was not up to it. Making non-committal noises, I suggested we get together with Mr Sheehan to finalise the choice of music. I made my excuses and was taken to a rehearsal studio to meet the Latvian choreographer. A small, blonde man shook my hand; he looked even more ill at ease than I was. He asked if I had any ideas. No, I did not. Did he?

'Well . . .' Obviously he had none. Offering me a chair, he started pacing up and down the studio, punching one fist into the open palm of his other hand, muttering, 'Ideas, ideas . . . they will come . . . good ideas . . .'

I felt sorry for the poor chap, but here was another problem to be discussed with Mr Sheehan. My optimism flew out the window. When I returned to the hotel, Jerry had news from Mr Hurok. With much glee, he told me that Hurok had received a call from Colonel de Basil asking where I was, as the company was leaving for Australia. Hurok had replied that I was under contract to MGM, making a film and not available. My heart sank in despair. The other news was that a house on Roxbury Drive had been rented for us from the mother of Gracie Fields.

I really could not have cared less! But that was not all. 'We can even buy a car now! What colour would you like?'

'Why does it suddenly matter what I like?' Tears stinging my eyes, I went into the garden behind the bungalow and cried my eyes out. All in all, it was a bad day.

In the days that followed, however, things started to fall into place at the studio, thanks to Mr Sheehan. The music question was sorted out. The 'no ideas' choreographer was replaced by a husband-and-wife team, Lenny and Garry, choreographers from Vienna. I liked them very much, as people and for their obvious professionalism. My Adrian outfits were ready – and they were lovely. I did a screen test, and found the director easy to get on with and very helpful. Now it was up to me. I had to stop brooding and try to do my best.

We moved into the Roxbury Drive house, where a brand-new pale green Pontiac graced the garage. Meeting Robert Young and the rest of the cast was a formal affair. There was none of the camaraderie I was used to in the ballet world. It was among the people in the make-up department that I found human warmth and friendship.

One lunchtime at the canteen, a little girl in a sailor suit approached me and asked, in that straightforward, endearing way children have, 'Are you the ballerina?' We chatted for a few minutes – her lovely little face was even lovelier than on the silver screen. Yes, it was Shirley Temple. I had heard so much from Akim Tamiroff about how amazing this child was – talented and easy to work with. Meeting her made my day!

When I was not on call for the next day's shooting and did not have to get up at five a.m. to be in make-up at six a.m., we would have dinner at the Tamiroffs. While Tamara was cooking *kotletki*, Akim helped me with my lines and gave me impromptu acting lessons in the form of exercises of his own invention, usually in Russian. One day he wanted me to reduce myself to tears. Each time I attempted it, I burst into nervous giggles with not a drop of tears! Finally Akim lost his temper and shouted at the top of his voice, 'Cry! Cry, damn you, cry!' I jumped out of my skin with fright and burst into tears. 'Aha!' shouted Akim, and then in a most caressing voice, 'Good, good . . . keep it up . . . good!'

Hearing the noise, Tamara burst into Akim's room and surveyed the scene. 'What are you doing to Irina?' she demanded. I was still sniffling and shaking.

'Hee, hee, hee,' chuckled Akim, well pleased with himself. 'Bring her a drop of brandy.' Dear, adorable Akim. He was such fun. I loved him and Tamara dearly.

For my part, I had no more problems during filming. I did not enjoy it, but it did not really bother me either. It was just a job, in novel and fascinating-to-observe surroundings. Before leaving Hollywood in the summer of 1940, I saw the rushes of the film. The best thing in it, I thought, was the Lipizzaner horse Florian! We packed our things in the green Pontiac and started on our three-day drive to New York.

BALLET WARS

As soon as we reached New York I went to stay with my parents in Sea Cliff for a few days. All was well with them, but Papa looked tired to me. There was a letter from Tassia, who was planning to come to New York in the near future. I rejoiced at the thought of seeing my best friend again.

As I had not had the chance, or time, to practise in Hollywood, I felt in great need of classes with Anatole Vilzak to get back in shape. I returned to New York and, during the week, took two classes a day, one in the morning and one in the afternoon. The weekends I spent with my parents. And I also celebrated my twenty-first birthday with them, finally! I was of age now. The following week I signed, myself, my contract with Sol Hurok. From then on I was under his personal management. He promptly asked me to go to South America, as a guest ballerina with Massine's company. I had to go but felt apprehensive. I did not like Mr Denham, the director of the company, and there were already three leading ballerinas in the company – Alicia Markova, Alexandra Danilova, and Mia Slavenska, whom I had never met. I did not think they would be overjoyed by my presence – one more to share roles with. Only Massine would be pleased, as apparently he had asked Hurok to get me to come. I would be dancing *Les Sylphides* and *Swan Lake*, and learning *Coppélia*, which I had never danced.

The tour lasted from June until August, with performances in Rio de Janeiro, São Paolo, Montevideo and Buenos Aires. Jerry, of course, came too, as Hurok's personal representative. I knew most of the company, and it felt good to be with 'my own people' again. Markova greeted me in a gracious and friendly manner. Slavenska was great – we immediately struck up a friendship. She was beautiful and fun. Danilova was haughty and icy, eyeing me with that sideways glance of hers. With our history, I could not blame her for being irritated by my presence. But worse was to come.

Massine made the mistake of asking Danilova to show me the Swanilda role in *Coppélia*. Danilova furiously declined and stopped talking to me altogether. She loved the role and already had Slavenska to share it with – now me as well! Slavenska promptly stepped in and said that she would be glad to work with me on the role, as did Igor Youskevitch, one of the outstanding leading artists and a brilliant partner. He danced the role of Franz in *Coppélia*, while Simon Semenoff mimed Dr Coppelius. My colleagues were wonderful. I learned the role very quickly, loved it and was ready to perform it in São Paolo.

On the day I was to perform, Slavenska hardly spoke to me and I could not think what was the matter. In the evening, a beautiful bouquet of flowers was delivered to my dressing room. The card read, 'Don't pay any attention to my mood today. I'm jealous. It will pass. Good luck for tonight. Love Mia.' That's how she was, Mia, a wonderful, generous person, a great artist and a good friend.

My debut in *Coppélia* received rave notices and Massine decreed that for the rest of the South American tour, the role of Swanilda would be exclusively mine. I was delighted to have a new ballet added to my guest performances, one so different in character and spirit from the old classics. It was gay, it was fun! Mia took it very well – after all, I was leaving at the end of the tour and she would dance it again, she reasoned.

But with Danilova I was firmly in the doghouse. She did not talk to me at all for a long, long time. As for Massine, I can only imagine the unpleasant scenes he had to endure. It happens in the best of families! Upon our return to New York, I had some good news from Sol Hurok. Colonel de Basil's company was to sail from Australia to Los Angeles, where they were to perform at the Philharmonic Auditorium, then come to New York for a season at the 51st Street Theatre, sponsored by Sol Hurok and Mr Behymer, a San Francisco impresario.

I was to join the company for these two occasions. When I told Hurok I would like to rejoin the company for good, he said, 'No, I have plans, big plans. There'll be a new, wonderful ballet company. I'll present it and that's where you should be. After New York, I'll wash my hands of de Basil's company. I don't see how, now that Europe is out of the question, he can survive financially. He has no backers, no future.' That was bad, horrid news! I simply did not want to believe it. *Surely the Colonel will think of something, will find a way! Hopefully the war will soon end.* Rejecting all negative thoughts, I looked forward to being reunited with my tribe and once more dancing all the roles I loved so much. Hurok told me that Balanchine was to choreograph a new work for the New York season, *Balustrade*, to Igor Stravinsky's Concerto for Violin and Orchestra, with scenery and costumes by Pavel Tchelitchev, a well-known Russian painter.

Things can't be that bad, I thought, *if the company can afford to mount a new Balanchine production.* Still, I wanted to know more about Hurok's new company and his big plans for it. He told me it had to do with Lucia Chase, a ballet artist in her own right, who was intimately associated with an already existing company called the Mordkin Ballet. She was a lady of determination, who wanted to create a great American company, to be called Ballet Theatre (later American Ballet Theatre), one that would present a strong, varied repertoire and promote young American dancers and choreographers. According to Hurok, there were no financial problems; Lucia Chase was able and willing to subsidise the development of the company.

I had no way of knowing how true Hurok's version of these events was. Soon after this conversation with him, my eyes were opened to his capacity to manipulate situations to his advantage. Perhaps they were just the tactics of a successful businessman. I asked Jerry about the proposed new company. He was rather evasive and economical with his comments, but told me that Anton Dolin was interested and involved in discussions with Lucia Chase, and that there was talk of Alicia Markova being asked to join the venture.

I decided to tackle Dolin next and find out more. Pat had great experience in ballet matters, and his views and advice were very much sought after. Before leaving for Los Angeles to join Colonel de Basil's company, I spent an evening with Dolin. According to him, everything was progressing well between Lucia Chase and Sol Hurok, except for one stumbling block – the director of the future company. Lucia Chase was an excellent demi-character dancer, Pat said, and wanted to continue to pursue her dancing career, which held a very important place in her life. She had tragically lost her husband and found herself a young widow with two small sons. In due course, she succeeded in two different but parallel ways of life – her private life with her sons and family, and her artistic life. Lucia Chase had no intention of being the director of the company. She just wanted to be one of the artists, with no special privileges. She already had a director and saw no reason for a change, but Sol Hurok wanted Jerry to take over the directorship.

'And that's the stumbling block!' said Pat, adding, 'I agree with Hurok. Jerry will be very good! He has experience, he has a way with dancers, and he's liked by Fokine and Nijinska, whom we'll need if we want to establish a strong repertoire to start with.'

I had to agree. Jerry would be an excellent choice. His six years of close association with our company and participation in running it with such success made him a great asset.

'But Lucia Chase doesn't want him. Hurok and I are working on it.' Pat was confident that all was going to plan and all difficulties between Lucia Chase and Hurok were ironing themselves out. He was also confident that Jerry would be accepted as director.

'In order not to bruise Jerry's ego, it's best if you don't meet Lucia Chase yet. She hopes that you and Alicia Markova will be our two ballerinas. She wants you badly!'

All these politics seemed frightfully complicated to me, and I tried not to dwell on it all. But the day after my chat with Pat, I could not resist asking Jerry, 'How are the negotiations progressing? Are you being appointed as the director of Ballet Theatre?'

His response was, 'There's a problem . . . Lucia Chase wants me but she doesn't want you!'

I felt contempt and pity for this person, who was so tormented by his touchy ego that he was not able to be straight with me. I could not resist needling him. 'Oh, that's no problem!' I said. 'You must accept the directorship. That's what you want. And I'll remain with Colonel de Basil. That's what I want. That way we're both happy.'

For a moment he eyed me with suspicion, then squeezed out a, 'Don't be silly!'

I did, of course, discuss the situation at great length with my parents. They understood my worry and sadness at not being part of Colonel de Basil's company any more. Papa thought that, due to the war and Sol Hurok's involvement with Ballet Theatre, the Colonel would face hard times. With Hurok monopolising the North American bookings, where would the Colonel take his company? South America?

Mother lamented that if I remained with the Colonel, I would be somewhere far away again. 'Please stay here, near us,' she kept insisting.

I really did not have much choice – I was still under contract to Hurok for the next two years. I had to face that reality and make the best of it. On the flight to Los Angeles I anticipated the joy and excitement of seeing my old friends and colleagues. It was as if time had not passed. I felt at home from the first class, the first rehearsal, and I performed my old roles as if I had never stopped doing so. There were a few new faces in the company who had gone to Australia to escape the war in Europe. Among them was one of the leading dancers, Yura (George) Skibine, a tall, blue-eyed, good-looking young man. He was assigned to rehearse *Les Cent Baisers* with me, with a view to partnering me in it sometimes. I found him taciturn, silent and rather uninterested in learning the role. I was intrigued and promised myself that I would work on this standoffish young man until I got a friendly response.

After a long interval, Toumanova, Riabouchinska and I, the so-called 'Three Baby Ballerinas', were reunited once again. It felt so right, how it should be, the trio complete again! Our Los Angeles performances passed with the usual success and get-togethers with friends, especially with my beloved Tamara and Akim Tamiroff. Back in New York we opened at the 51st Street Theatre to great reviews and full, enthusiastic houses. The predictions I was hearing from the Hurok 'camp' of gloom and doom for de Basil's company seemed to me incredible.

Balanchine's new ballet was not the success that was hoped for; it did not last long and was soon relegated to oblivion. Tamara Toumanova, at the end of the New York season, left the company yet again, this time to join Massine's company. My guesting was over and Tania Riabouchinska remained alone, loyal, like Lichine and the rest of our 'old guard'. I felt like a rat deserting a sinking ship, my artistic 'home', to which I owed so much. I felt rotten, ashamed of myself and angry with the world.

Once again there were sad goodbyes as the company, still half-heartedly managed by Hurok, departed for Mexico and then to Cuba. Some ten days later, Hurok asked me to go to Cuba, again as a guest artist. Jerry was to go as Hurok's personal representative, to investigate rumours that the dancers were protesting about cuts to their salaries and that some of them were threatening to strike.

What Hurok omitted to say was that he had withheld a sum of money from the Colonel, due to him by contract, and hence the dancers could not be paid in full. Not being able to afford even one square meal a day, the dancers rose mistakenly against the Colonel, who himself was in a desperate situation. Only upon arrival in Havana did I discover the devious plans forged by Hurok and Jerry to destroy and sink de Basil's company.

Surprisingly, Jerry, for a change, decided not to keep me in the dark. He asked me to take the side of the strikers and refuse to perform as well. He encouraged the striking dancers to hold firm while he talked privately with those whom Hurok wanted to join Ballet Theatre. I was disgusted at such cynicism and refused Jerry's request for me not to perform. We had a fierce row but I stood my ground. In no way did I want to be associated with these dirty dealings.

'You suffer from misplaced loyalties!' yelled Jerry. 'You put your parents first, Colonel de Basil second and me, your husband, in third place! What kind of wife are you?'

'Obviously the wrong kind!' I yelled back. 'Divorce me. It's the best solution for both of us!'

The word 'divorce' produced the effect of a boiling kettle being switched off. 'Don't be silly,' he said quietly and left the room.

Nothing was resolved. The subject was dropped. I went on performing. To cut a long, unsavoury story short, Colonel de Basil got wind of what was going on and filed a law suit against Hurok and Jerry, with charges of 'conspiracy and sabotage'.

Hurok, upon learning of this, instructed Jerry to leave Cuba immediately, in order to avoid being served with the papers, which a Cuban lawyer friend of the Colonel was preparing. To make certain that his instructions were carried out, Hurok sent down his 'right arm', Mae Froman, to collect Jerry and me. And that's how, returning to the hotel after class, I found Mae in our room helping Jerry to pack our bags and hurriedly explaining to me why we had to sail to Miami by the afternoon boat.

Efficient as ever, Mae not only had the tickets but also had a taxi waiting by the side door of the hotel to take us to the docks. 'Hurry, hurry up and change. We mustn't be seen leaving together,' urged Mae. 'Jerry and I will go to the taxi first with the luggage. You follow and try not to attract attention if you see anyone downstairs.'

Mae and Jerry went to the taxi. I had nothing to change into, as Mae had packed the lot. I was longing for a shower but contented myself with splashing my face with cold water. A thought crossed my mind: *What if I refuse to leave? More dramas? Upsetting my parents again? Oh hell, I'd better go.*

As I was leaving the room, I noticed quite a few oranges left on the table. I hurriedly put them into my headscarf and tied the corners. I always hated wasting food (still do). As I reached the bottom of the stairs at the back of the lobby, the knot on my scarf came undone and all my oranges rolled out, making their way along the slippery floor towards the feet of Papa Grigoriev, who was sitting in the lobby. He looked up in surprise. 'Oh, my angel . . .'

I had a moment of indecision . . . then rushed to pick up the oranges, gathering them back into my scarf and depositing the bundle in Papa Grigoriev's arms. The poor man looked totally bewildered as I said to him, 'It's for you!' I gave him a peck on the cheek and dashed through the side door to the waiting taxi.

'What took you so long?' asked Mae as the taxi drove off.

Bursting into laughter, I told them about the hiccup I had with the oranges. Mae and Jerry did not think it was funny at all. 'You see, Mae, what I have to put up with. Constant aggravation, stubborn as a mule!' Jerry was really annoyed.

We drove in silence until Mae burst into laughter. 'It must have been quite funny!' she said. Dear Mae . . . a lovely friend.

Eventually there was a court hearing in New York. Colonel de Basil lost the case on a technicality – he did not show up in court. How could he, poor man? He was in South America, battling on to obtain bookings for his company. Jerry was finally nominated managing director of Ballet Theatre and the 'defectors' from de Basil's company were brought over to join. Among them was Yura Skibine.

According to Charles Payne's 1978 book *American Ballet Theatre*, Jerry wrote a letter to Philip Richardson, the *Dancing Times* editor, at about this time. Payne reproduced the letter, which recounts the strike in Cuba, verbatim in his book. If genuine, then it totally misrepresents the facts in Jerry's favour – I did not refuse to perform, I did not threaten to return to my mother, and the Colonel was never rude to me. Although I knew nothing of the letter at the time, this constant need of Jerry's to manipulate the truth in his favour made me reluctant to believe anything he said. I felt oppressed by a constant feeling of insecurity and unrest.

As Dolin, Jerry and I stepped out of the lift, straight into Miss Chase's vast apartment on Park Avenue, she greeted me warmly and exclaimed, 'Finally! I've been longing to meet you for ages, but these naughty men have been hiding you from me!'

She laughed, slipped her arm through mine and ushered me into her living room. I immediately liked this good-looking lady, with her non-gushy, genuine warmth and expressive, beautiful eyes. By the time we sat down to dinner, my apprehensive feelings about the whole set-up had vanished. I had listened to Miss Chase's plans and learned that Fokine and Nijinska were to start working on two new productions for Ballet Theatre.

By the end of the evening, I felt a surge of enthusiasm at being part of the new venture. As time went on and I observed Miss Chase at work, she impressed me as a highly cultured, dedicated professional, who was wise, diplomatic and used her strength with gentleness and discretion. By the end of my first year with the company, I had learned to respect, admire and love her.

Soon after our first meeting I went to join and meet the rest of the company, who were already installed at Jacob's Pillow for the start of rehearsals. Jacob's Pillow, in Becket, Massachusetts, was the headquarters of Ted Shawn's company, Men Dancers. Dolin and Ballet Theatre leased the premises from Ted Shawn for the duration of our rehearsals, in preparation for our opening season in autumn. It consisted of a main long wooden building and rustic cabins, all surrounded by forests and fields. One covered rehearsal space and another big platform had been erected on the edge of the forest.

It was an idyllic place to work, surrounded by countryside and well away from the city. We all lived as if in a commune, taking turns at daily chores and having great fun. We rehearsed very intensely with Dolin, Antony Tudor and, upon her arrival, Mme Nijinska, who choreographed my role, Lise, in *La Fille mal gardée*. I was so happy to see her again and start working with her on this new (for me), famous ballet, in which my beloved teacher Mme Preobrajenska had enjoyed enormous success at the Maryinsky Theatre. It became one of my most loved roles – it was funny, gay, and gave me great scope in the comical scenes. Audiences everywhere loved it, and I achieved great personal success. Mme Nijinska was more than happy with me, which was so good for my morale and removed my feeling of insecurity at being thrown into a new company with people I hardly knew.

Mme Nijinska and her husband lived in a hotel in the little town nearby and were brought to rehearsals by car. Quite a few of us were billetted at Mother Derby's farmhouse, down the lane from the main compound. Mother Derby was quite a character – she reminded me of those cosy-looking grannies in children's books. She fed us well and we abided by her strict rules. Before meals she would send us into her garden to pick raspberries, which we later devoured with rich cream from her farm. We cleaned our own rooms. There was a bathroom, of sorts, but the toilet was in a shed outdoors.

There was much laughter and I found my American colleagues friendly, full of fun and easy to live and work with. I had a lovely little room with chintz curtains and a view of the fields beyond. Jerry was a rare visitor, as his work was at the office in New York. It was good to be in the country, away from the Russian Tea Room, enjoying the company of dancers my age, feeling free from restraint, light-hearted and relaxed. I hired a bicycle and pedalled up the lane to class and rehearsals. Some others followed suit, among them Yura Skibine, who also stayed at Mother Derby's, and who was becoming more and more friendly.

The weeks of rehearsals we spent at Jacob's Pillow went by in a happy, productive atmosphere. As I grew to know Lucia Chase better, I appreciated her more and more. She was truly one of us – so much so that one forgot that it was thanks to her that it was all happening! I found Lucia, as we all called her, most caring towards me. With unobtrusive sensitivity, she strived to make me feel welcome and at home. I was touched and grateful.

Fokine, who was to devise a new work for the whole company, based on the theme of Bluebeard, did not come to Jacob's Pillow. As usual, he worked out his choreography at home. He had carefully chosen and timed the Offenbach music and worked on it with Antal Dorati. It therefore took Fokine much less time to rehearse the dancers in a new production than it took other choreographers. There was no trial and error. The work, in its every detail, was stored in his mind – all Fokine had to do was to transmit it to the dancers. The few short weeks we spent in New York before opening night were more than sufficient for him to produce *Bluebeard*, complete, well rehearsed, polished and ready for its premiere.

There was much to do in New York: meetings with Marcel Vertes, the designer of the scenery and costumes for *Bluebeard*; costume fittings with Mme Karinska; and Fokine sent word that he wanted me at his home to talk about my role in *Bluebeard*. I was a bit surprised at that request but happy to satisfy my longstanding curiosity and see where, and how, he lived.

On the appointed afternoon, half an hour too early in my anxiousness not to be late, I stood gazing at Fokine's Tudor-style house in Riverdale, on the banks of the Hudson River. Speculating about what awaited me inside the house, I slowly paced up and down, checking my watch. At three o'clock exactly I rang the bell, hoping Fokine would notice my punctuality. A woman opened the door, all smiles. She showed me into a big room I assumed was Fokine's study, saying she would inform Fokine of my arrival. I stood in the middle of the room, fascinated by two life-sized paintings – one of Fokine in costume, the other a portrait of his wife – hanging on the wall opposite the door. I knew they were Fokine's work, having heard of them from his son, Vitale. They were truly beautiful! The diamond ring on Mme Fokine's finger drew my astonished attention – it looked so real – limpid and delicately sparkling. *Did Fokine insert a real stone into the painting?* Unable to restrain my curiosity, I climbed onto a chair to check. As I was poking my finger at the ring, I heard Fokine's voice behind me, his tone full of indignation, 'Fokine never fakes!' I almost fell, scrambling off the chair, blushing with acute embarrassment and wishing I could miraculously disappear. 'Satisfied?' he asked.

'It's beautiful,' I mumbled, glancing at him. The specs were down his nose, a good sign – he was amused. I relaxed a little but still felt like a fool.

Inviting me to sit down, Fokine asked me about Jacob's Pillow and how I was adjusting to the company. My answers were all positive and he seemed to be satisfied. Then, coming to the point of my visit, he outlined my role as Boulotte, Bluebeard's last wife. Boulotte had to be high-spirited, mischievous and funny. In the *pas de deux* for her and Bluebeard (Dolin), there was much playful, rough handling. I would be thrown, slide on the ground and roll to the footlights.

'Pat and I will have such fun doing that!' I exclaimed excitedly.

Fokine remarked, 'Vera Petrovna' (Mme Fokine) 'pointed out to me that you might get bruised.' Fokine's challenging look, so familiar to me by now, clearly asked, 'Are you going to complain?'

'Bruised?' I hastened to reply. 'You can break me into little pieces and I'll love it!'

He burst into laughter. For the first time ever, I saw and heard his laugh. For a moment, just a moment, he was off his pedestal.

Next day we started rehearsals. Once again, I had to marvel at the ease and speed with which the work progressed. Very occasionally, Fokine glanced at his notes, but all he had to do was to transmit it to us and work with us on his desired rendition of the ballet. From the first rehearsal, I knew that Boulotte would be one of my best and much-loved roles. *Bluebeard* met all expectations – a beautiful production in the grand manner, it was a huge success with the critics as well as audiences. It remained in the repertoire of Ballet Theatre for many, many years to come.

During our rehearsal period at Jacob's Pillow and in New York, we all had a chance to get acquainted with each other and bond into a harmonious group. I had been brought up on the Russian ballet tradition and Diaghilev's legacy, which were now deeply rooted in me, but it was soon evident to me that I needed to be diplomatic and above all keep an open mind about new trends and ideas.

The young American dancers in the company were vibrant, versatile and talented – some exceptionally so – achieving, in the years to come, great success and fame, among them Jerome Robbins, Nora Kaye, Donald Saddler and Maria Karnilova. These friends and colleagues are alas no more, except for Donald Saddler, whom I love dearly. He has warmed my heart with sixty-two years of unconditional friendship, which I treasure.

Although some of the dancers loved the old classics and the works of Fokine, they leant more towards Antony Tudor's style of choreography – with psychological themes and stiff, angular gestures. Tudor's ballets were beautiful and emotionally powerful. Two distinct camps emerged – the Antony Tudor camp and the Russian camp. The rest were neutral. Luckily, these personal preferences did not interfere with the good, friendly vibes within the company. The only person who openly resented what was later tagged the 'Russian invasion' was Agnes de Mille, several of whose works were in the company's repertoire. At every opportunity she would mutter, 'These bloody Russians!'

On one occasion years later, when I happened to be in New York, I was standing by her chair in the wings when someone mentioned that Mikhail Baryshnikov had been newly appointed artistic director of American Ballet Theatre. Agnes de Mille crossly exclaimed, 'Again, those bloody Russians!'

Jokingly, I tapped her on the shoulder and reminded her, 'Agnes, I'm Russian too.'

'Oh, nonsense,' she replied. 'You're one of us!'

Eccentric and witty, Agnes de Mille did some wonderful choreography for musicals and films, and was an excellent, eloquent speaker.

The good, friendly atmosphere in the company was largely due to Lucia Chase. She was one of us and never made us aware that she was the 'power behind the throne'. If she felt that one of the dancers deserved a chance to prove themselves, she would insistently point it out to Jerry. She was always right in her appraisal of a dancer's skills and talents. Interested in new ideas, she instinctively knew which new production had the potential for success.

The company was getting ready for its first season as Ballet Theatre, which took place in Mexico City. The Fokines were with us, as the premiere of *Bluebeard* was set for 27 October 1942 at the beautiful Palacio de Bellas Artes. Antal Dorati was now the musical director of Ballet Theatre, which gave me an added sense of security and familiarity.

Marcel Vertes came over to see to the lighting of his scenery for *Bluebeard*, and Sol Hurok arrived with Mae Froman. The Mexican audiences were always wonderfully appreciative, but when the curtain came back down on the premiere of *Bluebeard*, they went wild. The ballet was all we had hoped for and more. Fokine had produced, yet again, a superb work. Sol Hurok was ecstatic! Besides loving what he saw, he could also count on the ballet being a box office attraction. Pat was superb as Bluebeard. With his brisk movements and tongue-in-cheek humour, he made the role his very own, and to my mind was never equalled in it. Our 'rough' *pas de deux* was delightfully rough; Pat and I loved it, and so did the audiences. The bruises on my hips were a small price to pay for the joy I felt at dancing the role of Boulotte.

Encouraged by our successful new start, we now felt confident about our November season at the 44th Street Theatre in New York. Although by then I felt accepted by my colleagues, I missed my old tribe and often wondered how they were getting on in South America. I particularly missed Riabouchinska and Toumanova. In my heart and mind we were bound together, the three of us. I felt it was a great pity that life had separated us.

Back in New York, we had our last rehearsals with Nijinska for the premiere of *La Fille mal gardée*. I started to experience a serious case of butterflies, so anxious was I to please her and my parents, who were so excited to see me in my two new roles, Boulotte and Lise. As I was all tense and fidgety, nursing my fluttering butterflies, I admired the outward calm of Alicia Markova (whose real name was Marks – she was born in England). Only occasionally would she show her inner tension, with a biting remark in a quiet voice – so British. We Russians are loud! And, oh dear, so dramatic.

On the night of the premiere of *La Fille mal gardée*, I was warming up on the dimly lit, empty stage when Mme Nijinska appeared. She said she had come early to see that all was well with me and to say 'no down, no feathers'. She spoke softly, tenderly caressed my cheek and made the sign of the cross over my chest. I was deeply moved and wished that those who had been the victims of her sarcasm and bad temper could see her now and believe that she was not one hundred per cent dragon! Underneath the often-displayed horrid bad temper, there lurked a tender heart.

As I stood in the wings waiting for the curtain to go up and for my first entrance, an extraordinary feeling took hold of me, a sensation I had never experienced before and have never experienced since. Utter inner joy possessed my entire being, as if I were floating on a cloud, with invisible hands lightly supporting me. My dancing just happened all by itself – I was propelled into technical intricacies with an ease I'd never felt before. I was not pretending to be Lise, I *was* Lise, and hugely enjoying being alive.

The curtain came down and I was still in my dreamland, a bit disoriented. When the sound of tumultuous, prolonged applause gradually penetrated my consciousness, it was as if I had been rudely awoken from a dream and dropped from my magic cloud into the real world. For some reason I felt embarrassed and painfully shy about acknowledging the audience's ovation. The lasting memory of that performance never ceases to make me wonder what happened. Why? I still do not know the answer.

I was so happy to see how pleased everyone was with the ballet, the cast and me. I especially treasured the approval of Mme Nijinska and my parents. I loved dancing *La Fille mal gardée*. Whenever I think of it, it brings a happy grin to my old face!

10

LOVE

*O*ne night towards the end of our 44th Street Theatre season, after the last person left my dressing room, a man stepped forward to introduce himself. He was Ivanov from Moscow and in the film business. He enthusiastically expressed how much he had enjoyed my performance, then asked most politely if he could talk to me for a few minutes. I reluctantly invited him to sit down. He was on the small side, nondescript-looking and shabbily dressed by Western standards, but he did not lack self-assurance.

He started by telling me about the Soviet dancers and how they suffered from a lack of readily available toe shoes, tights, make-up, and so on. I sympathised and offered to take him to the specialist ballet shop Capezio and buy two dozen pairs of tights and two dozen pairs of toe shoes in various sizes as a present from me to those dancers most in need. He thanked me but declined my offer. 'You can do better than that!' he exclaimed. 'You must come home. You're Russian. You belong in Russia.'

'Yes, I'm Russian, but I don't belong in the USSR.'

Ivanov continued to argue his case. Feeling tired and hungry, I finally interrupted him. 'Look, my parents are here, my work with the greatest choreographers, my colleagues and friends are here! My life is in my suitcases and I love it! I don't want, nor ever will want, to go back to Russia – I mean the USSR!' I corrected myself.

He winced, sighed and got up to leave. As we said goodbye, I do not know why, but I felt sorry for him. At supper I told Jerry about my strange visitor from Moscow. Jerry looked mildly intrigued and commented with a smile, 'Well, you've collected a new admirer – a Soviet spy!'

I did not find this remark at all funny and felt even more sorry for Ivanov, being called a spy. 'All he did was express his feelings,' I told Jerry. 'In a way it was a compliment.'

'Are you stupid or naïve or both?' he asked impatiently.

'Both!' I snapped back.

Several days later, Ivanov reappeared at my dressing-room door. Greetings and compliments over, he brightly exclaimed, 'Our cultural attaché would like to meet you and put a wonderful idea to you. Would you consider coming to Leningrad for a few guest appearances?'

I was taken aback. To see St Petersburg, my birthplace, was tempting, but I replied, 'No, I couldn't possibly do that. Convey my thanks to the cultural attaché for his kind thought.'

But Ivanov insisted. 'Please meet him. No obligations. Just a chat.'

His pleading tone made me feel sorry for him again. Obeying my feelings, I said, 'Oh, all right, let's meet.' Now I was also curious.

'Great. Could you come tomorrow, at any time that suits you, to our office?'

But something clicked in my head. 'Your office? No! But I'm free to meet you both at the Plaza Hotel at four p.m., just for a cup of tea.'

For a moment he seemed indecisive, but then he said, 'All right, we'll be there.'

I decided not to say anything about my 'tea party' to Jerry, and secretly enjoyed having my own private little adventure. Next day at four p.m. sharp I was at the rendezvous. The attaché was cordial and not devoid of charm. I listened to his idea of me going to Moscow as a guest ballerina for a couple of performances. '*Swan Lake*, perhaps,' he ventured. When he finished, it was my turn to ask a few questions.

'I know of some people who were "invited". They went but never returned. Can you give me a guarantee that if I go I shall return?'

He laughed, took my hand and looked me in the eye. 'My dear, you'll love it so much there you won't want to return to the West!' His eyes were laughing. Ivanov's were not.

'Thanks for the charmingly put hint!' I smiled to him as I got up to take my leave.

'It was lovely to meet you,' they chorused, Ivanov adding, 'Perhaps we shall meet again.'

As I walked to the theatre and thought about the entire episode with the Soviets, it all seemed so bizarre. I felt uncomfortable, and regretted ever getting mixed up with these men. I was to encounter Ivanov again, months later, but I shall come to that – all in good time . . .

For the moment, I forgot the men from behind the 'Iron Curtain'. So many interesting things were being planned. We were to have another long season in Mexico. Fokine was to choreograph *Helen of Troy* with me as Helen and Dolin as Paris, to the music of Offenbach and with costumes by Marcel Vertes. Léonide Massine was to choreograph *Aleko* for Alicia Markova and Yura Skibine, to Tchaikovsky's Piano Trio in A Minor, with scenery and costumes by Marc Chagall. Sol Hurok had also asked for *Coppélia* to be included in our repertoire. Simon Semenoff staged it beautifully; once again, he was Dr Coppelius to my Swanilda, and Dolin was Franz.

Lucia Chase wanted to have copies of Alexandre Benois' sketches for his costumes for *Petrushka*. The original sketches were, at that time, on exhibition at the Harvard Museum if I am not mistaken. At Jerry's suggestion (which was really very nice of him), Lucia asked my father if he would go and copy all the sketches. Papa did so with great pleasure. Lucia then asked him to come to Mexico and assist Marc Chagall with the execution of his scenery for *Aleko* (Chagall always insisted on doing the scenery himself).

Papa took leave of absence from work and drove, with my mother, to Mexico City, joining us there a week after we arrived. A few of us took over what must once have been a large private house with a garden but had become a small hotel. I was a bit worried about how Jerry would get on with my parents, but to my relief they got along very well.

In spite of all the animosity over the years, Jerry – bless his heart – was obviously still trying to establish a friendly relationship. I was so happy to have my papa and mother with us. Mother so obviously enjoyed being backstage again, like in the good old days before my elopement. Poor Mama!

The months ahead promised to be busy for the whole company. I certainly had plenty to think about, learn and rehearse. Then unexpected extra work for me came in the shape of Señor Manuel Reachi, one of the producers from the Mexican film company Promesa Films. A longstanding balletomane, he approached Lucia Chase, Jerry, Pat and me with an offer to convert the film script he had into a story involving ballet performances, and make the leading lady a Russian ballerina. The film, which was to be called *Yolanda*, was a heavy melodrama set in Belle Époque Mexico. Besides my speaking role in Spanish, Pat and I were to dance the *pas de deux* from Act II of *Swan Lake*, the *pas de deux* from *Aurora's Wedding*, and an excerpt from *La Fille mal gardée* with the participation of the company.

Everyone liked the idea. At first, with memories of my Hollywood experience, I was hesitant, but not for long. It was a totally different set-up. Ballet Theatre was participating, I would be dancing with Anton Dolin – no worries, no aggravations, perfect! Learning the script in Spanish with a coach promised to be very interesting – I might even end up speaking passable Spanish. My leading man would be David Silva, a young Mexican who was a big star. The old husband would be played by Miguel Arenas, a distinguished actor. Financially it would work to everyone's advantage. Promesa Films was not stingy and Manuel Reachi was a considered, cultured gentleman.

However, Fokine had to cooperate and agree to rehearse *Helen of Troy* with me from five p.m. until seven-thirty p.m., after my day's work at the film studio. As the evening performances did not start until nine-thirty p.m., that would give me plenty of time to put on my make-up and warm up. On matinee days I would not be involved in filming. Fokine was wonderful. He agreed to work with me in the late afternoon and was very nice about it.

For some time, I had noticed that Fokine was becoming more approachable, more mellow, and that both he and Mrs Fokine were so much more relaxed in the way they communicated with us. While we were in Mexico, they even came with us, at Lucia Chase's invitation, on an excursion to Cuernavaca and Taxco. Fokine was in a playful mood and enjoyed walking around in his new purchase – a large sombrero.

Léonide Massine's arrival with his new wife, Tatiana Orlova, and their baby daughter was a happy event. Massine was beaming, so obviously proud to be a father. He had mellowed too; he was not 'dry toast' any more, but rather 'pumpernickel'! We, the old guard, gave them quite a welcome. The young American dancers who had never met him received him with spontaneous applause.

I once again had everything I could wish for in my working life, but something unexpected and disturbing crept into my private life. I was in love! Madly, romantically, uncontrollably in love. Oh yes, I had had a crush on Jerry when I was fifteen, but now I was twenty-three and the feeling was like nothing I had ever experienced before. Towards the end of our season in New York, I had become aware that my thoughts were dwelling more and more on Yura Skibine and the need I felt to be around him. I felt guilty. I was betraying Jerry's trust, even just in my thoughts. Jerry and I were temperamentally unsuited, and so far had just strung along, sometimes making each other miserable. We were both busy all day, so we did not have much contact with each other. His jealous nature and touchy ego were causes of aggravation to me, and I was in many ways, I realise now, not an easy person to live with. But I knew that, in his possessive way, he loved me and was devoted to me, so I felt guilty. I was not free, I had no business falling in love.

One day I was alone in wardrobe backstage, ironing my practice tunic. Engrossed in my thoughts, I did not hear the footsteps behind me. Two arms encircled my waist and a gentle kiss on my neck made me turn around. I gazed into Yura's eyes, and with a rush of affection I hugged him, my head on his chest as he gently stroked my hair. A feeling of tenderness, peace and happiness invaded my whole being. Neither of us spoke. Then a horrible smell of burning brought me back to earth. Oh dear! Turning around quickly, I grabbed the iron off my tunic and revealed a nasty-looking burn-hole right in the middle of it. We looked at each other and burst out laughing. That's how it started, my first, spring-like, romantic love for Yura. It was to alter the entire course of my life.

Meanwhile everyone anxiously scanned the newspapers each morning and listened to the radio for the latest news of the war. Since the Germans had turned on the USSR, the Russians had become popular. The ravages they suffered at the hand of the strong German Army, and their fierce resistance at Stalingrad, brought out feelings of sympathy and admiration.

Besides *Helen of Troy*, Fokine was due to produce one more ballet. Someone suggested that he should use Prokofiev's theme music written for the Soviet film *Lieutenant Kije*. Fokine did not like the story of the film, which was a satire on Tsarist times, and rejected it outright. But he heard in Prokofiev's music the soul of a simple soldier who, mortally wounded, crawls back to his village to die. Fokine wrote his own libretto, worked with Dorati on the score and, with Mstislav Doboujinsky's scenery and costumes, created a work that was deeply touching, stirring me to tears. It was to be premiered with the title *The Russian Soldier* in a gala charity performance at the Metropolitan Opera House.

Fokine felt strongly that he wished to have printed in the program, 'This ballet is dedicated, by Michel Fokine, to all suffering warriors.' He even demanded an official letter confirming this would be done. I did not see the rehearsals of this work, as I was busy on the film all day and then on my rehearsals for *Helen of Troy*.

Yura was not involved in the film, nor in *Helen of Troy*; he was working with Massine and Markova on *Aleko*. We hardly saw each other, except during performances and for a few short minutes in my dressing room as I was making up. We had to be very careful not to arouse any suspicion or gossip. It was not possible to solve our problem – not at that time, not yet. Too much was at stake. If word got out about us, Yura would be asked to leave the company immediately. And it would also be horribly humiliating for Jerry in his position as director of the company. My behaviour would be considered grubby, and rightly so.

I felt that what Yura and I had was so beautiful, so precious, that it must be handled with care, and with respect for Jerry. We had to be patient, wait for the right moment – if there is such a thing as the right moment. Pat's words would spring to mind: 'Don't rock the boat, not now!' When then? When could I ask Jerry for a divorce? *Patience*, I kept telling Yura and myself.

Overloaded with work, which I loved and enjoyed, I had to give it all my concentration and keep my feelings for Yura in a special, joyously serene, separate compartment of my heart. Self-discipline was a familiar occupation to me, although it was less so to Yura, who often showed signs of impatience and frustration. At least he was single. I was not. It became imperative to distance myself from Jerry. The work on the film provided me with a good excuse for doing so. I had to get up each day at five-thirty a.m., as the studio car would pick me up at six so that I was in the make-up department by six-thirty. We would start shooting at eight a.m.

As our performance did not finish until late, by the time I unwound, had supper and finally reached my bed, it was two a.m. All I had at my disposal were three-and-a-half hours' sleep before the shrill bell of the alarm clock under my pillow kicked me to my feet. I requested a bed in the small room next to the bathroom that we used as a dressing room. The reason I gave was that I would have a more tranquil sleep on my own and that I did not want to disturb Jerry at five-thirty a.m. Jerry accepted this as a sensible move. I felt relieved, at least for the time being, and could concentrate once more on my work and feel comfortable facing Yura in our ever so brief moments together.

Working on the film was a truly happy time with a group of friendly, fun people. My leading man, David Silva, behaved like a boisterous kid. He had a reputation for occasionally drinking one too many and breaking a chair or two in nightclubs. We became firm friends. Two of the young actors in supporting roles were devastatingly handsome and soon romancing two of our dancers.

My make-up lady, Dolores, who also did my hair and dressed me, looked after me like a loving nanny. One morning I kept dozing off in the make-up chair. Dolores put a mug of strong black coffee in front of me saying, 'Ah, *pobresita*, you're tired! Here, take this pill. It will give you energy.'

I obediently took the pill and drank the coffee. By the time Pat and I started shooting the *pas de deux* from *Aurora's Wedding* I felt like I could move mountains! From then on, each morning Dolores brought me a strong coffee and the magic pill. Its name was Benzedrine. Only recently I was reminiscing and mentioned the name of the magic pill to my daughter Irina. She informed me that it was an amphetamine, which gave me quite a shock! In those faraway days I did not know such things existed. I had heard only of opium, and vaguely of some mysterious stuff called cocaine. Whatever it was, it held no interest for me.

Another memorable day of shooting was on location in the country-side, by a small river. According to the script, I had to cross the river over a narrow makeshift bridge – just a plank with no railings. Halfway across, I was to lose my balance and fall in. As the little bridge lay high above the water and they did not want to run the risk of me hurting myself, they had my stand-in do the actual fall. On the first take she lost her balance, fell in the wrong place, hit her head on some big stone that was invisible in the murky water, and passed out! It created a big prob-lem, so I volunteered to do the fall myself. Reachi hesitated a little then, after I assured him I was a good diver and swimmer, finally agreed.

As a ballet dancer, my balance was better than that of my poor stand-in. I successfully reached the middle of the plank and fell in, pre-tending to be in trouble and letting the current take me to the spot we had agreed I would stop. The take was a total success and every-one breathed a sigh of relief, greeting me with applause as the director shouted, 'Cut!' I was having such fun! But now I had to stand in cold water up to my chest and wait for the solar panels to be moved for the next shot, and for the cameraman to move and adjust for the angle of the next take.

The director was conferring with David Silva on how to rescue me from the river. Meanwhile, Dolores noticed that I was freezing, my teeth chattering, having been left so long in the cold river. She alerted everyone and they sprang into action. A bottle of tequila was produced, tied to a rope, then thrown to me with instructions to take little sips to warm myself up. It worked. By the time the next shot was ready to go, I was drunk!

Nevertheless, the rescue went well. Dried and wrapped in a bath-robe, I was allowed to sleep it off in the car for a couple of hours. They teased me to bits for days afterwards! The ballet sequences pleased everybody. Taking into account that the film was made sixty-four years ago with one camera, I feel their efforts produced good results.

Being driven to the theatre from different locations after a day's shooting gave me time to relax, switch my thoughts and concentrate on the coming rehearsal with Fokine. At the first rehearsal he chore-ographed my beautiful entrance. It was demanding technically, but I loved the challenge. Satisfied, he sat down, looked at me sternly and said, 'Now I want you to do everything to the left.'

My mouth fell open in astonishment and dismay! 'But you know I'm not left-handed!' I protested.

'Are you a ballerina in this company?' he enquired sarcastically.

'Well, yes,' I replied lamely.

'A ballerina must be able to do everything to the left and right equally well!' His voice was dry, forbidding any argument. 'From the beginning, please, everything to the left!' With this command he motioned to our pianist to start playing. Swallowing my angry tears, I tried my best. 'Not too bad,' he said at the end, 'but you need some practice.'

Back in my dressing room, still fuming, I had started on my make-up when Yura popped in. I told him what had happened. 'You know what I think?' he said. 'Fokine wants to teach you a lesson.'

'Why?' I asked.

'So that your success here doesn't go to your head. Fokine likes and values you. Maybe he doesn't want you to rest on your laurels and imag-ine you have nothing more to learn, to work on, to search for. Think about it.'

The tender, loving hug Yura gave me made me feel better. As I resumed applying my make-up, I thought about what Yura had said.

I grudgingly admitted to myself that perhaps, indeed, all this attention had begun to go to my head. And, what's more, Yura must have noticed it too! I felt silly and ashamed of myself. From that night on, every spare moment – on the filmset, during performances, in every corner I could find – I practised to the left.

I did not tell Jerry about this 'to the left' business, afraid that he might say something to Fokine about it and give him the impression, correctly, that I was complaining. It would not have enhanced Fokine's opinion of me, so I kept quiet and practised. By the time we had a rehearsal on stage, I was comfortable and happy doing everything to the left. As I made my entrance, Fokine stopped me, saying with that challenging look of his, 'You can do everything to the right if you want.'

Oh, how I enjoyed replying, 'Thank you, but I'm very happy doing it to the left!'

I noticed Fokine exchange a look with his wife as his spectacles slid down his nose, the tip of his tongue between his teeth, a sign that he was pleased.

GOODBYE TO FOKINE

One night after the performance, I had a surprise visitor, the last person I ever expected to see in Mexico – Ivanov! He complimented our performance, then told me he was in Mexico City on business. 'Have you heard of our great ballerina Marina Semenova?' he asked.

'Yes, of course,' I replied.

'Our Embassy has received a film of Semenova dancing several roles. Would you like to see it? We can arrange a screening for you and any members of your company who care to come.'

I thanked Ivanov for his kind thought and expressed my genuine interest in seeing the great Soviet ballerina on film. I also pointed out to him that I was in no position to accept this kind of invitation on behalf of my colleagues. I suggested that he talk to our director about it. 'And here he is!' I exclaimed, as Jerry came in.

Ivanov repeated his invitation. Under the pretext that he had to check our schedule, Jerry asked Ivanov to phone him at the office the next day. Actually, Jerry wanted to consult Lucia. As Soviet Russia was popular at that time and many of us were curious to see Semenova dance, we accepted Ivanov's invitation. He met us at the Embassy gates at ten a.m. on the next matinee day (the only day I had a free morning). Quite a little crowd of Ballet Theatre dancers stood gazing at the imposing building of the USSR Embassy, with its high wrought-iron fence and gates. A uniformed guard stood by the sentry box, eyeing us with curiosity. He unlocked the gates and Ivanov asked us to come in one by one. As we filed in, the guard said loudly, in Russian, 'Anyone in possession of a firearm, please leave it here with me.' He then turned to Ivanov and asked him to translate.

My colleagues registered amazement at his request, but I could not contain my indignation. I turned to the guard and raised my voice. 'We're ballet dancers, not gangsters! Shame on you!'

Lucia put a hand on my arm to calm me while Ivanov hurriedly mumbled, 'Okay, okay,' and shepherded us inside. Their cultural attaché and two other officials met us in a very smart-looking projection room. Friendly greetings over, they invited us to partake of delicious small squares of Russian black bread piled with caviar, washed down with vodka. Only the boys indulged in a tumbler or two, but the atmosphere became quite jovial.

Finally the lights went down and we settled to watch Marina Semenova, whose performance was truly beautiful! We thanked our hosts for showing us their glorious ballerina and took our leave. We hurried out with Ivanov, anxious to get to the theatre on time, but the gates were locked and the sentry box empty. We waited a little while, then Jerry asked Ivanov to fetch someone to unlock the gate. 'It's all right, don't worry. Someone will come soon,' Ivanov reassured us.

'We're pressed for time. We have a matinee, remember?' put in Lucia, smiling sweetly.

'Well, we can always try to climb over the gates,' I suggested, eyeing the design of the wrought iron, looking for footholds.

'No, no! You mustn't do that!' said Ivanov, becoming agitated. 'Someone might start shooting by mistake.' The situation was becoming annoying, when a stony-faced guard finally appeared and let us out. We gave a hurried wave and were off. *Strange people, those USSR comrades*, I thought to myself, hoping it would be the last we saw of Ivanov. He was an uncomfortable acquaintance.

By now the film was completed, so my days returned to normal and rehearsals on *Helen of Troy* with Fokine demanded all my attention. It promised to be another masterpiece. He had only the Finale left to choreograph.

Meanwhile, Massine was progressing well with *Aleko*. It was great to see him in a happy and relaxed mood – parenthood had mellowed him visibly. Marc Chagall arrived about the same time as Massine, and immediately started painting the scenery for *Aleko*. My father assisted him, taking great pleasure in doing so. They were both Russian, which helped to establish a relaxed, friendly relationship right away. Whenever I had a minute, I loved watching them at work. Sprawled on the floor or perched on ladders, they would work mostly in silence, occasionally exchanging observations. During a break they would sit on little stools, have a coffee and talk of this and that, mostly art.

Chagall was a warm, friendly man, with an aura of sadness that intrigued me. He must have lived through hard times, but I did not know him well enough to ask him about it. Chagall's unusual insistence on painting the scenery himself turned out to be beneficial for Ballet Theatre; some years later, when *Aleko* was no longer performed, there was a financial crisis, and the scenery was sold for a hefty sum. The premiere of *Aleko* took place in Mexico City in September 1942. It was a great success for Massine, and for Alicia Markova and Yura Skibine in the leading roles. But that was to come, after a tragic loss to our art.

As Fokine neared the completion of *Helen of Troy*, he developed a thrombosis in his left leg. The pain he suffered was evident; he could not stand or walk but still conducted rehearsals, sitting down. Our boys carried him from the car up the long flight of stairs to the studio. In this way the ballet was almost completed; Fokine planned to polish the work in

New York, before its premiere at the Metropolitan Opera House. Mme Fokine now insisted on leaving immediately for New York. She did not trust our Czechoslovakian doctor friend, and had not allowed him anywhere near Fokine. She trusted only their own doctor in New York, and no amount of begging made her allow our doctor to see Fokine. We tried to make her see that a three-day journey on the train could only make Fokine's condition worse, but we succeeded only in making her quite hysterical. Fokine felt too sick to say anything and looked awful. There was nothing anyone could do but abide by his wife's wishes.

Lucia, Jerry and I took them to the railway station and installed them in their compartment. Fokine tried to put on a brave face, but he had aged, and his grey face was pinched with pain. We said our goodbyes, wishing them bon voyage. *Bon?* How could it be? I felt so sad for them both. As I stepped into the corridor, I heard Fokine's voice calling me back to their compartment. I approached the great man and he took both my hands in his. 'I just wanted you to know,' he said, 'I loved working with you.'

How precious those words were – and still are – to me. A lump rose in my throat, I burst into tears and did the unthinkable, hugged him, mumbling through my tears, 'Thank you, thank you, I owe you so much!'

Jerry knocked on the compartment window, making signs to me to get off the train. I quickly kissed Mme Fokine then, blinded by tears, joined Lucia and Jerry on the platform.

Fokine was very ill when he reached home. His doctor diagnosed pleurisy and put him in hospital. Pleurisy then turned into double pneumonia. On 22 August the company received the dreaded telegram informing us that Fokine had died a few minutes after midnight. He was only sixty-two.

Fokine's death was an irreplaceable loss to our art, and a dreadful shock to those of us who had worked with him since the early 1930s. He had guided, scolded and artistically nourished us, and we had had the privilege of being the creators of his new ballets. I was devastated. I admired, respected and loved him as a divinity. With Fokine gone, I felt there would be no more new, exciting roles for me to create. I sank into deep pessimism and felt there was nothing left to look forward to.

The unfinished Finale to *Helen of Troy* was somehow completed through the respectful efforts of Yurek Lazowski. In September we gave the whole ballet a trial performance, but it was painfully obvious to all that the Finale was not Fokine's choreography, and that the whole ballet lacked that Fokine polish and final attention to detail. Out of respect for Fokine, Lucia asked for the production to be abandoned.

To salvage the scenery and costumes, we gave David Lichine the opportunity to choreograph a shorter version with a new libretto. He accepted, and a light-hearted, frothy *Helen of Troy* was ready for our New York season, where it was quite successful.

The last new production to be premiered in Mexico was *Coppélia*. I loved the ballet, and enjoyed the same success in it as I had in South America. It lifted my sagging spirits and a measure of optimism returned to me regarding my artistic future.

My private life, on the other hand, was getting more and more complicated. Like any two people in love, Yura and I longed to spend time together; our brief moments at rehearsals and performances were not enough and we became reckless. During our lunch break, whenever possible, we would go out together, sit on a bench in the big square and munch on a sandwich, talking and dreaming about our future. But these outings did not escape Pat's eagle eye. 'Irina, you're playing with fire. What's going on between you and Yura?' he asked.

I told him and felt better for it; it helped to share my huge problem with a friend like Pat. He listened to me in silence, then said, 'Have you slept with Yura?'

'No. I have to be free first.'

'Jerry will be devastated. He adores you.' There was a tone of reproach in Pat's voice.

'You see it as adoration, I feel it as possessiveness. He often tells me when he's annoyed with me that he wishes he could put me in his breast pocket and only allow me out for performances. I don't want to be owned, I want to be loved!'

'Steady, my dear, your mascara is running.' Dear Pat, he could always make me smile. 'Well, it's your life, your decision, but please, don't create difficulties for our New York season. It's a very important one for all of us!'

'I promise I won't rock the boat until the final curtain.'

A nice Russian couple in Mexico City attended our performances regularly and always came backstage to say hello. They invited several of us to a luncheon party at their house the day after our last performance, which we gladly accepted. As we approached the house, someone on a frightfully noisy motorbike overtook us and stopped in front of the house. It was Ivanov! We exchanged surprised greetings at the gate, and I foolishly remarked how noisy his bike was and that I had never ridden on one.

'Hop on the back. I'll take you around the block,' Ivanov offered.

Oh, what fun, I thought to myself (that was as far as I thought), hopped on the back and held on to Ivanov as he roared up the avenue. At first it was fun, but as we gathered speed, I noticed we did not turn any corners, but were heading straight up the avenue. I felt more than uncomfortable – plain scared! Shouting, 'Stop! Stop!' I pounded his back with my fist, holding on to his waist for dear life with my other arm. He slowed down and stopped by the kerb.

'Did I scare you?' he asked, roaring with laughter.

'Yes, you did. Let's go back before we're both in trouble. And don't speed – I hate it!'

Jerry was there waiting as we stopped by the house. He was livid with rage – or was it worry? Or did he wish to drop me into his pocket and sew it up? He was rude to us both. On purpose, I thanked Ivanov profusely for the ride, brushed past Jerry up the steps and declared, 'It was such fun!' But all I really wanted to shout was, 'Let me breathe!'

The other guests were a charming, jovial crowd and my bad mood soon dispersed. The typically Russian lunch was a delicious treat, and we had a jolly good time at our end of the table. I noticed, with relief, that Jerry was entertaining and charming his companions at the other end by recounting stories of our travels – he was brilliant and funny. The storm had passed.

After lunch we moved to the living room and I saw Ivanov, who had imbibed more vodka than anyone else. He negotiated the distance from the door to the couch uncertainly, then dropped down next to me, put his head on my shoulder and burst into tears! 'Good God, what's the matter with you?' I asked in alarm.

'I received a telegram this morning requesting my immediate return to Moscow,' whimpered Ivanov.

'So? You must be happy to be going home.'

'I don't want to go!' he sobbed loudly.

Dismayed, then frightened for him, I whispered in his ear, 'Shut up. You'll get yourself into trouble!' He wiped his face with a rather grubby handkerchief. 'Now sit quietly. I'll be right back.'

I found our hostess and explained that Ivanov was in great need of coffee and asked her to help me steer him to a more secluded corner to sober up. Followed by amused looks from the other guests, we got him onto the veranda. As he sat down and emitted a loud hiccup, a large pot of coffee appeared – and so did Jerry. He gave Ivanov a disgusted look and stated the obvious. 'Drunk!'

'A little,' said our hostess coyly, giving a mug of coffee to Ivanov, who obediently took a sip.

Shaking his head in disapproval, Jerry turned his attention to me. 'Coming,' I said as he made to return indoors, 'in a moment.' A question was burning on my lips that only Ivanov could answer. When he looked more composed and our hostess had returned to her guests, I said to Ivanov reproachfully, 'You so-and-so, trying to persuade me to return to Russia – why?'

He looked at me apologetically. 'You must admit, I didn't try very hard. I like you, but that was my mission.' He looked sad. He was a good man. But the whole episode made we wonder who our hosts really were.

My parents had left Mexico City a week before our last perform-ance there. They were happy with their time spent with us, and I was relieved that they were oblivious to the turmoil going on inside me. But Jerry was not and, as soon as my parents left, he dropped his calm and somewhat distant attitude. He looked preoccupied and often asked me, 'Anything wrong?' I could not tell him, not yet, and so felt dreadfully guilty and shabby.

We said goodbye to Mexico City and arrived in Guadalajara on a hot afternoon. It was a biggish old city, not far from Lake Chapala. The old theatre was surprisingly big, with a beautiful auditorium and a large stage with an excellent floor. After our morning class, where Yura and I could exchange a few words, although most of my afternoons were free, he was always rehearsing, so there was no chance for us to get together. How frustrating!

We were told that there was a small village on the lake with a large, beautiful beach, so one day after class Pat, two other dancers, Jerry and I piled into our big old Packard car and set off. The beach was lovely, but the so-called village consisted of poor-looking mud huts, one bigger than the others with a sign saying '*Escuela*' (School). The entire place seemed deserted.

As soon as we settled ourselves on the beach, a bunch of little boys trying to sell us postcards appeared out of nowhere. One of them, cheekier than the others, with a wide smile and irresistible charm, knew a few words of English, probably picked up from tourists. We bought cards from all of them. Satisfied, the kids left, but not the little cheeky one, who sat himself on the sand among us and tried to make conversation. With our little Spanish and his very limited English, we got on famously.

'Me name Chico,' he informed us.

'Me name Bluebeard,' said Pat and shook his hand. Some mime was needed to explain to Chico what 'beard' meant. Pat assured Chico that at night he grew a blue beard. Chico's eyes stood on stalks. Jumping to his feet excitedly, he told Pat that he would sleep with him, to see his beard grow blue.

'It's *Bluebeard* tonight. Let's take him to the performance!' I suggested.

Everyone laughed and agreed. It turned out that Chico was eight years old and had never been to Guadalajara or anywhere outside his village. Theatre? What was that? But he was keen to find out. We told him we had to ask his parents' permission to take him with us.

We all followed him to his mud hut. The rickety door was wide open and two figures were sprawled on the earth, fast asleep. Chico rushed in, calling excitedly, '*Padre! Mamá!*' There was no movement, only snores. Chico shook each figure in turn. '*Despierte!*' (Wake up) he urged. A few tripped-up snores and a groan were the only response. Turning to us, he shrugged and said, '*Borracho!*' (Drunk), then pointed to the *escuela* further up the road.

We all followed, curious to see what would happen next. The noise of our approach brought a young woman to the open door of the school. Pointing his grubby finger at her, Chico commanded, 'Ask professor!' The young teacher smiled at us and asked in broken English how she could help.

Pat explained who we were – constantly interrupted by Chico's excited comments about the '*barba azul*' (blue beard) – and that we needed permission to take Chico with us and see our performance for himself. I pointed out that Chico would have to spend the night with us and we would bring him back in the morning.

'All right, you can go, Chico.'

Chico executed some kind of savage dance of joy.

'Won't his parents worry?' I asked.

'No, no, when you come tomorrow, they still sleep! Sad. Chico good boy, *muy inteligente!*'

'Who feeds him?'

'When mother drunk, I do.'

'Does he need to fetch anything from home for the night?' As soon as I asked, I knew it was a stupid question.

The teacher looked embarrassed. 'No, he has nothing.'

'We'll take care of what he'll need,' interjected Jerry. 'We must go now. We have lots to do before tonight.'

Chico was mostly silent in the car, his nose glued to the window – watching, discovering the world outside his village, occasionally asking a question. When we reached the city, he observed everything intently, with wonderment and a touch of fright. Our first stop was at a shop selling children's clothes. I was in charge of the purchases, while the others waited at a nearby café. As we walked into the shop, Chico assumed an air of importance and asked the saleslady, 'Do you have a nice shirt?' I decided not to interfere and let him choose two shirts and two pairs of shorts, underwear and pyjamas to his liking. The seriousness with which he made his choices was funny and moving at the same time. The purchase of sandals was another matter; Chico found footwear unwelcome. Only after I told him that everyone who wanted to see *Bluebeard* had to wear sandals did he agree to the purchase.

After we both consumed a large ice-cream, I took him to our hotel and asked the horrified person at the desk to bring a child's cot into our room. To pacify the man, I told him that it was just for one night and pushed a little something under the counter, which was most effective.

I braced myself for the next task and asked Chico to come into the bathroom and undress. He badly needed a good scrub but he eyed the tub with suspicion. At a loss for Spanish words, I unceremoniously lifted him in. Soaping and scrubbing him, then washing his hair was quite a battle. Soaking wet myself, I finally had the pleasure of seeing Chico clean and rather pleased with his image in the mirror. It was time for me to go to the theatre – I left Chico with Jerry, who would dress and feed him and take him to the performance.

The last intermission was almost over and I was about to leave my dressing room when Yura popped his head through the door and hurriedly handed me a letter. There was no time to read it, so I stuffed it in my handbag.

The curtain came up on *Bluebeard*. During my first entrance I had a chance to glance up at the box where Chico was sitting with Jerry. He was standing up, leaning forward, his little hands gripping the edge, his face intense with concentration. When Pat made his first entrance as Bluebeard, we heard Chico gasp. He was so excited he almost fell out of the box; Jerry caught him just in time, by the seat of his shorts!

Afterwards, the excitement and endless questions continued in Pat's dressing room. When Chico asked if he could touch the beard, Pat said, 'Yes, pull it down.' Chico pulled on the beard, which was attached to Pat's head by elastic, and pulled it down to Pat's chest. Startled, Chico let go of the beard, which slapped Pat's nose on its way up. Chico's merriment was something to behold! When we finally left the theatre to have some supper, Chico was fading rapidly. It had been a long day for him, full of excitement and unexpected discoveries.

Back at the hotel, I helped him undress and get into his pyjamas – another novelty! He spent a penny and I told him it was time for us all to go to sleep. Chico nodded, then curled up on the floor in the corner of the room.

'No, no! Come here!' I patted the cot. He sighed, closed his eyes and did not budge. I picked him up off the floor and tucked him in the cot. He caressed the sheet, murmured, '*Bonito,*' and fell fast asleep.

In the morning I woke up first and to my great alarm found that Chico had gone. Panic stations! Jerry dressed hurriedly then rushed out to look for him. Worried as I was about Chico, this gave me a chance to glance at Yura's letter without being caught. It was such a beautiful letter . . . I put it back into my handbag, looking forward to reading it properly in my dressing room later.

I was already dressed by the time Jerry returned. He had found Chico at the barbershop next door. Chico had some pesos in his pocket – a present from Pat – and upon waking had decided to spend some of it on a haircut! I found him truly amazing. He was so independent for a child of his age.

Mid-morning the three of us set off for Chapala, having made more purchases for Chico to take home. We delivered him back to the school hut, where his little friends were waiting with the teacher. They surrounded him immediately, all shouting questions at the same time, to Chico's evident delight.

We left the parcels in the care of the nice teacher, and I hugged Chico, who gave me a big kiss, holding my face in his hands. With tears in my eyes, I watched the little man run joyously towards the beach with his chums. I imagined the number of stories he would tell about all his adventures with Bluebeard in the big city.

Twenty-two years later I received a letter through the Royal Academy of Dance. To my great surprise it was signed 'Chico'! He reminisced about *Bluebeard*, telling me he still had the program from that performance. He had found out how to reach me from a ballet teacher friend of his who had just returned from a Royal Academy seminar in America. He wanted to thank me and Mr Pat for showing the little boy from Chapala that there was another world outside his village. He explained how, thanks to his village teacher, he had had a chance to get an education in the big city and that he was now an architect for a successful firm in Mexico City. It gave me a great thrill to hear from him and to know that the little escapade of so long ago had such wonderful results.

As we were leaving Chico's village, I reached into my handbag for a handkerchief but, as I pulled it out, Yura's letter slipped out and fell at Jerry's feet. As soon as we were back in the car, I was asked, 'And from whom might that be, the missive in your purse?'

'It's a fan letter,' I lied, my heart pounding.

'Must be very special for you to carry it with you!'

'No, I just forgot about it.' I started talking about Chico, hoping I would get away with it.

When we got back to the hotel, however, Jerry locked the door and angrily ordered me to sit down. He sat opposite me. 'Hand me that letter.'

'No, I won't.' How could I?

'Give. Me. The letter!'

'No!'

Now he was furious. 'I won't let you out of the room until you give me that letter!'

All I knew was that Yura's name must not come out. At a loss for how to proceed, I remained silent, just squeezing my handbag a bit tighter between my back and the armchair. Of one thing I was certain: Jerry would never use physical force against me or, for that matter, against anyone. It was not in his character. And thus we sat in silence, my mind blank as I stared out the window. The unexpected rescue came when someone knocked on the door. 'Who is it?' I called loudly.

'Pat.'

'Coming,' I chanted. Jerry had no option but to open the door and let him in. Pat wanted to know all about Chico. After a while, on the pretext of needing to spend a penny, I went to the bathroom and took my handbag with me, not daring to look at Jerry. Locking the door, I rapidly reread the beautiful note then tore it into little pieces and, full of regret, flushed it down the loo.

When I rejoined them, the look Jerry gave me told me clearly that he knew exactly what I had been up to in the bathroom. As for me, I could breathe again in the knowledge that the proof of my sin had gone down the drain. Even wild horses could not have dragged from me the name of the author of those tender words, meant for my eyes only. To what conclusions Jerry came after the letter episode, I do not know. He never mentioned the matter again, but the air was frosty, and cool politeness became the order of the day.

As soon as we arrived back in New York, Lichine started rehearsals for his version of *Helen of Troy*. It was so good to see him again. Working with him took me back to the 'good old days' of the early 1930s, although so much had happened and changed since then. Our very important season at the Metropolitan Opera House opened to a full house of glittering, enthusiastic spectators. The notices the next day were all that anyone could wish for. We were accepted and established as an important, major American company.

One of our early performances presented three Fokine ballets and was dedicated to his memory. *New York Times* critic John Martin appeared in front of the curtain as the lights went down and made a short speech honouring the great choreographer, at the end of which he asked the audience to stand with bowed heads while the orchestra played Chopin's Prelude in A major, Op. 28 No. 7. The curtain rose slowly to reveal the set of *Les Sylphides* and a dimly lit, empty stage. As the orchestra played the beautiful, peaceful melody, the dancers stood in the wings and total silence descended on the theatre. Only the sound of the prelude, like a gentle caress, bid Michel Fokine farewell. As the last notes faded away, the curtain slowly came back down. It was a deeply moving and fitting tribute to a great artist.

Sol Hurok was undoubtedly a past master at generating publicity. At the benefit performance in aid of the wartime charity Bundles for Russia, Fokine's *The Russian Soldier* was, of course, on the program. In front of the curtain, on either side of the stage, were two flags, one American, the other Soviet. I eyed the red flag with mixed feelings; the sight of it disturbed me deeply.

The Russian Soldier was an appropriate work for the occasion, but Sol Hurok had one more stunt up his sleeve that totally shocked me. At the end of the ballet, the wounded soldier is dying, the stage dimly lit, a spotlight on him. At that moment, to everyone's surprise, a man in Soviet uniform appeared on a platform above the dying soldier, waving the hammer and sickle, the spotlight now directed on him! Hurok's audacity in interfering with Fokine's work, adding his own choreography, profiting from the fact that Fokine was dead and in no position to protest, was shocking. On top of that, he ignored Fokine's strict instructions for the ballet to be dedicated to 'all suffering warriors'. Instead, Hurok had printed in the program, 'Dedicated to the gallant Russian soldiers of World War II.'

Hurok achieved the desired effect. The papers picked it up and people talked and argued about it for days. When I talked to Jerry about it, he did not look happy. All he had to say was, 'We need Hurok, so we must play ball with him.' Fokine would have been in a rage! I felt so sorry for Mme Fokine. Devastated as she was by her husband's death, this mutilation of Fokine's work, and the altered dedication, must have upset her a great deal.

DIVORCE

Meanwhile I was working with Massine again – he was staging his lovely *Boutique fantasque* for us. I had danced the Cancan Doll with Massine before, a few times when Danilova was indisposed, so these rehearsals were easy for me and I enjoyed watching the relaxed, mellow Massine working with his usual intensity. He was fascinating to watch, all his movements so expressive, with that inner spark that was always present in his work.

My parents came to the performances often, but these were the only times I could see them during that very busy New York season. I noticed that Papa at times brought his hand to his chest, as if in discomfort, but when I asked him if he was in pain, he said no, that he felt fine. I never quite believed him and remained concerned.

One afternoon, by chance, Yura and I found ourselves both free of rehearsals. Our longing to have a little time together was so great that, throwing all caution aside, I joined him at his lodgings. That afternoon we became lovers – it was so beautiful. But nothing was right, and it became imperative that I separate from Jerry with no more ado.

Rocking the boat? As far as I was concerned, it could not only rock, it could sink! Neither of us gave a thought to what would happen to us next. But the hand of fate took over and dealt our cards. Yura, along with several of our boys who were in the USA on quota visas waiting to receive US citizenship, was informed that the waiting time had been cut short and that his citizenship had been granted. This meant that as a US citizen he could be drafted into the army. General consternation!

Some of the American dancers were called to arms too. The draft letter stated the date and the place the boys were to report. This unexpected bombshell, painful as it was for Yura and me, at least clarified his immediate future. The awkward situation he would have been in once his involvement with me had come out was eliminated, as was the certainty of him being asked to leave the company, in which case I would have had no choice but to leave as well.

At this point, having ended our season in New York, we were to begin our US and Canadian tour. Yura was due to leave for the army in a few days, so I braced myself to tell Jerry that I wanted a divorce. But first I had to tell Pat. He did not try to stop me. He was kind and understanding, but warned me that Jerry would not be easy to deal with. Of that I was fully aware. Then I felt that I had to have a talk with Lucia, to put her in the picture. To my request to talk to her privately, she simply said, 'Hurry up and come over.'

We talked and talked all evening. Lucia listened to me with her comforting calm and understanding. At one point she asked, 'Where's Jerry now?'

'In the Russian Tea Room with Hurok, Richard Davis and the rest of them, as usual.'

'It must be very boring for you, you poor child,' she smiled, adding, 'Mind you, I like Jerry, but I felt from early on that you were ill matched.'

I asked Lucia if she would prefer, under the circumstances, for me to tender my resignation from the company.

'Oh, no, no, don't dream of leaving! It will settle down. I'll talk to Jerry. With Yura out of the way, he'll surely accept the separation more calmly.' On that point, however, I was not so sure. 'Why don't we room together on tour?' offered Lucia. What a generous, supportive gesture on her part! I accepted her kind offer with gratitude and, promising to phone her after my talk with Jerry, went back to the hotel to face the painful hours ahead of me.

When Jerry finally appeared, Richard Davis was with him and they settled in for a night cap. Sorting out my life would have to wait till morning! I went to bed, my nerves on edge, and pretended to be asleep until dawn. I dressed hurriedly and went to the sitting room, ordered a coffee from room service and sat down to wait for Jerry to surface.

It can never be pleasant to discuss divorce, since one must feel pain and inflict it. Our discussion of the matter, once Jerry got over his astonishment, turned horribly unpleasant, and we exchanged many wounding words. It ended with Jerry refusing to discuss the matter any further and, with a firm no to my request for a divorce, he walked out, banging the door. But I felt relieved. No more secrets, no more hiding my feelings. I was free to be myself again. I booked a room at the St. Regis Hotel then called Lucia and left a message telling her what had happened and where I would be.

I packed quickly and made my way to Pennsylvania Station, dropping my luggage at the hotel on the way. I wanted to tell my parents face to face that I had left Jerry, and the reason why. As I expected, they took the news calmly. I had a feeling that Mother was pleased, but my papa seemed a bit worried. In the mid-afternoon a car pulled up in front of the house. Bless her, it was Lucia. She had come to drive me back to New York and told me she had cancelled my booking at the St. Regis and I was to stay with her until we went on tour. My parents and I were deeply touched by her care and kindness.

I promised to phone my parents the next day and visit again before we left for our tour. Back at Lucia's, I called Yura, who was worried at not having heard from me all day. I told him why, briefly recounting my stormy morning with Jerry and his refusal to consider my request. Yura was relieved to hear that I had left the hotel and was staying with Lucia. 'Was my name mentioned?' he asked.

'I told Lucia and my parents about us, but no-one else.' When Jerry had asked me if someone else was involved, I had answered evasively, saying that since I had asked for a divorce, I considered myself free to have my own private life, and that I did not wish to discuss it. Yura and I agreed to meet the next morning at his place. He was due to leave for his army training course the day after.

I then called Sol Hurok. Since I was under contract to him, I felt it would be polite to let him know personally that Jerry and I were no longer together. I also wanted to instruct him to pay my salary to me and not to Jerry. Hurok took the news philosophically and asked me to stop by the office the next day. As I wanted to spend Yura's last day with him, I arranged to see Hurok the day after at three p.m. I hoped Jerry would not be there too.

To some extent I was aware that the days and weeks ahead would be tricky, but I had no idea what to expect or how it was all going to pan out. On that day I could think only of the pain of Yura's departure and of not knowing when or where we would see each other again. Lucia installed me in a lovely guest room. I felt safe, spoilt and infinitely grateful to have found in her such a supportive and sensitive friend. After a refreshing bath, I came downstairs and she coaxed me into having a drink before dinner. 'It will relax you,' she said kindly. 'You've had a heavy day.'

It was the first time I tried a dry martini. *Hmm . . . rather nice!* Then the phone rang – it was Pat. I whispered to Lucia that he knew about Yura and my intended talk with Jerry. She nodded, smiling at what Pat was saying, then said, 'Actually, she's staying with me. Why don't you come over and have dinner with us?'

Anxious to hear the dramas of the day, Pat arrived in no time. With his dry sense of humour, he told us that Jerry had called him mid-afternoon to ask if I was, by any chance, with him. When Pat said no, Jerry told him irritably that I could, as he knew, be unreasonable and stubborn, but this morning I had been unacceptably outrageous and had left the hotel, taking all my belongings! Pat had pretended to be astonished at hearing this, and Jerry did not volunteer anything further. I felt rotten that I had hurt and upset Jerry, but what could I do? I had to leave him – now Yura was my life.

Lucia refilled my glass, and I felt the gin going to my head; I had some wine with dinner and ended the evening in floods of tears. Feeling emotionally drained and in need of solitude, I hugged Lucia and Pat, thanked them for being there for me, and retired to my room. The night seemed endless. I was filled with gloomy thoughts and anxiety about the future. I didn't even know what tomorrow would bring! These thoughts went round and round in my head but I found no answers. All I knew was that I had created a mess, and that I might have to leave the company. That thought made me very sad. I had grown to love it, and had good friends and colleagues there, let alone Lucia and Pat, who both meant so much to me. Deep down I knew that my predictable, orderly life was over. I had burned my bridges. By morning, having had a good talk with myself, I felt exhausted but ready to face any eventuality.

Each morning that I stayed with Lucia, we had breakfast with her schoolboy son, a lovely young person, talkative and, like his mother, full of charm. His name was Alexander but I called him Sandy. As the years rolled by, our paths never crossed again, but whenever I thought of Lucia I remembered 'my little Sandy' with fondness.

But sometimes life can throw up some lovely surprises. In 1995, fifty-two years after that first breakfast, I received a letter from the chancellor of the North Carolina School of the Arts, asking me if I would consider coming to give some masterclasses to senior students in their dance department. The chancellor's letter was signed 'Sandy'! He added in his postscript, 'Remember, we used to have breakfast together?' Thrilled, I responded, 'Yes, yes, yes, I'm coming!'

And he was there to greet me at Winston–Salem Airport. I was looking out for my 'little' Sandy, but a tall, handsome man approached me shyly. 'Irina? I'm Sandy.' What a joyous moment! I had a most wonderful time with Sandy and his lovely wife, Sheila, who were both kindness itself. The school impressed me greatly – every aspect of the arts is taught there by great teachers, and my students were of a very high standard, ready to grace the stage with any professional company.

I am now in regular contact with Sheila and Sandy, who is writing a book about his amazing mother. Who better to tell us of her life at home, as an artist and as the founder of American Ballet Theatre than her son, Alexander Ewing? But way back then, when we had our first breakfast together, the future was not ours to see and I was preoccupied with the present.

I called my parents to put their minds at rest and then went to join Yura, promising Lucia to be back for dinner – staying with Yura at this point would have been indelicate and improper. It was a bittersweet day for us. The joy of being together, mixed with the pain of our impending parting for God knows how long, with no possibility of making any plans, made our day poignantly sad. Yura was going to write to me care of my parents, once he knew where I could reach him.

It was so hard to say goodbye. He tried to console me, reassuring me he would come back in one piece. I walked all the way back to Lucia's in a daze, my eyes blurred with tears, feeling lost. She was waiting for me. She had seen Jerry at the office and he knew I was staying with her – Hurok had told him. 'So, Irina is apparently with you!' he had said, shrugging his shoulders and adding nothing else.

Lucia and I had a quiet evening. She gave me a pill to make me sleep better; it worked fast and I sank into a heavy slumber, but in the morning I felt as if my head was stuffed with cotton wool. My morale at zero, I tried to pull myself together in anticipation of my meeting with Hurok. Breakfast with Sandy cheered me up – the beautiful simplicity of a child is so enchanting.

I felt in need of a class with Vilzak, so I walked to 57th Street, wondering the whole time how Yura was getting on. Vilzak's wonderful class and the good workout cleared my head and, at the appointed time, I stepped into Hurok's office ready for anything. He greeted me with, 'Ai-ai-ai! Why did you have to fall in love?'

'I didn't have to! It just happened!' I replied. 'Sorry to cause trouble.'

We discussed the situation, both of us hoping that Jerry and I would conduct our divorce in a civilised manner. Hurok produced an envelope from a desk drawer and handed it to me. 'Here's your cheque for the past month, as you requested. In future it will be simpler to deposit your salary directly into your bank account.'

'No, no, no!' I hurried to protest. 'I have no such thing as a bank account and I don't want a cheque. I want cash!'

Hurok looked at me in disbelief, then yelled at the top of his voice, 'Mae, Mae, come here!'

Darling Mae Froman appeared at a run. 'Sol, are you all right?' She looked at us in alarm.

Hurok got up from his desk and pointed at me. 'Sarah Abramovna' (his pet name for me) 'here has no bank account! Take her downstairs and open an account for her with her cheque, then teach her how to write one.'

'No,' I protested, 'I want cash!'

'And where are you going to keep so much cash? Under the hotel mattress?'

'Well, I'll put it in an envelope and pin it inside my girdle,' I insisted stubbornly.

Mae giggled. Hurok sighed, shook his head and raised his eyes to the ceiling. 'Mae, take her to the bank, open the account and bring me the particulars.' He won and I was denied the pleasure of feeling I had plenty of cash of my very own. He kissed me and patted my shoulder. 'Now go with Mae and be a good girl.' And so I became the possessor of a bank account, and of a lifetime of hassle – regularly being informed that I'm in the red again!

Back at Lucia's I found her packing her bag for the tour. As I packed too, my thoughts skipped from Yura to Jerry, from anxiety to sadness. Pat, Otis and Markova came to dinner that evening. Pat and Otis always brought cheer and laughter, and I tried my best to join in and not hang my troubles on other people's necks. Alicia, too, was in great form, and reminisced with Pat about their time in Diaghilev's company. It was such a nice evening, and I was grateful to them all that they did not bring up the subject of my matrimonial debacle.

Next morning I took the train for Long Island and spent the day with my parents. Mother was in great form, so obviously happy with the situation I had brought about. But my papa worried me. I still did not feel that all was well with him, in spite of his assurances that he was perfectly all right.

We were leaving for our tour the next day. I gave my parents our itinerary and asked them to enclose Yura's letters in their own, promising to write and call whenever I could. After dinner Papa drove me to the station to catch the last train back to New York. Lucia was already in bed when I arrived, but she was not asleep. She asked me about my day, then told me she had informed the office that we would be rooming together on the tour. A new phase in my life was about to begin.

LAST FURLOUGH

As we followed the porter to our carriage, I saw Jerry standing on the platform talking to a few members of our company. I felt nervous, not knowing what to expect, what his attitude would be when we came face to face, but as we drew level with him, he greeted Lucia and ignored me completely! I relaxed, hoping that his decision to ignore me would continue for as long as we were to be stuck in the same company. As the train pulled away from the station, I felt a sort of contentment. I was leaving the past in New York and rolling into the rosy future of my imaginings.

The company enjoyed great success in every town, and soon everyone settled into the routine of touring life. Lucia was a dream room-mate – great company, a good sport, with a good temperament. She was a most beneficial influence on me and my rather fragile emotions.

Weeks went by. I received several letters from my parents, with blue missives from Yura enclosed. Letters from soldiers were brief and censored, but Yura let me know that he had been promoted to sergeant and transferred to the Russian Section. All those who spoke foreign languages were needed as translators and for other duties, for which they were now trained in anticipation of being sent to Europe. They were stationed at Camp Ritchie, about an hour from Baltimore, in the Blue Ridge Mountains.

One night when I returned to the hotel after our performance, I found a telegram from Yura. His section was on standby to depart for Europe. His last furlough was from Friday evening to Sunday midnight but he must remain in the region – would I come? I stared at the telegram, my heart pounding. *Of course I will come – how can I not?* It was already Wednesday night. I showed Lucia the telegram and asked her for leave of absence from after the performance the next day until the following Tuesday.

'You'll have to ask Jerry,' Lucia said. 'He's the director. I know it's awkward.' She looked pensive. 'Call him now,' she suggested.

I took a deep breath and did just that. I apologised for disturbing him, stated my request and asked for an official okay from him as our director. Jerry's answer, delivered in an icy tone, was precise. 'No. You don't have my okay! If you disregard this, don't bother to return.'

The phone went dead. I turned to Lucia and said, 'I'll have to go over Jerry's head now. My contract is with Hurok, not Jerry. I'll call Hurok now. If he says I can go, Jerry can't do anything about it!'

Lucia nodded. I called Hurok at his home, but there was no answer. I would have to wait until morning and call his office. Meanwhile, I bought a ticket on the sleeper train to New York. No matter who said what, permission or no permission, no-one and nothing would stop me going to see Yura to say goodbye.

Sleep evaded me; thoughts kept hopping into my head like rabbits. At last morning came, and I got up with a feeling of defiance and a determination to follow the dictates of my heart. I rang Hurok's office as soon as I could.

'Sarah Abramovna, what can I do for you?' His kind voice was reassuring. I read the telegram to him and relayed my conversation with Jerry. He listened in silence.

'Please let me go!' I pleaded.

'Eh! Okay, go.' His voice was still kind.

'Do I come back?'

'Of course. Don't worry. I'll talk to Jerry.'

I felt immense relief and gratitude for Hurok's soft heart and understanding. Armed with my small overnight bag, I raced to the railway station as soon as the performance ended and took the night train to New York. Installed in my compartment I waited anxiously for the train to move. When it did, I felt like I was eloping again! As the train gathered speed and the wheels clacked rhythmically on the rails, I finally relaxed and turned my thoughts to Yura, hoping he had received my telegram and would meet me at Camp Ritchie Station.

And there he was! I saw him before he spotted me. He was thinner, with an unfamiliar short haircut and in uniform – it all looked so strange. A mixture of pity and sadness engulfed me as I saw his gaunt, tired face. Before I knew, I was lifted off the ground in a tight embrace. At that moment nothing mattered, nothing else existed, only the joy of seeing him, loving him and our being together. He put me down gently. 'Thanks for managing to get away. I suspect it wasn't easy.'

'No, but Hurok gave me the green light, bless him.'

As we walked out of the station hand in hand, we both had so many questions to ask each other – they leapfrogged as we gradually filled each other in on what all those weeks had been like since we last saw each other. We walked along a country road to the camp, forest on one side, a few houses on the other, some with bed and breakfast signs. As we approached the last house, which stood on a slope in a large garden, Yura veered towards the gate. 'Here we are,' he said. 'We have a nice room here and the landlady is charming. She had a son in the army and shows much sympathy for the boys in the camp.'

Yura was right. The landlady received us warmly and took us upstairs to a spacious, lovely room furnished in simple but cosy country style. The bathroom next door was immaculate, with an old-fashioned bathtub and bright cotton curtains. Our landlady disappeared, finally leaving us alone in the first room we ever shared – our room! I ran into his arms and time stood still. Ah, dear reader, the memory of that moment is deeply embedded in the heart of the romantic young woman I was then. Now, as I write these lines, a tender tear glides slowly down my old, wrinkled face . . .

The sun was low in the sky when we set off for a walk in the forest. All we had to do was cross the road and follow the little path across a simple field. The aroma of pine trees, the silence, the dense forest enclosing us, were enchanting. We strolled hand in hand, talking, dreaming of our future and falling into short companionable silences.

We came upon a fallen tree, so Yura lifted me up onto its trunk. Our faces level, he looked me squarely in the eyes, and gently shook my shoulders. As if reading my thoughts, he said, 'Stop worrying. Nothing can happen to me. I'll come back to you in one piece! I know it and so must you.'

I nodded vigorously, tears choking me. *I must not spoil our time together with tears and long faces*, I told myself. It was getting dark, so we walked down the road towards the camp. We were both starving, neither of us having eaten all day. Yura told me that the only place in the vicinity to get something to eat was at the bar facing the camp gate. The squat building looked more like a shed, but was festooned with multicoloured lights, and had long wooden tables and benches on the veranda. A group of soldiers from Yura's section hailed him and he introduced me – to funny, raucous comments. We all laughed as we joined them at their table. They were such a nice bunch of boys. The food was surprisingly good but we did not linger. I wished the boys God speed and safe return and, holding hands, Yura and I walked slowly back to the house and our welcoming room.

Our night was so gentle, loving and tender. Our future looked bright, our equal partnership in life seemed indissoluble, and growing old together would be such fun. These happy thoughts, like a lullaby, finally rocked us to sleep. How painfully precious was each second of the little time left to us before the long separation ahead! How long? It was impossible to tell. And then the dreaded moment was upon us. Sunday, eleven-thirty p.m. We were sitting on the bench in the garden, having come down from our room a little while earlier. 'Let's sit here for a moment,' Yura had said as we stepped out from the house.

We sat, wanting to say so many things, but only managing, 'Take care of yourself.'

'You too . . .'

'I must go,' Yura finally said, standing up. We moved towards the gate with his arm around my shoulder. As I have said, the French say *Partir, c'est mourir un peu* (to part is to die a little) – that's how it felt now, leaving each other. We hugged without words. I watched his figure disappear into the dark, the sound of his footsteps fading away. Silence . . . emptiness . . .

Back in our room I felt so alone. It was unbearable. I had to get out. I packed my bag hurriedly, gave the room one last glance and went out into the garden. *Now what?* My train to New York did not leave until seven a.m. I sat on the bench by the tree and stared into the night.

11

PAPA'S HEART

I rejoined the company with a heavy heart. Nothing was the same any more, and the bad vibes between Jerry and me were a disruptive element, preventing me from concentrating fully on my work. It would have been easier if he had kept ignoring me, but he changed his attitude to one of mocking hostility. It was soon clear to me that, as the guilty party, I would have to leave the company. I had a long talk with Lucia, who sympathised but did not want to lose me. She asked me to be patient. 'It will all settle down,' she said. 'Give Jerry time.'

But an unexpected turn of events swept all these problems aside. One day the phone rang in our room and Lucia answered. 'Jerry has a message for you,' she said, holding out the phone. He told me the terrible news that my papa had suffered a heart attack and was in hospital.

'I must go to my parents immediately,' I told him. 'Today.'

'Yes, of course,' he responded kindly. It was mid-afternoon, and Lucia and I had been about to have a rest before going to the theatre. 'Pack your bag,' said Jerry. 'I'll make all the arrangements. There should be a flight to New York tonight. I'll call you shortly.'

Lucia was sorry to hear the bad news about my papa. She also remarked, 'You see? Jerry really loves you. He'll be all right with you. Give him time.'

I then phoned Mother, but there was no answer – she must have been at the hospital. My packing did not take long, but the wait for Jerry to call back seemed interminable. So much had happened since that morning I had left Jerry. I had felt so many emotions – bad ones, good ones, happy ones, guilt, shame for causing pain and trouble – and now this, my papa! Was it my fault? I had given him so many worries! I was sinking deeper and deeper into gloomy thoughts, hating myself, when there was a knock at the door.

'I've sent a telegram to your mother with the time of your arrival at LaGuardia Airport,' said Jerry, handing me the ticket. 'You're on the late flight from Los Angeles to New York. I'll take you to the airport. You're only in the first ballet, so you'll have plenty of time.' I was truly grateful and told him so. He shrugged. 'I'll pick you up at your dressing room after the first intermission,' he said, then walked away. I relaxed and tucked the ticket into my handbag.

It was difficult to perform that evening – my mind was elsewhere. Jerry and I left the theatre and got into a waiting taxi. Neither of us spoke on the long drive to the airport. When we arrived, Jerry got out of the cab and asked the driver to wait for him. As we walked to the counter, I noticed he was carrying a parcel, but thought nothing of it. He saw me to the gate, then handed me the parcel and said, 'This is for you. Bon voyage. I hope your father gets well soon.'

He raised his hand in a farewell gesture and walked away, giving me no chance to thank him for all his help. I felt rotten; my guilt weighed heavily on my conscience. I owed Jerry a great deal and had repaid him poorly.

Installed in my seat, I closed my eyes, exhausted, but once the plane had taken off, my thoughts gradually turned to the package Jerry had given me. I took it down from the rack and opened it – and stared in amazement at the most beautiful handbag I had ever seen! *Why?* I did not deserve it. *Why this present? What shall I do?* As I put it back in its box, I felt utterly undeserving of such a present, any present from Jerry. That gorgeous bag remained in its box for two years before I decided what the hell and used it!

A friend of my parents met me at the airport and drove me straight to the hospital, reassuring me that Papa was making good progress.

I found Papa in a ward with three other patients, Mama sitting by his bed. My papa looked ashen, but was happy to see me. Mother, too, was obviously glad I had come. She was tense and looked tired. My heart went out to them.

A nurse came by to check Papa's pulse, so I asked her when I would be able to talk to Papa's doctor. She answered my numerous questions with good grace, saying that Papa was a model patient and that I was not to tire him with too much talking. As Papa was not a private patient, we had to adhere to the visiting hours, and so had to leave until that afternoon. As I kissed him goodbye, Papa asked me how long I could stay in New York.

'Until we go rollerskating again!' I answered, and at that moment I knew it would be a long time before I stepped on a stage once more. I could not leave my papa until he was fit and strong.

Mother, who had recently passed her driving test, drove us home – it was my first experience of her driving. She was a bit nervous, as was I, but we made it. The first thing I did was call Hurok's office to tell him I did not know when I would be able to return to the company, and that he should not count on me in the near future. He asked after my father and sent his good wishes, adding that he understood I would want to stay with my papa. But then he assumed a business tone and suggested we cancel our contract. I agreed. It freed me from my obligations to him and the company, and gave him a free hand in filling the void created by my absence. Under the circumstances, it was the best solution. With the pressure of the contract lifted, I felt able to dispose of my time as I wished. I asked Hurok to notify Jerry, Lucia and Pat not to expect me back. Then I wrote Jerry a brief note thanking him for his help and the handbag.

By the time I had unpacked and Mother and I had had a cup of coffee, it was time to return to the hospital. Papa greeted me with a big smile, took my hand, and urged, 'You must return to the company soon.'

'I don't have to, Papa,' I replied. 'They gave me a long leave of absence. All is well, so don't worry. Besides, it's good for me to have a rest and spend some time with you.'

Papa patted my hand and said, 'It's good to have you here.'

That evening I had a long talk with Mother – a rare occasion! There were no arguments, and she seemed less preoccupied with my career. Obviously other things were on her mind, the same as on mine. So I brought up the subject of their finances. Yes, she was worried. It was obvious that it would be some time before Papa would be able to work again, and they had very few savings. I told her not to worry. Since I had started receiving my whole salary, I had had very few expenses. Being on tour, eating on our train or at a drugstore, and sharing rooms with Lucia had enabled me to save a tidy sum of money.

'There'll be enough to see us through until Papa is well and can work again,' I said. 'I, too, will work again, so we'll be all right. I have a bank account now, and a cheque book.' Mother was impressed.

Lucia rang and we had a long talk – she was so understanding and supportive. At the end of the conversation she said, 'Please come back to us when you're ready. We'll keep in touch.' We did keep in touch. I saw her for the last time shortly before her death. I love and treasure her memory – she was such a great lady and, to me, a rare friend. But I never returned to Ballet Theatre. The current of life steered me towards different shores.

I loved my pretty room in my parents' house. It was so peaceful. Papa got better and it was a happy day when he was allowed to come home. His strength returned rapidly and he began to spend more and more time at his work table, painting. I loved to sit by him and watch, and began to enjoy my enforced holiday, suddenly realising that I was in need of a rest.

Papa was not happy about using my savings – he was a proud man – but my mother and I finally made him see sense. That out of the way, life in the little house went on in peace and good humour. Every day my thoughts flew to Yura. Where was he? How was he? I missed him so much!

Dear Pat telephoned each week without fail. One day, roaring with laughter, he told me that Jerry had received the unwelcome letter from Uncle Sam – he was drafted into the army! I was surprised, because I knew that at that time men of thirty-eight and over were not subject to the draft. 'But Jerry is forty! How come he was called up?' I asked.

With merriment in his voice, Pat put me in the picture. 'Listen to this,' he said. 'Jerry told me that when you got your Yugoslavian passport in Sydney, he had to renew his. He persuaded the clerk that his date of birth in the expiring passport was incorrect, a mistake he hadn't noticed at the time it was issued. The clerk obligingly altered the date from 1904 to 1907 in the new passport. Jerry did it because he was fed up with people saying he was twice your age; that way he could claim that when you were seventeen he was only twenty-nine. Now he bitterly regrets his little white lie!'

'I didn't know that. How silly of him! So what happened?' I queried.

'Well, when Jerry tried to persuade the bureaucrat interrogating him that the date in his passport was a mistake, the man was unsympathetic. He asked Jerry if he swore that the date was incorrect. Jerry said yes, but that it was just a mistake, that he had paid no attention. "Okay," said the bureaucrat, "you have two options. Either you go to jail for perjury or you join the army. Which will it be?" Jerry chose the army!' Pat was highly amused, and I must admit, so was I.

Later I heard that Jerry was put in the Russian Section as a translator, since he spoke several languages. How would a man like him, whose ego did not permit him to accept being second-in-command, cope with standing to attention, saying 'yes, sir' and not being the boss, I wondered. It must have been anathema to him. Another thought crossed my mind – both Yura and Jerry would be in the Russian Section. Would they bump into each other? I hoped not!

Now that all the obstacles were removed, I could eventually have returned to Ballet Theatre, but something held me back – I did not feel happy at the prospect of returning. With Fokine dead, I knew that there would be no new productions in that grand style of his, which had given me the most important successes of my career. Massine? He was not with the company. Tudor? He had his style, his group of dancers, his tribe. I needed time out, to rest, to enjoy being at home, then I would consider going back. I did a long set of barre exercises on the veranda every morning and tried to keep in shape. I often thought of my friends in the company, and I missed Lucia greatly.

I became deeply religious for a time, influenced and inspired by our Russian priest, Father Vassili, who was calm and kind. He conducted beautiful services in the little church the Sea Cliff Russians had built, and I never missed one. Reciting set prayers learned from childhood was not enough – I had to talk to the Almighty in my own words, pouring out my heart and humbly asking for His help. I did not have to be in church to pray – in my room or on a walk by the sea was just as good. It gave me a feeling of peace and renewed hope.

Papa continued to recuperate and started to go for short walks, even to drive for short distances. The time had come for me to think seriously about what I was going to do about resuming work. Our finances would soon need a boost! As if in answer to my ponderings, Léonide Massine called. His relationship with the Monte Carlo company had gone pear-shaped and he was working on a new project, which was the reason for his call. He arranged to come the next day and discuss it with me. The possibility of working with Massine again filled me with joy!

When he arrived he gave me a present – I almost fainted with surprise! It was Worth's perfume, Je Reviens, and a big bottle too. Since Massine did not have a reputation for gift-giving, I was amazed and deeply touched.

Massine's dream was to have a company all of his own. He proposed to have a go at it, at first on a small scale. Several dancers, among them André Eglevsky and Yurek Lazowksi, had already agreed to join him. So did I. The first program would be comprised of short extracts from the classical repertoire, his own ballets and some new numbers he would choreograph on us. He would employ a small twenty-piece orchestra to travel with us on tour.

Massine called his company Ballet Russe Highlights, which would be under the management of the impresario Fortune Gallo. The opening performance would be in New York and then we would go on tour. The other ballerina would be Avdotia Istomina, a lovely soloist, and rehearsals were to be held in the big studio at Massine's house in Long Island. It all sounded perfect! But there was the thorny question of remuneration. I had never negotiated a contract myself and knew that I would be too embarrassed to ask for decent money and would accept whatever Massine offered me. So I told him that my agent would discuss the terms. But the truth was, I had no agent! Now I had to produce one in a hurry.

Massine seemed surprised that I had an agent, and didn't look too happy about it. 'Oh well,' he said, 'you ask your agent to call me tomorrow morning. What's his name?'

I started to blush, then remembered Jules Ziegler from the Louis Shurr Agency. Jerry had got him to negotiate my terms for *Florian*, so hoping for the best I gave Massine Ziegler's name.

'So, good,' Massine said. 'We start rehearsals next week. I'll telephone you.'

As soon as Massine had left in the Lincoln car he'd had for many years, I hurried to grab the phone book and searched frantically for the phone number of the Louis Shurr Agency. Luckily Jules Ziegler was in the office. He was surprised to hear from me, but greeted me cordially. To my plea to take me on and negotiate my contract with Massine, he said, 'With pleasure. What's it all about?'

I put him in the picture and told him that I had told Massine he was my agent. 'He's expecting you to call him in the morning. Sorry!' I explained how it had all happened and the fact that Massine was notoriously tight and hated parting with his pennies. 'I'd like a better financial arrangement for a change.'

Jules laughed. 'You've come to the right person. Count on me, I'll skin him!'

I was shocked by such an expression, but he promised to call me after he had spoken to Massine. 'These American agents have no respect for a great man like Massine,' I complained to my papa. 'I only wanted a bit more money, not his skin!'

Jules told me the next morning that the bargaining had started. Massine resisted, Jules insisted. By mid-afternoon they were on and off the phone, still not arriving at a sum acceptable to both parties. Finally, at the end of the day, Jules called to tell me that Massine had agreed to pay me a sum that satisfied Jules and made me feel – *Wa-oo!* – rich! But embarrassed.

When I turned up for the first rehearsal, I wondered if Massine would seem annoyed with me. But he did not, and never mentioned anything concerning my pay. The program he devised was excellent in its variety; the new numbers he choreographed were beautiful and effective. I loved the Russian peasant number he staged for me and Lazowksi to the tune of the popular song '*Yablotchko*' (Little Apple) – it was funny, gay and fast, a show-stopper. All in all, there were twenty numbers, with only one intermission; we changed backstage at breakneck speed! The tour was an artistic success, but did not meet Massine's financial expectations. The expenses were far greater than the profits, but his desire to have his own company was so great that he decided to chance a second tour later in the year.

In the last ten days before the end of the tour, my ankles and insteps started to swell up, as if full of water. I could hardly tie the ribbons of my toe shoes around my ankles, which looked awful! I spent the hours before going to the theatre lying down with my legs up on pillows, trying to ease the swelling. Dancing on them was uncomfortable and even painful.

'Hold on till the end, don't let me down! Just a few more days,' Massine urged me. As the last curtain came down, he looked at my deformed ankles and shook his head, saying, 'As soon as you get home, go to your doctor.'

I did not have a doctor in Sea Cliff, so Papa called his, who was kind enough to see me right away. Tests, cardiograms, questions – it was worrying and boring and I was getting depressed. Finally the verdict came: an enlarged and strained heart – six months of total rest and no physical effort of any kind. To me it sounded like a death sentence. For a dancer not to do a class every day is unthinkable. I was devastated! My poor parents looked shocked and worried. Mother kept saying that it was Colonel de Basil's fault, that he had exploited and overworked us; I kept defending him, so we had a few clashes.

My first great love, Yura Skibine, and me in Aurora's Wedding, *Ballet Theatre, 1942.* (Maurice Seymour, Chicago)

As Lise in a Ballet Theatre production of La fille mal gardée, *1940.*

Pat Dolin and I take to the stage once more, at an American Ballet Theatre gala celebration in New York.

Jerome (Jerry) Robbins and me at the launch of Sono Osato's book, Distant Dances, *in 1980.* (Steven Caras, © 1980)

Sono Osato (left), Natalia Makarova (right) and I caught up in 1979.

Mikhail Baryshnikov, Sono Osato and me at the launch of her book. (Steven Caras, © 1980)

With Vera Zorina (Eva Brigitta Hartwig, left) and my agent at the time, Jules Ziegler, at Sardi's in New York, 1944.

The dear free spirit Yul Brynner. He and I starred in Dark Eyes *on its tour of England in 1948.*

In my Russian costume for Dark Eyes.

Anna Volkova in Aurora's Wedding*;
she often replaced Riabouchinska in some
of her roles.* (Maurice Seymour, Chicago)

*With David Gale, who contributed so
much to the development of English
ballet students.*

*Cecil and I always enjoyed our dinners
with Peter Ustinov.*

Tamara Tchinarova as Zobeide, with Martin Rubinstein as the Golden Slave in a 1944 revival of Fokine's Scheherazade *for the Australian Borovansky Ballet.*

With my friend and colleague since childhood Tamara Tchinarova Finch in 2000.

Mrs Mary and Dr Joseph Ringland Anderson (centre) in 1935. Dr Anderson's films of our company are among the few recordings of our performances in existence.

Pat Dolin and I cuddle some gorgeous koalas, 1938. I fell in love with these beautiful animals the minute I saw them.

In Australia to work with the Australian Ballet in 1986; (left to right) the late Sir Robert Southey, me, Lady Marigold Southey and the late Noël Pelly.

With my dear friends the late Dr Raymond and Mrs Pamela Lister, who befriended me and 'adopted' me as one of their family. (Daniel Ray Studios)

Bob and Helen Gifford, the most caring, loving friends I'm so lucky to have.

Dear Cecil and me on our wedding day, 28 May 1949, in Sheridan, Wyoming.

My dear husband, Cecil Tennant. (Boris Chaliapin, 1976)

Cecil's family home in Yorkshire.

Cecil (left), Vivien Leigh and Laurence Olivier (right) during the Old Vic tour of Australia in 1948.

At the theatre in 1950 with Laurence Olivier, Vivien Leigh and Cecil.

My three children, Victoria (left), Robert (centre) and Irina (right), enjoy the sun.

Pat Dolin with me and the three children, Robert (left), Irina (centre) and Victoria (right) in 1958. He had just appeared as St George in the Christmas pantomime St George and the Dragon. *Karsavina's son played the dragon.*

With Irina (left) and Victoria (right) in 1978. (Jennie Walton)

My daughter Victoria's two children, Katya and Nikolai, in 2005.

My daughter Victoria.

My daughter Irina.

Irina's daughter, Natasha.

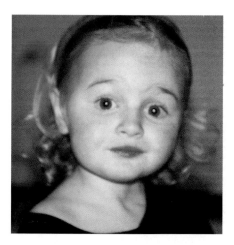

Natasha's daughter, Zoe.

My son, Robert, all grown up and winner of the P&O Ferries Formula Ford 1600 race in Thruxton in 1980.

Robert's sons Finn (left) and Laurie (right) in 2005.

Robert's son Hugh in 2005.

With Mme Tamara Karsavina in London, thirty years after I first saw her dance.

The three 'Baby Ballerinas' – Tamara Toumanova (left), me (centre) and Tania Riabouchinska (right) – at a party given by Riabouchinska in Hollywood in 1980.

With Serge Lifar in 1987, a few months before he died.

With Roman Jasinski, who was one of the Ballet Russe de Monte Carlo's first leading dancers.

There was no immediate financial worry – Jules Ziegler did well by me – but I began to wonder if I would ever be able to get back in shape and dance again. That thought gave me nightmares. For a long time now, there had been no letters from Yura – that was another worry. I lost my grip and became a miserable mess. I prayed, I cried, and I began to stuff myself with food. Soon I could not fit into any of my clothes and was spending all day in my nightshirt, praying and eating, eating and praying. My parents did not hassle me, but waited patiently for me to sort myself out.

One day, though, Papa had had enough of me wallowing in misery. He stuck me in front of Mother's big dressing-table mirror and asked, 'What do you see?' I stared and stared at myself in silence. 'Irischka, what do you see?'

Disgust with myself swelled inside me and I finally answered, 'I see a fat woman with a sour expression on her ugly face.'

'It's not you, is it?' he said.

I looked at Papa full of remorse. He had just recovered from a heart attack and what was *I* doing? Giving him another one? I felt like a selfish, self-centred, gutless, disgusting fatso! Bursting into sobs, I hung onto my papa's neck, blubbering, 'Sorry, sorry, sorry!'

From that day on I got a grip on myself and gradually came to my senses. Papa was great, cheering me up with his kind sense of humour and encouraging me to stick to the diet I had imposed on myself. A month later I was able to fit into my clothes again. My ankles and feet were improving too, and I at last received a letter from Yura. It contained little information about his whereabouts, but it was loving and he seemed in good spirits. It was such a joy to hear from him, and such a relief to know that he was all right. Mother cheered up too, and stopped cursing Colonel de Basil.

My head cleared and I was able to think calmly about my situation. What if my dancing days *were* numbered? Well, I could give classes, teach at a school of dance. I knew I would be able to provide for myself. But how about my papa with his bad heart? He might be all right, but he might not.

It became imperative in my mind to provide Papa with some measure of financial security. As an adult I fully realised what misery we had lived in, in the years following our flight from Russia, and now I was determined that my parents would never have to go through hard or worrying times again. Going back to the ballet company would not achieve my aim. What would? I thought of Jules Ziegler. No matter how much I disliked the idea of having an agent, I had to admit that the deal he had made for me with Massine was amazing. I decided to talk to him and see if he had any suggestions for earning the kind of money a ballet company could not or would not, at that time, offer its leading artists.

I made an appointment to see Ziegler, and took the train to New York. He listened patiently to my worries, and I begged him not to spread it around that I was having health problems. He nodded then glanced at his watch. 'I'm hungry, aren't you?' he asked. 'Let's go around the corner to Sardi's. I'll tell you what we can do over lunch.'

Everyone who was anyone on Broadway patronised Sardi's. After the opening night of a musical or play, all involved would gather at Sardi's and anxiously await the early editions of the newspapers, to read the notices and hear the critics' verdict. The walls of the restaurant were solidly hung with caricatures of Broadway stars, sketched by Alex Gard, a Russian refugee and ex-naval officer.

'Look, I have a couple of ideas,' said Jules, sipping his gin and tonic after we had ordered our food. 'If you're ready to start working, I can easily get you a contract for the next month's music hall program at the Roxy Cinema. With your name they'll grab you! And the money I'll get for you will be a sizeable amount.'

My heart sank. Cinema, music hall – what a come-down. I knew exactly what to expect if I went for it – one number four times a day, five times on Saturdays and Sundays, stuck among rockettes, comedians, clever poodles, acrobats and magicians, all performing between showings of the featured film. *Well*, I told myself, *if the great Preobrajenska, my beloved teacher, could dance in the same circumstances on a visit to London, so can I!* Things were radically different, of course, from Preobrajenska's day, and no self-respecting ballerina would dream of performing somewhere like the Roxy Cinema now, but in the circumstances there was no room for sitting on high horses. I had to swallow my pride, cash in my chips while the going was good, and ignore the disparaging remarks I would earn from many people. All this flashed through my mind while the waiter placed the food in front of us.

'And what's your second idea?' I asked Jules, eyeing my sole meunière without enthusiasm.

'It's a musical comedy. They're hoping to start rehearsals in a couple of months. Most of it's already cast. The mature leads are a singer, Gertrude Niesen, and Frank Parker, but they're looking for a juvenile lead. Can you sing?'

'No!' His stupid question irritated me.

'Hmm . . . that's all right,' said Jules brightly. 'They could make the character a dancer instead of a singer.'

'What's the musical about?' I asked.

Jules explained that it was a comedy – a naval base full of sailors, lots of beautiful girls, lots of funny songs – Jackie Gleason was the lead comedian. My heart sank even lower. I had no doubt that all of them were wonderful people, but what would I be doing among them? Our arts were poles apart; I simply did not fit into this ribald musical. I told Jules what I felt.

He seemed to understand but pointed out, 'That's where the money is, so think about it. Meanwhile, I'll suggest you for the part to Dave Wolper, the producer.'

'Anything else you can suggest?' I asked tentatively.

'No, not at present.'

I sat staring at Jules, thinking that I did not like either proposal, but the anxiety of being in no position to help my parents if the need arose became a fixation. A little voice in my head said insistently, *What the hell, don't be choosy. Go for it!* There was no time to shillyshally. I had to give Jules an answer. 'All right, if you can get me the Roxy and the part in the musical, I'll take them.'

'Great!' said Jules, looking satisfied. 'Let's go to my office and sign the agreement.'

As I left his office, having signed up as his client, he was already on the phone to the Roxy. He was to call me the next day with the news. Sitting on the train on the way home, I worked out how I would explain it all to my parents. After dinner, as we sat in the living room, I told them I had been to see Jules Ziegler.

'Oh, why?' exclaimed Mother, and Papa looked up from his book in alarm. I explained to them that if I sat around much longer doing nothing, I would go bonkers. My ankles seemed all right again, and a bit of work would do me good and keep me in practice. They looked doubtful. But when I told them about Ziegler's idea of a month at the Roxy, they were horrified. It took the rest of the evening to argue my case. They were far from convinced by my arguments, but reconciled themselves to the fact that if the job at the Roxy materialised I would take it on. I omitted to tell them about the vague prospect of the musical. There was no point upsetting them even more with something that might never happen.

Ziegler phoned the next afternoon. The Roxy was interested; I was to come to his office the next day and he would take me to meet the director of the show. The next day at the fixed hour we were shown into the director's office. As soon as we were introduced, I felt at ease, and settled down in my armchair, curious to learn about this new world so far removed from mine. The director paid me some effusive compliments and turned out to be quite a balletomane.

The men must have worked out the conditions beforehand – the contract was ready on the desk. The director read it to me; I was to have my name in lights at the front entrance, and my own dresser; I would devise the number I would perform, in consultation with the resident choreographers; I would receive half my pay on signing the contract and the rest on the day of the last performance. When I heard the financial terms I was stunned – they exceeded my craziest dreams! But I forced myself not to show my astonishment and excitement.

'Does that mean I meet with your approval?' asked the director. 'Any questions?' His manner was most charming. I looked at Jules, took my time and, watched by two smiling faces, signed the contract. I could hardly believe it was that simple!

A new challenge, a new experience, was waiting for me, for better, for worse. I felt alive again.

A DIFFERENT STAGE

The Roxy: a memory I do not relish! The day after I signed the contract, I was to meet the choreographers to discuss how to present my number – a decision had to be made pronto. The Roxy, like a conveyor belt, churned out entertainment for cinemagoers. I met Jules at his office and he took me to the Roxy's stage door, where the director's secretary was waiting. First she took me to my assigned dressing room, which was spacious but Spartan, with a worn-out couch that was a comfort when I had to spend almost all my waking hours inside those walls.

We then proceeded to a large studio, where a pleasant surprise awaited me. The choreographers I was to meet turned out to be Lenny and Garry, the couple I had worked with on *Florian*. What a great relief! They were very good at what they did, and I got on well with them. We greeted each other warmly, with hugs and happy exclamations.

They then outlined their idea for my number – I would appear at the top of a tall, wide staircase with three half-landings, on either side of which would sit six harpists, all dressed in electric blue chiffon evening gowns. They would be my orchestra, and would play 'Rhapsody for Strings', which had been newly composed for a hugely popular film of the time. It was light, romantic and most suitable for a ballet variation. I would dance my way down, zigzagging between the harpists, then spend the rest of the variation covering as much as possible of the vast stage, which would be lit in moonlight tones. My costume would be an ankle-length pale fuchsia skirt with a brighter fuchsia bodice. It sounded all right to me, and the idea of the harpists was certainly a novelty. However, I could not help voicing my misgiving that my 'arty' number, sandwiched between a magic act and three slapstick comics, would look a little out of place.

'But so you are!' Garry laughed.

I felt like kicking him, but he was right, of course. I would have to brace myself and expect many dismayed and disappointed remarks to come my way.

'So what do you think?' asked Lenny.

'I like your idea very much. When do we start rehearsing?'

'Next week, Monday nine a.m. We'll have all the harpists here by then. It'll be smooth sailing, you'll see!' Garry and Lenny looked cheerful, and so did Jules.

We all moved off to the wardrobe department, where my measurements were taken and arrangements made for a fitting on Monday. Jules and I then went to lunch, leaving Lenny and Garry to discuss the details of my costume with the wardrobe staff. Over lunch, Jules pointed out to me that I would have to move to New York for the duration of my Roxy engagement, since it was not practical to commute from Long Island. 'Which hotel will I book you into?' he asked. 'Any preference?'

That possibility had crossed my mind already, so I had been on the look-out and had noticed a small hotel a few doors away from the Roxy stage door. 'Yes,' I replied, 'there's a hotel near the stage door. It's handy and probably cheap. Let's try there.'

Jules raised his arms in horror. 'You can't stay there,' he said. 'It's horrible! The street is horrible, noisy, full of cheap clubs. No, no, not for you!'

'I only need a bed for a few hours' sleep. I'll spend all my days in my dressing room. Why waste money on a good hotel?'

'But you'll be earning good money. Why stay in a horrid place?'

'I'm earning it to keep it, not to spend it, remember?!'

'But, but . . . oh dear, you're worse than Massine!' At this, we both burst out laughing.

After lunch, Jules returned to his office, saying he would come to the rehearsal on Monday and not to tell anyone where I would be staying in New York, if I really was going to insist on my silly idea. It was a pleasure to get back to Sea Cliff – to get away from the city and the traffic – to breathe fresh air was such a relief. My parents listened to my account of the day with interest, and pronounced my choice of hotel practical and time-saving. Thank God my parents were not snobs!

On the said Monday I got to the Roxy early, installed myself in my dressing room, then went to the rehearsal studio. The harps, harpists, Lenny and Garry were already there when I arrived. As we were introduced, I noticed how lovely these young musicians were and, after they played for us, I admired their skill and musical sensitivity. Lenny and Garry had worked out the choreography well and transmitted it to me smoothly. For a few hours I plunged into the work I loved, my body feeling alive again and my ankles doing well. The music sounded so enchanting, I almost forgot where I was and why!

Jules popped in then left again, satisfied that all was well. My costume fitting in the afternoon also went well, so I returned to Sea Cliff pleasantly tired. There a letter from Yura awaited me – so welcome, so treasured. I had a nice dinner with my parents, wrote a reply to Yura, and slept better than I had in a long time.

Two days before the we were due to start at the Roxy, we were all called for a very early morning rehearsal, and I saw for the first time what my number would be like – I thought Lenny and Garry had done well by me. The other numbers were good, and were well suited to the Roxy. I came on after a magician and was followed by three comedians, with whom I became good friends in the days to come. Jules, who watched the dress rehearsal from the vast auditorium, was satisfied.

When I was finally free to leave the rehearsal, Jules came with me to the hotel next door, to see if there were any vacancies, which there were. The man at the desk informed us that acts from the Roxy often stayed at his establishment. We inspected the room: it was small and basic, with heavy old furniture – a bed, bedside table, dressing table, one chair, hanger behind a curtain – but oh, luxury, a tiny bathroom of my very own! It was . . . sort of clean. I looked at Jules triumphantly. 'What more do you need?' I asked. While he looked at me with silent disgust, I booked the room for a month and moved in the next day.

My parents were coming to see the first of the first four performances the next day, so I asked the stage doorman to show them to my dressing room when they came in after the show. All was done and ready, but what would tomorrow bring? Butterflies started to flutter in my stomach.

My first night in the hotel was ghastly! The noise from the narrow street below was deafening – loud voices of customers emerging from the sleazy nightclubs added to the din of the all-night traffic – and the flicking neon lights from across the street hit my eyes mercilessly through the flimsy, sad-looking curtains in my room. They were projected onto the walls and ceiling – red, blue, orange – on and on, all night! *Bloody hell!* I reflected. *Jules would have a good laugh if he could see me now!*

First thing in the morning I ran to the drugstore and bought an eye-mask and some earplugs. Armed with my purchases and nursing a splitting headache, I returned to my room, swallowed a Kalmin tablet and went to the theatre.

The loudspeaker in my dressing room was soon calling me, so I crossed myself and hurried on stage, hoping I would not stumble on the staircase and make an even bigger fool of myself by sliding all the way down on my bottom. The harpists looked lovely. We wished each other luck then took our places.

The curtain went up, the beautiful sound of harps filled the auditorium, and I appeared at the top of the staircase. Out of the vast black abyss facing me, where no human was visible, came a whistle followed by a ripple of giggles – quite a change from the reception I was used to! Steeling myself against the hurt I felt, I danced my variation, giving it my all – one must, regardless of what churns inside.

The lukewarm applause at the end was far from encouraging, although the harpists, Lenny, Garry and Jules all said the number looked beautiful. One of the three comics called out, 'Well done, kiddo,' but I already knew the Roxy was a big mistake. It paid well, though – somehow that did not make sense to me.

I waited for my parents back in my dressing room, dreading their reaction. They arrived looking bewildered and sad but tried not to show it, complimenting me on my performance and saying they liked the number. 'But,' my papa finally said, 'it's not the Roxy's usual fare.' They were tactful and did not stay long; I was glad to be left alone, and braced myself for the next performance.

There was a knock at the door and the three smiling faces of the comedians appeared. 'Hi, we're going out for a bite. Can we bring you something?' I was touched by their kindness – at this stage they were total strangers. I thanked them for their offer, then handed them my thermos, which I had forgotten to fill up with coffee that morning.

'Which one are you?' I asked the nearest. 'Nolan, Denis or Marti?' I had heard their names over the loudspeaker.

'I'm Marti,' he said. Pointing to the short one, he added, 'That's Denis, and Nolan, he's the one with the business head!'

'Hi,' I said. 'Thanks for your kind words backstage. It helped.'

'I meant it.'

'If you could have this filled with black coffee, no sugar, and get me a bun, any bun, I would be so grateful,' I said, pointing to the thermos.

It became a routine. Every time the boys went out between shows, they brought me coffee and buns. Other times they sat in my dressing room talking and laughing, making my days bearable and even fun.

As that first day progressed, I was fascinated to notice the change in the audiences' reactions: at the second show they were polite; at the third warm; at the fourth quite good, and much more appreciative of my offering. But at weekends, the eleven a.m. show was the worst of all, a disaster! I was whistled at and booed, while ribald remarks rained on me from the balconies and feet stomped on the floor. Classical ballet was clearly not their cup of tea. I learned to live with it and not get too upset. Going on stage became a job – art flew out the window. I hated that feeling, but there are times in life when one can't be too choosy.

The last show of all was a huge relief, the last cheque a huge satisfaction! Some time later, I bumped into Igor Youskevitch as I came out of one of Vilzak's classes. 'How could you prostitute your art?' he threw at me as he walked away.

It was heaven to be back in my lovely room at my parents' house, away from New York and from the stresses of the past month. Papa resumed going to work twice a week at Bobri's design studio; the rest of the week he had plenty of work he could do from home. My ankles continued to behave, and I went to New York with Papa on the days he drove in, so I could take one of Vilzak's classes. The rest of the week I did a long set of barre exercises at home on the veranda each day; Papa had installed a proper barre for me there. The doctor chided me for starting work against his advice, but on the whole I was satisfied with my ticker.

My preoccupation with long-term financial security became fanatical. I knew Lucia Chase would always welcome me back to Ballet Theatre, but what if the musical Jules Ziegler had talked about did materialise? *What to do? Follow my heart, or follow my head and 'prostitute my art' again?* I did not want to broach the subject of the musical with my parents yet. After all, nothing was certain. Three weeks went by, then one morning, when Papa and I were about to set off for New York, Jules phoned with news about the musical, which was to be called *Follow the Girls*. The producer, Dave Wolper, was interested in meeting me, and changing the character from a singer to a dancer would be no problem. Did I want to meet Wolper?

'Could I have a couple of days to think it over?' I asked.

'No,' Jules replied. 'Rehearsals are due to start in ten days, so yes or no?'

'What would the conditions be if the producer and I like each other?'

'I've worked it out. Can you come to my office now?'

Seated in his office later that morning, I settled down to hear what Jules had to say. He pulled a memo towards him and started reading: '1. Star billing to be shared with Gertrude Niesen and Frank Parker; 2. Paid rehearsal time (standard); 3. If show successful, subject to out-of-town performances before opening in New York, regular contract for a year at $2000 per week; 4. Costumes to be executed by Mme Karinska; and 5. Approval of choreography for own dance numbers. How does that sound to you?'

I could hardly believe my ears. 'Two thousand a week? That's not possible!'

'On Broadway it is,' retorted Jules. At that moment the phone rang and made me jump. 'Yeah ... put him on ... Hi, Dave ... yes,

I talked to her . . . it took a bit of persuading, but she'll meet with you . . . lunch? Good idea. I'll ring her now and call you back.' Jules hung up, all smiles.

'He's really keen to meet you, proposes to have lunch with you and me at Sardi's tomorrow. Come on, let's go – you've got absolutely nothing to lose.'

Nothing, I thought to myself, *but my reputation*, which had already been mucked up by the Roxy in some people's eyes. 'All right, Jules, I'll come.' Yet again I was about to plunge into unfamiliar waters.

'How was your day?' Papa asked when I joined him at Bobri's. As we drove home, I told him about the possibility of being in a musical comedy and what Jules had to say. When I mentioned the amount of money Jules would ask for on my behalf, Papa remained silent for a while then said, 'Irischka, money is not everything in life. There are more important things than money.'

I knew what Papa was driving at. 'Papa, if Fokine were alive and with the company, I wouldn't hesitate to go back to Ballet Theatre, but he's dead. Perhaps this is a good moment to make a bit of money for a rainy day. Something will turn up for me in the ballet world again, something exciting, I know it will!'

Papa did not comment. We fell silent, each of us wrestling with our thoughts and feelings. Mother took my news in her stride and expressed contentment in the fact that by doing the musical I would remain near them in New York. Up in my room that night, I started a letter to Yura. I missed him so much and wondered what advice he would have given me in my present situation.

The next day, as Jules and I entered Sardi's, a man approached and greeted Jules. 'Dave, meet Baronova.' We shook hands and I was immediately aware that Wolper was looking me over – a horrid sensation.

We proceeded to a table, where a slight, grey-haired man was sitting. He stood up as we approached. 'Ah,' he said, 'Miss Baronova, how nice to meet you.' His eyes did not inspect me, and his friendly manner was pleasing.

'Harry Delmar, our director,' said Dave Wolper.

We talked in general terms about their musical and my possible participation in it. They told me that the choreographer for the entire show was Catherine Littlefield, which cheered me up. 'Could you work with Catherine?' asked Wolper.

'I've met her. I know of her work, and I think she's a lovely lady,' I answered noncommittally

As the lunch came to an end, Mr Wolper asked me if it would be in order for him and Jules to discuss the contract. Time was passing, and if they could agree on terms he would like to have the contract signed in the next couple of days. My heart in my throat, I said, 'Yes, it's in order,' even managing a light-hearted laugh.

The men put me in a taxi for the station and turned their steps towards Jules's office. I did not hear from Jules until the next evening. 'Wolper agreed to all our conditions,' he announced. 'We're ready to sign tomorrow at four p.m. at my office.'

I told my parents the news – none of us really knew what I was getting into, perhaps for a whole year. We sat around in a rather subdued mood, each of us engrossed in our private thoughts. *But the pay is good!* I thought to cheer myself up. The truth was, my whole being longed to be back where I belonged, in a ballet company.

The next day, uncertain whether to laugh or cry, I signed the contract, committing myself to a novel experience, and determined to make the best of it. When Wolper left, Jules went into practicalities. I would have to move to New York, but that was not pressing – it would only become an issue after the out-of-town tour, before the opening in New York. 'But the show might not make it,' I ventured. 'It might be a flop.'

'It *will* make it,' responded Jules. 'Wolper has already made the deal with Shubert's New Century Theatre.' Jules obviously believed the show would be a success. 'My secretary will engage a dresser for you and line up some flats to look at,' he added.

That's service, I thought, amazed. I thanked him for all his efforts and, a bit dazed, made for home. My parents showed neither pleasure nor displeasure at the news that I had signed. Papa just said, 'I hope it goes well for you.' Mother said, 'Oh well.'

Trying to look cheerful, I struck a ballet pose and chanted, 'And I might earn lots of pennies for a change.'

Mother giggled, Papa remained pensive. I was pensive too when I went to bed. In the morning I had a call from the stage manager, to advise me that I had an appointment with Catherine Littlefield the next day at the theatre. From the word go, I knew I was in good hands with Catherine. Her sister, Dorothy, acted as her assistant, and both were calm, friendly and highly efficient. Catherine brought a pianist, who played the three pieces that had been suggested by one of the three composers and the musical director for my three numbers. They were the popular 'Montezuma', a classical flamenco and music specifically composed for my number with the sailors. Catherine wanted me to approve them, but she knew the musical comedy business, I did not. If she approved the music, it was fine with me. I told her so.

'Oh good!' she exclaimed. 'I can see you'll be easy and a joy to work with!' We were to start work on the first number that same afternoon. Meanwhile, the stage manager handed me the script so that I could learn my lines. The 'heart-throb' of the show was Frank Parker, and most of my dialogue was with him, along with short exchanges with Gertrude Niesen and a few others. Learning lines did not bother me – I always had a good memory. It was my accent. Would I be understood?

'Don't worry. Delmar will see to that,' the stage manager reassured me. And he was right.

It took two days to devise my two solo numbers and three hours to devise my number with the sailors. They were a jolly lot of chorus boys, friendly and likeable. I found myself getting interested in how this jigsaw puzzle was going to be put together, and decided to observe the director and the cast closely, especially my co-stars, whom I was yet to meet.

My impressions of my first meeting with the cast have never changed. Gertrude Niesen was short, blonde and tarty-looking, with a lovely deep singing voice. She was self-centred, tough and hoity-toity, and was always accompanied by her father–manager. He was an unpleasant-looking man with a permanent smelly, slimy, chewed-up cigar between his bulbous lips. During the entire year I spent with the show, I only ever heard his voice arguing or complaining, never once in greeting or with a friendly word. His daughter never talked to me, apart from the words she was required to say to me by the script during the performance. She knew how to put across a song, was very good in the role, and was a big success.

Frank Parker was short, with a beautiful tenor voice, but he was no matinee idol. He was unpretentious, charming and easy to work with. The rest of the cast were a nice, friendly bunch. The chorus girls were tall, highly professional, beautiful-looking women who dreamt of being stars one day. But the cast was not a 'tribe', as we were in our ballet company. There was no easy, relaxed camaraderie. They came to the theatre, gave their performance and went away to get on with their individual lives. In the ballet we had a large repertoire and were always rehearsing new productions while travelling around the world. I found that to do the same thing night after night in a rather undistinguished show was not very inspiring. It became automatic, like a monotonous job.

My parents came to opening night. They were not impressed, but they acted supportive, for which I was very grateful. I had gone for a bit of financial security – I got it. One can't have one's cake and eat it too! By the time we arrived in New York, I had my own dresser, Beatrice Winters, a black American. She was portly and in her forties, with a beautiful coffee-coloured face. A strong bond developed between us: she called me her 'baby', I adored her. She looked after me like a nanny – in and out of the theatre, she guarded me from people she did not approve of; she would glare at them and scare them away. She became a dear, close friend, and my parents loved her dearly too.

I moved into my own flat, which Jules's secretary had found for me, in an old brownstone house – 23 East 69th Street, between Madison Avenue and Park Avenue. My landlady lived on the ground floor; on the first floor it was just me. I had a large living room and bedroom, a bathroom, a good kitchen and a nice little entrance hall. My very first, my very own lovely flat. I was so thrilled to feel grown-up and independent. I was twenty-six years old – about time I felt grown-up!

At that time Jules also introduced me to his lawyer friend, who told me he could obtain a legal Mexican divorce from Jerry for me, which would be recognised in the United States. Jerry's consent would not be needed, and I would not be required to go to Mexico, so I asked him to go ahead with it. I wanted to be a free woman for Yura's return. I missed him, worried about him and scrutinised the newspapers every day for news from Europe.

I had heard from my dear buddy Tassia. She was closing her school and moving back to New York with her mama and her poodle very soon. One evening there was a knock on my dressing-room door and there she was, my dear, dear Tassia. She had come straight from the station – we could hardly wait for the show to finish, we had so much to talk about! While I was on stage, she wasted no time making friends with Beatrice. By the end of the evening they were getting on like a house on fire. It was so good to have my old friend with me again. She stayed with me until she found a flat for herself, her mama and her poodle, who both arrived in due course.

Tassia volunteered for entertaining the American troops overseas. As soon as she had installed her mama and poodle in her flat, she went off in her smart-looking uniform to Italy. She reappeared at my door sooner than expected, with her arm in a sling. 'What happened?' I cried in alarm.

'Too much chianti! I lost my balance on stage, got entangled in the back curtain, and fell and broke my arm.'

I was delighted to have her back. With her around, life was more cheerful. She came on Sundays to my parents' house, and they were always happy to see her. Tassia's husband, a naval officer whom she hardly ever saw, and whose existence she had almost forgotten, came to New York from San Francisco to say hello. Tassia's poodle usually growled at him, but on this rare visit he bit him. Furious, her husband gave Tassia an ultimatum: the poodle or him. Tassia chose the poodle, and she and her husband never saw each other again!

The show people often visited the military hospitals. Several times, some of us from *Follow the Girls* went to Mitchel Field Air Force Hospital near New York. The sight of the badly wounded, burnt, traumatised young men brought home to me the ghastly reality of war. Talking to the personnel, I discovered that volunteers were welcome to chat with some boys, read to those incapable of doing so and generally give a helping hand where it was needed. As I had some free mornings and afternoons, I enlisted as a volunteer. It was not easy to see so much suffering, but it made me feel useful, and nearer to Yura. Unless you lost a loved one, it was hard to feel that the United States was at war. Life went on as usual with plenty of everything, but some suffered and shed tears.

ENDINGS

My Mexican divorce came through, and I felt satisfied as I put the document in a drawer. It occurred to me that it would be polite to inform Jerry that we were now free of each other, so I wrote him a short note. Assuming that he would be in communication with his old friend Richard Davis, I addressed the envelope care of him. When I told Tassia about it, her comment was, 'Poor Jerry. He'll be heartbroken!' What could I say? Nothing. I could only feel guilty and sort of sad.

During this time I often had supper with Mme Karinska. I enjoyed her company, and that of her equally eccentric, interesting friends. On one particular occasion, she introduced me to a friend of hers from Hollywood, Ray Milland the film star. He was on location in New York, filming *The Lost Weekend*, in which he portrayed an alcoholic, later winning an Oscar for his rendition. He was a tall, handsome man with a most pleasing manner. He told me that he was Welsh, and recounted funny stories of the time he served in the British Cavalry Regiment before turning his steps to Hollywood.

A week or so later, Mme Karinska was working late and called to ask if I would come over after the performance for a bite to eat with her. Soon after I arrived, a dreadful-looking Ray Milland appeared. He was unshaven, not with a five o'clock shadow, but with at least a ten o'clock shadow! 'Just finished shooting on Third Avenue, saw your lights on and here I am, begging for a drink,' he said. He had his drink, but we were all so tired that we did not linger.

Before we parted, Ray asked Mme Karinska and me to have supper with him on his last night in New York. As it turned out, he was only in town a few days longer. On his last night he picked Mme Karinska up in a chauffeur-driven limousine, then rolled up at the stage door of the theatre. Ray strolled through the stage door and down the corridor to my dressing room, shown the way by the impressed stage doorkeeper, and gaped at by members of the cast who were on their way out. As I settled myself down in the limousine, Mme Karinska laughed and said, 'That'll set their tongues wagging!'

Of course I had heard of the famous El Morocco nightclub, but I had never been there. It was very posh – the maître d' had the prim and solemn manner of an English butler. The seats were covered in zebra skin, there was subdued lighting and a large dance floor. People in evening dress sat at the tables, looking rich and debonair, while a pretty girl wandered among them, taking photographs that she later offered to interested patrons. We had a most enjoyable supper, then Ray and I danced a couple of times and he danced a lively foxtrot with Karinska. We went home in the limousine and parted in high spirits, wishing Ray bon voyage and success with the rest of filming.

The next morning Tassia appeared at my flat brandishing a news-paper. 'Wait till you see this!' she laughed as she opened the paper to the gossip page. There, the much-feared gossip columnist Louella Parsons spread her hearsay and poison. Many marriages and careers suffered at the hands of this troublemaker. 'Read this!' Tassia cried.

Intrigued by her hilarity, I took the paper and began to read: 'IRINA BARONOVA AND RAY MILLAND SEEN DANCING AT EL MOROCCO. IS MISS BARONOVA THE NEXT MRS MILLAND?'

'What?!' I exclaimed in disbelief, although still somewhat amused.

'His wife might clock him on the head with a rolling pin when he gets home,' giggled Tassia.

'Oh, she must be used to this sort of gossip by now,' I replied, dismissing the whole incident as of no consequence.

A while later Ray Milland rang. 'I'm at the airport,' he said. 'Just wanted to warn you, in today's Louella Par –'

'I know, I know, I read it!'

'I hope it won't cause any embarrassment. I'm really sorry.'

'Oh, forget it,' I reassured him, then joked, 'Will you get a sour reception when you get home?'

Ray laughed. 'No, my wife doesn't pay attention to gossip columnists.'

That afternoon as I walked down Madison Avenue, I stopped to look in the window of a pet shop. Two wire-haired terrier puppies were on display, rolling playfully over each other. I could not resist going in to see these adorable pups at closer quarters. The result – I walked out of the shop with a lovely yapping furry companion in my arms, my first doggy. I called him Jicky, the name of my favourite Guerlain perfume. I had just got home and settled down to play with the little fellow when Tassia walked in. 'What on earth?' she exclaimed. As I explained myself, Jicky, excited by the new arrival, did a huge piddle in the middle of the living-room carpet. Tassia looked at me mockingly. 'I told you years ago, think first, before giving in to your impulses!'

We argued as I mopped up the puddle. I had to admit that in many ways Tassia was right. I was condemning Jicky to life in a flat and to solitude and boredom most of the time. Dogs were not allowed in ballet classes or in theatres, and walking on a leash around city streets cannot be called good exercise. 'But *you* have a dog. *He* looks happy,' I argued.

'Yes, but I also have my mother,' Tassia countered. 'She's always with him if I'm not home. Dogs need companionship.'

Meanwhile, Jicky tugged at the mop and made funny growling noises, dear little man – I knew I could not give him away for good. 'Tassia, Jicky's coming on Sunday to meet my parents. I know they'll fall in love with him too. Maybe they'll suggest he stay with them. That way, I'll see Jicky often, and he'll have a garden to run around in, and constant loving company.'

'Good idea,' approved Tassia. There were several days left till Sunday, so Tassia, like the good sport she was, sat in my flat with Jicky until I returned from the theatre. As I hoped, my parents fell in love with Jicky and suggested he live with them. And so Jicky lived happily into old age, loved and cherished by my parents. I returned to my flat on Monday feeling rather sad. The only reminders of my few privileged days with a doggy were the stain in the middle of the living-room carpet and a few others in the bedroom.

Weeks melted into weeks, months into months. I worked, and waited until the blessed day when the world heard that the war in Europe was over. Some months later, the nation was greatly shocked to learn of President Franklin D. Roosevelt's death. Consternation and sadness were reflected in people's faces. Harry S. Truman succeeded, and soon everyone was sure that victory would soon be declared on all fronts. The excitement in the air was palpable as we all prepared to welcome the boys home.

All I wanted was to be completely free of any commitments by the time Yura returned, so I asked Jules Ziegler to tell Dave Wolper I would not be signing on for the second year of *Follow the Girls*. I persuaded Papa that it was a sensible thing to accept just over half of my considerable savings, after much argument and with the help of my mother. He was ill at ease about it, but it was the best thing for everyone's peace of mind. I had plenty left to ensure that Yura and I could take as long as necessary to make solid decisions concerning our future.

I felt happier than I had been in a long time, and even found performing in the show each night fun. Nothing mattered – Yura was coming back. His most recent letter, written soon after the Americans entered Paris, had described his joyous reunion with his parents and told how much he was looking forward to his approaching demobilisation. I was in seventh heaven!

After my last performance in *Follow the Girls*, having said goodbye to the cast, I was taken to Sardi's by the producer, the director and the Littlefield sisters; Jules Ziegler joined us there. We parted with hugs and kisses, promising to keep in touch. When I got home, I could not unwind for a long time. There I was, on the brink of a new life, free of Broadway, free of immediate financial worry, with my own flat in which to welcome

Yura, and with the exciting prospect of shaping our future together. When I finally went to bed, dawn was peeping through the curtains.

It was late when I woke up. I turned on the radio and it was clear that something was going on. There were excited voices, hoots, loud exclamations, a totally happy-sounding bedlam! I listened more intently. *Yes! Yes! Yes! The war is over!* I called my parents and Tassia. We were all ecstatic. I danced all the way to the kitchen, made myself some coffee and looked in my mailbox. Among a couple of missives was a letter from Yura. My heart did a *pirouette*!

As I unfolded the single page, a newspaper clipping slipped out. I pushed it to the side, anxious to read the letter first. No words of endearment preceded my name. He addressed me in dry tones: 'Irina. This was sent to me by a friend. You betrayed my trust, you betrayed what we had – so precious, or so I thought. Apparently you did not feel the same way. As we shall not see each other again, best of luck. Yura.'

I could not believe what my eyes were reading. I choked. I felt like I had been stabbed in the guts. I pulled the clipping towards me – it was Louella Parsons' gossip column. I sat in a daze. *Some Victory Day! Who is that stupid, malicious, so-called friend who sent Yura that rubbish?* I just could not think. But for Yura to believe it! His trust in me proved to be fragile. My hurt soon turned into bitter, fierce anger. That's how Tassia found me when she came to fetch me for an outing we had planned. 'You look terrible!' she cried. 'What's the matter with you?'

I pushed the letter and the cutting towards her. 'Read, read!' I insisted.

Her reaction was explicit. 'What the hell? Who is this friend?'

'I don't know. It'll crop up, I'll know.'

But that was not important. The harm was done. What was so shattering was that Yura thought so little of me as to believe so readily in gossip. His short, cold letter of dismissal, sent without having checked with me first, was deeply humiliating. Had I been living all this time in a fantasy world, in the delusion that nothing could ever change our beautiful relationship? It seemed so. I just could not take it in. It felt like a bad dream, a nightmare.

'You'll respond to the letter? You must!'

'I don't know, Tassia. I don't know anything any more.' My anger subsided and despair took over. Tears, silent tears, flooded my eyes.

Tassia made some coffee and we sat in silence. After a while, she asked if I would like to be left alone. No, I would not. I was grateful to have my soul mate with me. As I sit at my desk writing this, sixty years later, I have no memory of the rest of that day, nor of the night.

The next morning I was surprised to find myself sitting in the armchair, with Tassia asleep on the couch. My thoughts started to function, bringing reality into focus. *Have some pride*, I told myself. *Pull yourself together. Don't allow yourself to fall to pieces.* Tassia stirred, open her eyes, took one look at me and said, 'God, you look awful!'

'So do you,' I returned the compliment.

'Are you going to see your parents?' Do you feel up to it?'

'Yes, I must. They, too, had been looking forward to Yura's return.'

Jicky greeted us at the door, jumping up, his tail wagging in delight. But my papa immediately sensed that I was not my usual cheerful self. When we had settled down, he asked me what was troubling me. I showed them Yura's letter and they were stunned. But Mother still said, 'It's partly your fault. You shouldn't have put yourself in a position that could provoke gossip.'

'Why should going to supper with two people provoke gossip?' I asked.

'It depends who those people are,' she replied. 'And stop playing at being a naïve little girl!' Mother was getting edgy, but I did have to admit to myself that she was right, and that made me feel angry with the whole world.

While Tassia went out to the garden to play with Jicky, Papa intervened, trying to placate me. 'Irischka, war is ugly. Yura's been through some tough times. He must be physically and emotionally tired and vulnerable. Try to understand him. When he returns it might all sort itself out.'

It was kind of Papa, but it did not help much, although I pretended it did. I did not feel like I could, or even wanted to, discuss the matter any further. For the rest of our stay we talked lamely of other things, knowing perfectly well what was on everyone's mind. I took Jicky for long walks and thought about where my future work should be. I decided, once I felt more calm, to talk to Lucia Chase. To be back where I belonged, doing what I loved, would be healing.

When I got back to New York there was a letter in the mailbox with a French stamp. My heart leapt, only to fall in a depleted heap when I saw that the writing on the envelope was not Yura's, but Jerry's. *Oh, now what?* I had some errands to run, so I decided to read it later.

When I finally braced myself to open it, I was surprised by the endearing, warm tones in which he addressed me. It was a long letter, humorously recounting his experiences in Paris (so, he was there too . . .). He wanted to know how things were with me, and to tell me that he thought about me and missed me. He ended his letter by saying he would be demobbed and back in New York within four to six weeks, and asked if I would consider giving us another chance at 'being miserable together'. I was utterly surprised by the letter and its content. His idea of getting back together was preposterous, but it was a nice, forgiving gesture on his part.

Tassia, her arm now healed, was giving private lessons at the studio of a friend of hers, so I did not see her till the next evening. I gave her Jerry's letter to read, but she expressed no surprise as she put it down. 'He really loves you . . . after all the ups and downs, he doesn't want to give up on you. I find it touching.'

We talked about Jerry for a while, then Tassia changed the subject, telling me she had seen an advertisement for an army surplus depot that was selling jeeps at low prices. 'We should go to driving school and get driver's licences, then see if we can get a jeep.' I thought it was a great idea, so we joined a driving school the next day. Having a goal to work towards helped me keep a grip on myself.

I composed several replies to Jerry and flung them all in the wastepaper basket; they were stilted and inadequate. I shared my problem with Tassia. 'Look, it's simple,' she said. 'Say, "Okay, let's try again." Irischka, you owe it to him.'

I was taken aback. 'But I don't feel love for him . . . sort of affection, possibly . . . but that's not good enough. Besides, I couldn't bear anyone near me as long as Yura is in my daily thoughts.'

'In that case, just say you need time to think about it, that his letter was quite a surprise and you can't give him a quick answer.'

I finally posted a letter along those lines to Jerry. I did not tell my parents about his letter; I knew only too well the effect it would have – enraging Mother and worrying Papa.

Meanwhile, my driving lessons were going well, but Tassia was rotten at reverse parking, always hitting, scraping or mounting the kerb, or driving straight into the car parked behind, hitting its bumper bar. Our instructor was in despair, but Tassia just giggled and assured him she would be okay for the test. At the end of our last lesson we gave the instructor a bottle of whiskey and a bottle of gin. He, in turn, promised to try to fix us up for the test the next day with an examiner who was his pal. He obviously succeeded, and the forty dollars (twenty from each of us) that Tassia innocently placed on the examiner's seat helped too. We both passed with flying colours! Mind you, in those days the traffic was nothing compared to today's. To drive around town was orderly and easy.

An old friend of Tassia's, Allan, who was lame and therefore had not been drafted, knew exactly where to get a surplus jeep, having purchased one himself, and offered to take us there. I emerged from the depot's huge parking lot the proud owner of a brand-new jeep. Allan was most helpful, filling in papers for me and dealing with registration and insurance, all of which was Chinese to me.

Tassia, however, decided to wait to make her purchase. She had been offered the chance to open her own ballet school in Houston, Texas, where there were also budding plans to start a local ballet company, for which Tassia might be offered the post of ballet mistress and artistic director. It sounded very interesting and, depending on the results of her negotiations, she, her mama and her poodle might be moving to Houston. Once again, my dear friend would be far away, and I would miss her terribly. However, it was a great opportunity for her, so we both kept our fingers crossed.

The next weekend, feeling a bit nervous, I drove the jeep to Sea Cliff. My new acquisition was much admired by my parents and their friends. Tassia was not able to come, so I planned to stay there for the best part of the week. One afternoon the phone rang and I answered.

'Irina.' I froze. 'It's Yura.' I could not speak. 'I'm in New York. I want to see you.'

'Yes, of course,' I finally managed to say. 'I can be back at my flat in two hours.'

'See you there,' he replied, then hung up.

I tore downstairs, my knees like jelly, my heart pounding. 'Mama, Papa, Yura's back! It was him on the phone. I must go . . . now . . . he's coming to my flat.'

Excited but anxious, my parents exclaimed, both at the same time, 'Calm down. Take it easy. Are you safe to drive? Be careful!' Ten minutes later I was on my way, two hours later I was home. The thought that so unexpectedly, so suddenly, Yura would be there in my flat, made me more and more nervous. How would we greet each other, what would we say? I tidied myself up and went to the window to watch out for him, trying hard to compose myself. A taxi pulled up and there he was! I backed away from the window, trying to control the pain, the joy, the panic, all these feelings merging one into the other. The doorbell rang.

For a moment we stood staring at each other. The next moment we were in each other's arms. *Oblivion!* Then, slowly, reality began to creep in. My pride, my pain, took over. Gently, I pushed him away. We stepped into the living room, where, grabbing my arm, he turned me around to face him. The slap on my face was so hard it made me reel sideways. Enraged, I slapped him back with all the strength I possessed. For a moment we stood there, glaring at each other in disbelief.

'I'm sorry,' he whispered.

My rage was gone, but a deep feeling of loss had taken its place. 'Sit down,' I said. He dropped into an armchair. I sat facing him. 'What happened to us?' I asked. 'Where are those two people who were standing in the forest at Camp Ritchie with so much love and hope? Were they just a dream?' He listened to me in silence. 'I don't know anything any more.' I added.

'Neither do I.' I wanted to put my arms around him, but instead fetched Jerry's letter and asked him to read it. Having done so, he carefully put it down on the table beside him, then asked, 'Did you reply?'

'Yes.'

'What did you say?'

'That I needed time to think about it.' We sat in silence. I hoped Yura would say, 'Write again and say no,' but he said nothing. What he was thinking I will never know. I broke the silence and asked him who had sent him that rubbishy gossip.

He shrugged. 'Richard and Roger.' They were an elderly gay couple who had befriended some of our dancers at Ballet Theatre.

'Nice friends you've got!' I could not resist saying.

Silence. We had nothing to say. Trust was broken. The beautiful dream was lost. Only pain remained, and silence. Yura gave me a long look, got up and slowly went into the hall, picked up his kepi and walked out, quietly closing the door.

I sat staring at the door, unable to move, frozen in my grief. And so ended my first real romantic, strong love. I felt my heart was broken forever. But nothing is forever. It mended, in time, perhaps just marked by a scar.

JERRY AND THE BOYS

My parents were saddened by the outcome of my encounter with Yura. Tassia was non-committal, but I was grateful for her discretion and her tact in not returning to this painful subject. I did not want to talk about it, and could not. My only escape from my badgering thoughts was Vilzak's classes, which I attended twice a day. I had been taught from childhood to concentrate, to control and be aware of my body, muscles, tendons, posture and positions, and to use each exercise with understanding and application, so the self-discipline required to do the classes was second nature to me. All other thoughts would switch off automatically; for three hours a day I was transported into the world I loved, that could not be taken away from me.

I saw Lucia and Pat when they were in town, and shared my sad tale with them. Days went by. Tassia told me she had heard that Yura had gone back to Paris. Strangely enough, this was a relief. There was a distance separating us now, some kind of closure. The torment of being in the same city had disappeared, at least. More days went by.

Late one afternoon, as I was about to leave for dinner at Tassia's – her mama was cooking – the phone rang. It was Jerry. My greeting must have sounded quite flat, as he asked me if I was well. When I asked him how he knew my phone number, he said Hurok's office had given it to him. Jerry was back at a camp near New York, waiting to be demobbed. Family members could visit the day after next between seven and eight-thirty p.m. In a friendly, jovial voice, he asked if I could possibly come. I hesitated, at a loss for what to say, but he picked up on it.

'Irischka, stop turning round and round in your head whether you should come or not. Whatever happens between us, I'll always be your friend. Don't complicate things, just say you'll come.'

'I'll try . . .' I said, far from sure that I meant it.

'Thanks for your letter,' he added. 'We'll talk about it when I see you, not on the phone.' I wished there was nothing to discuss, but apparently there was – I owed Jerry that courtesy.

Tassia's poodle greeted me as usual, wagging his short tail and proffering his paw to shake. Tassia and her funny, delightful mama greeted me with their usual bonhomie, glasses of chianti in hand. They told me delightedly that the news from Houston was good, and they might be on their way to Texas in a month. Tassia needed a solid, interesting position with a future and, although I knew I would miss her very much, I was thrilled for her.

After dinner I told them about Jerry's telephone call. 'Of course you must go!' they exclaimed. Mama gesticulated so excitedly she knocked over her glass. The wine spilled down her frock and dripped onto the floor, to the poodle's delight – he promptly licked the floor clean.

'Tassia, he'll get drunk!' I cried in alarm.

'Nooo, he's used to it,' was her nonchalant answer. I had to laugh – I was astonished to find that I still could.

As I was leaving, Tassia offered to come with me to visit Jerry. 'Would that help?' she asked.

'Yes it would,' I replied. 'If you come with me, I might go.'

'We'll go. Now sleep, and don't worry so much.'

But I did not sleep well and I did worry. *What if something works out with Jerry? Mother will be furious, Papa sad. Could I face it all over again?* Nine years down the track, I was still afraid of my mother! A feeling of rebellion arose in me, as if I were a teenager once again.

On the appointed day, in a messy state of mind, nervous and apprehensive, I was about to get into the jeep when Tassia asked me, 'Would you like me to drive?'

'No, you direct me,' I replied quickly. The last thing I needed was my darling friend's erratic driving! But she was good at directions, and I was hopeless at them.

At the massive gates of the camp we gave Jerry's name and were directed to a huge tent, where a crowd of men was assembled to see the visitors. Tassia and I stopped at the entrance, trying to spot Jerry, but he saw us first, and appeared as if out of nowhere with Borislav (one of our dancers), Misha (Eugenia Delarova's brother), and another man I did not know who looked almost Jerry's age.

While a delighted Borislav and Misha hugged Tassia and introduced her to the other man, Jerry and I greeted each other awkwardly. He seemed more relaxed than I was; he gave me a peck on the cheek and introduced his 'brother in arms', Dima. Then it was my turn to be hugged by my laughing friends Borislav and Misha.

I was glad they were there. It made this first meeting with Jerry after almost three years a bit easier. Tassia enticed the boys into playing a game of ping-pong at one of the tables set up inside the tent, leaving Jerry and me to sort ourselves out. He was thinner, and had developed a nervous twitch at the side of his mouth. 'Tired?' I ventured, for something to say.

'No, not really,' he replied. 'We had an easy time in Paris, saw Boris Kochno and Bérard, some other friends too. They're all right – they didn't have it so bad during the occupation. And how are you?'

'All right. I've got a jeep.'

'Wonderful! Bravo! So you drive legally now.' We both laughed, and it eased the tension between us. Hurok had told him about my adventures at the Roxy and about *Follow the Girls*. Apparently Hurok didn't approve.

'No-one approved,' I said, 'and I hated it, but I had my reasons.' I was starting to get irritated.

Jerry noticed and tried to placate me. 'Hurok also told me you were a big success in Massine's Highlights.'

'Oh, it was really wonderful to work with Massine again.' *Enough about me*, I thought, so I asked Jerry to tell me what sort of time he had in the army. As soon as I asked, I regretted it. It was a stupid question; it sounded flippant and out of place. Luckily, at that moment the others joined us, and Jerry was spared from answering. The boys now told me that they were being released into 'civvy street' in two days' time. They also told me they had nowhere to go. They were not sure how long it would take them to find jobs, so they had to be careful with their meagre savings. This problem offered me a chance to delay sorting out my issues with Jerry.

'Look, boys,' I said. 'I've got a large living room in my flat. If you can provide sleeping bags, you can camp there for a few days. It'll give you time to sort yourselves out.'

The three men promptly and gratefully accepted my proposal. Jerry looked at me quizzically and asked, 'Am I included in this kind offer?'

Tassia, who was leaning on the back of my chair, pinched my neck. 'Well, yes,' I replied. 'If you have a sleeping bag.' I hoped my answer would make it clear to him that nothing was settled in my mind regarding his idea for us to be miserable together again. He understood all right, and Boris and Misha exchanged amused glances – they knew, of course, what the score was.

After a slight pause, Jerry smiled and replied, 'Thanks, the sleeping bag will do fine.'

I looked at those four men and thought, *What am I getting myself into?* I did not want them in my flat – I wanted Yura! I resented those four I had invited, but why? I grew angry with myself, with Tassia, with the world. Jerry's voice interrupted my thoughts. 'So, Irischka, I'll phone to tell you when we'll be arriving.'

'All right.' My reply lacked enthusiasm. I wanted to go, to get out of there. 'Tassia,' I said, 'we must go now. It's time.'

We said our goodbyes, but I was struggling all the while to be polite. When we got to the gates, Tassia said, 'Well done, Irischka.'

'Not well done at all,' I barked back. 'You made me do it!'

'Don't blame me if you're so easily influenced,' she retorted. We drove back in silence.

The next morning I set off for Sea Cliff, to face my parents and tell them about the recent turn of events. As I expected, Mother hit the roof in a big way, but Papa's dismayed, sombre expression spoke louder than her angry screams. My rebellious streak rose to the surface. 'Mama, please stop!' I cried. 'This argument is pointless. I'm twenty-six, it's my life, and I have the right to make my own decisions!'

'The right? The right? Look where your right to make decisions has got you – mess after mess after mess! And now this – I forbid you to have any truck with that man ever again!'

I was trembling with anger. In some ways Mother was right, but in others she was being unfair. 'Mama,' I said, 'you cannot forbid me from making my own choices in life, even if they may prove to be wrong. I appreciate your advice when you give it in a calm, friendly mood, but screaming at me achieves nothing!'

'Calm down, both of you,' Papa interjected, himself becoming increasingly distressed.

But Mama continued to glare at me. 'If you're going to go against my wishes, don't come here any more.'

History was repeating itself. I hugged Papa, said, 'See you at Bobri's,' ignored Mother, climbed into my jeep and drove back to New York, fuming all the way.

'How did it go?' Tassia asked when I phoned her.

'Badly!' I replied.

'It will grind and become flour,' she said, trying to comfort me.

By the time Jerry called to let me know when the boys would be coming, I had fallen into emotional apathy. I did not care one way or the other. *Whatever happens, let it be. Who cares?* I did not.

I warned my landlady about my visitors, but she did not mind at all. Tassia was there for my moral support when the boys arrived, and there they were, bundles and all, spilling out of two taxis, still in their uniforms. We watched from the living-room window as my landlady greeted them on the front steps. 'What a nice lady!' remarked Tassia, and I agreed that I was very lucky.

With broad smiles, all talking at the same time, thanking me for letting them stay for a few days, the boys invaded my home. 'Ah, you have a piano,' cried Dima with delight.

'He's quite a musician,' said Misha, then added, 'Nice place you have here.'

'I'm hungry,' wailed Borislav, making a beeline for the kitchen.

Meanwhile, Jerry walked around slowly, inspecting the flat. 'You have two beds in your room,' he said.

'Yes, the other one is Tassia's. She often stays overnight.'

I suggested that Jerry, being the oldest, should sleep on the couch. It was extra long and wide, so I was sure he would be comfortable. I knew it was not what he wanted to hear but, if he was disappointed, he didn't show it. 'The boys can find their own spots on the floor,' I added. Dima bagsed the spot by the piano, Misha behind the gramophone cabinet, and Borislav under one of the windows.

At that moment the doorbell rang. 'It must be Richard,' said Jerry as he made for the door. 'I asked him to drop by.' He and Richard Davis were very happy to see each other again, but I was not at all happy – my home was being taken over!

A few days passed. We started getting used to each other; the boys, to my surprise, proved to be rather tidy and clean. But it soon became clear that it would take longer than a few days for them to fit in to civvy street again, and that it might be some time before I would get my home and my privacy back. The three boys spent their days contacting friends and putting out feelers for jobs. Jerry and Richard met every day, mostly at my place, to discuss what Jerry should do. He had lost interest in the ballet world; he wanted to go into business, any business.

I felt rather disoriented in this communal existence – my only escapes were going to Vilzak's classes twice a day, visiting Papa on the days he worked at Bobri's, and seeing that the fridge was well stocked. There were no set times for meals: we usually ate separately, but sometimes Misha cooked and we all ate together. Jerry and Richard dined at the Russian Tea Room; they kept asking me to join them, but I could not face it and kept refusing, to their growing annoyance.

Tassia, meanwhile, was busy packing, sorting out her affairs and seeing her friends before leaving for Houston. I felt sad to see her go, and realised just how dependent on her I had become for company and moral support. There was still my papa, of course, but he had taken up a stance of neutrality. The time I spent with him was always good, but I found that having constantly to avoid mentioning either Mother or Jerry was unnatural and tedious.

Borislav, Misha and Dima were now so totally at home in my flat and so used to having me around that they were rapidly reverting to barracks language and behaviour. Dima banged loudly on the piano and sang ribald songs while the others, including Jerry, joined in. They walked around in their underpants and became increasingly messy. Their initial restrained, polite behaviour had vanished. I chose to be patient and ignored their antics, hoping they would be gone in a few more days. But the day of reckoning came sooner than I expected.

When I came home from class one morning the noise coming from my flat was deafening. As I walked in, a nasty smell hit my nostrils. Misha shouted something from the bathroom to the others, provoking general hilarity – the bathroom door was wide open. As I walked past it, the shock of what greeted my eyes made me flush with anger. Misha was sitting on the toilet, underpants around his ankles, smoking and flicking the ashes into the sink. 'You're disgusting!' I shouted angrily, closing the door with a bang.

Misha immediately pulled the door open again and, staring at me with an idiotic smile, gave out a long, loud fart! Attracted by my angry voice, the others had appeared, and were obviously enjoying the scene. They laughed their heads off and teased me, imitating my anger and calling me hoity-toity. I saw red! I faced them as calmly as I could and kept my voice steady as I said, 'Okay, chaps, I've had enough. You came for a few days, you've stayed for a few weeks, it's time to push off. You have a week to find alternative accommodation. Meanwhile, I'll relieve you of my presence. I'll take possession of my flat again in one week's time!'

My little speech reduced the boys to astonished silence. When I went to my room to pack a small bag, Jerry followed me. 'You can't do that to the boys,' he said reproachfully.

'If you don't like it, you can go too!' I said. I threw a few more things into the bag, shut it and walked out of the flat. Installed in my jeep, I asked myself, *Now what?* I needed to cool off, so I went to a delicatessen I liked on Sixth Avenue and treated myself to cheesecake and iced coffee. Feeling better, I drove to Bobri's studio to see Papa and tell him I would not be at my flat for a week. *Where shall I stay?* I asked myself as I parked in front of the studio. I could not go to Sea Cliff; Mother didn't want me around – I was in disgrace. *Oh well, first things first, I'll think about that later.*

When I told Papa what had just happened at the flat, he chuckled with amusement.

'Papa, it wasn't funny!' I cried.

'Irischka, you're not losing your sense of humour, I hope?'

I reflected for a moment. 'You think I was unfair?'

'Perhaps a bit . . . Those men have been through tough times. They need to unwind, readjust. It takes time.' After a pause, Papa asked where I would be staying in the coming week.

'Perhaps there'll be a room at that motel we pass on the way to Sea Cliff,' I ventured.

'This is ridiculous! You have a room at our house. I'm going to call your mother right now.' With these words, Papa made for the phone in Bobri's office. *Dear, dear Papa.* I felt apprehensive, but he emerged from the office with a satisfied smile. 'It's all settled,' he announced. 'You're coming home. Mother is delighted. She really missed not seeing you, but was too stubborn to admit it. I made her promise not to harass you.'

'By rubbing my nose into yet another mess of my doing?'

We both laughed. I told Papa that I was taking Tassia and her mother to dinner – they were leaving for Houston the next morning. 'That's all right,' he said. 'Give them our love and drive over after dinner. We'll wait up for you. Jicky will be happy to see you too.'

I hugged my papa – with so much gratitude and endless love – then drove to pick up Tassia and her mother. I had shed my resentment and anger and felt so much better, thanks to Papa's wise words and his understanding, compassion and kindness. My dinner with Tassia and her adorable mama was happy and tearful: happy at Tassia's big chance for success in Houston; tearful at the thought of not seeing them again, perhaps for a long time to come. I took them home, gave them one last hug, and a pat and kiss to the poodle, then drove to Sea Cliff. Mother received me with a warm embrace, and I felt that the subject of our latest feud would not be brought up again. I was grateful to be back in my pretty bedroom and not stuck in some motel – I slept better than I had in a long time.

That week I missed going to Vilzak's classes, but it was good to spend some time with my parents in peace. Mama kept her promise and never raised the subject of Jerry again during this particular period of my life.

A week later, I drove back to New York, not sure what I would find at my flat. The first thing I saw on the hall table were the three spare keys I had given the boys when they moved in. There was also a thank-you note from them, which made me feel slightly guilty for throwing them out. The living room was spick and span, and there was a beautiful bunch of flowers on the coffee table. My conscience was troubled.

On the way to the bedroom, I noticed Jerry's bulging canvas bag under the hall table, a reminder that our talk about our unresolved relationship was now inevitable. *What should I do? What should I decide? Tassia said I owe it to him to give it another chance. 'It'? What's 'it'?*

The phone rang and interrupted my complicated thoughts. 'Ah, good, you're back,' said Jerry's voice. 'Where were you all week?'

'At my parents'.'

'Oh dear!' Jerry heaved a sigh. 'Irischka, it's time you gave me an answer one way or another. I've given you plenty of time to think it over.'

'You're right. Let's thrash it out. The sooner we do it the better, for both of us.'

'Good, I'm coming over.'

It was not very romantic, more like some business deal to be discussed. Oh well, I had had romantic love, and where had it got me? The first thing I asked Jerry when he arrived was where Borislav, Misha and Dima had got to. Misha and Dima, shaken by my angry outburst, had sprung into action. Misha invested his savings in a one-way ticket to Paris. Besides some business connections he had made there, he preferred the Parisian way of life. He had left midweek. Dima contacted a cousin in Chicago, who invited him over. Borislav, Jerry said, would eventually work for him. Meanwhile, he was staying with some Serbian friends.

'You have some definite plans, then?' I was genuinely interested. Richard's brother, Bernard Davis, owned a big factory near Philadelphia that manufactured high-quality upholstery fabric. It appeared that Bernard, who was about to acquire a small warehouse and office space in New York, had offered Jerry a job promoting his products and finding new customers. Jerry would deal with the paperwork and contact people in the trade, while Borislav would visit them and show them samples. It sounded like a good beginning – three cheers to Richard for having Bernard as a brother!

Then I told Jerry my plans: I could soon be guesting with Ballet Theatre, but my secret hope, now that the war was over, was that Colonel de Basil's company would resurface from South America and I could rejoin my tribe. Jerry and I discussed our lives frankly, and at length. He told me about his affair, which I was aware of, with the beautiful young talented actress Dorothy McGuire. It started soon after our separation but ended sadly and unexpectedly for him, according to his side of the story. When he was in camp awaiting departure for Europe and Miss McGuire was in Hollywood filming, he opened the paper to read that she had just been married in a surprise wedding ceremony in Hollywood. It was quite a shock, he told me, but he spoke of her in the nicest terms. I liked that. We talked about our existing feelings – in general and for each other. Friends? We were certainly not strangers!

'I'll always love you, no matter what happens,' he said. 'How about it? Shall we try to be miserable together again?' He took my hand in his with the look of a dog begging for a bone (or should I say leftovers?). At that moment I felt touched, and that I indeed owed it to him to try seriously at giving us another chance. And so started the new experience of a relationship 'on crutches'!

I had good news from Tassia. She had opened her school and it had aroused great interest among young students. Discussions were underway for the formation of a committee to look at the possibility of opening a Houston Ballet Company. Tassia was delighted. I had some news for her too. I was soon to depart for London, to appear in a ballet–comedy play with Léonide Massine! The idea of guesting with Ballet Theatre was on hold – the possibility of working with Massine again was too wonderful to miss.

It had all come about quite unexpectedly. I received a telegram from Caryl Brahms and S. J. Simon, the co-authors of a murder-mystery novel, A Bullet in the Ballet. It was based on the real, eccentric characters within our company, of whom they were devotees and friends. The story they invented was based around the dancer playing the much-coveted role of Petrushka in Fokine's ballet getting shot in the last moments of a performance.

The book was hilariously funny, especially to us, as we could recognise the original for each character in it. There had been plans to make a film of the book, but these had been abandoned with the declaration of World War II. However, Brahms and Simon turned the book into a stage play and found an impresario to back it. All had high hopes for a run in London after an extensive tour of England. The impresario was Julian Braunsweg, who was no stranger to me. His short, pudgy figure and smiling face were always around in the prewar days.

When I got my telegram, which expressed a hope that Massine and I would head the cast, I rang Massine immediately. After his Highlights venture, he was at a loose end, so he sounded happy to do something out of the ordinary that would combine ballet and acting. He thought it could be very interesting.

Once I had Massine's assurance that he would be accepting the offer, I hurried to Western Union to send a telegram to Brahms and Simon – saying that I accepted their invitation and would be thrilled to return to London. That evening, when Jerry returned from his office at the warehouse, I excitedly showed him the telegram, and told him that I had wired my acceptance. Jerry's expression changed from surprised interest to great displeasure and gloom. 'So,' he said, 'you didn't consider it necessary to discuss the matter with me first, before wiring them your consent?'

For me it was at last payback time for past grievances. I answered him with a question. 'And you didn't consider it necessary to consult me first, before telling me that you and I were leaving our company, did you?'

'Under the circumstances, there was nothing to discuss,' he snapped, nervously lighting a cigarette.

'Wasn't there?' I persisted. 'Your over-sized ego never gave a thought to the fact that you were taking me away from my company, my repertoire, all that I loved and had worked so hard for. You didn't think you owed me the courtesy of discussing those matters, so get off your high horse. You're not in a position to complain!'

I felt better for having voiced this hurt, which I had bottled up for so long. Jerry stabbed out his cigarette and got up to pour himself a drink. I observed him with detachment, but a feeling that two wrongs do not make a right was starting to bother me. After a reflective silence, Jerry asked, 'Would you like me to negotiate your contract for *A Bullet in the Ballet?*'

It was an unexpected gesture of reconciliation. 'Yes, please,' I responded. 'Thank you.' Discussing contracts always embarrassed me, so I was really glad to let Jerry do it. Besides, he knew Brahms and Simon well from the old days, and talking business with them would be easy for him. My answer pleased Jerry, who relaxed and called Richard to tell him my news. For some reason Richard became frightfully excited and insisted on taking us out for dinner.

As much as I often did not appreciate Richard's almost constant company, I have to admit that he always stuck by Jerry as a loyal best friend, without ever showing me anything but courtesy and respect, no matter what I was up to! I appreciated that character trait, and it changed my attitude towards him. I strove to make him feel welcome and to stop myself looking bored when he embarked on sad stories of how his heart had been broken by the latest 'Cinderella'.

That night I finally agreed to dine again at the Russian Tea Room. The idea of *borscht* and *piroshki* proved stronger than my reluctance to face the usual gossiping patrons occupying the first three booths. I was greeted with ahs and ohs – to my surprise, everyone seemed delighted to see me! Halfway through dinner, Jerry remarked that I might be away for several months. 'I don't like that,' he mused.

'I know what,' exclaimed Richard, 'we'll come to visit you!' As far as he was concerned, this settled the matter. For the rest of the evening, he was making all sorts of plans, getting increasingly enthusiastic about the thought of going to England. Jerry looked amused, but did not reject the possibility of such a visit.

Massine and I were to start rehearsals in London in early September. While he sailed with his family in August, I decided to fly, as I wanted some free time to catch up with my English friends. Darling Beatrice Winters, my dresser from *Follow the Girls*, insisted on sorting out my clothes and helping me pack. We were as close as ever and I shared all my tribulations with her. Jerry did not like Beatrice and she did not like him either – she thought him most unfriendly. As for Jerry, he resented our closeness and affection. But the packing proceeded smoothly – Jerry kept out of the way.

I spent my last weekend with my parents, who were pleased that I would soon be working with Massine again. They promised to send food parcels as soon as I let them know what was scarce in rationed

England. I already had masses of different-sized nylon stockings, chocolate bars and tinned ham packed in my luggage.

Jerry and Richard saw me off at LaGuardia Airport, Richard promising they would be there for opening night, Jerry looking gloomy. As for me, I could hardly wait to see my beloved London again.

POSTWAR SHOCKS

I was quite unprepared for the shock I experienced on my arrival. The London I knew, the way of life there, had changed – the way it was before was relegated to memory. I felt displaced and bewildered.

Julian Braunsweg met me at the airport and drove me to the furnished flat that had been rented for me in Swiss Cottage. My heart broke at the sight of buildings demolished by bombs, ragged skeletons of once-lovely houses, gaping holes where houses I could remember had once stood, all reduced to rubble. I felt unworthy of these Londoners, who had been through such suffering and deprivation, caught up in the horrors of war. All that time, I had had it so good under the wing of the United States eagle.

Baron d'Erlanger (Uncle Freddie) was dead now, as was Captain Bruce Ottley. Other friends had retired to the country, their London homes either destroyed or requisitioned. Everything was rationed, and the black market was thriving. By hook or by crook, I managed to visit most of my friends; their stiff upper lips were very much in evidence – they were getting on with life calmly, and with that typical English sense of humour.

As soon as Massine and his family had arrived and settled in, the whole cast got together for a read-through. We met the producer–director, Marcel Varnel, and the leading actors: Ivy St Helier, whose role was a take-off on Mme Tchernicheva; and Charles Goldner, who played a hilarious caricature based on Colonel de Basil. I became firm friends with Charles Goldner and his lovely wife, Maureen, who were warm and generous of heart. They sort of adopted me, and made sure I never felt lonely. Charles, a character actor of repute, was Hungarian, buoyant and funny.

The other characters in the play were based on the eccentricities of Papa Grigoriev, the dancers and some of the mothers. The script depicted the company's intrigues and jealousies with humour, and included the murder of the star and a whodunit mystery. Massine and I were greatly amused and impressed by how closely our ballet company had been observed by Caryl Brahms and S.J. Simon, who depicted our individual characteristics and painted them with a humorous brush.

It was difficult at this time to secure a theatre in London, as many were under repair or closed. Julian Braunsweg kept reassuring us with a big smile that all would be well. We wanted to believe him and worked enthusiastically – we already had firm bookings for a provincial tour. Massine held auditions for the dancers required for the ballet sequences, and rehearsals started in earnest. Every morning Massine and I would do a class together for an hour, before the others gathered for the rehearsal. It was bliss working with Massine again, and the cast were all lovely people and a joy to work with. We embarked on our tour with great expectations.

As promised, Jerry and Richard turned up at the first city of our tour for opening night. The performance went very well, but the stagehands put some of the scenery in the wrong places during the first act, so that the actors were confused about their entrances and exits. To crown it all, the front drop curtain came down too early and knocked Charles on the head, sending his wig flying. We were all very upset and expected bad notices in the papers the next day, but to our amazement and relief, they were all excellent. All proclaimed *A Bullet in the Ballet* by far the funniest play they had seen in a long time, and that with the ballet sequences the whole performance was unforgettable. The authors, director, actors, dancers, Massine and I all received rave reviews. Of course we were delighted, but it did make us wonder whether we should leave in all the mistakes and mishaps! Fortunately, good sense prevailed.

A week later we all set off for the next town on our tour and Jerry and Richard returned to New York. The tour was very successful, but it was drawing to an end and there was still no news of a theatre in London. When we arrived at our last town, Julian Braunsweg, minus his smile, announced that sadly he was unable to find an available theatre in London and so regrettably the show must fold. Maureen and Charles invited me to stay with them in their lovely little London house until Braunsweg could provide me with my return ticket to New York. As for Massine, Dame Ninette de Valois asked him to remount a few of his ballets for her company, the Sadler's Wells Ballet (which later became the Royal Ballet). He and his family remained in London.

I left London with a heavy heart. The state of the country had made a deep impression on me and given me much food for thought. I stayed with my parents for a few days then started sorting out my immediate professional future. Jerry's business at the warehouse was not making any headway – he looked preoccupied and dispirited.

In mid-April 1946 I picked up the phone and, to my great surprise, heard Colonel de Basil's voice. 'Hello, Irischka?'

'Wassily Grigorievich! Where are you?'

'In New York on business for a few days. I must see you urgently.' He went on to explain that it would help him enormously if I came to join his company as a guest for their forthcoming seasons in Cuba and especially in Rio de Janeiro. I was thrilled at the thought of being with my tribe again. The Colonel arranged to come over that evening to discuss it.

I was so happy that I would finally see the Colonel after all these years, and looked forward to hearing about my friends and colleagues, whom I missed so much. But Jerry was home before the Colonel arrived, and he was not happy. 'You can't do that!' he cried. 'You've been talking to Lucia about guesting with Ballet Theatre.'

'It could all fit in nicely. I know Lucia will cooperate. She'll understand my attachment to the company that nurtured me and was "home" for me.' I was starting to get irritated, but the Colonel's arrival put a stop to any argument.

I hugged this tall, lanky man with all the affection I had felt for him from the age of fourteen. His eyes, almost invisible behind the thick lenses of his spectacles, did not betray his feelings, but his warm hug told me that he was happy to see me too. Jerry shook his hand with a forced smile.

I asked after the Colonel's wife, Olga Morosova, who had taken on many leading roles in the absence of ballerinas. His face lit up. 'Ah, she's wonderful,' he said. 'Her legs are like champagne.'

I glanced at Jerry, who smirked and asked, 'So why do you need Irina?'

The Colonel looked at Jerry reproachfully. 'Don't be silly, Jerry, I'm not blind or stupid. I had to keep the company going, and someone had to dance the leading roles.' He told us about the difficult and sometimes desperate times the dancers had been through during their wartime tour of South America. Now he had great hopes and plans for the future of the company. He suggested that I dance *Swan Lake*, *Les Sylphides* and *Scheherazade*, before proceeding with the company to Rio. He could not offer me much financially in Cuba, but in Rio he could do better. My desire to join *my* company was so great, I would have done so without any pay at all. But I felt that I would have to talk to Lucia before giving my answer to the Colonel. He made me promise to give him a definite answer the next day, although I knew all the time that, no matter what, I would be with him on that flight to Cuba.

Jerry made no further comments about my decision, just shrugged and made himself scarce when Beatrice came to help me pack. My parents were somewhat taken aback and a bit worried. As I hugged them goodbye, Mother said, 'Don't let that terrible man exploit you again.'

On the first leg to Miami, I enjoyed the Colonel's company, but secretly I could not quite share his optimistic ideas about the company's glorious future. Things had changed. There was now serious competition, and it became clear to me that my poor Colonel was in for a few shocks and hard times.

As we emerged from the aircraft into the humid heat of Cuba, the first familiar face we saw was that of Vova Grigoriev, who had come to meet us. My heart jumped for joy! In the hotel lobby, Mme Tchernicheva and Papa Grigoriev were waiting for us. We hugged, tears in our eyes.

Next morning, hardly able to contain my excitement, I dashed to the theatre early, to meet up with my old colleagues and join them in Mme Tchernicheva's class. I was in for a rude awakening. The Colonel was not alone in living in the past – so was I! In my foolish dreams I had imagined I was returning to my tribe, but in reality I had returned to a company of strangers. Most of the old tribe had drifted away during the war years, in search of better venues and better pay. The Colonel had had to replace them with local talent from the countries he visited. Some tried hard and did their best, while others were not only bad dancers, but also bad pedestrians. There were a few good dancers who shared the leading roles with Morosova. I knew them slightly, but the company I had rejoined had nothing in common with the company I had known and loved, except for the repertoire, Colonel de Basil and the Ballet Russe name.

It was most distressing to see a great ballet company reduced to such a state. The war alone could not be blamed for this: intrigues, egos, jealousies, treachery and the whims of the powerful Sol Hurok had done enough damage to spell the end of a once-unforgettable company. But there I was, my head somewhat cleared of my illusions, determined to enjoy my friends and lose myself in the joy of performing. Mme Tchernicheva rehearsed and coached me, just like in the old days. It felt so good!

During the first *Swan Lake* rehearsal, a young man stood quietly by the door of the studio, watching, responding to the music with tiny movements. I asked Mme Tchernicheva who he was and learned that he was William McDermott, the company's orchestral conductor and also a brilliant pianist. The courteous, friendly and careful way he checked that I was comfortable with his tempos endeared him to me immediately. He was one of the best conductors I had the privilege to work with; his cheerfulness and humour made his company a sheer delight.

As the years went by, William and I kept bumping into each other, in England, the United States, Switzerland. We have corresponded for years, and in our old age we are firm friends, regularly exchanging our views, illnesses, grumps and memories by airmail. His letters are hilarious and a mine of information. I wish he would write a book about his times and tribulations with ballet companies and their prima donnas – it would be quite an eye-opener. It all goes to show that you never know when or where you might meet someone special – I met William in Cuba!

My performances in Cuba went well. The company was friendly and made my guesting a pleasure, but I shut my eyes to the situation they were in and tried not to dwell on it.

The Colonel told me that his friends in Rio de Janeiro were keen to have me stay with them. They were an American couple, Ben and Helen Foster, who lived in a large, beautiful apartment in Copacabana. He hoped I would accept their invitation, as it would help him financially not to have the expense of my hotel accommodation. Put that way, how could I refuse?

Helen Foster was at the airport to meet the Colonel and me when we landed. She was a tall, voluptuous, good-looking lady with a merry face and a warm, bubbly manner. I liked her immediately. The Fosters' apartment was truly beautiful, as was the view from the large windows onto the long strip of beach and up to the huge statue of Christ high up on the rock.

Ben Foster was home waiting for us and was just as welcoming as his wife. He looked much, much older than her, but was just as jolly. They showed me to my gorgeous bedroom and I felt so grateful for their kind invitation. It was good to escape the anonymity of a hotel and I told them so. We got on like a house on fire from the word go, and our friendship lasted for many years.

Every morning Helen came with me in her chauffeur-driven car to watch our class and rehearsals. In the evenings she sat in my dressing room or watched the performances from the wings. She loved ballet, and revelled in the backstage life of the dancers. Ben watched from his seat in the stalls.

I was glad to see a few people I had met on my previous visit to Rio, among them a most charming man, Nelson Siabra. An adoring friend of Mia Slavenska and George Zoritch, he was quiet, with impeccable manners, and much liked by everyone. I was really glad to see him again.

My season in Rio went very well, and the Colonel was pleased with his company's success. On the spur of an exuberant moment, I invited the whole company to the Copacabana casino for supper after the closing performance. Nelson Siabra and the Fosters were, of course, included in this invitation. When my last day with the company arrived, I felt somewhat sad and melancholy. After the curtain came down for the last time, I rushed off to the casino, to arrive at my party ahead of the others and check on the arrangements. Everything looked lovely under the starry night and the soft lights. The flowers on the long table exhaled a beautiful aroma, the waves broke gently on the beach, the band played softly – everything was perfect.

Soon my guests started to arrive. I noticed the effort the girls had put in to look their best. In their simple, modest gear they were more attractive than the other patrons in their expensive gowns. I wanted to hug them all! When everyone was seated, I made a little speech, thanking the company for making me so welcome and finishing with, 'Now eat, drink and be merry!'

Oh boy, did they eat? Oh dear, did they drink? Merry? They danced into the wee hours! As the clock ticked away and the corks kept popping, an exhausted-looking Mme Tchernicheva and Papa Grigoriev took their leave. I hated to say goodbye to them, and became tearful. Colonel de Basil soon made to leave too. Ben Foster, who was wilting, offered to drop the Colonel at his lodgings, telling Helen and me that he would send the car back for us. Helen was in no hurry to leave. The Colonel was coming to the airport with the Fosters to see me off, so I did not feel that our hug was a final goodbye.

As I sat down again, in quite a sagging, reflective mood, my eyes roamed over our by then rather messy-looking table. It suddenly occurred to me that with all the extras the bill would be considerably more than I had catered for. I had brought some money from New York and had what the Colonel had paid me, but would that be enough? Panic seized me. I dashed to the powder room and locked myself in a toilet, frantically emptying my bag and counting my money. It soon became obvious that I would not have enough for all the extras.

Oh Lord, that's all I need! I visualised myself missing my flight, washing dishes in the casino kitchen. The embarrassment, the degradation, the scandal!

My knees turned to jelly as I made my way to the maître d's desk. Trying hard to look nonchalant, I requested the bill and asked to see the manager. The maître d' bowed gallantly and said with a big smile, 'The bill is already settled, Señora, by Señor Siabra.' I froze in astonishment and stared at the maître d'. He bowed again, as if to dismiss me.

Feeling weak with relief, I went to find Nelson, who was rumba-ing with Helen. When the band stopped playing, I dashed to his side, pulled at his sleeve and whispered urgently, 'Nelson, I must talk to you about the bill.' I intended to send him a cheque from New York.

'Shhh,' he said, his index finger touching his lips. 'It's my small gift to you for all the pleasure you've given me.'

Ah, those were the days!

It was sad saying goodbye to the Colonel at the airport. He was so full of hope and projects for the company and urged me to return permanently, but I had my doubts and reservations. I was not to know that that day at Rio de Janeiro airport was the last time I would hug the Colonel. I never saw him again.

DARK EYES AND YUL BRYNNER

As I recall it, a friend of the Fosters (whom they called Pickle Puss!) was connected with Pan American Airways and managed to get me onto the very first non-stop flight from Rio to New York, which spared me changing planes in Miami. In those days planes were comfortable – there was plenty of leg room, the seats were wide and the passengers were not packed in like sardines, their legs crippled at the end of the trip. That was before greed took over. Nowadays one has to be seriously rich to travel in comfort. I often caught up with Ben and Helen Foster again in New York and when Ben died, Helen moved to Portugal and was a frequent guest at my home in England.

Jerry greeted me gloomily on my return. 'You're hardly ever home,' he complained.

'So? What do you want me to do?' I asked uncertainly.

'I want you to stay home.'

'And stop performing?'

'Yes!' was his curt reply.

He hasn't changed, I thought. *He still wants to keep me firmly tucked in his breast pocket.* That was not my idea of a shared life. Where was the give and take? *Life in a suffocating breast pocket? No, no, no!* I felt touchy and could not face a confrontation with Jerry, so I made no reply to his grumpy request. I let it be . . . for the moment. For almost a year, I stayed at home.

But on that day I was not even half unpacked when Richard appeared with a box of chocolates and lots of questions about my guesting with de Basil's company. As I dug into the chocolates and answered Richard's questions, it occurred to me that Jerry had shown no interest in my time with de Basil. He had asked me no questions. Was it resentment or indifference? I, in turn, learned from the conversation between Jerry and Richard that the warehouse enterprise was still not doing well. I was sorry to hear it.

When I next had the chance to have a long talk with Lucia, she said, 'Don't worry, things may change and Jerry will find his feet and a lucrative occupation.' This advice did not help me much. As it eventually turned out, there was no need to worry any more – the situation changed abruptly. A few days later, Bernard Davis closed the New York venture and Jerry lost his job.

Since Jerry had no prospect of earning money in the immediate future, he brought up the subject of our respective financial situations. He was almost broke. I told him where I stood – I had enough in my current account to last us a few months, but I was not prepared to touch my savings under any circumstances.

He laughed at my financial arrangements and suggested that he had better take over. I consented to let him deal with my current account, but not my savings account, which was strictly my baby.

He got offended, I got cross. We plunged into a filthy row, which was most unpleasant. After we had cooled off somewhat, Jerry asked me, 'And what happens when your current account runs dry and I'm still out of work?'

'I don't know,' I replied innocently. 'What do you want me to do?'

'Be useful,' he barked. 'Go back to work!'

I was delighted to be released from the breast pocket! The expression on my face, whatever it was, infuriated him and we had another verbal battle. A couple of days later, to my surprise, Jerry came home in a cheerful mood and told me that he had talked to the Marquis de Cuevas, who would be delighted to have me as a guest with his ballet company – the contract would be ready to sign in a couple of days. I was furious! That was the one company I had never even considered joining. I liked the Marquis; he was a charming eccentric, but as weak as they come, and was used and manipulated by his entourage. From what I had heard, the company was a wasp's nest. *Besides, was I consulted? No! Here we go again.*

Trying to keep my calm, I replied to Jerry, 'So, you've found yourself a job – you're my manager now? Well, the answer is no, I'm not interested. I'll go back to work, but *I'll* choose where and with whom, not you!' With that I walked out of the flat, not wishing to discuss the issue any further. Later on, I rang Jules Ziegler and arranged to see him the next day.

Jules greeted me with a big grin. 'In trouble again?'

'Yes,' I replied, and told him about my latest predicament.

His first question was, 'What about Ballet Theatre?'

'It doesn't fit in right now.' I explained why, then said I had heard about Summer Stock and asked him what it was. He informed me that it was a long-established venue where new plays were tried out and where actors of repute liked to explore new roles. One rehearsed one week, performed for a week, then moved on to the next venue. It sounded to me like an interesting experience.

'There's no big money in it,' he warned me.

'I don't care. That's the least of my concerns.'

Jules thought for a moment. 'I might have something just right for you,' he exclaimed. 'A comedy called *Dark Eyes*, by Elena Miramova and Eugenie Leontovich' (the wife of actor Gregory Ratoff) 'is to be performed this summer. It's about three young Russian women who find themselves in an American family. They already have Uta Hagen and Paula Laurence. Let me check if the third Russian part is still open.' He got right on the phone while I waited, fingers crossed. 'You're on!' he cried when he had hung up. 'They're delighted to have a genuine Russian.'

I too was delighted with this stroke of luck. Rehearsals were to start at the end of the following week in a place called Yardley, Pennsylvania, a dear town four miles from Trenton. I rushed home to tell Jerry I was being 'useful' again, but my news sent him into a state of utter exasperation for ruining his plans. And he was not pleased with my idea of travelling the circuit in my jeep, thus leaving him with no wheels. I am a little ashamed to admit that I enjoyed observing his discomfiture in silence. My parents were intrigued by my news and pleased that our circuit would include the Hamptons on Long Island and that they would be able to come to our performances there.

Uta Hagen was already in Yardley, where she would be appearing in *Angel Street* during our rehearsal week. Paula Laurence and I met in New York, got on well and decided to travel together in my jeep. She had not been in one before and looked forward to it. I collected her on the morning of our departure and we merrily set off with our luggage and costumes (which we had to provide ourselves) piled up behind us. When we arrived in Yardley, we met Uta, a lovely, gregarious person, who was having first-night butterflies. We watched her performance in *Angel Street* that night.

We became an inseparable trio, off stage as well as on. We travelled the circuit in my jeep, laughing all the time (what bliss it was to laugh!) and enjoying performing in *Dark Eyes* immensely. The character of the Russian émigré, Prince Nicolai, was played by Adia Kuznetzoff, a well-known gypsy basso who had appeared in many Hollywood pictures and on radio shows. It was his first time at Summer Stock – it was so funny to see this giant of a man falling to pieces with nerves before each performance. It was a wonderful surprise for me to find him in Yardley – we had often met at the Tamiroffs' house whenever I had been in Hollywood. Those weeks at Summer Stock in 1947 were happy and carefree. We were away from it all and just having fun.

Once we were on the road, Jerry and Richard came to see a performance at one of the Hamptons. Richard, who knew the authors, became very excited, loved the play, and started nagging Jerry to help him take it to London. Jerry had the right managerial experience and contacts in London, Richard had the money. As there was nothing else in the offing, Jerry finally agreed to try. He found two willing co-producers in London, Bill Linnit and Jack Dunfee, who ran a well-known theatrical agency in London. Jerry and Richard flew to England to clinch the deal and engage Charles Goldner to direct the play.

Soon our US tour was over and preparations started in earnest for our London season. We were to bring the four 'Russians' with us, but the other actors would be engaged in London – the play's American family was to be replaced by an English one. I was very happy to go to London, and so put Ballet Theatre on the backburner once again. We would be opening at the Strand Theatre at the end of 1947, after a short provincial tour. Uta, Paula and Adia had other engagements and were not available, but we did not have much time to find replacements. Eugenia Delarova (Massine's ex-wife) gladly accepted the offer to replace Paula Laurence, while Uta suggested Polly Rowles, a lovely well-established actress, for her role. As for Adia's part, both Uta and Paula suggested Yul Brynner: 'He's divine,' they chorused.

I asked who he was. A struggling actor in his late twenties, they told me, a Russian who spoke English and French like a native, but with an Eastern lilt, with a voice of deep velvet, who played the guitar and sang gypsy songs like a true gypsy. It was quite a recommendation from the enthusiastic Uta and Paula. I was delegated the task of phoning him and luring him into meeting Jerry and Richard. Uta and Paula were right – the voice at the other end of the phone was like a velvety caress.

After introducing myself, I explained the reason for my call. His response was guarded, and he did not seem that interested. It took some persuasion on my part for him to finally agree to meet us at my flat the following week. When he heard at that meeting that Uta and Paula had recommended him, he did relax a little – they were his friends. But when they started to discuss the terms of the offer, I left them to it and sat in the kitchen, trying to remember why the appearance of this total stranger rang a distant bell in my memory. *This seriously balding man of average height, with slightly Asiatic looks and almond-shaped eyes – why do I have a feeling I've seen him before?*

I was interrupted in my reflections by being called back into the living room. They had reached an agreement and Yul would give a definite answer the next day, after talking to his wife. It transpired that his wife was Virginia Gilmore, a film actress, and that they had a baby son called Rocky. Yul called the next day to say that he would sign on, and Richard invited him and his wife to dinner at the Russian casino the next day to celebrate.

Yul's wife had beautiful, Grace Kelly-type looks. Unassuming and reserved, she seemed preoccupied and did not talk much. But when I asked her about her baby, she brightened up. I confessed to her that I, too, would love to have a baby but that, sadly, it did not look likely.

At that point the gypsy band burst into its first song and Yul started to hum under his breath. Suddenly it all came back to me – where I had seen him before, long ago. I turned to him and asked cautiously, 'Yul, were you in Paris in the early thirties?'

'Yes.'

'Did you play with a gypsy troupe at Russian charity balls?'

'Ye-e-s, my mother and sister were in that troupe. Why?'

'Oh, what a handsome young boy you were, with a great mop of unruly hair!'

Yul looked at me, puzzled and reproachful. 'Do you have to mention my hair?' he scolded. 'How do you know all this?'

I reminded him of that particular occasion and our brief encounter, and also of the humiliation I felt when he told me I looked younger than I told him I was. We had a good laugh and shared the story of our first encounter with the others. The atmosphere at our table then became

424

a little more jovial. We gave the Brynners a lift home and, as Virginia climbed out of the jeep, she asked me if I would like to see little Rocky. *Yes, I would.* In a very small room, a tiny angelic-looking chap stood up in his cot, holding onto the railings. Seeing his mum, he stretched out his arms with happy sounds, asking to be picked up. As Virginia picked him up, my heart squeezed like a sponge. I envied her. But I was surprised and saddened for little Rocky when I heard from people who knew the Brynners that their union was heading for the rocks. When I asked why, everyone had the same answer: 'Yul is a free spirit!'

After a tearful weekend with my parents – Mother was unhappy that I was going abroad again – and a cheerful phone call to Tassia, on a cold winter's day in 1947, Eugenia, Polly, Yul and I sailed for England. Jerry and Richard were flying over in a few days and would meet our ship in Southampton. It was great to have an old friend like Eugenia along. Polly was rapidly being russified, and Yul, in great spirits, was getting friendlier by the minute. Even as we stood on deck, waving goodbye to Jerry and Richard, I felt Yul's arm around my waist as he drew me to him. The first thought that shot through my mind was, *Ah, the free spirit!* My second thought was, *That feels rather nice.* But at the same time, somewhere from the depths of my subconscious, came Pat's voice saying, *Don't rock the boat!* Then my thoughts were drowned out by Eugenia saying, 'Let's unpack and get ready for dinner.'

We three girls shared one cabin; we were pushed for space, but we spent a carefree and relaxing six days on the ship. Once dinner was over, Yul would fetch his guitar, sit in the lotus position on the floor of the lounge, and sing gypsy songs, along with French and English songs. He delighted not only us, but the other passengers too. They would crowd around, even sitting on the floor if they had missed out on a nearby table or sofa. Yul became the most popular passenger in second class, and even first-class passengers would drop in to listen to him. I was developing a sort of crush on him myself . . . or was it just his guitar and his gypsy songs that fascinated me?

When, after our arrival in England, I recounted to Jerry and Richard how divinely Yul sang, and his popularity on the ship, I noticed Jerry bristle at my enthusiasm. From then on, his attitude to Yul became unfriendly, which created bad vibes all round, especially between Jerry and me – again. It was so monotonous and tedious!

We had a great reunion with Maureen and Charles Goldner, and having him as director was of huge benefit to me. The leading English actor was Edwin Styles, a tall, middle-aged, distinguished-looking man and an absolute dear. Eugenia and Edwin fast became friends and soon after companions. We met the English producers, Bill Linnit and Jack Dunfee. Linnit was a serious, solid, professional gentleman of the old school who inspired confidence and respect. Dunfee, on the other hand, was a dashing eccentric. Sporting large sideburns and clad in tailor-made shirts reminiscent of the Edwardian era, he was always to be seen around town in his convertible sports car, invariably with a gorgeous young lady at his side. The other English actors they brought to the play were a pleasure to meet and work with.

While we were rehearsing in London, Jerry, Richard and I stayed in the Grosvenor House Hotel in Park Lane, which was hugely expensive. Eugenia, Polly and Yul, on Charles's recommendation, took themselves to the Hotel Pastoria just off Leicester Square, a small, old-fashioned, cosy, slightly bohemian establishment run by the Pastori family. A happy friendship quickly developed among the threesome and the Pastoris. The place became like a home away from home, and of course Yul and his guitar were very popular there. It sounded like such fun – I was most envious!

Jerry came with us on our provincial tour, while Richard returned to New York, planning to reappear for our London opening. The tour went well – *Dark Eyes* was not a great success as a play (one had seen better comedies), but it was well received, and the critics were good to us.

Some of our old friends kept asking me when they would see me dance again. I was asking myself the same question. When would I finally be able to do what I wanted most in my life, dance? It became increasingly clear to me that Jerry and I were a handicap to each other. I could not get to do what I wanted most and, as long as I was around, he could not concentrate on going after what his ego was striving for. This 'miserable together' life was destroying us both. One of us had to put an end to it, however painful that might be.

Back in London, we stayed at the Waldorf Hotel, next door to the Strand Theatre. It was handy for me but I still envied the others back at the Pastoria. Richard returned, so each night while I performed, he and Jerry did their own thing. Not long after opening night, they planned to see a show and then explore the nightclubs, so I was to have supper without them. That was fine by me!

At the end of the performance, I decided to join Polly and Yul, who always had their supper at the Pastoria. Of course Yul, by popular demand, brought down his guitar, and everyone had a great time. It was late when I got back to our hotel and Jerry was already in. 'Where the hell have you been?' he asked in an unpleasant tone.

I told him where I had been and that I had enjoyed my supper and had a lovely time. He listened in silence, then came out with acid remarks that did not spare any one of my friends in residence at the Pastoria. It was not exactly a lullaby to send me peacefully into the arms of the sandman, but the straw that broke the camel's back. By the next afternoon my mind was already made up. I asked Jerry to come to my room (by then we already had two adjoining rooms with a bathroom between). To hide my nerves, I sat at the dressing table, pretending to file my nails. Jerry came over and sat on the windowsill to face me. I had the impression that he knew what was coming.

'I don't feel we can go on like this,' I said, feeling awful. 'I know I can't.' Jerry remained silent, so I continued. 'We must separate.' I kept my head down, a lump in my throat. Silence. I looked up at him.

Finally, he asked calmly, 'Have you given this serious thought? Is it what you really want?' I nodded, tears choking me. 'All right, then,' he said. 'Good luck. Be happy.' Then he calmly returned to his room.

I went to the theatre and sat, empty-headed, in my dressing room until it was time to start my make-up. I could not concentrate. My feeling of unreality – or was it anticlimax? – was most disturbing. What I had thought would be so painfully difficult had turned out to be so simple, without argument, without harsh words. In less than five minutes our relationship was over.

I was absentmindedly putting on my navy suit for the first act when my dresser came in with my freshly laundered blouse. 'Oh, the blouse . . .' I said. 'I almost forgot.' Only the knock on my door and a cry of 'Five minutes, please' made me pull myself together and attempt to concentrate.

The performance over, I bade Polly and Yul goodnight, as usual, then went back to the hotel. Uncertain of what Jerry's next move might be, I went to my room with some apprehension. All was quiet. The door to his room was open, but he was not there. None of his stuff was in the bathroom. I opened his wardrobe – it was empty. He was gone. I closed the connecting door and locked it. *No more hurting each other. It's over. It's finished. Now what?* Those were my thoughts as I sat on my bed, not quite sure what to do next.

After a while, I dialled Richard's room. There was no answer. I called the desk, pretending I had forgotten his room number, but as I suspected he had checked out that evening. They were both gone.

Only then did it occur to me that I had 'rocked the boat' without thinking through the impact my actions my might have on the run of our play. Had I, yet again, acted on impulse without thinking responsibly first? Tassia sprang up in my mind's eye, laughing as she cried, *Think first, Irischka. Think first!* Had I created problems for Bill Linnit? Would the Davis–Severn (by now Jerry's surname was Severn) production still work? I had strong doubts. Was this all terrible timing on my part?

Embarrassing as it might be, I decided I would call Bill Linnit in the morning and put him in the picture. With that thought I went to bed, but sleep was slow to come. When it did, it was scattered with nightmares. I woke up early, with a splitting headache. My first thought was, *I must get out of here. I hate this room. I hate this place.* But all I managed to do was take some headache pills and go back to bed.

When I woke up again, I thought how happy my mother would be when she and Papa got my letter with this latest news. She would be triumphant! And I imagined the tongues wagging in the Russian Tea

Room. All sorts of rubbish went through my head until I got up and called Bill Linnit. He took my news calmly. 'Don't worry now,' he said. 'Let's wait and see what happens.'

Next I called Polly. She became very excited at hearing my tale and insisted on coming over. I had just managed to get dressed when she appeared, with Yul in tow. We all seemed to be talking at once, until Polly decreed that I must move to the Pastoria to be with them. Yul phoned immediately to see if they had a room, and they did. My two friends helped me pack, with a humour that helped lift my spirits and, before I knew what had hit me, we were on our way to the Pastoria.

Eugenia was in the lobby when we arrived. When I told her why I was moving in with them, she was appalled. 'You're crazy!' she cried. 'How could you do that to Jerry? He adores you. You're despicable!' Two days later she checked out from the hotel and did not speak to me again for twenty years. I was shaken by her violent outburst, which I felt was out of place. Nevertheless, I was sorry, and sad to have lost her friendship.

It was quite a change to find myself in the company of light-hearted, unregimented, spontaneous friends. I began to look forward to each new day, and felt happy to be alive. But meanwhile, there was no news from either Jerry or Richard. Bill Linnit's efforts to locate them failed; the two partners had just disappeared, ignoring their commitment to Linnit and Dunfee. It was very embarrassing. We were approaching the end of May 1948 when Linnit and Dunfee, after having valiantly kept the play going on their own, found themselves in no position to sustain the expenses any longer. We were regretfully advised that we would have to close in two weeks' time. As I stood in the wings with Eugenia, awaiting our cue, she hissed, 'It's all your fault!'

She was right, and I was stuck in front of all our actors with a huge sense of guilt. Jerry and Richard were teaching me a lesson at the expense of other people, without even bothering to contact or come to a settlement with Bill Linnit. It seemed disgraceful to me, if not plain dishonest. My feeling of regret at having caused Jerry pain left me – embarrassment and anger remained.

A letter from Boris Kochno arrived and diverted my angry thoughts into happier channels. He was coming over from Paris with Bébé Bérard and they were hoping there would be room for them at our inn. To see these dear people again after all these years was emotionally uplifting and morale-boosting. It was especially good to see Kochno, my mentor and companion in so many adventures. They liked Polly and immediately fell in love with Yul. Every night Boris would join Yul in his gypsy songs while Bérard, the romantic old softie, would let a tear or two slide down into his beard. They returned to Paris just before the play closed, and urged us to visit them. I wanted so much to see Paris again. Polly and Yul were keen too, so we all promised to visit Paris before returning to America.

After the last performance, Bill Linnit and his lovely wife had us all over for supper at their house. It was a lovely gesture on their part, given that *Dark Eyes* had not been a happy experience for Bill. He had remained a true gentleman throughout the saga.

The next morning the three of us purchased our tickets to Paris. Polly planned to fly direct to New York from there, but Yul and I wanted to return to London. I wanted to see something more of my old friends before returning to the United States, Yul wanted to talk to theatrical agents about the possibility of him finding work in England – he was particularly keen to get into films. We sat on the floor in my room and counted our money. Financially it looked feasible, even after we took into account the cost of our return plane tickets to New York.

It felt so simple, so natural, that my friendship with Yul was sliding into a light, happy love affair. By the time we left for Paris, we were sharing our nights as well as our days. I felt like a dog let off its lead – free! Free to run in any direction, wagging its tail, with no-one calling it to heel.

Paris brought back so many memories of my childhood. I wanted to roam around it as I had used to with my papa, but the first thing I did was dash to see Mme Preobrajenska. My beloved teacher was about to start a class, but she hugged me close and gave me a warm welcome. Yul and I showed Polly the beautiful sights of Paris and enjoyed our evenings with Kochno and Bérard. I got a bee in my bonnet that I wanted to see the sunrise while sitting under the Arc de Triomphe and looking down the length of the beautiful Avenue des Champs-Elysées. I did, and Yul kept me company.

But all good things come to an end. Polly left and it was time for Yul and me to return to London. Back at the Pastoria, we took stock of our finances. We were in trouble, having greatly overspent in Paris. It was evident that we could not stay at the Pastoria for more than a week. What to do? It seemed that the only thing to do was to get back to the United States before our plane-ticket money dwindled as well.

The next day, as we were walking along Piccadilly towards the airline offices to purchase our tickets, I recognised a tall, blue-eyed man walking towards us. 'Noel!' I cried.

'Irina!'

We stopped, delighted and surprised to see each other. It was Noel Langley, the well-known scriptwriter, who had co-written the script of *Florian* and whom I had often seen on the MGM lot in Hollywood when I was making the film. I introduced him to Yul and he asked what we were doing in London. 'Oh, it's a long story,' I replied.

'I want to hear it. Let's go and have a drink somewhere and you tell me all about it.' Noel had a calm but rather abrupt manner – I always had the impression that he was like a dormant volcano that could erupt without warning.

Installed in a pub on Shaftesbury Avenue, we told Noel our story and he told us his. He was going through a difficult time with his wife, who had buzzed off to South Africa. He was living in Kingston-on-Thames with his four children, a housekeeper and a maid-cum-secretary. He had no spare rooms in the house, but he did have a very big yard, a gypsy caravan occupied by a young journalist friend, and a huge army surplus tent, in which we were very welcome to stay for as long as we wanted. Destiny works in strange ways!

With much gratitude, we promptly accepted Noel's kind offer and arranged to appear at his house the following afternoon. With no hotel expenses, we could put off returning to the United States for a little longer. We thanked Noel profusely and dashed off to pack and to tell the Pastori family the reason for our hurried departure.

I had, of course, already written to tell my parents about my separation from Jerry and my move to the Pastoria. Now I scribbled a quick note telling them Noel's address and that I would be sharing a tent in his yard with Yul. As I ran out to post it, I thought of my papa and mother. *Poor things, they'll think I've gone totally round the bend!* Probably, but it was so exciting, the thought of living in a tent!

The next afternoon we descended upon the Langley household with all our luggage and a large number of food parcels that we had purchased with our ration coupons and with some 'under the table' help from Pastori Jnr. We also had the latest parcel from my parents, which included a big tin of ham. All the food had been stuffed into an old potato sack by the chef at the Pastoria and tied up at each end with rope. It provoked a furore of delight when the Langley children found bars of chocolate and boiled sweets.

We had a hilarious time erecting the huge tent, with everyone under the sun helping and Noel directing. For bedside tables we had two beer crates, for beds two old mattresses dragged from the attic and our sleeping bags. We strung a rope across one corner on which to hang our clothes. Noel provided us with two torches. We could share Noel's bathroom and use the downstairs toilet if we were caught short in the middle of the night. It was perfect. Life was fun!

I made firm friends with the youngest of the Langley children, an angelic-looking four-year-old with blond hair and blue eyes. He was a continual source of delight and refreshing company. Noel was in the process of writing a new play, so sometimes at dinner he would explode into oratory, venting his frustrations with life or with people. There was never a dull moment in that unlikely household: we had poltergeists, so a priest came in to exorcise the premises; the children were always getting sick; and the long summer nights were filled with the sounds of Yul's guitar, sad gypsy songs and raucous English ones.

Yul's excursions to theatrical agencies were unproductive, and his finances dwindled alarmingly. He wrote frantic letters to his agent in New York, then one day got some good news. There was a musical, to be called *Lute Song*, in preparation and his agent was trying to get him the lead. The next day Yul dashed to London and that evening, as we all sat in the garden, he sang '*Otchi Cherni*' (the gypsy song 'Dark Eyes') and informed me, 'Tra-la-la-la-la, I have to leave, tra-la-la-la-la, tomorrow, ta-di-da-da, tra-la-la-la-la, farewell, my love, farewell.'

How not to laugh? We all did, and wished him luck. As I helped him pack, I asked if he had bought his plane ticket that day. 'No, I bought it last week,' he replied.

'Why didn't you tell me?'

'I didn't want to upset you.'

He was catching the early morning train to London and would collect the rest of his luggage from the Pastoria before proceeding to the airport. I saw him off at the gate and then, since the railway tracks ran right by Noel's yard, I stood there waiting for the train to pass. As it came into view, I started waving, and as it flashed by I had a glimpse of Yul waving back. The free spirit was gone, bless him.

The next time we saw each other was twenty-eight years later. By then he had shaved off his remaining hair, had starred in films and was the King of Siam in *The King and I*. He had pinched my little white radio when he left Kingston, but he did replace it twenty-eight years later with a great big modern one! I still use it. I shall always remember him with a smile and affection.

V

A NEW LIFE, 1948–1967

12

FREEDOM

No sooner had Yul left than it turned cold and started to rain. I went down with tonsillitis and was running a high temperature, so Noel's doctor sent me to hospital to have my tonsils out, a most unpleasant experience! The hospital bill ate into what I had saved for my return ticket to New York, and I was broke. Much as I hated to dip into my New York savings account, it seemed I had no other alternative but to do so. Not having a clue how to go about it, I asked Noel's advice. He asked me why I needed extra money, so I told him it was for my plane ticket.

'Don't be silly, I'll lend you what you need,' he kindly offered.

I thanked him but declined the offer. I never borrowed money from anyone and was not prepared to start doing so. Proud? Yes. Noel tried to reason with me, pointing out that once you start dipping into your savings, before you know it there will be none left. 'What shall I do then?' I asked.

'If you won't take my money, then earn it.' He went on to tell me that a new production of his play *Farm of Three Echoes* was going into rehearsal. In two or three weeks' time he could give me the part of the tart from Bloomfontaine. He had bookings for the tour and was waiting for a theatre in London. He would let me go as soon as I had saved up enough to get myself to New York. 'Mind you, I can't pay you much on the road,' he warned me.

I could hardly believe my luck! Noel seemed to be sent to me from heaven. His kindness and understanding touched me deeply, and I accepted his offer with gratitude and relief.

Noel seemed a little surprised. 'Good for you!' he laughed, with a scrutinising look. The next day he produced a script and said, 'Learn your lines.'

'How about my accent?' I asked.

'In that role it won't matter.'

At this time a letter from my parents brought disturbing news. Jerry was in New York and had phoned them to ask if they wanted my piano and gramophone cabinet. If so, he would have them delivered to their house, which he did. My parents heard that he had made arrangements with my landlady to pass on the flat to some friends of his, telling her that I would not be returning from England for some time and would no longer be needing the flat. What he had done with the rest of my furniture or with my clothes and personal belongings, they did not know. 'What's going on?' they asked worriedly. 'When are you coming back?'

Their letter stunned me! I could understand Jerry's anger at me, and even his sabotaging the play, but his desire to take even my flat away from me in this underhand, malicious way took me by surprise. I hurried to pacify my parents, writing to assure them that I would be with them for Christmas and that I had no intention of remaining in England. I dressed up the fact that I would be touring with Noel's play as good experience for me, omitting to tell them the real reason. I expressed my shock and surprise at their news about my flat, and told them I would sort it out on my return.

Having posted my letter express, I went for a slow walk along the Thames, my thoughts in turmoil. *What a mess!* As I passed by a pub, I caught sight of a notice stuck in the window announcing 'Casual help wanted'. I stopped in my tracks. *Well, why not?* I mused. It was the possibility of earning pennies. *Every little bit helps.*

Gathering up my courage, I walked boldly into the pub. A couple of customers were sitting at the counter, perched on high stools. Unsure of what I should do, I sidled up to the end of the counter, where the till stood. A man holding a tray approached and said, 'Yes, Miss?'

'I'm here about the notice in your window.'

'You're looking for a job, then?'

'Yes, a temporary one, for the next three weeks.' I felt uncomfortable and started blushing.

'Where do you come from?' the man asked with undisguised curiosity.

'You mean my accent?'

'Yes, I can't quite place it. Are you Swedish?'

'No, I'm Russian.'

The man's eyes lit up with interest. 'Oh really? Come, why don't we sit down.'

We sat at a table and the man plied me with questions. We talked and talked – he was fascinated by my story, or those bits of it I chose to tell him! We ended up on first-name terms and I got the job. My duties would be to sweep the floor, clean the tables and wash glasses. I told him I did not know anything about mixing drinks, so he asked if I could help him with making sandwiches. The deal was struck and I started early the next morning.

That evening, very pleased with myself, I told the Langley household about my new career at the pub. They all declared me nuts. Perhaps I was, but I was earning enough pocket money to keep me going without having to dip any further into my plane-ticket money. The people at the pub were nice, the work did not require a university degree, I was spared the boredom of doing nothing, and I had an amusing time with my new experience.

Three weeks later, after fond goodbyes to all at the pub, I started riding to London each morning with Noel, to rehearse his play, *Farm of Three Echoes*. Griffith Jones was the star – he seemed to me to be permanently depressed and preoccupied, rather like the character he was portraying. The female lead was Muriel Pavlow, who was petite, lovely-looking and seemed too young to be married, although her husband came with her on the tour. The rest of the cast, all of whom were nice enough, kept themselves to themselves, and there was not that feeling of cama-raderie that I was so used to in the ballet world. On that particular tour I missed it more than ever.

I stayed in digs, to save my pennies, while the others stayed in hotels. The winter was upon us and it was a beastly cold one. I was con-stantly running out of the shilling coins needed to keep the small gas fire going – one coin for an hour of heat. At night it took all my courage to undress in front of that meagre fire, slip into my woollen ballet tights, a flannel shirt, two jumpers and mittens, and get into bed, hoping not to encounter damp sheets.

Three weeks before the end of the tour Noel did not seem any closer to getting a theatre in London. He was in a bad temper and the cast was worried, but I was not. I would be going back to New York and, *oh bliss*, my lovely warm room at my parents' house.

On the day we arrived in Hull, one of the last stops on our tour, I went straight to the theatre as usual, and asked the stage doorkeeper where I would find the nearest digs. 'Just up the street, about two-hundred yards on your left, you'll see a "bed and breakfast" sign,' he told me. It was handy at least. They gave me a room, which was big and bare. Due to the damp, the old wallpaper was parting company, in places, with the wall. There was no gas fire, and only a bare light bulb hanging from the ceiling to illuminate the sadness of the room, but there was a sink. *Never mind, it's near the theatre – a great convenience.*

I slept through the night but as the rainy grey dawn was creeping through the bare window I was awoken by a strange noise. I sat up in bed and listened. It came from the direction of my suitcase, which I had left open on the floor. The tissue paper in which I had carefully wrapped my belongings was rustling. *Who's going through my suitcase?* Then it struck me. *Mice!* I had always been terrified of mice (and birds), and still am. *Oh my God!*

Too terrified to get out of bed, I picked my slippers up off the floor and threw them one after the other into my suitcase – some movement, more noises, and then silence. But I was still too afraid to get out of bed. In despair, I pounded the bed with my fists and burst into tears, drowning in self-pity. As I shed my last tear, wiped my eyes and stopped sniffling, I became angry with myself. *Self-pity indeed! You got into this situation all by yourself, so now get out of it all by yourself, stupid cow!* It helped. I got out of bed, bravely picked up the case and threw it on top of the bed, dressed myself at top speed, threw my belongings into the case, buckled it up and flew out of the room. I had to get out of that house – I could not face another encounter with mice.

The landlady was standing at the foot of the stairs in her dressing gown. 'What was all that noise?' she enquired, obviously displeased with me.

I told her I could not live with mice, paid her and walked out. Where else was there to go but my dressing room? The stage door was locked, and it was much too early for the stage doorkeeper to be on duty, so I sat on my case by the door and hoped that the small café over the road might open soon. How I longed for hot coffee!

Later, somewhat comforted by the café having been opened, I was taking out my money to pay for a cup of coffee and a bun when I spotted, in one of the compartments of my wallet, the stack of ration coupons I had been saving to give to Noel before I left. An idea sprang into my mind, and I took them out and divided them into three equal bunches, each containing coupons for food, sweets and cigarettes. As I put them back into my wallet, I said to myself, *Oh, it'll never work!* But then I thought, *You'll never know unless you try.*

I took my coffee and bun back to the stage door and waited until ten a.m., when the doorkeeper arrived – he was very surprised to find me on the doorstep. I told him my sad story, not only about the mice, but that I was saving for my plane ticket back to New York. He was full of sympathy. 'Shall I help you find some more digs?' he asked kindly.

'No, but you could help me in a much better way,' I said endearingly.

'How?'

'By letting me stay in my dressing room at night.'

'But it's against the regulations,' he exclaimed, astonished by my request.

'Maybe you could make an exception,' I pleaded. He looked perplexed, so I took the first batch of ration coupons out of my wallet and coaxed him with a smile. 'And to show my gratitude,' I said, 'I'll give you all these coupons.' The dear man pursed his lips and looked uncertain. 'If I'm caught,' I added, 'I'll say that I was hiding and that you knew nothing about it.' I produced the second batch of coupons. 'You can have these too.'

I was feeling like a crook and, embarrassed at having started this dubious experiment, was about to give up and turn it all into a joke when the doorman reached for the coupons and stuffed them in his pocket. 'I guess my missus will be pleased to have these,' he grinned. 'All right, stay. But not a word to anyone.'

I hugged him, amazed that my scheme had worked. For the next four days, my dressing room was my home. I slept in the well-worn chair, with my *doumka* on which to lay my head, and my winter coat to keep me warm. I started each night with a thermos full of coffee and a supply of buns from the café over the road. There was a sink, so I could brush my teeth and more or less keep clean, and I had two books to read.

Each morning I had the stage all to myself to do a class; in the afternoons I sat by the doorkeeper's desk and listened to his stories of the hardships his family had been through during the war. One afternoon his 'missus' came by, curious to meet me, and thanked me for the coupons. I gave her the last batch, abandoning my plan to bribe the next stage doorkeeper. These people had been kind to me, and it was the least I could do in return. In the last two towns of our tour I stayed in digs, and thankfully had no more encounters with mice.

On the final night of the play, Noel took us all to supper. It was very sad saying goodbye to him – I will never forget his amazing kindness to me and I always cherished his friendship. Back in London, I dropped my case at the Pastoria and dashed to buy my plane ticket. It was Monday and I was lucky enough to get a ticket for Thursday. I had saved enough for the ticket and my hotel bill with a few pounds left over. I was so pleased with myself!

After a proper dinner and a wonderful hot bath, it was such a treat to get into a comfortable bed. I slept like a log. *What bliss!* Next day, after repacking my luggage (I am very particular about packing), I called a few friends to say goodbye, washed my hair and set it in curlers, then settled down to read my book. The phone rang. 'This is Ealing Studios. Sir Michael Balcon wishes to speak to you, please hold.' *What on earth can he want?*

'Irina?'

'Yes, Sir Michael. How did you know I was here?'

'Noel Langley told me. You're off to New York in a few days?'

'Yes, Thursday. Why?'

'We're starting work on a new film, *Train of Events*. There's a character in it who's a concert pianist. I thought of you. Would you be interested?'

'But, Sir Michael, I can't play the piano like a professional!'

'That doesn't matter,' he laughed. He briefly told me the plot – there were four disconnected episodes explaining why the people involved happened to be on a train that is involved in a crash. 'Valerie Hobson and John Clements have already signed up for the episode I had you in mind for. Are you interested?'

In the state of mind I was in then, always worrying about money and saving, my first thought was not about the part in the film, but the fact that, if I did it, I would not have to dip into my savings when I returned to New York. 'Well, yes,' I replied. 'But I'm off on Thursday.'

'That's all right. If it works out, depending on us getting a labour permit for you, we won't start shooting that sequence until mid-January.' We discussed finances, and his offer was more than I expected. How could I refuse? 'Do you mind doing a screen test?' Sir Michael asked, as an afterthought.

'Not at all,' I answered.

'If I send you a few pages to learn overnight, can you do the test tomorrow?'

'Yes, of course,' I replied, rather bewildered.

'Good! You'll get the pages by six o'clock. A car will pick you up at six in the morning. See you tomorrow.'

I could not settle down to my book again, so I decided to go for a short walk and get some fresh air. As I started to take out my curlers, the phone rang again. 'Miss Baronova? Mr Tennant for you.' *Oh dear, how embarrassing.* A mutual friend had told me to call him and I never had.

'Hello, hello,' he said cheerily. 'Why didn't you call me? Ogden wrote to me and said you'd call. I was looking forward to meeting you.' The voice sounded jolly and friendly. Embarrassed, I made some silly, non-valid excuses. 'What are you doing now?' he asked.

'Taking the curlers out of my hair.'

'Well, hurry up and come to my office,' he commanded. 'It's just around the corner from you, in St James's Street. We must finally meet!'

'How did you know where to phone me?'

'Oh, I know everything,' he laughed.

'All right,' I said. I'll be with you shortly.' *What a nice man,* I thought.

Half an hour later I was standing in front of an imposing building, where a plaque saying 'Myron Selznick Agency' indicated the way. The receptionist announced my arrival and almost immediately the very tall, elegant, handsome Mr Tennant came out to greet me. I had never met anyone as tall as him, and had to bend back my neck just to look him in the face.

'Ah, finally we meet,' he said with a broad smile and showed me into his office. As I sat down, eyeing him with astonishment, he perched himself on the corner of his desk. 'So, you're doing a screen test tomorrow? Good luck.'

'How did you know?' I asked in amazement.

'As I told you before, I know everything,' he chuckled. 'I also know that you're off to New York on Thursday. I hope it works out with the film and that you'll be back in January.'

We talked about the film, what it was about and who the other actors were. The entire time we talked, I had the impression that he was looking at me with a measure of amusement. *What does he find so funny about me?* I wondered.

Suddenly he shouted out, 'Olive, Olive – come here for a minute!' A lady wearing imposing-looking tortoiseshell spectacles stuck her head in the door. 'Come and meet Miss Baronova, the funny Russian who never phoned . . . and this is Miss Harding.' He smiled at us both.

We chatted for a little while longer and then I got up to take my leave. Promising this charming man to phone him if or when I returned, I went back to the hotel to await the arrival of the script I had to study for the next day. I was sitting downstairs, having a glass of wine with Pastori Jnr, when the script arrived. I declined dinner – I was getting butterflies in my stomach and could not face food. Instead, I got into bed and started memorising my lines.

The alarm sounded most unpleasant at four-thirty in the morning. By six a.m. I had made my way downstairs to wait for the car, but it was already waiting for me. I arrived at Ealing Studios, was shown into a dressing room, then whisked off to the make-up department. At nine a.m. I was taken onto the set and introduced to Sir Michael, the director and the cameraman. I was scared stiff, never having done a screen test before, but after a while I relaxed, turned my head to the left and right, walked about as asked, and did not fluff my lines when required to go through the scene with the actor who was there to do it with me. To my embarrassment, the actor turned out to be John Clements, whom, due to my nerves, I did not immediately recognise. At last, the ordeal was over. Sir Michael was noncommittal and said he would call me in the morning, after they had all looked at the screen test.

Feeling a wreck, I was driven back to the Pastoria. I called Noel but he was not in. I called Bill Linnit. 'How did the screen test go?' he asked.

Everybody seems to know everything in this town, I mused. 'Bill, if it comes to anything, will you do the contract for me?'

'Yes, of course,' was his kind reply.

That settled, I lay down and went to sleep. Hunger woke me up. I had an early dinner downstairs then went back to bed, feeling rotten. Sir Michael called in the morning. The test was good, he said, and they would apply immediately for my labour permit. Who was my agent? he wanted to know. I told him it was Bill Linnit. 'Good,' he said, 'I'll be in touch with him. Well, hope to see you soon,' he added, wishing me bon voyage.

I thanked him and hung up with a sigh of satisfied relief. Harold Good, my dear old friend, took me to dinner and offered to drive me to the airport the next morning. As the aeroplane took off, I was thinking how strange, how unpredictable life was, and wondering what 1949 would bring.

After an eventful, chaotic year, and my happy-go-lucky existence, which had brought unwelcome problems in its wake, it was so good and reassuring to see my parents, to be with them again in their home, in my room. They were the only people in my life who represented constancy and solidity. I came to see that events and people might come and go, but my parents would always be there for me. We might argue and quarrel, but we would never forsake each other. In short, I was happy to be home. There was a Christmas tree on the low round table in the living room – it smelt so good – and, *oh*, my piano and my gramophone! I was glad they had found a niche for them in this cosy room. My papa even made my favourite Russian Christmas sweet, *koutia*, from barley, honey, vanilla and nuts. What a treat!

There was so much to tell them that I talked myself hoarse. When I told them about my experiences at the pub and about sleeping in my dressing room, Papa laughed, shaking his head at his wayward daughter. But Mother, somewhat disapprovingly, cried, 'Oh, *Gospodi*!' (Oh, God!). I talked to Tassia on the phone. She was doing splendidly, as was her mama. My darling Beatrice came to spend the day, and seeing my Russian Sea Cliff friends was like being in another world. My soul was resting.

After Christmas I went to New York for the day. Beatrice came with me to my old flat – I wanted to sort out what had happened to my belongings. The landlady was surprised but delighted to see me. We had a long talk and it transpired that I had met the couple who were now living in my flat. He was a Russian actor from Hollywood, and they had brought their own furniture from California. 'What happened to mine?' I asked. The landlady did not know. 'And my clothes and so on?' She did not know either. The flat was empty when the others had moved in. Well, that was that, there was nothing I could do.

'You could sue Mr Severn,' the landlady suggested.

'No, it's not worth it,' I replied. 'Stirring mud? No.' Out of curiosity, as we were leaving I asked the landlady if she knew Mr Severn's whereabouts.

'Yes, from what I hear, Mr Severn has gone with Mr Davis to the South of France.'

Beatrice grumbled all the way to the bus, but I felt like laughing. What at? I could not really tell.

It was lovely to get out at Sea Cliff Station, breathe in the crisp fresh air and hear the snow crackle under my boots. It was so good to be away from it all. We saw the New Year in at a friend's house. It was a jolly party, and everyone brought something delicious for supper. The Russians are good at partying – there is always much laughter, singing and dancing into the early hours of the morning. Doggy Jicky was allowed to come, and had a ball, with everyone feeding him bits and spoiling him rotten.

Back home, as we bade each other goodnight, my papa hugged me tight and said, 'It's time you looked seriously at your life. You've been dissipating it, Irishenka. Get it together again! May this New Year bring you peace and happiness in what you do best – dance.' He kissed me and we all went to bed.

I lay in bed for a long time, thinking about what Papa had said. Yes, he was right. As soon as possible I had to get back into dancing. I did miss it so much . . . And no more men in my life. Enough is enough, they are only trouble. With these good intentions, I finally fell asleep.

ENGAGED

In the first week of January I was on pins and needles, waiting for news from London. Finally, on the fifth, a telegram arrived. It read, 'LABOUR PERMIT GRANTED STOP YOU ARE EXPECTED FOR COSTUMES ON THE 13TH STOP REGARDS CECIL TENNANT.'

I was puzzled. Of course it was very nice of Cecil to let me know, but I would have to hear it from Bill Linnit or Sir Michael Balcon. I immediately wired Bill Linnit, asking him to confirm the news I had heard from Cecil Tennant. I received his reply the next morning. 'LABOUR PERMIT GRANTED STOP REPORT STUDIO ON 13TH STOP AIR TICKET ON THE WAY STOP REGARDS BILL.'

Here I was once again, embarking on an adventure instead of seriously resuming my career. When I showed the telegrams to my parents, I swore to them that I was straying for the last time. I started to pack half-heartedly, absolutely certain that I would be back by the end of February, or at the latest by the very beginning of March 1949, in time to celebrate my thirtieth birthday with my parents.

A studio car met me at the airport in London and took me to the Pastoria. In my room I found a most beautiful basket of flowers – no, not from the studio, nor from Bill, but from none other than Cecil Tennant! *How very nice*, I thought, and I called right away to thank him.

'Ah, welcome back,' came his cheerful voice. 'Did you have a nice flight? Look, I'm sorry, I can't take you out for dinner tonight – I have to see Michael Redgrave on business – but tomorrow I'll pick you up from your hotel at seven p.m. Relax now. See you tomorrow.'

I sat with my mouth open in astonishment. *What a funny man*, I thought. *He didn't ask if I was free or wanted to come out to dinner, he just assumed all these things.* However, he did sound so nice, friendly and different that I looked forward with pleasure to seeing him the next evening.

There was so much to attend to the next day, and I had to hurry not to be late for my dinner date. And there he was – punctual, smart and smiling. He took me to the Savoy Grill, which held many memories for me from the prewar days. My brief mood of nostalgia was diverted by my charming companion and, as our dinner progressed, I felt as if I had known him for a long time. We ended on first-name terms.

On the way back to the Pastoria, although it was hardly on the way, Cecil drove to New Scotland Yard and stopped the car right under the bright lights in front of the gates. We were in the middle of a discussion he obviously did not want to interrupt. What a place to stop! I thought it rather funny. We finished our discussion then he said, glancing at his pocket watch (I had never seen one like it, nor have I since), 'Bedtime for you. You have an early call in the morning.' On the way to the hotel he informed me that he would pick me up from the studio the next day and take me to dinner in Soho.

'But, Cecil, I don't know what time I'll be finished.'

'Not to worry. I'll find out.' We shook hands and bade each other goodnight. As he pulled out, he called through the open window, 'See you tomorrow!'

What a lovely person and a perfect gentleman, I thought to myself as I brushed my teeth. I felt so pleased that I would be spending the next evening in his company again.

By then I was somewhat familiar with how things work in a film studio. The day passed in fittings, make-up tests, working out with our hair stylist which style would be good for which outfit or hat. At the commissary at lunchtime I met Valerie Hobson, who came over to the table where I was sitting alone and introduced herself, saying, 'I'm Valerie Hobson. We'll be working together. Can I sit with you?' Her simple, unpompous, friendly approach was so refreshing. She was a big star, very beautiful and totally natural. We talked about a scene we had together, and about the film in general.

I also met the lady pianist who was going to coach me on the piece of music I had to play in the film, or rather make it *look* like I was playing it. I would be on stage, with a symphony orchestra and with John Clements in the role of the conductor. It proved to be quite a challenge, learning to have my fingers in the right place, if not always on the right note!

As promised, when I was free to go, Cecil was there waiting for me. We had a very good dinner at a Hungarian restaurant, where horsemeat was disguised as goulash but tasted delicious. We ended the evening, yet again, in front of New Scotland Yard. We talked about our respective families and he listened, fascinated, to my story of our risky escape from Russia. I, in turn, learned that he was the youngest in the family, and had four sisters and two brothers. The eldest sister had died at the age of seven, before he was born; the eldest brother was killed in the trenches on the last day of World War I. His father was dead, his mother (whom he called 'the old cheese') was a bridge fanatic and practically lived at Crockfords Club, a casino, never missing a day.

There were lots of aunts, cousins and nephews. They all sounded rather eccentric to me, and funny. As for Cecil, he had grown up in Yorkshire and then been sent to Eton College. He started adult life as a chartered accountant with Price Waterhouse. While doing the books at the Myron Selznick Agency, he became friends with Mr Selznick, who then persuaded him to drop accountancy and join the agency. Myron thought he could make Cecil into a fine agent and offer him a more interesting life. Cecil was indecisive about the wisdom of going into show business, and could not make up his mind until Marlene Dietrich walked into the office and passed his desk with a husky 'hello'. That did it! He joined Myron Selznick. When Myron died, he left the business to Cecil, who by then ranked as one of the top agents in the business.

When World War II was declared, he immediately volunteered to join the Coldstream Guards. He survived Dunkirk, and on D-Day he was in command of his tank division, which after the debarkation pushed north-east through Belgium and Holland. Demobilised with the rank of major, he returned to head his agency.

It also came up in our conversation that he was nine years older than me, but our birthdays were only a week apart. Cecil's demeanour to me was strictly respectful. By no word or gesture did he permit himself any familiarity. As he dropped me at my hotel that night, he said, 'See you tomorrow. I'll pick you up at the studio.'

This time it felt right and not at all odd. For the next nine days, the routine did not change. Cecil picked me up after work, took me to dinner followed by a chat while parked outside New Scotland Yard, and I was in bed by nine, learning my lines for the next day. After our ninth evening spent together, as we bade each other goodnight, Cecil said, 'Tomorrow I'll take you to dinner at my sister Esmee's. She's very keen to meet you.'

By then I knew that he shared a flat with his sister, and I was pleased at the thought of meeting her. She was quite a few years older than Cecil – there was another sister between her and him. She greeted me warmly and I immediately felt at ease in her company. Esmee was a very good-looking woman. She was separated from her husband and had a daughter in her late teens.

After dinner, which was most enjoyable, Esmee made coffee then disappeared under the pretext of a slight headache. Cecil poured the coffee, then reclined in his armchair and asked, 'Aren't you tired of so much travelling all your life?'

'No, I love it. But I must admit that at times I wish I could unpack and throw all my suitcases away,' I laughed.

'Do you like children?'

'Yes, I love kids and dogs.'

Cecil looked pensive. 'Would you like to marry again?'

'Maybe, one day. Who knows?'

He looked deadly serious as he voiced his next question. 'How would you like to be married to me?'

Was it a hypothetical question or was it his funny way of proposing to me? I was not sure. To be on the safe side, I responded lightly, 'Oh, I'd like it very much!'

'Good!' cried Cecil. Then he got up, walked towards me, lifted me up so I was standing on the sofa, kissed me on the forehead, put me back down again, went back to his armchair, then called out, 'Esmee, Esmee, come here!' She appeared instantaneously. 'We're engaged,' Cecil announced, grinning.

You could have knocked me down with a feather! This funny, loveable Englishman was like no-one I had ever met. Making delighted noises, Esmee produced a bottle of champagne. As Cecil got up to open it, I watched them in a pleasant daze. Was I in love with Cecil? Yes, I was. It had crept up on me, without me noticing, or I had not perhaps allowed myself to acknowledge it. Had I not promised no more men? Had I not decided that they were trouble? But there I was, throwing my good resolutions away and letting my feelings take over.

It was later than usual when Cecil took me back to the Pastoria – we did not stop at New Scotland Yard. This time, as we said goodnight, Cecil kissed me on the forehead, saying there would be much to sort out the next day at dinner. As I went to my room I hummed, *A fine romance, without wishes* . . . My dear, funny Cecil, his strictly proper ways were so endearing. I loved him more by the minute!

A sense of unreality still persisted the next day. That evening at dinner, Cecil informed me that his lawyer had told him my Mexican divorce was not legal in England. To obtain one was a lengthy procedure and would require Jerry's consent and signature. Did I know where to find him?

'No.'

In that case, the lawyer had suggested that I go back to the United States and establish six weeks' residence in Reno (a favourite with film people) or the Virgin Islands, get a local lawyer to petition for my divorce, and insert an ad in the important international newspapers saying that I would hold my husband financially responsible for me, including for my legal costs, until he sign his consent to a divorce. 'That's the quickest way to go,' Cecil advised.

'But what if Jerry never sees the ad?' I asked.

'Apparently it always gets to the husbands. If they miss it, friends usually inform them,' Cecil laughed.

However, there was a hitch. Cecil did not want me to stay in Reno, nor the Virgin Islands. He considered these places frivolous, with their casinos, nightclubs and the rest, and most unsuitable. He asked his lawyer to find another small, quiet place for me to go, where the law would apply to my case and where I could secure a quick divorce.

The invalidity of my Mexican divorce was unpleasant news! After dinner, parked outside the now-familiar New Scotland Yard, Cecil had more news for me. Before he met me, he had rented himself a flat in the same street as his office and was due to move in there in a few days. Being in the corner building, it faced St James's Palace, and the flat was very nice. But there was a hitch. All the flats in the building were strictly for bachelor men, and neither women nor married couples were allowed to live in them. He would be moving into the flat the following week, but would start looking for a suitable flat for when we were married. Meanwhile, it would be more proper if I did not come to his flat, out of respect for our families. Would I mind if we did not sleep together before we were married?

My education in the British way of life had begun. I expressed my amusement at the concept of flats that were strictly for bachelors only. But the respect in which he held my family endeared me to him even more. I felt that his commitment to me was based on a strong feeling of honour, and I greatly admired and respected him for this. 'Of course I don't mind,' I answered. 'Our wedding night will recapture its meaning.' We both laughed, I heartily, Cecil in a slightly embarrassed manner.

'Oh, by the way,' he said, 'we're having lunch on Sunday with my mother. Aunt Aggie lives with her. They're sisters, both great characters.'

On Sunday morning, as I was getting ready, the prospect of meeting my future mother-in-law made me feel quite nervous. *What if she doesn't approve of her son's choice?* Cecil was all smiles when he picked me up. He told me that his mother's first name was Helen but that her friends called her Daisy. Aunt Aggie was Mrs Garnett. Their flat was in Draycott Place, just off Sloane Square.

A very tall, imposing-looking lady opened the door. She wore a large picture hat, adorned with silk roses and a bunch of fake cherries! *Wow* – I was mesmerised. Giving me a slight push to enter, Cecil made the introduction, 'Mother, this is the girl I am to marry.'

His mother looked me up and down, then said, 'I can see why you want to marry her.' Then she turned to me and said, 'But I can't see why you want to marry him!'

I relaxed. This lady was something else! She introduced me to her sister. Aunt Aggie looked older than Mrs Tennant, but actually was the younger of the two, I discovered later. The family maintained that she had given birth to twenty-two children, including three sets of twins – no wonder she looked like a little old lady! She, too, eyed me with interest, but said nothing.

The door to the inner sanctum opened a crack, and a mousy-looking face with tufts of white hair looked in. 'Lunch is served, Madam,' she said.

Cecil smiled at her. 'Hello, Louie. Come meet my future wife.'

A tiny figure emerged and vigorously shook my hand.

'That's Cook,' said his mother. 'She's been with me forever.'

In the conversation over lunch, there was mention of me being Russian. Aunt Aggie looked alarmed at this. The disclosure that I was a ballerina on top of being Russian brought an exclamation of disapproval. 'Oh dear,' sighed Aunt Aggie.

'Did you see our Ballet Russe before the war, at Covent Garden?' I enquired.

'No, what's that?' was the answer.

'She never went anywhere,' chuckled Cecil's mother. 'Too busy making babies! Now she sits at home painting ladies in crinolines being handed a rose, and reading murder stories,' she added with scorn.

I had a hard time not laughing. My future family promised to be entertaining! When we left, Mrs Tennant gave me a kiss and said, 'Welcome to our family,' at which Cecil looked pleased. I gave Aunt Aggie a kiss – she looked startled.

As we got into Cecil's car, he decided to go and see if another of his sisters, Helen, was home. Helen had a small business she ran from home, selling very special tea to private clients. She did the deliveries in her very ancient Rolls Royce. Helen was home, and she obviously knew all about me and our engagement. She greeted us with cries of, 'Congratulations, you two! It's all very sudden, wot?'

Another lady appeared, all excited and exuberant. Descending on Cecil, she kissed him on both cheeks, then fell on me, smothering me in her embrace and exclaiming, 'C'est magnifique! I am so happy to meet you. I saw you in the ballets. You are magnifique!'

'That's Fabienne Hillyard, my best friend. She's French,' explained Helen, interrupting the lady's effusiveness. I noticed Cecil's smile disappear and a shadow of worry – or was it displeasure? – cross his face. I wondered what was bothering him. Helen was tall, thin, angular and loud, so different from her sister, Esmee. As for Fabienne, she was the epitome of French femininity.

The tea was jolly, but Cecil obviously did not want to linger. Once outside he said, 'Let's go to Esmee's flat so we can talk. I have something to discuss with you.' I was intrigued. Esmee was out, so Cecil poured himself a whisky and soda and asked if I would like a sherry. I declined and he sat down in an armchair looking tense. 'How do you envisage our future?' he asked.

'Happy!' I smiled cheerfully.

'I want you to know what I'm expecting of you.' His look was stern. 'I expect you to give up your ballet career for good, and any other form of work. I also don't want you, for five years, to see anyone from or have anything to do with the ballet world.'

I was shocked. 'But they're my friends, some of them close friends, the best friends I ever had! How can I turn my back on them?' I protested, totally bewildered.

'I will not discuss this any further. I'll give you forty-eight hours to think about it and give me an answer.'

Is our marriage off? As far as Cecil was concerned, the subject was closed and the ball was in my court. *Yes, I need to think and search deeply within myself. Like my papa told me, it's time for me to think seriously about my life. I must try not to make any more mistakes.* 'All right. You're asking a lot of me. Yes, I'll think about it. Now, please take me back to the Pastoria.'

No, I did not want any dinner. Pulled down from my rosy clouds into the real world of complicated human beings, all I wanted was to be alone and sort out the disarray of my feelings. I could not bear the thought of losing Cecil. At the same time, I had to be as honest with him as he had been with me. As we stopped in front of the Pastoria, Cecil looked at me with infinite kindness, patted my hand and said, 'I shall wait for your call. I do love you . . . but marriage is a serious step to take. We must have the same goals.'

The first thing I did on entering my room was rip up my letter to my parents, which I had started earlier that morning, telling them about

Cecil. Perhaps there would be nothing of importance to tell them after all. *So I have forty-eight hours to come up with a yea or nay. It's like some kind of business deal,* I thought bitterly. The entire day had been an unusual experience to say the least, ending with this most unexpected ultimatum. I had to sleep on it first, then think. My night was hardly restful.

Next morning at the studio, as I was being made up, in walked a young man who approached me shyly and said, 'Good morning. You're Irina Baronova?'

'Yes.'

'I'm Tamara Tchinarova's husband. My name's Peter Finch. We arrived recently from Australia.'

What an amazing surprise! The thought of seeing Tamara again, a colleague and friend since my earliest days in ballet, was a real joy. Another surprise: Peter Finch, the young Australian actor noticed and praised by Laurence Olivier during his tour to Australia with Vivien Leigh, was in England to film one of the episodes in *Train of Events*. We chatted and exchanged telephone numbers.

It felt strange not to see Cecil after I finished work that day, and to have dinner alone at the Pastoria. My thoughts were in turmoil. Back in my room I called Tamara. We had a long talk and made plans to meet. It was so good to hear her voice and hear about the events in her life. Talking to Tamara brought back so many memories of that golden past, and reminded me how fanatically devoted I had been to my art. *Had been?* I caught myself thinking in the past tense. It acted like a wake-up call, and I realised it was time to face some facts.

I threw myself across the bed and stared at the ceiling. *What a disjointed life I have led these past years,* I thought. Was I deliberately avoiding a return to Ballet Theatre? If so, why? I did love my art and always would, but I had to admit that my devotion to it, since Michel Fokine's death, had waned considerably. Other things in my private life had begun to take on greater importance, deservedly or not.

It had never entered my head that I would, or could, leave the stage! Of course, one day it would come naturally, when my knees started to shake and everything else started to sag, but I never thought about it, except on those rare occasions when I was a guest in a family home. I would observe them, enjoy their children, and think with regret that I would never know that kind of life. *Well,* I would console myself, *one cannot have everything in life, and I have been given so much to be grateful for.*

My thoughts probed into the deepest nooks and crannies of my being. I had to be honest with myself, no matter how unpleasant the result might be, in order to give Cecil a fair response and not to risk messing up his life. My thoughts started to swell to typically Russian, dramatic proportions! I was getting nowhere and I was tired. *But the question is simple, there's no need to procrastinate,* I thought crossly. *What do I want more: another fifteen to twenty years on the stage, or this extraordinary chance life is giving me, to have Cecil as a husband, to have, God willing, children, a family, a home, to grow old together, to steer that 'rocking boat' of mine into calmer waters and drop the anchor, to experience what more there is to life besides my art, besides success and applause?* What did I want? I knew the answer in a flash. I was seriously in love with Cecil and looked up to him with deep respect. The thought of losing him was unacceptable. I wanted him for keeps.

I looked at my clock. It was almost eleven p.m. It had taken me twenty-eight hours to come to a decision and have an answer for Cecil. I stretched for the phone, then thought, with an inner grin, *No, I'll call him in the morning. Let him sweat!* I slept like a log.

Next morning, as soon as I was out of make-up, I called Cecil, who was just finishing his breakfast. 'You win! Do you still love me?' I asked.

'I'm going to marry you, aren't I? I'll pick you up at the studio.'

All was well in my world. At the end of the day, Cecil greeted me with a hug and a kiss and a big, happy grin. 'I missed you,' he said. We had dinner at Wheelers, famous for its oysters and fish. I told him about Peter Finch and that he was married to my old friend and colleague, but quickly added that, as far as I knew, she had no intention of resuming her career. Cecil smiled. 'We must get together, then. Laurence Olivier thinks Peter Finch has a great future.'

I was relieved. For some reason best known to Cecil, he was all right with me seeing Tamara. That was all that mattered to me. Then Cecil told me his lawyer had found a place for me to go to in order to obtain my divorce from Jerry – a small town in Wyoming farming country called Sheridan. I had to be there no later than 15 April 1949 to establish my six-week residency. A local lawyer had already been contacted, and could arrange for my case to be heard on 28 May. I was amazed at the speed and efficiency with which Cecil had dealt with the matter. I would soon have finished my work on the film, and there was much to plan and discuss. Cecil told me he had asked his lawyer to have lunch with us the following week, to finalise our plans. As Cecil had some packing to do – he was due to move into the bachelor flat the next morning – there was no visit to New Scotland Yard.

When I arrived at the hotel, a letter from my mother was awaiting me. Her news saddened and worried me: Papa had suffered a mild heart attack but did not need hospitalisation, just a few days in bed and a strict diet. He would have to take it easy for a while, and in the future work more from home. My poor, dear papa.

I called Cecil to share my worry with him. He was very understanding and tried to cheer me up. When I told him that I had not yet told my parents about our engagement, he advised me not to tell them in a letter, that it would be too much of a shock, but to wait until my return to New York, so I could tell them face to face, discuss it with them properly and answer all their questions. I felt, too, that that would be best.

Feeling a bit better after talking to Cecil, I sat down to write to my parents. Under the circumstances, I felt more than ever that I had to keep my promise and be back with them for my birthday. Cecil was most understanding, and promised to despatch me to them in good time. Our lunch with Cecil's lawyer was most productive, although I did not understand half of what they said! Everything was under control, Cecil reassured me.

On my last day, I said goodbye with a sense of relief to all at Ealing Studios. Although it had been a pleasant experience, it had interfered with something much more important – the unexpected turn in my life. Now I was free to grasp my new role in life fully and make the necessary emotional adjustments. Cecil started to introduce me to his close friends, such as the Rhodes family – Stanley, Joan and their three lovely daughters, Penny, Ginny and Annabel – who were the most happy-go-lucky, wonderful people. We would have many hilarious times with them in the years to come. Then there were the Baker-Carrs, who were so warm and loving.

The close theatrical friends to which Cecil exhibited me first ('Meet my funny Russian!') included Laurence Olivier and Vivien Leigh. I felt intimidated as Cecil and I entered Durham Cottage, the Oliviers' home in London, but their welcome to me was most warm and gracious. They were the most glamorous, beautiful people I had ever seen, which made me feel even more intimidated and inadequate. As time went by, however, I also came to be considered their close friend, and grew to admire and love them dearly.

I also met Annie and Tom Bushell. Tom was an actor, and a close friend of Laurence Olivier, to whom he acted as a sort of aide-de-camp during the making of his films. Annie was lovely and friendly. They lived in the cottage that stood on the premises of the Oliviers' country home, Notley Abbey. The last friend of Cecil's I met before leaving for New York was Roger Furse. A well-known painter and designer, he was a close friend of the Oliviers, and designed many of the costumes and sets for their plays and films. He was a lovely, gentle, bearded man, and I liked him enormously right away. When I saw how much my handsome future husband's friends loved him, my chest swelled with joy and pride!

The time for my departure was rapidly approaching. I was bemoaning the fact that we would not see each other for two months when Cecil, who was not happy about it either, said, 'I know what I can do. I'll fly over for a long weekend to see you and meet your parents before you leave for Sheridan. Besides, it will show respect for your family, my coming over to meet them.'

'Oh, that would be wonderful!'

I knew my parents would appreciate his gesture enormously, and that once they met him they would stop worrying that their daughter had once again acted rashly. As Cecil was seeing me off at the airport, he suddenly said, 'Would you ask your mother for me if she would go to Sheridan with you? I hate the thought of you being there alone.'

'Of course I will. How sweet of you. She'll be so pleased.'

My dear, dear Cecil. I did love him so!

A DIVORCE AND A WEDDING

I was overjoyed to see my happy parents, who came to meet me at the airport. It appeared to be Papa's first outing in the car since his latest heart attack, but he had insisted on coming. He looked thinner, but well and in high spirits. Jicky gave me a tremendous welcome. My parents wanted to hear about the film, and more about Tamara Tchinarova, as they knew from my letters about my surprise meeting with Peter Finch. They also wanted to know more about that nice Mr Tennant. I answered their questions, leaving Mr Tennant for the grand finale.

'Now, brace yourselves,' I said. 'I have wonderful, exciting news for you!' I looked at Papa and Mama, whose faces had become tense and serious. I could read their thoughts as if they were written in bright lights on their foreheads: 'What's she done now?'

'Your future son-in-law is coming over from London to meet you, and he's that nice Mr Tennant.'

There was a moment of stupefaction, then Mama, with a deep sigh, squeezed out, 'Oh, *Gospodi!*'

Papa scratched his ear pensively. 'Well, tell us about it,' he said with a worried look at Mother.

And so I did, without sparing any details. As my unlikely tale unwound, their faces relaxed, and at times they even smiled, amused at what they were hearing. When I finished, they were full of questions and decided that Cecil sounded rather nice. Not an adverse word crossed their lips. I was greatly surprised, but also greatly relieved.

Mother was delighted by Cecil's request for her to accompany me to Sheridan, and Papa quickly smiled his approval. Before going to bed, I wrote to my dear Cecil and, at my parents' request, sent him their warm regards. I also wrote to Tassia, to keep her up to date.

In the morning, through sheer habit, I went onto the veranda to do my barre. Halfway through, it occurred to me that I did not have to do it any more. I did not have to keep fit. I would never dance again! My heart pinched and I shed silent tears. I knew then that it would not be easy to reconcile myself to my decision. In the days that followed, I tried not to dwell on it, but rather to imagine what life would be like in my new role of housewife, as it was described in passports. My imagination was not up to it. I gave up! Papa and I spent a lot of time together; Mama was in a contented mood. I counted the days until Cecil's arrival.

Finally there he was. He conquered my parents in no time at all, with his natural charm and easy manner. Jicky, too, decided that the tall man in the house was acceptable, and the two of them became great friends. Papa pulled Cecil's leg gently about Scotland Yard, and Mother declared that he was not at all like English 'dry toast'.

The visit was a success! We spent two light-hearted, happy days during which Cecil informed us of the further arrangements he had made. Everything in Sheridan was being taken care of by the most obliging local lawyer, who would meet me and my mother at the airport in Sheridan on 14 April. As for Cecil, he had to be in Hollywood on business in mid-May, and planned to get hold of a car to drive to Sheridan, to arrive two days before the case was due to be dealt with in court. Cecil suggested we get married the same day, and then that Mother should fly back while he and I drove across America to Sea Cliff. There we would have a nice celebration with Papa, who unfortunately had been forbidden by his doctor to travel by plane. The train trip was much too long for him to undertake so soon after his heart attack, mild as it had been.

I was sad at the thought of not having Papa with me on such an important day, and asked Cecil why we could not get married in Sea Cliff. His plea was that driving across from Sheridan to New York would be the only time we would have three days for the honeymoon, as after the few days with Papa he would have to go back to work, with no chance to get away again for some months.

Seeing me so upset, Papa came up with an idea. He asked if Cecil would consent to having the Russian priest bless our union in a short private service in Sea Cliff on our return. Cecil, taken aback, thought for a moment (I knew he was Church of England, but he was not a keen churchgoer).

'Oh please, Cecil,' I burst in. 'That way Papa will be part of our marriage,' I pleaded.

'Yes, of course. Would you arrange it, Michael?' Cecil asked, turning to my papa. I was so grateful to Cecil for his understanding. Having our marriage blessed in our little church by Father Vassili would mean so much more to me than 'I pronounce you man and wife' spoken by someone like the 'cigar man' who had married Jerry and me. I knew my papa felt the same way I did.

As we were seeing Cecil off at the airport, he said, 'Why don't you take Jicky with you to Sheridan? He could come back with us in the car. It would also be easier for Michael.'

Gosh, my parents were lucky to have such a son-in-law! Russian friends and the neighbours across the street insisted that Papa dine with them every day while Mother was away, and also promised to keep a close eye on him. In our little Russian colony in Sea Cliff, people were always ready to help each other. They took great interest in my forthcoming marriage, and there was much talk buzzing around about 'Irina's tall Englishman', of whom they heartily approved.

It was a small aircraft that flew us on the last leg of our journey to Sheridan. As we made our descent, my nose was glued to the window. I saw a very small town with what looked like one main street, surrounded by farmland, with lots of cattle and some forest. It looked lovely and peaceful.

As we landed, a jolly youngish man approached us – he was my lawyer. He could not have been nicer, helping me to get a most fed-up-looking Jicky out of his cage, and carting our cases to his car. On the way to the only hotel in town, I asked him what the chances were of receiving

Jerry's signed consent. He thought they were good and told me I should not worry anyway – he would obtain my divorce one way or another.

The hotel was a pleasant surprise. A two-storey, elongated building at the end of the main street that was crossed by railway tracks, it had a big veranda and a garden. The lawyer told us that cattle wagons were transported on that line, and that only a few went by in the evenings.

The owners of the hotel, Mr and Mrs Diaz, were waiting for us in the spacious lobby and welcomed us warmly. They were a middle-aged, cosy-looking couple. The dining room off the lobby looked impeccable, with white linen tablecloths and fresh flowers on each table. They only served breakfast and dinner – at lunchtime we could have light meals at the local bar, halfway up the street. The hotel also had a bar, but it served only drinks.

Having been informed of the amenities, we were shown to our room on the first floor. As impeccable as the rest of the place, our room was large and bright, with heavy oak beds, old-fashioned and very inviting. Jicky was welcome there. We assured the Diazes that he would not cause any trouble.

Having noticed that my lawyer (sorry, no matter how I try, I cannot remember his name!) wore a wedding band, I invited him and his wife to join Mother and me for dinner. He was delighted to accept.

Mother was in great spirits. Leaving her to unpack her case, I took Jicky for a walk, curious to discover what things of interest the main street held for us. *Hooray!* There was a cinema, with a change of program every three days. *Great!* There was that bar, looking exactly as they do in Hollywood westerns. There was a corner drugstore, a clothing shop that also sold cowboy boots and hats, a grocery shop, and a small bakery displaying a large urn and dispensing hot coffee. At the very end of the main street stood the imposing red brick Court House. *Aha, my reason for being here.* I looked at it with respect.

After a most enjoyable dinner with my lawyer and his very nice wife, the Diazes joined us for coffee and I felt our time in Sheridan would not be lonely. It was not! The ads in the newspapers also produced the desired result. The signed letter from Jerry, not contesting the divorce, was on my lawyer's desk two weeks later. The divorce hearing was set for 28 May.

Every other day there was a letter from Cecil. On his way to Hollywood from London, he spent three days in Sea Cliff with my papa – another lovely gesture on his part. We talked on the phone to Papa regularly. The weeks passed by peacefully and pleasantly.

Cecil called me from Hollywood to say he would be driving to Sheridan on the morning of 27 May. He wanted to meet me alone first, to have some time with me before going to the hotel. Where could he meet me? I suggested the drugstore and explained where it was. He replied, 'See you there at one p.m. Can hardly wait!'

Neither could I. On the stroke of one p.m. a grey Cadillac pulled up in front of the drugstore and there he was! The wait was over. How good it was to hug him and be hugged. We had a cup of coffee – he needed it, having driven a mile a minute to cover the distance in time.

At the hotel, Mother, the Diazes and our lawyer were waiting to greet Cecil. Mrs Diaz very kindly prepared a delicious cold lunch for us all, and everyone was excited and merry. After lunch, Cecil told me he had two wedding rings for me to choose from, and made to go to his room to fetch them. I got up to go with him but he stopped me. 'No, you can't come to my room. It wouldn't be proper.' He brought the rings downstairs and I chose the plain, simple one that is on my old finger now. After dinner Cecil suggested a walk in the fresh evening air. Romantically, we sat on the railway fence, watching the trains go by, and I discovered that Cecil loved trains.

The next morning, Cecil drove Mother and me to the Court House, where our lawyer was waiting. The hearing was at ten a.m. Mother and I went in while Cecil waited in the car. He seemed a bit tense. The judge was an elderly man and looked very stern. I stated my name, hand on the Bible, and he asked me pertinent questions. The judge then turned to Mama who, never having been in such company, was so intimidated and nervous that when he asked her name, she forgot it and called to me, 'Irina, help!'

'Lydia Baronova,' I whispered.

'I am Lydia Baronova, her mother,' she said, putting her trembling hand on my shoulder.

After a short discussion between the judge and the lawyer, of which I did not understand a word, the judge banged his mallet on his desk and said, 'Divorce granted.'

I managed to say, 'Thank you, your honour,' and, with a pleased-looking lawyer, walked out to the impatiently waiting Cecil. I was legally a free woman! But not for long. In two hours' time I was due to tie the knot with Cecil in the Diazes' sitting room, where a justice of the peace was to unite us. There, everyone – including Jicky – would assemble, and afterwards, amid the beautiful flower arrangements, we would celebrate the occasion with champagne.

Back from the Court House, we dashed to our respective rooms to change. Everyone was at the hotel by one o'clock except Cecil. We waited . . . 'Shall I ring the bar downstairs?' suggested the lawyer. 'Perhaps Cecil got nervous.' He rang the bar and, indeed, Cecil was there. When he appeared a couple of minutes later, he looked slightly embarrassed but was grinning.

I wanted to take in and remember every moment of the following brief minutes as we were formally united. I did, and my memory of them has never faded and never will.

MARRIAGE, BIRTH AND DEATH

Wedding celebrations over, Cecil and I said our fond thanks and farewell to the Diazes, who drove Mother to the airport. I hugged the lawyer and his wife, then Cecil and I climbed into the Cadillac and set off on our three-day honeymoon, driving across America. By nightfall we spotted somewhere to stay. Cecil had thought of everything – out of the boot he produced a large picnic basket crammed with food. After we had seen to Jicky's needs and partaken of a delicious supper, Cecil asked if I minded if he used the bathroom first. I did not mind at all, and took Jicky out for a last pee.

Cecil was in bed in no time at all, looking exhausted by the emotions of the day and the long drive. When I emerged from the bathroom in my glamorous new nightgown, Cecil was fast asleep and snoring gently! *Poor lamb*, I thought, *he must be so tired.* I crept in beside him, careful not to wake him up. I felt at peace and was soon asleep myself.

In the morning I was awoken by a gentle tap on my shoulder to the delicious smell of frying bacon. 'Time to get up. Good morning. Breakfast's almost ready.' Cecil was in great form, cooking bacon and eggs. Jicky, attracted by the smell of bacon, jumped hopefully around Cecil's legs. I had discovered one more thing about my dear funny husband. He liked cooking and was good at it too. As I climbed out of bed, Cecil remarked, 'Pretty nightie.'

'Wasted!' I responded, laughing.

After breakfast, we packed up and by eight a.m. were on our way. Cecil refused to let me drive to give him a rest, and drove solidly the whole day. It was a lovely day. We talked non-stop and laughed a great deal. At nightfall we again found somewhere to stay. It was the second night of our honeymoon. I do not have to describe it – it was an exact repetition of the previous night. When I emerged from the bathroom, Cecil was asleep, snoring gently. I wondered if I lacked sex appeal, and decided to ask him in the morning.

As we were eating our bacon and eggs, I asked him. Cecil thought it was terribly funny, and laughingly said, 'Don't be silly, Kinnikins' (that is what he called me in private from then on). 'You'll see, it will all be fine when we get back to London.'

London? Well, I thought, *in that case there's no point wearing my pretty nightie.* I put it back in my nightbag with my old pyjamas. Again, we had a glorious, fun day. Jicky was as good as gold, and at nightfall we found somewhere to stay for our third and last night. It was the same scenario as on the two previous nights.

The next day, towards evening, we arrived at my parents' house. It was a joy to see my papa looking so well and so much stronger. My parents put us in their bedroom and moved themselves downstairs onto the veranda. It was really so sweet of them.

Cecil was impressed by our little church, constructed at weekends through the efforts of all the Russians at Sea Cliff. I pointed out to him the onion-shaped dome, which I had painted gold, perched on the roof while Mama watched from below, worried I might fall off.

The blessing service, conducted so touchingly by Father Vassili, must have stirred something deep-seated in Cecil's heart. He stood there with a pensive expression, listening to Father Vassili's melodious voice. When it was over, Papa and Mother embraced us and wished us happiness. Papa had tears in his eyes and a big smile on his face. In the afternoon, my parents threw a party for us, and Cecil met all our dear Russian friends.

'You Russians are funny,' said Cecil to me afterwards.

'You English are funny too!' I answered.

He agreed with a grin. And so began our married life.

When we returned to London, Cecil managed, with great difficulty, to persuade the superintendent of his bachelor-flat building to let me stay until we found another flat. The man gave us a week, no more, to find somewhere else. We found a very nice one on two floors in Hans Road, facing one side of Harrods. Then we dashed to auctions, looking for additional furniture. That was great fun!

What was no fun at all was when I had to start shopping for food. I did not know the names of fish, nor what they looked like raw, nor did I know the differences between cuts of meat. My cooking skills were limited, so Cecil took over until I improved. I had a great deal to learn, but I applied myself very seriously.

Gradually, I met all Cecil's friends, and we often went away for weekends. We met Cecil's brother Geoffrey and his wife, Sylvia, who lived in Harrogate, Yorkshire. We also met two more of his aunts, Nelly, who wore no hat, and Agnes, who wore hats like Cecil's mother, even at breakfast. Agnes lived nearby.

I often took my mother-in-law to lunch, and then afterwards to the cinema, where she commented loudly on the goings-on on the screen, to the great annoyance of the other spectators! I met Cecil's elder sister, Beryl. She had a husband, also named Cecil, a dog, and a parrot that imitated her commanding voice to perfection, often fooling her husband and the dog by yelling their name followed by, 'Come here immediately!' The called one would appear on the double!

It was a pleasure to meet Beryl's two sons by a previous marriage and their wives: Douglas and his very eccentric wife, Elspeth; and especially Tony Riley-Smith and his wife, June. Tony and June were a most delightful young couple, and in later years became very close and dear to me. Cecil was only ten years older than Tony, and they enjoyed each other's company very much. We had great times staying with Tony and June at their estate on the Isle of Jura.

All the same, it was not easy for me to adjust to the English way of life and behaviour. Many times I would put my foot in it and feel embarrassed. Cecil took it all in his stride, teasing me about it, but I learned fast.

In January 1950, we were overjoyed to discover that I was pregnant. With great excitement, we started to plan and prepare for our first baby. My doctor, Dr Cavadias, our ballet doctor, recommended Mr O'Sullivan, who was well-known in the medical profession, to take care of me and deliver my baby. Mr O'Sullivan was a dear, and Cecil was happy for me to be under his care.

My papa sent me a design and colour scheme for the future nursery. He and Mama were happy for us, and looked forward to becoming grandparents. But we had to find another flat, since ours had only one bedroom and a small dressing room. By a stroke of luck, my mother-in-law fell out with her sister, Aggie. Aunt Aggie asked Daisy, 'How is Disraeli these days?'

'You are not to be lived with!' declared Daisy, exasperated that her sister could be so out of touch as to think Disraeli was still prime minister! True to her word, she despatched Aggie to live with one of her many offspring, rented a bedsit for herself, and offered Cecil and me the flat in Draycott Place, with Louie, her lifelong cook, into the bargain. We grabbed the offer with gratitude.

There would be room for the nursery and a nanny, which Cecil insisted we absolutely must have. As soon as Daisy and Aggie moved out, we started doing up the nursery. We had the good luck to 'inherit' a wonderful nanny from Dr Leslie's family. He was a paediatrician, and eventually looked after our baby. His children had grown up, and their nanny was ready to take on a new baby. Her name was Hilda Wood. She was middle-aged and had trained in her youth at the famous Norland Institute for nannies. They all wore grey uniforms and gathered in Hyde Park for a natter while their little charges slept in their prams. That kind of nanny is a thing of the past!

Nanny Wood, after interviewing us – not the other way round – consented to be our nanny, and moved in several days before my baby was due. She then prepared, arranged and instructed us in her ways and requirements. My mother flew over for the birth, and soon she and Daisy were comparing their legs and debating whose legs were more beautiful. Both pulled up their skirts but, since Daisy's legs were obscured by bloomers that came down to her knees, Mother won that beauty contest hands down!

My waters broke and labour started on 29 September, at around eight p.m. On the double, Cecil drove me to 29 Welbeck Street, at that time a highly regarded private clinic. Cecil was not allowed to stay – it was not done in those days. The prospective fathers returned home and were summoned by telephone after the baby was born.

The hours ticked away; I was still in labour. Gosh, it hurt! I groaned, pushed and groaned and finally begged Mr O'Sullivan to 'Do something!'. I was offered some gas to sniff, which I immediately rejected, deciding I would rather groan than miss a moment of my baby's birth. Finally, after some twelve hours of labour, on 30 September, my baby was born.

'Congratulations, it's a beautiful little girl!' exclaimed Mr O'Sullivan with delight. Pain instantly forgotten, all my being was enveloped in utter joy! I held my baby in my arms and gazed upon the most beautiful little doll-like face, my little daughter, a miracle. A huge wave of love rose in me towards this precious *babka*, our girl!

Cecil flew into the room like a meteor. 'Where's my daughter?' he demanded in great excitement. As he held our little daughter, he grinned from ear to ear, then looked lovingly into her tiny face and said softly, 'Hello, Victoria, I'm your daddy.'

My mother and Nanny arrived shortly after. I was sitting in a happy daze, on a rosy cloud, and I suspect Cecil was sharing it with me! In those days one did not get up and get on with it as they do now. After giving birth, one was kept in bed for eleven days before being allowed to go back home.

The nursery looked so pretty when I arrived home, all pale yellow and white, now with my baby asleep in her frilly crib. I soon discovered, to my slight annoyance, that Nanny was the boss. I nursed little Victoria every four hours; sitting in the nursery on a low chair, holding the little bundle, was sheer bliss.

Soon my mother flew back home happy and content, armed with snapshots of Victoria. But my mother-in-law was still around, and Nanny did not appreciate her regular visits. The first thing Daisy always did when she arrived was yell from the hall, 'Nurse, bring the child!' And then she would make Victoria cry. One day I suggested that Victoria might be afraid of her hat and asked her to take it off. Mumbling, 'What nonsense,' she removed the 'orchard' from her head, at which Victoria stopped crying and gave her a smile. From then on 'the old cheese' always removed her scary hat before yelling, 'Nurse, bring the child!'

As for our cook, dear old Louie was blind as a bat but refused to wear spectacles – she said they spoiled her beauty. Loud crashes were often to be heard from the kitchen. One morning the crash was followed by some new, strange noises. I dashed to the kitchen and found Louie, who yet again had missed the stove with the kettle and was now kicking it all over the floor as if it were a football, muttering, 'F— you! F— you!' I dashed to tell Cecil.

'Cecil, Cecil, Louie's kicking the kettle!'

'That's all right, Kinnikins. Ignore it,' he said calmly.

Cecil was very busy with his illustrious actors, bringing home scripts to read in search of suitable vehicles for each of them. He was also helping Larry with his Laurence Olivier Productions Ltd, and agonising over whether to accept an offer from MCA (Musical Corporation of

America) to merge with them, which would mean selling the Myron Selznick Agency to MCA then continuing under their banner and expanding into Europe. His discussions on this matter were with Lew Wasserman, the brilliant head of MCA in America, whom Cecil liked very much, and who was highly regarded by all who came in contact with him. After deliberation and consultation with his clients, Cecil decided to merge with MCA.

My life, meanwhile, revolved around my little daughter and home, which filled my life and made me happy. On Sundays, Nanny's free day, Cecil was always home, helping me take care of our little treasure, playing with her and proudly pushing the pram down the street to the park, to the amused glances of passers-by. Men were not supposed to push prams – it was a woman's job.

In the summer of 1951 we took a brief holiday near Dartmouth in Devonshire. It was very nice, but it was not much fun on the beach – the sea was freezing! When we returned to London, I was able to let my parents know that we would all be coming to stay with them from December to the beginning of April. I could hardly wait to show my precious Victosha to my papa.

We were travelling to America with the Oliviers, who were taking their two productions, Shaw's *Caesar and Cleopatra* and Shakespeare's *Antony and Cleopatra*, for a long season in New York at the Ziegfeld Theatre, opening on 19 December 1951. The plays would alternate on consecutive nights. It was quite a venture, and Larry had asked Cecil to accompany them.

Besides, Vivien was worrying Larry – her health and strange moods were of great concern to those closest to her. It was truly amazing that she never forgot her lines and always gave a brilliant performance, in spite of the fact that her mental state was sometimes alarming and unpredictable. Cecil was able to calm her when no-one else could. She trusted him and relied on him when she was going through a phase of being scared and wary of everyone else. I watched these periodic events with sadness, as I had grown to be so fond of Vivien and Larry, and admired them both enormously as actors. We sailed at the beginning of

December. The Oliviers had a great send-off and then Vivien, who was looking very tired, went to their state room, where she spent most of the voyage.

Cecil and I had an adjoining cabin with Victosha and Nanny. When Nanny, on the second day out to sea, became hopelessly seasick, we would take the little one on deck, where Cecil and Larry, her adoring godfather, would take turns pushing the pram around. Victosha would happily throw all her toys out of it, while I would bring up the rear, picking them all up again.

When we arrived in New York, the press were waiting for the Oliviers en masse. We left them to it and drove to Sea Cliff – in a car that a chauffeur from the New York office had delivered to Cecil – into the arms of my overjoyed parents. Victosha and Nanny had my pretty room, and happily installed themselves in it. Jicky excitedly participated in everything.

My papa and his little granddaughter were firm friends from the word go! They played together in the playpen, walked around hand in hand, and Papa would watch her eat, afterwards presenting her with a piece of chocolate, under Nanny's disapproving gaze.

But papa was not looking well, and I noticed that he often touched his chest, as if he were in some discomfort. When I asked him if he was in pain, he denied it. He enjoyed his granddaughter, and obviously did not want to talk about his health. So I worried in silence.

Cecil drove to New York each day, returning for dinner. The Oliviers' few performances out of town were to occur in Philadelphia, and Cecil wanted me to come with him. I asked if he would mind me calling Henry and Esther Clifford, since they were colleagues from my Ballet Russe days. They lived just outside Philadelphia in a house as sumptuous as their house in Florence. Cecil did not mind, and suggested I invite them to the opening night.

The Cliffords were delighted to hear from me, and invited us to stay with them. I did not expect Cecil to accept their invitation, but to my surprise he did. He was received by them with open arms and became quite relaxed. Ballet was never mentioned. Henry and Cecil got on like a house on fire, and we had a lovely time with them. Meanwhile, the Oliviers were a hit and the press for their shows was excellent.

When we returned to Sea Cliff, we got busy with preparations for Christmas. Papa decorated a beautiful Christmas tree, little Victoria's first, at which she stared in delighted amazement and clapped her hands. My darling Beatrice came to spend a Sunday in the New Year, meeting both Cecil and Victoria. 'She's my baby,' said Beatrice to Cecil, as she pointed at me.

'She's my baby too,' said Cecil with a grin. Beatrice thought he was just great.

At the same time, we found out that I was pregnant again – my second baby was due in mid-August. We were thrilled to bits! The only cloud in my blue sky was a slow but visible deterioration in my papa's health. The heart specialist did tests. By the end of February the diagnosis was bad: Papa had coronary thrombosis. In those days there was nothing the medical profession could do about it. Papa took it stoically, and continued working as usual at the work he loved.

As the day of our departure approached, my heart grew heavier and heavier at the thought of going so far away from my papa. Two days before we left, Mother stayed in bed, crying non-stop! Cecil and I thought she was crying about Papa, so we went to talk to her.

'No, no,' she said, 'I'm not crying because of Michael. I just can't bear Irina being so far away.' She took Cecil's hand and pleaded, 'Promise me, promise me you'll find work for Michael in London and move us there.' Cecil looked at me helplessly. I was shocked! How could she want to impose the strain and stress of moving to London and starting a new job on my papa? Now she was sobbing, still demanding, 'Promise me, Cecil. Promise.'

'All right, all right, Lydia, I'll do my best,' said Cecil. 'Now get up and stop crying, and don't upset Michael,' he added in a serious voice. In a while Mother appeared, bright as a button. I was badly embarrassed by her behaviour in front of Cecil.

The morning of our departure, Papa asked Cecil and me to step into his workroom to have a word. 'I know my days are numbered,' he said. 'I know you'll look after Lydia. Let her live near you when I'm gone, but never, never, let her live with you. She's a very difficult woman.' Then he hugged us both, saying to Cecil, 'I know Irina's happy. Thank you.'

I felt devastated by Papa's words, but was determined not to upset him by cracking up. He held Victoria in his arms as we put the luggage in the car. He had taught her to say *Dedouska*, 'Grandfather' in Russian. Once Nanny was seated in the car, Papa kissed Victoria and said, 'Bye bye.' She hugged his neck tight, kissed his cheek and said, 'Bye bye, *Dedouska*.' Papa's eyes filled with tears as he deposited Victoria on Nanny's lap.

When I approached Papa to say goodbye, we looked in each other's eyes. There were no words to express to each other how we felt. At that moment I knew that I would never see him again. He embraced me tenderly and made the sign of the cross over my chest, saying, '*S Bogom*.' Then he led me to the car.

As we moved off, I turned to look back at my parents, who stood on the porch, waving to us. My eyes locked with Papa's and I had to clench my teeth to stop myself making a sound that would frighten Victoria. I kept my eyes locked on Papa's, then the car turned the corner and he disappeared from my sight. The words have not yet been invented that could describe my sorrow, the devastation I felt, so I shall not even try. Three weeks later, my mother telephoned. Papa had dropped dead while getting ready to go to work. He was only fifty-seven years old. *Why? Oh God, why?*

I am still waiting for an answer.

13

FAMILY LIFE

The news of my papa's death was no shock to me, but it provoked a deep, deep sadness that no tears could wash away. When I talked to my mother, she seemed calm and collected. I told her I would fly over for the funeral. 'I don't think you should,' she said. 'Ask your doctor first.'

Not be at Papa's funeral? It was unthinkable! But Cecil agreed with her and called Mr O'Sullivan himself. 'On no account must she go,' was his response. I was in my sixth month of pregnancy, and the flight and emotional strain were to be avoided. 'She must think of her baby,' Mr O'Sullivan insisted.

As he put the phone down, Cecil saw my dismay. 'I'm certain your father would agree with Mr O'Sullivan, Kinnikins. You must think of our baby and yourself now.'

'It feels terrible to think of not being by Papa's coffin, by Mama's side.'

'I'll be there. I'll help your mother. Stop worrying and be sensible.'

I had no choice but to be sensible, and sadly resigned myself to it. I was immensely grateful that Cecil would be there by my mother's side. The next day he was on the flight to New York. He returned a week later with the following news: Mother wanted to move to England as soon as possible, and wanted to bring the car as well – a huge Lincoln. Close friends helped her sell the house, deal with business matters, pack and get on the ship to Southampton. 'Kinnikins,' said Cecil, 'I told Lydia she will live with us.'

'Oh? After what Papa said to us?' I was taken aback.

'She's had a hard life. She had to leave her home and family. Have a heart, Kinnikins.' I wished my heart was as kind as his! 'I have some sad news, too,' he continued. 'Just before Michael passed away, Jicky was attacked in the street by an alsatian and his neck was broken. He died . . .' Cecil put his arms around me and rocked my tears away.

With the approaching arrival of our second baby, and the forthcoming arrival of my mother, we realised that our Draycott Place flat would no longer be big enough and that we would have to move again. We found a flat in Mount Street, just off Berkeley Square, in Mayfair. It was on two floors, with plenty of room for everyone and a large, light room that would be great for a day nursery.

Dear old Louie decided to retire when we moved, and go to live with some family she had in the north of England. The Tennants gathered together and gave her a dinner party at a nice restaurant. She was ever so pleased, received presents and got sloshed! Great fun was had by all.

Cecil found a cook through an agency who would come to do lunch when required and dinner every night. Nanny cooked Victoria's food – the way it ought to be done! Once all of that was sorted out, we moved to Mount Street. It turned out that Valerie Hobson lived across the street and also had a Norland nanny, who happened to be a friend of ours. Nanny was delighted. She and Valerie's nanny would wheel their prams around Hyde Park together each morning and afternoon.

Once we were installed in our new home, Cecil decided to send Victosha, Nanny and me to the Hotel Portmeirion in Wales, a very well-known, fashionable hotel with bungalows and huge pointy papier mâché figures all over the premises. There was a beach nearby where Victosha could play and we could all enjoy a bit of fresh air before Mother's arrival and before it became unsafe for me to be too far away from Mr O'Sullivan. Cecil would join us at weekends; he was not only very busy in the office, but also very concerned, as was Larry, about Vivien's health and future ability to work. Her state of mind and behaviour now often gave Larry and Cecil cause for concern.

There are parts of Britain that are very beautiful, and Wales is one of them. The hotel was great, and the gaudily painted figures amused my little daughter no end. I rested with my feet up most of the day, having become by that stage huge and clumsy.

One weekend, Cecil arrived looking tense. As his mother had been having health troubles and suffering from anaemia, the first thing I asked was, 'How's Mother?'

'She's dead,' was his short reply.

It was my turn to wipe his tears. Apparently his mother had had a stroke the day before, and four hours later was dead, never having regained consciousness. The funeral was to be held in Yorkshire, where she was to be buried next to Cecil's father.

We cut our holiday short, packing up and returning to London to drop Nanny and Victosha at the flat before driving up to Yorkshire, where the family was gathering at the house of Cecil's brother. On the day of the funeral, as everyone was about to leave for the church, Cecil's sister Helen threw a fit of hysterics, yelling and sobbing, 'I can't bear it, I can't face it, I can't go.'

They asked me if I would stay at home with her, which I was happy to do. I was actually relieved not to have to go to my mother-in-law's funeral when I had not been able to attend my own dear papa's. As soon as everyone left, Helen calmed down very quickly, poured herself a large gin and tonic and instructed me on the different brands of tea until the family returned hours later. And I wondered why Cecil thought the Russians were funny!

By mid-July my mother had phoned with the date of her arrival. On the given day, on a lovely sunny morning, we drove to Southampton to meet the ship. The office chauffeur came with us, in order to deal with Mother's car and drive it to London. I stood on the dock apprehensively, not knowing in what shape mother would be or what to expect. And finally there she was – calm and comforting *me*, saying how happy she was to be with us in England.

On the drive to London she complained about the cabin she had had on the ship, about the other passengers, about the rough crossing. When we arrived home, she showed signs of displeasure that her room was upstairs, next to Nanny, Victoria and the new baby's room. 'Oh, I'm put with the children,' she remarked acidly. I told her it was the only room we had. 'Oh dear, it's rather small!' she exclaimed when she entered it. It was not a promising start to our cohabitation!

Nanny maintained that it was beneficial for a child to spend an hour a day alone in the nursery, and would lock Victoria in and leave her there. I felt sorry for Victosha, so while Nanny was in her own room, I would look through the keyhole to see what my poor little thing was doing. First she would try unsuccessfully to open the door, then she would walk around, climb on a chair, gaze out the window and doze off. How boring it must have been for her! I could not stand it, and would push magazines under the door for her to look at, which she did, sitting on the floor in front of the door. When I heard Nanny coming, I would quickly go in and remove the magazines, saying to Victosha, 'Your hour's up, darling . . . and here's Nanny.'

I did not dare stand up to Nanny, intimidated as I was by her superior knowledge (so I thought) of how to bring up children, but in secret I did not agree with some of her ways. Her devotion, kindness and love for her little charges was admirable, and I always knew that they were safe with her, but at times I thought to myself, *Brother! I wanted children for myself, not for Nanny!*

My second baby was due any day . . . then overdue by eleven days! Mr O'Sullivan ordered me into the Welbeck Street clinic and punctured the amniotic sac. Nothing! Next afternoon, Cecil took matters into his own hands. He put me in the car and drove me up and down a very bad piece of road. I felt as if I were in a cocktail shaker!

Safely back at the clinic by seven p.m., I went into labour. But I also felt very hungry, so I did not tell the nurse that my baby was coming until after I had eaten dinner. 'Oh dear, you shouldn't have eaten. You are a naughty girl!' she exclaimed, and ran in to call Mr O'Sullivan.

I phoned Cecil. 'It's coming! It worked! It's coming!'

'Make sure it's not a redhead,' was his joyous command.

The birth was easy and swift. Just after midnight, a beautiful nine-pound baby girl with a great mop of carrot-coloured hair made her much-anticipated appearance. Once again, I was overwhelmed by a special, extraordinary feeling of joy, wonder and love for that angelic-looking little bundle.

Once again, Cecil stormed in and cried, 'Where's my daughter?' I passed our daughter to him to hold. He looked at her intently, and with a big, amused smile said, 'Hello, Carrots! It's your daddy.'

Mid-morning the next day, Victoria, Cecil and Nanny came to visit and 'Carrots' was introduced to her big sister. Victosha looked at the new baby with interest and then, stroking her head, declared with all seriousness, 'I like her!' Soon we stopped calling her Carrots, and gave her her real name, Irina.

Eleven days later we were home. Cecil purchased a huge double pram in which both children could ride in comfort on our outings to Hyde Park. Aunty Nelly phoned from Yorkshire with her congratulations, but added at the end, 'I'm still waiting for you to produce a boy.' It was very important to her that the Tennant name should be perpetuated, and we were her only hope. There were no male Tennant children in the family, and Aunty Nelly was getting impatient with me. Silly old bird, adorable Nelly.

FAMILY DRAMAS

'Guess who's coming for drinks tomorrow?' asked Cecil one evening when he came back from the office. I made a few guesses, all of them wrong. 'Your hero,' he cried, 'Clark Gable! He's bringing Grace Kelly and we'll be taking them to dinner at the Savoy Grill.'

That truly was an exciting experience. I loved Clark Gable on the screen and I had met him fleetingly in Hollywood. This big man with his teasing eyes and disarming smile became my screen idol, especially after I saw him in *Gone With the Wind*. I was thrilled to bits!

'I'll bring the children down to meet him, just for a few minutes,' decreed Nanny.

'I must go to the hairdresser,' said Mother.

At six p.m. the next day, the bell rang and there he was, with the beautiful Grace Kelly. They were a real pleasure – charming, easy to talk to and fun. As we were having drinks, Nanny poked her head through the door. 'Can we say goodnight?' she asked.

Victoria, who was two years old, was very social and always loved talking to our guests. She marched in, clad in her new dressing gown, stared for a moment at Miss Kelly, then made a beeline for Clark Gable. 'Do you like my new dressing gown?' she demanded.

'Yes, very much,' he solemnly replied.

Victoria beamed. 'And I like your moustache,' she said.

Irina, whose hair by then had turned golden, was in her all-in-one night attire and shyly eyeing Miss Kelly, who was trying to coax her from Nanny's arms onto her knees. Nanny transferred Irina to Miss Kelly's lap and Irina stared as only little ones do, then grabbed her earring, trying to pull it off.

Victoria did a little curtsy as she said goodnight to our guests (little girls were always taught to curtsy to grown-ups in those days). We all kissed the children goodnight and Gable complimented Nanny on her charges. She beamed as she took our daughters to bed. 'What adorable children,' chorused Kelly and Gable, which made Cecil and me swell with pride.

For some time now, Cecil and I had been discussing the possibility of moving to the country. We both felt that our children would be happier there, with many more possibilities and a greater variety of things to do than in London, where they were cooped up in the flat and taken on monotonous outings to Hyde Park. We wanted a big garden for them, with space and freedom to indulge in their hobbies, such as they might be. Was it possible?

Cecil started to investigate, looking for a nice place within commuting distance of his office. He came across a house that was on the market, twenty-five miles from London, on the Wentworth Estate in

Surrey, which was the site of the Wentworth Club, a famous golf course. That fact was a big attraction for Cecil, who was a keen golfer. The house stood by the fourteenth green! We had to go to see it.

The house was called Little Courtenay and stood in an acre of lovely garden bordered by big rhododendron bushes and on a big cul-de-sac secluded from the private road. It had the right number of rooms for our needs, and one that would make a perfect playroom for our children. We loved the house, and without further ado Cecil got on with the business of buying it.

Mother loved the country and was delighted at our news, but Nanny was not. She was not at all keen on the idea of living in the country. She liked to be in London and in the company of the other nannies who gathered daily in Hyde Park. With great regret, she handed in her resignation, offering to stay with us until the day we moved. She had no difficulty finding another position with a lovely family, and in the end she left us a week before we moved. Fond as I was of Nanny, I was secretly relieved that she wanted to stay in London. *When we move, I told myself, I'll be the boss in the nursery and enjoy my children to the full! No more nannies!*

When I broached the subject with Cecil, he agreed that it would be much more fun without a nanny. 'We can get an au pair to help out instead,' he suggested. He found an agency and applied for a mother's help. Two days later, a very young Geordie arrived. Her name was Sadie, and it was her first time away from Newcastle. Shy to start with, she soon became used to us, and was a great help. She was wonderful with our girls.

We moved to Little Courtenay the day after Irina's birthday, which we celebrated with a birthday cake, balloons, hats and lots of noise, all of us sitting on packing cases. For the next ten years, Little Courtenay was to be our wonderful happy home, a home in which my children grew from little angels into little devils, where there was never a dull moment – tears, drama and anxiety intermingled with a great deal of fun and many happy days. Of all the homes I lived in, it is the one I loved most.

At the end of 1953, a few months after we moved, we had great news – I was pregnant again! My third baby was due in August 1954. We were all so happy, except for Mother, who did not exhibit much patience with little people. Upon hearing the wonderful news, she lifted her eyes to the ceiling and said, 'Oh, *Gospodi!*' What a damper!

We acquired a cook by the name of Irene, who had a little dog. The doggy was sweet, but Irene was a tough, outspoken woman. She was, however, a great cook. I was scared of her. If I was coming down from the bedroom and heard her coming, I would hide inside the long curtains of the landing window and not emerge until she disappeared into the kitchen.

Irene had to go when Cecil asked her to cook his steak a bit more, as he did not like it rare. She pushed the plate away, saying, 'If you don't like it, cook it yourself!' That did it – goodbye, Irene. The agency sent a new cook, who was a shifty-looking person, but with the arrival of our third baby fast approaching, we decided to try her out.

At this time, Cecil was much occupied with Vivien and Larry. Her hysterical spells, which would start without warning, were becoming more and more frequent, and were always immensely difficult to deal with. She would become violent as well as verbally abusive, turning her hostility on Larry and growing suspicious of everyone around her. Cecil was still the only person she trusted and who could manage to pacify her to some extent.

The heart-breaking situation was taking its toll on Larry, whose nerves were always on edge. Emotionally drained, he became sombre and remote. What was incredible was that Vivien continued to perform as brilliantly as usual, never going wrong or forgetting her lines, except for two ghastly occasions when she went berserk. One of these was on the Hollywood set of *Elephant Walk*, in which she was replaced by Elizabeth Taylor. With endless difficulty, she was brought back home under sedation, which kept failing, by Larry, Cecil and two nurses. The other incident occurred in New York much later, in 1963, when she was starring in a musical based on the play *Tovarich*. She lost the plot on stage, and the understudy had to take over.

Those times were worrying and sad for Cecil, and also for me, since I was sometimes present or called upon to assist when poor Vivien was suffering the hell induced by her sick mind. In her delusional state, she turned her attentions to Peter Finch, which brought misery to his wife, my friend Tamara.

It was not long now until our third baby was due. Our Victoria was almost four, and we called her Totosh. Irina, who was almost two, was Pingle or Wingle. Both these nicknames were given to them by Cecil. Our little daughters were a constant source of joy and amusement. My mother, who adored Cecil and soon saw that he was not going to fall under her thumb, restrained her natural desire to rule the roost, and unpleasant clashes were few and far between. When they did occur, they were between her and me, mostly about how to bring up my children and how to run my house. If I complained to Cecil and asked him to talk to Mother, he would grin and say laughingly, 'No, you talk to her, Kinnikins. She's your mother!'

It was understood that if our third baby was a boy, he would be named Robert – it was a tradition in the Tennant family that the first boy bore that name. So Cecil and I were concentrating on girls' names in case we should have another girl. I went to Mr O'Sullivan for regular check-ups but, as we now lived in the country, he suggested that a Dr Vernon deliver my baby in the King Edward VII Hospital in Windsor, just a few miles away. Baby's room was ready, and I had a bed in there for myself since, experienced mum as I was, I knew I would sometimes have to sleep with the little mite and attend to its needs.

On the evening of 8 August, I went into labour and was whisked to hospital. Dr Vernon was alerted and I faced a night of not-much-fun labour. By six in the morning the baby was ready to be born, but could not make up its mind whether to make its grand appearance head-first or feet-first. It kept shifting its position, to the mounting despair of Dr Vernon and to my discomfort and worry. If the baby's antics continued, it ran the risk of being strangled by the umbilical cord. Dr Vernon rushed to call for assistance. By the time he came back, the head was down again. 'Push, push, push . . . that's good . . . Puuuuuush!' yelled Dr Vernon.

It was about seven a.m. when I heard the blessed words, 'Congratulations, you have a lovely little boy.'

No, I did not get used to having babies, or become blasé about it. The same feeling of magic and profound happiness enveloped me and, as I gazed into that little face, I was bursting with love and tenderness for my little son. He looked like a naughty little pixie. He had brown hair, and looked more like Cecil and his brother, Geoffrey; the girls were more like me.

Cecil rushed in and cried, 'Where's my son?'

His son was being weighed, naked and kicking his little legs for all he was worth. Cecil bent over him, 'Hello, Berts, it's Daddy,' he said gently, all smiles, catching the little hand in his. Then he gave me a kiss and said, 'Aunty Nelly will be pleased.'

She was indeed! As soon as it was possible, we took Berts to Yorkshire to introduce him to his Great-aunt Nelly. She gave our Robert the christening mug that had been inscribed and given to his uncle Robert who, at twenty-one, had been killed on the last day of World War I.

While I was still in hospital, I felt so well that I decided to twist everyone's arm so they would let me go home sooner than the prescribed eleven days. My little girls were brought in to meet their baby brother – they peered at little Robert with great curiosity and asked if they could hold him. Sitting on my bed, they both had a turn at holding him, while I looked at the three of them, thinking how blessed I was to have these three beautiful little monkeys. My arm-twisting succeeded, and on the sixth day I was home.

Three weeks later, Victoria fell very ill, with an extremely high temperature that would not come down. My poor little Totosh was listless, burning and miserable. Tests showed that she had contracted paratyphoid, a very infectious disease, which our doctor had to report to the health authorities. She was taken immediately to the isolation ward for infectious diseases at King Edward VII Hospital, then a health inspector arrived and told us that paratyphoid could be transmitted through food handled by a carrier of the disease. Everyone in the house had to undergo tests, and I had to stop nursing Robert and switch to bottles.

Each room in the house was fumigated in turn, and the rest of us were quarantined, allowed no contact with the outside world until the test results were known. It was a terrible wrench, leaving little Victoria at the hospital. She was too young to understand why Mummy and Daddy were leaving her there. It was heart-breaking to hear her crying and calling for us as we walked away. I alone was allowed to visit her each afternoon, after first undergoing a thorough disinfection and changing into hospital garb. Victoria settled down, and put up with the medication and constant tests very bravely.

At home, a kind neighbour did our shopping for us, leaving it on the doorstep. Finally, the inspector arrived with the results of all the tests. With a shock, we learned that our cook was the carrier of the disease. She had to leave immediately, and was sent to a special place run by the health authorities for cleaning up carriers. Later, under investigation, it came out that the cook knew she was a carrier of the bug. She had never been sick herself, but had infected members of the other families she had worked for before coming to us, always leaving them abruptly and leaving a false address for a non-existent brother. No wonder I thought she was shifty!

Poor Sadie, our mother's help, was under suspicion of having become a carrier, so she had to go to a hospital in London. The rest of us were clear and out of quarantine. As for Victoria, she had to undergo three consecutive tests before she could be pronounced cured. We were overjoyed when the first two tests were clear, since we assumed, of course, that the third one would prove clear as well. On the Saturday morning of the third test, certain we would be bringing Victoria home, Cecil and I raced to the hospital with fresh clothes for her and went straight to the matron's office. 'I haven't received the results yet,' she said dryly, 'so I cannot allow you to take Victoria home.'

'Aren't the results ready?' asked Cecil with some irritation.

'They're probably ready, but it's the weekend, and there's no-one there to deal with it. Come back on Monday.' Her manner was dismissive.

Cecil flew into a rage – I had never seen him so cross! 'This is disgraceful!' he shouted. 'We're taking Victoria home now!'

'You cannot do that without my permission,' was the haughty reply.

'Your permission? I can tell you what you can do with your permission!' snapped Cecil. With that, we marched to Victoria's room with a now very cross matron on our heels. 'You're coming home, Tito-Toto!' exclaimed Cecil, scooping Victoria into his arms and hurrying out towards the exit. As I half skipped, half ran after them, the matron still in pursuit, I waved to Victosha, who was rather bewildered by the commotion. As we drove off, we could hear the fading screams of matron. Merrily, we drove home! Irina was thrilled to have her big sister home again – she wanted to hug her all the time, and would not let her out of her sight.

On the Monday, the hospital rang to tell me that Victoria's belongings, including her books and toys, would have to be fumigated before I could fetch them. And so ended the first big crisis in our family. Now we had to find a new mother's help and a new cook. In the interim I thought we had managed quite well without help. Cecil, who loved cooking and was good at it (but so messy!), produced wonderful meals on weekends. Mine during the week were somewhat inferior, but I was learning.

Mr Ford, our gardener, suggested that his wife could take on washing the nappies, which was a great help. Disposable nappies did not yet exist, and we, like most people at that time, did not have a washing machine. Each morning I would deliver a bucket-load of nappies soaking in water to Mrs Ford and collect the clean ones. Mr Ford had a friend in our garden, a robin, which he fed bits of bread from between his teeth, the robin perched happily on his hand, pecking at the bread. I was amazed that our garden always looked so impeccable since, most of the time, when I came across Mr Ford he was fast asleep in his wheelbarrow!

Through Mrs Ford I found Janet, a local girl in her late teens who was willing to come and help me with the children. She took a fancy to Cecil, and kept asking him if she could be his caddie when he played golf on weekends.

One morning Victoria was browned off with her father and Robert, who was sitting in his highchair. 'Big Chief Running Water and his son, Little Drip!' she cried.

At that moment Janet came in and, with a flirtatious grimace, rolling her eyes, asked Cecil, 'Can I be your caddy today?'

'How dare you talk to my father like that!' cried Victoria.

Janet, furious, flew out of the room. We were secretly delighted at Victoria's intervention. Soon after, Cecil went to the nursery to fetch something and heard Janet grumbling aloud, 'Who the hell does she think she is?' Cecil sacked her on the spot, and we never saw her again.

It was not long before we found two new daily helpers, both local ladies. Miss Chapman, a middle-aged, gentle, sweet person, came as a cook and cleaner, and Maureen, a young, just-married woman who was a pleasure to have around, came as a mother's help.

Victoria started kindergarten, and soon Irina insisted that she, too, wanted to go to 'school'. On Irina's very first day, Victoria got out of the car and ran into the schoolyard. I took Irina by the hand, ready to take her in. 'No, I want to go alone, like Victoria!' she protested, removing her hand from mine and walking bravely into the yard. I soon saw a teacher approach her and take charge – only then did I turn the car around and go home. They were growing up.

OLD FRIENDS AND A CURSE

One Sunday morning, Cecil passed me a section of the newspaper he was reading and remarked that there was an article in there about Anton Dolin. Surprised that he mentioned it to me, I read it avidly. Dolin was in town! I did miss my wonderful friend so much. As if he read my thoughts, Cecil said, 'Why don't you call him and ask him over for a weekend?'

I could not believe my ears! What had happened to produce this volte-face in Cecil? Had I passed the exam? Was it safe now for me to see my old colleagues? I was not sure what to say, so I settled for, 'Oh, that would be nice, but I don't know how to reach him.'

'That shouldn't be difficult to find out. Surely he'd like to see our children.'

'Yes, he would. That is if he's not cross with me for not being in touch for so long.' I looked reproachfully at Cecil.

'I'm sure he understands and will be delighted to hear from you. I'll find out his number for you tomorrow.' He went on reading his paper.

I knew then I was out of 'quarantine'. True to his word, the next day Cecil gave me Pat's telephone number. I called Pat, quite prepared for a cold reception. 'Pat, it's Irina.'

'*Doushka*!' (Darling!) 'So the ban is lifted?' he teased. Of course he knew, as did Lucia, what the situation was, as I had written to them both to explain why they would not hear from me for a bit – a long bit! Pat and I talked for ages and, to my surprise, he told me he had known Cecil for ages, and that he had called Cecil several times since our marriage to find out how I was. He accepted my invitation to come over the next weekend. I was overjoyed, and could hardly wait to have my precious friend back in my life. Pat not only came back into my life, but firmly installed himself in the lives of my children, who adored him, calling him Uncle Peter. He loved them too, and to the end of his life showed his care for them, made them laugh and was always there for us all.

A little while later, Maureen, my mother's help, had to leave us, as her husband had been posted to Mauritius. This time we thought of getting a mother's help from Finland: Finnish girls were eager to spend a year in England to learn the language. Anja, who was from a small town, was lovely-looking, orderly, calm and dignified. We liked her very much, and she obviously liked us, since she offered to stay with us for a second year. When the time finally came for her to return to Finland, she got a friend of hers to come and take over. And then we had another friend take over after that.

Eventually two friends arrived from Orsara di Puglia, a small village in Italy: Pasqualina, as a cook; and Lucia, as a mother's help. They were great in their work and loud in their arguments, which I was often called upon to sort out. Italian songs filled the kitchen, and most delicious Italian dishes emerged from it.

Pasqualina was tall and fat while Lucia was small and thin – two comical characters who spoke a most comical English. They collected two Yugoslav suitors: Stan, big, rough and loud; and Nicolai, small and quiet. Stan fancied Lucia, Nicolai fancied Pasqualina, then decided they had made a mistake and swapped. It worked fine, and they all decided to get married.

The girls had a bitter quarrel over the purchase of their wedding dresses. Pasqualina, to outdo Lucia, spent all Stan's savings (not her own!) to buy a super dress with a long train. Lucia maintained that it was crazy to spend a fortune on a dress that was to be worn only once. When they returned from their shopping expedition they were no longer on speaking terms.

'*Madama, Madama*!' yelled Lucia to me. 'Pasqualina *stupido*! Gotta *molto* expensive dress. Whata she tink, she is Principessa Margareta?'

Lucia and Nicolai had a quiet, simple wedding at a registry office, but Pasqualina had to have a grand church wedding. She asked Cecil to give her away, Victoria and Irina to be bridesmaids and Robert and Irina to carry her long train as she came down the aisle. All was arranged according to her wishes, much to Cecil's annoyance, since the wedding would interfere with his golf.

On the big day, we gathered in the church with Stan and friends of the happy couple, to await the arrival of the bride with Cecil. When they appeared, Pasqualina proudly slipped her arm through Cecil's while the children fussed, arranging her long train under Victoria's directions. The organ intoned the wedding march and they started down the aisle. As they advanced, Irina and Robert kept losing hold of the train and it would drop to the floor. In several of their attempts to catch it, Robert stepped on it, which made Pasqualina stumble backwards, much to the amusement of the congregation, and to mounting giggles from Robert and Irina. And Lucia's voice could be heard saying, 'Looka, Principessa Margareta!'

Lucia insisted on staying with us until we found a new cook, only then joining Nicolai in the small town in which he worked. Now the children were older, I no longer needed a mother's help. Through Lucia, who still had friends in Orsara di Puglia, we found a married couple willing to move to England to work for us as cook and gardener. As our dear Mr Ford was wanting to retire, it sounded perfect. And so two adorable young people, Rocchina and Tommaso Poppa, arrived from Italy, leaving their village for the first time. Both were small in stature and both had a sunny disposition. They truly became part of our family, much loved by us all, and for many years their home was with us.

One night Cecil and I were returning home from dinner at film-maker Alexander Korda's, where the other guests had been the Oliviers, the Redgraves, and Noël Coward, who as usual kept us in stitches. As we entered the gates, we saw a police car at the front door and several policemen, one of them with an alsatian that was sniffing in the bushes. My heart dropped. As I rushed out of the car, my first question was, 'Are the children all right?'

'Yes, yes, they're all right, fast asleep. You've been burgled,' answered a man in plain clothes.

Once I knew the children were all right, the rest did not really matter, as far as I was concerned. But imagine, with three adults and three children in the house, no-one heard a thing! While the kids slept and the adults watched TV in their respective quarters, the burglars entered our room through our bedroom window, which was above the porch roof. Later, my mother noticed that the lights were on in our bedroom, went to switch them off, then noticed our room had been ransacked, with drawers on the floor, wardrobe doors open and mess everywhere. Mother had called the police and alerted Tommaso and Rocchina.

I went straight in to check on the children, but they were all sleeping peacefully. I then discovered that the yobbos had relieved me of all my coats and fur pieces, and some jewellery I had foolishly left in my dressing table drawer. Cecil sustained a few smaller losses. The police asked us not to touch anything, as in the morning they would come to take fingerprints. After they had left, Cecil grumbled, 'That bloody inspector polished off my whisky, and his dog almost bit me!' upon which he waded through the mess, went to bed and in no time was asleep. Men are amazing! I could not sleep a wink.

As so often happens, we shut the stable door after the horse had bolted. We installed grilles on all the windows and glass doors, and acquired a puppy bull terrier we named Rocket. He grew into a divine character, adored by us all and spoiled to bits by Cecil. Rocket was very possessive – if anyone got too near to any of us, they would be growled at and, if they were not careful, attacked. With his Roman nose, slanty eyes and broad shoulders, he grew up to be very powerful. Highly intelligent, he was my great and constant companion.

Soon after the burglary, Cecil had to go to Paris on business and asked me to go with him. I wanted Cecil to meet my beloved teacher, Mme Preobrajenska, and this trip seemed like the perfect opportunity. As it was only for three days, we thought that the children would be all right in the care of Mother and Rocchina.

When we arrived in Paris, I called Mme Preobrajenska. Since Cecil and I had a couple of hours free between meetings, Madame invited us to come to her flat. She had tea ready for us, and her parrot, Popka, eyed us, cocking his head. We were so happy to see each other, and she obviously liked Cecil, to whom she chatted coquettishly, half in French, half in English. When it was time for us to leave, she commanded Cecil to bend down and gave him a kiss. It made my day!

There was much for us to do and worry about when we returned home. Vivien was cut up about the unexpected (for her, at least) selection of Marilyn Monroe to star with Larry in the film *The Prince and the Showgirl*. Vivien was angry that she was not playing the part she had already created on stage. It did not help her fragile state of health, and she became once again irritable, nervous and agitated.

However, she was there with Larry to meet Marilyn and her husband, Arthur Miller, when they arrived in England. The press was also there en masse, storming Marilyn and paying hardly any attention to Vivien. This infuriated her even further, which made everyone tense. The atmosphere in the Oliviers' car was cool as they drove the new arrivals to their rented home in Virginia Water (a stone's throw from us). Marilyn was intimidated by the presence of Vivien Leigh, Vivien was simmering with irritation with everyone, and Larry and Arthur Miller were ill at ease.

Two more people came over from America with Monroe: the producer of the film, Milton Greene, a photographer by profession and a close friend of Marilyn's; and Paula Strasburg of the Actors Studio (the method-acting school), Marilyn's new coach, in whom, as it turned out, she believed more than in Laurence Olivier's direction. That lady's blatant interference made work on the film impossible, and forced Larry to prohibit her presence on the set.

It was a hellish experience for Larry, working with Marilyn Monroe. She was invariably late for work, or would not turn up at all, her husband calling to say she was indisposed. When she did appear, she could not remember her lines. An enormous amount of time was wasted, and time was running out.

Larry begged Cecil to stop at Marilyn's house on his way to the office each day, to drag her out of bed and see that she was driven to the set. Cecil obliged. At times, the barrage of abuse from Miss Monroe from beneath the covers, like 'Get the f— out of my room!', became too much for Cecil, and he would phone me to come over and help persuade Marilyn to get up. You had to coax her gently, with patience, and ignore the foul names she called you. We both felt very sorry for her. The poor girl was so messed up, so dependent on pills to face going to work, to wake up, to go to sleep, and so confused by people under whose influence she fell. Was she deep down shy and insecure? The Marilyn Monroe we saw and loved on the big screen was a talented, beautiful, sexy actress oozing charm, an idol, a creature apart, like no other. What a contrast! When the shooting of the film was finally over, everyone's sighs could be heard in Timbuktu!

It always amazed me that, even when Vivien was going through a hysterical, manic phase, she always remembered to send a greeting and a present to her close friends on their birthdays, at Christmas, or on their opening nights. Her friends were very important to her, and her loyalty to them was total. Irina, being her goddaughter, was never forgotten, no matter what state Vivien was in. On one occasion, as Christmas was approaching, I had a call from Vivien. 'What would Irina like for Christmas?' she asked. As I took time to reply, she continued, 'I know,

Irina and Victoria keep asking when they can have a pony. I'll give her a pony, and you and Cecil can get Victoria one too. They can start riding together!'

Vivien had made her decision! A couple of hours later she informed Cecil that she had made arrangements with a place selling ponies, and that we should take our girls to see if the ponies were suitable and to their liking. And so, that Christmas, Robin, Irina's pony, and Kismet, Victoria's pony, joined our family. Our daughters became very good riders, and to this day never miss an occasion to jump into the saddle.

Robert's passion was, and still is, cars – he takes after his father. They would spend hours with their heads under the bonnet, fiddling with the engine, Cecil explaining to Robert the workings of the motor. After *The Prince and the Showgirl* had been released, Larry presented Robert with a scale model of the Rolls Royce that had been used in the film. It was Robert's pride and joy.

On our home front all was well, but to the problems and dramas caused by Vivien's illness was now added a real worry about Larry's own emotional and physical health. He was constantly under great stress, having to deal with Vivien's hysterics, furies and depressions. The doctors, predicting that he would crack up himself and be unable to work, strongly advised a separation from Vivien. 'How can I turn my back on a sick woman?' Larry agonised.

At that time, Vivien was having another episode. At the end of his tether, Larry asked Cecil and me to come over to Notley Abbey for the weekend to lend him support. During this period, Vivien's rage centred primarily on the fact that she had ordered several outfits from Dior but had been told by Cecil and Larry that she could not have them since, according to the law of the time, no-one was allowed to send more than £300 out of England. Cecil had already tried to pacify Vivien, promising her that she could have one outfit, the payment for which he would arrange through his office in Milan. But this did not work. Vivien still demanded to have all of her dresses, and started shouting abuse at Cecil, yelling that she would pay for them all, even if it meant she would have to go to jail.

Cecil tried again to reason with her, gently and calmly, which threw her into a livid, frightening rage. She showered him with filthy words of abuse and stormed around the living room, finally collapsing onto the little sofa, curling up on the cushions, closing her eyes and seeming to doze off. Larry, Cecil and I sat in silence, shaken by the scene we had just witnessed.

Suddenly Vivien sat up and angrily fixed Cecil with her cat-like green eyes. In a low, husky voice, she hissed, 'When I die, I'll take you with me!' then fell back onto the cushions as if in a deep sleep. I felt as if an icy hand had gripped my entire being. I glanced at Cecil, who was staring at Vivien, ashen-faced. Larry, his head in his hands, was swaying back and forth on the big sofa. There was evil in the room. None of us changed our position. No-one said a thing.

Soon after, Larry moved out, Vivien moved to the flat in Eton Square, and Notley Abbey was for sale.

14

BALLET AGAIN

*D*ame Margot Fonteyn took me aback one day when she phoned to ask me to join the Royal Academy of Dancing (which became the Royal Academy of Dance in 1999), of which she was the president. She also wanted me to give masterclasses and mime classes for the teacher's training course, a course that took three years to complete. 'Oh, Margot,' I said, 'I can't. You know I promised Cecil not to have anything to do with dancing any more.'

'Hmm,' she replied. 'Can I come for lunch on Sunday?'

'Yes, of course. That would be lovely!'

'Good. I'll make Cecil change his mind! See you Sunday then.'

As I put down the receiver, I smiled to myself. *That should be fun!* On Sunday Margot breezed in, beautiful and elegant as usual. She was sweet with the children and charmed Cecil, with whom she was very persuasive. Cecil melted, and finally said, 'Would you like to do it, Kinnikins?'

'Yes, once a week, I would like it very much.'

'But you must be back in time to fetch the children from school!'

'I promise she will,' laughed Margot.

And that's how my happy association with the RAD started. Even my little son fell under Dame Margot's spell and asked if she would wait for him to grow up, because he wanted to marry her!

Soon after Dame Margot's visit, she invited the children to a matinee performance of *The Sleeping Beauty*. We had a box to ourselves and the children watched transfixed. When the seven beautiful ladies appeared in their pink tutus, Robert's eyes went out on stalks! That night, as I attended to his bath, he told me he wanted to marry the seven pink girls. I asked him, laughing, 'What on earth are you going to do with seven wives?'

Without hesitation he replied, 'Bath them and beat them!' And a romantic he remained.

At about this time, all three children came down with the measles. Dr Connell, Dame Ninette de Valois' husband, came to look after them. On his visits, he would joke with Cecil that if they caught the measles from the kids it might do their manhood harm. Believe it or not, they both caught them! When everyone had recuperated, the men with no harm done, we had Dame Ninette and Dr Connell for dinner one night. Cecil suggested we shut Rocket in the nursery during dinner; I suggested that Rocket might get offended. So Rocket remained with us, lying quietly under the table. As dessert was served, I remarked to Cecil, 'You see how good Rocket is, not bothering anyone?'

I lifted the tablecloth to look at our darling pooch and froze in horror. Rocket was busily chewing Dame Ninette's beautiful Asprey handbag into little pieces! *Oh my God! The ghastly embarrassment!* Dame Ninette was not amused. The next day, I dashed to Harrods in search of the biggest bottle of perfume I could find. I had it delivered to her home with a card from Rocket begging for her forgiveness, but it took some time for her to forgive and forget.

But life merrily went on. We learned that the Marquis de Cuevas's ballet company was having a season in London and the guest artists were Léonide Massine and Tamara Toumanova. I wanted so much for Cecil to meet Massine, Tamara and her mama. With photos of the children in my handbag, we attended a performance. When Massine appeared on stage, I felt such a pang! Oh, memories . . . He danced the 'Faruca' from his ballet *Le Tricorne* as brilliantly as ever, and received a standing ovation. Toumanova, beautiful as ever, was superb with him in the 'Black Swan' *pas de deux* from *Swan Lake*. The passing of the years had not touched either of them. They still looked young and still were great.

During intermission, we met Serge Lifar in the foyer. With his usual exuberance, he started to demonstrate to Cecil how he had manoeuvred during his duel with the Marquis de Cuevas, finally drawing blood from the Marquis' hand. With the imaginary sword in his hand, Lifar jumped from one seat to another, to the amusement and alarm of the surrounding audience. Cecil looked slightly bewildered!

After the performance, I had a lovely reunion with Massine backstage and introduced him to Cecil. I showed him photographs of our children, which he looked at with interest before saying with a smile, 'Children are a very precious thing in life, aren't they?' Then he turned to Cecil and said, 'You have very beautiful children. Congratulations!'

'What a nice man,' said Cecil as we left Massine's dressing room.

In Toumanova's dressing room we were greeted with exclamations of surprise and delight. After complimenting Tamara on her performance, I showed her the photos of my children, which she and her mama admired with noisy excitement. Mamotschka hugged me and said, 'You no dance any more. You have more children!'

While I talked to Tamara, Mamotschka made Cecil sit by her on the sofa, where she told him in her broken English, 'My Tamarotschka has wonderful husband. Every day he bring presents to Tamara, me, Papa! We have everythink. We never go church now, nothink to ask from God! Nothink!'

Amused, Cecil replied, 'You should go to church, Madame, to say "Thank you, God".' When we got into the car, Cecil said, 'You Russians are funny!' and shook his head in disbelief.

'Yes, but they're not boring. They're my tribe, and I love them.' It was quite an evening.

The year 1960 saw the dissolution of the Oliviers' marriage, and the 'Golden Couple' became history. All their friends remained loyal to them both. Neither was at fault; her illness was the culprit.

Vivien purchased a lovely place in the country called Tickerage Mill. It was not big, but it had a beautiful garden, a lake, and enough grounds to make it entirely secluded. It was reached by a long private road. Jack Merivale, who had acted with Vivien in the 1960 New York production of the play *Duel of Angels*, became her constant companion, totally devoted to her, as she became to him. Bless him – she was not alone. Her illness continued with the same pattern, but Jack bore it with stoicism and patience. Larry eventually married the wonderful actress Joan Plowright, a down-to-earth, lovely person who gave him children, love and peace.

The newspapers' interest in the Olivier drama evaporated, replaced by a sensational new event in 1961: the Kirov Ballet Company's leading dancer had defected to the West. At the Paris airport of Le Bourget, he had escaped his keepers and requested political asylum. His name was Rudolf Nureyev. Every major ballet company offered him a contract. His technique was sensational, of a kind never before seen in the West, his personality electrifying. Rudolf Nureyev came to London, and Dame Ninette de Valois made things happen the way she wanted, getting him for the Royal Ballet and forming the Fonteyn–Nureyev partnership. The rest is history.

When Nureyev first arrived in London, a friend of ours, a devoted balletomane, invited the great dancer to his house, which was not far from ours. He brought Nureyev over for a drink and to meet me, a fellow Russian. When they arrived, we were all at the door to greet them, including Rocket. Nureyev took one look at him and said to Cecil, 'Your dog looks like a Japanese pig!'

Cecil, offended for Rocket, replied, 'You don't look so hot yourself!'

Not a very good start to the evening. Nureyev looked tense. No wonder – he was in a new country, surrounded by strangers, and his English was very basic. He talked mostly in Russian to Mother and me.

Cecil handed him a whisky and soda and he promptly spilled it all over the armchair. As Mother fussed about wiping it, he stretched out his glass to Cecil and demanded, 'More!' Cecil poured him another one. There were several 'more's, and Rudolf became rather moody, confessing to me that he was homesick and missed his mother, but could not survive in 'that regime'. I felt so sorry for him. Later, when I knew him better, I discovered that he was a moody, difficult young man, but what an artist he was!

In 1962 a call from Paris brought sad news: Mme Preobrajenska had fallen and broken her hip, and was in the American Hospital in Neuilly. We all knew her financial situation was precarious, so her old students in Paris started to seek donations to pay for her hospital bills, while Anton Dolin and I started a collection, sending letters to all the people we knew, as well as to all the ballet schools and artistic organisations. The response was tremendous! The moneys went into a *fonds de secours* established in Paris in Madame's name, and they dealt with the bills.

At her advanced age, the shock was great, and Madame did not heal well. Her mind faltered, and she had to be transferred to a nursing home, never to return to her own flat. We started a second collection, and I went to Paris to help my colleagues sell the flat and deal with her belongings. An auction was organised, headed by Serge Lifar and me, and we received many amazing donations.

I visited Madame in the nursing home. After a while she recognised me, and to my amazement said, 'You're the one with that tall, tall husband.' I told her of my love and gratitude for all she had done to give me a chance in life. She listened intently, patted my cheek and said, 'You're a good girl,' then spoke no more, looking vaguely at nothing. Her tiny, old, lonely, sad little figure, lying in bed, helpless, was devastatingly sad. Our great and much beloved teacher died on 27 December 1962, never to be forgotten by any of us.

SUMMER HOLIDAYS

But time marches on. The children were growing, and our lovely house had become too small for our needs. And then a terrible thing happened: Rocket escaped onto our road, was hit by a motorcycle and was badly injured, his hip knocked out of joint. The vet was pessimistic about his recovery, so in despair, we took him to the veterinary research institute, where the chief surgeon proposed to strap Rocket's leg and hip by the same method used for cows. He had never tried it on a dog, but it was the only chance Rocket had. Of course we gave our consent.

For three weeks we took turns staying by Rocket at night, to make sure he did not attempt to get to his feet. We carried him out in our arms for his needs, and prayed silently for his recovery. When our vet told us the experiment had worked, and that Rocket was saved, Cecil burst into tears of relief! I am glad to say he cried in front of the children, so that they saw there is no shame in showing one's feelings, and that it is not always necessary to maintain a stiff upper lip.

Cecil had heard that the widow of aviation pioneer Lord Brabazon (whose car registration plate was FLY 1) was selling their house, which was called Grangewood and stood on the other side of the Wentworth Club. We made an appointment with Lady Brabazon and went to see it. The house was great – with a few alterations and additions it would provide all the accommodation we needed. It stood in fourteen acres, partly garden, partly woodland, and had a cottage, which could be very useful. The children would have all the space in the world for their hobbies and games.

After much deliberation, we decided to buy it, to the great excitement of the children, and put Little Courtenay up for sale. I loved our old house, and could not help feeling sad. Many, many years later, it became the home of Sarah Ferguson, when her marriage to Prince Andrew, the Duke of York, ended in divorce. It feels strange – I still think of it as my home!

And so Grangewood became our new home. While alterations were in progress, we started moving in some of our possessions and furniture. As parts of the house were under construction and could not be locked at night, Cecil, Robert and Irina went to sleep there every night, armed with their sleeping bags. It was an adventure for the kids, who really loved it, as did Cecil! Finally the house was ready and we moved in. (Several years later, after we left it, Grangewood was bought by Ringo Starr.)

Irina was planning to have lots of little animals. Mother already had a cat, which the children had rescued from the bushes, where it had been thrown and abandoned as a small kitten. There had also been two tortoises, but they had not survived, and Robert had two budgerigars.

The first new addition to the household was a hamster, which Irina called Sir Barnabas Barnacle, A.C.N.B. (All Cock, No Balls!). Then she acquired a beautiful grey long-haired guinea pig she called Fred. He looked so lonely, we got him a wife. Tommaso built Fred and his wife a big two-storey hut with ramps and a fence all around it. Oh dear. Soon Irina had their babies to attend to, and by the end of the third year, the hut was home to forty-three guinea pigs!

There was a white bunny too. Not content with that lot, Irina bought two more hamsters, which lived in a large cage in her room. She let them out each day to run around, and on one such occasion, one of them escaped into my bathroom and promptly disappeared down the plughole of my bidet! We had a hard time enticing him out again.

At times the girls unknowingly brought fieldmice from the ponies' field back to the house in their hoods. The mice then scampered all over the house. I was terrified of them; my mother fed them chocolates! I always had to ask Tommaso to get rid of the mice – I could not stand them in the house.

Robert kept his budgies in his room and would also let them out to fly around. Whenever he had difficulty catching them to put them back in the cage, he would call Irina and me for help. I have a thing about touching feathers, and I do not enjoy chasing birds as a form of exercise!

Cecil suggested I join the local ladies at their sewing parties, which were held once a week at the house of our neighbour, Lady Stewart-Richardson. I did join, and tried my best at sewing press-studs on dolls' clothes for the school fete, and listening to the ladies' gossip, which was sometimes quite salty! Then the vicar would appear for tea, and the ladies would pretend to be little saints. But it was not for me. I soon gave up.

One day I asked our village cobbler, a dear old boy, 'Tell me, tell me, you hear all the gossip, what are the ladies saying about me?'

'Well, they say they tried their best, but had to give up on you!'

Victoria's interest was books. She was an avid reader. Even on overseas holidays, riding in the car, she was always buried in a book instead of looking at the view. She knew what she wanted: to be an actress. She later achieved her dream with success after attending the Central School of Acting. Very independent, she had her own ideas. In good company she was great fun.

As for Robert, he avoided making friends with boys his age, preferring the company of his father. He teased my mother and they often clashed, which usually resulted in Mother confiscating his favourite toy car, upon which he would rush to her room and confiscate her favourite perfume.

He also liked to wait for Mother to take Rocket for his walk in the woods. It was not a fenced area, so Rocket had to be on a leash, to keep him off the road. Robert would position himself in his bedroom window then, as soon as Mother reappeared from the woods, he would shoot his toy airgun, which was very loud. Rocket, startled by the bang, would start running, pulling Mother flat on the ground and dragging her on her stomach across the large lawn towards the house.

Robert also liked to frighten Tommaso by throwing bread and butter knives near him from his window while Tommaso was planting tulips. Robert would roar with laughter as Tommaso screamed to me, '*Madama, Madama*, Roberto try kill me!'

One day the girls and I were waiting for Robert in the car. It was time for me to take them all to school and Robert was late. I asked Victoria to go inside to fetch him, and soon she rushed out again, screaming, 'Mummy, come quickly, Robert's killing Granny!' The fight was about Robert's scarf. Mother wanted Robert to put it on, Robert did not. Neither would give in!

Each year we all went abroad during the children's summer holidays, each time to a new place. We usually travelled in two cars, and I often got lost, since I was unable to keep up with Cecil. Each holiday was a great adventure, with lots of cultural interest, and great fun on the beaches.

One time we went to Ireland, where Laurence Olivier came to join us for a few days. Then it was Elba, where Peter Ustinov arrived in his sailing boat, on which we all had great fun. On Sicily we had a ball with the Rhodes family. We also visited St Tropez before it became spoiled. In Italy we stayed in lovely little cabanas right on the beach in Salto di Fondi. It was a great place to stay, as from there we had an easy drive to Monte Cassino, where the great battle of World War II had taken place. In Rome we all got the shivers when we visited the Colosseum. Standing inside, we remembered the atrocities that had taken place there during the Roman Empire, when people were thrown in to be savaged by lions. In Naples, Cecil took us all for a walk in the slums. He walked beside the children in silence, letting them observe for themselves and understand that there were a lot of very poor people in the world and that not everyone was as lucky as we were.

We also visited Corfu, where Roger Furse and his wife had bought a house. They were spending more and more time there, and always trying to persuade us to visit. Cecil acquired a motorboat, which he dragged all the way across the Continent to Greece. When it was unloaded from the ferry at Corfu, I drove the car up to our rented villa with Victoria, leaving Cecil, Robert and Irina to take the boat to the villa by sea. As Victoria and I arrived at the villa, a little boy came running up, and with the help of Roger Furse, who translated, we discovered that I had left with the boat's engine keys in my purse.

When we drove down in a hurry to deliver the keys, we found Cecil furious and Robert and Irina in their bathing costumes in the middle of the square. The heat was so intense that they had stripped down in front of the café customers, who were all eating watermelons. Finally, seeing them safely start the engine and get into the boat, we drove back up to the villa. They had not far to go to cover the distance, so we all stood on the veranda looking out to sea, watching out for them. But they were nowhere to be seen! Eventually, a small boat appeared, towing behind it, with great difficulty, our motorboat, which had conked out as soon as they had left the bay. They had been drifting out to sea until the man in the little boat had seen their desperate waves and come to rescue them.

A few days later the boat was stolen from its mooring in our little private bay. The day after, Tommaso found it in a neighbouring bay with all the electrical wires ripped out. Once we had it back, the mechanics took a long time to discover what had been wrong with the boat to start with. We never got a proper ride in it, and carted it all the way across the Continent and back to England again. Once we arrived back home, Cecil sold it immediately, saying, 'That bloody boat!'

Mother made great friends with one of the teachers at Robert's school by the name of Bertil. He was Austrian, and gave French and art classes. They became friends unexpectedly after he told me one day that he would like to learn Russian. I said that my mother gave Russian lessons, and would be glad for him to come and study with her. He did and they became bosom friends, even though he was only my age.

Bertil came along on our Corfu holiday to tutor Robert in Latin. Mother preferred to come with him in his car, especially as they were to stop for a couple of days in Vienna to see Bertil's aunt, arriving at the villa a few days after us. They were more than a few days late, and when they finally appeared, both of them were hanging onto only half a steering wheel, scratched, bleeding and bruised. We soon learned that Bertil had swerved to avoid a sheep on a small Yugoslavian road and, being a dreadful driver, had overturned the car into a ditch. Pulled out by shepherds, they had to wait for the car to be patched up before they could continue, and then had to stop the night somewhere. In the little town they reached, all the accommodation was full. They finally found a place with one room left, and had to share a bed. Bertil was embarrassed, apparently; Mother not at all! Bertil wrapped himself in a sheet like a mummy, and lay down carefully on the edge of the bed, which made Mother giggle. Only in the morning, when they came downstairs to pay the bill, did they realise they had spent the night in a bordello! Every summer after that they drove to Vienna, had adventures and by the end of the holiday were no longer speaking to each other!

Another holiday to remember we spent in Spain, at the village of Figueres, in a brand-new pension, just opened by our English friends the Asquiths. We were their first guests. It was a lovely little village, right on the sea, and the food was superb. Each year, Cecil's method was to get himself burnt to a crisp on his first day on the beach, then suffer for a couple of days, flat on his back and unable to touch his burnt skin. Then he would assure us that from then on he would tan and never burn again. On this occasion, he proceeded to get burnt as usual.

As he lay in our room in agony, I took the children in the car to explore other beaches outside Figueres. We came upon a very small, peaceful, totally deserted beach at the other end of which, rising right out of the sea, elevated on the rocks, stood a beautiful white house. As the children and I played on the beach, we all decided how nice it would be if we could only have a house like that, right on the beach. At that moment, I saw a man emerge from the house and come down towards us. Something about him looked familiar to me. Then I saw him waving and calling, 'Irina, Irina!' Good God, it was Dalí! It was his house in Portlligat that we had been admiring. He told us that Gala, his wife, was in the house and would love to see us all.

The first thing we saw as we entered the house was a huge brown bear carved out of wood, standing on his haunches, with chains and coloured beads around his neck. The children were amused. Gala appeared and we had a lovely reunion. She asked us into their sitting room while Salvador went to fetch some cold drinks for us all. There an extraordinary sight greeted us; the children seemed frightfully embarrassed as they looked with disbelief at the chairs around the coffee table. They were also carved from wood, undoubtedly to order from Dalí's design. The back of the chair represented the lower part of a woman's torso, with her legs wide open and showing every detail of a woman's anatomy. One sat between her legs! The children, their eyes on stalks, were not keen to follow Gala's invitation to sit down, then Robert started muffled giggles. Dalí remained totally oblivious to the effect his furniture produced on my children, and calmly and sweetly poured them cold drinks. Gala looked at me, grinned and winked. Fun was had by all. It was great to see this extraordinary couple, who never ceased to astonish and fascinate.

They said they regretted not meeting Cecil, as they would be off the next day to Paris. I regretted it too – Cecil would have been fascinated, if not shocked. The children spoke of their experience for days and days afterwards, each time killing themselves with laughter. Ah, those holidays. They are great memories.

BACK IN THE USSR

At the beginning of April 1967, Cecil came home one evening asking me to guess where he had to go in a few days' time. He wanted me to go with him. I mentioned several places, to which, with a smile, he shook his head. Then, with a big grin, he announced that we were going to Russia. He explained that he had been invited by the Soviet film-makers to come and see their almost-finished version of *War and Peace*, which they hoped could be released in the West through Cecil's office. The films went for eight hours, four of which were already playing at a Moscow cinema. The remaining four were still being edited.

After my initial delight at the opportunity to see the country of my birth, I asked Cecil if he was certain that I could come with him. White Russians were not liked in the Soviet Union, and I was sure that I would not be welcome. I advised Cecil to tell them who I was. Cecil laughed. 'I told them already,' he said, 'but I didn't have to. They already knew everything about you, and probably more than even I do.'

My mother was glad that I would be able to see Russia, but she begged me not to try to discover the fate of any of the Baronov family since, if any of them were still alive, it could only bring them a great deal of trouble.

The Soviet Embassy's cultural attaché saw us off at the airport. Cecil and another man from the embassy walked in front of me and the cultural attaché, who asked me what kind of passport I had. 'British,' I replied.

'Ha,' he said. 'The minute you cross into Russia your British passport doesn't mean anything. You were born in Russia, and as far as we're concerned you're Russian.'

I did not at all like what he said, and got a bit worried. However, my desire to step on the soil to which I belonged overcame all my doubts. During the flight, I told Cecil of the attaché's remark, and Cecil asked me never to go anywhere without him or be out of his sight. We were met and lodged in Moscow at the Metropole Hotel, which apparently had not changed since before the Revolution. They were beautiful rooms, big and comfortable, except there were no telephones and, if one wished to make a call, one had to go down to the reception desk with one's passport, have one's passport number and particulars taken down, and then answer an interrogation as to who one was calling and why. Also aware that the rooms were almost certainly bugged, Cecil begged me not to forget to keep my mouth shut. I solemnly promised not to, but I found my promise hard to keep!

We saw the first part of the film in the cinema, and it truly was superbly made. The next day we were taken to the studio to see the last four hours of the film. As the introductions were made and people heard my perfect Russian and realised that indeed I was a Russian from the West, they shut up like clams, and would not address a word to me for the rest of the day. Poor things, they were afraid.

Cecil promised to take me to Leningrad, where I was born, after he finished his business talks in Moscow. I wanted very much to follow my mother's directions and find the house she had lived in as a child with my grandparents. I did not particularly like Moscow, except for certain former palaces, and of course Red Square and the Kremlin, which are very impressive. But Leningrad was magnificent, truly the Venice of the north.

Although not everything was in good condition, and many of the churches were ruined or transformed into stables or warehouses, one could still see how beautiful they must have been. The magnificent palaces, such as the Winter Palace, which makes Buckingham Palace look like a little cottage, were truly impressive.

We spent a day visiting the Hermitage, the most amazing collection of paintings and other unique and precious pieces. One particular piece that sticks in my mind was a present from Queen Victoria to the father of Nicholas II. It was an enormous solid gold cage standing as high as a man, with birds perching at various levels inside, each one a jewel, with real precious stones for eyes. We were really impressed, and fascinated to see so much treasure still left after so much had been pillaged or sold abroad by the Bolsheviks. It was a very emotional visit for me.

Around the end of May or beginning of June, Cecil asked if I would arrange things at home to come with him to the get-together in France of the Companions du Beaujolais, a syndicate of which he was a member, which acquired a special kind of Beaujolais wine from France. As none of them spoke French and I did, they reckoned I could be very helpful. We all went to France and had a jolly good time. It was interesting to see all the vineyards and wine cellars, and to learn something about that delicious liquid.

Soon after we returned home, the phone rang and Larry's shaken voice told Cecil that Vivien was dead. Jack Merivale, who had been her companion for the past seven years, found her dead on the floor when he returned from performing in a play in Guildford on 7 July 1967.

TRAGEDY

The date was 12 July 1967: the day of Vivien Leigh's funeral at St Mary's in London, a sad morning to wake up to. Immersed in our respective thoughts, Cecil and I busied ourselves with getting dressed. He was ready first. He sat on my dressing-room stool and watched me for a moment, then, as I got my suit out of the wardrobe, suddenly said, 'Kinnikins, I don't want you to come to the funeral.'

'Why?' I asked in astonishment.

'Funerals are not a place for women,' Cecil said firmly.

'But everyone will be there. It will be very odd if I'm not there with you,' I protested.

'I don't care,' he said, shrugging his shoulders. 'I don't want you to be there.' His tone of voice prohibited all further argument. I hung my suit back in the wardrobe, wondering what it was all about. 'I think the time has come for you to meet Brian Chilver,' Cecil announced. 'We'll be having lunch with him on Monday.' His tone was more relaxed now, if a bit pensive.

'Who's Brian Chilver?' I enquired, rather puzzled.

'He's my accountant and advisor on private matters.'

I was even more puzzled, having learned by then that my husband's financial matters were not 'the little woman's' business. By the same token, he never asked me what I was doing with my savings, which I had transferred from my New York account. It did seem strange to me, but I assumed it was the normal way in England, and did not dwell on it or question it. 'Oh, all right,' I answered, deciding it was not a good time to ask questions.

This strange conversation became even stranger when Cecil suddenly said, 'If anything happens to me, I'd like you to marry again.' That floored me!

'What are you talking about? Don't be silly! Why?'

'It would show that you liked being married,' he answered with the hint of a smile.

He can't be serious, I thought and, trying to turn it into a joke, said, 'And you must promise me that if anything happens to me you'll remarry too!'

Cecil smiled again but said nothing, and we went down to breakfast. I was still turning Cecil's comments around in my head when he kissed the children and me and drove away to London and what was going to be an emotionally difficult day.

Once he had left, my thoughts turned to Vivien, how her dreadful illness had destroyed a glorious life. How destiny had bestowed on her a life one can only dream of – love, incredible success, adulation all around her – and then brutally taken it all away, leaving her suffering in an unreal world of mental chaos.

The comings and goings of the day distracted my thoughts into other channels. I thought with pleasure of our forthcoming summer holiday, this time exploring Corsica. A young man friend of Victoria's arrived for a natter and a game of tennis. Victoria was by then two months short of her seventeenth birthday – how time flies! Then Irina's friend Benjy popped in. Talkative and mischievously witty, he made her laugh. She was almost fifteen, and rather mischievous herself. Robert was soon to be thirteen, a teenager! He was hanging around teasing Irina and Benjy. The young ones occupied, I settled down to write letters, and the day went peacefully by.

Victoria's friend was going to stay for dinner, but Benjy was ready to go home. I had just got my station wagon out of the garage to drive him home, when Cecil rolled in in his E-type Jaguar. His car was a big attraction with the kids, who loved it, but I hated it. Smoke was billowing from the left rear wheel, smelling of burning rubber. 'What's wrong with your beastly car?' I asked Cecil when he stopped.

'Don't be rude to my little E-type, Kinnikins. I was naughty and drove a bit too fast. It's all right, it happens sometimes,' he said, getting out of the car and greeting the kids, who now, very excited, were inspecting the Jaguar from all sides.

I was shocked at how tired Cecil looked. His face was yellow, as if he had jaundice. 'You must have had a terrible day,' I said. 'Go and change, relax and have a drink while I take Benjy home.'

He smiled and remained on the porch, watching the kids. 'They love my car. I'll take Benjy home.'

'Yes, yes, Dad!' chorused Irina and Robert.

I protested. 'No, Cecil, you're tired. I have my car out. I'll take Benjy, you go in and relax.'

But it was to no avail. They piled into his car. 'We'll be back in thirty minutes,' Cecil said to me with a grin. And off they went.

Poor Cecil. He must have had an awful day, I thought as I went back to the kitchen to ask Rocchina not to start cooking dinner before Cecil got back. That would give him the chance to relax in peace with a drink. I called to Mother that dinner would be a bit later, then went out into the garden. It was a beautiful summer's early evening. The sun was still not ready to set; its now more gentle rays were throwing a lovely glow on our beds of roses. As I slowly strolled around, admiring an especially big tree, I thought how lucky I was to have my dear, beloved children, a husband, a soul mate in the wonderful dear person that Cecil was, a happy home, a family, all those things I had never imagined or thought I could have. *And here I am, blessed with so much!*

I glanced at my watch. Half an hour had passed and they were still not back. I went indoors to phone Benjy's parents. 'Oh, they're still here,' said Benjy's mother. 'Robert wanted a swim in the pool, and Cecil had a drink with us. They're about to leave now. You worry too much,' she laughed.

I went to ask Rocchina to delay our dinner a bit longer, poured myself a sherry and sat down to wait, feeling so utterly fulfilled and happy. It was twenty to eight. Suddenly, it was as if a dagger had been stuck into my chest, causing me pain and terror. I had a moment of knowledge, of certainty that something terrible had happened.

I tore out the door and started running up the road, tormented and scared. The road was uphill, straight and empty. I ran past our neighbour Rita, who was in her garden, and shouted to her to go to my house and tell them that something had happened, that I was running up the road. Then a man appeared, coming slowly down the hill. I stopped him, asking him if he had seen an accident up the road.

'Yes, I did.'

'Were there two children?'

'Yes . . .'

I took off, my guts shaking with fear. As I reached the brow of the hill, I saw two ambulances, a police car, and a twisted heap of metal lying grotesquely on its side in the ditch. I made for the ambulance nearest to me, in which I could see my children. Robert was lying down, Irina sitting, the attendant standing by the still-open door. Two men, police officers, barred my way, grabbing my arms. 'You can't go there, Madam,' they said.

Trying to get away from them, I shouted, 'Let me go, get away. They're my children!'

'No, you're not allowed to approach them. Get into our car. We'll follow them to the hospital.' They pulled me towards the car and I furiously resisted.

The ambulance attendant came to my rescue. Hurrying over, he asked the two policemen to let me go to my children. 'She's their mother, for Christ's sake!' Reluctantly, they let go of me and I ran to the ambulance, asking the attendant how my husband was.

'We mustn't waste time talking,' he replied. 'We must hurry to the hospital. They'll tell you there.'

I jumped into the ambulance and took my children's hands in my trembling ones. Irina, covered in scratches and bruises and dirt from the road, looked dazed, shocked but calm. She squeezed my hand, saying, 'Don't worry, Mum. We're all right.'

Robert's head was smeared in blood, his clothes torn in places, one leg bleeding through his trousers. He had a vague look in his eyes, which kept closing, as he slipped in and out of consciousness. But he, too, realising I was there, managed to squeeze my hand and say, 'Don't worry, Mum, we'll be all right.' My heart was tearing for my poor, poor children.

'How's Daddy?' I asked Irina.

She must have been in pain, as her face contracted as she tried to move. 'Don't worry, Mum,' she said. 'It'll be all right.' The poor child was trying to reassure me, in spite of the trauma she had been through and the state she was in.

The ambulance stopped and people emerged from the hospital, rolling out stretchers. I jumped out, wanting to run to the ambulance in front of ours, to see Cecil, but his ambulance did not stop. It kept going, and disappeared down the path among the trees. I anxiously asked the ambulance attendant where they were taking my husband.

'He'll be examined by the doctors now. They'll come out and talk to you when they're ready,' was his reply. My heart sank. *He must be badly injured*, I thought to myself.

The children, behind curtained-off spaces, were being examined. Nurses were trying to clean the bits of asphalt from their bodies. I asked one of them if she could phone our home and tell them what had happened and that I wanted my daughter Victoria to come over right away. She hurried to do so, and returned to tell me that she had spoken to a lady who said she was my mother and had passed on the message that I wanted Victoria with me.

Robert was wheeled away to have his head X-rayed. I kept asking if anyone knew what was happening with my husband and getting the same answer: 'The doctors are with him. When they're ready, they'll come and talk to you.'

Irina was lying still, silent, uncomplaining. Robert was wheeled back and they told me he had no fracture, but that pieces of glass were lodged in his head – they would make their way out on their own. I asked for Robert to be seen by a head specialist. They told me they did not have one at the hospital. 'I'll find a specialist then,' I suggested.

'You're not allowed to bring in anyone from outside this hospital,' was the man's terse answer. 'Besides, your son does not need one. It would be a waste of time.'

I argued that it was better to be safe than sorry. The man was not impressed. Then and there I made up my mind that Robert would be seen by a specialist, no matter what they said. *Try and stop me!*

My anxiety about Cecil was reaching breaking point, as the time passed and the doctors still did not come and tell me what was happening. At that moment, my mother appeared. 'Where's Victoria?' I asked. 'Why isn't she here? I need her!' I demanded, raising my voice.

Calmly, Mother said, 'I told Victoria to look after Rocchina, who's having hysterics.' As I held my head in my hands in despair, a nasty sound escaped from my throat. 'Behave yourself!' ordered Mother. 'At a time like this you need me, not Victoria!'

I saw red. Losing all control, I turned to her and shouted, 'I don't need you! I need my daughter!' In my anger and frustration, I was ready to attack her physically. I was stopped in that shameful, unforgivable act of hitting my mother by the appearance of a nurse through the door by which the doctors were expected. I ran to her and grabbed her shoulders. 'You must know. Tell me, please tell me. How is my husband?'

'The doctors are just—'

I stopped her. 'You know. I know you know. Tell me!' I let go of her and stood still. 'Tell me, please.'

A soft look of sympathy came into her eyes.

'He's dead?' I whispered.

The nurse slowly inclined her head. The next moment my head was in her lap and I was gulping for air . . .

A vision flashed through my numb mind: Vivien's angry, cat-like green eyes looking at Cecil, her husky, hissing voice saying, 'When I die, I'll take you with me!'

She did.

My poor children – their lives and mine were shattered to pieces. We were now on a slippery road into the unknown.

EPILOGUE

From that terrible day, which will haunt me to the end of my existence, life as I knew and loved it ended abruptly. It became an existence, as I groped in the dark, making mistakes to the detriment of my children, not helping their emotional states, nor the difficult teenage period of their lives. Never having been a teenager, a real, normal teenager, myself, I was at a loss. Forgive me, my children, forgive me.

I am eighty-six now. When I lost Cecil I was forty-eight years old. The years in between have held some moments of joy – given to me by my children – and a great deal of stress and worry. I avoid dwelling on those years and do not like talking about them, which is why I have not included them in my memoirs.

After several displacements, first to Malta, then Switzerland (for financial reasons), I was finally given the green light to return to live in England. I lived in London, near the River Thames, in a lovely district called Barnes. My mother and I settled down there in a small cottage, which I considered would be my last address.

The monotony of my existence was broken by an invitation from the Royal Academy of Dancing to become one of their vice presidents. Thanks to the then chief executive, David Watchman, who sensed my need to function, I started to travel all over the world, to the ballet schools registered with the RAD, which are in over sixty different countries, giving mime classes and talks.

Another invitation that followed, and led to one of my happiest memories, came in 1986 from Maina Gielgud, who was then the artistic director of the Australian Ballet. She asked me to fly to Melbourne and coach the company in Fokine's *Les Sylphides*. I was very impressed by the high standard of the dancers and by the extraordinarily warm way in which they received me into their midst. I have never been so spoilt as I was by the company's then chief executive, Noël Pelly. Now I have the honour of being the patron of the Australian Ballet School, under the directorship of Marilyn Rowe and the administration of John Barren, which makes me feel adopted by the Australian ballet world. I had come full circle, starting with ballet and ending again in the ballet world. Such was my destiny.

My mother lived with us, then me, for forty years. She died in 1992, at the age of ninety-three. No, she suffered no illness; she fell down the stairs. Poor Mama, how I regret now that I did not make better friends with her. I know she loved me – perhaps too much! I loved her too, my mama.

Victoria, Irina and Robert grew up into adulthood and took to their wings, on their own journeys of destiny. We are very close and they are very caring towards me, my beloved children. Bless them!

They have brought much joy into my life by making me a grandmother. The first to do so was Irina. Her daughter, Natasha, was born in 1972. She is now a beautiful young woman with a daughter of her own, my great-grandchild, Zoe. She is an angelic-looking, bright, funny little monkey, now aged three.

After Natasha was born, there was a gap of twenty years before the rest of my grandchildren made their appearance. Next was Hugh, now thirteen, Robert's son, followed by two more boys, Robert's sons Finn, now nine, and Laurie, now five. Three wonderful chaps.

Victoria has given me two grandchildren, Katya, now seven, a beautiful, bright child, and Nicolai, a fearless, lovely little man of five. They all bring sunshine into my life, and I love them to bits!

Me? No, I never married again. I am 'old widow Tennant', now put out to pasture! I graze in a most beautiful spot in the country I fell in love with in 1938 – Australia. So, after all, Barnes was not to be my last address. On the instigation and insistence of my daughter Irina, at the age of eighty I packed up once again and arrived in Byron Bay, where Irina was living.

I feel privileged to be allowed to end my days in this enchanted place, so peaceful and beautiful, where I am aware that there is another world besides the busy human one. Outside my veranda the birds enchant me at sunrise and sunset with their calls and songs, the crickets and tiny jade-coloured tree frogs wake up to greet the night, and I hear the garden come alive with the wanderings of nocturnal creatures.

Sitting on my veranda at the end of the day, I sip my bourbon and soda, always in awe of the vast view out over the valley below me, ending in the ocean. At sunset, the ever-changing sky turns from orange to pink to pale blue to deep navy, and thousands of stars appear, so bright, seeming so low, that I have the impression I could touch them. The moon rises out of the sea like a huge orange ball. It is magic!

I count my blessings.

ACKNOWLEDGEMENTS

First of all, thanks to Peter Wilmoth, who started it all with his article about me in the *Sunday Age*.

My profound thanks and gratitude to the Penguins, in particular to Clare Forster, Nicola Young, Nikki Townsend, Sally Bateman, Daniel Ruffino, Fran Haysey, Tammie Gay and Robert Sessions. Clare Forster read Peter Wilmoth's article and expressed her interest, without which this book would not have been published.

My huge thanks to Liz Friend, for her endless patience and heartfelt enthusiasm in figuring out my writing, and correcting my spelling and occasional grammatical mistakes, for four long years.

To my children, Victoria, Irina and Robert, for their constant interest, encouragement and support, and for believing that I could do it. And extra special thanks to my daughter Irina, for giving me of her time to help with matters connected with my writing. Thanks also to my granddaughter Natasha, for her intense interest and encouragement.

My gratitude to Clement Crisp, for consenting to write the Foreword, for which I am deeply grateful.

Thanks to Kathrine Sorley Walker and the late Vicente García-Márquez, whose splendid books on our Ballet Russe company – *De Basil's Ballets Russes* and *The Ballets Russes: Colonel de Basil's Ballets Russes de Monte Carlo, 1932–1952* – helped me in checking certain dates.

To Sono Osato and her husband, Victor Elmaleh, for a lifelong friendship and most generous hospitality whenever I visited New York. And my love to Donald Saddler, whose friendship I cherish.

My gratitude to Tamara Tchinarova Finch, a lifelong friend and colleague, for her extraordinary care of my mother and me while we lived in her house.

Thanks to Mrs Pamela and the late Dr Raymond Lister, for all their love and care in adopting me as one of their family. And my big love to Bob and Helen Gifford who, from neighbours across the street, became most cherished friends.

My thanks for the happy times I have had with the Royal Academy of Dance to the president, Dame Antoinette Sibley, for inviting me to become one of the vice presidents, and to the chief executive, David Watchman, who felt my need for action and sent me travelling all over the world on behalf of the RAD.

My profound love and thanks to my 'little friend' Sandy, Alexander Ewing, who grew up to be the chancellor of the North Carolina School of the Arts, and who remembered the breakfast companion of his schooldays by inviting me to guest-teach at that magnificent school.

My thanks to Dr Joseph and Mrs Mary Ringland Anderson, who became part of our ballet tribe and allowed us to become part of their family, which made our stay in Australia one of unforgettable memories.

The memory of the late Sir Robert Southey will always be in my loving thoughts, as the little boy who played with us in the Ringland Anderson's pool and much, much later as the chairman of the Australian Ballet. And my thanks to Lady Marigold Southey, for her friendship and hospitality.

I thank Maina Gielgud, for giving me one of my happiest memories, by inviting me to coach the Australian Ballet company and work with its superbly talented dancers. And also I fondly remember the late Noël Pelly, the Australian Ballet's then chief executive, for the kindness and care with which he showered me.

I extend my grateful thanks to the director of the Australian Ballet School, Marilyn Rowe, and to the committee and the administrator,

John Barren, for asking me to be the patron of the Australian Ballet School, which gave me the warm feeling of being accepted into the Australian ballet world.

And on behalf of all my colleagues in Colonel de Basil's Ballet Russe, I extend my immense gratitude to Dayna Goldfine and Dan Geller, for the magnificent documentary they have made on our company and our times, *Ballets Russes*.

It has not always been possible to trace and acknowledge copyright material. The author and publisher would be pleased to hear from any copyright holders who have not been acknowledged.

Text design by Nikki Townsend copyright Penguin Group (Australia).

Front jacket photograph by Spencer Sitier, Irina Baronova as the Siren in David Lichine's *The Prodigal Son*, taken during the Covent Garden Ballet Russe's 1939 tour of Australia, reproduced courtesy of the National Library of Australia.

Back jacket photograph: Irina Baronova in Michel Fokine's *Les Sylphides*.

Front cover and page 197 drawings by Sir Daryl Lindsay, Irina Baronova as the Queen of Shemakham in Fokine's *Le Coq d'or*, reproduced courtesy the Australian Ballet School.

Page ii photograph by Maurice Seymour, Chicago, Irina Baronova in *Swan Lake*.

Page 13 drawing by Sir Daryl Lindsay, *Les Cent Baisers* seen from the manager's box.

Typeset in 11/16 pt Berling by Post-press Group, Brisbane, Australia.

Irina Baronova escaped Bolshevik Russia in 1919. At the age of thirteen, she became a founding member of the highly influential Ballets Russes de Monte Carlo, directed by George Balanchine. In 1949 she met and married Australian theatrical agent Cecil Tennant. She is now vice-president of the Royal Academy of Dance in Australia and a founding patron of the Australian Ballet.

INDEX